THE VESTRY BOOK

OF THE

UPPER PARISH

NANSEMOND COUNTY, VIRGINIA

1743-1793

WILMER L. HALL

Editor

Southern Historical Press, Inc.
Greenville, South Carolina

This volume was reproduced from
A personal copy located in the
Publisher's private Library

All rights reserved. No part of this publication may be reproduced,
stored in a retrieval system, transmitted in any form, posted
on to the web in any form or by any means without
the prior written permission of the publisher.

Please direct all correspondence and orders to:

www.southernhistoricalpress.com
or
**SOUTHERN HISTORICAL PRESS, Inc.
PO Box 1267
375 West Broad Street
Greenville, SC   29601**
southernhistoricalpress@gmail.com

Originally published: Richmond, VA. 1949
ISBN #0-89308-824-2
All rights Reserved.
Printed in the United States of America

PREFACE

Shortly before his death on April 3, 1939, Dr. C. G. Chamberlayne, editor of several parish record books published by the Library Board, completed and deposited in the Virginia State Library a handwritten transcript of the vestry book, 1743-1793, of the Upper Parish, Nansemond County, Virginia. In choosing this volume, which has not hitherto been published, as the subject for his next contribution to the series, he was following a general plan of giving precedence to parish books from those Virginia counties whose early public records have been lost. Since the parishes of the Established Church in colonial Virginia were also local governmental units, their records are, in a real sense, official, important and revealing.

The original volume was formerly in the collection of parish record books in the library of the Protestant Episcopal Theological Seminary at Alexandria, Virginia, and was among those which were borrowed and photocopied by the Virginia State Library in 1924-1925, and returned. With other parish record books there, it was deposited in the Archives Division of the Virginia State Library in 1931. Although the photoduplicated copy shows that the original was in poor condition in 1925 (many edges of leaves in the earlier part were crumbled away), the original suffered further deterioration in later years, with the result that the photocopy, in the beginning, is more complete in certain small details of the text than is the original.

Early in 1944, the present editor, having about completed the publication work on which he was then engaged, turned to Dr. Chamberlayne's transcription of this vestry book with the intention of using it, with a minimum expenditure of time for checking and editing, as the text for the printed volume (Dr. Chamberlayne, who wrote very legibly, was accustomed to have typesetting done directly from his handwritten transcripts of these parish books). However, when assistants undertook to check the original volume with Dr. Chamberlayne's transcript, they noted many obvious errors and some serious omissions in the latter which Dr. Chamberlayne, had he lived and his health permitted, would doubtless have corrected on re-examination or in editing. It was also the case that Dr. Chamberlayne had followed his customary practice of making (except for his uniform handwriting and with some judicious inconsistency which every editor of such manuscripts must exercise more or less in view of the inconsistencies of the clerks) a virtual facsimile of the original with respect to arrangement, the formation of words, various uncertainties, the use of obsolete symbols, etc. In consideration of these matters, of the great change that type makes in manuscript, of the fact that no manuscript can be duplicated in print except by photographic reproduction, and of the desirability of providing a more legible text by appropriate modernization, it was decided to make a typescript of the original and to edit it with reasonable thoroughness. The original volume, however, was in no condition for repeated handling on account of the brittleness of the paper, loose leaves, and dilapidated binding. Therefore, the leaves of the book were "restored," and fastened temporarily (the old binding could not be reused), in fourteen parts, in acid-free folders, pending an improvement in the binding industry, circumstances which resulted in the postponement of the completion of the typescript and the editing. In the few instances where the photocopy of 1925 supplements the present original, the additional details have been enclosed in square brackets, with explanatory footnotes.

The pages of the original volume were unnumbered and the book may have contained additional proceedings, especially at the beginning. Before "restoration," the book was carefully collated, and page numbers supplied in pencil, with the exception of three blank pages at the end. Judging by these blank pages and the infrequent meetings after 1786, when the parish was virtually in collapse, it seems unlikely that the book formerly included other matter at the end although the last numbered page ([287]) contains a partial record (three returns) of processioning, all appaently dated in 1793. Of these 287 pages, six ([28], [126], [142], [170], [238] and [239]) are blank, and two ([149]-[150], or one leaf) are mostly torn away. In accordance with Dr. Chamberlayne's method of detailing the texts of all of his contributions to the series, each supplied page number, in brackets, is shown in order on a separate line in the printed volume, although such insertions interrupt the continuity of the text; for this information makes many things more apparent to the student than footnotes would do: why balances are carried and brought forward at particular places; why the clerks sometimes resort to unusual arrangements; whether there are omissions on account of lost or misplaced leaves, as on

p. [1]; blank and mutilated pages within the text; etc. In addition, of course, the make-up of pages provides a quick and exact guide for persons who wish to refer to the original or who desire photocopies of particular data.

Four loose leaves (eight pages), being mostly a sketchy account of the parish taken from the vestry book, were laid in the volume. These pages were evidently written much later than the conclusion of the vestry book by the then possessor of the volume (possibly the clerk for the Upper Suffolk Parish, St. Paul's Church, Suffolk) in response to an inquiry. Judging from a similarity of language in a brief mention of Lower Suffolk Parish which occurs in this sketch and in Bishop William Meade's *Old Churches, Ministers and Families of Virginia*,[1] the information may have been compiled for Bishop Meade who later obtained the original vestry book which was doubtless deposited with the other parish books accumulated for the purpose of this work at the Seminary at Alexandria.[2]

The editor has used the utmost care, in spite of numerous problems and perplexities, to have the printed text conform to the original in all the essentials of accuracy. To modernize the text of such a manuscript completely would impair its intrinsic character; to achieve accuracy at the same time would be unlikely if not impossible. The editor might well perpetrate many errors if he should, for example, try to clarify, by punctuation or rearrangement, many confused returns of processioning; or to seek to reconcile, by insertions or corrective footnotes which would overwhelm the text, the innumerable variant spellings, especially of personal names whose identity seems obvious or is strongly presumptive. In attempting a judicious modernization of the original text, he has striven primarily for greater clarity and legibility in his arrangement, insertions, corrections and footnotes, with only a minimum of interpretation. The text of the original varies considerably in form, and the handwriting of the clerks varies greatly in style and legibility; but great pains have been taken to preserve essentially the writer's arrangement (with slight modifications for

---

[1] 1861 edition (Philadelphia, J. B. Lippincott & Co.), v. 1, p. 289. This edition, of which all later editions are merely reissues, is the one hereafter cited as Meade. J. C. Wise published a separate index in 1910. The few important variations in the 1861 edition from the edition first published in book form in 1857 are in v. 2.

[2] According to a report on these books in *The Virginia Magazine of History and Biography* (hereafter cited as *Va. Mag.*), v. 3, p. 85-86, the parish books used by Bishop Meade were deposited at the Seminary "at his death", which occurred in 1862.

clearness and general uniformity), paragraphing (when indicated by indentions, separating lines, spacing, or mode of entry), spelling (sometimes doubtful), capitalization (often conjectural), and, for the most part, his punctuation (or lack of it). Braces, often used by the clerks for various purposes, have usually been discarded in favor of the indentions which they imply except in those cases where they clarify the arrangement; and those retained have been rightly turned where reversed. Dashes at the end of lines, dots and dashes from items in accounts to corresponding numbers in columns of figures, and meaningless dots or periods and colons which seem to have fairly dripped from the clerk's pen in the earlier part of the book, are omitted. Likewise excluded are horizontal marks and lines which are drawn across some pages; also vertical lines which are ordinarily, but not always, used to separate columns of figures, these lines being replaced by the punctuation employed in their stead by the clerks in other instances.

The text has been rendered in modern type, no obsolete characters being employed. The sign for "per", sometimes combined with the superior letter "r", has been replaced by the word for which it stands; the short instead of the long "s" has been used; peculiar marks made as substitutes for signatures have been expressed, as nearly as possible, by conventional letters with descriptive footnotes; the circumflex has been omitted; the abbreviation for pounds (weight), usually loosely written like "ll" has been given as "lb"; the forms "y^e" (often used) and "y^t" (seldom used) have been shown as "the" and "that" respectively.

The elimination of the per mark and the circumflex have presented some problems. In the earlier part of the original, the former symbol is used not only to represent the word "per" but also, if the circumflex be disregarded, such parts of words as "pre" in "present," and "par" in "parish," "pro" in "procession," etc.; but since the circumflex has also been used in these words, the per mark has the effect of the letter "P" or "p" and has been so rendered, with the omitted letters indicated by the circumflex supplied in brackets, except in cases where the symbol stands for the syllable "per," as in "persons." Throughout the printed text, the per mark, sometimes indistinguishable in form from "P" or "p," has been rendered by that letter when per is not meant. The omission of the circumflex, which occurs frequently in the earlier part of the original book, has the effect of making the clerks responsible for certain peculiar and erroneous spellings of which they are not justly chargeable; but, in the permutations of their orthography, these may be regarded as a very minor variation in the prevalent practice of contraction; indeed there is sometimes uncertainty whether a carelessly made mark, at the end of abbreviated words, is intended for the circumflex or the customary superior letter.

Various other changes of small moment and infrequent occurrence have been made in the interest of uniformity, and in order that certain particularities and peculiarities of the clerks should not distract attention or pose typographical problems: punctuation which is presumably indicated by the make-up of lines or occasional spacing within lines has been mostly ignored; interlineations have been brought down to the line; the apostrophe has been substituted for the comma and period in the few cases where the former is the appropriate punctuation; the occasional capital letter within or at the end of words and abbreviations has been changed to lower case; pen flourishes and lines, even where significant in composition, have not been reproduced; and a few other adjustments have been made. The editor has, however, retained the clerks' superior letters, after the style of the previously published volumes of this series, rather than elected to exercise his discretion and attempt consistency in bringing them, or most of them, down to the line; but he has omitted dots, dashes, colons or commas usually placed under them. The clerks not only employed superior letters to indicate abbreviations but also, on occasion, for other reasons, including punctuation. To bring them all down without supplying additional letters would result in many peculiar and mistaken words. Examples are "Cur^t" for "Current"; "ball^e" for "balance"; "ward^s" for "wardens"; "sexton^s" for "sextoness," etc. There are no doubt minor errors in interpreting the clerks' intentions in regard to raising letters, if indeed those functionaries always acted with considered purpose.

Editorial insertions or queries are indicated by enclosure within square brackets. Since it is unnecessary and inexpedient to call attention to all clerical errors, "[*sic*]" has been used sparingly, and especially to indicate mistakes which might be considered particularly editorial or typographical. For the most part, the reader will have to rely on the accuracy of the transcription, although it is more than probable that there are some editorial mistakes, and observe the usually obvious meaning of the text, it being practically impossible to correct all of the inconsistencies of the clerks or to detect all of their errors. A preliminary index, indispensable for the proper editing of such a work, has made it possible to point out various errors, to decipher certain names which are virtually illegible, and to provide other identifications.

The introduction is designed to be a brief history of the Upper Parish, drawn largely from the vestry book itself and arranged topically for coherence. Otherwise it is the product of what is considered a reasonable amount of investigation of accessible sources although it is likely that exhaustive research in various depositories would yield additional information. While this account is inseparably a part of the history of the Established Church in Virginia, it is necessarily limited in its treatment of that vast and complicated subject which has been dealt with comprehensively by various historians. Likewise it is incidentally a part of the history of Nansemond County.

Owing to the great variations in spelling in the text, especially of the names of those who were evidently the same persons, variants have been combined in index entries or, in cases of doubt, related by *See also* references. The index is also designed as a guide to various classes of persons such as ministers, clerks and readers, vestrymen, physicians, sheriffs, etc.

The editor wishes to make grateful acknowledgment of his indebtedness to the late Dr. C. G. Chamberlayne whose transcript has been useful in many ways; to Dr. G. MacLaren Brydon, Historiographer of the Diocese of Virginia, whose suggestions concerning the introduction have been very helpful (his *Virginia's Mother Church* had not been published when the introduction was written); to Mr. W. J. Van Schreeven, Head Archivist of the Virginia State Library, who has been a liberal critic of the manuscript of the introduction and who has also, as well as his assistants, greatly aided in the location of obscure source materials; to Mr. Robert B. Tunstall, Chairman of the Library Board of Virginia, and Mr. R. W. Church, State Librarian, who have reviewed the manuscript of the introduction; to Miss Martha Winfrey, Executive Secretary of the Virginia State Library, who found opportunity intermittently to execute the typescript in collaboration with the editor and to assemble much pertinent information; and to Mrs. Frances McGovern, Miss Virginia Jones, Miss Marjorie Connell and Miss Emily Terry of the library staff who have helped variously in typing, proof-reading and indexing.

WILMER L. HALL

Virginia State Library, Richmond
February 15, 1949.

CONTENTS

	PAGE
PREFACE	v
INTRODUCTION	
Formation of the Parish	xiii
The Vestry and Its Record	xviii
Religion in the Parish	xxii
Ministers	xxxii
Churches and Chapels	xlix
Poorhouse	lv
The Revolution and Its Consequences	lxiv
THE VESTRY BOOK	1
INDEX	265

INTRODUCTION

Formation of the Parish

Bishop William Meade in his *Old Churches, Ministers and Families of Virginia* states "There were settlements in Nansemond at a very early period. The Acts of Assembly in dividing counties and parishes are nearly all of its early history that can be gotten. A vestry-book of the upper parish, commencing in 1743 and continuing to 1787 [*sic*], contains all the statistics I can get. These are painfully interesting."[3] In spite of his indefatigable efforts to locate and secure parish records for the purpose of his book, Bishop Meade apparently was unaware of the existence of the vestry book, 1749-1856,[4] of Suffolk Parish (the Lower, or Lower Suffolk, Parish) of Nansemond County which is now in the office of the clerk of the Circuit Court of the city of Suffolk, Virginia (photocopy in the Virginia State Library). However, in addition to the vestry book of the Upper Parish, he did secure, by dint of inquiry, the copy of a portion of an old vestry book of Chuckatuck Parish in Nansemond County, containing the proceedings of the vestry from 1702 to 1709.[5]

Bishop Meade's lament over the dearth of materials for the early history of Nansemond County, amply warranted by the destruction which the local public records had suffered by fire in 1734 and 1779,[6] is even more justified today, inasmuch as a fire in 1866 is reported to have de-

---

[3] Meade, v. 1, p. 282.

[4] There are no entries in this vestry book from 1784 to 1825.

[5] Meade, v. 1, p. 305. In the Suffolk Parish vestry book, 1749-1856, p. 76 of the photocopy, there is reproduced a letter from Jno. R. (or B.) Purdie to James H. Godwin, dated Smithfield, September 15, 1856, which quotes part of a letter from Bishop Meade, asking Purdie's good offices in obtaining for him the Chuckatuck book, probably in the possession of Godwin whose address Bishop Meade did not know. This was undoubtedly the James H. Godwin who was long a prominent vestryman, and secretary or treasurer of the vestry, of the Suffolk or Lower Parish, representing the territory on the north side of the Nansemond River, formerly Chuckatuck Parish. The schedule of inhabitants of Smithfield, Va., U. S. Census of 1850, shows John R. Purdie, a physician, living in that town.

[6] *The Statutes at Large; Being a Collection of All the Laws of Virginia . . .* by William Waller Hening, v. 4, p. 448. (This work (13 v.: v. 1-12, Richmond, 1809-1823; v. 13, Philadelphia, 1823) is hereafter cited as Hening); *The History of Nansemond County, Virginia*, by Joseph B. Dunn (1907), p. 31, 45. (This work is hereafter cited as Dunn.)

stroyed all of the records then in the clerk's office.[7] Under the circumstances, this vestry book of the Upper Parish is particularly important as a primary historical source; for the vestries of the Established Church in colonial Virginia had important powers and duties in local government, and were clothed by law with large control over both civil and religious affairs.

There must have been earlier records of the Upper Parish which have not survived, for the parish had had a century of existence prior to the beginning of this vestry book. Nansemond County was formed from the territory which was organized first as Elizabeth City County, one of the eight original shires created in 1634.[8] In 1636, that part of Elizabeth City County south of the James River became New Norfolk County which was divided in 1637 into Upper Norfolk and Lower Norfolk counties.[9] The name of Upper Norfolk County was changed by law to "Nansimum" in 1646[10] although it may have been so-called earlier.

An act of the January 1639/40 session of the Assembly in relation to the boundaries of Isle of Wight, Upper Norfolk and Lower Norfolk counties also established coterminous parishes of the same name.[11] At the March 1642/43 session, Upper Norfolk County was divided into three parishes: South, East and West.[12] It is not certain when the South Parish

---

[7] *Virginia Local Public Records: Housing Conditions in the Offices of the Clerks of County and City Courts of Record, 1929.* Report of Special Committee of the Virginia State Bar Association to Coöperate with the State Library Board. Reprinted from *Annual Report of Virginia State Bar Association, 1929* (Richmond, 1930), p. 6.

[8] Hening, v. 1, p. 224.

[9] *Virginia Counties: Those Resulting from Virginia Legislation,* by Morgan Poitiaux Robinson (*Bulletin* of the Virginia State Library, v. 9, no. 1/3, Jan./July, 1916), p. 59, 62, 70, 85. (This work is hereafter cited as Robinson.) These dates are based on local records since the acts and proceedings of the Assembly for these years have not been preserved.

[10] Hening, v. 1, p. 321. Robinson (p. 85, note 52, and p. 198) gives 1642 as the date of the establishment of Nansemond County, based on an act (not in Hening) of the General Assembly, passed in 1647, which relates to the boundary between Nansemond and Isle of Wight counties as established by an act of 1642 which he assumed is not in Hening. However, there is an act in Hening (v. 1, p. 247), passed at the March 1642/43 session, relating to the boundaries of Isle of Wight, Upper and Lower Norfolk counties, which is similar to the partial act of 1647 printed in Robinson (p. 198) when the new name of the county would probably have been used.

[11] The act, which is not in Hening, is printed in Robinson, p. 197-198.

[12] Hening, v. 1, p. 250-251. The portion of this act relating to these parishes is as follows:

    For the better inabling of the inhabitants of this collony to the religious worship and service of Almighty God which is often neglected

became the Upper Parish, the East Parish became the Lower Parish, and the West Parish became Chuckatuck Parish, but there is a record of a grant of land in the Upper Parish, June 3, 1656, and in the Lower Parish, October 5, 1658.[13] The name Chuckatuck was probably bestowed concurrently; it was certainly in use by 1663 when the Assembly ordered that the vestry be fined "for not swaring churchwardens."[14]

The extent of the Upper Parish underwent various changes, partly due to vague boundaries. The long boundary dispute between Nansemond and Isle of Wight counties naturally affected the area of the Upper Parish; in fact, it appears from a proposal of the inhabitants of the Lower Parish of Isle of Wight County to the Assembly, that part of the Upper Parish was at one time within the latter county.[15] This boundary controversy extended

> and slackened by the inconvenience and remote vastnes of parishes, It is therefore enacted and confirmed by the authority of this present Grand Assembly, that the county of Upper Norff: shall be divided into three distinct parishes (vizt.) one on the south side of Nansimum River, The bounds of the parish to beginn from the present gleab to the head of the said river, on the other side of the river, the bounds to be lymitted from Cooling's Creek including both sides of the creek upwards to the head of the Westerne Branch and to be nominated the South parish.
>
> It is also thought fitt and confirmed that the east side of Nansimum River from the present gleab downewards to the mouth of the said River be a peculiar parish to which the gleab and parsonage house that now is shall be appropriated and called the east parish.—The third parish to beginn on the westerly side of Nansimum River to be lymitted from Coolings Creek as aforesaid and to extend downewards to the mouth of the River including all Chuckatuck on both sides and the Ragged Is[l]ands and to be knowne by the name of the West parish.

[13] Virginia State Land Office *Patents*, No. 3, 1652-1655 [*i.e.* 1653-1656], p. 385; No. 4, 1655-1664, p. 352.

[14] *Journals of the House of Burgesses of Virginia* (hereafter cited as *Jour. House Bur.*) 1659-1693 (Richmond, 1914), p. 27. The statement in *Va. Mag.*, v. 12, p. 447, that "In 1640, a patent was granted to Epaphroditus Lawson, in Tarrascoe Neck, Chuckeytuck parish, Nansemond county" is derived from a patent of 1693 (erroneously given as 1692) which is referred to in the next sentence of the article and which mentions these names (*Cf.* Virginia State Land Office *Patents*, No. 8, 1689-1695, p. 275). Neither Nansemond County nor the West Parish, the predecessor of Chuckatuck, had been established in 1640.

[15] *Jour. House Bur.*, 1695-1702 (Richmond, 1913), p. 12, records the following action on April 25, 1695:

> And upon Consideration of the Reporte of the s^d Comittee upon a Proposition of the Inhabitants of the Lower parish of the Isle of Wight County, that that part of the upper parish of Nanzimond County which lies within the Said County of Isle of Wight may be joyned to the lower parish of Isle of Wight the house agreed with the Comittee that

practically to the end of the colonial period, although all of the changes did not affect the Upper Parish. There was also the question of the boundary line with North Carolina which was not determined until 1728. It appears that, for reasons of economy, the Lower and Chuckatuck parishes were united officially in 1737 under the name of Suffolk Parish though some sort of union seems to have existed previously.[16] Of several petitions to the Assembly for adding parts of the Upper Parish to other parishes, one from the inhabitants of the Upper Parish, praying for the union of a part thereof to Suffolk Parish, was rejected in 1742.[17] However, at its September, 1744 session, the Assembly acted favorably on a petition from Nansemond County "setting forth, That when the dividing Line was run between the Parish of Suffolk, and the Upper Parish, in the said County, it was in Order to make the Number of Tithables near equal in both Parishes; but since the Division thereof, great Numbers of People have settled in the Upper Parish, by which means the Number of Tithables amount to more than Twelve Hundred; whereas in the Parish of Suffolk, they amount to no more than Six Hundred, and sometimes under that Number; and praying that the Parishes aforesaid may again be divided, and that the Division be as followeth: To begin at the Head of Pugh's Creek, thence down the same to Nansemond River; thence down the River to the Mouth of the Western Branch; thence up to the Branch to Isle of Wight County Line a small Distance below Everard's Mill: Which Division will make the Number of Tithables in the said Parish of Suffolk, to be within One Hundred and Nineteen of the Upper Parish."[18] The resulting bill, which was amended,[19] was passed as "An Act for

> the bounds of the s^d parishes Continue as now they are Setled according to the Act of Assembly made at James City the 20th day of October 1673 & therefore
> Ordered that the s^d Proposition be rejected.

The act of October 20, 1673, does not appear in Hening, nor is it referred to in *Jour. House Bur.* of that date. However, in Hening, v. 2, p. 318, there is an act, passed at the September 1674 session of the General Assembly, which refers to the long dispute between the inhabitants of the two counties, and established the boundary line between Isle of Wight and Nansemond, with the express provision that the parishes on this dividing line should not be changed.

[16] *Executive Journals of the Council of Colonial Virginia* (hereafter cited as *Exec. Jour.*), v. 4 (Richmond, 1930), p. 411-412. Cf. *William and Mary College Quarterly Historical Magazine*, 2d series, v. 5, p. 30-34; Hening, v. 8, p. 287-289.

[17] *Jour. House Bur.*, 1742-1749 (Richmond, 1909), p. 43.

[18] *Ibid.*, p. 95-96.

[19] *Ibid.*, p. 100.

dividing the upper parish in Nansemond county, and adding part thereof to Suffolk parish", effective November 20, 1744.[20] This act set forth the general reasons for the division and established a boundary line between the two parishes. According to this boundary, the Upper Parish, for approximately the entire period of this vestry book, included all the large, general area of Nansemond County south of Brewer Creek on the east side of Nansemond River and the Western Branch on the west side of Nansemond River to the North Carolina line. In 1786, that part "lying south of the rivers Blackwater and Nottoway" was added to Southampton County.[21] The town of Suffolk, established in 1742, was in the Upper Parish, not in Suffolk Parish as the name might lead one to suppose.

[20] Hening, v. 5, p. 269-270. The text of this act is as follows:

    I. Whereas, by reason of the small number of tithables in the parish of Suffolk, in the county of Nansemond, occasioned by a division of that parish, from the upper parish, in the said county, at a time when the lands in the said upper parish, were not fully settled; but since the said division, great numbers of people have settled therein: And as the inhabitants of the said parish of Suffolk, are, for the most part, very poor, and the levies large and burthensome; for the better regulating of the said parishes,

    II. Be it enacted, by the Lieutenant Governor, Council, and Burgesses, of this present General Assembly, and it is hereby enacted, by the authority of the same, That from and after the twentieth day of November, next ensuing, part of the parish called the upper parish, in the said county of Nansemond, be annexed to, and made part of the parish of Suffolk; and that the bounds thereof, for the future, be established in manner following; that is to say, to begin at the head of Duke's creek, thence running down the said creek, to Nansemond river; thence down the said river, to the mouth of the Western branch; thence up the said Western branch its several courses, till it intersects Isle of Wight county line; which shall always hereafter, be reputed, deemed, and taken, to be the bounds between the said parishes.

    III. Provided always, That nothing herein contained, shall be construed to hinder the collector of the said upper parish, as the same now stands intire, and undivided, to make distress for any levies, which shall be due from the inhabitants below the said line, after the said twentieth day of November, as by law he might have done, if this act had never been made. Any law, custom, or usage, to the contrary thereof, in any wise, notwithstanding.

    An article on the Gregory family in *Va. Mag.* for October, 1908 (v. 16, p. 202) gives the following explanation of this boundary: "By the Act of the General Assembly of September, 1744, that part of the Upper Parish which was below the following lines was added to the Suffolk Parish, to-wit: 'beginning at the head of Duke's Creek' (now known as Brewers Creek and which is about three and one half miles down the river from Suffolk town) ... The said Duke Creek was on the east side of Nansemond River."

[21] Hening, v. 12, p. 69.

The Vestry and Its Record

In general, vestries were self-perpetuating during most of the colonial period and were in the hands of the ruling class, the men of property and education. Bishop Meade hardly exaggerated when he stated "The vestries were the depositaries of power in Virginia. They not only governed the Church by the election of ministers, the levying of taxes, the enforcing of laws, but they made laws in the House of Burgesses; for the burgesses were the most intelligent and influential men of the parish, and were mostly vestrymen . . . Nor were the vestries represented in the popular branch of the Government only. We will venture to affirm . . . that there was scarce an instance of any but a vestryman being in the Council . . ."[22] He might have added that members of the vestry were also often civil officers of the local government and judges of the county courts, who were appointed by the governor. It might well happen that all local authority would be exercised by the same prominent men, none of whom was elected by the people. When there was more than one parish in a county, however, local authority would not be centralized in the same body of men.

The vestry made up the parish budget, and levied and apportioned the taxes for parish expenses; employed ministers and other church officers (clerks and lay readers were usually the same persons); built and repaired churches and chapels; took care of the poor, of orphan and illegitimate children, including the rudimentary education of pauper children; kept records of births, marriages and deaths; presented offenders and collected fines for offenses against morality and church discipline; appointed persons to establish and maintain the boundary lines of owners of land, known as processioning, and kept a record of their reports; and exercised other powers necessary for the management of parochial affairs. Such duties and powers are usually explicit in this vestry book.

There is no doubt that the vestrymen of the Upper Parish were, on the whole, "conspicuous and prosperous" as has been said of Andrew Meade, first of those listed in the vestry book, who was for years a representative of Nansemond County in the House of Burgesses, a member of the county court, and an officer in the militia.[23] Colonel William Byrd helped to

---

[22] Meade, v. 1, p. 151.

[23] *Andrew Meade of Ireland and Virginia; His Ancestors, and Some of His Descendants and Their Connections* . . . by P. Hamilton Baskervill (Richmond, 1921), p. 23-27. (This work is cited below as Baskervill.)

perpetuate his memory as the genial and generous host to the commissioners for running the boundary line with North Carolina in 1728.[24] Members of this family, his descendants, also served as vestrymen of the Upper Parish and held various offices.[25] Other prominent families, who were numerously represented on the vestry, were the Norfleets, Bakers, Sumners and, most of all, the Riddicks. Lemuel Riddick and Willis Riddick, undoubtedly the vestrymen, represented Nansemond County for many years in the House of Burgesses. It was customary for vestrymen to be succeeded by their sons or to be chosen from the same families. It is also the case that various lists of justices of the county court for Nansemond County read like lists of vestrymen of the Upper and Suffolk parishes.

As a detailed record of the business transactions of the vestry in the exercise of its various functions, this vestry book, though satisfactory in many respects, yet leaves a great deal to be desired. Much is omitted or only implied. Sometimes the lacking information may be supplied from other sources; sometimes it has probably been lost with the destruction of the local public records; sometimes it has no doubt perished with those to whom it was self-evident. On the whole, however, the book is a fairly adequate record of the discharge of duties prescribed by law; and it also contains much incidental information in regard to the life of the parish.

As has been noted, an effort was made in 1742 to add part of the Upper Parish to Suffolk Parish; and when such a division was made, in 1744, three members of the vestry of the Upper Parish were taken thereby into Suffolk Parish and had to be replaced.[26] Several other vestrymen were chosen in the next decade to take the place of deceased members but there was evidently a widespread dissatisfaction with the vestry and apparently a growing dissension within that body which may have been caused, at least in part, by the decision to build a new church at considerable expense. In 1749, the Assembly gave careful consideration to a "Petition of the Freeholders and Inhabitants of the upper Parish of Nansemond County, for dissolving the Vestry of that Parish, and making a new Election of Vestrymen in the said Parish", which its Committee of Propositions and

---

[24] *William Byrd's Histories of the Dividing Line Betwixt Virginia and North Carolina*, with Introduction and Notes by William K. Boyd (Raleigh, N. C., 1929), p. 68, 69, 78, 83. (This work is cited hereafter as Byrd.)

[25] Baskervill, p. 30, 33.

[26] *Vestry Book of the Upper Parish* (the printed text herewith), p. 14-15. (Cited hereafter as *V. B.*)

Grievances at first regarded as reasonable, but which, on further consideration, was rejected.[27] It appears, however, that the situation continued to worsen. On May 16, 1755, the House of Burgesses received "A Petition of several of the Vestrymen and other Freeholders in the upper Parish in Nansemond County, setting forth, That several of the Vestrymen of the said Parish are ancient, weak and infirm persons, That some others refuse to appear at the Vestries when legally called, and that there has been for some past, a Disagreement amongst the Members, so that the Petitioners imagine the Business of the said Parish is neglected, and praying that an Act may pass for dissolving the said Vestry, and that they may be impowered to elect twelve other Men, for Vestrymen of the said Parish," and "Ordered, That a Bill be brought in pursuant to the Prayer of the said Petition, and it is referred to Mr Riddick to prepare and bring in the same."[28]

Lemuel Riddick, burgess from Nansemond County and undoubtedly the vestryman of the Upper Parish, presented a bill, as directed, but, after a second reading, it was committed to Riddick and Anthony Holladay, the other Nansemond burgess and doubtless the vestryman of Suffolk Parish, amended, and passed as "An Act for dissolving the vestry of the upper parish in the county of Nansemond."[29] The preamble of this act, which somewhat changes and softens the language of the petition, states "it hath been represented to this Assembly, by several of the vestrymen and others of the upper parish, in the county of Nansemond, that many of the vestrymen of the said parish are old and infirm, and thereby rendered unable to perform their duty, and that others of the said vestry have refused to act as vestrymen, and have prayed to be dissolved." The act itself, after dissolving the existing vestry, provided that the "freeholders and housekeepers of the said upper parish, shall meet at some convenient time and place, to be appointed and publicly advertised, at least one month before, by the sheriff of the said county of Nansemond, before the first day of August next, and then and there, elect twelve of the most able and discreet persons of the said parish, to be vestrymen . . ."; and made the actions of the previous vestry in regard to the parish poorhouse binding on the new vestry, which was given specific authority "to levy a reasonable allowance"

---

[27] *Jour. House Bur.*, 1742-1749 (Richmond, 1909), p. 373, 378, 379.
[28] *Jour. House Bur.*, 1752-1758 (Richmond, 1909), p. 258.
[29] *Ibid.*, p. 261, 265, 267, 268, 272, 279; Hening, v. 6, p. 518-519.

for the education and maintenance of poor children placed therein.[30] The concern of the act with this parish venture indicates perhaps a leading cause of disagreement and dissatisfaction, probably due to the expense of the undertaking. The organization meeting of the new vestry immediately took up the matter of securing the coöperation and support of Suffolk Parish in this enterprise.[31]

It seems useless to speculate further as to the causes and results of this upheaval which has some curious aspects. Prior to the election, the only two vestrymen who had long absented themselves from meetings were John Norfleet, if still a member, and Lemuel Riddick himself, although the latter apparently had discharged some routine parish business. The election did not result in the choice of "twelve other Men". Of former members, it appears that six were returned and that several others were later appointed to vacancies. Most of the newly elected members bore the names of families prominent in the life of the vestry. In fact, in the absence of information as to parish politics and personalities, it seems that little was accomplished by the election of a new vestry.

The vestries seem to have been diligent and conscientious in promoting the religious life of the parish. They built and maintained a "handsome brick church" in Suffolk, the center of population, and erected chapels of ease, as needed, to serve remote sections. They strove constantly to provide the services of a minister, taking action to fill vacancies in the rectorate promptly rather than to economize by depending for long periods on lay readers, as was sometimes done elsewhere. They employed lay readers, who were regularly the clerks of churches and chapels, to conduct services at the various places of worship in the absence of the minister. But the vestries endeavored not only to encourage righteousness; they also sought, as their record shows, to discourage wickedness by punishing violators of the laws against vice. As appears later, they strove valiantly to maintain the parish under the great difficulties and discouragements incident to the American Revolution.

A very important duty of the vestry of each parish was the processioning of the bounds of every person's land which determined the record of land titles. Every fourth year, upon the order of the county court, the vestry, having divided its parish into precincts of convenient size, appointed

---

[30] Hening, v. 6, p. 518-519.
[31] *V. B.*, p. 99; *cf.* below, p. lx.

two freeholders of each precinct to conduct the processioning and report in writing to the vestry, which reports, or returns, were required "to be registred in particular books to be kept for that purpose, by the clerk of the vestry" and to be certified by the churchwardens. The law declared that processioning "at three several times" should be considered sufficient to fix boundaries unalterably.[32]

Processioning orders and returns are a notable feature of this vestry book, nearly half of it being devoted to such records. The volume therefore served both for entering the proceedings of vestry meetings and for registering the records of processioning. However, it is doubtful that it was the only register used for this purpose: all legal requirements were not met; in no case are there returns for all orders, in some cases there are few corresponding returns, and in one instance (the orders of November 23, 1743) there are no returns at all; and there is a reference in an order of August 31, 1747, to "the Register Book",[33] which moreover makes manifest the necessity of other records of the setting up of precincts, etc.

Whatever the reasons for using this vestry book for records of processioning, the result has been to provide for its period the names, and to some extent the location, of most of the land holders of the Upper Parish. At most processionings, the parish was divided into twenty-eight precincts or districts. Numbers 2 and 26 of the orders of November 23, 1743, constituted the part of the Upper Parish which was added to Suffolk Parish[34] in 1744, but the number of precincts was soon readjusted to twenty-eight. The order of April 14, 1784, shows an increase to thirty precincts to take in land which had "before been neglected."[35] The three returns at the end of the book are an incomplete record of processioning for which the vestry was no longer responsible.

Religion in the Parish

The rites and doctrine of the Church of England were brought to Virginia by the first settlers, and the laws and regulations of the early years of the colony had much to do with the maintenance of the orthodox

---

[32] Hening, v. 5, p. 426-428; and cf. Hening, v. 3, p. 529-531.
[33] *V. B.*, p. 24.
[34] *V. B.*, p. 24-25.
[35] *V. B.*, p. 252.

form of worship and with religious observance.[36] There can be little doubt, that the Anglican Church was established as a matter of course in the area of Nansemond County with the first permanent settlements and in conformity with existing law. It is probable that the first settlers, being few and widely scattered, were unable to build churches and enjoy the regular service of ministers, but that they met in private houses or rooms set apart for divine worship.[37] No church is mentioned in the act of 1643, dividing Upper Norfolk County into three parishes, although "the gleab and parsonage house that now is" were appropriated to the East Parish.[38] It seems evident from this that there was then a minister in Upper Norfolk County. It is probable that a church was soon built in the South or Upper Parish, perhaps the "old brick church" of a century later which must have been erected in the early years of the parish.

The church labored under severe handicaps in a sparsely settled land of great plantations. Parishes were very large, life isolated, and ministers difficult to obtain. The General Assembly took cognizance of such conditions in the act dividing Upper Norfolk County into parishes but the South or Upper Parish was nevertheless of great extent.

The laws enjoining religious observance and conformity to the canons of the Church of England in a time when religion was often more nominal than real provided fertile ground for pious Puritans, some of whom had settled in Upper Norfolk, or Nansemond, County. In 1642, these zealous nonconformists applied to Boston for Puritan ministers. Three came who preached to good crowds and, it is said, gained their strongest foothold in this county.[39] But they were soon obliged to leave, for a new and stringent act of 1643, probably aimed at them, required that all ministers should be "conformable to the orders and constitutions of the church of England, and the laws therein established, and not otherwise to be admitted to teach or preach publickly or privatly, And that the Gov. and Counsel do take care that all nonconformists upon notice of them shall be compelled to

---

[36] *Cf. Separation of Church and State in Virginia; a Study in the Development of the Revolution* by H. J. Eckenrode (Richmond, 1910), p. 5-9. (This work is cited hereafter as Eckenrode.)
[37] *Cf.* Hening, v. 1, p. 122-123.
[38] Hening, v. 1, p. 251.
[39] Eckenrode, p. 8-9; Dunn, p. 19; *Contributions to the Ecclesiastical History of the United States of America* by Francis L. Hawks. 2 v. (New York, 1836-39) V. 1: *A Narrative of Events Connected with the Rise and Progress of the Protestant Episcopal Church in Virginia*, p. 49-50. (This work is cited hereafter as Hawks.)

depart the collony with all conveniencie."⁴⁰ However, the Reverend Thomas Harrison, who had been minister of Elizabeth River Parish in Lower Norfolk County, preached openly in Nansemond as a Puritan for a number of years thereafter, and is said to have ministered to a flourishing church of that faith. It appears that he was summoned before the Colonial Council for nonconformity in April, 1645, but was not ordered to leave Virginia until 1648 after he had refused to use the Book of Common Prayer in accordance with an act of Assembly of 1647, designed to check a growing Puritanism, which provided moreover that in the case of ministers who did not read the "appointed and prescribed" prayers, the parishioners should be exempted from the payment of tithes.⁴¹ But there may have been other considerations in the banishment of Harrison, who, as a member of Cromwell's party, was a political undesirable in loyalist Virginia.⁴² It is said that the Reverend Thomas Bennett was another recusant minister in Nansemond County who became head of an Independent congregation and was banished in 1648.⁴³ Religious independence was then regarded as political disloyalty. It appears that these Independents in Nansemond County were generally suppressed with the further banishment of their teachers and the persecution of their adherents, a number of whom left the colony. Nevertheless it seems that many remained to provide a fruitful field of labor for the Quakers who became active in Virginia in the period of comparative toleration following the Puritan Revolution.⁴⁴

It was not only that the Quakers advocated democracy in church government, the equality of opportunity for religious expression, and the renunciation of the ritual of the Established Church; in the beginning, many members of this sect were fanatics who mocked the rulers and institutions of the colony, interrupted established forms of religious worship, and refused obedience to the law of the land. It appeared that the authorities had to deal with no mere question of religious conformity but with an

---

⁴⁰ Hening, v. 1, p. 277; Eckenrode, p. 9.

⁴¹ *Va. Mag.*, v. 53, p. 306-307; Dunn, p. 19; Hening, v. 1, p. 341-342; Eckenrode, p. 11.

⁴² Hawks, v. 1, p. 57-58; *Va. Mag.*, v. 53, p. 302, 304.

⁴³ *The Colonial Church in Virginia* . . . by Edward Lewis Goodwin (Milwaukee, 1927), p. 250. (This work is cited hereafter as Goodwin.)

⁴⁴ Dunn, p. 21, 23; *The Struggle of Protestant Dissenters for Religious Toleration in Virginia* by Henry R. McIlwaine. Baltimore, 1894 (*Johns Hopkins University Studies in Historical and Political Science*, 12th ser., iv), p. 28. (This work is cited hereafter as McIlwaine.)

attempt to subvert the authority of the civil government as well.⁴⁵ Although some Quakers were prosecuted and punished under existing law,⁴⁶ a special enactment against them was evidently considered necessary. Accordingly the General Assembly of March 1659/60 passed "An Act for the suppressing the Quakers" which imposed a heavy fine on any masters of vessels bringing Quakers into the colony; provided that all Quakers "as have beene questioned or shall hereafter arrive" should be apprehended and banished, proceeded against if they should return, and prosecuted as felons upon a third entrance; prescribed severe fines for persons entertaining Quakers or permitting assemblies of this sect in or near their houses; and prohibited the publication or distribution of their literature.⁴⁷

Following the Restoration, there were determined efforts to bring about the strict regulation and maintenance of the Established Church in Virginia. Most parishes were not supplied with ministers and many lacked glebes and churches. Few ministers of ability would forego good livings in England for a precarious service to vast, sparsely settled parishes in the colony where they would ordinarily be controlled by hardfisted and cautious vestries who exercised the right to employ ministers temporarily and not present them to the governor for induction and permanent tenure as the law and church system contemplated. Those ministers who did come were often lacking in qualifications and perhaps in character.⁴⁸ Authorities resigned themselves perforce to endure unworthy ministers in the knowledge that if all such were turned out the ranks of the clergy would be too badly depleted. Even the redoubtable James Blair, commissary or deputy in Virginia for the Bishop of London, was induced by "the want of Clergymen to fill the vacancies" to be forbearing in cases of clerical ill conduct unless "notoriously Scandalous."⁴⁹

Thoroughgoing measures indeed seemed necessary at a time of religious decline in the Church of England. Accordingly, the General Assembly, in

---

⁴⁵ Dunn, p. 23; McIlwaine, p. 26-27; Goodwin, p. 99.
⁴⁶ *Southern Quakers and Slavery, a Study in Institutional History*, by Stephen B. Weeks (*Johns Hopkins University Studies in Historical and Political Science*, extra volume XV), p. 14-16 (This work is cited hereafter as Weeks); cf. *Minutes of the Council and General Court of Colonial Virginia* (Richmond, 1924), p. 506.
⁴⁷ Hening, v. 1, p. 532-533.
⁴⁸ Eckenrode, p. 12-14; Hawks, v. 1, p. 88-90.
⁴⁹ *Papers Relating to the History of the Church in Virginia, A. D. 1650-1776*. Edited by William Stevens Perry (1870), p. 250-251. (This work is cited hereafter as Perry.)

1660-1662, passed many important laws which pretty well fixed the character of the church to the Revolution. The principal enactments, which dealt largely with subjects of earlier legislation, provided that vestries should each be limited in number to twelve persons, who were required to take the oaths of allegiance and supremacy and subscribe to be conformable to the doctrine and discipline of the Church of England, and have authority to fill their own vacancies; that the duties of vestries should consist of making and proportioning levies for building and repairing churches and chapels, providing for the poor, maintaining the ministers, whose salaries were fixed, and managing parochial affairs in general; that two churchwardens, chosen from each vestry, should be responsible for presenting offenders against morality, keeping up the churches and their ornaments, and conducting other business of the parish; that parishes should provide glebes, houses and maintenance for ministers; that churches or chapels of ease should be built; that lay readers should be appointed; that all ministers should present evidence of ordination by an English bishop and subscribe their conformity to the Church of England, the governor and Council being empowered to silence all other persons teaching or preaching publicly or privately; that Sabbath observance and church attendance should be enforced; that ministers should preach every Sunday; that the whole liturgy should be read, and no other catechism than that of the Church of England taught; and that no marriages should be solemnized or considered valid except when performed by lawful ministers.[50]

That religious conditions in Nansemond were considered bad and deserving of special legal action is revealed in an order of the General Assembly of September 10, 1663, in response to a report by a jury of inquest for the county: "Whereas there was presented to the Grand Assembly by the Jury of Inquest in Nanzemund Countie a list of severall persons, who contrarie to the Lawes of this Country, Some had totally absented themselves from the Church, and hearing of Divine service; Some onely neglecters to Come to Church, Some Quakers some that under pretence of marriage, Lived unlawfully together in fornication, the Court itselfe for not ordering the severall Vesstries to divide the parishes into precincts, for bounding of Lands, and the vestrie of Chuckatuck for not swaring Churchwardens, It is therefore Ordered that the severall persons,

---

[50] Hening, v. 2, p. 25, 29-30, 44-48, 49-52.

Court, and Vestrie be fined soe much as the perticular acts, against breach is by them made, doe impose upon them, and That the Court of Nanzemund doe ascertaine and issue out warrants to the Sherriff to Collect the same this present yeare, and that the Grand Jury Sherriff and Clerke of the s^d Countie be paide their reasonable penny worths out of those fines and that the rest be imployed at the discretion of the Court for pious uses in the same Countie."[51]

Fresh laws providing for the regulation of Quakers or other separatists, but not the banishment of those already in the colony, were passed at the March 1661/62 and September 1663 sessions of the General Assembly, but it seems that these were laxly enforced; in fact, the law of the latter year provided that, if convicted Quakers or other separatists should give security not to meet in unlawful assemblies (defined by the law as five or more persons aged sixteen or more), they should be discharged from all penalties.[52] Apparently the authorities did not interfere with the individual's religion unless he combined with others against the laws of the colony; it was against organized opposition to the government and institutions that the laws were evidently directed.[53]

Notwithstanding the efforts of the General Assembly, the Quakers continued to flourish and hold gatherings. Evidently they were tolerated by custom. In 1672, George Fox, the founder of the Society of Friends, visited Virginia. He held "large and precious" meetings in various places in Nansemond County, including the Upper Parish, which attracted many prominent people. It is apparent that the effects of Fox's labors were lasting and that Quaker sentiment remained strong in the county.[54]

This sect, which grew less aggressive with the passage of time, did not threaten the supremacy of the Established Church. It seems that the Toleration Act of William and Mary, passed in 1689, did not receive any formal statutory recognition in Virginia before 1699 but it is said that the Quakers had obtained practical recognition of their rights under it as early as 1692.[55] It appears that they increased rapidly in Nansemond County and were practically unmolested, except in the case of some obstreperous individuals who defied the laws and defamed the Established Church; in

---

[51] *Jour. House Bur.*, 1659-1693 (Richmond, 1914), p. 27.
[52] Hening, v. 2, p. 48, 180-183.
[53] McIlwaine, p. 21, 23; Dunn, p. 23.
[54] Weeks, p. 37-40; Dunn, p. 23, 25.
[55] Weeks, p. 149.

fact, it seems that their preachers, working amid a sympathetic population, made many converts.[56]

Quakers constantly protested their taxation for the support of the Established Church and some of them in Nansemond were distrained for refusing to pay what they termed "church rates" and "priest's wages."[57] Among the earlier protests to the General Assembly was one from Nansemond County. On August 20, 1736, the House of Burgesses "Resolved, That the Proposition from the County of Nansemond, from the People in that County, called Quakers, to be exempted from the Paiment of Parish Levies, except for the Maintenance of the Poor, be rejected."[58]

The activities of the Quakers in Nansemond County are responsible for providing an insight into religious conditions in that county during the first part of the eighteenth century. The Reverend Alexander Forbes, minister of the Upper Parish of Isle of Wight County, who had also officiated at a church in Nansemond County, stated in a letter to the Bishop of London, dated July 21, 1724: "In Nansimond a large Populous & wealthy County, the Quakers do sensibly encrease not only in offspring but also Proselytes; and so many are the offended Persons there high and low, at the Ministry of the Church, that I think, there wants but little more, than a learned, talkative, and Subtle Quaker Preacher to persuade a great number of them to Quakerism."[59] In this account, Forbes includes a statement on the "doleful Theme" of "the most unworthy and scandalous carriage of some Ministers of the Church who by their corrupt Conversation and vicious practice do demolish more in one year, than even a Wise Master Builder could re-edify in a much longer space of time: whose behavior is such that it greatly tends to confirm Atheists in their Infidelity and contempt of Religion, yea, to make Proselytes thereto, or to any party besides the Church of England, so that on occasion taken from these Men's offensive Carriage, the Doctrines of our Church, the discipline, and Ministry thereof have been lately reproached, slandered and impugned by a Quaker Teacher and that openly in the face of the County Court of Nansimond, and such are the natural fruits that do arise from the wicked lives of spiritual Guides in any such Church whatever, for when there is

---

[56] McIlwaine, p. 32; Dunn, p. 27; Perry, p. 333; and *cf. Exec. Jour.*, v. 4 (Richmond, 1930), p. 13, 67, 150.
[57] Weeks, p. 150-151.
[58] *Jour. House Bur.*, 1727-1740 (Richmond, 1910), p. 261.
[59] Perry, p. 333.

such obvious contradiction between the Doctrine and Practice of these men; even miracles could not maintain the Credit of that Church where such lewed and Profane Ministers are Tolerated or Connived at."[60]

Colonel William Byrd also, when running the dividing line with North Carolina in 1728, was moved by the presence of the Quakers to certain reflections on the state of religion in Nansemond County. He noted that that sect was quite strong in the Upper Parish, no less than two meeting houses being observed. In his sprightly manner, he remarked that "That persuasion prevails much in the lower end of Nansimond county, for want of Ministers to Pilot the People a decenter way to Heaven"; and he made the following comment on the situation: "The ill Reputation of Tobacco planted in those lower Parishes makes the Clergy unwilling to accept of them, unless it be such whose abilities are as mean as their Pay. Thus, whether the Churches be quite void or but indifferently filled, the Quakers will have an Opportunity of gaining Proselytes. Tis a wonder no Popish Missionaries are sent from Maryland to labour in this Neglected Vineyard, who we know have Zeal enough to traverse Sea and Land on the Meritorious Errand of making converts. Nor is it less Strange that some Wolf in Sheep's cloathing arrives not from New England to lead astray a Flock that has no shepherd. People uninstructed in any Religion are ready to embrace the first that offers."[61]

Byrd, who liked to jest at the expense of the clergy, was not speaking idly when he referred to the interdependence of tobacco and religion. According to a historian of the Quakers, "Dissenters were strongest in those counties that did not produce good tobacco, for the clergy of the Established Church were paid in this, went to the counties where the best was grown, and left the poorer counties to Dissenters and others."[62] Since the annual salary of the parson was fixed by law at 16,000 pounds of tobacco, the quality of that commodity had much to do with the supply and ability of ministers in the various parishes. North of James River, where the tobacco was better, parishes were more regularly supplied with ministers, and probably better ministers.[63] The land in Nansemond County, not being adapted to the cultivation of good tobacco, ministers there re-

---

[60] Perry, p. 332.
[61] Byrd, p. 68.
[62] Weeks, p. 153.
[63] McIlwaine, p. 34.

ceived a scant living. Alexander Forbes of the adjoining county of Isle of Wight had also referred, as follows, to the value of clerical salaries in his letter of July 21, 1724: "My Living (as of all ministers in the Colony) is 16,000 pds Tobacco valued by our antient laws at 80 lb. current money, i. e. about 65^{lb} Ster^g ... But the value of livings is very unequal because of the unequal value of Tobacco in different places of the Colony; on the North side of James River in many Parishes their Tobacco is sold at 20 sh^s per Hundred, so that Ministers' Salaries in those Parishes are worth 160 p^{ds} per ann^m and sometimes much more when Tobacco sells at the highest rate, and they have this advantage that their Tobacco seldom goes so low but that they have a competent living thereby. But on the South Side of James River the value of Tobacco is much inferior; for in most Parishes it rarely exceeds 10 sh^s a hundred and very often doth not amount to above one half that sum; so that instead of 80^{lb} we have but 40^{lbs} most commonly; except it be in some few Parishes."[64] It was less difficult to find ministers for the so-called "Sweet Scented" parishes where the tobacco was more valuable than for the "Oronoko" ones where the commodity was inferior. Writing to the Bishop of London in 1724, Commissary James Blair stated "We are in very great want of Clergymen, having now no less than five sweet scented Parishes and about double that number of Oranoco ones vacant, and the Presbyterians taking advantage of the want of Ministers are very busy, fitting up meetings in many Places where they had none heretofore."[65] Like Byrd, Blair observed that, a religious vacuum having been created, dissenting preachers rushed in.

Forbes and Byrd painted a dark picture of religious conditions in Nansemond County and its Upper Parish compounded of neglect and an unworthy ministry. It appears that Forbes was "not a mere complainant, but a very faithful and laborious man",[66] but his indignant indictment of "some Ministers of the Church" was probably influenced particularly by the character and conduct of his near neighbor, the Reverend Thomas Bayley, minister of the Lower or Newport Parish in Isle of Wight County, who also had Chuckatuck Parish, in Nansemond, under his care, preaching in the latter on a week day or sometimes on Sunday.[67] Bayley, who has

---

[64] Perry, p. 329.
[65] Perry, p. 318.
[66] Meade, v. 1, p. 302.
[67] Perry, p. 275; Meade, v. 1, p. 302.

been described as "a most notoriously wicked man"[68] must have been well known throughout Nansemond County, whose other parishes had probably experienced his ministrations at times; for he seems to have been one of those peripatetic preachers who sought the customarily liberal compensation for supplying vacant pulpits. Perhaps Alexander Forbes also had Bayley in mind when he wrote: "But it often falleth out, that we have void Parishes which are supply'd by Ministers invited thereto by the Parishioners, or else who offer themselves to serve such Parishes on some day of the Week they find most convenient. Where I must admonish your Lordships, that such proceeding is not always regulated in due and decent manner, for some undertake to serve so many vacant Parishes that they must of necessity neglect their own. I have also heard lately of a very unseemly and offensive contention at a certain Church before Sundry Spectators, between two ministers striving together which should be employed to supply the Vacancy."[69] It appears that there were "many grievous complaints" against Bayley who was "so very scandalous for drunkenness & fighting & quarreling publicly"; that he was charged before the Colonial Council of "many notorious immoralities & other offences", and turned out of his parish; that no parish at last would accept him; that he was "fined by King George County Court in 1726 for swearing twelve oaths in one day"; and that he was finally compelled to leave the country, on which occasion Governor Gooch wrote to the Bishop of London: "Was I to give your Lordship a Character of Mr Baylie a Clergyman who gos home in this Fleet, I could not say worse of him than he deserves."[70]

After the first quarter of the eighteenth century, the population of the colony increased rapidly, pushing the frontiers westward to the mountains and into the Valley of Virginia. Various dissenting sects developed, particularly in the midland and western counties, and increasingly challenged the Established Church. But it appears that there were, for many years, few dissenters in Nansemond County in addition to the Quakers[71] although

---

[68] Meade, v. 1, p. 302.
[69] Perry, p. 330.
[70] *The Colonial Clergy of Virginia. Addendum to Goodwin's List.* By G. MacLaren Brydon [Richmond, 1933], (typewritten volume of numbered leaves), l. 6. (This work is hereafter cited as *Colonial Clergy*); Perry, p. 252; *Exec. Jour.*, v. 4 (Richmond, 1930), p. 89; Goodwin, p. 249; *Va. Mag.*, v. 32, p. 224, 229.
[71] McIlwaine, p. 25, 30, 32, 33.

other sects were established there before the Revolution while Quakerism declined. The entire number of dissenters in the Upper Parish in 1778, when they were exempted by law from levies to support the Established Church, was comparatively small.[72]

Religion was in a low state in the eighteenth century. Among the English clergy, religious decay "manifested itself in formalism, sloth, and greed for preferment and emoluments, combined sometimes with gross laxity of life and conformity to the vices which permeated society."[73] In reaction to the religious and moral decline of the age, and to the formalism and rationalism of the Church of England, there came the evangelical revival which spread throughout the English colonies in America and has sometimes been called the "Great Awakening of 1740" although not confined to that year.[74] The formalism of the Anglican Church in Virginia could not prevail against the fervor of dissenters who came preaching a different and vital religion although many new parishes were organized and a more adequate supply of ministers was obtained. As for the character of the colonial ministers, there were some who fully justified the bitter observation of Bishop Meade, their severest critic, that there was "most evil living among the clergy."[75] The deeds of these unworthy ministers, often perpetuated in public records, brought discredit to the entire order. It appears, however, that the majority were good men. As a class, they seem to have performed faithfully the offices of the church and to have ministered to a society which "produced a noble breed of men in this age."[76]

The Upper Parish, however, was unfortunate in several of its ministers and Bishop Meade had grounds for his pessimistic conclusion in regard to its religious life: "The misconduct of several of the ministers, and several other circumstances, had combined for a long time to bring the Church and religion to a sad condition."[77]

MINISTERS

Information in regard to the early clergy of the Upper Parish is meagre and confused. There are apparently long periods in which the parish was without a minister although perhaps served at such times and to some

---

[72] *V. B.*, p. 240.
[73] Goodwin, p. 92.
[74] McIlwaine, p. 43-44.
[75] Meade, v. 1, p. 16.
[76] Eckenrode, p. 35-36.
[77] Meade, v. 1, p. 290.

extent by clergymen from other parishes. It is also the case that the names of parishes with their incumbent ministers were sometimes given erroneously in occasional, contemporary lists sent to the home authorities in England. Various sketches of individual clergymen admittedly embody much of conjecture. Under the circumstances, any account of the early ministers must be incomplete and may be, in some degree, inaccurate.

It seems probable that services by a minister were held in the area which became Nansemond County as early as 1635, or even earlier, since there was a land grant in that year on Nansemond River to George White, "Minister of the word of God," no doubt the same George White "of Nansamund Clarke" who seems to have been compensated for officiating in Lower Norfolk County in 1637.[78] That he was in the colony prior to 1635 is indicated in the proceedings of the Privy Council on the investigation of charges against Sir John Harvey, governor of Virginia, dated December 11, 1635, in which the governor denied that he had silenced "Mr. White, a minister" "for cursing of those of his parish"; but added: "That he could never see any orders albeit he had two years time to show his orders."[79]

The Reverend Roger Green, scholar, probable author, and leader in settling that part of Virginia on Roanoke River, was evidently in Nansemond County in 1653[80] but there is apparently no record until 1680 of the names of ministers in the particular parishes of the county.

"A list of the Parishes in Virginia," dated "June the 30th 1680,"[81] shows Mr. John Gregory as minister of the Upper Parish, Mr. John Wood as minister of the Lower Parish, and Mr. William Housden as minister of Chuckatuck Parish "who serves in Isle of Wight alsoe." There seems to be only the barest speculation in regard to Gregory's identity.[82] A list dated July 8, 1702,[83] shows the Upper, Lower and Chuckatuck parishes in Nansemond County but not the names of ministers. Possibly all three parishes were then without ministers. A list of February 25,

---

[78] *Va. Mag.*, v. 3, p. 188; *The Lower Norfolk County Virginia Antiquary*, v. 1, p. 82.
[79] *Va. Mag.*, v. 8, p. 405.
[80] Goodwin, p. 274-275; Hening, v. 1, p. 380-381.
[81] British Public Record Office, London (hereafter cited as P.R.O.) C.O. 1: 45 (photocopy in Archives Division of Virginia State Library); *Va. Mag.*, v. 1, p. 243.
[82] *Cf.* Goodwin, p. 275.
[83] "A List of the Parishes, Ministers, Tithables, Clergy, &c . . . in Virginia, July the 8th 1702," in *Va. Mag.*, v. 1, p. 373, 376, from P.R.O. C.O. 5: 1312, no. 38ii.

1704/5,[84] gives the names of James Burtell as minister of the Upper Parish and William Rudd as minister of the Lower Parish, but shows no minister for Chuckatuck Parish. But Burtell may have served the latter also for it appears that he appointed Chuckatuck Parish Church and July 5, 1705, as the place and date of a public disputation with the Quaker, Thomas Story. It seems that he is best known because of his controversy with Story who called him "the French Priest," meaning a Huguenot;[85] but he was also among the majority of ministers who opposed Commissary James Blair in his bitter and successful controversy with Governor Francis Nicholson who sought to exercise the right of presentation and induction of clergymen which would have given ministers permanent tenure instead of employment by the year.[86] According to the above-mentioned list, which is marked to indicate such information, neither Burtell nor Rudd had been inducted; in fact, the explanation of the symbols states that parishes so marked had "made excuse for not Inducting." An account of 1714[87] gives the names of Mr. Ransford,[88] minister of the Lower Parish, and Mr. Wallice,[89] minister of Chuckatuck Parish, but shows no minister for the Upper Parish. Thomas Hughes was minister of the Upper Parish, 1716-1719. It is stated that he received the King's Bounty[90] on January 31, 1715/16, coming to Virginia in 1716; and that he was minister in Abingdon Parish, Gloucester County, Virginia, probably from 1719 to 1744, and perhaps longer.[91]

A list of 1726[92] indicates that a Mr. Jones was then minister of Upper, Lower, and Chuckatuck parishes. This must have been Nicholas Jones who appears in 1729 as minister of Lower and Chuckatuck parishes, a Mr.

---

[84] "A List of the sev'll parishes within this her Matys Colony of Virginia with the names of the present Ministers thereof," dated "Feb: 25th 1704[/5]," P.R.O. C.O. 5: 1314 no. 43(iii) (a). (Photocopy of Library of Congress transcript in Archives Division of Virginia State Library.)

[85] *Colonial Clergy*, l. 15.

[86] Perry, p. 141-142, 142-143, 162-163.

[87] "The present State of Virginia for the year 1714 with respect to the Countys in particular," P.R.O. C.O. 5: 1317, p. 265 (Photocopy of Library of Congress transcript in Archives Division of Virginia State Library); *Va. Mag.*, v. 2, p. 9.

[88] Giles Rainsford as given in Goodwin, p. 301.

[89] Or Wallis, Samuel, according to Goodwin, p. 314.

[90] A payment toward traveling expenses to clergymen licensed to the colonies.

[91] Goodwin, p. 280; Meade, v. 1, p. 329.

[92] "The present State of Virginia with respect to the Colony in General," 1726. P.R.O. C.O. 5: 1320, p. 107 (Photocopy of Library of Congress transcript in Archives Division of Virginia State Library).

Smith being shown then as minister of the Upper Parish.[93] It appears that Nicholas Jones, recipient of the King's Bounty for Virginia, December 6, 1723, served in this section for a number of years,[94] being shown as minister of the Lower Parish in 1735 when Joseph Smith is given as minister for both the Upper and Chuckatuck parishes.[95] Possibly this was the Joseph Smith who received the King's Bounty for Virginia on September 21, 1727, and who has been identified as the unworthy clergyman referred to by Governor William Gooch in various letters to the Bishop of London in 1728-1738. Of "Mr. Smith," Governor Gooch wrote that he was "so very mean in appearance, in pocket so poor, and so little to say for himself, that no Parish would receive him"; that he was too infirm to serve the large parishes of Virginia; that, through the influence of the governor, he was being employed in 1728 in Williamsburg as lecturer and reader; that his "ignorance of the World very visible in his Conversation, and his great heedlessness in doing the duty of his Function" strongly prejudiced people against him; that the governor would be obliged to compel a parish to accept him; that he later (this letter is dated April 20, 1738) surrendered a parish rather than "submit himself to an Hearing in the Commissary's Court," having been "charged with grievous Crimes, and is such a Sott, and so weak in mind as well as Body, that he is neither fitt nor able to Serve a Cure"; and that the governor with some difficulty "prevailed with the Vestry to allow him something annually towards his Maintenance, and what it falls short must be made up some other way." The name of this parish is not given and it is stated that nothing is known of Smith beyond the references in Governor Gooch's letters, one of which gives the information that he died on May 12, 1738.[96]

From this characterization, it seems strange that this was the Joseph Smith who was serving as minister of the Upper Parish in 1729 and of both the Upper and Chuckatuck parishes in 1735, but this possibility is not contradicted by the known chronology of an unacceptable minister by the

---

[93] "The present State of Virginia with respect to the Colony in General Anno 1729." P.R.O. C.O. 5: 1322, p. 245 (Photocopy of Library of Congress transcript in Archives Division of Virginia State Library).

[94] Goodwin, p. 283; *Colonial Clergy*, l. 47; Meade, v. 1, p. 248.

[95] "A List of the Counties, Parishes and present Ministers of Virginia, Mar. 25, 1735." Fulham Mss. Virginia. Box III, No. 85 (Photocopy of Library of Congress transcript in Archives Division of Virginia State Library).

[96] *Va. Mag.*, v. 32, p. 221, 221, footnote, 223, v. 33, p. 51-53; Goodwin, p. 308.

name of Smith. On July 10, 1728, Governor Gooch had written "I shal at last I hope provide for Mr Smith, he is now gone to a Church upon tryal, where I have used great Interest with the Vestry to accept of him."[97] In 1734, Governor Gooch sent a Reverend Mr. Smith to St. George's Parish, Spotsylvania County, but his preaching was so much disliked that the vestry decided not to receive him as minister.[98]

When the vestry book opens, the Reverend William Balfour was minister of the parish. He may have been serving in that capacity since 1738 for Governor William Gooch had written the Bishop of London on August 25, 1738, stating that he had had a letter "from Mr Balfour wherein he desires me, now he is in Possession of a Parish, to Acquaint Your Lordship with it, Your Lordship having promised him, upon a Line from me setting forth his Settlement here, to procure for him the Royal Bounty, which he had not when Your Lordship Ordained him."[99] It appears that he received the King's Bounty for Virginia January 23, 1738/39.[100]

Governor Gooch had added in his letter "He is a very honest deserving Man, and I dare say will prove a diligent Minister,"[101] but this amiable prophecy was not fulfilled. At its meeting on April 16, 1745, the vestry ordered a special meeting at the Middle Chapel "to Enq^r in to the Behaviour of the Revd Wm Balfour Minister; who hath Bin Guilty of Drunkenness, p[ro]fane Swaring a[nd] Many Other Indecensess & hath failed in p[er]forming his Service at Church [&] Chapple Severall times, Therefore it is Ordered that the Church Wardens Serve the Said Mr Balfour with a Copy of this Order, And req^r that he [be] p[re]sent at Said Vestry to Answer Such things as Shall be Then & there said to his Charge."[102]

Evidently Balfour did not wish to face these charges as this meeting was not held, and he disappears from the scene. On December 4, 1745, the

---

[97] *Va. Mag.*, v. 32, p. 226.

[98] *St. George Parish, Spotsylvania County, Vestry Book, 1726-45* (photocopy of original manuscript in Archives Division of Virginia State Library) meeting of October 14, 1734; *History of St. George's Parish, in the County of Spotsylvania, and Diocese of Virginia* by Philip Slaughter (1890), p. 17; Meade, v. 2, p. 69.

[99] *Va. Mag.*, v. 33, p. 55.

[100] *Va. Mag.*, v. 33, p. 55n; Goodwin, p. 247.

[101] *Va. Mag.*, v. 33, p. 55.

[102] *V. B.*, p. 15-16.

vestry made an allowance to his executor for salary for eleven months.[103]

The parish was without a minister until it secured the services of the Reverend William Webb who was received by the vestry on August 31, 1747.[104] It appears that he had recently arrived in the colony, having been licensed for Virginia March 16, 1746/47 and having received the King's Bounty for Virginia April 7, 1747.[105] There is speculation as to whether he might have been one of the two of this name at Oxford in 1728 and 1730.[106] On the basis of the record in the vestry book, he served the parish faithfully for some thirteen years, taking an active part in its business affairs and being a constant attendant at vestry meetings, whose proceedings he invariably signed. He seems to have merited Bishop Meade's encomium, a "minister without reproof."[107]

Following the death of its minister, the Reverend John Mackenzie, the vestry of Suffolk Parish, on March 24, 1754, "agreed with the Revd Mr Webb to preech Sermonds in the S^d p[ar]ish, till Discharg^d by the Vestry, and that he preech the first Sermon, on Fryday Next at the Church on this Side the River and on Fryday Following at Chuckatuck Church, & after that to preech once a month." However, this turned out to be a short engagement since the vestry of Suffolk Parish soon secured a minister, the Reverend John Agnew, and paid William Webb for three sermons.[108]

It is stated that William Webb was the only one in a convocation of the clergy to oppose sending the Reverend John Camm to England to present an appeal to the king to veto the so-called "Two Penny" act.[109] If, as seems likely, his refusal to support this course was based on a conviction of the unwisdom of appealing to the English government over the heads of the colonial authorities, he nevertheless displayed rare courage

---

[103] *V. B.*, p. 16.

[104] *V. B.*, p. 24. On June 30, 1746, the vestry had ordered the churchwardens to "make a present to the Revd Mr Beckett in Gratuation to him for his Trouble in Coming into this p[ar]ish and preaching one Sermon three pistoles."—*V. B.*, p. 19. This was probably Rev. J. (or Thomas) Beckett who seems to have served at various times in several parishes and whose character also was not above reproach. *Cf.* Goodwin, p. 249; *Colonial Clergy*, l. 6; Meade, v. 1, p. 459, v. 2, p. 44, 76, 77; *Va. Mag.*, v. 32, p. 219, 332.

[105] Goodwin, p. 315.

[106] Goodwin, p. 315.

[107] Meade, v. 1, p. 290.

[108] *Suffolk Parish, Nansemond County, Virginia, Vestry Book, 1749-1856* (photocopy), p. [20], [21].

[109] Perry, p. 466.

and foresight in opposing a policy which was otherwise advocated unanimously by an assemblage of clergymen who were outraged by the law, but a policy which, as subsequent events proved, was to have such disastrous consequences for the clergy and the Established Church.[110]

William Webb evidently resigned as rector of the Upper Parish to become, on September 25, 1760, master of the Grammar School of the College of William and Mary, a post to which he had been elected by the college authorities on August 14, 1760.[111] The parish accounts of November 28, 1760, provided for the payment of his salary and allowances for three-fourths of the year.[112]

In the months while the parish was without a rector, the vestry sought the temporary services of various ministers. On November 28, 1760, it provided payment "To the Revd Mr Colmer for a Sermon Preach^d in the Church"[113] and ordered the churchwardens to "Aply to Mr Agnew and a Gree with him to Preach in our Church & Chapels."[114] However, it is probable that no such agreement was made because the parish secured a minister a few days afterward in the person of the Reverend Patrick Lunan who was "Receiv^d by this Vestry As Minister of this Parrish" on

---

[110] On account of a shortage of tobacco, the General Assembly, in 1755 and again in 1758, had passed a general but temporary law which permitted the payment of obligations due in that commodity at a commutation rate of two pence per pound. The clergy consequently received no compensating benefit by the rise in tobacco prices and considered, moreover, that these laws, which had not received royal sanction, violated the act of 1748, approved by the king, which had fixed their salaries in terms of tobacco. Their remonstrances against the law of 1755 had come to nought but, after the passage of the second of these "Two Penny" acts, a considerable number of them met in convocation at the College of William and Mary, drew up an appeal to the king, and chose Camm as their agent to present it at court. Camm, who has been called "an able and insinuating man" (Eckenrode, p. 23), was successful in having the acts of 1755 and 1758 disallowed, but this royal interference in local affairs aroused great bitterness in the colony, led to a pamphlet and newspaper controversy in which the clergy were violently assailed, provided grounds for unpopular suits to collect unpaid balances of clerical incomes, injured the prestige of the Establishment and the authority of the crown on which it sought to depend for protection, encouraged dissenters, and helped prepare the way for the Revolution.

The most celebrated of the court actions was the so-called "Parsons' Cause" in 1763 which brought Patrick Henry to public notice.

[111] *William and Mary College Quarterly Historical Magazine*, v. 3, p. 61, 130.

[112] *V. B.*, p. 151.

[113] *V. B.*, p. 152. This was probably Davis Colmer who, while chaplain to the Virginia Regiment in 1763, absconded, owing debts to several persons. *Cf. Jour. House Bur.*, 1761-1765 (Richmond, 1907), p. 247; *Colonial Clergy*, l. 19.

[114] *V. B.*, p. 153.

December 8, 1760, and subscribed to an understanding as to the times and places at which he should preach.[115] It appears that he had been licensed for Virginia December 23, 1759, and had received the King's Bounty for Virginia January 29, 1760;[116] and it is stated that he had served on trial for three months in St. Andrew's Parish, Brunswick County, in 1760, and had been rejected by the vestry.[117] The circumstances of his employment by the Upper Parish are not stated but, in the light of events, it seems that he must have been inducted by the governor, making him in effect the incumbent for life who could not be displaced by the vestry.[118]

Thus began the turbulent ministry of the Reverend Patrick Lunan who indeed seems to have achieved some sort of record in his time for clerical profligacy. During the early years of his ministry, there is only negative evidence of a lack of religious leadership, manifested in less frequent vestry meetings, which were rarely attended by the minister; but there must have been ample reason to question his rectitude long before the vestry took official action against him. Finally, at a special meeting on September 22, 1766, an outraged vestry "Ordered that A petition be drawn up to the Revd Commissary Robinson Seting forth the general behaviour & pray releif Against the Revd Patrick Lunan Which Pettion being drawn up by Lemuel Riddick With fourteen Charges[119] Alledg^d Against the Said Lunan & receiv^d in Vestry Was Approv^d of And ordered that Lemuel Riddick Wait on the Said Commissary with the Said petition & Cause the Said Lunan to be properly prosecuted thereon & Such Expences as May Arise by Occasion thereof is to be paid by the parrish."[120]

The vestry book does not disclose the result of this appeal to Com-

---

[115] *V. B.*, p. 153-154.
[116] Goodwin, p. 288.
[117] *Colonial Clergy*, l. 50; *cf.* Meade, v. 1, p. 478.
[118] The Reverend Gronow Owen, the minister who had served on trial in St. Andrew's Parish with the Reverend Patrick Lunan and is said to have also met with the disapproval of the vestry, had been inducted into that parish by the governor. Owen, an unworthy minister, continued as rector there until his death in 1769.—*William and Mary College Quarterly Historical Magazine*, v. 9, p. 161; *Colonial Clergy*, l. 61.

For brief discussions of the tenure of the clergy with respect to temporary employment, presentation, collation, induction, and visitation see Eckenrode, p. 10, 17-19, 21-22; Meade, v. 1, 149-151; *Va. Mag.*, v. 32, p. 214-216; Goodwin, p. 93; also "Godwin et al. v. Lunan," cited below, p. xl, n. 125.

[119] For charges against Lunan, as set forth in a report on his case before the General Court in October, 1771, see p. xli.

[120] *V. B.*, p. 177-178.

missary William Robinson, but since this deputy of the Bishop of London lacked the power to discipline or punish the clergy, any direct action on his part would have had no effect on a contumacious cleric; and a previous commissary had held that he did not possess the requisite powers to proceed judicially against an unworthy minister.[121]

On December 30, 1767, the vestry ordered that David Meade and Thomas Gilchrist, two of the vestrymen, should "Apply to Mr Attorney General & Mr Benj^a Waller & present them with the Alegations drawn up by the Vestry of this parish Against the Revd Patrick Lunan Minister of this parish And have there advice Concerning turning out the Said Lunan And the Said Mr Meade & Mr Gilchrist proceed according to the advice of the Said Attornies."[122] It appears that these representatives consulted the attorney general and George Wythe and obtained the advice that there was "cause of prosecution & that the same can be supported by the Laws of this Country." Consequently the vestry, at its next meeting on March 5, 1768, appointed David Meade to employ "such attornies as he may see fitt to manage said prosecution at the expence of this parish," which finding and instruction were embodied in as order signed by Jerimiah Godwin, churchwarden.[123]

Although there was no tribunal recognized as competent to punish unworthy ministers, there were precedents which indicated that, in the absence of any other authority, jurisdiction would fall to the General Court, the highest court of the colony, which had been concerned at times with ecclesiastical affairs.[124] Accordingly the case of the churchwardens and vestry of the Upper Parish against Lunan was brought before the General Court.

The report of this case by Thomas Jefferson[125] shows that the plaintiffs filed a libel in the General Court, as a court of ecclesiastical jurisdiction,

---

[121] Eckenrode, p. 28.
[122] *V. B.*, p. 184.
[123] *V. B.*, p. 186.
[124] *Cf.* Eckenrode, p. 28.
[125] "Godwin et al. v. Lunan" in *Reports of Cases Determined in the General Court of Virginia. From 1730, to 1740; and from 1768, to 1772* by Thomas Jefferson (Charlottesville, 1829), p. 96-108. (This work is cited hereafter as *Jefferson's Reports.*)

Jefferson's argument, but not his entire report of the case, is reprinted in his *Writings*, v. 1 (1892), p. 399-412, and in his *Works* (Federal Edition), v. 2 (1904), p. 16-35, both edited by P. L. Ford.

against Lunan "charging that he was minister of the gospel of Christ, regularly ordained, according to the rites of the church of England; that he was received to the care of the said parish; that he was of evil fame and profligate manners; that he was much addicted to drunkenness, in so much, as to be often drunk at church, and unable to go through divine service, or to baptize or marry those who attended for those purposes; that he officiated in ridiculous apparel unbecoming a priest; that he was a common disturber of the peace, and often quarrelling and fighting; that he was a common and profane swearer; that on the 10th of July 1767, and at other times, he exposed his private parts to view in public companies, and solicited negro and other women to fornication and adultery with him; that he neglected the parochial duties of performing divine service, preaching and administering the sacrament of the Lord's supper; that he had declared he did not believe in the revealed religion of Christ, and cared not of what religion he was so he got the tobacco, nor what became of the flock so that he could get the fleece." The libellants therefore "prayed that the said Patrick Lunan might be corrected, punished and deprived, or otherwise, that right and justice might be administered. The defendant pleaded to the jurisdiction of the court, and on that plea it came to be argued in October 1771."[126]

This case engaged the services of a number of distinguished lawyers, including George Wythe and Thomas Jefferson for the libellants; Richard Bland who, Jefferson states, "came to the bar as a volunteer in this cause";[127] and John Randolph, attorney general, for the defendant. It does not appear that Lunan was tried on the charges brought against him, the arguments of counsel being directed solely to the matter of determining the ecclesiastical jurisdiction of the court. Wythe sought to prove that the court possessed ecclesiastical jurisdiction, including the power to deprive ecclesiastics of their parishes. Jefferson, although he considered the ecclesiastical jurisdiction of the court established beyond a doubt, yet "conceived it did not follow thence that they might deprive the defendant of his parish, because visitation and deprivation are no parts of the office of an ecclesiastical judge." His argument, which constitutes the bulk of the

---

[126] *Jefferson's Reports*, p. 96-97.

[127] *Ibid.*, p. 108. Jefferson identifies him only as "Colonel Bland" but he was undoubtedly Richard Bland who had previously opposed the clergy vigorously in the controversy over the "Two Penny" act.

report, is a historical and legal dissertation on the kinds of parochial establishments and their patronage. It sought to prove that the churches of Virginia were of a class of which the king was patron, but that the members of the General Court, acting as the king's chancellor, might exercise the right of visitation "not indeed sitting on this bench as a court of chancery, but as a court of visitation at any other time or place, at which you shall think proper to call the incumbent before you." Colonel Bland, in contradiction to Jefferson, maintained that the churches of Virginia were of a kind peculiar to themselves and contended that, as a result, the right of visitation was in the vestries. It appears that John Randolph, attorney general, confined himself entirely to answering Wythe as the others "had declared against the jurisdiction of the court in this particular case, and so far were in favor of his client," but "he contended further that this court had not a general ecclesiastical jurisdiction."[128]

The court adjudged that "they possessed ecclesiastical jurisdiction in general, and that as an ecclesiastical court they might proceed to censure or deprive the defendant, if there should be sufficient cause. But on the importunity of the Attorney General, a re-hearing was granted."[129]

No further account of this case has been found, which is probably due to the destruction of the great mass of the records of the General Court in 1865; but it appears from a statement of Richard Bland, probably made in 1773, that the court "disaffirmed their jurisdiction in such cases."[130] At any rate, Lunan was not deprived of his parish and seems to have continued on his robustious and uninhibited course.[131]

---

[128] *Ibid.*, p. 97, 108.
[129] *Ibid.*, p. 108.
[130] *To the Clergy of Virginia* by Richard Bland (1773?), p. 2.
[131] In *The Virginia Gazette* (Williamsburg, Purdie & Dixon), December 3, 1772, p. [2], and December 10, 1772, p. [3], there is the following notice:

Suffolk, November 16, 1772.

Mess. Purdie & Dixon,
Gentlemen,
 I keep a Tavern in the Town of Suffolk, and have always behaved so as to give Satisfaction to my Customers. In the Month of September last the Reverend Patrick Lunan came to my House, and stayed four Days, treating every Person that would condescend to drink with him, until his Account amounted to two Pounds fourteen Shillings and ten Pence current Money. When I demanded my Money, he refused Payment: I brought a Petition against him in this County Court; he employed an Attorney, and took Shelter under the Act of Assembly where no more Credit than twenty Shillings is to be given to any one

Thrown back on its own resources, the vestry, at the time of making the parish levies on November 25, 1772, decided, Lemuel Riddick dissenting, to provide no tobacco to pay the salary and perquisites of "the Revd Patrick Lunan present Minister of this parish on Account of his Ill behaviour and Neglect of duty in the Churches."[132] Since Lemuel Riddick had drawn up the original indictment of Lunan by the vestry for presentation to the commissary, his dissent from this decision must have been due to his disbelief in the advisability of this action rather than any concern for Lunan. There were ominous provisions in the law that the minister was "entitled to all the spiritual and temporal benefits of his parish" and was authorized to "maintain an action of trespass, against any person or persons whatsoever, who shall disturb him in the possession and enjoyment thereof"; and that "if the vestry of any parish shall neglect or refuse to levy the tobacco due to the minister, or other parish creditors, in such case, all and every the vestrymen of the parish neglecting, or refusing, shall be liable to the action of the party grieved, his, or her executors, or administrators, for all damages which he or she shall sustain by such refusal or neglect."[133] At its next meeting, on January 2, 1773, the vestry recorded its opinion "that the Church W^{ds} Refuse the Revd Patrick Lunan admittance in any the Churches or Chappels in this parish to preform divine Service on Account of his Ill behaviour & Neglect of duty," to which Lemuel Riddick, Willis Riddick and Thomas Norfleet dissented.[134]

Pursuing its policy of dispensing with Lunan's ministrations, the vestry sought the services of temporary substitutes. On March 15, 1774, it "orderd that the Ch: Wardens do apply to & agree with the Reverend Mr John Agnew to preach once a Month at Suffolk Church & also at the Cyprus Chapel & to agree with the Reverend Mr Burgess to preach once a Month at the Holy Neck Chapel."[135] The record shows no service by the latter

---

Person. The Attorney, at the same time, declared he acted by the particular Direction of his Client. I now desire of you, Gentlemen, to insert this in your Gazette, that thereby others in my Situation may know how to treat him, the said Mr. Lunan, for the future; and you will oblige   Your humble Servant,
                            William Dixon.

[132] *V. B.*, p. 218.
[133] Hening, v. 6, p. 89, 90.
[134] *V. B.*, p. 221.
[135] *V. B.*, p. 225. John Agnew was still minister of Suffolk Parish; and Henry John Burgess (Burges) was then minister in Newport Parish, Isle of Wight County. —Goodwin, p. 245, 256.

but the parish accounts of December 17, 1774, include an item of £ 10 in payment to Agnew for five sermons.[136] It was also ordered, on March 21, 1775, that the Reverend Mr. Duncan should be paid "the Sum of £ 6 for 3 Sermons preach'd at Suffolk Church & Cyprus Chapel."[137]

At the latter meeting, however, the vestry "reciev'd the Reverend Wm Andrews as Minister of this Parrish for one Year," and agreed "to pay him the sum of £ 128 Current Money for Services hereafter Mentioned, He is to perform One Sunday at Suffolk Church, One Sunday at Holy Neck & the Next Sunday at Suffolk Church, And the Next Sunday at the Cyprus Chapel and so to Continue the year out, Good friday and Christmas to preach at Suffolk Church."[138] Evidently the vestry was well satisfied with Andrews because on December 19, 1775, he was "Recieved as Minister of this Parrish."[139]

It is stated that Andrews was a native of Ireland who, after having been some time in America, returned in 1770 for ordination, being licensed by the Bishop of London for New York, June 10, 1770; that he was appointed missionary to the Indians by the Society for the Propagation of the Gospel, being stationed (1770-1773) at Schenectady, N. Y., where some of his relatives probably resided; that he opened a grammar school in the fall of 1771; that ill health and perhaps other causes led him, in 1773, to resign his charge there and migrate to Virginia; that he resided for a time at Williamsburg; and that he became minister of Nottoway Parish, Southampton County.[140]

---

[136] *V. B.*, p. 226.

[137] *V. B.*, p. 228. This was probably Rev. William Duncan whose name appears in an assessors book of the Isle of Wight County for 1778 as a "recusant" who had declined or neglected to take the oath of allegiance to the state and was therefore subjected to double taxes.—*William and Mary College Quarterly Historical Magazine*, v. 25, p. 170.

[138] *V. B.*, p. 227-228.

[139] *V. B.*, p. 231.

[140] *Va. Mag.*, v. 41, p. 20-21 (sketch by Brydon); *Annals of the American Pulpit* by William B. Sprague, v. 5 (1869), p. 91, footnote; *American Loyalists. Transcript of the Manuscript Books and Papers of the Commission of Enquiry into the Losses and Services of the American Loyalists held under Acts of Parliament of 23, 25, 26, 28 and 29 of George III. preserved amongst the Audit Office Records in the Public Record Office of England 1783-1790. Volume 58. Examinations in London. Memorials, Schedules of Losses and Evidences. Virginia Claimants in two books (Book i).* Transcribed for the New York Public Library, 1901 (microfilm copy in Archives Division of Virginia State Library; cited hereafter as *American Loyalists*, v. 58) p. 378. Bishop Meade states "in the year 1776, the Rev. William

In the meantime, it appears that the vestry had been making every effort to get rid of Lunan. At the meeting on March 21, 1775, at which Andrews was first received, it had "Order'd the Church Wardens apply to Mr Lunan to give up the Gleab & to have it put in repair for the Reverend Wm Andrews As it appears to this Vestry that it is of not much Use to the said Mr Lunan and that there is much danger of the House being destroy'd by fire and of its going to ruin On Account of some person to Live in it it appearing that Mr Lunan is Seldom at home and in Case he refuses to give up the Gleab to take possession."[141] The vestry evidently prosecuted him on various charges and, in turn, was probably sued by him for the "temporal benefits" assured by law to the minister of the parish. The vestry finally compounded his claims in a settlement which must have appealed to this clergyman who was, so to speak, minister with portfolio but without the emoluments of office, ordering, on September 30, 1775, "that the Ch Wardens do pay to the Reverend Patrick Lunan the sum of £ 100 the Money that was Levied Last fall &c In June 1777 to pay the sum of £ 100 more and in June 1778 to Recieve the Last payment of £ 100 more Exclusive of Interest Which makes the sum of £ 300 Likewise to discharge the said Lunan of all costs that may or shall accrue from Lawsuits that are Commenc'd by the Parrish against the said Lunan on his giving a proper Relinquishment of all Immunities emoluments or Claims that he the said Lunan hath or ever shall have in or against this parrish as a Minister."[142] In consideration of this settlement, Lunan, with witnesses, signed the following relinquishment: "Septr 30th 1775 The Reverend Patrick Lunan, claiming to be Rector of the Upper parish in Nansemond, appeard this day in Vestry, & hereby Relinquishes all Right, Title & Claim as Rector of the said Parish."[143]

These sums were duly paid[144] and the claims of this tenacious clergyman came to an end. Apparently he continued to reside in the parish since an action, which evidently commended itself to the vestry, provided a

---

Andrews takes the place of Mr. Agur in Nottoway parish," Southampton County (Meade, v. II, p. 307-308) which must have been in error as to the date. No vestry book of Nottoway Parish of this period is known to be extant.

[141] *V. B.*, p. 228.
[142] *V. B.*, p. 228.
[143] *V. B.*, p. 229.
[144] *V. B.*, p. 238, 239.

record on March 14, 1782, of a payment "To Mr Patrick Lunan for burying a poor Woman."[145]

Like various other Anglican ministers who would not renounce allegiance to the king, the head of the Established Church, the Reverend William Andrews refused to support the independence of the colonies; and being an uncompromising and outspoken loyalist, who asserted afterward that he had always included the king and refused to include the Congress in reading the prescribed form of prayer, he had his troubles as rector of the Upper Parish, apparently being threatened in the church with death by an ardent patriot on one occasion in 1776 because of his intransigent orthodoxy.[146]

It was probably due to his difficulties that he soon accepted the ministry of Albemarle Parish, Sussex County, tendered to him by resolution of the vestry of that parish on July 18, 1776, "upon the special conditions that he accommodate himself at his own expence, with a House to reside in, till Miss^rs Willie Our late incumbents Widdow removes from the Glebe, which is expected at Xmas, and allso that he will submit to be upon the same foundation with the rest of the Clergy in this Government, as the common Wealth of Virginia"; and this formal invitation of the vestry also instructed the churchwardens to "Write to Mr Andrews the contents of this resolution and request him to remove and perform divine service in this Parish as soon as possible."[147] It seems that he assumed the duties of his new position on October 1, 1776,[148] but soon returned to his previous charge, since the vestry of the Upper Parish, on December 28, 1778, provided £400 for his salary,[149] an increase which must have reflected, in part at least, the influence of inflation and the lack of a glebe.[150] But this seems to have marked the end of his ministry there and, indeed, the end of the ministry of the Established Church in the Upper Parish so far as the vestry book shows. If the parish thereafter enjoyed any services by clergymen of its faith, these must have been compensated by voluntary contributions since the laws of the Revolutionary state government had put an end

---

[145] *V. B.*, p. 247.
[146] *American Loyalists*, v. 58, p. 378-379.
[147] *Albemarle Parish, Surry & Sussex Counties, Virginia, 1742-1787 . . . Vestry Book* (photocopy of original manuscript in Archives Division of Virginia State Library), pt. II, p. [296].
[148] *Ibid.*, p. [299]; *Colonial Clergy*, l. 2; and cf. *V. B.*, p. 229, 236.
[149] *V. B.*, p. 240.
[150] The glebe had been "rendered totally unfit for the reception of a Clergyman." Cf. p. 65, 68.

to the levying of taxes for religious purposes and for the payment of ministers' salaries.

It appears that Andrews was appointed minister of Portsmouth Parish by the vestry in 1779, a position which not only provided a better living than that of the Upper Parish but also afforded, in troublous times, a better opportunity to flee the country.[151] But in Portsmouth as at Suffolk, he evidently experienced some of the harsh consequences of his freely expressed views, declaring later that he was knocked down in the street in 1780 during a celebration of the Declaration of Independence for publicly stating that that instrument was "both improper and impolitick."[152] He stated that he proffered his service to the British force under General Benedict Arnold which occupied Portsmouth in January 1781; that he was appointed chaplain to the garrison there; that his influence as rector and his knowledge of the country made him useful in promoting the royal cause; that he joined the British army under General Cornwallis and was continued as chaplain at Yorktown; that after the surrender there he went immediately to Portsmouth in order to remove his distressed family to New York, and was thereupon imprisoned, tried for his life, but not convicted, and banished; and that these things happened when his wife was suffering from an "obstinate disorder" of which she died, leaving two small children.[153]

Much might be added to Andrews' condensed account of what happened to him after Yorktown. It appears that he was paroled and delivered to the civil authorities for trial; and that his case was referred to the governor and Council of State which received pleas in his behalf from those who upheld his steadfast character as "a worthy clergyman" whose Christian and humane principles had been constantly demonstrated in his service to American prisoners of the British, declared that his only fault was "differing in opinion from us," set forth the distressing condition of his family, and represented his wife as being "a bigot" in favor of American independence.[154] But there was also a complaint from local officers that Andrews, having returned to Norfolk County after the surrender of the

---

[151] *American Loyalists*, v. 58, p. 378, 379, 382.
[152] *Ibid.*, p. 379.
[153] *Ibid.*, p. 372-373, 377, 379-380.
[154] *Official Letters of the Governors of the State of Virginia*, v. 3 (Richmond, 1929), p. 90; *Calendar of Virginia State Papers and Other Manuscripts* (cited hereafter as *Calendar*), v. 2 (Richmond, 1881), p. 589, 613. Andrews had evidently married again as it appears that a former wife had died in 1775.—*Colonial Clergy,*

British army at Yorktown, was performing some of his ministerial functions there, and that his influence might have bad effects on the allegiance of the people to the American cause. These officers therefore suggested that he should be suspended or silenced.[155] Andrews, apparently conforming to a suggestion made by the governor through these officers, applied on April 16, 1782, for a passport to leave the state "where my conduct has been lately obnoxious."[156] On April 24, 1782, the Council of State gave permission "to the Reverend William Andrews, his Wife Children & one servant" and to several others "to go to New York no more to return to this State."[157] It seems that Andrews was unable to avail himself of the permission so given, evidently being in the custody of the law on a charge of treason from which a passport did not absolve him. Since it appeared that the executive had the certain power to pardon those accused, but not convicted, of treason, the governor and Council decided to dispose of Andrews' case by this means. On June 15, 1782, the Council considered "a representation in behalf of the Reverend William Andrews now under confinement,

---

l. 2. In his evidence before the Commission of Enquiry into the Losses and Services of the American Loyalists, Andrews stated that his wife was "remarkably rebelliously inclined," and that the interest and influence of her family had enabled him to stay in Virginia.—*American Loyalists*, v. 58, p. 379. He had evidently married Elizabeth Conner (Connar). Cf. *Albemarle Parish, Surry & Sussex Counties, Virginia. Parish Register, 1739-1778* (photocopy of original manuscript in Archives Division of Virginia State Library) pt. II, p. [59; or, under a different pagination, 159]; *American Loyalists*, v. 58, p. 381.

[155] *Calendar*, v. 3 (Richmond, 1883), p. 410-411. The original, undated letter in the *Executive Papers* in the Archives Division of the Virginia State Library is endorsed on the back to the effect that it was answered on January 25, 1782. Therefore the marginal annotation of December 1782, instead of 1781, in the *Calendar* is erroneous and misleading. A copy of this answer has not been found but it is apparently referred to in Andrews' letter of April 16, 1782, to the governor complaining that the information therein had been long withheld from him. This error seems to have given rise to the belief that Andrews soon returned to Norfolk (Portsmouth Parish was in Norfolk County) and resumed his "professional labors without interference" after having been granted permission to leave the state. Cf. *The Revolution in Virginia*, by H. J. Eckenrode (Boston and New York, 1916), p. 285. (This work is cited hereafter as *Revolution in Virginia*); *Va. Mag.*, v. 41, p. 21. Andrews may have also opened a school in Portsmouth; and he may have conducted one there previously. Cf. *Calendar*, v. 2, p. 589; *American Loyalists*, v. 58, p. 373.

[156] Original letter in *Executive Papers*. Cf. *Calendar*, v. 3, p. 131, where the date of the letter is erroneously given as April 15. Prior to this date, apparently, Andrews had appeared before the governor and Council of State. Cf. *American Loyalists*, v. 58, p. 376; *Calendar*, v. 2, p. 589, 613.

[157] *Council Journals from Decr 1st 1781 to [November 16th 1782]* (manuscript volume in Archives Division of the Virginia State Library), p. 132.

on a charge for high Treason" and advised "his Excellency to grant him, the said William Andrews, a pardon, on condition that he leave the State no more to return."[158]

Andrews went with his children to New York[159] and thence to Great Britain where he later presented a claim for £1754 to the Commission of Enquiry into the Losses and Services of the American Loyalists for losses suffered by reason of the American Revolution and his support of the royal cause: income and property (including books and slaves); and expenses due to imprisonment, trial and journeys from Virginia to Great Britain.[160]

CHURCHES AND CHAPELS

When the vestry book opens, in 1743, there is mention in processioning orders 3 and 4 of "the Brick Church", the principal place of worship, which was already old and no longer near the center of population of the parish. The landmarks of that day now provide an uncertain and perhaps erroneous location for this church but recent investigations have located the site on the Western Branch of the Nansemond River about seven miles north of Suffolk.[161]

It is probable that the condition as well as the location of this old church influenced the vestry in its decision to build a new church and to levy funds at various times for its construction. The vestry met on September 1, 1746, in order "to Appoint a place for the Building & Eretting a Church for this p[ar]ish and to Agree Upon the Dementions, &c" but, several members being absent, deferred action until October 7, 1746, when a majority agreed to build "a New Brick Church in the Old field of James March Convenient to a good Spring." Several vestrymen were delegated to attend to the details of acquiring the site, providing "A plan of a Church of the Valeeu of & Not Exceeding five Hundred pounds", and advertising the undertaking.[162]

---

[158] *Ibid.*, p. 182; *cf. Calendar*, v. 3, p. 193-194. It appears that his pardon, signed by Governor Benjamin Harrison, was dated June 17, 1782. *Cf. American Loyalists*, v. 58, p. 380.

[159] This city was not evacuated by the British until after the signing of the definitive treaty of peace in 1783.

[160] *American Loyalists*, v. 58, p. 373-377, 380-382.

[161] *V. B.*, p. 2-3; and *cf.* processioning orders No. 2 and No. 3 on p. 58, and return on p. 82; *Colonial Churches of Tidewater Virginia*, by George Carrington Mason (Richmond, Va., 1945), p. 181. (This work is cited hereafter as Mason.)

[162] *V. B.*, p. 19, 20.

There was evidently much dissatisfaction, perhaps shared by several vestrymen, with this decision to build a new church, probably deriving from both the location and the levies for expenses. At its meeting on April 29, 1747, the Colonial Council had before it "the Petition of several Inhabitants of the upper Parish of Nansemond praying Releif against an Order of Vestry for levying 16000 w^t of Tobacco to build a Church &c" and "Ordered That the Churchwardens of the said Parish be summoned to answer the Subject Matter of the said Petition the next Court of Oyer and Terminer." The churchwardens appearing on June 10, 1747, the Council, "having heard the Parties on both sides and duly Considered the Subject matter of the s^d Petition", ordered "That a Map of the Parish be drawn and laid before this Board in next October Court in Order to fix the most Convenient place for building a new Church And that they may proceed in the mean Time in making the Levies for defraying the Expence thereof."[163]

Although the vestry continued to levy tobacco toward the expense of building a new church, the proposed location was evidently abandoned in favor of the town of Suffolk which had become a center of population. On October 14, 1748, the vestry declared "that a handsome brick Church ought to be Built in this Parish", and appointed the Reverend William Webb, minister, David Meade, Jethro Sumner, Daniel Pugh and Josiah Riddick, vestrymen (of whom any three could act) as directors for carrying out the undertaking. The directors were instructed to apply to Jethro Sumner, who does not seem to have been present at the meeting, and Margaret, his wife, "and Endevour to purchase two Acres of Land at the head of Suffolk Town." The church was to be built according to "the Plan already drawn" and to be completed in four years. The right to build a private gallery "in one of the Crosses or wings of the Church Oposite to the front Door" was given Lemuel Riddick for £20, "which money is to be Laid out for Church Ornament"; and a similar privilege was accorded David Meade "on the Oposite Wing" in return for "A sufficient bell for the said Church and fiting the same."[164]

The directors reported at the next meeting of the vestry on March 28, 1749, that Jethro Sumner had "refused to sell the said Land at a moderate Price" and were "Impowered to treat with any other person or persons for

---

[163] *Exec. Jour.*, v. 5 (Richmond, 1945), p. 233, 238-239.
[164] *V. B.*, p. 46-47.

the purchase of Two Lots of Land in any part of Suffolk Town that they shall think proper."[165] Since there is no separate record in the vestry book of payment for a site, the land was probably purchased from Daniel Pugh who became the builder of the church.[166] On May 23, 1751, some of the specifications affecting walls and windows were changed,[167] indicating that the building had not then progressed far. It seems to have been completed by July 26, 1753, when the vestry ordered that Daniel Pugh should be paid "the Ball^e due for the Building the Church in Suffolk", and reconciled its account with him.[168] However, various changes and improvements continued to be made. At this same meeting the vestry ordered "that John Watson & Alexander Cairnes, have Leave to Build a Pew in the South end of the Parish Galere" for which they were to pay "Six Pound Sterling, to be laid out in Ornaments for the Church"; and this money was evidently used, in part at least, to buy "A foilio Bible And two foilio prayer books."[169] In the course of time, an adjoining lot was purchased;[170] the church yard seems to have been fenced in several times;[171] a pipe organ was installed;[172] a communion cloth and marble font were bought;[173] and probably "A sufficient bell" secured.[174] The "handsome brick Church" must have been realized both in appearance and appointments. A recent investigator has stated that it "stood on the west side of what was formerly known as Back Street, but is now called Church Street, the existing

---

[165] *V. B.*, p. 48. Jethro Sumner and his wife Margaret, to whom certain lots were reserved when the town of Suffolk was established on fifty acres of which he was part owner in right of his wife, were probably dissatisfied with the prices previously paid. He had evidently felt aggrieved by the act of the General Assembly in 1742, which established the town and set the price of the land at £3 an acre. In order to quiet the claims of his wife Margaret and to dispose of various controversies and doubts concerning titles, the General Assembly in 1744 had directed that a further sum of £100 should be paid him by the trustees appointed for the town (Hening, v. 5, p. 199-202, 241-244). In 1746, the House of Burgesses rejected a petition of Jethro Sumner in which he stated that he had not been paid all of this sum. (*Jour. House Bur.*, 1742-1749 (Richmond, 1909), p. 208). In 1761 or 1762 the vestry paid £12.10s. for a lot adjoining the church site (*V. B.*, p. 156).

[166] The cost of the site may have been included in his contract. An adjoining lot was bought from him in 1761 or 1762 (*V. B.*, p. 156).

[167] *V. B.*, p. 54-55.
[168] *V. B.*, p. 88, 89.
[169] *V. B.*, p. 88-89, 93.
[170] *V. B.*, p. 156.
[171] *Cf. V. B.*, p. 128, 133, 184.
[172] *Cf. V. B.*, p. 86, 91, 159, 162, 201, 206, 220.
[173] *V. B.*, p. 86.
[174] *Cf. V. B.*, p. 241.

Western Avenue having been cut through its site in modern times."[175]

The occupancy of the new church probably marked the virtual abandonment of the old brick church, whose ornaments were brought to Suffolk.[176] On October 14, 1748, the vestry had voiced its "Opinion the Old brick Church is useless" and ordered "that the Ministor do not Preach any more there, but that he Preach two Sundays, at the middle Chapple and one at the Sommorton Chappell untill such time as the upper New Chappell is Built."[177] This order, which must have provoked prompt protests from parishioners living near the old church, was revoked at the next meeting of the vestry on March 28, 1749,[178] and the church and its services were evidently maintained until 1753, after which it seems that the building gradually fell into ruins although apparently accounted for many more years as one of the parish churches.[179]

The vestry book lacks explicitness in identifying and locating some of the various chapels of ease which were built for the convenience of those living at a considerable distance from the parish church. The financial account and proceedings of the vestry, November 3, 1744, refer to the Lower Chapel, the Upper Chapel, the Middle Chapel and Somerton Chapel.[180] The Lower Chapel disappears from the record; it may have been in that part of the Upper Parish which was united to Suffolk Parish on November 20, 1744.[181] The Middle Chapel is mentioned until 1752 but was probably abandoned after the completion of the new church in Suffolk in 1753, when Henry Gwin, who had been serving as sexton, was allowed 5 s. for "bringin down the Ornam^{ts} of the Chapell."[182] Although the vestry book, until 1778, contains references to "the" chapel, it is apparent in a number of instances that the clerks or vestries thus referred

---

[175] Mason, p. 183.
[176] V. B., p. 91.
[177] V. B., p. 47.
[178] V. B., p. 48.
[179] Cf. V. B., p. 218, 221.
[180] V. B., p. 12-14.
[181] Mason (p. 184) states: "It is apparent from the vestry record that the Lower Chapel soon became known as the Middle Chapel, perhaps to distinguish it from the Old Brick Church, which was the Lower Church of the parish"; and he gives (p. 185) the site of the Middle Chapel as now being "in a cornfield on the east side of State Route 53, nearly opposite the present Liberty Spring Christian Church and about three miles north of Whaleyville", in what would have been considered the middle section of the parish. So far as the meager record of the Lower Chapel shows, the two chapels were then coexistent.
[182] V. B., p. 91.

to whatever chapel they had in mind; but in the beginning, at least, the Middle Chapel seems to be identified sometimes with "the" chapel.[183]

The Upper Chapel, which appears in the vestry records until 1754, was evidently replaced by a new chapel, ordered by the vestry on December 19, 1747, to be located "at a place Called Holy Neck on the Back swamp."[184] This order gives the dimensions of the proposed chapel and specifies that a gallery is to be constructed at one end. It appears from the proceedings of the vestry, October 14, 1748, that this "upper New Chappell" had not then been built but it is referred to as Holy Neck Chapel in processioning order No. 12 of October 21, 1751.[185] It must have been completed about this time for the parish account of November 30, 1752, provides payment to the clerk of Holy Neck Chapel for service for thirteen months.[186] It is said that the name was traditionally derived from the fact that the Indians held religious rites at the place and regarded the spot as sacred.[187] The vestry book mentions Holy Neck Chapel until December 28, 1778, but it probably fell into disuse soon afterward. It is said to have been used later by other sects.[188]

It has been stated that the Upper Chapel, whose site lies "about a quarter mile east of Somerton village", "soon came to be known as Somerton Chapel"; and that Holy Neck Chapel "succeeded Somerton Chapel as the upper chapel of ease for the parish and, being situated only three miles northwest of Somerton village, also came to be known as Somerton Chapel."[189] An upper chapel, near Somerton, may have come to be known as Somerton Chapel many years before the beginning of the vestry book,[190] but the Upper Chapel of the vestry record seems to have been coexistent with Somerton Chapel until 1754 when it was evidently replaced by Holy

---

[183] *Cf.*, for example, *V. B.*, p. 14, 16; and references in the index to services of Henry Gwin.
[184] *V. B.*, p. 28.
[185] *V. B.*, p. 47, 61.
[186] *V. B.*, p. 85.
[187] Mason, p. 185-186.
[188] Mason, p. 186.
[189] Mason, p. 185, 186.
[190] In "An Act for relief of certain persons, who were sufferers in the loss of the Records of the county of Nansemond", passed at the August 1736 session of the General Assembly, there is confirmation of title to land purchased in 1721 "in the place called Summerton, in the old field where Summerton chapel now stands" (Hening, v. 4, p. 529); and Colonel William Byrd in his "History of the Dividing Line, Run in the Year 1728" (Byrd, p. 104) refers to Somerton Chapel as being left by the surveyors on the Virginia side of the boundary with North Carolina.

Neck Chapel. There is the possibility that the names were sometimes used indiscriminately in the vestry book, and it appears that the same clerks and sextons are often recorded under these various names at different times. It is also the case that Somerton Chapel is not mentioned in the preaching agreements with ministers recorded in 1760, 1774 and 1775,[191] which might indicate its discontinuance unless this neighboring chapel was maintained for occasional and lay services. Taken at their face value, the frequent references to each, often in the same parish account, seem to show that Somerton Chapel, which is mentioned in the vestry book until 1777, and Holy Neck Chapel were distinct.

At its meeting on November 30, 1752, the vestry considered "The Petition of the Inhabitants over Black Water and Notaway" for a small chapel to be "Built over Notaway River", and appointed two of its members to "Go and View some place over Notaway Convenient for that Purpose, and make Return of their Proceedings."[192] These men having reported that James Cary's land was the most convenient site, the vestry, at its meeting on July 26, 1753, ordered the churchwardens to apply to him for the purchase of one acre, prescribed the dimensions of the proposed chapel, specified that it should "be Finish'd in the same Maner as Summerton C[hape]l is", and stipulated that it should be completed by the last day of July, 1754.[193] In 1758, the vestry ordered that a ferry should be kept over the Nottoway River to the chapel on Sundays and it appears that such service was compensated until 1762.[194] In 1760, it was agreed that the minister should preach there four times a year.[195] Nottoway Chapel seems to have thrived until 1765 when its name disappears from the vestry book. The territory in which it was located was added to Southampton County in 1786.[196]

Cypress Chapel, the last to be built, was ordered by the vestry on November 29, 1758. It was to be "of the Same Demensions of that at Notaway", and to be completed by the last of October, 1759. The minister and four vestrymen, of whom any three could act, were commissioned to "Agree with Thos Harrel for one Acre of Land" for the site and to

---

[191] V. B., p. 153-154, 225, 227-228.
[192] V. B., p. 87.
[193] V. B., p. 88, 89.
[194] V. B., p. 124, 158.
[195] V. B., p. 153.
[196] Hening, v. 12, p. 69.

"Advertise the Said Chapell to be Built by the Lowest Undertaker by the Time Afore Said."[197] Since a clear title to this land could not be obtained, the vestry ordered, on January 1, 1759, that a like quantity of land should be acquired from John Norfleet.[198] It was no doubt completed before November 28, 1760, when three members of the vestry were ordered to inspect it "And See Wheather it be done Agreeable to the Articles."[199] This chapel which served the southeastern part of the parish is said to have "stood on the south bank of Cypress Swamp, only a mile west of the great Dismal Swamp . . . [and] about eight miles due south of Suffolk."[200] The name of this chapel disappears from the vestry book after 1778. In later years, the building or location was used by other denominations.[201]

Poorhouse

Vestries were charged by law with the care of the poor which included provision, more or less, for maintenance, medical attention, clothing, funeral expenses, etc. It seems that this provision for the poor grew increasingly burdensome, not only on account of legitimate subjects for charity but also because of large numbers of vagrants and vagrant poor who became charges on the parishes. These became so numerous and troublesome that the General Assembly, at its 1748/49 session, amended and strengthened the law for the restraint of vagrants effective after June 10, 1751.[202]

In its discharge of this very important and growing duty of poor relief, the vestry of the Upper Parish had a reason and an incentive to try an interesting and promising experiment: an almshouse where the poor of the parish might be concentrated, supervised, put to work, and pauper children schooled. William Cadowgan of the Upper Parish had, by his will dated January 1, 1675 (*i. e.* 1676), devised certain properties for the benefit of the parish: the plantation, where he then lived, for a glebe; the rents and profits of his land, appurtenances and stock at Somerton for the benefit of the poor and for other charitable uses until such time as a relation of his name should appear in Virginia and claim this property; and the rents and

---

[197] *V. B.*, p. 128.
[198] *V. B.*, p. 129.
[199] *V. B.*, p. 153.
[200] Mason, p. 187.
[201] Mason, p. 187.
[202] Hening, v. 6, p. 29-33.

profits of 700 acres of land also for the latter purposes. In 1742, the Assembly had considered reasonable a "Petition of the Churchwardens and Vestry of the Upper Parish, in Nansemond County, for selling certain Lands therein mentioned, devised by the Will of William Cadowgan, deceased, to charitable Uses; and for purchasing other Lands, of equal Value, to the same Uses", but had not given the petitioners the desired legal authority.[203] In 1752, the minister, churchwardens and vestrymen of the Upper Parish petitioned the Assembly again, setting forth the terms of Cadowgan's will affecting the parish and stating "That the said Lands given for a Glebe, are so barren, that no Minister, for many Years, hath lived thereon; That the other Lands given for the Benefit of the Poor, are likewise so poor, that the Profits arising thereby, is not sufficient to pay the Quitrents thereof; And that no Person of the Name of Cadowgan, hath ever appeared to claim the same; And praying that an Act of Assembly may pass, impowering the Churchwardens of the said Parish, to sell the said Lands, and to apply the Money arising from the Sale of the Glebe Land, in Purchase of another Glebe, and the Money arising from the Sale of the other Lands, for building a House for the Reception of the Poor of the said Parish, and such other charitable Uses, as the said Vestry shall think fit."[204] The resulting act, couched in similar language, vested all of these properties in the vestry and granted the prayer of the petitioners with a proviso that any relation of the name of Cadowgan who should appear in Virginia and claim the property at Somerton should be paid the entire proceeds of such sale.[205]

In pursuance of this act, the vestry ordered, on May 14, 1752, that a committee of its members should "Sell the Land at Wickams And Sumerton in Such Lots or parcels as they Shall think fitt for Six Months Credditt"; and that several other members and the minister should "Sell the Gleab Land for Six Months Credditt."[206] At the next meeting of the vestry, on October 14, 1752, "The Trustees for selling the Glebe Land Reported . . . that they had Attempted to sell the Glebe Land, But could

---

[203] *Jour. House Bur.*, 1742-1749 (Richmond, 1909), p. 29, 44.
[204] *Jour. House Bur.*, 1752-1758 (Richmond, 1909), p. 45. There are occasional references in the vestry book (cf. p. 23-24, 48, 50, 57, 88, 93) to income derived from the "Poors Land" and the payment of quitrents thereon. It seems to have been mostly woodland (cf. Hening, v. 6, p. 267) from which tar and lightwood were sometimes obtained.
[205] Hening, v. 6, p. 266-268.
[206] *V. B.*, p. 173.

not from the uncertainty of the Bounds", and it was "Ordered that the Surveyor of the County, Survey the Said Land According to a Survey made in behalf of the said Parish, as Appears by a plan now on the Surveyors Book. And that the Church wardens have the same Done between this and the Laying the Next Parish Levy"; and it was also "Ordered that the Surveyor with the Church Wardens, Survey the Land at Wickham Taken up by Blake and Cadowgan, According to the Patent, in Order to Assert what Quantity of Land belongs to the Parish."[207] There seems to have been considerable difficulty and delay in establishing the bounds and title to this glebe and finding a buyer but the land was evidently sold in 1758.[208] There is uncertainty as to the outcome of the effort to secure and dispose of the 700 acres, evidently at Wickhams, which, of all these properties, remained unsold on October 19, 1769, when the vestry "Ordered that the Church Wardens Inquire where the Said Lands Lie in Whose possesion the Same is And apply to Some Noted Attorney for his advice as to the title and make report to the Next Vestry."[209] But the vestry book throws no further light on this matter.[210]

The vestry had not awaited the sale of these properties to carry out its purpose of erecting a poorhouse. On May 14, 1752, it ordered that the house should be built "A Greeable to the plan deliver^d to the Vestry this Day by Lemuel Riddick", and located near Suffolk on three acres of land to be given by Daniel Pugh for the purpose.[211] It appears that the minister and vestrymen, who were delegated to carry out this undertaking, agreed soon afterward with Josiah Riddick "to Build the Said House for the

---

[207] *V. B.*, p. 83-84.
[208] *Cf. V. B.*, p. 88, 92, 104, 122, 128.
[209] *V. B.*, p. 196; and *cf.* p. 125.
[210] In "An Act for dissolving the vestry of the upper parish in the county of Nansemond" (Hening, v. 6, p. 518-519), passed at the May 1755 session of the General Assembly, in which the actions of the vestry in regard to the poorhouse were made binding on the new vestry to be elected, it is stated that the vestry "have sold the said lands and applied the money arising from the sale, in erecting a house for the reception of divers poor persons, who receive relief from the said parish, and for educating and maintaining several poor children, and have ordained and established sundry good and convenient rules and orders relating to the said house, and the poor received, employed, and educated therein"; but the statement in regard to the sale of the lands is not borne out by the vestry book. This act specifically gave the new vestry "full power and authority to levy a reasonable allowance in their parish levy, for the education and maintainance of the poor children, now placed, or to be placed in the said house", indicating, perhaps, that there had been doubt or disagreement as to this policy.
[211] *V. B.*, p. 173-174.

Sum of One Hundred and Fifty Nine Pounds Currant Money"; but the vestry, at its next meeting on October 14, 1752, having declared its "Opinion on more Mature Consideration that it would be More convenient if the Said House was Built on a Lot in Suffolk Town Belonging to Josiah Riddick Lying on the Main Street", all parties agreed that the house should "be Built on the Said Lot According to the Said plan, Except the Partition wall in the Length of the House to be Built with Brick one & half Brick Thick & Plaistered, In Consideration of the Said Riddicks finding the Lot and Building the Said House there, he Instead of the Sum Aforesaid, is to Receive Two Hundred Pounds Currant Money . . . and that the Said House be Compleatly Finished by the Last Day of June Next . . ."[212] It appears, however, that the work was much delayed. On March 25, 1754, the vestry decided "that the Alms House that is to be Built in Suffolk town be Raised two feet in the Walls All Round So that the floors be ten feet from the Ceiling for Which the Under taker Josiah Redik Is to Receive Twenty three pounds moore."[213] The vestry received the house, "finished According to Agrement", on November 14, 1754; ordered that it be furnished; gave instructions that the churchwardens should "at Chrismas Next or Some Convenient time Soon After Convei into the Said House All the Poor persons that now is or Hereafter Shall be Maintaind at the Parrish Expence there Be Supported"; and appointed Samuel Wallis[214] "As Overseer and Master", who was also to "Teach Eight poor Children Which Is to be Sent into the Said House by the Church Wardens To Read Rite &c." For all of his services, Wallis was to receive annually "the Sum of Twenty Pounds Current Money His Own Children Accomadated And Liberty To take in And School ten Children besides the Poors Accordin as he Can Agree With there Parents &c Dureing the time As he Shall be Continued."[215]

It is probable that the example of the Upper Parish had its influence in the passage of a general law authorizing the establishment of poorhouses

---

[212] *V. B.*, p. 84-85.
[213] *V. B.*, p. 92-93.
[214] Or Wallice, as his name sometimes appears in the vestry book.
[215] *V. B.*, p. 97. A Samuel Wallis was ordained for Virginia, August 8, 1709, and received the King's Bounty for Virginia, September 8, 1709. A "Mr. Wallice", thought to be the same minister, is recorded as being in Chuckatuck Parish, Nansemond County, in 1714. (*Cf.* Goodwin, p. 314; above, p. xxxiv.) It is probable, however, that this minister would have been too old for the overseer and teacher who is referred to in this vestry book until 1770.

or workhouses in the various parishes of the colony, but this act was the direct result of a petition from the minister, churchwardens and vestry of Bruton Parish to the May 1755 session of the Assembly which set forth "That the Charge of providing for the Poor of the said Parish, hath always been burthensome to the Inhabitants thereof, and of late Years hath much increased, which they conceive is owing to the great Number of idle Persons, that resort to the City of Williamsburg (situate in the said Parish) in publick Times, who lurk about the Town, and Parts adjacent, till they gain a Settlement, and then become a Charge to the Parish. That there is a House belonging to the Parish, at the Capitol Landing, which might easily be converted into a Workhouse, where the Poor might be more cheaply maintained, and usefully employed; provided the Officers of the said Parish had sufficient Power to compel them to live there; and praying, that an Act may pass to empower them to compel the Poor of their Parish, to dwell and work in the said House, under such Regulations and Restrictions, as this House shall direct."[216] The Assembly ordered that a bill to this end should be brought in, which, on its second reading, was referred to a committee of which Lemuel Riddick, burgess from Nansemond County and no doubt the vestryman of the Upper Parish, was chairman. This committee amended the bill which was then passed in due course as "An Act for employing and better maintaining the Poor."[217]

This detailed act authorized the vestry of every parish, or, for reasons of prohibitive expense, the vestries of two or more conveniently situated parishes in unison, to provide land and a house or houses "for the lodging, maintaining, and employing of all such poor people as shall be upon the parish, or who shall desire relief from the vestry or churchwardens" although it appears that exceptions might be made in the case of those incapable of labor because of sickness or old age; to provide materials and equipment for the employment of the inmates, and to use the proceeds of their labor toward their support; to include in parish levies a reasonable allowance for the education of poor children placed therein; and to appoint overseers to manage these establishments under "proper rules and orders." The law furthermore required that the churchwardens of every parish

---

[216] *Jour. House Bur.*, 1752-1758 (Richmond, 1909), p. 260.
[217] *Ibid.*, p. 268, 274, 276, 279, 293.

should keep a register of those receiving relief; and that persons on relief should wear a badge showing the name of the parish.[218]

Availing itself promptly of the legal permission to unite with another parish in establishing a poorhouse or workhouse, the vestry of the Upper Parish, on August 23, 1755, "Ordered that the Church Wardens do Treat with the Vestry of Suffolk Parrish to See upon what Terms they will Agree To Joyn there Poor with ours In our Poors house before the Laying of our Parrish Leivie."[219] Neither the vestry book of the Upper Parish nor that of Suffolk Parish contains any further reference to this matter. Among possible reasons for the failure of this proposal may have been the relatively generous endowments for its poor which Suffolk Parish enjoyed by reason of various donations to the former Lower Parish; the wish and, as it turned out, the obligation to employ these charity funds locally; and the difficulties and dissension caused by their use. On complaint of various inhabitants of Suffolk Parish, involving the renting of lands donated for the poor, the vestry of Suffolk Parish had been dissolved by the General Assembly in 1749;[220] and, despite the opposition of some of the vestry and other inhabitants of that part of the parish formerly called Chuckatuck Parish, the vestry was again dissolved by law in 1759 on account of the misapplication of funds intended by their donors to be used only for the poor in that part of the parish formerly known as the Lower Parish.[221]

Samuel Wallis remained as overseer of the poorhouse for a number of years although under somewhat different conditions. On January 17, 1756, the vestry ordered that he "be Continued in the Poors house the Ensueing year at Ten pounds Current money and that there is A woman as an asistant Imploy^d when Occasion Requires By the Church wardens and that he have Liberty to take in and School Fifteen Children Besides our Poor them Not Exceeding Eight"; and that the churchwardens "take Cear to Buy and Provide Such Meteirals and other Instruments to Imploy the Said Poor People In Such work as Shall be thought Proper For the Benifit of the Parrish."[222]

---

[218] Hening, v. 6, p. 475-478.
[219] *V. B.*, p. 99.
[220] *Jour. House Bur.*, 1742-1749 (Richmond, 1909), p. 273, 298; Hening, v. 6, p. 214.
[221] *Jour. House Bur.*, 1758-1761 (Richmond, 1908), p. 9, 105-106; Hening, v. 7, p. 303-305.
[222] *V. B.*, p. 103-104.

Evidently the business did not proceed to the satisfaction of the vestry. On March 28, 1758, it appointed the minister and four of its members "Vissators" who should "make Enquiry What Number of Children will be Nesasary to keep In the House how Many the master may take on pay And of them who are fit to Leave the House to Inform the Court In order to have them Bound to trade & all times to report to the Vestry the State & Condition they find the affairs of the House & to Se the Law And Orders of Vestry Punctaly fulfiled and they are to meet as often As they think Nesasary & any three of them at any time is Sufficient To make Any Such Inspection or Inquiry."[223] Future developments indicate that this board of visitors was not continued long.

Results were apparently not commensurate with expenses which must have been unduly burdensome because the vestry continued to make allowances, as formerly, to various individual poor persons. On January 1, 1759, the vestry declared that "A Sufficient Number of Children Cannot be got to be Educated In the Said house and that Continueing the Said Mr Wallice Will be Runing the parrish to Expence without haveing the Desierd Good Efect", and ordered the churchwardens to discharge Mr. Wallice; to employ "Some Sober Careful person to Look after the Said House Goods poor and other things Belonging to the S^d House"; and to "Rent out Any Room or Rooms . . . that may be thought Not usefull for Such poor as Shall be Sent to the Said House", the proceeds to be used for the benefit of the poor of the parish or for other charitable uses.[224] Although the discharge of Mr. Wallis or Wallice ended this venture in public education, the vestry continued to avail itself of his services for a less ambitious policy, paying him at various times for teaching certain poor children.[225]

The poorhouse was apparently continued in this manner for a decade, funds being allotted for its maintenance and also for various individual poor people. But matters did not go satisfactorily. On October 19, 1769, the vestry declared that it had "Strictly Examin^d the present state of the Poors House & are of Opinion that its Necessary to make Several Rules & orders for the well Goverment of the Same And has ordered that each Member Consider the mater relateing thereto" before the next meeting

---

[223] *V. B.*, p. 124.
[224] *V. B.*, p. 129.
[225] *V. B.*, p. 162, 198, 202; and *cf.* p. 207.

"When the Parish Leivie will be laid And that proper Notice be given in Church."[226]

On November 22, 1769, the vestry considered the "present state order & Condition of the persons in the poors house & the regulations thereof" and adopted a series of resolutions: "that the Said house at present is not under such goverm^t as the Law design^d & required and that . . . it is highly Necessary" to adopt "proper & Legal rules & orders" for its "better goverment"; that, since it was inconvenient for distant churchwardens to inspect the house as often as necessary, "a Certain Number of the Vestry Liveing Convenient to the s^d house be appointed as Visitors" who should "at least once in three Months To Visit Inspect & Inquire into the state & Condition of the Said house and the poor therein and the behaviour & actions of the overseer thereof & to make such rules & orders as they from Time to time shall think Necessary & Convenient The same Not being repugnant to the Law or any order of this Vestry And to report to the Next Vestry an account of there proceedings"; that "a proper person be appointed as an Overseer . . . Constantly to attend his duty as the Law requiers who is to have all the authority over the poor as is directed by the Act of assembly"; that the churchwardens should procure materials "Sufficient to Imploy the poor and all Vagarent People that may be Imploy^d in the poors house", the proceeds to be used for the "benifitt of the Poor in the said house or as Shall otherwise be directed by the Vestry"; and that a levy be made "towards defraying the Charge of the Said poor & to reimburse the Church W^{ds} What they may in the Mean time advance for the use & purposes aforesaid." Visitors were thereuopn appointed and ordered to "agree with a proper person to be overseer" who should receive, "besides all Necessary Expences a Sum Not exceeding Twenty Pounds per Anum."[227]

John Miles was appointed overseer soon afterward[228] but the poorhouse did not prosper. On February 2, 1771, the vestry, declaring that "the parishoners are dissatisfied at the Same and often Complaining of the Expence" and that experience had shown that it did not answer the desired purpose, ordered that the churchwardens should "place the poor now in the s^d House as well as all Such as Shall become as Charge in this parish out

---

[226] *V. B.*, p. 196.
[227] *V. B.*, p. 198-200.
[228] *V. B.*, p. 202.

to Such persons as to them Shall Seem Convenient to be paid for & Setled by this Vestry"; that, as soon as the poor should be removed, the house should be "rented out for the benifitt of the Poor" of the parish; that John Miles, the overseer, should be discharged; and that the furniture in the house, belonging to the parish, should be sold.[229]

It seems that these plans were not carried out in their entirety. On November 25, 1772, the vestry agreed "to reverse an order made bearing Date Febuary 2^d 1771 Concerning Renting out the poors House and that the Said house be restablished as formerly"; and ordered the churchwardens to "provide Furniture and Necessaries As Shall Seem to them Convenient for the poors House & employ the poor in Such Work as they Shall think proper."[230] But it appears that the poorhouse remained a burden, for the vestry, on December 17, 1774, again reversed itself and ordered "that the Poors house be discontinued As it is the Opinion of this Vestry that it be rather an Incumberance to the Parrish & that the said House be rented out by the Ch: Wardens & the furniture sold."[231]

In the meantime a glebe had finally been bought in place of the barren land devised by Cadowgan, still apparently unoccupied by the minister to whom the vestry annually made an allowance of tobacco as recompense. On February 2, 1771, the vestry declared that it "thinks its Necessary to purchase a Gleabe for the Minister" and appointed an early date for the consideration of the matter.[232] At this meeting on February 11, 1771, the vestry acted favorably on the offer of Captain Mills Riddick "to Sell his Lands with the Apurtenances on the White Marsh to this parrish as a Gleab", and it was ordered that he should "Resurvey his Said Plantation and if the Surveior Shall return that the Said Land Contains the Number of Acres prescrib'd by Law Sufficient for A Gleab then & In such Case it is agreed by Said Vestry to pay unto Said Capt Riddick in Consideration of the same ... Five Hundred pounds Current Money In three payments Anualey", with interest. It was also agreed that Captain Mills Riddick should "deliver up the posession of the Said Land & premises on the Tenth Day of Decemb^r Next in Good Order & to Execute a deed Good & Suffi-

---

[229] *V. B.*, p. 203-204.
[230] *V. B.*, p. 219.
[231] *V. B.*, p. 227.
[232] *V. B.*, p. 204.

cient for the Same."[233] This business was evidently consummated since the payments for this glebe were made.[234]

The vestry and other inhabitants of the Upper Parish presented a petition to the October 1778 session of the Assembly setting forth "That the Glebe in the said Parish is rendered totally unfit for the reception of a Clergyman by the principal Houses thereon Viz. the Dwelling house & Kitchen being consum'd by fire, & that it wou'd be very inconvenient & at this time very expensive to build proper houses on the said Glebe for the use of a Minister, And your Petitioners further shew that in pursuance of an Act of Assembly in that behalf made, the Vestry of the said Parish did purchase a Lot of Land & thereon did erect & build a house in the Town of Suffolk in the County aforesaid as a work house for the reception of the poor of the said Parish, which work house has been found by experience not to answer the good purpose expected from it"; and praying "that a Law may be passed impowering the Vestry of the said Parish to sell the said Glebe & Work house with the Land thereto belonging by publick Auction for the most that can be got for them & to apply the money arising from such sales to the necessary uses of the said Parish." This petition[235] is endorsed: ". . . ref^d to Religion[236] 20th Nov. 1778. Nov. 27th 1778. Reasonable as to the disposal of the Workhouse & Rejected as to the other part of the Petition." The resulting law accordingly instructed the vestry "to sell the workhouse and lands thereto belonging in the town of Suffolk" and to apply "the money arising from such sale . . . towards lessening their parish levy."[237]

The vestry availed itself of this authorization without delay. On December 28, 1778, it ordered the churchwardens to "advertise & sell the Poors House & the Land belong^g to it to the Highest Bidder."[238]

THE REVOLUTION AND ITS CONSEQUENCES

As the American Revolution was a phase of a democratic upheaval affecting the whole of the western world, so the struggle for the separation of church and state was part of the democratic revolution in Virginia. It

---

[233] *V. B.*, p. 204-205.
[234] *V. B.*, p. 207, 220, 224, 227.
[235] Original manuscript in Nansemond County petitions in Archives Division of the Virginia State Lbrary.
[236] *I.e.* Committee for Religion of the House of Delegates.
[237] Hening, v. 9, p. 527.
[238] *V. B.*, p. 242.

was an age in which the whole order of society was questioned; in which the forces of the old conservatism and the new democracy were joined. The Established Church in Virginia came to its end mainly as the result of political and social revolution and the eventual triumph of the evangelical denominations.

The history of the disestablishment of the church is long and involved. The principal legal steps, extending from 1776 to 1787, were the broad assertion of religious liberty in the Declaration of Rights; the suspension and then prohibition of levies for the support of the clergy; the abolition of taxation of dissenters for the benefit of the church; the ending of all taxes for religious purposes; the abrogation of former laws in regard to the church; the enactment of the long-pending bill for religious freedom; the transfer of poor relief to elected overseers of the poor; the liberalization of the marriage law to establish the legality of marriages performed by non-Anglican ministers; the defeat of a general assessment bill to provide state support for all Christian denominations; and the enactment and repeal of the law incorporating the Protestant Episcopal Church.

As would be expected, the vestry book of the Upper Parish adds little to the general history of disestablishment but the effects of these measures are apparent in its record; nor does it give any direct information about the war which came at an early date to disrupt the peaceful life of the parish.

Actual hostilities in Virginia may be said to have begun around Norfolk in the last part of 1775 by the fugitive royal governor, Lord Dunmore, who was supported by warships, and a mixed force of British troops, loyalists and Negroes. The battle of Great Bridge was fought on December 9, 1775, Norfolk was destroyed in January and February, 1776, and Portsmouth, across the Elizabeth River from Norfolk, was occupied by British troops. Suffolk, accessible to the Virginia authorities and less exposed to attack, became an important post for colonial troops defending that vital region and, in time, the chief depot of military supplies in Virginia.[239] Suffolk was also the refuge of homeless fugitives from Norfolk and vicinity, and the town was badly overcrowded.[240] Since the British fleet often blockaded Chesapeake Bay, South Quay, in the Upper Parish, also became an important depot for foreign trade destined for the supply of

---

[239] *Revolution in Virginia*, p. 89-90, 263; *Calendar*, v. 8, p. 87, 93, 113, 114, 117, 119, 126, 141-142.
[240] Dunn, p. 43; *Calendar*, v. 8, p. 178.

Suffolk.[241] Disorganization in the parish may be indicated by the failure of the vestry to meet between December 19, 1775, and February 11, 1777.

It appears that there was inevitably much sickness among the troops stationed in and around Suffolk.[242] That certain results of this were a charge against the Upper Parish is shown by an entry in the vestry book, at the meeting on February 11, 1777, when payment was provided to the sexton of Suffolk Church for burying some soldiers.[243] These troops were undoubtedly a turbulent lot, probably little better disciplined than those who had by rapine aided the enemy in the destruction of Norfolk. At the October 1777 session of the General Assembly commissioners were required to "ascertain the damages sustained by the burning of any houses in the town of Portsmouth by the troops of this commonwealth, and the damages to the proprietors of any houses used as barracks by the said troops" in Norfolk, Portsmouth, Suffolk and Great Bridge.[244]

Whether due to war time conditions or not, it appears that the property of the parish suffered much damage at this time. On January 17, 1778, the vestry provided a considerable sum for repairing the church.[245] It was also stated in the petition of the vestry and other inhabitants of the Upper Parish to the October 1778 session of the Assembly that the glebe was "rendered totally unfit for the reception of a Clergyman by the principal Houses thereon Viz. the Dwelling house & Kitchen being consum'd by fire."[246] In this petition the distressed parish had sought permission to sell both its glebe and poorhouse and to apply the proceeds to "necessary uses" but were denied the right to dispose of the former.

The parish was undoubtedly in financial straits. The last installment of £100 had just been paid to the Reverend Patrick Lunan, the poorhouse had always been burdensome, expenses were increasing, dissenters had been exempted by law from taxation to support the church, and levies for the payment of ministers' salaries had been suspended since January 1, 1777.[247] In regard to the latter, the vestry, on January 17, 1778 (the next meeting subject to the law), had exempted dissenters from strictly religious ex-

---

[241] Dunn, p. 43.
[242] *Calendar*, v. 8, p. 130, 141-142.
[243] *V. B.*, p. 236.
[244] Hening, v. 9, p. 428.
[245] *V. B.*, p. 239.
[246] See above, p. lxiv.
[247] Hening, v. 9, p. 164-167, 312, 387-388, 469, 578-579.

penses but had continued to tax others for the support of the church which was, however, then without a minister.[248] On December 28, 1778, the vestry drew up the parish expenses in two parts, one having to do with poor relief, for which tithables were taxed, and the other covering the salaries of the minister and readers, and other expenses pertaining strictly to the church, which presumably were to be met from other sources.[249] This was the end of the ministry in the Upper Parish so far as the vestry book shows. At the next meeting on December 30, 1779, a comparatively small amount for the support of the church appears in the parish accounts;[250] thereafter the fiscal authority of the vestry seems to have been reduced to levying and administering funds for the poor. On December 28, 1780, the hard-pressed vestry ordered that the churchwardens "Sell the Houses &c on the Glebe assoon as Convenient to the best advantage."[251] Since it is improbable that the dwelling and kitchen had been rebuilt, this must have referred mostly to other buildings on the glebe.[252] As appears afterward, this was probably a bootless venture.

In the meanwhile, the war had come home to the parish. The British invaded Virginia in May, 1779, occupied Portsmouth, and sent out raiding parties in various directions, one of which captured Suffolk on May 13. A small force of militia under Colonel Willis Riddick, no doubt the vestryman, had attempted to oppose the raiders before Suffolk but had been dispersed. The place had then been abandoned to the enemy who captured or burned the stores and vessels there. The fire, spreading widely, destroyed most of the town, including the court house and the clerk's office, with all of the county records.[253] During the next two years, Nansemond County and Suffolk suffered further invasions by the enemy and were occupied at various times by American forces.[254]

The destruction of war and the effects of political measures brought

---

[248] *V. B.*, p. 239-240.
[249] *V. B.*, p. 240-242.
[250] *V. B.*, p. 243-244.
[251] *V. B.*, p. 246.
[252] The law had provided for such outbuildings as a barn, stable, dairy, meat house and corn house. *Cf.* Hening, v. 6, p. 89.
[253] *Revolution in Virginia*, p. 262-263; Dunn, 43-45; *The Virginia Historical Register* . . . edited by William Maxwell, v. 4 (Richmond, 1851), p. 189.
[254] Losses suffered by the county and many of its inhabitants during various invasions by the enemy are set forth in a collection of original manuscripts from Nansemond County on this subject, mostly dated in 1782, in the Archives Division of the Virginia State Library.

irreparable disaster to the parish. The Anglican Church had nearly gone to wreck during the war and subsequent laws severed all remaining connection with the state on which it still depended. Indeed this connection had become in reality a disadvantage since the church, still bound to the state without consequent benefit, was not free to organize itself in accordance with new conditions. As an established church, it was subject to constant attack.

Incorporation of the Protestant Episcopal Church, which was requested by a convention meeting in Richmond on June 3, 1784, seemed to offer a means of adjusting conditions to the existing state of affairs. The Protestant Episcopal Church in America, as successor to the Church of England, was being organized and the Anglican branch in Virginia wished to join the new communion.[255] Despite some opposition, "An act for incorporating the Protestant Episcopal Church" was passed at the October 1784 session of the General Assembly at a time of conservative reaction following the war.[256] This law incorporated the minister and vestry of each parish; assured to them the ownership of all the property of the former Established Church therein and the right to acquire other property; provided that, in any vacant parish, two members of the Episcopal Church might act to bring about an election of vestrymen by and from its Episcopal body; stipulated that vestrymen should be elected every three years by contributing members of the Episcopal Church and should subscribe, before entering on their office, "to be conformable to the doctrine, discipline, and worship of the Protestant Episcopal Church"; set forth general rules for holding vestry meetings, deciding questions and filling vacancies; required, under penalty, that a report of property and revenue should be made every three years to the county court, which should, in the case of annual revenue in excess of £800, inform the governor and, through him, the General Assembly; repealed former laws in regard to the Established Church; dissolved all vestries "on the day before the Monday in next Easter week" (the time for holding the first triennial election); and authorized the Protestant Episcopal Church in Virginia to regulates its religious concerns, including the removal of unworthy ministers, in conventions to be held when desired and to consist of two persons from each parish, one being the minister, and at least forty delegates; and directed that vestries which had

---

[255] Eckenrode, p. 78-80.
[256] Eckenrode, p. 91-92, 101-102.

been negligent in meeting their legal demands should lay their parish levies and provide for the poor.[257] This law, which may be said to have completed disestablishment although it maintained a tentative connection between the church and state, gave much encouragement to the Episcopal Church. The title to ecclesiastical property was vested in the church authorities who were empowered to regulate their church affairs without legislative interference.

In accordance with this law, the Upper Parish elected a new vestry, half of which were previous members, which met and organized on April 18, 1785, when the vestrymen subscribed themselves to be members of the Protestant Episcopal Church and promised "to be conformable to the Doctrine, Discipline, and Worship of the Same." Willis Riddick and Richard Baker, vestrymen, were chosen as delegates to attend the convention in Richmond which met on May 18-25, 1785, to organize the Protestant Episcopal Church in Virginia.[258]

At this vestry meeting, it was also recommended "that the Church Wardens do Advertise to procure a Minister for this parish."[259] But ministers were scarce. Deprived of their salaries, harassed for a living, and dispersed during the war, many had left their charges and taken up other work.[260] There is other evidence of the determination of the vestry to rehabilitate the religious life of the parish. At its meeting on October 11, 1785, the vestry "Ordered that Each of the Vestrymen assist in the numbering the Episcopalians in the upper Parish of Nansemond; and present a Subscription to the people professing that Religion; in order to See what Sum of Money can be raised, and make report of their Success to the next Vestry."[261]

Other legislative measures came to effect a complete disestablishment of the Episcopal Church: the long-debated assessment bill for the support of all Christian denominations, advocated by the Episcopalians who still believed that religion could not exist without state support, was defeated; the act "for establishing religious freedom" was passed; poor relief and processioning were transferred to locally elected overseers of the poor, thus

---

[257] Hening, v. 11, p. 532-537.
[258] *V. B.*, p. 257-258.
[259] *V. B.*, p. 257.
[260] Eckenrode, p. 64, 65, 75; Meade, v. 1, p. 17.
[261] *V. B.*, p. 258.

ending the last vestige of the civil authority of vestries; and the law incorporating the Protestant Episcopal Church was repealed.

The next meeting in the vestry book, November 17, 1786, was of the overseers of the poor for Nansemond County, a body which apparently included only one vestryman of the Upper Parish. Judging by the number of overseers present[262] and several references, the Upper Parish was apparently one of the districts of the county, Suffolk Parish probably being the other.[263] This meeting seems to have been called to effect a settlement of accounts with the Upper Parish, to allot funds to the poor of the county, and to make a county levy to meet requirements.

As appears from the various amendatory acts themselves, the laws relating to poor relief and its overseers proved indefinite, inadequate and unsatisfactory.[264] One of the unforeseen results of these acts became apparent when the overseers of the poor in Suffolk Parish proceeded to apply the considerable donations for the support of the poor of that parish to such relief for the whole county, including the Upper Parish. The inhabitants of Suffolk Parish considered that this action was contrary to the intention and design of the donors; and that it was unduly burdensome since it subjected the parish to a general assessment with the county whereas they could support their own poor at small expense. Accordingly, they petitioned the House of Delegates at its October 1791 session, praying for a law to empower the overseers of the poor in that district to make assessment within the parish for the support of their own poor, and to coöperate with the vestry in assessment and the distribution of donations.[265] The resulting act directed the overseers of the poor in the district to make a separate adjustment and assessment for the parish of the charges for poor relief but gave no authority to the vestry in such matters.[266]

Great opposition to incorporation had developed and many petitions for its repeal came to the legislature. Advocates of repeal contended that the incorporation law violated the Declaration of Rights and the act establishing religious freedom; that it continued the connection of church and state; and that it reserved the property of the old establishment,

---

[262] The law (Hening, v. 12, p. 27, 272) provided for three from each district.
[263] *V. B.*, p. 258-261; *cf.* Hening, v. 13, p. 280.
[264] *Cf.* Hening, v. 12, p. 272-275, 573-580, 712-713; v. 13, p. 262-264.
[265] Original manuscript in Nansemond County petitions in Archives Division of Virginia State Library.
[266] Hening, v. 13, p. 280.

acquired by common taxation, to the new Episcopal Church to the prejudice of the other churches.[267]

Defenders of the Episcopal Church tried to forestall and to prevent repeal, submitting many petitions to that end to the legislature. In its remonstrance, the Episcopal convention of 1786 recommended "to the several parishes to present petitions of a similar nature."[268] Among the many parishes, mostly in the conservative tidewater and southside sections, which lodged such protests, was the Upper Parish:

"The petition of the Vestry men and Inhabitants of the Upper Parish in the County of Nansemond Humbly Sheweth, that your petitioners are well pleased with, and very easy under the Act of Assembly passed for Incorporating the Protestant Episcopal Church in this State; that we are informed, & verily believe, that a vigorous attempt will be made to induce your Honbl^e Body at Your Next Meeting in this present Year 1786, for the Repeal of said law, that we humbly conceive there is no Sect or Society under Heaven that are in any manner injured by the operation of that law which we are well pleased with, And that any Sect or Sects of Christians, on application to the General Assembly, May, we make no doubt have their Church or Churches inco[r]porated: Your petitioners pray your Honbl^e body to refuse all Solicitations that may be made to You for the purpose of repealing the said law, (knowing that the many bad consequences which will attend the repeal of that Salutary law must occur to you on reflection without their being enumerated here)."[269]

However, the opposition of the other sects and various liberal elements was too strong, and the law was repealed in January, 1787. The new act provided for the "Saving to all religious societies the property to them respectively belonging", which were authorized to appoint trustees to administer the same, and repealed "so much of all laws now in force, as prevents any religious society from regulating its own discipline."[270] Some doubt arising as to the authority of vestries and trustees in the management of the property of the Episcopal Church, the General Assembly provided, in 1788, that the latter should be considered as successors to the former

---

[267] Eckenrode, p. 116, 119, 125.
[268] Hawks, v. 1, p. 13; Eckenrode, p. 116-118.
[269] Original manuscript in Nansemond County petitions in Archives Division of the Virginia State Library.
[270] Hening, v. 12, p. 266-267.

in holding and managing property left for charitable purposes or for the use of individuals.[271]

With the repeal of the incorporation act, all churches became independent of the civil authority as to doctrine, discipline and means of support. The Episcopal Church finally stood on the same footing as the other churches in the state.[272]

Newly elected members of the vestry were certified on September 13, 1790, as "Lawfully chosen to serve as Trustees & Vestery Men for the upper parrish of Nansemond County." Seven members who were present at the time subscribed themselves "to be conformable to the Doctrin Discipline and government of the protestant Episcopal Church of Virginia", but seem to have transacted no other business.[273]

At the last recorded meeting, on April 21, 1791, the vestry seemed determined to maintain the parish in spite of all handicaps. It ordered "that the Church Wardens take an Acco^t of the Church property in this Parrish both real & personal & make an immediate Report thereof to the Treasurer of the Convention, also that he be informd that at present there is no minister in this parrish"; "that the Church Wardens do collect by Subscription what Money they can to be sent to the Treasurer of the Convention to be apply'd to the Generall purposes of the church agreeable to the requisition of the last Convention"; "that Mr Arch^d Richardson & Docter Joseph Hay be appointed to represent this parrish, as Laymen in the next convention to be held at Richmond in May Next"; and "that each Vestryman with the Church Wardens open Subscriptions for the purpos of Raising Money for to Repair the Church & Chappills of this Parrish."[274]

The property of the parish was in ruinous condition. Although the church in Suffolk had escaped destruction by fire in 1779, it was severely damaged during the war, and both church and chapels probably suffered greatly from abuse and neglect then and in succeeding years. Evidently the effort to raise funds by subscription to repair the church and chapels was, in the main, unsuccessful. Accordingly, there was presented to the House of Delegates, at its October 1792 session, "The Petition of the

---

[271] Hening, v. 12, p. 705-706.
[272] Eckenrode, p. 129.
[273] *V. B.*, p. 261-262.
[274] *V. B.*, p. 262.

inhabitants of the upper Parish", signed by 81 persons and including the names of those who must have been vestrymen at the time, which set forth:

"That the Episcopal Church in the Town of Suffolk, was in the late War between Great Britain an America, so torn to pieces and mutilated that it has become quite unfit for use, and the houses on the Glebe of the said Parish are quite decayed and fallen down.

"Your petitioners therefore humbly pray, that an Act may pass, authorizing the Vestry of the said Parish, to raise by way of lottery, a sum of money, not exceeding one thousand pounds, for the purpose of rebuilding the Church in the said Town of Suffolk, and to make such necessary repairs and improvements upon the Glebe land thereunto belonging, as the said Vestry shall judge most necessary and proper."[275]

This petition, with the requested amount reduced to £400, was considered reasonable and the Committee of Propositions and Grievances, to which it had been referred, was ordered to prepare and bring in a bill accordingly.[276] But no further action is apparent. It was not an age in which legislators would have advanced moralistic objections to this method of raising funds; legislative sanction of lotteries for religious and other purposes was then quite customary. Perhaps the current agitation to dispossess the Episcopal Church of its glebes, eventually successful, was largely responsible for the failure of this request.

The plight of the parish now appeared hopeless, a condition which soon seemed to extend, for a time, to the whole Protestant Episcopal Church in Virginia which was prostrated by further legislation affecting its status and property, external hostility, internal apathy, crippling poverty, and other circumstances.[277] The agitation for the confiscation of the glebes and other property led the General Assembly in 1799 to repeal, specifically and by title, previous acts relating to the church, the reason given being that this body of law "manifestly tends to the reestablishment of a national church."[278] Thus the earlier guarantees to the church were withdrawn

---

[275] Original manuscript in Nansemond County Petitions in Archives Division of Virginia State Library.
[276] *Journal of the House of Delegates . . . of Virginia*, October 1792 session (Richmond, 1792), p. 24, 34.
[277] Meade, v. 1, p. 17-18, 30-31; Eckenrode, p. 1147; *Colonial Churches in the Original Colony of Virginia*, 2d ed., rev. and improved (Richmond, Va., 1908), p. 34, 45, 46.
[278] *The Statutes at Large of Virginia*, by Samuel Shepherd, v. 2 (Richmond, 1835), p. 149.

and the way prepared for the confiscatory act of 1802 which provided for the sale of the glebes and related property of "the late protestant episcopal church."[279]

The Upper Parish, among others, seems to have given up in despair. The church in Suffolk went completely to ruin, and was finally torn down and its bricks used for other purposes.[280] It is said that during the final stage of the decay of the old church, boys took reeds from its pipe organ and blew them up and down the streets.[281] The writer of the notes on the parish[282] states that "a very beautiful crimson Communion cloth, with rich gold lace" and the "old Bible & prayer book belonging to the old church" were then in St. Paul's Episcopal Church in Suffolk, but he was unable to account for the disappearance of the plate and the marble font. It is stated that the Bible is still in use in the present St. Paul's Church and "bears the date 1751."[283] It appears that the old church yard continued to be used as a burial ground for a long time and, since many of the graves were dug through the foundation of the structure and a street was cut through the site, no trace of the building is now evident.[284]

The glebe was no doubt taken from the Upper Parish under the confiscatory act of 1802, and the chapels passed out of the possession of the church into the hands of other denominations.[285]

The parish seemed to have gone down in ruin but its life was not extinct. Identified with Suffolk Parish, served vicariously by various ministers, the parish, with St. Paul's Church in Suffolk as a center, was at length revived as the Upper Suffolk Parish.

WILMER L. HALL.

---

[279] *Ibid.,* p. 314-316.
[280] The date of the demolition of this ruined building is uncertain. Mason (p. 184) states "about 1802" although some of the bricks "had already been used to build the Union Chapel at Suffolk in the year 1800" where one of the pews of the old church is said to have been installed. The writer of the notes on the parish (see Preface, p. vii), evidently referring to the same building, states: "I recollect this Church from 1810 to 1820, but in a very dilapidated condition, no windows or floors. In 1820 the wal[l]s were thrown down, the bricks sold, and the money arising from the sale of the bricks, was reserved, and expended for a bell, which now hangs over St. Paul's Episcopal Church in Suffolk." Dunn (p. 47) also says that "It was pulled down in 1820." Apparently the remains of the old church were utilized from time to time over a number of years.
[281] Mason, p. 184.
[282] See Preface, p. vii; and above, footnote 280.
[283] Mason, p. 183.
[284] Mason, p. 184.
[285] Dunn, p. 47; writer of the notes on the parish; Mason, p. 186, 187.

The Vestry Book
of the
Upper Parish
Nansemond County, Virginia, 1743-1793

At a Vestry held At Mr Edwd Doughties March 27th 1744[1] for the Up^r P[ar]ish of Nansemond County

Present
- Col^o And: Meede
- Mr Wm Butler
- Mr Jno Winborn
- Mr Jno Norfleet

Edwd Norfleet
Col^o Danl Pugh } Ch Wds:
Capt Jethro Sumner

Col^o Danl Pugh haveing in his hands Rec^d for fines fifty Shil Cur^t Money:

And Out of the Said fines hath Distributed as Foloeth Viz^t

To Mourning Busskin	£ 0 : 18 : 9
To Sarah Wood	1 : 2 : 10
To Rebeckah Nash	0 : 8 : 5
	2 : 10 : 0

Col^o Danl Pugh and Capt Jethro Sumner Are Continued And Sworn Church Wardens Untill Easter Next

Danl Pugh } Ch: Warden[s]
Jethro Sumner

At A Vestry held at Suffolk Town in the Up^r P[ar]ish of Nansemond County Novem: the 30th 1743

---

[1] This meeting bears a later date than the one next recorded on the same page of the vestry book. It is probable that the dates are correct (subsequent orders for quadrennial processioning seem to substantiate the date of the next meeting) and that the clerk copied the proceedings of the two meetings in reverse order. Matters were not always entered chronologically.

Present And[r] Meede   John Gregorie
         Edw[d] Norfleet   John Norfleet
         Lem[l] Riddick   Dan[l] Pugh   } Church Wardens
                              Jethro Sumner

Pursuant to An Ord[r] of Court Dated Novemb: 23[d] 1743 for the respective Vestrys to appoint P[ro]cess[rs] in their p[ar]ishes The Vestry hath p[ro]ceeded as folloeth

[2]

Ord[d] that Robert Gouldie And Lemuel Riddick Gen[t] in p[re]sence of the Inhabitants of the Town of Suffolk p[ro]cess[i]on all the Bounds of Land belonging to Said Town and the Severall Lotts therein Contained and Make Return of their p[ro]ceedings as the Law Directs

2

Ord[d] that John Milner Jun[r] & John Hines in p[re]sence of the Inhabitants p[ro]cession all the Bounds of Land on the North Side the Western Branch to the Extent of the p[ar]ish Including all the Land in the Said Bounds You Are to go round every Mans Land & renew the Land Marks, & return to the Vestry An Acco[t] of every Mans Land You p[ro]cess: w[th] the Names of the p[er]sons p[re]sent at the Same; & what Land in Youre p[re]cinct you Shall faile to p[ro]cession, You Are to give an Acco[t] w[th] the p[ar]ticular reasons of Such faillure, & If Any if Any [sic] refuse to have their Land p[ro]cess[d] You Are to Certifie the same to the Church Wardens w[th] in Tenn Days from Under Youre hands &c

3

[O]rd[d] that John Jones & John Moore in p[re]sence of the Inhabitants p[ro]cession [a]ll the bounds of Land on the North Side the Western Branch as the rode [r]uns from the Brick Church to Poorter Bridge including all the Land in the Said Bounds; You Are to go round every Mans Land and [re]new the Land marks and return to the Vestry An Acco[t] of every [m]ans Land You p[ro]cess: & the Names of the p[er]sons p[re]sent at the same [an]d what Land in Yo[r] p[re]cinct You shall faile to p[ro]cess: You Are to give An Acco[t] [wi]th the p[ar]ticular reasons of Such faillure, And if Any refuse to have their [l]and p[ro]cess[d]

You Are to Certifie the same to the Church Wardens [wit]hin Tenn
Day's from Under Youre Hands &c

4

Ordered that William Babb & William Norfleet in p[re]sence [o]f
the inhabitants p[ro]cession all the Bounds of Land on the west side the
Southern Branch and on the South side the Church Road as [i]t runs from
the Brick Church to Jernagans Bridge including all the Land in the Said
Bounds You Are to go round Every mans Land and [r]enew the Land
Marks & Return to the Vestry an Acco^t of every mans Land you p[ro]-
cession and the Names of the p[er]sons p[re]sent at the Same, And what
Land in Youre p[re]cinct you Shall faile to p[ro]cession [yo]u Are to
give An Acco^t wth the p[ar]ticular reasons of Such faillure And if Any
Refuse to have their Land p[ro]cessioned you Are to Certifie the Same to
the Church Wardens within Tenn Days from Under Your Hands &c

[3]
5

Ord^d that James Lawrance and Exum^2 Scott in p[re]sence of the
Inhab[itants] p[ro]cession all the Bounds of Land, beginning at Pattersons
Neck So up the Indian Creak & runn to the Extent of the County, Along
the Count[y] Line to Everits Creek. You Are to go round every mans
Land and renew th[e] Land Marks and return to the Vestry An Acco^t of
every mans Land You p[ro]cess and the Names of the p[er]sons p[re]sent
at the Same and what Land in Yo^r p[re]cinct you Shall faile to p[ro]-
cession You Are to give An Acco^t wth the p[ar]ticular reasons of Such
faillure; & if Any refuse to have their Land p[ro]cess^d You Are to
Certifie the Same to the Church Wardens Within Tenn Day's from Under
Yo^r Hands &c

6

Ord^d that Robt Archer & Edward Eley in p[re]sence of the Inhabitants
p[ro]cession all the Bounds of Land In the Upe^r Side the Road from
Jernagans Bridge to Poorters Bridge to the Extent of the County Including all the Land in the Said Bounds: You Are to go round every mans
Land and renew the Land Marks and return to the Vestry An Acco^t of
every mans Land You p[ro]cess and the Names of the p[er]sons p[re]sent

---

^{2} This name may be spelled Exam.

at the Same and what Land in Yo[r] p[re]cinct You Shall faile to p[ro]cession You Are to give An Acco[t] w[th] the p[ar]ticular reasons of Such faillure, and if Any refuse to have their Land p[ro]cess[d] You Are to Certifie the Same to the Church Wardens w[th]in Tenn [days] from Under Yore Hands &c

7

Ord[d] that Henry Wright & Peter Butler in p[re]sence of the Inhabitants p[ro]cession all the Bounds of Land, from Jernagans Bridge runn to Speights Runn So up to William Battles &c Michael Kings Sen[rs] Including all the Land in the Said bounds, You Are to go round Every mans Land and renew the Land marks and return to the Vestry An Acco[t] of every mans Land You p[ro]cession And the Names of the p[er]sons p[re]sent at the Same, and what Land in Yo[r] p[re]cinct You Shall faile to procession you Are [to] give An Acco[t] w[th] the p[ar]ticular reasons of Such faillure, And if Any refuse to have their Land p[ro]cessioned You Are to Certifie the Same to the Church Wardens w[th]in Tenn days from Under You[r] Hands &c

8

Ord[d] that William Harrison & Jn[o] Harrisson in p[re]sence of the Inhabitants p[ro]cession all the bounds of Land from William Walters plantation to the Beaverdam Swamp by Hunters plantation; thence on the North Side Sum[r]ton Roade to John Poorters thence to Sum[r]ton Swamp; thence to the head of the Meadow Branch thence to the County Line; Thence to Luke Hares plantation, Thence to the first station Including all the Land in the Said Bounds, You are to go round every mans Land and renew the Land marks; and return to the Vestry An Acco[t] of every Mans Land You p[ro]cession And the Names of the p[er]sons p[re]sent at the same And what Land in Yo[r] p[re]cinct you shall faile to p[ro]cession, You Are to give An Acco[t] w[th] the p[ar]ticular reasons of Such faillure, & if Any refuse to have their Land p[ro]cessioned You Are to Certifie the Same to the Church Wardens w[th]in Tenn Day's from Under Youre Hands &c

[4]   9

[Or]d[d] that William Rawles Jun[r] & John Hare, in the p[re]sence of the Inhabitants [pro]cession all the Bounds of Land; Beginning at John Poorters Joining Sum[r]ton [S]wamp on the North Side Sum[r]ton Road to the Knuckle Swamp Including [a]ll the Land in the Said Bounds, You Are to go round every mans Land & Renew the Land Marks & return to the Vestry An Acco^t of every mans Land You p[ro]cession & the Names of the p[er]sons p[re]sent At the Same and what Land in Yo^r p[re]cinct You Shall faile to p[ro]cess: you Are to give An Acco^t wth the p[ar]ticular reasons of Such faillure, And if Any Refuse to have their Land p[ro]cessioned You Are to Certifie the Same to the Church Wardens wthin Tenn Days from Under Yo^r Hands &c

10

Ord^d that Jacob Langstone & Theophilus Jones in p[re]sence of the Inhabitants p[ro]cession all the Bounds of Land on the North Side Sum^{r}ton Swamp & the South Side the Road from Thomas Jones to Jno Jenkins, Including all the Land in the Said Bounds: You Are to go round Every mans Land renew the Land marks & Return to the Vestry An Acco^t of every mans Land You p[ro]cession & the Names of the p[er]sons p[re]sent At the Same; And what Land in Yo^r p[re]cinct you Shall faile to p[ro]cession You Are to give An Acco^t wth the p[ar]ticular Reasons of Such faillure And If Any refuse to have their Land p[ro]cessioned, You Are to Certifie the Same to the Church Wardens from Under Yo^r Hands &c

11

Ord^d that James Eley & Henry Coor in p[re]sence of the Inhabitants p[ro]cession all the Bounds of Land, from Sum^{r}ton Creek on the west Side the Road from Sum^{r}ton Creek By Coors to South Keey Road Including all the Land in the said Bounds: You Are to go round every mans Land & Renew the Land Marks, & return to the Vestry An Acco^t of Every mans Land you p[ro]cession wth the Names of the p[er]sons p[re]sent At the same and what Land in You^r p[re]cinct You shall faile to p[ro]cession you Are to give An Acco^t wth the p[ar]ticular reasons of such faillure: & If Any refuse to have their Land process^d, you Are to Certifie the Same to the Church Wardens wthin Tenn Days from Under Yo^r Hands &c

12

Ord^d that Joseph Rogers & Edwd Boyt in p[re]sence of the Inhabitants p[ro]cession all the Bounds of Land from Sum^{r}ton Creek on the South Side the road from Said Creek By Coors to South Key rode, Includeing all the Land in the Said Bounds You Are to go round every mans Land and renew the Land marks & return to the Vestry An Acco^t of every mans Land You p[ro]cession & the Names of the p[er]sons p[re]sent at the Same, And what Land [in] you^r percinct you Shall faile to p[ro]cession You Are to give An Acco^t wth the p[ar]ticular reasons of Such faillure, And if Any refuse to have their Land p[ro]cess^d You Are to Certifie the Same to the Church Wardens wthin Tenn Days from Under Yo^r Hands &c

[5]   13

Ord^d that Thomas Jones and George Keene in p[re]sence of the Inha[bitants] p[ro]cession all the Bounds of Land on the South Side South Key Road begining at Thos Jones plantation from thence as the path runs from Jno Jen[?]³ to James Hollands to South Key road down the South Side the Said road to Robt Yeats Bridge Includeing all the Land in the Said Bounds, You Are to go round every Mans Land & Renew the Land Marks and return to the Vestry An Acco^t of every mans Land You p[ro]cession with the Names of the p[er]sons p[re]sent At the Same & what Land in Yo^r p[re]cinct you shall faile to p[ro]cess you are to give An Acco^t wth the p[ar]ticular reason of Such faillure and if Any Refuse to have their Land p[ro]cess^d You Are to Certifie the same to the Church Wardens wthin Tenn Days from Under You^r Hands &c

14

Ord^d that Culbert Hedgpath & Joseph Holland in p[re]sence of the Inhabitants p[ro]cession all the Bounds of Land; Begining at Henry Hollands plantation so Down the North Side King Sale Swamp to the County Line; from thence to the head of the Meadow Branch, so to Robt Yeats Bridge: from thence on the North Side South Key Road to Henry Hollands p^{l}tation, Including all the Land in the Said Bounds: you Are to go round every mans Land and renew the Land Marks and return to the Vestry An Acco^t of every man[s] Land You p[ro]cession & the Names of the p[er]sons p[re]sent At the Same; and what Land in Yo^r p[re]cinct You Shall faile to p[ro]cess. You Are to give An Acco^t with the p[ar]ticular Reason of Such faillure, & if Any refuse to have have [sic] their

---

³ Jenkins undoubtedly. A fragment of the edge of the page is missing and not shown in the photocopy. *Cf.* procession order No. 10, p. 61.

Land p[ro]cess^d You Are to Certifie the Same to the Church Wardens wth in Tenn Day's from Under Your Hands &c

15

Ord^d that Carr Darden & Jacob Darden in p[re]sence of the Inhabitants p[ro]cession all the Bounds of Land, on the South Black Water & Nottaway Rivers to the Extent of the County & Country Lines including all the Land in the said Bounds, You Are to go round every mans Land & renew the Land marks And return to the Vestry An Acco^t of ever[y] mans Land you p[ro]cession & the Names of the p[er]sons p[re]sent At the Same, and what Land in Yo^r p[re]cinct you shall faile to p[ro]cess: you Are to give An Acco^t wth the p[ar]ticular reasons of Such faillure, And if Any refuse to have their Land p[ro]cess^d you Are to Certifie the Same to the Church Wardens wth in Tenn Day's from Under yor Hands &c

16

Ord^d that Thos Shivers & Henry Lawrance in the p[re]sence of the Inhabitants p[ro]cession all the Bounds of Land, from the going Over Wickam Swamp to the Country Line so to King saile Swamp up the said Swamp to the first station Including all the Land in the Said Bounds: You Are to go round every mans Land and renew the Land Marks & Return to the Vestry an Acco^t of every man[s] Land you p[ro]cess: and the Names of the p[er]sons p[re]sent At the Same, And what Land in Yo^r p[re]cinct You Shall faile to p[ro]cess: You Are to give An Acco^t with the p[ar]ticular reasons of Such faillure; And if Any refuse to have to have [sic] their Land p[ro]cessioned You Are to Certifie the Same to the Church Warden[s] With in Tenn Day's from Under Your Hands &c

[6]   17

[Or]d^d that Mosses Hall & John Cross p[ro]cession all the Bounds of Land, from [the] Knuckle Swamp on the West Side Searum Road to the Extent of the County [in]cluding all the Land in the Said Bounds, You Are to go round Every mans Land [a]nd renew the Land Marks, and return to the Vestry An Acco^t of every mans Land You p[ro]cession and the Names of the p[er]sons p[re]sent at the Same, and what Land in yor p[re]cinct you Shall faile to p[ro]cession You are to give An Acco^t wth the p[ar]ticular reasons of Such faillure, and if Any refuse to have their Land p[ro]cessioned You Are to Certifie the Same to the Church Wardens w^{th}in Tenn Day's from Under Youre Hands &c

18

Ord^d that James Brinkley & Thomas Wilkins in p[re]sence of the Inhabitants p[ro]cession all the Bounds of Land, from the Sipruss Swamp On the East Side Orapeak road to the Country Line Including all the Land in the said Bounds; You Are to go round every Mans Land and renew the Land Marks and return to the Vestry An Acco^t of every mans Land You p[ro]cession and the Names of the p[er]sons p[re]sent At the Same; And what Land in Your p[re]cinct You Shall faile to p[ro]cession You Are to give Acco^t wth the p[ar]ticular reasons of Such faillure; And if Any refuse to have their Land p[ro]cessioned you Are to Certifie the Same to the Church Wardens w^{th}in Tenn Days from Under Yo^r Hands &c

19

Ord^d that John Baker & Joseph Griffing in p[re]sence of the Inhabitants p[ro]cession all the Bounds of Land, Begining At the Sipress swamp thence on the West Side Orapeak Roade to the Country Line, thence to Raby's Swamp to the head thereof thence down the Road to the Draggon Swamp to the Siprus Swamp to Orapeak Road, Including all the Land in the Said Bounds, You Are to go round every mans Land and renew the Land marks and return to the Vestry An Acco^t of every mans Land You p[ro]cession wth the Names of the p[er]sons p[re]sent at the Same, and what Land in Youre p[re]cinct you Shall faile to p[ro]cession you Are to give An Acco^t wth the p[ar]ticular reasons of Such faillure, And if Any refuse to have their Land p[ro]cessioned you Are to Certifie the Same to the Church Wardens w^{th}in Tenn Day's from Under Yo^r Hands &c

20

Ord^d that John Cole Junr & William Horten in p[re]sence of the Inhabitants p[ro]cession all the Bounds of Land, from the Knuckle swamp to Barbecue Swamp Betwene Sum^rton road & Smiths road Including all the Land in the Said Bounds, You Are to go round every mans Land & renew the Land Marks, and return to the Vestry An Acco^t of every mans Land You p[ro]cess: And the Names of the p[er]sons p[re]sent at the Same, & what Land in Yo^r p[re]cinct You Shall faile to p[ro]cession,

You Are to give An Acco^t wth the p[ar]ticular Reasons of Such faillure. And If any Refuse to have their Land p[ro]cessioned, You Are to Certifie the Same to the Church Wardens within Tenn Days from Under Yo^r Hands &c

[7]   21

Ord^d that Robert Peele and Job Hairell in p[re]sence of the Inhabitants p[ro]cession all the Bounds of Land, from the Country Line to Adam Raby's Swamp up the Said Swamp to the Road as the road runs to Smiths Road and as the Road Runs to the Country Line, Including all the Land in the Said Bounds you Are to go round every Mans Land renew the Land Marks and return to the Vestry An Acco^t of every mans Land You p[ro]cession, And the names of the p[er]sons p[re]sent At the Same, And w^t Land in Yo^r p[re]cinct You Shall faile to to [sic] p[ro]cession, you Are to give An Acco^t wth the p[ar]ticular reasons of Such faillure, and if Any refuse to have their Land p[ro]cessioned You Are to Certifi[e] the Same to the Church Wardens within Tenn Day's from Under Yo^r Hands &c

22

Ord^d that William Hunter & Joseph Pery in p[re]sence of the Inhabitants p[ro]cession All the Bounds of Land from Barbecue Swamp Down Nubies Road to Fran: Copelands Branch down the S^d Branch to Bakers Mil[l] run up the Said runn to the Mouth of the Beaverdam Swamp up the Said Swamp to the Bridge So up Sum^{r}ton Road to Barbecue Swamp Including all the Land in the Said Bounds, You Are to go round every mans Land And renew the Land Marks And return to the Vestry An Acco^t of every Mans Land You p[ro]cession And the Names of the p[er]sons p[re]sent At the Same & w^t Land in Yo^r p[re]cinct You Shall faile to p[ro]cession You Are to give An Acco^t wth the p[ar]ticular reasons of Such faillure, And if Any refuse to have their Land p[ro]cess^d You Are to Certifie the Same to the Church Wardens wthin Tenn Days from Under Youre Hands &c

23

Ord^d that Jno Rountree & Abra: Lassiter in the p[re]sence of the Inhabitants p[ro]cession all the Bounds of Land, from Nuby's Rode Down Barbcue & the Siprus Swamp to the Desert down the Desert to the pocosson up the pocosson to the head of Fran. Coplands Branch, Including all the Land in the Said Bounds, You Are to go round Every Mans Land & Renew the Land Marks, And return to the Vestry An Acco[t] of every mans Land You p[ro]cession and the Names of the p[er]sons p[re]sent At the Same And w[t] Land in Yo[r] p[re]cinct you Shall faile to p[ro]cess: you Are to give An Acco[t] with the p[ar]ticular reasons of Such faillure, And if Any refuse to have their Land p[ro]cess[d] you Are to Certifie the Same to the Church Wardens w[th]in Tenn [days] from Under Yo[r] Hands &c

24

Ord[d] that Henry Skiner & Jn[o] Long in the p[re]sence of the Inhabitants p[ro]cession all the Bounds of Land, on the West Side the Beaverdam to Fran: Copelands Branch, dow[n] donn [sic] the S[d] Branch to Bakers Mill run donn [sic] the Said run & Creek to Pughs Creek, Including all the Land in the Said Bounds, You Are to go round every mans Land & renew the Land Marks, & return to the Vestry An Acco[t] of ever[y] Mans Land you p[ro]cess: & the Names of the p[er]sons p[re]sent at the Same, & w[t] Lan[d] in Yo[r] p[re]cinct You Shall faile to p[ro]cession you Are to give An Acco[t] w[th] the p[ar]ticular reasons of Such faillure, And if Any refuse to have their Land p[ro]cess[d] You Are to Certifie the Same to the Church Wardens w[th]in Tenn Day's from Under Yo[r] Hands; &c

[8]   25

Ord[d] that Rob[t] Baker & Nathanill Bemond in the p[re]sence of the Inhabitants p[ro]cession all the Bounds of Land, Betwene Maj[r] Pughs mill Creek and Keatons Creek up the Branch betwene Keetons and Gumbs to the Desert Including all the Land in the Said Bounds, You Are to go round Every mans Land and renew the Land marks, And return to the Vestry An Acco[t] of every mans Land You p[ro]cession And the Names of the p[er]sons p[re]sent at the Same And what Land in Yo[r] p[re]cinct You Shall faile to p[ro]cession You Are to give An Acco[t] w[th] the p[ar]ticular reasons of Such faillure, And if Any refuse to have their Land p[ro]cess[d] You Are to Certifie the Same to the Church Wardens w[th]in Tenn Days from Under Yo[r] Hands &c

26

Ord[d] that Robert Jassey And Edw[d] Coffield in p[re]sence of the Inhabitants p[ro]cession All the Bounds of Land, from Keetons Creek

Down to the Extent of the p[ar]ish Including all the Land in the Said Bounds: You Are to go round every mans Land and renew the Land Marks And return to the Vestry An Acco^t of every Mans Land You p[ro]cession And the Names of the p[er]sons p[re]sent At the Same, And what Land in You^r p[re]cinct You Shall faile to p[ro]cession You Are to give An Acco^t wth the p[ar]ticular reasons of Such faillure And If Any refuse to have their Land p[ro]cessioned You Are to Certifie the Same to the Church Wardens wthin Tenn Days from Under Youre Hands &c

27

Ord^d that Mills Riddick & James Booth in p[re]sence of the Inhabitants p[ro]cession all the Bounds of Land on the East Side the Beaverdam Up to the pocossen, Including all the Land in the Said Bounds, You Are to go round Every mans Land and renew the Land Marks [a]nd Return to the Vestry An Acco^t of every Mans Land You p[ro]cession [a]nd the Names of the p[er]sons p[re]sent At the Same, And what Land in Yo^r p[re]cinct You Shall faile to p[ro]cession You Are to give An Acco^t wth the p[ar]ticular Reasons of Such faillure, And If Any refuse to have their Land p[ro]cess^d You Are to Certifie the Same to the Church Wardens wthin Tenn Days from Under Yo^r Hands &c

28

Ord^d that William Rice & Jno Roggers in the p[re]sence of the Inhabitants, p[ro]cession all the Bounds of Land, from the Knuckle Swamp Bridge on the South Side the Swamp up the East side Sum^{r}ton road to the Country Line, so Along the Line to Smiths road So Down Smiths Road to the Knuckle Swamp so Down the South Side thereof to the first Station Including all the Land in the said Bounds, You Are to go round every mans Land & renew the Land Marks And return to the Vestry An Acco^t of every mans Land You p[ro]cession And the Names of the persons p[re]sent At the Same and w^t Land in Yo^r p[re]cinct You Shall faile to p[ro]cession You Are to give An Acco^t with the p[ar]ticular Reasons of Such faillure, And if Any refuse to have their Land p[ro]cessioned You Are to Certifie the Same to Church Wardens Within Tenn Days from Under Yo^r Hands &c

Edwd Norfleet: C^l Vestry   Danl Pugh } Ch: Wds
                                 Jethro Sumner

[9]

At A Vestry held At the Court house for the Up p[ar]ish of Nansemond County Novemr the 3d 1744[4]

Present: The Revd Wm Balfour Minister
Capt Wm Wright   Edwd Norfleet
Colo And{w} Meede   Capt Lem{l} Riddick
Mr Wm Butler   Colo Danl Pugh   ⎫
Mr Jno Norfleet   Capt Jethro Sumner   ⎬ Church Wardens

Dr

To the Revd Wm Balfour his Sallery	16000	
To D{o} for Cask	640	
To D{o} for Gleeb	2000	
To Jno Lester for Keeping a p{o} wom: 4 months	161	
To Robert Fry as C{lk} for 11 months	734	
To Wm Shettleton as Reader @ Up{r} Chap{l}	800	
To Mr Nathan{ll} Wright for Insolv{ts}	1734	
To James Baker for the Trouble of his house in Looking after Rachel Wrench in Child Bed &c	900	
To D{o} for Keeping and Nursing her Child	466	
To Colo Osheal his Charge for Keeping Saml Smith Till Chrismas Next	600	
To John Gwin for Horse Blocks & Cleaning the Yard & Road @ Lower Chap{l}	240	242[75]
To Jno Carr Keeping Jno Blith 2 m{o} @ 800{lb} Tob{o} per Ann:	134	
To Christ{o} Sanders for Keeping D{o} 8 m{o}	520	
To Eliza Farrow for Keeping for Keeping [sic] Grace Armsted 2 m{o} ½	125	
To Thos Williams for Keeping Fran{s} Collings 2 m{o}	134	
To Edward Norfleet as Usual	2000	
To Wm Johns for Mooving a poor woman	40	
To Theo{s} Pugh for Sarah Hoods pasage to New England	1000	
To Wm Yeats for Burying Mary Robinson	500	

[4] The bracketed matter in the proceedings of this meeting mostly appears in the photocopy of 1925.

Down to the Extent of the p[ar]ish Including all the Land in the Said Bounds: You Are to go round every mans Land and renew the Land Marks And return to the Vestry An Acco^t of every Mans Land You p[ro]cession And the Names of the p[er]sons p[re]sent At the Same, And what Land in You^r p[re]cinct You Shall faile to p[ro]cession You Are to give An Acco^t wth the p[ar]ticular reasons of Such faillure And If Any refuse to have their Land p[ro]cessioned You Are to Certifie the Same to the Church Wardens wthin Tenn Days from Under Youre Hands &c

27

Ord^d that Mills Riddick & James Booth in p[re]sence of the Inhabitants p[ro]cession all the Bounds of Land on the East Side the Beaverdam Up to the pocossen, Including all the Land in the Said Bounds, You Are to go round Every mans Land and renew the Land Marks [a]nd Return to the Vestry An Acco^t of every Mans Land You p[ro]cession [a]nd the Names of the p[er]sons p[re]sent At the Same, And what Land in Yo^r p[re]cinct You Shall faile to p[ro]cession You Are to give An Acco^t wth the p[ar]ticular Reasons of Such faillure, And If Any refuse to have their Land p[ro]cess^d You Are to Certifie the Same to the Church Wardens wthin Tenn Days from Under Yo^r Hands &c

28

Ord^d that William Rice & Jno Roggers in the p[re]sence of the Inhabitants, p[ro]cession all the Bounds of Land, from the Knuckle Swamp Bridge on the South Side the Swamp up the East side Sum^{r}ton road to the Country Line, so Along the Line to Smiths road So Down Smiths Road to the Knuckle Swamp so Down the South Side thereof to the first Station Including all the Land in the said Bounds, You Are to go round every mans Land & renew the Land Marks And return to the Vestry An Acco^t of every mans Land You p[ro]cession And the Names of the persons p[re]sent At the Same and w^t Land in Yo^r p[re]cinct You Shall faile to p[ro]cession You Are to give An Acco^t with the p[ar]ticular Reasons of Such faillure, And if Any refuse to have their Land p[ro]cessioned You Are to Certifie the Same to Church Wardens Within Tenn Days from Under Yo^r Hands &c

Edwd Norfleet: C^l Vestry   Danl Pugh } Ch: Wds
     Jethro Sumner

Ord^d that Isaac Rambow be Clerk of the Middle Chap^l Sallery as Usuall begining 21st of October 1744

[O]rd^d that Hen^ry Skiner be Clerk of Sum^rton Chap^l for which [for] which [sic] He is to Attend the Same Every Saboath at 1200^lb [To]b^o per Ann:

[The] p[ar]ish being Indebted the Sum of fourty Nine Thousand [and] thirty two pounds of Tobacco and there being 1278 tithables [in] the Said p[ar]ish wch Sum being p[ro]portioned on Every Individuall tithable [A]mo^ts to the Sum of 39^lb of Tobacco per p^o wth a Dep^o due the p[ar]ish [81]0^lb of Tob^o to be Allowed at the Laying the Next p[ar]ish Levie &c

[Ord]^d that Mr Edwd Wright Sher^ff Collect of 1278 tithables in this [paris]h the Sum of 49032^lb of Tob^o and pay Unto the Severall Creditors [of] this p[ar]ish their Sums of Tob^o Due unto them, According to the Above [Settle]m^t and Late Act of Assembly[5] & Acco^t wth the Church Wardens & [Vestry] at the Laying the Next p[ar]ish Levie, giving Bond & Security as [the] [La]w Directs

Exa: [per] E. Norfleet C^l vestry

      Danl Pugh } Ch: Wardens
      Jethro Sumner

[11]

[At A Ve]stry held at Suffolk Town for [the] Up p[arish] of Nansemond County [De]cem: the 29[th] 1744[6]

Present Mr Wm Balfour Minister
          Mr Wm Butler   Mr Jno Winborn
          Capt Lem^l Riddick Edwd Norfleet
          Mr Jno Norfleet   Mr Jethro Sumner Church Warden

[Th]is Day the Vestry Mett and Whereas Capt Wm Wright Capt Jno Gregorie [a]nd Mr Jno Milner Late Vestry men in this p[ar]ish Are by

---

[5] Sections XXVIII-XXX of "An Act, for reducing the Laws made, for amending the Staple of Tobacco; and for preventing frauds in his Majesty's Customs, into one act of Assembly" (Hening, v. 5, p. 138-139), passed at the May 1742 session of the General Assembly, defined the duties of sheriffs or other collectors in regard to collecting and disbursing parish and other levies, fees, etc., payable in tobacco.

[6] The bracketed matter in the proceedings of this meeting mostly appears in the photocopy of 1925.

Act of Assembly[7] [ta]ken into Suffolk p[ar]ish Wherefore this Vestry have thought fitt to Elect [in] their Rooms Mills Riddick, D[t] Hening Tembte Now Sworne & Take [th]eir places Accordinly Likewise Christ[o] Norfleet to be quallified next [V]estry

         W[m] Balfour Minister
         Jethro Sumner Church Warden

 At a Vestry held at M[r] Edw[d] Doughties for the Up[r] p[ar]ish of Nansemond County Ap[l] 16[th] 1745[8]

Present: M[r] W[m] Butler
    Cap[t] Lem[l] Riddick Edw[d] Norfleet
    M[r] Mills Riddick
    Cap[t] Hening Tembte Cap[t] Jethro Sumner Ch: Wd
    M[r] Jn[o] Winborn

This Day Christopher Norfleet haveing Taken the Oaths Appointed for a Vestry [M]an & Signed the Test Takes his place Accordingly

[T]he Vestry have Made Choice of M[r] David Meede and M[r] Daniel [P]ugh as Vestry men in the Roome of Col[o] And: Meed & Col[o] [D]aniel Pugh Dec[d]

Cap[t] Jethro Sumner & M[r] Mills Riddick are Elected & Sworn Church Wardens Untill Easter Next

Ord[d] the Executers of Cap[t] Dan[l] Pugh Dec[d] Do Acco[t] with the p[re]sent Church Wardens for the fines Due in the Hands of the Said Dec[d]

            Bourn Over

[12]

Brought Over

Ordered that this Vestry will Meet Againe on the Eighteenth Day of Ma[...][9] next at the Middle Chap[l] to Enq[r] in to the Behaviour of the

---

[7] Hening, v. 5, p. 269-270. This act for adding part of the Upper Parish to Suffolk Parish became effective November 20, 1744. See Introduction, p. xvi-xvii.

[8] The bracketed matter in the proceedings of this meeting mostly appears in the photocopy of 1925.

[9] In the original, only "Ma" shows, the final letter or letters at the edge of the page having been lost; in the photocopy, "Mar" seems to show but the apparent "r" is probably the first stroke of "y". The word is doubtless May since March would defer the meeting for almost a year. The vestry book contains no record of a meeting on May 18, 1745, March 18, 1746, or May 18, 1746, but on December 4, 1745, the vestry provided that the executor of the Rev. William Balfour should be paid eleven months salary (See p. 16).

Rev[d] W[m] Balfour Minister; who hath Bin Guilty of Drunkenness, p[ro]fane Swaring a[nd] Many Other Indecensess & hath failed in p[er]forming his Service at Church [&] Chapple Severall times, Therefore it is Ordered that the Church Wardens Serve the Said M[r] Balfour with a Copy of this Order, And req[r] that he [be] p[re]sent at Said Vestry to Answer Such things as Shall be Then & there said to his Charge

Jethro Sumner }
Mills Riddick } Ch: Warde[ns]

At a Vestry held at the Court house for the Up[r] p[ar]ish of Nansemond Co[unty] Decem: the 4[th] Day 1745[10]

Present: W[m] Butler   Lemuel Riddick   Jethro Sumner
          Edw[d] Norfleet   Hening Tembte   Mills Riddick
          John Winborn   Jn[o] Norfleet   Church Wardens

M[r] Daniel Pugh Came into the Vestry and toock the Oaths and Subscrib[ed] the Test and Then Took his place in the S[d] Vestry

	D[r] lb Tob[o]
Parish	
To M[r] Jn[o] Woddrap Execu[r] of the Rev[d] William Balfoure for 11 months Sallery	14667
To D[o] 4 per C[t] for Cask	586
To D[o] for a Gleeb	2000
To Edw[d] Norfleet for being Clk of the Vestry & Reader	2000
To M[r] Isaac Rambow Reader at the Chap[l]	800
To M[r] Hen[y] Skiner D[o] Sum[r]ton	1200
To Hen[y] Gwin for Cleaning the Middle Chapple	250
To Susana Tayloe for Cleaning Sum[r]ton D[o]	150
To D[o] for Keeping Margrett Horten 5½ months	550
To Jn[o] Lester for Keeping Mary Jordan 8 D[o]	333
To Peter Butler for Keeping Gladman 13 months	1108
To D[o] for Burying D[o]	300
To Docter Christopher Wright for Medd[s] Adm: to R: Babb	575

---

[10] The bracketed matter in the proceedings of this meeting appears in part in the photocopy of 1925.

To D⁰ for Attendance & Med⁸ for Joell Brown a Saylor, p[ro]vided the Church Wardens Sue Capᵗ Lewis Merideth & Recover So much of him: Other ways to be refunded	450
To Jaˢ Lacey for Boarding a Sick Man	350
To John Gwin	150
To Wᵐ Horten for Keeping a poor Child	1085
[To] D⁰ for Keeping Mary Harriss 5½ months	456
[To] Jn⁰ Denby for D⁰ 6½ D⁰	542
[To] D⁰ Sarah Whinard 9 months	600
[To] Garritt Cotter D⁰ Reb: Champion 3½ D⁰	250
Bourn Over	28402

[13]

Brought Over	28402
To Jaˢ Lassiter Sʳ D⁰ 3 D⁰	200
To The⁰ Jones for Keeping Ann Boyt 5 D⁰	300
To Mʳ Nathˡˡ Wright his Accoᵗ	282
To Richᵈ Webb for Boarding R: Rack 13 months	1300
To Edwᵈ Doughtie	300
To Mʳ Mills Riddick his Accoᵗ	1000
To Edwᵈ Wright Sherᶠᶠ, for Insolvents, after Accoᵗing for Last Years Dep⁰	555
To Joshua Ward for Keeping Grace Armstead	1000
To John Blith	117
To Christopher Sanders for Keeping Jn⁰ Blith 9 months	600
To Christ⁰ Jackson for the Copy 4 Lists Tithab:	80
To John Cole for Keeping Grace Armsted 1 month	67
To Jethro Sumner his Accoᵗ	4784
To 7215ˡᵇ of Tob⁰ Levied toward the Building a Church to be paid by the Collector to Jethro Sumner & Mills Riddick Church Wardens and by them Sold for Cash and to Accoᵗ wᵗʰ the Vestry at Laying the Next p[ar]ish Levie	7215
	46402
To Edwᵈ Wright Sherᶠᶠ for Collecting 46402ˡᵇ of Tob⁰ @ 6 per Cᵗ	2785
	49187

Ord^d that John Campbell be Reader to the Church & Chaples of this p[ar]ish & that he officiate in Course at Each Every Sabboth Day

The p[ar]ish being Indebted the Sum of forty nine Thousand one hundred Eightie Seven pounds of Tob^o & there being 1139 Tithables in the Said p[ar]ish wch Said Sum being p[ro]portion'd on Every Tithable Am^ts to the Sum of 43^lb of Tob^o per & 210^lb of Tob^o to be paid the p[ar]ish Collec^r Next Year &c

Ord^d that Edwd Wright, Gen^t Collect of 1139 Tithables in this p[ar]ish the Sum of 49187^lb of Tob^o and pay unto the Sev^l Creditors of this p[ar]ish the Sums of Tob^o Due unto them According to the Above Settlem^t and Late Act of Assembly[11] and Acco^t wth the Church Wardens & Vestry at Laying the Next p[ar]ish Levie giving Bond & Security as the Law Directs

Jethro Sumner } Church Warde[ns]
Mills Riddick }

[14]

At a Vestry held at the Court house for the Upper p[ar]ish of Nans^d County Apriel the 1st 1746

Present Jno Norfleet   Edwd Norfleet
         Capt Hen^g Temple [sic]   Capt Jethro Sumnr } Ch. Wds
         Mr Danl Pugh   Capt Mills Riddick }
         Christo^r Norfleet

Capt Jethro Sumner and Capt Mills Riddick Are Continued and Sworne Church Wardens Untill Easter Next

Jethro Sumner
Mills Riddick

At a Vestry held at Suffolk Town June the 30th 1746 for the Upper p[ar]ish of Nans^d County

Present Wm Butler   Hening Temple [sic]
         Jno Winborn   Daniel Pugh
         Chris^o Norfleet   Jethro Sumner } Ch. Wds
                              Mills Riddick }

---

[11] See p. 14, footnote 5.

Mr David Mead being Elected and Chosen a Vestry Man hath Taken the Oaths Appointed for the Same And Taken his place Accordingly

Aded: David Mead & Lem^l Riddick

Ord^d the Church Wardens make a present to the Revd Mr Beckett in Gratuation to him for his Trouble in Coming into this p[ar]ish and preaching one Sermon three pistoles and that they Bring in Their Charge at the Laying the Next p[ar]ish Leavey

Ord^d this Vestry Meet Againe at this place the first Munday in September Next

          Jethro Sumner Ch^d w^d
          Mills Riddick

[15]

At A Vestry held at Suffolk Town 7^{ber12} 1st 1746

Present Wm Butler   Christ^o Norfleet
    Lem^l Riddick   Edwd Norfleet
    Jno Winborne   Jethro Sumner Ch^d W^d
    Wm Baker

The Vestry having this day Met According to the Last Appointment with intent to Appoint a place for the Building & Eretting a Church for this p[ar]ish and to Agree Upon the Dementions &c. And there appearing but a bare Vestry this Vestry doth not think proper to Enter Upon So Weaty an Affair Without a fuller Vestry. Therefore Its Ord^d that this Vestry Meet Again at this place on the first Munday in Next Month in Order to Consult On the Aforesaid Affair

          Jethro Sumner Ch^d w^d
          Mills Riddick

At a Vestry held at Suffolk Town for the Upper p[ar]ish of Nans^d County October 7th 1746

Present Mr Wm Butler   Mr Danl Pugh
    Mr Jno Winborn   Mr Jno Norfleet
    Capt Wm Baker   May^r Lem^l Riddick
    Mr David Meade   Christ^o Norfleet
     Edwd Norfleet   Capt Jethro Sumnr } Ch. W^{ds}
            Capt Mills Riddick }

The Majority of this Vestry being Agreed for the Building a New

---

[12] *I. e.* September. The year then began on March 25.

Brick Church in the Old field of James March Convenient to a good Spring; Sixty foot Long & Thirty foot Wide or Other Dementions as May be Agreed On hereafter; and the Said James March at this time Consenting to Make Conven^s [?] of two Acres of the Said Old field or Land as Abov[e] Said; Ord^d that Mr David Meade Mr Mills Riddick Mr Jethro Sumner Mr Danl Pugh & Mr Edwd Norfleet Meet on Friday Next at the Plantation of the S^d March and Lay out the Said two Acres of Land in the Convenienteth place on the Said plantation—and its further Ordred the Church Wardens prepair a Deed of Sale for the S^d Land against the Next Court. Ordred that the above S^d persons provide A plan of a Church of the Valeeu of & Not Exceeding five Hundred pounds to be produc'd at the Next Vestry and that they Advertize the Undertaking of the S^d Church on the third Munday in November Next at the Middle Chapple

Jethro Sumner
Mills Riddick

[16]

Att a Vestry held at Suffolk Town January 24 1746[/47] for Laying the parish Levy

Present Jethro Sumner & Mills Riddick Gen^t Churchwardens

William Butler
Lemuel Riddick
Hening Tembte   } Gen^t of the Vestry
Christopher Norfleet
&
David Meade

Edward Norfleet the present Clerk being Sick and not able to Attend & doe the duty of Clarke of this Vestry and Lemuel Riddick Offering to Officiate as Clarke without any sallary or Allowance is Appointed Clarke of this Vestry & keeper of this Parish Register

Ordered that Edward Norfleet Deliver to him the parish Regester

The upper P[ar]ish of Nansemond County for the year 1746 is D^r

	lb Tob^o
To John Campbell Reader at the Church & Chappell	1000
To Edward Norfleet Gen^t for keeping the parish Register &c 14 months	1533

To Susanah Tayloe for Cleaning the Upper Chappell	0150
To Henry Gwin for Cleaning & attending as Sexton at the midle Chapell	0250
To John Long for keeping Mary Jordan one y^r to wit 1745 Last y^r omitted	0500
To John Lester for keeping &^{c} Mary Jordan 6 m^o at 750 per y^r	0375
To William Horton for Keeping Mary Harris 9 m^o at 1000 per y^r	0750
To Wm Horton for Keeping & Clothing Eliz^a Hackett 14 ½ m^o at 800 per y^r	0966
To Theophilus Jones for keeping Ann Boyt for 5 m^o & 17 days at 1200 per y^r	0550
To D^o for his Extrodinary trouble Looking after her in her Ilness and burying her & finding & provideing for her funerall	0400
To John Blythe for his Maintenance	0350
To John Denby for Keeping Mary Harris 5 ½ M^o at 1000 per y^r	0458
To Richard Adkins for keeping Babbs Child 1 Year	0750
To John Gwinn for Clearing the Road to the middle Chappell 150 for Clearing the Spring & Chappell yard 25 for 12 benches & white oak Blocks 300	0475
To Elizabeth Farrow for keeping Grace Annstead 2 M^o & 3 Weeks 800 per y^r	0175
To John Cole of Tuckers Neck for keeping Grace Anstead 11 M^o at 800 per y^r	0733
To Richard Webb for keeping Richd Rack 13 M^o & 20 Days	1375
To Doct^r Christopher Wright for Performing an Operation on Mary Brinkly	1000
To Edward Doughtie per his Acco^t	0090
To Christopher Jackson Clerke as per his Acco^t	0202
To Hening Tembte for Medicines for Richd Rack	0150
To Doct^r Robert Brown for Phissick &^{c} for Robt Frazier	0660
	12892

[17]

The upper parish of Nansemond County	D^r
Brought over from the other Side	12892
To Mr Edward Wright Late Sheriff for 42 Levys Insolvent the last Year at 43 lb Tob^o per pole	01806

To Ballance due from the parish to the S^d Sherif Last year	00210
To James Lacey for Maintaining Fenol Brown 9 M° 17 days	00950
To Thomas Jones a poor man for Maintenance of himself & family	01500
To Jethro Sumner Gen^t Churchwarden for his Acco^t for disburstm^{ts} for the poor	03952
To Mills Riddick Gen^t Church warden his Acco^t for Disburstments for the poor & 3 Pistoles paid the Revd Mr Beckett	02419
To James Sumner 1 Levy overlisted Last Year	00043
To 16000 lb Tob° to be paid to & Sold by the Church wardens for the time being in July Court next for Ready money to the highest bidder & the Church wardens to Acco^t with the Vestry when Required which money is to be Applied towards Building a Church	16000
To Mr David Meade for 5/ paid for the advertiseing the building a Church	00050
	39822
To the Collector 6 per C^t on 39822 lb Tob° for Collectining	02389
	42211
To a Ball due to the parish to be paid by the Collector next P[ar]ish Levy	197
	42408

The parish being D^r the Sum of 42211 lb Tob° to Sundry Persons as Stated in the Above Acco^t its Ordered that Mills Riddick Gen^t Collect from Every tithable in this parish (to wit) 1116 Each the Sum of thirty Eight Pounds of Tobacco & therewith Discharge the Above Debts which Amounts to   42408
He first Giving bond & Security as Usuall

Jethro Sumner Gen^t one of the Church wardens rendered his Acco^t of the one half of the 7215 lb Tob° Levied the Last Levy towards building a Church which was Sold for 9/11 per C^t amounts to   17..17..8
which he Acknowledges now to have in his hands.

Mills Riddick Gen^t one of the Church wardens Rendered

his Acco^t of the Sale of one half of 7215 lb Tob^o Levied the Last Levy Towards building a Church which Sold at 9/11 per C^t amounts to 17..17..8 which he Acknowledges to have in his hands

Ordered the above Sum of 17..17..8 in the hands of Jethro Sumner Remain in his hands untill Otherways Ordered by this Vestry

Ordered that the Above Sum of 17..17..8 in the hands of Mills Riddick remain in his hands untill otherways ordered by this Vestry

Truely Entered by me   Signed { Jethro Sumner
  Lemuel Riddick Clerk Vestry   Mills Riddick

[18]

Att a Vestry held at the House of Mr Josiah Riddick in Suffolk Town for the upper parish of Nansemond County on Easter Tuesday the 21 of April 1747.

Present Jethro Sumner
           &   } Gen^t Church wardens
         Mills Riddick
         William Butler
         John Winbourn
         William Baker
         Lemuel Riddick } Gen^t of the Vestry
         Hening Tembte
           &
         Daniel Pugh

Josiah Riddick Gen^t being duely Elected a Vestryman for this Parish (in the room of Edward Norfleet Gen^t Deceased) who having taken the Oaths to the Goverment the Oath of Abjuration and Subscribed the Test & the Oath of a Vestry man hath taken his place in the Vestry

Jethro Sumner and Mills Riddick Gen^t are Appointed Church wardens untill Easter next they having taken the Oath of a Church warden prescrib'd by Law

Jethro Sumner Gen^t one of the Church wardens Reported he had Security for payment of Tenn barrels of Tarr for Lightwood Sold of the poors Land its therefore Ordered that as Soon as the Said Tarr is Received the Said Sumner pay unto Ann Hains the Sum of five barrels of the Said

Tarr & to Ruth Whale the other five barrels or that he Lay the Same out for provision or Cloths for them as he thinks proper

<table>
<tr><td>Truely Entered by
Lemuel Riddick Clerke
of the Vestry</td><td>Signed {</td><td>Jethro Sumner
Mills Riddick</td></tr>
</table>

[19]

At a Vestry held for the upper parish of Nansemond County (at Suffolk Town) August 31. 1747.

Present Mills Riddick Gen^t Church warden

John Norfleet
William Baker
Lemuel Riddick   } Gen^t of the Vestry
Hening Tembte
Daniel Pugh
& Josiah Riddick

added John Winburn
& Christopher Norfleet } Gen^t

The Reverend Mr William Webb is Received by this Vestry as Minister of this parish

Lemuel Riddick & Christopher Wright are Appointed to procession the bounds of Land in Suffolk Town, being the bounds Mentioned in the former Order in the Register Book Distinguis'd by the Number 1.

The bounds formerly N° 2 is now aded to Suffolk parish

Ord^d Jonathan Roberts & Jonathan Nelms Procession all the Lands in the bounds N° 3 According to Law.

Ordered that Christopher Norfleet & Edward Moor procession all the Lands in the bounds N° 4 According to Law

Ordered that Thomas Milner Junr & Joseph Lawrence Procession all the Land in the bounds N° 5 According to Law.

Ordered that John Best & William Bateman procession all the Lands in the bounds N° 6 According to Law

Ordered that Abraham Ballard & Elisha Ashburn procession all the Lands in the bounds N° 7 According to Law.

Ordered that Abraham Carnall & John Skinner procession all the Lands in the bounds N° 8 According to Law

Ordered that James Coupland & Jn° Porter Procession all the Lands in the bounds N° 9 According to Law

[20]

Ordered that Jacob Jones & Frederick Jones Procession all the Lands in the bounds N° 10 According to Law

Ordered that Henry Daughtry & Thomas Shivers Procession all the Lands in the bounds N° 11 According to Law

Ordered that Abraham Riddick & John Lawrence Son of George Procession all the Lands in the bounds N° 12 According to Law

Ordered that John Winbourn Jun' & John Ralls Procesion all the Lands in the bounds N° 13 According to Law

Ordered that Stephen Dardan & James Holland the son of John Procession all the Lands in the bounds N° 14 According to Law

Ordered that William Hart and Joseph Curle Procession all the Lands in the bounds N° 15 According to Law

Ordered that William Sanders & James Uzell procession all the Lands in the bounds N° 16 According to Law

Ordered Joshua Peel & Daniel March procession all the Lands in the bounds N° 17 According to Law

Ordered that James Lacitor Jun' & Joshua Spivy Jun' procession all the Lands in the bounds N° 18 According to Law

Ordered that Arthur Gorlay & George Bains Procession all the Lands in the bounds N° 19 According to Law

Ordered that Joseph Baker & Francis Duke Procession all the Lands in the bounds N° 20 According to Law

Ordered that Richard Tayloe & Samuel Smith Procesion all the Lands in the bounds N° 21 According to Law

Ordered that Henry Gwinn & James Bandy Procesion all the Lands in the bounds N° 22 According to Law

Ordered that Robert Rowntree & James Spivy Procession all the bounds of Lands N° 23 According to Law

Ordered that Daniel Pugh & Moses Riddick Procession all the bounds of Land in N° 24 According to Law

Ordered that John Duke & Thomas Duke Procesion all the Lands in the bounds N° 25 According to Law

The Bounds N° 26 is now aded to Suffolk Parish

[21]

Ordered that Willis Riddick & Jotham Lacitor Procession all the Lands in the bounds Nº 27 According to Law

Ordered that John Haslip Joseph Horton Junr Procession all the Lands in the bounds Nº 28 According to Law

Truly Entered by   Signed by Mills Riddick Ch,w^d
Lemuel Riddick C. Vestry

At a Vestry held for the upper parish of Nansemond County at Suffolk Town the 19th Day of December 1747 for Laying Proportioning[13] the parish Levy

Present. The Reverend Mr Webb Minister

John Norfleet,   John Winbourn
William Baker,   Lemuel Riddick   } Gen^t of the Vestry
Daniel Pugh &   Josiah Riddick

Jethro Sumner
Mills Riddick   } Church wardens

The upper parish of Nansemond County to Sundrys In the year 1747 is   D^r
Viz^t

To the Revd Mr Wm Webb for his Sallary from the 31 day of August Last untill 31 day of this Ins^t at 16000 per y^r	5333⅓
To D^o for an Allowance for a Glebe at 2000 per y^r	666⅔
To D^o for Conveniency 4 per C^t on 6000	240
To Susanah Tayloe for Cleaning the upper Chappell	150
To Henry Gwinn for Attending at the Middle Chappell as Sexton 250 & for repairs to the Chappell 150	400
To William Horton for keeping Mary Harris	1200
To John Blythe for his Maintenance	350
To Richard Webb for keeping Richard Rack	1200
To Elizabeth Farrow for keeping Grace Anstead 11 Months at 800 per y^r	726
To John Kerr for keeping Mary Sap 5 M^{ths} 1 Week at 100 per m	575
To D^o for a p^r Shoes	

---

[13] "Proportioning" is interlined, with a caret after "Laying".

To Arthur Gourlay for Salavateing &c Mary Kelly & Mary Brinkly	2300
To John Gwinn for Cleaning the road & Spring &c	150

[22]
Brought Over

To John Langston 1 Tithable over Charged Last y^r remitted	38
To Rachell Lester for Looking after Mary Jordan and provideing for her funerall	400
To Humphry Griffin for a Coffin & Diging a Grave for Mary Brinkly	150
To Mills Riddick Church warden for Disburstm^{ts} for the poor 1447 To D^o for Insolvents Last y^r ball due to him 1331	2778
To Jethro Sumner Church warden his Acco^t for Disburstments for the Poor	2780
To 20000 lb Tob^o Levied towards building a Church to be paid by the Collector to the Church wardens for the time being in July next & by them Sold for ready money at Publick & to Account with the Vestry when required for the same	20000
	39437
To the Collector 6 per C^t on 39437	2366
To the Sherif for Q^{ts} 800 Acres Glebe & poors Land 168 and 6 per C^t for Collection	178
To John Cambell Reader at the Church & Chappells 1000 6 per C^t on D^o for Collection	1060
	43041
The parish C^r by 39 lb Tob^o on 1107 Tithables	43173
due to the parish	132

Ordered that Mills Riddick Gen^t Collect from every Tithable in this parish the Sum of thirty nine pounds of Tobacco & there with Discharge the above Debts due from the Parish

Jethro Sumner & Mills Riddick Gen^t Church wardens Rendered an Acco^t of the Sale of Sixteen thousand Pounds of Tobacco Levied the Last year towards the building a Church which Sold for 80..6..8. the Said Mills Riddick & Jethro Sumner Each acknowledged they had Each of them one half in their hands.

Ordered that the Said Money Remain in the Hands of the Said Mills Riddick & Jethro Sumner untill otherways Ordered by this Vestry

[23]

Ordered that William Baker, John Winbourn, Lemuel Riddick, Christopher Norfleet, & John Ralls or any three of them Indeavour to Purchase two Acres of Land from Hardy Ralls at a place Called Holy Neck on the Back swamp for a place to erect & build a Chappell on, for the use of this Parrish and that a Deed be made to William Baker Gen[t] in Trust for this Parish and that the Same be recorded as Soon as Possable and the Said William Baker, John Winbourn, Christopher Norfleet John Ralls & Lemuel Riddick are hereby Appointed Directors & Trustees for Carrying on the building a Chappell at the Said Holy Neck as Soon as they Can get a Sufficient Deed for the Land the Chappell to be of the following Dimensions to be built with a good Fraime, Plank Walls, & Well Shingled of the Length of fifty feet. the Wedth Twenty Six feet, the Pitch fourteen feet. with a Galire at one End the whole to be Compleated as Soon as Can be after the Usuall Manner of building Chappells that the Said Trustees Imploy some Person or Persons to build the Same & that as often as they Shall have Occasion of Money for Carrying on the Said Work they Draw on the Church wardens for Money for that Use and that the Said Trustees Account with the Vestry when required and Render an Acco[t] of their Actings & doings

 Truely Entered by   Signed William Webb.
  Lemuel Riddick   Cl Vestry

[24]

At a Vestry held for the upper parish of Nansem[d] County. April 12th 1748 at the House of M[r] Rawlins

 Pressent. The Reverend M[r] W[m] Webb Minister
    Mills Riddick one of the Churchwardens
    Jn[o] Winbourn
    Lemuel Riddick
    Christopher Norfleet } Gen[t] of the Vestry
    Daniel Pugh &
    Josiah Riddick

John Winbourn and Lemuel Riddick are appointed & Sworn Churchwardens untill Easter next

Mills Riddick rendered an Acco^t of fines by him Rece^d Since Easter Last of 6..5...0.

Ordered that the Said Mills Riddick pay unto Ann Hains out of the Said Sum 30/.

Ordered that the Said Mills Riddick pay to Gertrude Frost the Sum of thirty Shillings out of the S^d Sum & to Ruth Whale 15/ & to Judith Hare 15/ & to the Widdow Keene 35/.

Lemuel Riddick Promised to pay Sarah Johns fine for having a Bastard Child 50/ Its ordered that he pay unto Issabella Flint, out of the Said Sum Twenty five Shillings & to the Widdow of Samuel Wells twenty five Shillings More

Ordered that the Clerk of the Vestry Deliver unto the Reverend Mr Webb the Parish Register

Truly Entered   Signed, Will: Webb.
    Per Lemuel Riddick Clerk of the Vestry.

[25]

Pursuant to an order of Vestory Dated August 31: 1747 We the subscribors being Appointed by the said order, have processioned all the bounds of Land Contained in the said Order begining at Henry Hollands his Land processioned pres^t the said Henry and Henry Holland Elder and Likewise Isaac Flesmny [sic][14] Likewise Ja^s Sumners and Capt William Bakers and Henry Hedgpeths William Butler William Johnson and Joseph Holland John Holland and Joseph Holland and Henry Johnsons Land present Capt Wm Baker and William Johnson Thence John Butlers and John Daughtrys and James Johnson William Moores and John Peirce Moses Hares present John Peirce Thence William Harisons Land and John Harisons Anne Foulks and John Kings and Chrstopher Sanders his Land John Harison and William Harison John Winbernes John Bradlys Culbirt Hedgpeth's Son Hedgpeths Land present John Winborne and John Hedgpeth John Carr John Copeland and William Cleny James Holland and Stephin Darden present John Carr and John Copeland, Including all

---

[14] Doubtless intended for Fleming.

the bounds of Lands Contain^d in the said Order peasably and Quietly processioned by us the Subscribers

Stephen Darden
Ja^s Holland

In obedience to an Order of Vestry Dated August the 31: 1747 Prosessioned the Line Between Nathaniel Pruden and Henry Wright Likewise the Line between Henry Wright and Peter Buttler and the Line of Buttler and James March and the Line of March and Elisha Ashburn and the Head line of James March and John Ashburn and the Line of John Gwins and David Meads and the line of John Gwin and Wm Moore and the line of David Mead and William Moore and the line of David Mead and James March and the line of David Mead and Daniel Doughtey and the line of David Mead and Mary Lackey and the line of Daniel Doughtey and James March and the line of Frances Forsett and James March and the line of Frances Forsett and William Battle and the line of William Battle and Abr^m Ballard—Present Nathaniel Prudent, Peter Buttler, William Moore, John Gwin Jame[s] March, Elisha Battle.

Abr^m Ballard
Elisha Ashburn

According to the Order we have processioned all the Land Within the bounds the oners of the Land there present, only the Chapple Land John Barfield and John Landing was at the doing of that and Capting Sumners Land William Rogers was at the doing of that it is all don peasable and quietly with out Distur[b]ance.

Febuary the 18th 1747[/48]   John Haslep
Joseph Horton

[26]

In abedience to a Order of Vestry Granted August the 31: 1747 We that are Appouinted Procesions of the West side the Southern branch of Nansem^d River and on the South side the Church Rode to Jernigans bridge and Beginning at a Line between Jethro Sumner and Samuel Jordan and a Line between Thomas Norfleet and Jethro Sumner and a Line between Jethro Sumner and Christopher Norfleet and a Line between Jethro Sumner and Pugh and a Line between Pugh and David Rice and the head Line between Jethro Sumner and Pugh and Rice and Ward and the Owners in Present and Richard Webb and a Line between Rice and Ward and a Line between Ward and Wm Balb [sic]^15 and a line between Ward and Richd Webb and a Line between Richard Webb and Thomas Hair and a line between Hair and Christopher Norfleet and a Line between Norfleet and Harning Tembty and a Line between Tembty and Thomas Hair and a line between Tembty and Richard Webb and a Line between Tembty and Mikel Forrer and a line between Tembty and Jeremiah Godwin the oners in present and Mikel Forrer Richard Webb and a Line between Tembty and Bodys and a line between Godwin and John Hansell and a line between Hansell and Edward Moore and a Line between Hansell and Richard Babb and a Line between Babb and John Jones the s^d persons in present then a line between Christepher Norfleet and Thomas Norfleet and a Line between Thomas Norfleet and John Norflet a line between John Norfleet and William Norfleet and a Line between William Norfleet and Thomas Norfleet and a line between William Norfleet and Christepher Sander and a line between John Norfleet and Christepher Sander and a line between Christepher Sander and Daniel Doughtie and a Line between Doughtie and John Best and a line between Daniel Doughtie and John Norfleet at the Mill and the oners in present &c.

           Christopher Norfleet
           Edward Moore

  In Obediance to an Order of Vestry August the 31: 1747 We have procession the Lines of Lands between Capt William Baker and the Country Line and also between the said Bakers and Thomas Core Senr and the lines between Thomas Core Senr and Junr also between Abraham Riddick and Thomas Core Senr and Between Thomas Lawrence and Abraham Riddick and John Butler and between John Lawrence and Henry Lawrence and b[e]tween George Lawrence and Henry Lawrence and the Lines between Mich^l Lawrence and Mr David Mead and between Mr Mead and John Pender and between Mich^l & Thos Lawrence and Thomas Shiffers and the Lines between Thomas Shiffers and Abraham Riddick Given under our hands This 4 Day of March 1747[/48]

           Henry Daughtry
           Thomas Shiffers

---

^15 Doubtless intended for Babb.

[27]

At A Vestry held for the upper Parish of Nansimond County August the 31th 1747 Ordered that William Sanders and James Uzzell prossesion all the bounds of Land from the going over of wickam Swamp to the County Line so to Kingsail swamp, up the s^d Swamp to the first Station which said Lands we have done acording to order to wit Possesioned the Line between Mr Henry Holland Junr and Stephen Darden also the Line between the said Holland and John Hedgpeth and also the Line between the said Holland and William Holland Senr and also the Line between the said Holland and Wm Sanders also the Line between the said Sanders and Thomas Whitfield to Eliz^h Vaughan also between the said Whitfield and the said Vaughn also between the said Vaughns and Wm Sanders also between William Sanders and Thomas Whitfield also the line between William Sanders and John Thomas also the Line between the said Thomas and John Whitfield also the line between the said Whitfield and Mr Isaac Fleming also the line between John Whitfield and Thomas Whitfield also between Thomas Whitfield and the said Fleming also the line between the said Fleming and John Hedgpeth also between the said Hedgpeth and Thomas Whitfield also the line between Mr Fleming and Mr Baker White also the line between the said White and Stephen Darden also between the said Darden and Samuel Job then possesioned the line between Joseph Holland and Bryun Daughtry Senr also between the said Holland and William Sanders also between the said Sanders and William Vaughn also between the Said Vaughn and Bryun Daugtry and the Line between William Vaughn and Lewis Daughtry and between Lewis Daughtry and Bryun Daughtry also between the said Daughtry and Mr William Baker also between the said Baker & Lewis Daughtry also between the said Baker and Bryun Daughtry Junr also the Line between the said Baker and John Daughtry also between the said Baker and Mr John Milner also between the said Milner and John Daughtry also the line between the s^d Milner and Thomas Scutchin also between the said Milner and Archilus Weeks then possesioned the line between John Daughtry and John Scutchins also between the s^d Cutchens [sic] and Thomas Scutchens also between the s^d scutchens & Olover Worrell also between the said Worrell and John Daughtry also the Line between the said Worrell and William

Vaughn also the line between the said Worrell and Thomas Vaughn also the line between the said Vaughn and James Uzzell also the Line between the said Uzzell and William Sanders

Sertified under our hands   William Sanders
            & James Uzzell

[28 blank][16]

[29]

Nansemond upper Parish, March the first 1747/8

this is to Sartifie that we the subscribers have fulfild a Order of Vestry to us Derected and have processioned all the bounds of Land in our Presink the Oners of the Land being Present only the line between John Skinner and Jacob Hanton not procession the oners of the Land not Appeiring

            Henry Gwin
            James Bandy

In Obedience to an Order of Vestry held for the upper Parrish of Nansimond County August 31 : 1747 We the subscribers have Processioned the bounds of every Mans Land within our presint Peacably and Quietly Given under our hands March 1747/8

            Thos Milner
            Jo^s Lawrence

In Pursuance to an Order of Vestry bearing Date August 31th 1747 We have Possessioned all the Land of the South side of Black water and Notaway River in Nansemond County Except some small peices of Lines which we Could not get at for freshes as John pope Simon Evrits George Williams's Daniel Williamses Joseph Carls James Bakers John Hollands Robt Cars William Wiggins Joshaa Williamses Mary Harts John Harts Wm Harts James Cary's Wm Bakers Saml Warrans John Drews Thos Woodlys Richard Stringfields Richard Williamses Daniel Battens Thomas Edwards John Weatherly Michal Lawrance Michal Dawtery Jacob Durdens Mosses Durdens Robert Cars Senr Car Durdens Robert Durdens James Garners Thomas Lawrance Jesse Browns John Lawrence all in Presence Except Mosses Durden.

March the 12th 1747/8   William Hart
            Joseph Curl

---

[16] The right-hand and left-hand margin of this page is ruled with a vertical line as if the page was intended for a financial statement.

[30]

Pursute to a Order of Vestry held August the 30[17] Day for Procesioning we have Compleated with the sade order as followes beginning at Robert Parkors line between him and his Father and Robert is present, between Robert Parkors and John Rodgers and Both present between William Roders [sic] and Jethro Sumnles [sic][18] and William Rodgers present between Joshua Peelle and the Chapel Land and John Cross present Joshua Peelle and John Cross present between Rodgers and Benjamin Rodgerz [sic] and Both present bet[w]een John Purves and John Purves's Son James Purves Jeen Shavass and James Purves and Both present between Danniel March and Abraham Odome and Both Present between James March and John Heair and Both Present between Daniel March and Poll Pender

Feb^r the 26 Day 1747/8   Joshua Peelle
                                    Daniel March

We the Subscribers make a return of bounds from the Kneukle swamp to Barbi[c]ure betwen sum^t Road and Smiths Road, Beginning at Josept Bakers line Jn° Porter and James Webb being P^ts and then to James Webbs line John Porter being present then to Wm Henrys line Thos Gwin Samuel Baker Ja^s Baker present then to James and Samuel Bakers and John Smiths line and they all present then John Porters line and Thos Webb and William Hairs line they being all present then to John Webbs line James Baker and Samuel Baker being present then to William Birds Aaron Byrds Ja^s Harrell Adam Harrell and Edward Byrds and they all present then to William Bawls[19] Junr line John Hare and William Bawls[20] Edward Byrd and Adam Harrell present then to Francis Dukes line Philip Draper and Thos Duke present then to Philip Draper line and John Webbs line, James Webb being pr[e]sent then to John Byrds line William Wharton and Jacob Byrd being present then to Jacob Byrds line and Joseph Wharton they being present then to John Byrd son of John Byrd William Wharton being present then to James Bakers Line to the first Station.

February the 18: 1747[/48]   Quietly Possessioned by us Joseph Baker
                                                                                            Francis Duke

---

[17] This date should be August 31.
[18] Doubtless intended for Sumner.
[19] Probably intended for Rawls.
[20] Probably intended for Rawls.

[31]

In Obediance to an Order of Vestry pursuant to an Order of Court dated 31st of August 1747 We the subscribers have proceeded as followeth and Possessioned all the lines of Land in our respective Precinct as follows Imprimis Robert Archer and Thomas Godwin present James Copeland and William Collings 2^d the Line between Thomas Godwin and John Barkley 3^d the line between William Collings and Robert Archer 4th the line between Robert Archer and Phillip Alesbury 5th the line between the said Alesbury and William Collings 6th the Line between John Barkley and William Collings 7th the line between John Barkley and Robert Archer 8th the line between James Copeland and John Stokes 9th the Line between s^d Stokes and Doctor Tembte 10th the line between the said Copeland and Tembte 11th between the said Copeland and John Wyat 12th between said Copeland and Thomas Gay all the above lines was Possessioned in present of the Owners of Land and Edward Eley and John Barkley also present the line between Thomas Gay and John Wyat between said Wyat and Francies Powell between said Powell and William King between said King and John Wyat between said King and Thomas Gay between said Gay and John Wyat between said Gay and Henry Wright Juner between John Osheal and John Eley between John Eley and John Wyat between said Wyat and Michael Eley between said Wyat and Edward Taylor between said Taylor and Joseph Hollaway between said Hollaway and John Parker between said Parker and William Scott between said Scott and William Mackclenny between said M^{c}clenny and Samuel Osborn between said Soborn [sic] and John Simons between the said Simons and William Moore betwen Francis Powell and John Bradley between said Bradley and John Wyat between said Wyat and Doctor Tembte, between John Stocks and James Baker between said Stocks and Thomas Howard between said Howard and James Baker between said Bake[r] and John Barkley between said Baker and John Holland between said Holland & Jeremiah Godwin between said Godwin and David Nelmes between said Godwin and John Best between John Holland and William Bateman between John Holland and John Best between said Best and Daniel Doughtie between said Doughtie and John Holland between said Doughtie and John Willson between said Wilson and John Holland between said Willson and John Stocks between the said Stockes and John Holland between said Stockes and Thomas Howard

John Best
William Bateman

[32]

This is to Sertifie you that we have purseastioned all the Land in our Limated Bounds

The Names of the Men

Thomas Joanes	Who was p[r]esent
Feathearick Joanes	Isac Langston
William Joanes	John Boyte
Jacob Joanes	Jacob Longston
John Rawls	Isac Langston
Theophilus Joanes	John byte, still
Arter Joanes	Mical Joanes
John Langston	Jacob Langston: Still
Jacob Langston	Isac Langston Still
Mical Joanes	John Boyte Still
George Joanes	Mical Joanes Still
John Porter	Jacob Langston Still
Willaim Boyte	John Boyte Still
George Garnagan	Jacob Langston Still
Wm Howel	Mical Langston Still
John Willson	John Boyte Still
John Hair	Jacob Langston Still
James Coplan	George Gornagan
Franses Rawls	Mical Natson
Richard parker	George Garnagan Still
Robert Parker	William Howel
Moses Boyte	George Garnagan Still
Rebeaco Boyte	William Howel Still
Lydia Ken	Arter Joanes
	Isac Langston Still
	Jacob Langston Still
Assigned by us	John Byte Still
mark	William Byte
Jacob II Joanes[21]	
his	
Fredireck Joanes	

---

[21] His mark, written like the letters "I I", each letter bisected by a short horizontal line, probably represents "J J", his initials.

[33]

Joshua Spivey and James Lacitter haveing Possessioned a line between Eley Brinkley and John Cleeves Eley Brinkley and John Cleeves present and a line between Micall Brinkley and John Cleeves Eley Brinkley and John Cleeves present and a line between Michall Brinkley and Eley Brinkley John Cleeves and Eley Brinkley present and a line between Michall Brinkley and Humphry Griffin Michall Brinkley and Humphry Griffin Juner present, and a line between Joshua Spivey and Michall Brinkley Humphry Griffin and Michall Brinkley present and a line between Humphry Griffin and Jonah Mackclary Michall Brinkley and Humphry Griffin Junr present and a line of Michall Brinkley Michall Brinkley present and a line between Michall Brinkley and John Brinkley Michall Brinkley and John Brinkley present and a line of Jonah Mackclarys William Brinkley present and a Corner tree between John Brinkley and Jean Riddick John Brinkley present and a line between Richard Brothers and Peter Brinkley Peter Brinkley present and a line between Peter Brinkley and Thomas Wilkins Peter Brinkley present and a line between Thomas Wilkins and Richard Brothers Thomas Wilkins Present and a line between Thomas Wilkins and Henry Brinkley Thos Wilkins and Henry Brinkley present and a line between Peter Franklin and Thomas Wilkins Henry Brinkley Thomas Wilkins present and a line between Peter Franklin and Edward Arnall Peter Franklin Thomas Wilkins present and a line between Richard Brothers and John Brinkley Peter Franklin and Thos Wilkins present and a line between Henry Brinkley and Peter Frankley [sic] Henry Brinkley present and a line between Henry Brinkley and Jean Riddick Henry Brinkley present and a line between James Brinkley and Thomas Brantun James Brinkley present and a line between James Brinkley and Jean Riddick Henry Brinkley present and a line between James Lacitter and Thomas Brantun James Brinkley present and a line between James Lacitter and John Meltere James Brinkley present and a line between Joshula [?]^{22} Spivey & Jesse Riddick Joshua Spivey present and a line between Jesse Riddick and Humphry Griffin Joshua Spivey present and a line between Joshua Spivey and Joseph Griffin Joshua Spivey present and a line between Michall Brinkley and Joseph Griffin Humphry Griffin present and a line between Michall

---

^{22} *I. e.* Joshua. The clerk apparently misspelled the name inadvertently and, attempting a hasty correction, left the word partly illegible.

Brinkley and Humphry Griffin Humphry Griffin present a line between Humphry Griffin and Joseph Griffin Humphry Griffin present and a line between Richard Brothers and Willis and William Wilkason Richard Brothers present and another line between Richard Brothers and John Brinkley Richard Brothers

Brought over

[34]

Present and a line between Richard Brothers and James Sumner Richard Brothers present.

Joshua Spivey
James Lacitter

In Obedence to an Oder of Vestry made the 31 of August 1747 We the subscribers have acordingly meet and have processioned Every mans Land within the bounds Mentioned

Epharem Peals Land don	Present Wil^m Peal
Wil^m Peals Land don	Present Epharem peal
Cader Rabys don	Present Jacob Sumner
Jacob Sumners don	Present Cader Raby
Alexander Everas don	Present Wil^m Evera
Robert Peals don	Present him Self
John Pearces don	Present Robert Peal
Susana Taylors don	Present Wil^m Pearce
John Harrells don	Present Job Harrell
John bakers don	Present Job Harrell
Arthor Gorelys don	Present John Baker
Edward and James [?][23] Bakers don	Present Them Selves
Martha Smiths don	Present John Smith
Moses Harrells don	Present Richard Nusom
Richard Nusoms don	Present him Self
Weddow Harrisons	Present Richard Nusom

Richard Taylor
Samuell Smith

---

[23] It appears that the clerk may have written "Samuel" and carelessly corrected it to "James".

[35]

Persuant to an Order of Vestry Dated August 31: 1747 We the subscribers have Processioned all the Lands in our bounds in the following manner

At the Processioning of the lines between Easter Pugh and Daniel Pugh present Thomas Brown

At the Processioning the lines between Easter Pugh and Thomas Spivy present Daniel Pugh and John Campbell

At the Porcessioning the lines between Thomas Spivy and Aaron Lacitor present Daniel Pugh and John Campbell

At the Processioning the lines between Aaron Lacitor and John Campbell Present Daniel Pugh

At the Processioning the lines between John Campbell and Willis Riddick Present both Parties

At the Processioning the lines between Willis Riddick and John Riddick present Soloman Riddick

At the Processioning the lines between John Riddick and Joseph Stallings Present Soloman Riddick Joseph Stallings Junr

At the Porcessioning the lines between John Riddick and Joseph Stallings present Soloman Riddick Joseph Stallings Junr

At the Processioning the line between Joseph Stallings and Wm Stallings present both Parties

At the Processioning the line between Wm Stallings and Mills Riddick present Wm Stallings and Joseph Stallings Junr

At the processioning of the lines betweent Mills Riddick and Lemuel Riddick present John Stallings and Wm Stallings Junr

At the processioning the Line between Lemuel Riddick and James Booth present James Booth

            Willis Riddick
            Jotham Lacitor

[36]

Pursuant to an Order of Vestry Wee the Subscribers have meet on the Several Lands and Procestioned all the bounds beginning as followeth

Prosestioned the line between John Denbigh and Joseph Price present both Parties

Prosestioned the line between Thomas Price and Joseph Price present both Parties

Prosestioned the line between Henry Skinner and Thomas Price present both Parties

Prosestioned the line between Henry Skinner and John Hamleton present Henry Skinner and Thomas Price

Prosestioned the line between John Hamleton and Christopher Jackson Present Henry Skinner and Thomas Price

Prosestioned the line between Christopher Jackson and Daniel Pugh Present Henry Skinner and Thomas Price

Prosestioned the line between Rachal Lester and David Mead present Mansfield Torlington

Prosestioned the line between Rachal Lester and Sarah Johns present Mansfeild Torlington

Prosestioned the line between David Mead and Sarah Johns present Mansfeild Torlington

Prosestioned the line betwen David Mead and John Watson present both Parties

Prosestioned the line between David Mead and Josah Riddick present both Parties

Prosestioned the line between David Mead and Esther Pugh present Mansfield Torlington

Prosestioned the line between David Mead and Daniel Pugh present Mansfeild Torlinton

Prosestioned the line between David Mead and Jethro Sumner present Mansfeild Torlinton

Prosestioned the line between Daniel Pugh and Christopher Wright Present both Parties

Prosestioned the line between Christopher Wright and Hester Pugh Present Mansfield Torlinton

Prosestioned the line between Hester Pugh and Thomas Spivey present Joseph Stallings Thomas Spivey

[37]

Prosestioned the line between Josiah Riddick and Thomas Spivey Present Joseph Stallings and Thomas Spivey

Prosestioned the bounds of Lands between the Widdow Johns and Daniel Pugh Present John Watson Josiah Riddick and Joseph Stallions

Prosestioned the line between John Watson and Daniel Pugh present both Parties

Prosestioned the line between Hester Pugh and John Watson present Daniel Pugh Josiah Riddick and Moses Riddick

Prosestioned the line between Daniel Pugh and Mathew Parker present Ephraim Parker

Processioned the [line] between Daniel Pugh and Ephraim Parker present both Parties

Processioned the line between Mathew Parker and Epharim [sic] Parker present both Parties

Processioned the line between Hester Pugh and Daniel Pugh present Christopher Wright

Processioned the line between Joseph Booth and Jotham Lasetor present both Parties

Processioned the line between Jotham Lasetor and Moses Riddick present both Parties

Daniel Pugh
Moses Riddick

[38 and 39]²⁴

February the 28th 1747[/48]

This return According to Order is to Sertify what Lands have been purcessioned, and what has not and who present

the line between Jeremiah Godwin and Joⁿ Norflit
No Person present But the oners thereof

the line between Jeremiah Godwin and Hening Temty
No Person present But we & the oners

the line between Joⁿ Norflit and Jon^a Roberts
No Person present But we and the oners

the line between John Norflit and the Gleeb
Niclous Perit present

the line between Jon^a Roberts and the Gleeb
the same Person present

the line between Jon^a Roberts and Hening Temty
Elisha Norflet present

---

²⁴ In the following return, the records of those present, as printed here in alternate lines, appear in corresponding lines on p. [39] of the original.

the line between Nicholus Perit and the Gleeb and
the same Person present

the line between Nich⁵ Perit and Benjn Wainwright
the same person present

the line between Jon^a Roberts and Benjn Wainwright and
Nicholus Perit present

the line between David Nelms Junr and Jon^a Roberts and
Peter Green Present

the line between David Nelms and Peter Green and
No person present But the oners and we

the line between Peter Green and John Jones and
No Person present But the oners

the line between Peter Green and John Pinner and
No Person present But the oners

the line between John Jones and George Frith and
James Jones present

the line between George Frith and Chris^r Sanders and
No Person present But the oners

the line between Christopher Sanders and John Pinner and
No Person present

the line between Christopher Sanders and David Nelms and
No Person present

the line between Jo^n Pinner and David Nelms and
No Person present

the line between David Nelms and Peter Mason and
Jo^n Thomas present

the line between Jeremiah Godwin and David Nelms and
No Person present

the line between Peter Mason and Jonathan Roberts and
Jo^n Thomas present

the line between Jonathan Roberts and John Thomas and
No Person Present

the line between Jon^a Roberts and Jeremiah Godwin and
No Person Present

the line between Jeremiah Godwin and Peter Mason and
No Person Present

the line between Jeremiah Godwin and Jon^a Nelms and

James Jones present
  the line between Jo^n Thomas and Jon^a Nelms and
Jo^n Pinner present
  the line between Jo^n Thomas and Jeremiah Godwin and
No person present
  the lands of Boyds no one Appraed to Purcessioned so not Dun
  the Land of Cunyerds so called no one appeared so not Dun
  the Land of Tuckers no one Appard and Joseph Godwins not Dun
  As Witnen our hands
                                        Jonathan Roberts
                                        Jonathan Nelms

[40]

Feberay the 2^d Day 1747[/48]

James Spivey and Robert Rountree began to posesion the bounds of Land appointed for them Robert Booth and Abraham Lacitor son of John not agreeing to have one line posesioned a line between Thomas Harrell and Robert Booth a line between Thomas Harrell and Joseph Perry a line [between] Robert Booth and Abraham Lacitor Thomas Newby and Thomas Harrell present a line between Abraham Lacitor and Thomas Newby a line between Thomas Newby and Joseph Perry a line between Thomas Newby and Jesse Lacitor a line between New [sic] and Thomas Price a line between Newby and Thomas Norflet Thomas Newby present a line between George Spivey and Jesse Lacitor Abraham Lacitor present, a line between Joshua Spivey and Jesse Lacitor a line between Jotham Lacitor and Abraham son of Robert Abrham Lacitor present a line between John Lacitor Sener and Robert Roundtree a line between John Roundtree and John Lacitor Sener a line between John Roundtree and Robert Roundtree John Roundtree present a line between John Waterridge and John Roundtree John Roundtree John Waterridge and John Roundtree present a line betweent Abraham Lacitor son of Robt and Robert Roundtree Abraham Lacitor present a line between Joseph Booth and Jotham Lacitor a line betweent Joseph Booth and Jesse Lacitor Joseph Booth present a line between John Denby and Thomas Newby a line between Denby and Jesse Lacitor a line between Denby and Edward Giles a line between Denby and Joseph Price John Denby Joseph Price present a line for Henry Larrans, a line between Larrans and John Lacitor Henry

Larrans and John Lacitor present a line between Joseph Perrey and Jesse Lacitor a line between Perrey and John Lacitor a line between Perrey and Henry Larrans James Boys and Jesse Lacitor present a line between Jesse Lacitor and James Boys Jesse Lacitor present

Feberary the 26th Day 1747[/48] We made an end of Posessioning the bounds of Land order by the Vestry

John Lacitor and Joseph Booth could not agree to have a line Posesioned between them

James Spivey
Robert Roundtree

[41]
In Obbediance to an order Vestre Dated August 31: 1747 To Posseson the bounds of Land Begining at John Porters Joyning Summerton Swamp on the Northside of Summerton Road to the Knuckels Swamp Wee the Subscribers have Possesioned all the said bounds of Land beginning at John Porters According to order, & Possesioned his Line in Presents of him James Copeland & John Folks & a Line between John Porter & Wm Harrell in Presents of them & James Copeland Thomas Rawles John Folks and a line between John Porter & Thomas Rawles in Present of them James Copeland John Folks and a Line between James Copeland and Thomas Rawles in Presents of them John Porter John Folks and a line between John Porter Senr & William Moore in Presents of John Porter Junr James Copeland William Rawles son of W^m in Presents of Wm Rawls James Copeland Jhn^o [sic] Porter Thomas Rawls John Folks and a line between Wm Rawls Senr and Wm Rawles son of John in Presents of William Rawls James Copeland John Folks and a line between Wm Rawls son of John & John Hare in Presents of them James Copeland John Porter & a line between John Hare & John Folks in Presents of them James Copeland John Porter and a line between John Folks & Robert Parker in present of them James Copeland John Porter

James Copeland
John Porter

[42]
At a Vestry held for the upper Parish of Nansimond County at the House of Mr Rawlins in Suffolk Town the 14th of October 1748

Present the Reverend Mr Wm Webb Minister

John Winbourn } Church wardens
Lemuel Riddick }

William Baker   ⎫
Mills Riddick   ⎪
Daniel Pugh   ⎬ Gent. Vestry
Josiah Riddick ⎭

added David Mead Gen^t

William Coupland having been Chosen a Vestryman at the Last Vestry in the Room of William Butler Gent. Deceas'd and having this Day in Vestry taken the Oaths to the Goverm^t the Oath of Abjuration & Signed the Test also the Oath of a Vestryman, took his Place in the Vestry

The Upperish of Nansimond County for the year 1748
To sundry Persons is   Dr
Viz^t

To the Reverend Mr William Webb his Salary	16000
To Ditto in Leiu of a Glebe	2000
To Ditto for Cask 4 per C^t on 16000	640
To John Camble Reader	1060
To Henry Wright for Dreshing &c to Richd Pain	200
To Susanah Tayloe for Clea[n]ing the upper Chappell	150
To Richard Webb for keeping Rack	1200
To Ditto for Repairing the Church	300
To Mrs Mary Doughte for keeping Leatch Ten months	850
To Sarah Johns for keeping Elizabeth Green 4 m 17 days at the Rate of 1000 per Year	383

[43]

To Thomas Williams for keeping Grace Anstead 9 m. at 1000	600
To William Horton for keeping Mary Harris 1 Year	1200
To John Gwin for Clearing the Roads to Church the Spring &c	150
To John Simon for keeping Mary Sap 9 m. at 100	900
To Ditto for 1 p^r Shoes 45^lb & ½ [?][25] y^ds Country Cloth 12	57
To James Purvis a poor man 500 lb^s Tobacco	500
To Christopher Jackson for Copy List Tithables 2 years	138

---

[25] Practically illegible but looks like a fraction.

To Mills Riddick for Insolvants Last year	1294
To Henry Gwin Sexton at the Middle Chapple	250
To the Sherif for Quitrents Glebe 800 Acres 22	176
To the Collector 6 per C^t	1680
To 20000 lb^s Tob^o Levied towards Buildings a Church }	21200
To Collection on Ditto 6 per C^t 1200	
	50928
C^r By 44 lb^s Tob^o on 1175 Tithables	51700
A depositum due to the parish	772

Ordered that Capt Anthony Holladay Sherif (he first giving bond and Security to the Church wardens) Collect from every Tithable in this Parish forty four Pounds of Tob^o and therewith Discharge the above Creditors

Turn over

[44]

The Vestry being of Opinion that a handsome brick Church ought to be Built in this Parish, the Reverend William Webb, David Mead, Jethro Summner, Daniel Pugh and Josiah Riddick are appointed Trustees and Directors for Carrying on and Building the said Church and purchaseing Land for that purpose and that they observe the following Directions Viz^t

that they apply to Mr Jethro Sumner and Margret his Wife and Endevour to purchase two Acres of Land at the head of Suffolk Town and that a Deed for the same be made to David Mead Gent. Intrust for this Parish and when they have made the s^d Purchase, they draw on the Churchwardens, for money for that Purpose, and that the Church be Built According to the Plan already drawn by Mr Rand, that Publick notice be given for Persons to undertake the Building of the same, and that the Church be Compleated in four years, and that any three of the said Trustees have power to make any Agreement as well as if the whole Five were present Lemuel Riddick Proposeing to the Vestry that he would give Twenty Pounds for Liberty to build a Galire in one of the Crosses or wings of the Church Oposite to the front Door, It is therefore Agreed that the said Lemuel have Liberty to build the said Galare on his Paying or Securing to be Paid the said sum of Twenty pounds which money is to be Laid out for Church Ornament, and that the Churchwardens for the time being make a Deed to the said Lemuel his Heirs and Assigns for the same, It is also agreed that David Mead Gen^t have Leave to Build a Galare on the Oposite Wing of the said Church and that the Churchwardens for the time being make a Deed to him his Heirs and Assigns for the same he finding or securing to the said Churchwardens to be found A sufficient bell for the said Church and fiting the same

[45]

The upper parish of Nansimond County in money	D^r
To Lemuel Riddick Church warden for Disburstment for the Poor, And provideing for the sacrament	7 : 4 : 2 ½
To Doctor Goarlay for Medicens &c to Harmon	4 : 10 : –
To Mills Riddick Late Church warden for Disburstment for the Poor	3 : 12 : 2
To Mrs Webb for Surplus	6 : 18 : 9

Ordered that Mills Riddick Deduct out of the money in his hands the above sum due to him

Ordered that Lemuel Riddick Deduct out of the money in his hands belonging to the Parish, the money due to him and Doctor Gorlay as above Stated, and to Mrs Webb.

Ordered the Churchwardens for the time being in July Next, Sell the Said Twenty Thousand pounds of Tobacco at the Court house of this County at Publick sale, and that they receive the money Arising by the said Sale and Account with the Vestry for the same when required which said sum of Tobacco the Collectors Ordered to pay the said Churchwardens

The Vestry is of Opinion the Old brick Church is useless, and therefore order that the Minister do not Preach any more there, but that he Preach two Sundays, at the middle Chapple and one at the Sommorton Chappell untill such time as the upper New Chappell is Built

Harrell Bly is appointed Reader at the Middle Chappell that he's to have 1000 lb^s Tobacco per year

John Campble reader at summerton, to have 1000 lb^s Tobacco per year

Truly Registered   (Signed)   William Webb
    Per Lemuel Riddick
       Cl. Vestry

[46]

At a Vestry held on Eauster Tuesday the 28th of March 1749 at the house of Mr Edward Miles in Suffolk Town.

Pressent the Revd Wm [Webb] Minister

John Winbourn
& } Churchwardens
Lemuel Riddick

Mills Riddick
Christopher Norfleet
David Meade } Gent of the Vestry
Daniel Pugh
Josiah Riddick

John Winbourn & Lemuel Riddick is Chosen and Sworn Churchwardens untill Easter next.

four barrells of Tarr being paid unto Lemuel Riddick by Jon Rales for Light wood burnt on the poors Land. Ordered that sd Lemuel pay unto Ann Palmer for the support of her Children.

Aded Jethro Sumner
& Hening Tembte } Gent Vestrymen

The Trustees appointed by the Last order of Vestry to treat with Jethro Sumner & Margerit his Wife, for the Purchase of two Acres of Land whereon to build a Church; Reported to the Vestry this day that the said Sumner refused to sell the said Land at a moderate Price therefore its ordered the Trustees are hereby Impowered to treat with any other person or persons for the purchase of Two Lots of Land in any part of Suffolk Town that they shall think proper & for their further Direction they are to Observe the aforesaid Order of Vestry.

It appearing to the Vestry that its Necessary for the Ease & Convenientcy of Severall persons in this parish that the Last Vestry for preventing the Minister's attendance & preaching at the old brick Church ought to be Revoked and it is now further ordered that the Minister Preach at the said Church as formerly.

William Webb Minister

[47]

At a Vestry held at the house of Edward Miles in Suffolk Town for the upper Parish of Nansemond County, July 17: 1749.

Present the Reverend Wm Webb Minister
  Lemuel Riddick Churchwarden
  Wm Baker
  Jethro Sumner
  Mills Riddick   Vestrymen
  Daniel Pugh
  &
  Josiah Riddick

Ordered that the Churchwardens be Impowered to give five pounds Apprintice fee with Joseph Palmer Orphan of Truman Palmer and Charge the same to the parish.   William Webb

At a Vestry held for the upper Parish of Nansemond County at Suffolk Town the 16th day of October 1749.

Present The Reverend Wm Webb Minister
  John Winbourn & Lemuel Riddick Church{ds}
  Wm Baker
  Jothro Sumner
  Hening Tembte
  Christ° Norfleet
  Daniel Pugh
  Miles [sic] Riddick

The upper Parish to sundry persons, for the year 1749 is	Dr
To the Reverend Mr Webb his Salary	16000
To D° for Cask 4 per C{t}	640
To ditto for a Glebe	2000
To Jn° Campbell reader at the upper Chapple	1060
To sarah Johns for Keeping Richard Rack 9 m. 1000 per	800
To Edward Miles for keeping Elizabeth Green 9 m. 1000	800
To David Nelms Junr for keeping Grace Anstead 1 yr 800	900
To D° for making Cloth	
To Mary Doughte for keeping Leitch 1 yr	1000
To Susanah Taylor for Cleaning upper Chapple 9 months	110
Carried over	23510[26]

---

[26] This addition is in error and should be 23310; but the total of 29330 is correct. Since the figures of the various items are quite legible, the clerk must have made a compensating error in adding in the amount carried forward or given the right total without correcting the sub-total.

[48]

Brought over	23510
To Wm Horton for keeping Mary Hairs 1 y^r	1200
To Jn° Gwin for horse block, Clearing the road, Spring &c	320
To Richd Webb for a ball due Last	200
To Jn° Karr for keeping Mary Sap 4 weeks	100
To Henry Gwinn Sexton	250
To D° for transporting Sarah Johns a poor Woman out the parish	100
To Jn° Wright for 4 List Tithables 80	80
To Wm Baker for p^d the Clerk for Recording deed for Chappel Land	86
To Mills Riddick for 2 Levies overcharged last year 44	88
To Josiah Riddick for 2 D°	88
To Willis Riddick for 1 D°	44
To Daniel Pugh for 1 D°	44
To Mary Ralls for Cleaning Chappell 3 months	60
To Anthony Holladay Sherif for Insolvants &c last year	2534
To Joⁿ Cole for Cleaning the Church	250
To Garrot Cotter for burying Edward Newby	400
To the Sheriff for Q^{ts} poor & Glebe Land	176
	29330
To 25000 lb Tobacco to be paid the Churchwardens and by them sold in July Court next for money towards building Church & other Cash Charges	25000
	54330

	£	S	d
To Doctor Robert Brown for Phisick for poor People	10	0	0
To Dr Christopher Wright for Do.	6	10	0
To Jethro Sumner ball. due	0	8	0
	16	18	0

Brought down	54330
To the Collector at 6 per C^t	3258[27]
	57588
C^r By 1151 Tithables at 50 per pole	57550
Due to the Collector	38

---

[27] This amount is not quite 6% of 54330.

Ordered that Mr Anthony Holladay Collect from each tithable in the Parish 50 lb Tobacco & therewith Discharge the Parish Debts According to the above Settlement.

Ordered that Lemuel Riddick out of the Parish money in his hands pay the money debts above Stated.

William Coupland one of the Vestry being dead William Moor is this day Chosen a Vestryman in the room of the said Coupland. Ordered the Churchwardens give notice to the s^d Moor that he appear at the next Vestry in order to be Quallified[28] as a Vestryman.

William Webb

[49]

At a Vestry held for the upper Parish of Nansemond County at Suffolk Town the 21 Day of May 1750.

Present the Revd Wm Webb Minister

Lemuel Riddick Churchwarden

Jethro Sumner
Mills Riddick
Daniel Pugh } Gen^t Vestrymen
Josiah Riddick
Wm Moor

Abraham Odam not beening allowed for keeping Jonathan Watson a poor Criple Boy Last year, it is ordered that Lemuel Riddick pay unto the said Abraham Odam five pounds out of the Parish Money in his hands, in full, for keeping the said Boy untill this day

Lemuel Riddick ordered to pay Mary Ralls 5/ for washing Surplice Twice

Daniel Pugh and William Moor are appointed and sowrn [sic] Churchwardens untill Easter next.

William Webb

[50]

At a Vestry held for the upper Parish of Nansemond County at Suffolk Town November 5th 1750.

Present the Reverend Wm Webb Minister,

Daniel Pugh and William Moor, Churchwardens,
John Winborn, Wm Baker, Lemuel Riddick and

---

[28] The last syllable of this word is partially blotted, with the spelling uncertain but probably as given here.

Christopher Norfleet, Gen^t of the Vestry. Added Mills Riddick, & Josiah Riddick

James Cary Junr is appointed Clerk of the Vestry in the room of Lemuel Riddick who hath Resigned.

The upper Parish of Nansemond County for the year of our Lord 1750 is D^r

	Tobacco
To the Revd William Webb his Salary	16000
To D^o for Cask 4 per C^t	640
To D^o for a Glebe	2000
To John Campble Reader at the Chapple 8 Months	704
To Wm Shickleton Clerk at the upper Chapple	750
To Henry Gwinn Sexton	250
To Mary Ralls Sextonest at the upper Chapple	250
To D^o for washing Surplice	50
To Elisha Ashborn for burying the Corps of George Blake	298
To Thomas Williams for keeping John Palmmer	600
To D^o for D^o Grace Amsted 2 months	133
To D^o making Cloths for Palmmer and Amsted	80
To David Nelms J^r for keeping Grace Amsted	460
To John Cole Sexton at the brick Church	350
To John Gwinn for Clearing the Road & Spring	150
To Elizabeth Farrum for keeping Grace Amsted 3 ½ months	231
To Mary Doughte for keeping Leach	1000
To Robert Pruer a Levy over Charged	50
To John Simon for keeping Mary Sap 3 months	300
To D^o for burying D^o	150
To Wm Horton for keeping & burying Mary Harriss	450
To Nathan Wyat for keeping Gertrude Bell	1200
To Robert Rogers 2 Levies over Charged in the year 1748	88
To Henry Gwinn for mending the Chapple	50
To D^o for washing the Surplice	75
To James Howard 1 Levy over Charged in the year 1748	44
To Abraham Odam for keeping Jonathan Watson 6 months	250
To Edward Miles for keeping Elizabeth Green 4 ½ months	374

[51]

	Tobacco
Brought over	
To Edward Miles for keeping a Sick Portoguese called Anthony and for burying another Called Frank	500
To Elizabeth Green for 6 months board	500
To Aaron Almand Clerk at the Middle Chapple 5 ½ Months	702½
To John Wright 4 List of Tithables	80
To Capt Holladay Late Sheriff his Acc^t for Insolvants & Ballance due Last year	3725
To 25 M. towards the Church to be paid the Church wardens and by them sold for Cash in July Court next	25000
	57520[29]
To the Collector at 6 per C^t	3450
	lb 60970

	Dr
The upper Parish in Cash	
To Robert Willis for keeping and burying Robert Darnal	£ 3..18..2
To Doctor Gorlay for Phisick &c for Willis's Daughter	6.. 0..0
To sarah Johns for keeping and burying Rack	3.. 0..0
To Wm Moor disbursed for the poor	7..10..6
To Daniel Pught for D^o	3.. 8..9
To D^o towards the Church	180.. 0..0
To Mills Riddick a Ballance due him	0.. 5..8
	204.. 3..1

The Parish being Indebted unto several Persons Cash Acc^t Its ordered that they be Discharged in the following manner Viz^t Daniel Pugh having sold 25 [!] lb Tob^o for 175 £ He is to Discount so much out of the 180 £ due to him towards building the Church and its ordered that Lemuel Riddick pay the Ballance, to wit, five pounds to the said Daniel out of the money in his hands also that the said Lemuel pay the other Cash Demands now Levied, due from the Parish.

---

[29] Assuming that the figures of the various items are correct (they seem to be quite legible) this addition is in error, and should be 57484½.

Mills Riddick produced his account how he had paid the Parish Money which he formerly had in his hands and its ordered that the said Account be registered.

[52]

There being 1180 Tithables each is to pay 52 lb Tob⁰ and a Depositum of 390 due the Sheriff. ordered Josiah Riddick Collect from every Tithable 52 lb Tob⁰ and therewith Discharge the Parish Credits he giving Bond and Security to the Churchwardens for that Purpose.

Truly entered by Ja^s Cary Ju^r Clerk

       Sign'd William Webb.

1748 the Vestry of this Parish D^r to Mills Riddick		C^r
To Cash paid Wm Baker by order	39..15..0	
To D⁰ paid Daniel Pught by D⁰	12..0..0	
To my Acc^t for maintaining the Poor this year	5..1..8	
To going to and from W^{ms}borgh & attending the Council	1..10..0	
	58..6..8	

At a Vestry held in Suffolk Town May 23^d 1751 for the Upper Parish of of [*sic*] Nansemond County.

Present the Reverend William Webb Minister
  Daniel Pugh & William Moore Church W^{ds}
  John Winbourn Lemuel Riddick ⎫
  Jethro Sumner Christopher Norfleet ⎬ Gentlemen Vestrymen
  & Josiah Riddick   ⎭

Richd Webb is Appointed Clerk of this Vestry in the Room of James Cary Junr who hath removed out of the Parish, who took the Oath of Clerk of the Vestry

It Appearing to this Vestry that the Trustees Appointed by former Ord^r of Vestry for Imploying workmen to Build a Church in this Town, hath Agreed with Daniel Pugh Gen^t to Build a Church, & that in the Articles Agreed on, the Said Church was to be two and a half Brick thick to the Water Table & two Brick thick from the Water table up. It is now Agreed that the Said Pugh make the Wall of the Weadth of three Brick thick from the foundation to the Water table and two and a half Brick thick from the Water table up, for which the Said Pugh is to have a further Allowance after the Rate of Thirty Shillings for every thousand Bricks the said Wall will take more by this Alteration and that Instead of Square Arches to the Windows they have Compass heads, and that a Reasonable Allowance be made for it

Daniel Pugh & Wm Moore is Appointed & Sworn Ch: W^{ds} till Easter Next.

Daniel Pugh Acknowledged to have in his hands five Pounds for Sarah Johns and Ann Nails fines for haveing Bastard Children.

William Moore Acknowledged to have in his hands fifty Shillings Sarah Hines fine for haveing a Bastard Child,

Carried Forward

[53]

Brought forward

Ordered the said Daniel Pugh pay to Issabella Flint fifty Shillings of the Said fine, and to Sarah Metcalf fifty Shillings, and that William Moore pay to John Coupland fifty Shillings.

Truly Enter'd by Richd Webb C^l Vestry

Sign'd William Webb

At a Vestry held in Suffolk Town October the 21st 1751 for the Upper Parish of Nansemond County

Present The Revd William Webb Minister
   Daniel Pugh & Wm Moore Ch. W^{ds}
   John Winbourn William Baker ⎫
   Lemuel Riddick Jethro Sumner ⎬ Gent^n Vestrymen
   Josiah Riddick & David Meade ⎭

The upper Parish of Nansemond County for the Year of Our Lord 1751 is

	D^r
	Tob^o
To the Revd Wm Webb his Salary	16000
To D^o for Cask 4 per C^t	640
To D^o for Shrinkage 4 per C^t	640
To D^o his Allowance for Glebe	2000
To Elizabeth Cotter for keeping and Burying J^no Conaway And for Damiage Done to a Bead	3 :16 :9

To John Giblin for Burying John Tibbs		300
To Doct' Arthur Gourley for Medicens and Attendance to John Conaway	2 :10 :–	
To Elizabeth Osheal for Burying Poor Man	1 :10 :–	
To Sarah Johns for keeping Rob' Taylor	2 :15 :–	
To Doct' Thomas Edmonson for keeping Widdow Green Nine Months at 1000 per Year		750
To D° for Bord & Medicens for Wigmore	4 : 7 :1	
To David Nelms for keeping Grace Annstead[30] Seven Weeks at 800 per Year		108
To D° for keping Joseph Whitney 3 ½ Months		240
To Lemuel Riddick for Copy 3 Acts & 4 Lists		172
To Peter Mason for keeping Joseph Whitney Eight Months and Making Cloths		630
To Daniel Pugh his Disbursments for the Poor	5 :17 :6 &	44
To W'" Moore for D°		1667
To Henry Gwin Sexton at Middle Chapel	250	
To D° for Washing the Surplus	75	325
To John Cole Sexton at Brick Church	250	
To D° for Washing the Surplus	50	300
To Ruth Rawles Sextones at upper Chapel	250	
To D° for washing the Surplus	50	300
Carr'd Over	£20 :16 :4	24116

[54]

Brought Over	£20 :16 :4	24116
To Aaron Almond Clerk at Brick Church and Middle Chapel		1500
To W'" Sheckleton Clerk at upper Chapel Tenn Months		832
To Mary Doughtie for keeping John Leatch And Makeing Cloths		1050
To John Gwin for Cleaning the Chapel Road & Spring		100

---

[30] This name may be spelled Armstead.

To John Camble for keeping Two Poor Children	600
To Elisha Ashborn for keeping Wilsons Child 9 M^ths	450
To Wm Moore for keeping Richd Pain five weeks	100
To D° for keeping Grace Annstead[31] Nine Months And three Weeks at 800 per Year	670
To Thos Williams for keeping John Palmer 500 ⎫ To D° for Makeing Cloths 40 ⎭	540
To Doct^r Wm Flemming for Medicens and Attendance to Robt Taylor 14 :— :—	
To Josiah Riddick for Insolvents Last Year	2040
To Wm Baker for hinges for the Chapel	100
To James Cary former Cl of this Vestry	500
To Richd Webb Pres^t Clerk	500
To John Scott for Makeing a Leg for Taylor	100
To 30 M Towards the Church to be Sold by the Church W^ds at July Court for Cash	30000
	£34 :16 :4 63190[32]

John Rawls is Appointed Vestryman in the room of Christo^r Nofleet Deceas'd

The Vestry Adjourned Till Monday Next in this Town

According to the Above Adjourm^t the Vestry met and Proceeded as followeth. Viz

To Daniel Pugh for paying the Q^ts of the Poors Land 800 Acres Two Years	2 :0 :8
	Tob°
The Parish being Indebted the Sum of	63198
To the Collector @ 6 per C^t	3792
	66990

There being 1204 Tithables in this Parish which being Proportioned Amounts to 56 lb Tob° per pole, there being a Depositum of 1024 in the Sherif's hands to be Accounted for at the Laying the Nex Parish Levy

---

[31] This name may be spelled Armstead.

[32] This addition is in error since the final figure, which seems very plain, should be 8. The correct total, 63198, is given next below.

[55]

The Parish being Indebted the Sum of £36:17s:– and there being a Ballance of £25:10s:4d in Lemuel Riddicks hands, And £11: 2s:11d in Daniel Pugh's hands, It's Order'd they Discharge the Several Creditors their Cash Acct[83]

Ordered that Josiah Riddick Gen^t Collect from Every Tithable in this Parish 56 lb Tob^o and therewith Discharge the Parish Credits, he first giveing Bond and Security for that Purpose

N° 1

Ordered that Alexander Cairnes and Mathias Jones in Presence of the Inhabitants of the Town of Suffolk, Procession all the Bounds of Land Belonging to the S^d Town and the Several Lots therein Contained, and Make Return their Proceedings as the Law Directs

N° 2

Ordered that Joseph Godwin and Peter Mason in Presence of the Inhabitants Procession all the Bounds of Land on the South side the Western Branch as the Road runs from the Brick Church to Poorters Bridge Including all the Land in the Said Bounds, you are to go Round Every Mans Land and Renew the Land Marks, and Return to the Vestry an Acco^t of Every Mans Land you Procession with the Names of the Persons Present at the Same, and What Land in Your Precinct you Shall fail to Procession you are to give an Acco^t with the Particular Reasons of Such failure, and if any refuse to have their Land Processioned, you are to Certify the same to the ChW^{ds} within Tenn Days from Under Y^r Hands.

N° 3

Ordered that Richd Webb and Thos Norfleet in Presence of the Inhabitants Procession all the Bounds of Land on the West side the Southern Branch and on the South side the Church Road as it runs from the Brick Church to Jarnagans Bridge Includeing all the Land in the Said Bounds, you are to goe Round Every Mans Land and Renew the Land Marks, and Return to the Vestry an Acco^t of Every Mans Land you Procession, with the Names of the persons Pres^t at the Same, and what Land in your Precinct you Shall fail to Procession, you are to Give an Acco^t with the Particular Reasons of Such failure and if Any Refuse to

---

[83] The figures in the original seem to be quite plain but the amounts stated as being on hand are not sufficient to discharge the indebtedness.

have their Land Processioned you are to Certify the Same to the Church Wardens within Tenn Days from Under Y^r Hands.

N° 4

Ordered that Thos Pinner & Robt Lawrance in Presence of the Inhabitants Procession all the Bounds of Land, begining at Pattesons Neck, so up the Indian Creek and Run to the Extent of the County, along the County Line to Everits Creek. Including all the Land in the Said bounds, You are to go Round Every Mans Land and Renew the Land Marks, and Return to the Vestry an Acco^t of Every Mans Land you Procession with the Names of the Persons Pres^t at the same and what Land in You Prec^t you Shall fail to Proc^n You are to give an Acco^t with the Particular Reasons of such failure, and if any Refuse to have their Land Process^d You are to Certify the same to the Church Wardens within Tenn Days from Under Your Hands &c

[56]   N° 5

Ordered that John Berkley & Henry Wright Junr in Presence of the Inhabitants Procession all the Bounds of Land on the Upper side the Road from Jarnagans Bridge to Poorters Bridge to the Extent of the County, Includeing all the Land in the Said Bounds you are to go Round Every Mans Land and Renew the Land Marks, and Return to the Vestry an Acco^t of Every Mans Land you Procession, and what Land in your Prec^t you Shall fail to Proces^n you are to give an Acco^t with the particular Reasons of Such failure, and if any Refuse to have their Land Process^d You are to Certify the same to the Church W^{ds} within Tenn Days from Under Your Hands &c

N° 6

Ordered that Elisha Ashborn & John Gwin in Presence of the Inhabitants Procession all the Bounds of Land, from Jarnagans Bridge run to Spight's Run, so up to Wm Battles and Michael Kings Sr Includeing all the Land in the said Bounds, you are to go Round Every Mans Land and Renew the Land Marks, and Return to the Vestry an Acco^t of Every Mans Land you Procession, With the Names of the persons Pres^t at the same and what Land in Your Prec^t You Shall fail to Procession, you are to Give an Acco^t with the particular Reasons of Such failure, and if any Refuse to have their Land Processioned, you are to Certify the same to the Church Wardens within Tenn Days from Under Your Hands &c

N° 7

Ordered that John Butler and Henry Butler in Presence of the Inhabitants Process[n] all the Bounds of Land, from W[m] Walters Plan[n] to the Beverdam Swamp by Jn[o] Butlers on the North side South Key Road to the flat Swamp thence to the Meadow Branch, thence up S[d] Branch to the County Line, thence to the first Station, Includ'g all the Land in the S[d] bounds you are to go Round Every Mans Land and Renew the Land Marks and Return to the Vestry an Acco[t] of every Mans Land you Procession, with the Names of the Persons Pres[t] at the same, and what Land in Y[r] Prec[t] you Shall fail to Procession you are to give an Acco[t] with the Particular Reasons of such failure, and if any Refuse to have their Land Proces[d] you are to Certify the same to the Church Wardens within Tenn Days from Under Your Hands &c

N° 8

Ordered that James Winbourn and W[m] Harriss Jun[r][34] [in][35] Presence of the Inhabitants Procession all the Bounds of Land from John Poorters to Sum[n] Road. thence the North Side Summ[n] Road to the Bever dam Swamp by Cap[t] Hunters, thence up the Swamp to South Key Road by Jn[o] Butlers on the South side to the flat Swamp, thence Down the East Side the S[d] swamp, to James Coupland's, thence to the first Station, Includeing all the Land in the S[d] Bounds, you are to go Round Every Mans Land and Renew the Land Marks and Return to the Vestry an Acco[t] of Every Mans Land you Proces[n] with the Names of the Persons Pres[t] at the same, and what Land in your Prec[t] you Shall fail to proces[n] you are to give an Acco[t] with the Particu[r] Reasons of Such failure, and if Any Refuse to have their Land Process[d] you are to Certify the Same to the Church Wardens within Tenn Days from Under your Hands &c

[57] ### N. 9

Ordered that John Hare & W[m] Rawls in Presence of the Inhabitants Procession all the Bounds of Land, Begining at John Poorters Joyning Summerton Swamp on the North side Sum[n] Road to the Knuckle Swamp; Including all the Land in the Said Bounds, You are to go Round Every

---

[34] The names, James Winborne and William Harrisson, are signed to the return as recorded (See p. 69).

[35] This word, which is undoubtedly in the original, has been obliterated by a blot.

Mans Land and Renew the Land Marks, and Return to the Vestry an Acco^t of Every Mans Land you Procession, with the Names of the persons Pres^t at the same and what Land in Your Prec^t you Shall fail to Procession, you are to give an Acco^t with the Particular Reasons of Such failure, and if any Refuse to have their Land Processioned you are to Certify the same to the Ch. W^{ds} within Tenn Days from Under your Hands &c

N° 10

Ordered that Jacob Langston and Isaac Langston in Presence of the Inhabitants Procession all the Bounds of Land, on the North Side Sum^n Swamp, and the South side the Road from Thomas Jones's to John Jenkins's Including all the Land in the Said Bounds, you are to go Round Every Mans Land and Renew the Land Marks, and Return to the Vestry an Acco^t of Every Mans Land you Procession, with the Names of the Persons Pres^t at the same, and what Land in your Prec^t you Shall fail to Procession, you are to give an Acc^t with the Particular Reasons of Such failure, and if any Refuse to have their Land Proces^d you are to Certify the same to the Church W^{ds} within Tenn Days from Under your Hands, &c

N° 11

Ordered that Abraham Riddick and & [sic] John Lawrance in Presence of the Inhabitants Procession all the Bounds of Land, from Sum^n Creek on the west side the Road from Sum^n Creek by Coors, to South Key Road, Including all the Land in the Said Bounds, You are to go Round Every Mans Land and Renew the Land Marks, and Return to the Vestry an Acco^t of Every Mans Land you Procession with the Names of the Persons Pres^t at the same, and what Land in your Prec^t you Shall fail to Procession, you are to give an Acco^t with the Particular Reasons of Such failure, and if any Refuse to have their Land Processioned You are to Certify the same to the Church W^{ds} within Tenn Days from Under Your Hands &c

N° 12

Ordered that Edward Howell & Henry Daughtree in Presence of the Inhabitants Procession all the bounds of Land, from the East Side Summerton Creek Road at Coors, up the Said Creek to Holy Neck Chapel thence on the west side to South Key Road, Including all the Land in the Said Bounds You are to go Round Every Mans Land and Renew the Land

Marks, and Return to the Vestry an Acco^t of Every Mans Land you Procession with the Names of the Persons Present at the same, and what Land in Your Precinct you Shall fail to procession you are to give an Acco^t with the Particular Reasons of Such failure, and if any Refuse to have their Land Processioned, you are to Certify the same to the Church W^ds within Tenn Days from Under Your Hands &c

[58]   N° 13

Ordered that Thos Jones Junr and Henry Jones in Presence of the Inhabitants Procession all the Bounds of Land on the South side South Key Road, Begining at Thos Jones's so along the Road to the Chapel thence along the East side the Chapel Road to South Key Road from thence to the first Station, Including all the Land in the Said Bounds, you are to go Round Every Mans Land and Renew the Land Marks and Return to the Vestry an Acco^t of Every Mans Land you Procession, with the Names of the Persons Pres^t at the same, and what Land in your Prec^t you Shall fail to Procession, you are to give an Acco^t with the Particular Reasons of Such failure, and if any Refuse to have their Land Processioned, you are to Certify the same to the Church W^ds within Tenn Days from Under Your Hands &c

N° 14

Ordered that James Holland Junr and Joseph Holland Junr In Presence of the Inhabitants Procession all the Bounds of Land, Begining at Henry Hollands Plantation, so Down the North side King Sale Swamp, to the County Line, from thence to the head of the Meadow Branch, so to Robt Yeats's Bridge, from thence on the North side South Key Road to Henry Hollands Plantation, Including all the Land in the Said Bounds You are to go Round Every Mans Land and Renew the Land Marks and Return to the Vestry an Acco^t of Every Mans Land you Proces^n with the Names of the Persons Pres^t at the Same, and what Land in your Precinct you Shall fail to Process^n you are to give an Acco^t with the Particular Reasons of Such failure, And if any Refuse to have their Land Process^d you are to Certify the same to the C[h]urch W^ds within Tenn Days from Under Your Hands &c

N° 15

Ordered that Robt Darden and Thomas Edwards in Presence of the Inhabitants, Procession all the Bounds of Land, Between Black water and

Notaway, Including all the Land in the Said Bounds you are to go Round Every Mans Land and Renew the Land Marks and return to the Vestry an Acc^t of Every Mans Land you Procession with the Names of the Persons Present at the same, and what Land in Your Precinct you Shall fail to Proc[e]ssion You are to give an Acco^t with the Particular Reasons of Such failure, and if any Refuse to have their Land Processioned, you are to Certify the same to the Church W^{ds} within Tenn Days from Under Your Hands &c

N° 16

Ordered that John Holland and John Hart in Presence of the Inhabitants Procession all the Bounds of Land, Over Notaway River and to the Extent of the County and Country Lines, Including all the Land in the Said Bounds you are to go Round Every Mans Land and Renew the Land Marks, and Return to the Vestry an Acco^t of Every Mans Land you Procession, with the Names of the Persons present at the same, and what Land in Your Precinct you Shall fail to Proces. You are to give an Acco^t with the Particular Reasons of Such failure, and if any Refuse to have their Land Processioned You are to Certify the same to the Church W^{ds} within Tenn Days from Under Your Hands &c

[59] ### N° 17

Ordered that John Wheatfield and John Daughtree in Presence of the Inhabitants Procession all the Bounds of Land, from the going over Wickam Swamp, to the Country Line, so to King Sale Swamp up the Said Swamp to the first Station, Including all the Land in the Said Bounds, you are to go Round Every Mans Land and Renew the Land Marks and Return to the Vestry an Acco^t of Every Mans Land you Procession, with the Names of the Persons Present at the same, And what Land in Your Precinct you shall fail to Procession you are to give an Acco^t with the Particular Reasons of such failure, and if any Refuse to have their Land Processioned, You are to Certify the same to the Church W^{ds} within Tenn Days from Under Your Hands &c

N° 18

Ordered that John Pulver[36] and John Cross in Presence of the Inhabitants, Procession all the Bounds of Land, from the Knuckle Swamp on

---

[36] This name may be a mistake for John Purvis who signed the return as recorded (See p. 80).

the west side Searum Road, to the Extent of the County Including all the Land in the said Bounds, You are to go Round Every Mans Land and Renew the Land Marks, and Return to the Vestry an Acco^t of Every Mans Land you Procession, with the Names of the Persons present at the same, and what Land in your Precinct you shall fail to Procession you are to give an Acc^t with the Particular Reasons of such failure, and if any Refuse to have their Land Processioned you are to Certify the same to the Church W^{ds} within Tenn Days from Under Your Hands, &[c]

N° 19

Ordered that Jesse Riddick & Moses Spivy in Presence of the Inhabitants Procession all the Bounds of Land, from the Cyprus Swamp on the East side Orapeak Road to the Country Line, Including all the Land in the S^d bounds You are to go Round Every Mans Land, and Renew the Land Marks, and Return to the Vestry an Acco^t of Every Mans Land you Procession, with the Names of the persons Pres^t at the same, and what Land in Your Prec^t You Shall fail to Process^n you are to give an Acco^t with the particular Reasons of such failure, and if any Refuse to have their Land Processioned You are to Certify the same to the Church W^{ds} within Tenn Days from Under Your hands &c

N. 20

Ordered that Moses Harrell and James Raby in Presence of the Inhabitants Procession all the Bounds of Land, Begining at the Cyprus swamp, thence on the West side Orapeak Road to the Country Line, thence to Raby's Swamp to the head thereof, thence Down the Road to the Draggon Swamp, to the Cyprus Swamp to Orapeak Road, Including all all [sic] the Land in the Said Bounds, You are to go Round Every Mans Land and Renew the Land Marks and Return to the Vestry an Acco^t of Every Mans Land you Procession, with the Names of the Persons Pres^t at the same, and what Land in y^r Prec^t you shall fail to Procession, you are to give an Acco^t with the Particular reasons of such failure, and if any Refuse to have their Land Processioned You are to Certify the same to the Church W^{ds} within Tenn Days from Under Your Hands &c

[60]

N. 21

Ordered that Joseph Baker and Francis Duke in Presence of the Inhabitants Procession all the Bounds of Land, from the Knuckle Swamp, to Barbecue Swamp Between Summerton Road and Smiths Road, Including all the Land in the S^d Bounds you are to go Round Every Mans Land and Renew the Land Marks, and Return to the Vestry an Acco^t of Every Mans Land you Procession, with the Names of the persons Pres^t at the same, and what Land in Y^r Precinct you shall fail to Procession, you are to give an Acco^t with the Particular Reasons of Such failure, and if any Refuse to have their Land Processioned you are to Certify the same to the Church W^ds within Tenn Days from Under your Hands &c

N° 22

Ordered that Wm Pierce and Edwd Baker in Presence of the Inhabitants Procession all the Bounds of Land, from the Country Line, to Adam Raby's Swamp, up the S^d Swamp to the Road, as the Road runs to Smiths Road, and as the Road runs to the Country Line, Including all the Land in the Said Bounds, you are to go Round Every Mans Land and Renew the Land Marks, and Return to the Vestry an Acco^t of Every Mans Land you Procession with the Names of the Persons Present at the same, and what Land in you[r] Prec^t you Shall fail to Procession, you are to give an Acco^t with the Particular Reasons of Such failure And if any Refuse to have their Land Processioned, you are to Certify the Same to the Church W^ds within Tenn Days from under Y^r Hands.

N° 23

Ordered that Joseph Perry and Jacob Price in Presence of the Inhabitants Procession all the Bounds of Land from Barbacue swamp Down Newby's Road to Francis Couplands Branch, Down the Said Branch to Bakers Mill Run up the Said Run to the Mouth of the Bever dam Swamp up the Said Swamp to the Bridge, so up Summ^n Road to the Barbacue Swamp, Including all the Land in the Said Bounds, you are to [go] Round Every Mans Land and Renew the Land Marks, and Return to the Vestry, an Acco^t of Every Mans Land you Process^n with the Names of the Persons Pres^t at the same and what Land in Y^r Prec^t you Shall fail to Procession You are to give an Acco^t with the Particular Reasons of Such [failure] and if any Refuse to have their Land Processioned, You are to Certify the same to the Ch: W^ds within Tenn Days from Under Y^r Hands &c

N° 24

Ordered that George Spivy & Abraham Lasitor in Presence of the Inhabitants Procession all the Bounds of Land, from Newby's Road, Down

Barbacue and the Cyprus Swamp to the Desert down the Desert to the Pocosson, up the Pocosson to the head of Francis Couplands Branch, Including all the Land in the Said Bounds, You are to go Round Every Mans Land and Renew the Land Marks and Return to the Vestry an Acco^t of Every Mans Land you Procession with the Names of the Persons Present at the Same, and what Land in Your Prec^t you Shall fail to Procession you are to give an Acco^t with the Particular Reasons of Such failure, and if Any Refuse to have their Land Processioned, You are to Certify the Same to the Church w^{ds} within Tenn Days from Under Your Hands &c

[61] N° 25

Ordered that Danl Pugh & Moses Riddick in Presence of the Inhabitants Process^n all the Bounds of Land, on the West side the Bever Dam, to Francis Couplands Branch, Down the Said Branch to Bakers Mill Run, Down the S^d Run & Creek to Pughs Creek, Including all the Land in the S^d Bounds, You are to go Round Every Mans Land & Renew the Land Marks, and Return to the Vestry an Acco^t of Every Mans Land You Process. with the Names of the Persons Pres^t at the Same and what Land in Y^r Precinct you shall fail to Process^n you are to give an Acco^t wth. the Particular Reasons of Such failure, and if any Refuse to have their Land Process^d you are to Certify the Same to the Church Wardens within Tenn Days from Under Y^r Hands, &c

N° 26

Ordered that John Northcott & John Brewer in Presence of the Inhabitants Procession all the Bounds of Land, Between Pughs Mill Creek, & Keatons Creek, up the Branch between Keetons and Gumbs's to the Desert Including all the Land in the S^d Bounds you are to go Round Every Mans Land and Renew the Land Marks, & Return to the Vestry an Acco^t of Every Mans Land you Procession with the Names of the persons Pres^t at the Same and what Land in your Prec^t you Shall fail to Process^n you are to give an Acco^t with the Particular Reasons of such failure, and if any Refuse to have their Land Process^d you are to Certify the Same to the Church W^{ds} within Tenn Days from Under your Hands &c

N° 27

Ordered that Moses Rawlins & Aaron Lasitor in Presence of the Inhabitants Procession all the Bounds of Land, on the East Side the Bever Dam up to the Pocosson, Including all the Land in the S^d Bounds. you are to go Round. Every Mans Land and Renew the Land Marks and Return to the Vestry an Acco^t of Every Mans Land you Process^n and the Names of the Persons Pres^t at the Same and what Land in Your Prec^t you Shall fail to Process. you are to give an Acco^t with the Particular Reasons of Such failure, and if any Refuse to have their Land Process^d you are to Certify the Same to the Ch. W^{ds} within Tenn Days from Under Your Hands &c

N° 28

Ordered that John Rodgers & James Roberts in Presence of the Inhabitants Process^n all the Bounds of Land, from the Knuckle Swamp Bridge on the South Side the Swamp, up the East side Summ. Road, to the Country Line, so along the Line to Smiths Road, so Down Smiths Road to the Knuckle Swamp, so Down the South side thereof to the first Station, Including all the Land in the S^d Bounds, you are to go Round Every Mans Land and Renew the Land Marks, and Return to the Vestry an Acco^t of Every Mans Land you Procession and the Names of the Persons Pres^t at the same and what Land in Your Prec^t you Shall fail to Procession you are to give an Acco^t with the Particular Reasons of Such failure, and if any Refuse to have their Land Processioned, you are to Certify the same to the Ch. W^{ds} within Tenn Days from Under Your Hands &c

Truly Entered by   Sign'd by William Webb
    Richd Webb Cl Vestry

[62]

At a Vestry held in Suffolk Town March the 31st 1752 for the Upper Parish of Nansemond County

Pres^t {
The Revd William Webb Minister
Daniel Pugh & William Moore Ch. W^{ds}
David Meade   Josiah Riddick } Gent^n Vestrymen
Henning Tembte & John Rawls
}

Daniel Pugh Acknowledged to have in his Hands Seven Pound Tenn Shillings Due to the poor of the Parish

Ordered the said Daniel Pugh pay to Sarah Ozburn Twenty Shillgs and to Mary Babb Twenty five Shillings, to buy her one Cow & Calf But that the Property thereof Remain in the Church W^ds hands Till other ways Ordered by this Vestry, And to John Coupland Forty Shillings, and to Rebecca Hine Twenty Shillings, and to Kesiah Slatter Twenty five Shillings, And to Mary Spight Twenty Shillings.

Daniel Pugh and William Moore are Continued and Sworn Chur: W^ds Till Easter Next.

Thomas Sumner is Appointed Vestryman in the room of Jethro Sumner Deceas'd.

Truly Enter'd by   Sign'd by William Webb
    Richd Webb Cl. Vestry

By an Order of Vestry we have Process^d the Line Between John Gwin and Wm Moore & the Line Between Wm Moore & David Meade and also the Line between David Meade & John Gwin, the Party's Pres^t; the Line between John March & David Meade & between David Meade and Wm Lakey Pres^t Josiah Gwin Wm Gwin & Thos Jordan & Peter Watkins, Process^d the Line Between John Ashburn & Jno March and John Hine & between Peter Butler & Richd Hine & Between Butler and Henry Wright & between Jno March & Peter Butler & Henry Wright & Between Henry Wright & Nathan^l Pruden Pres^t John March & Ja^s March & Richd Hine & Nathl Pruden Ja^s Hine Wm Wright and the Line Between Nathl Pruden & Henry Wright and the Line between Henning Tembte & Michaell King and also the Line Between Elisha Ballard & Forset & also Between Elisha Ballard & Jno March, Pres^t Francis Forset Elisha Ballard and James March

                                      Elisha Ashburn
                                        John Gwin

[63]

Pursuant to an Order of Vestry we the Subscribers have gone Round Every Mans Land and Renewed their Land Marks, Begining at James Couplands a Line Between the said Coupland and John Rawls Present the two Propriet^rs Thos Winborne and John Coupland, Thence a Line between John Porter & John Ballard Pres^t the said Porter & John Harrisson Senr Thence a Line Between William Harrisson & John Harrisson Pres^t John Rawls Ja^s Coupland & Thomas Winborne, a Line of John Harrissons

Binding on Surpless Land Pres^t John Porter & James Harrisson a Line Between W^m & John Harrisson Present the Two Proprietors Wm Harrisson Junr John Harrisson Junr & Ja^s Harrisson. Joseph Bakers Land Process^d Pres^t John Skiner and William Baker John Skiner's Land Process^d Pres^t the said Skiner and Joseph Baker a Line Between Ephraim Hunter & Oliver Worrell Pres^t John Worrell a Line Between John Ballard and John Butler Pres^t the said John Butler & Jno Harrisson Junr a Line Between John Butler and John Harrisson Pres^t the two proprietors. a Line Between Jno Winborne Senr and William Harrisson Junr Pres^t William Shitleton all the Bounds of Land containing in the said Order Quietly Processioned without any Objections by

Feby 8th 1752   James Winborne
                William Harrisson

To Obedient to an Order of an Vestry to us Directed we have Processioned the Lines, Daniel Battens Lands Process^d Robt Williams Pres^t Thos Edwards Land Process^d Richd Williams Pres^t Richd Williams Land Process^d Danl Batten Pres^t Christo^r Reynols Land Process^d Richd Williams pres^t John Hay's Land process^d Richd Williams Pres^t James Massigal, Land Process^d Danl Battin Pres^t Maj^r Lemuel Riddick's Land Process^d Thos Lawrance Son of Mich^l Pres^t Ja^s Gardiner's Land Process^d Thos Lawrance Pres^t Ja^s Gardiner Junr Land Process^d Thos Lawrance Pres^t Robt Dardan Land Process^d Joshua Gardiner Pres^t Thos Lawrance Land Process^d Ja^s Gardiner Pres^t Carr Dardan Land Process^d Robt Car Pres^t Moses Dardan Land Process^d Michaell Daughtree pres^t Michaell Daughtree Land Process^d Jacob Dardan Pres^t Robt Car Land Process^d Car Dardan Pres^t Jacob Dardan Land Process^d Mich^l Daughtree Present

                Robert Dardan
                Thomas Edwards

[64]

I John Whitfield and John Daughtrie Doth make our Return to Honourable Court, of Every Mans Land in our Ord^r Henry Holland Junr Land & Wm Holland Land both at Pres^t and Stephen Dardan Land & William Baker Land, William & Isaac Flemming at Pres^t & Isaac Flemming Land & he at Pres^t and William Sanders & Ja^s Uzzell Land both at Pres^t & Jo^s Holland and Wm Vaughan Land and both at Pres^t and Elizth Vaughan and John Whitfield Land and Both at Pres^t and Lewis

Daughtree and Bryan Daughtree Land Lewis Daughtree at Pres[t] and Tho[s] Vaughan & Oliver Worrell Land and both at Pres[t] & John Cuchin & John Daughtree Land and John Cuchin's at Pres[t] & Tho[s] Cuchins and John Milner Land Tho[s] Cuchin's & William Bryant at Pres[t] Culbert Hedgepeth Land & Henry Holland at Pres[t] we have Process[d] all the Land Marks that was in our Ord[r]

          John Whitfield
          John I[37] Daughtrey

 To Obedient to an Ord[r] of an Vestry to us Directed we have Process[d] the Lines
A Line Between M[r] David Meade & Mich[l] Lawrance Jethro Dardan Pres[t] a Line between M[r] Meade and John Pinder John Lawrance and Paul Lawrance Pres[t] a Line Between Tho[s] Shivers & Mich[l] Lawrance Geo: Lawrance Tho[s] Shivers Pres[t] a Line Between Abraham Riddick and John Butler Tho[s] Shivers & George Lawrance Pres[t] a line Between Abraham Riddick & Tho[s] Shivers John Lawrance Pres[t] A Line Between Rieddick [sic] and Tho[s] Lowther Thomas Shivers & George Lawrance Pres[t] A Line Between Lowther & Riddick George Lawrance and Tho[s] Sh[i]vers Pres[t] A line between Lowther's John Lawrance and Paul Lawrance Pres[t] a line of Tho[s] Core John Norris & Tho[s] Low[t]her pres[t] A Line Cap[t] Baker's he Pres[t] A Country Line Cap[t] Baker Pres[t] a line Between Geo: Lawrance and Mich[l] Lawrance Jn[o] Lawrance Pres[t] A line Between Geo[e] Lawrance & Paul Lawrance Jn[o] Lawrance Pres[t] A line between John Lawrance & Paul Lawrance

          Abraham Riddick
          John Lawrance

[65]

Pursuant to an Order of Vestry to us Directed we have Process[d] all the Lands in the bounds Mentioned in the said Order Viz A Line Between Lemuel Riddick and the Plantation that Richard Smith live on Pres[t] the Said Lemuel Riddick John Streator Richard Smith John Cross Lemuel Riddick Jun[r] a Line between the Said Riddick and William Landing the same persons Pres[t] and W[m] Landing a line between the s[d] Riddick and John Bearfield all these s[d] Persons pres[t] a line between the s[d]

---

[37] This is written like "I", bisected by a short horizontal line. It probably represents his mark and "J", the initial of his given name.

Riddick and Hugh Goff all the aforesaid Persons pres^t a line Between Robt Parker and James Long Robt Parker Pres^t and Adam Harrod a line Between Edmund Bird and Robt Parker Pres^t Joseph Horton a line Between Richd Parker and John Cole Junr pres^t John Bird a line between John Bird and John Cole Pres^t Richard Parker a line Between John Cole and Wm Everat Pres^t the s^d Cole and the S^d Everat, a line Between Wm Peal and Francis Parker Pres^t William Peal, a line Between Moses Horton and John Taylor pres^t Saml Horton a line Between Peter Parker and Joseph .orton Pres^t Peter Parker, a line Between Richd Parker and Peter Parker Pres^t Peter Parker, a line Between Richd Taylor and Edwd Baker pres^t Richd Taylor, a line Between Charles Russell and Francis Parker Pres^t Charles Russell, a line Between Charles Russell and Robt Smith Pres^t Robt Smith, a line Between John Roger and Wm Roger pres^t John Roger, a line Between James Roberts and John Rogers Pres^t the S^d Rogers and Roberts, all the Said Lands in Quiet and Peaceable Procession as Witness our Hands this Sixth Day of March 1752

         James Roberds [sic]
         John Rogers

[66]

Pursuant to an Order of Vestry we the Subscribers have Process^d all the Said Lands within the Bounds of the said Order Begining at Henry Hollands Process^d a line between Stephen Darden and Joseph Holland Pres^t Moses Darden, a line [between] Henry Holland's and Stephen Darden pres^t Solomon Holland & Jno Baly a line Between James Holland and Joseph Holland Pres^t John Hedgepeth and James Sumner, a line between James Holland and John Holland Pres^t Jno Hedgepeth & Ja^s Sumner a line Between John Winborne & Jno Holland Pres^t the S^d Winborne & Jno Faulk a line Between Jno Winborne and Culbert Hedgepeth Pres^t John Hedgepeth Ja^s Sumner and Solomon Holland a line Between John Winborne & Wm Harrisson Pres^t the s^d Winborne & Jno Faulk a line between John Winborne & James Holland Pres^t the Said Winborne & John Faulk, a line Between John Faulk and Capt John King Pres^t the said John Faulk and Wm Harrisson a line Between Christo^r Sanders & William Harrisson Pres^t the said Wm Har..sson & Ja^s Harrisson a line Between Capt John King and William Harrisson Pres^t John Harrisson and Peter Butler a line Between Peter Butler & Jno Harrisson

Pres^t Ja^s Harrisson & the S^d Peter Butler, a line between W^m & Jno Harrisson & Jno Carr Jno Carr & Jno Harrisson a line Between John Carr & Joseph Holland Pres^t Jo^s Holl^d & Jno Carr a line between John Holland & Jo^s Holland a line between Henry Johnson & Jo^s Holland Pres^t Jo^s Holland a line Between Jo^s Holland & Wm Johnson, Jos. Holland a line Between Ja^s Holland & John Carr Pres^t Jno Carr. a line between Culbert Hedgepeth & Jo^s Holl^d Pres^t Jo^s Holl^d a line Between Capt Wm Baker & Joseph Holland Wm Baker Junr Edwd Hare and Ja^s Sumner a line Between Capt William Baker and Henry Hedgepeth Pres^t Wm Baker J^r Henry Hedgepeth. a line Between Capt Baker and Ja^s Sumner Pres^t Wm Baker Junr Henry Hedgepeth a line between Isaac Fleming & Ja^s Sumner Pres^t Edwd Hare & Ja^s Sumner a line Between Henry Hedgepeth & Ja^s Sumner Pres^t Edwd Hare Ja^s Sumner so Including all the Lands within the S^d bounds Contain^g in the S^d Order peaceable & Quietly by us the Subscribers, March the 3^d 1752

James Holland
Joseph Holland

[67]

In Obedience to an Order of Vestry w[e] have Process^d all the Land in our Prec^t as followeth

Process^d a line between John Wilson and Mary Douthtie in Presence of John Holland and James Holland

Process^d a line Between John Holland and John Wilson in the Presence of John Best and William Beatman

Process^d a line Between John Wilson and Thomas Stokes in the Presence of John Holland John Best

Process^d a line Between John Holland and Mary Doughtie in the Presence of John Best and James Holland

Process^d a line Between John Best and John Holland in the Presence of James Holland

Process^d a line Between John Holland and William Beatman in the Presence of James Holland

Process^d a line between David Nelms and Jeremiah Godwin in the Presence of John Best

Process^d a line Between Jeremiah Godwin and Wm Beatman in the Presence of John Best

Process^d a line Between Jeremiah Godwin and John Best Only the owners Present

Process^d a line Belonging to Jeremiah Godwin in the Presence of John Best & William Beatman

Process^d a line Between Thomas Stokes and Jane Baker in the Presence of John Best and William Beatman

Process^d a line Between Jane Baker and John Holland in the Presence of Edward Eley and James Holland

Process^d a line Between John Barkley and Jane Baker in the Presence of Edward Eley and James Holland

Process^d a line between John Barkley and Robert Archer in the Presence of John Holland and Thomas Godwin

Process^d a line Between John Barkley and William Collans in the Presence of Edward Eley and Robert Archer

Carr^d Over

[68]

Bro^t forw^d

Process^d a line Between Thomas Godwin and William Collins in the Presence of Edward Eley and Robert Archer

Process^d a line between Robert Archer and William Collins in the Presence of Edward Eley

Process^d a line Between Thomas Godwin and Robt Archer in the Presence of Edward Eley

Process^d a line between Robert Archer and Philip Elsbury in the Presence of Edward Eley and Thomas Godwin

Process^d a line Between Philip Elsbury & William Collins in the Presence of Robert Archer and Thomas Godwin

Process^d a line Between John Eley and Daniel Osheal in the Presence of Edward Eley and Michael Eley

Process^d a line Between John Eley and John Rodes in the Presence of Michael Eley and Edward Eley

Process^d a line Between John Wyatt and Henning Tembte in the Presence of Francis Powell and Jessy King

Process^d a line Between Henning Tembte and James Coupland in the presence of John Rodes and Joshua King

Process^d a line Between Henning Tembte and Thos Stokes in the Presence of John Rodes and Joshua King

Process^d a line Between Jane Baker and Thomas Stokes in the Presence of John Rodes and Joshua King

Process^d a line Between Thomas Gay and James Coupland

Process^d a line Between Thos Gay and John Wyatt in the presence of Francis Powell and James Parker

Process^d a line Between John Wyatt and James Coupland in the Presence of Francis Powell and James Parker

Process^d a line Between Henning Tembte and Francis Powell in the Presence of John Wyatt and James Parker

Process^d a line Between Francis Powell and William King in the Presence of John Wyatt and James Parker

Process^d a line Between William King and Thomas Gay in the presence of Francis Powell and John Rodes

Carr^d Forw^d

[69]

Process^d a line Between William King and John Rodes in the Presence of James Parker and Joshua King

Process^d a line Between John Rodes and Thomas Gay in the Presence of Francis Powell James Parker & Jessy King

Process^d a line Between Thomas Gay and Henry Wright in the Presence of Francis Powell John Rodes and James Parker

Process^d a line Between Thomas Gay and Henry Hobgood in the Presence of Francis Powell James Parker Jessy King

Process^d a line Between John Butler and Augustin Simons in the Presence of John Simons

Process^d a line Between Samuel Ozburn and William McClenney in the Presence of Edwd Taylor & Saml Parker William Ozborn

Process^d a line Between William McClenney and Sarah Scott in the Presence of Samuel Parker and Joseph Scott

Process^d a line Between William Scott and Sarah Scott in the Presence of William McClenney and Edward Taylor

Process^d a line Between Sarah Scott and John Parker in the Presence of Samuel Parker and Joseph Scott

Process^d a line Between Wm Scott and John Parker in the Presence of Edward Taylor and Samuel Parker

Process^d a line Between John Parker and William Devoll in the Presence of Charles Gay and Edward Taylor

Process^d A line Between William Devoll and Michael Eley in the Presence of Samuel Parker and Edward Taylor

Process^d a line Between William Devoll and Edward Taylor in the Presence of Samuel Parker

Process^d a line Between Edward Taylor and Michael Eley in the Presence of Samuel Parker

Process^d a line Between Edward Taylor and John Rodes Only Edward Taylor Present

Process^d a line belonging to William Ozborn in the Presence of Matthew Pierce

          John Barkley
          Henry Wright

[70]

To Obedient to an Order of an Vestry to us Directed we have Processioned the Lines, a line Between Abraham Riddick and Thomas Shivers Present A line Between Abraham Riddick and Thomas Shivers Pres^t a line Between Thomas Lowther and John Pinder Joseph Rodgers Pres^t a line Between John Rodgers and and [sic] Joseph Roggers they Present a line between Boothe and Pinder Thos Shivers and Abraham Riddick Pres^t A line Between William Baker and Bryant Daughtry and William Baker Pres^t a line Between Capt Baker and Thos Howard they Present, a line Between Henry Daughtry and John Butler Thos Shivers & Abraham Riddick Pres^t a line Between John Rawls and William Howell Mich^l Watson Pres^t a line between John Watson and Edward Howell William Howell Pres^t a line Between Edward Howell and & [sic] Saml Watson William Howell Pres^t a line Between Baker and Boothe Henry Daughtry Pres^t and Abraham Riddick Thos Shivers a line Between Riddick and Shivers a line Between John Roggers and Robt Roggers James Wiggins Pres^t a line Between Edward Howell and Jo^s Roggers Joseph Roggers Pres^t a line Between Henry Daughtry and Edward Howell Robert Roggers Pres^t a line Between John Jenkins and Edward Boyt William Boyt Pres^t a line Between Edward Boyt and William Boyt a line Between Henry Jones and Edward Boyt a line Between Henry Jones & Thos Jones Henry Jones and Samuel Watson James Howell Saml Watson A line Between William Homes and Henry Jones a line Between James Howell and Henry Jones,

          Henry Daughtry
          Edward Howell

[71]

Pursuant to an Order of Vestry we the Subscribers have Process^d all the Lands within the Bounds of the said order Begining at Thomas Jones's Line binding on the Parish Land[38] present Henry Coupland and Moses Jones & John Keen, a line Process^d between Henry Coupland and George Keen Pres^t the two Proprietors a line Betwen Henry Coupland and John Hare Process^d Pres^t the s^d Hare & Jno Keen a line Between Henry Jones and Peter Howard Process^d Pres^t the two Proprietors and James Howard a line Between Peter Howard and James Howard Process^d Pres^t the two proprietors a line Between James Eley and James Howard Process^d Pres^t Peter Howard and Ja^s Howard a line Between Thomas Howard and John Ballard Process^d Pres^t Thomas Howard a line Between Bryant Daughtry and John Ballard Process^d Pres^t William Daughtry Ja^s Howard and Thomas Howard a line between John Ballard and Joseph Holland Process^d Pres^t James Eley and Peter Howard a line Between W^m and Henry Holland Process^d Pres^t the two Proprietors, a line Between Henry Holland Senr and Henry Holland Junr Pres^t the two Proprietors a line Between Robt Holland and John Everit Pres^t Robt Holland a line Between James Winborne and John Everit Pres^t Robt Holland a line Between James Winborne and Charles Jenkins Process^d Pres^t Robert Holland a line Between Henry Coupland and Robert Brewer Pres^t Henry Coupland, a line betwee[n] John Rawls and Robt Brewer, Henry Holland John Rawls and John Winborne a line between William Holland and the Orphans of Luke Rawls Deceas'd, Process^d Pres^t John Winborne and John Rawls a line Between John Winborne and William Holland Process^d Pres^t Jno Rawls and Henry Holland and the Proprietors a line Between Henry Holland and Willm Holland pres^t the two proprietors a line Between John Winborne and William Collins Pres^t John Winborne and Wm Holland a line Between William Harrisson and John Winborne Pres^t the two Proprietors a line of Mainers and John Faulks Process^d Pres^t John Winborne a line between William Harrisson and James Holland Process^d Pres^t John Winborne and John Faulk, a line Between Ja^s Holland & John Winborne Pres^t the two Proprietors

Carr^d forw^d

---

[38] The last three letters of this word are very faint as if they had been erased for a possible substitution.

[72]
Continued

a line Between James Holland Son of Henry and James Holland Son of John, Process^d Pres^t John Winborne, a line Between James Holl^d Son of Henry and Joseph Holland Pres^t John Winborne
So Including all the Said Lands within the Said Bounds by the aforesaid Order are peaceably and Quietly Process^d without any Molestation by us the Subscribers.

March the 4th 1752   Thomas Jones
                           Henry Jones

In Obedience to an Order of Vestry we the Subscribers have Process^d the Land in our Precinct in Maner and form following Jeremiah Godwin's Land Process^d by his Order Elisha Norfleet's Land Process^d he being Pres^t the Glebe Land Process^d by the Ch.^{wds} order, Jonathan Roberts his Land Process^d he being Pres^t the Land of Nicholas Perritt Process^d he being Pres^t the Land of Capt Tembte Process^d by his Order the Land of Benjamin Weignrights Process^d Jonathan Roberts being Pres^t The Land of John Jones Process^d he being Pres^t the Line between John Jones and Capt Tembte the Land which was formerly call^d Boyts Land by the s^d Tembte's order and John Jones Pres^t the Land of David Nelms Junr Proc^d by his Order the Land of Peter Green Process^d he being Pres^t the Land of George Frith Process^d his Wife Pres^t the Land of John Pinner Process^d he being Pres^t the Land of Christo^r Sanders Process^d his Son Pres^t the Land of William Nelms Process^d he being Pres^t the Land of David Nelms Senr Process^d he being Pres^t the Land of Peter Mason Process^d he Pres^t the Land of John Thomas Process^d his Son being Pres^t the Land of Jonathan Nelms Process^d he being Pres^t the Land of Maj^r Tucker no Procession Tucker not Appeared the Land formerly Call'd Conyears no Procession, no one Appeared the Land of Joseph Godwin Process^d he Pres^t

                           Peter Mason
                           Joseph Godwin

[73]
This to Certify you that we have Marked all the Lines that is in the Bounds that we were to do.

The Names of the Men that owns the Land	Who was Present
Thomas Jones	Thomas Boyt Present
Frederick Jones	Jacob Jones
William Jones	Theophilus Jones
Theophilus Jones	Arthur Jones
Jacob Langston	John Streator
Jacob Jones	David Sumner
James Rawls	John Rawls
John Rawls	James Rawls
Arthur Jones	Arthur Jones Still
George Jones	Theophilus Jones Still
George Jarnagan	Hardy Rawls
William Howell	James Coupland
John Watson	John Hare
William Boyt	William Howell
Hardy Rawls	Arthur Jones Still
James Coupland	David Sumner
John Hare	These are the Men that were Present
Edward Boyt	
George Keen	
Lemuel Riddick	
David Sumner	
Francis Parker	
Robert Parker	
Isaac Langston	
	Jacob Langston
	Isaac Langston

[74]³⁹

Acording to order we have Process^d all the Land in the Precinct Before Mentioned, Begining at Thomas Milners in the Presence of John Wilkison and Thomas Milner and George Frith's in the Presence of Nicholas Perritt Thomas Milner & George Frith, John Wilkison's in the Presence of John Lawrence Samuel Lawrence George Frith Nicholas

---

³⁹ In the return on this page, it appears that the spelling "Lawrance" has been corrected to "Lawrence" in most cases, but the changes to one spelling or the other are sometimes difficult to decipher.

Perritt and Thomas Milner Nicholas Perritt's in the Presence of John Lawrence Samuel Lawrence John Wilkison Nicholas Perritt & Joseph Dardan, James Almond's in the Presence of Samuel Lawrence John Lawrence John Wilkison & Joseph Darden, John Lawrence's in the Presence of John Lawrence Samuel Lawrance Nicholas Perritt Jn⁰ Wilkison and Joseph Darden Robert Lawrence's in the Presence of John Wilkison John Lawrence Samuel Lawrence Nicholas Perritt and Joseph Dardan, Samuel Lawrence's in the Presence of Nicholas Perritt Samuel Lawrence & Joseph Dardan, Exum Scott's in the Presence of John Lawrence Samuel Lawrance Thomas Pinners in the Presence of Exum Scott & Saml Lawrance Mourning Scott's in the presence of Exum Scott and Saml Lawrence, Margaret Joanna Godwin's in the Presence of John Woodrope Cordial Norfleet Margaret Godwin and Ann Lawrance, Ann Lawrance's in the Presence of John Woodrope Cordial Norfleet and Ann Lawrence, Elizabeth's[40] in the Presence of John Woodroph and Cordial Norfleet John Woodroph's in the Presence of Cordial Norfleet and John Woodroph, Being all Quietly Process^d

Given Under our hands this Seventh Day of March 1752

Thomas Pinner
Robert Lawrance

[75]

Pursuant to and [sic] Order Vestry to us Directed we have Process^d all the Lands in the Bounds Mentioned in the Said Order Viz
A Line between Lemuel Riddick and John Cross Pres^t the Said John Cross and the Said Lemuel Riddick and John Streator and Wm Cross a line between Lemuel Riddick and David Sumner Pres^t Jn⁰ Streator and Robert Sumner and William Cross, a line Between William Cross and William Roggers Pres^t Robert Roger, a line Between John Cross and Benjamin Rogger Pres^t Jethro Roger, a line Between Benjamin Rogers and John Purvis Pres^t William Cross a line between William Savage and William Rogers Pres^t Benjamin Rogers a line between William Purvis and James Purvis Pres^t Robert Roger a line Between Robert Roger and James Purvis Pres^t James Savage a line Between Daniel March and Abraham Odam Pres^t James Odam a line Between John Hare and Daniel March Pres^t William Purvis a line between John Johnson and James Ellet Pres^t

---

[40] Probably Elizabeth Norfleet. *Cf.* returns on p. 185-186, 209.

William Purvis and John Hare all the Said Lands in Quiet and Peaceable Processions as Witness our Hands the Sixth Day of March 1752

John Cross Senr
John Purvis

[76]

In Obedience to and [sic] Order of Vestry we William Pearce and Edward Baker have Processioned all the Land within our Bounds and no Interuption John Smith's Land Done Pres^t him Self and James Long, James Long's Done Pres^t Moses Harrell, William Henry's Pres^t the Same Constantine Harmons Land Done Pres^t the Same Moses Harrell's Land Done Pres^t the same John Harrell's Land Done Pres^t Job Harrell & John Baker Job Harrell's Land Done Pres^t the same, John Baker's Land Done Pres^t the same Arthur Gorley's Done Pres^t Ephraim Peal and John Baker, Ephraim Peal's Land Done Pres^t the same, William Peals Land Done Pres^t the same, Kedar Raby's Land Done Pres^t William Peal and Jacob Sumner Alexander Averi's Done Pres^t the same, Robert Peals Done Pres^t Joseph Parker, Jesse Peal's Done Pres^t the same, William Pearce's Done Pres^t Robert Peal, Jonathan Tayloes Done Pres^t Richard Tayloe Edward Baker's Done Pres^t James Long and Samuel Baker, Samuel Baker's Done Pres^t the same Richard Tayloe's Done Pres^t the same.

his
William M[41] Pearce
Mark

his
Edward E Baker
Mark

[77]

An Account of the Lands procession'd from the Pocosson to the Beverdam in the Year 1752.

Renewed the Line between Jotham Lassetor & James Boothe in the Presence of both Parties and Henry Riddick

The Line between Mills Riddick and Jotham Lassetor in Presence of Jotham Lassetor and Henry Riddick

---

[41] This is made like the letter "M", with the middle strokes extending below the line of the name and crossed.

The Line Between James Boothe & Lemuel Riddick in Presence of Ja⁵ Boothe

The Line Between Lemuel Riddick and Mills Riddick in Presence of James Riddick and Henry Riddick

The Line Between Mills Riddick and William Stallins in Presence of William Stallins

The Line Between William Stallins and Joseph Stallins in Presence of Both parties

The Line Between Joseph Stallins and John Riddick in Presence of both Parties

The Line Between John Riddick and Willis Riddick in Presence of Willis Riddick and Samuel Riddick

The Line Between Willis Riddick and John Cambell in Presence of Willis Riddick and Samuel Riddick

The Line Between John Cambell and Esther Pugh in presence of John Cambell

The Line between John Cambell & Aaron Lassetor in presence of both parties

The Line Between Moses Rawlings and Aaron Lassetor in Presence of John Cambell and Thomas Field

The Line Between Moses Rawlings and Edward Bates in Pres⁵ of John Cambell

The Line Between Edward Bates & Joseph Stallins in Presence of Thomas Field

The Line Between Edward Bates and John Cambell in Presence of John Cambell

The Line Between Edward Bates and Josiah Riddick in Presence of Thomas Field

The Line Between [. . .]⁴² & Esther Pugh at a place Call'd Hickmons in Presence of Thoˢ Field

Carr^d Over

[78]

Brought Over

The Line Between Edward Bates and Esther Pugh at a place Call'd Jerico in Presence of John Cambell

---

⁴² Name omitted in original. *Cf.* return on p. 109-110.

The Line Between Aaron Lasseter and Daniel Pugh in Presence of John Cambell

The Line Between Daniel Pugh & Moses Rawlings in Presence of John Cambell

The Line Between Aaron Lasseter and Esther Pugh in Presence of John Cambell

The Line Between Esther Pugh and William Woodward in Presence of Daniel Pugh & Thomas Brown

The Line Between Daniel Pugh & William Woodward in Presence of Thomas Brown

Moses Rawlings
Aaron Lasseter

In Obedience to an Order of Vestry we the Subscribers have Accordingly Mett and Procession d all the Lands on the North side the Southern Branch, and on the South side of the Road as it Runs from the Brick Church to Jarnagans Bridge; Present Jethro Sumner, Christopher Norfleet, David Rice, Senr Henning Tembte, Elisha Norfleet, William Norfleet, John Best, Thomas Sumner, John Jones, Moses Sanders, Martha Frith, Jeremiah Godwin, Edward Moore, & John Hansel,

Richard Webb
Thomas Norfleet

[79]

By Virtue of an Order of Vestry Pass'd, that we the Subscribers have Procession'd the following Lands, one Line done Between Wm King and Elisha Ballard, William King & Elisha Ballard & Jesse King Present, one Line Done Between William King & Michael King William King & Michael King & Jesse King Present, one Line Done Between William Moore & John Perritt, William Moore & Thos Pearce and John Pearce, Present, one Line Done Between William Moore and John Coupland, William Moore & Thos Pearce & Wm King Present, one Line Done Between Wm Moore & Thos Pearce, William Moore and Thos Pearce & William King & James Butler Present, one Line Done Between William Moore & James Butler, William Moore and James Butler, Thos Pearce, William King Present, one Line Done Between James Butler and Thos Pearce, James Butler and Thos Pearce, William King Pres^t one Line Done Between Willm King and Thos Pearce, These pres^t one Line done Between John and Henry Butler & Wm King, John & Henry Butler & Wm King Thos Pearce & John Pearce these Present, one Line done Between Thos Pearce & Edward Moore These pres^t one Line done Between John Coupland & William McClenney these present, one Line Done Between William McClenney and John Kerr, these Pres^t one Line done Between John Kerr, and John Coupland and John Pearce Pres^t one Line Done Between John Coupland & Peter Butler, John Coupland John Pearce Pres^t one Line Done Between James Johnson & Nathan Wyatt, James Johnson Pres^t one Line Done Between James Johnson and Wm Butler these Pres^t one Line Between John King & John Harrisson not Done, one Line Between John King & Wm Beasley.

John Butler
Henry Butler

[80]

Joseph Perry and Jacob Price Processioned the Land Marks from Spikes's Run to Barbacu and from Summorton Road to Newby's, Pres^t William Hunter, Mansfield Tarlinton, Peter Walkins [sic], James March, John Denby, Christopher Norfleet John Skinner, Henry Gwin, & Edward Pryor.

Joseph Perry
Jacob Price

At a Vestry held in Suffolk Town October the 14th 1752[43] for the Upper Parish of Nansemond County.

    The Revd William Webb Minister
    Daniel Pugh & William Moore Gent^n Ch: W^ds
    John Winbourne, David Meade } Gent^n Vestrymen
    John Rawls & Thos Sumner }
    Added Josiah Riddick Gent^n

The Trustees for selling the Glebe Land[44] Reported to this Vestry, that they had Attempted to sell the Glebe Land, But could not from the uncertainty of the Bounds, It is Ordered that the Surveyor of the County, Survey the Said Land According to a Survey made in behalf of the said

---

[43] For the proceedings of the meeting of May 14, 1752, which were mislaid in the clerk's office and copied into the vestry book after those of November 16, 1764, see p. 173-174.

[44] Appointed at the meeting on May 14, 1752. See p. 173.

Parish, as Appears by a plan now on the Surveyors Book. And that the Church wardens have the same Done between this and the Laying the Next Parish Levy;

Ordered that the Surveyor with the Church Wardens, Survey the Land at Wickham Taken up by Blake and Cadowgan, According to the Patent, In Order to Assert what Quantity of Land belongs to the Parish,[45]

[81]

Whereas at a Vestry held May the 14th last It was Agree'd and Ordered that William Webb, Daniel Pugh, Josiah Riddick & Lemuel Riddick or any Three of them Should Agree with some workmen to Build a house Pursuant to the Act of Assembly[46] Lately Made for that Purpose, Viz^t for the Reception of the Poor of the Parish, and that the House should be agreeable to a plan then Shewn the Vestry, and Set on a piece of Land which Daniel Pugh then offered to give the Parish for that Purpose, and whereas soon afterwards the Said Trustees did Agree with Josiah Riddick to Build the Said House for the Sum of One Hundred and Fifty Nine Pounds Currant Money, & Whereas the Vestry are of Opinion on more Mature Consideration that it would be More convenient if the Said House was Built on a Lot in Suffolk Town Belonging to Josiah Riddick Lying on the Main Street which he bought of Charles Smith, It is Agreed by & Between the Vestry & the Said Josiah Riddick with the free and Mutual Consent of the Said Trustees that the Said House Shall be Built on the Said Lot According to the Said plan, Except the Partition Wall in the Length of the House to be Built with Brick one & half Brick Thick & Plaistered, In Consideration of the Said Riddicks finding the Lot and Building the Said House there, he Instead of the Sum Aforesaid, is to Receive Two Hundred Pounds Currant Money, and that he Before he Receieves the Said Sum, Make a Deed of Bargain and Sale to the Church wardens of the Parish for the Said Lot for the Uses Aforesaid, and that the Said House be Compleatly Finished by the Last Day of June Next, and the Money Paid when the House is finished, and that the Aforesaid Trustees give their Bond for the payment of the said sum of

---

[45] At the meeting on May 14, 1752, this land was also ordered to be sold. See p. 173.
[46] See p. 173 and footnote 93.

Money, on the Said Josiah Riddicks Giveing Bond to Perform the work aforesaid; Agreeable to this Order.

Truly Entered by   Sign'd   William Webb
     Richd Webb Cl Vestry

[82]

At a Vestry held in Suffolk Town Novr the 30th 1752 for the Upper Parish of Nansemond County

Pres^t The Revd William Webb Minister
     Danl Pugh & Wm Moore Gent^n Ch: Wardens
     John Winbourne Mills Riddick ⎫
     Henning Tembte David Meade ⎬ Gent^n Vestrymen
     Josiah Riddick & John Rawls ⎭

The Upper Parish of Nansem^d County for the Year of our Lord 1752 is   Dr Tob^o

To the Revd Wm Webb his Salary	16000
To D^o an Allowance for a Glebe	2000
To D^o 4 per C^t for Cask	640
To D^o 4 per C^t for Shrinkage	640
To Aaron [Allmand] Clerk at Brick Church and Mid^e Chapel	1500
To Wm Shittleton Clerk at Holy Neck Chapel 13 Months	1128
To John Cole Sexton at Brick Church 250 ⎫	
To D^o for washing the Surplus & Mending 100 ⎬	350
To Henry Gwin Sexton at Middle Chapel 250 ⎫	
To D^o for washing the Surplus 75 ⎬	325
To Ruth Rawls Sextones at Holy Neck Chapel 250 ⎫	
To D^o for washing the Surplus 50 ⎬	300
To Wm Moore for keeping Grace Anstead & Cornelus's Children	1454
To Edward Miles for keeping Wilsons Child	900
To Thos Williams for keeping John Palmer	250
To Saml Job for keeping two poor Children	300
To Josiah Riddick A ball^e Due for Insolvants Last Year After the Last Years Depositum Deducted	854
To James Lacy for keep^g Peter Vaughan 10 ½ Mo^s @ 800 per Y^r	693
To John Campbell for keeping Peter Vaughan & Jno James	300
To Jno Gwin for keeping Wilsons Child & Clear^g the Cha^l Road & Spring	1400

To Mary Doughtie for keeping John Leatch	300
To Elisha Ashborne for keeping Jane Wilson	400

Carrᵈ forward

[83]   Tobacco

Brought forward	29734
To Richᵈ Hine for keeping Ann Hine	1000
To Coˡ Riddick for Copy 4 Lists Tithables	69
To Richᵈ Webb for keeping the Parsh. Register one Yʳ	1000
To 25 M for the use of the Parish to be Paid to the Church wᵈˢ and by them Sold for Cash at July Court Next	25000
To 8 M to be paid to the Church Wardens and by them Sold for Cash for the Use of the Organs	8000
	64803
To the Collector @ 6 per Cᵗ	3890
	68693
The Parish Cʳ By 1183 Tithables at 58 per Pole	68614
Depositum due to the Collector	79

The Upper Parish in Cash   Dʳ

To Lemuel Riddick for a Ballᵉ of his Accᵗ For a Communion Cloth and Marbel Font	£28..10
To Wᵐ Moore his Accᵗ for Disbursments for the Poor	8..15..3
To Doctʳ Wᵐ Fleming for Medicines &	4..7..11
To Mary Doughtie for Burying Jnº Leatch	1..10
To James Lacy for Clothing a Poor Child	1..1..6
To Doctʳ Robᵗ Brown his Accᵗ &	1..4
To Samˡ Job for Burying Cornelus 30/	
To Dº for Carrying Poor Children to Court 5/	1..15
To David Nelms Junʳ for keeping & Burying Joseph Whitney	1..16..6
To Elisha Ashborne for Burying Jane Wilson	1..10
To Edwᵈ Bromegom Admiʳ of Judith Bromegom for keeping Robᵗ Taylor in Salevation	4..10
To Danˡ Pugh his Accᵗ for Disbursments for the poor	5..5..2
To Hardy Rawls for Services done at Upper Chapel	1..10

To John Rawls for Tarring the Chapel	2..15
To John Giblin for Burying a Poor Man	1..10
	£66..0..4

[84]

Ordered that Willis Riddick Sher'f, Collect from Every Tithable in this Parish fifty eight Pounds Tobacco and therewith Discharge the Parish Credits, he first giving Bond and Security to the Church wardens for that Purpose;

Order'd that the Churchwardens sell Thirty three Thousand Pounds of Tobacco at July Court Next, for Cash, and therewith Discharge the Parish Credits now Levied due from the Parish

Order'd that George Waff keep a Ferry from Suffolk Warf to Saml Jordans Point, for the use of the Church and Vestry, And that he have 1200 lb Tobacco per Year;

The Petition of the Inhabitants over Black Water and Notaway, Sheweth forth that they Desire to have a Small Chapel Built over Notaway River; It's Order'd that Co^l Baker and Wm Moore Gentlemen, Go and View some place over Notaway Convenient for that Purpose, and make Return of their Proceedings;

Order'd that Richd Webb have 500 lb Tobacco for keeping the Register, for the Ensuing Year;

Order'd that Aaron Almond be Allowed 4 per C^t on the Tob^o Levied for him the Ensuing Year;

Truly Enter'd by   Sign'd by William Webb
    Richd Webb C^l of the Vestry

[85]

[At] a Vestry held in Suffolk Town Apr^l the 24th 1753 for the Upper Parish of Nansemond County;

    The Revd William Webb Minister
    Danl Pugh & William Moore Gent^l Ch: W^{ds}
    William Baker John Winborne ⎫
    John Rawls & Josiah Riddick   ⎬ Gent^l Vestrymen

Danl Pugh Produced his Acc^t of Money Rec^d the Year past

		S	d
Of Ann Oneil her fine	£2	. .	10
of John Rawls for Tar Burnt of the poors Land	4		
	£6	. .	10

It's Order'd that Danl Pugh doe pay to

		S	d
Henry Gwin out of the above Money	£3	. .	0
To Sarah Midcalf	1	. .	0
To Mary Spight	1		
To John Coupland		:15	
To John Parker Near Mr Moores		:15	
	£6	. .	10

William Baker & Josiah Riddick are Appointed Church Wardens for the Ensuing Year;

It is the Opinion of this Vestry that the Churchwardens doe Take the Advice of some Attorney Concerning the Title of the Glebe Land;

William Baker and William Moore hath this Day Reported that James Cary's Land is the most Convenientrest place to set a Chapel on, over Notaway.

 Truly Enter'd by   Sign'd by William Webb
  Richd Webb C^l Vestry

[86]

At a Vestry held in Suffolk Town July the 26th 1753 for th[e] Upper Parish of Nansemond County;

Present The Revd William Webb Minister

  William Baker & Josiah Riddick Genl Ch: ward^s
  Mills Riddick Henning Tembte ⎫
  Danl Pugh & Wm Moore   ⎬ Gen Vestrymen
  Added David Meade Gentleman ⎭

Order'd that the Churchwardens pay to Daniel Pugh the Sum of £57..15S..—d out of the Money in their hands, being the Ball^e due for the Building the Church in Suffolk.

Order'd that John Watson & Alexander Cairnes, have Leave to Build a Pew in the South end of the Parish Galere Eight feet Nine Inches at the front, and back to the End Wall, and that the Vestry make them, (or either of them) a title to the Said Pew, And that in Consideration thereof, they Pay to the Churchwardens the Sum of Six Pound Sterling, to be laid out in Ornaments for the Church.

Order'd that the Churchwardens Apply to James Cary Sen[r] to Purchace one Acre of Land, whereon to Erect and Build a Chapel, and that they Agree with workmen to Build the Said Chapel Agreeable to the following Dimentions, The Length thereof to be Thirty feet, the Breadth Twenty four, with a good Frameing, Tenn feet Pitch between Sill and Plate, with two Dores, Two windows in Each side and one in the East end, and that the said windows is to have Eighteen Lights [o]f Glass in each, Eight Inches by Tenn, and th[at] [t]he said Chapel be Finish'd in the same Maner as Summerton C[hape]l is, and that it be finish'd by the Last Day of July Next;[47]

    Truly Enter'd by   Sign'd by William Webb
       Rich[d] Webb Cl Vestry

[87]
D[r] the Uper parrish to Daniel Pugh per Contra C[r]

	£	s
1753 To Building the Church		
1753 By Cash for Sundry[s]	536:	5
As per Agreement 540		
To Sundry Aditions		
As per Agreement 54		
Tobacco Sold		
By Ball: due to Daniel Pugh	57:	15
£594	£594:	0

Daniel Pugh

At a Vestry Held In Suffolk Town Novemb[r] the 19th 1753 For the Up[r] Parrish of Nansemond County
  Pressent The Rev[d] William Webb
      William Baker & Josiah Redik   Ch Wds
        Daniel Pugh   William Moore ⎫
        John Winbourn   Mills Redik   ⎬ Gentlemen
    Added David Mead   Tho[s] Sumner ⎭ Vestry Men
                                     Cary[d] Over

---

[47] In this paragraph, certain letters, obliterated by blots, have been supplied in brackets.

[88]

The Up^r Parrish of Nansem^d County	D^r
for the year of our Lord 1753	
To the Revd William Webb His Sallary	16000
To D^o An An [sic] Allowance for a gleab	2000
To D^o 4 per C for Caskque	640
To D^o 4 per C for Srinkage	640
To Aaron Allmand Clerk of Suffolk Church	1500
To D^o 4 per C for Srinkage	60
To Thos Johnson Sexton of Suffolk Church Due at Chrismas	600
To Mary Rawls Sexton^s of the uper Chapell	300
To William Shekelton Clerk of Holy Neck Chapell	1000
To Colⁿ Lamuel Redik for Recordin four List of thydables	225
To William Moore for Work Done	1186
To Stephen Dardan for keeping Sarah Cornelus 10 months	437
Soloman Redik. Aaron lasater and John Giles Patrol^{rs} are alow^d there Leivies for the year 1752	174
To James Lacey for Boardin Peter Vaughan	800
To John gwin for keepin John Wilson an orphan	1200
To John Best for Carrying the Chain Over the gleab Land	90
To John gwin for keeping Rebeckah Hynes 7 Months	467
	27319

[89]

Brought Forward	27319
To James Jones for Carrying the Chain over the gleab	90
To Richard Hynes for keepin An Hynes 11 Months	754
To Richard Webb Clerk of the Vestry	500
To Richard Hynes Over Charg^d a leivie for the year past	58
To John Ashbourn Over Charg^d 2 D^o for the year past	116
To the Shereif for Insolvents	2030
To the Shereif A Depositum due from the year 1752	79
To 12 M^o thwards the Buildin Notaway Chapell To be Sold by the Churchwardens at July Court for Cash	12000
The Parrish being Indebted the Sum of	42944[48]

---

[48] This addition is in error and should be 42946. The figures of the various items which make up this total are quite legible.

To the Collect^r at 6 per C	2577
	45521
By Crd on 1308 Thydables Amounts to at 35 pounds per Thydable	45780
A Depossitum due to the Parrish	259

Cary^d Over the Cash Account

[90]

The Up^r Parrish D^r In Cash for the Year of our lord 1753

	£ : s
To Docktor Jesse brown for Medicines for W^{im} Hedgbirth	8 : 14
Col^n W^{im} Baker^s Account for Sarah Cornelus	1 : 2 : 6
Col^n Lemuel Rediks Account for Sundries Deliver^d by the Church Wardens Order	0 : 19 : 3
To Dockt^r Robert Brown for Medicines for Rebeckah Hynes	15 : 6
To John Scott for Sundries of Work done in the Church	1 : 18 : 2
To W^{im} Moore for Sundries of work done	5 : 7 : 11
To John Bird for Burying Barna bird	1 : 10
To An Nail for takeing Care of Mary Miles	2 : 3 : 4
To John Ashbourn Account paid to Dockt^r Fanin for Henry gwin	1 : 15
To Docktor Flemings for Medicines for Henry Gwin	3 : 12
To D^o for Harmon Miles	0 : 16 : 3[49]
To Edward Giles for makeing the Church Lader	0 : 14 : 6
To James Lacey for Cloathin Peter Vaughn	1 : 6 : 1½
To John Best for bringin the Ornaments of the Brick Church to Suffolk	0 : 5
To Nickolas Perrit for Atendin the Surveior And Markin Trees on the gleab	0 : 6
To Capt Northcott for burying John dudle [sic][50]	1 : 10
To Thos Johnson for Atendance when Seting up the Organ	1 : 1 : 8
To Henry Gwin for bringin down the Ornam^{ts} of the Chapell	0 : 5 : 0
To Sarah Watkins for Washing the Cirplis 3 times	0 : 7 : 6
	£34 : 9 : 8½

---

[49] The first number in this sum seems to be 6 (perhaps 16), partially blotted and erased. Judging by the total, the character O was evidently intended.

[50] Perhaps this name is intended for Dudley.

[91]

Tis Ordered that Willis Redik Sherreif do Collect from Every Thydable in this Parrish thirty five pounds of Tobacco P^r thydable And therewith Discharge the Parrish Creddits In Tobacco first giveing Bond and Security to the Church Wardens as Useal for that Purpose

Tis Ordered that the Church wardens do Bring A Suit in Chancery Against John Norpleet [sic] to Determine the bounds of the gleab Land

Aaron Allmand Is Apointed Clerk of the Vestry in the room of Richard Webb And Acordinly Sworn

Mr John Watson Haveing Paid back to Col^n W^{im} Baker   £   s   d
Church warden the Sum of   20 : 4 : 8
And Desires his Accounts may be Strictly Examined
And an Abstract Enter^d on this Record Tis Ordered
that the Revd W^{im} Webb And Capt Daniel Pugh do
Examine them and Make there Report to the Next Vestry

Mr Josiah Redick Haveing Render^d in his Ac^t As
Church Warden and Acknowledg^d to have In his hands
the Sum of   28 : 9 : 5¾
                                                                 ─────────────
                                                                  £48 : 14 : 1¾
Tis Ordered that the Church Wardens do pay the
Sum of   34 : 9 : 8½
And therewith Discharge the Parrish Credits In Cash

    Truly Entered By   Sign^d By
      Aaron Allmand Clk Vestry   William Webb

[92]

At A Vestry Held in Suffolk Town March the 25th 1754 for the Up^r Parrish of Nansemond County

Pressent Revd William Webb

Josiah Redick		Church War^d
David Mead	John Winbourn	Gent:
Daniel Pugh	Hening Tembtey	Vestry
Thos Sumner	W^{im} Moore	Men

It is the Opinion of this Vestry that the Alms House that is to be Built in Suffolk town be Raised two feet in the Walls All Round So that the floors be ten feet from the Ceiling for Which the Under taker Josiah

Redik Is to Receive Twenty three pounds moore then he was to have for Buildin the Said House

It is the Opinion of this Vestry that A foilio Bible And two foilio prayer books be Sent for And to be paid for out of the money Mes^{rs} Watson & Cairnes Is to give the Parrish for the Priviledge of Buildin there Galeary And for the Use of the Church in this town

 Truly Regerist^d by   Sign^d By William Webb
  Aaron Allmand
  Clk Vestry

[93]

 At A Vestry Held In Suffolk Town May the 6th 1754 For the Uper Parrish of Nansemond County

 Pressent The Revd William Webb
   Col^n W^{im} Baker & Josiah Redick Ch: War^{ds}
   M^{rss} David Mead W^{im} Moore
   Danil Pugh John Rawls ⎬ Get: Vestrymen
   & Thos Sumner

 Mr Josiah Redick Produced His Account Render^d in his Acc^t

As Church Warden	£	s	
To the Qtrs of the Poors Land two year 700 Acres	1	15	6
To 2½ Barrells Corn deliver^d tho^s Jones	1	0	0
To 5 y^{ds} Ozenbrig^s & 1 Quart Brandy to D^o	0	6	3
To 2 Weeding Hows to D^o	0	7	6
To 7 y^{ds} Ozenbrigs Deliver^d Richard Payn	0	7	0
	£3	16	3
Per Contra Credit	£	s	d
By Cash from John Rawls for Lightwood	2	17	9
By John Penders fine	0	5	0
By Cash from Richd Matthews daughter	5	0	0
By Olive Morgans fine	2	10	0
By Rebeckah Dues fine	2	10	0
By Purvis fine	2	10	0
By part of Sarah green^s fine	1	15	0
	17	7	9

	3 : 16 : 3
Ball: Due	£13 : 11 : 6
Cary Over	

[94]
Brought Over

Tis Ordered that Mr Josiah Redick do pay Out of the Said money being Sum on the Other Side or Ballance of

	£ s
	13 : 11 : 6
To Henry gwin	2 : 0 : 0
To Thos Jones	1 : 10 : 0
To William Lam	4 : 1 : 6
To Sarah Midcef	1 : 10 : 0
To Sarah Osburn	1 : 10 : 0
To John Rawls Son of Thos	1 : 10 : 0
To Mary Bab	1 : 10 : 0
	£13 : 11 : 6

Col^n William Baker And Mr Josiah Redik Are Continued And Sworn Church Wardens for the Ensueing Year

Truly Regeristed By   Sign^d By William Webb
    Aaron Allmand Clerk Vestry

[95]
At A Vestry Held In Suffolk Town Octo^{br} the 1st 1754 For the Uper Parrish of Nansem^d County

Pressent The Revd William Webb
        M^{rss} Josiah Redik   Ch: War^d
        David Mead   Hening Tembtey ⎫
        Mills Redik   Daniel Pugh   ⎬ Gentlemen
        Thos Sumner   ⎭ Vestrymen

Mr William Hunter Is Elected and Chosen A Vestry Man In the Room of Coll^n Baker Deceas^d

Nickolas Maggett Is apointed Clerk of Notaway Chappell at one thousand pounds of Tobacco per year

Mr Thos Sumner Is Apointed and Sworn Church Warden In the Room of Coll^n William Baker Decas^d Untill Easter Next

    Truly Registred By   Sign^d By William Webb
        Aaron Allmand Clk Vestry

[96]

At a Vestry held in Suffolk Town for the Upper Parish of Nansemond County Novemb^r the 14th 1754

                Present

William Webb: Clk[51]	Henning Tembte
Josiah Riddick	John Rawles
David Mead	William More
Mills Riddick	Thomas Sumner
Daniel Pugh	William Hunter
John Winburn	

To the Revd William Webb	16000
To D^o an Allowance for a Glebe	3000
To D^o An Allowance of 4 per Ct for Caskue And D^o for Srinkage	1280
To D^o for Searching for Searching [sic] for a Pattent	34½
To Willm Shekelton Clk of the Up^r Chapell	1000
To Aaron Allmand Clk of Suffolk Church	2000
To D^o An Allowance of 4 per Ct	80
To Edward Cary for Officeateing as Clk at Notaway Chapell	160
To Nickolas Magett Clerk of Nottaway Chapell 1 ½ mo^s	125
To John Milner for a Survei	430
To Col^n Godwin for Services in the Suit of the Church Ward^{ns} Against Narney	52
Cary^d Forward	24161½

[97]

Brought Forward	24161½
To Jean Baker Allowd a Leivie for the year Past	35
To John Gwin for keepin Rebeckah Hynes	800

---

[51] He may have acted as clerk, at least in the first part of the meeting, and made the initial entries of this meeting in the vestry book; for the handwriting, spelling and arrangement differ in the beginning from the characteristic writing of Aaron Allmand.

To Dº for keepin Jno Wilson an Orphan	1200
To Richard Hynes for keepin An Hynes	800
To Stephen Dardan for keepin Sarah Cornelas	150
To Wm Moore for keepin Grace Amisted	868
To Mary Rawls Sextons of Sumrt Chapell And Washin the Cirplis	300
To Jno Jenkins for Cleanin Sumrt Chapel Well	20
To Thos Johnson Sexton of Suffolk Church due at Chrisms	800
To James Cary for Sundries of Work done at Nottaway Chapell	350
To George Worf for keepin Suffolk fery one year	1500
To Majr Willis Redik for Insolvents after the Last years Possitum deducted	966
To James lacey for keepin Peter Vaughan 5 mon: @ 800 per year	335
To Josiah Vaughan for keepin Peter Vaughn	800
To 24000 Pounds of Tobacco towards Dischargein of the Alms House and Other Charges To be Sold at July Court for Cash by the Church Wardens	24000
	57085
To the Sherreif for Collection @ 6 per Ct Amounts to	3641[62]
	60726
Parish Crds on 1319 thithables Amounts to at 46 ps per Pole	60674
A Depossitum due to the Sherreif	00052

[98]

The Uper Parrish of Nansemd County Dr In Cash 1754

	£ : s
To Jno Milner for A Copy of two Plots	0 : 10 : 0
To Sarah Watkins for Washin the Cirplis 4 times	0 : 10 : 0
To Mary gwin for Makein Cloaths for Rebeckah Hynes and John Wilson	0 : 13 : 6
To Stephen Dardan for Buryin Sarah Cornelus	1 : 10 : 0
To Edward Giles for Makein Dyals Coffin	0 : 8 : 0
To Robert Willis for Buryin dyal	1 : 2 : 0
To Dº for Caryin Buntley to Dockter Browns	0 : 12 : 6

---

[62] This amount exceeds 6%.

To Dock{tr} Flemin for Medicines for the Widow Harmon	0 : 15 : 0
To Docktor Jesse Brown for Medicines for Jean Savage And Susanah Bond	8 : 0 : 0
To Henry Redik for Buryin Johnson	1 : 10 : 0
To Josiah Redik for Sundries Delivered the Poor And Sundrie aditions to the Alms house	35 : 8 : 6
	£50 : 19 : 6
Crd By Coln Baker to Josiah Redik	3 : 10 : 3
	47 : 9 : 3

Tis Ordered that the Money that was In Col{n} Bakers Hands be paid to Mr Josiah Redik To wards Dischargein His Account £3 : 10s : 3d

Tis Ordered the Church Wardens do take the Sum of £31 : 18s : 3 Upon Intrest it being the Ballance due to Mr Josiah Redik for Buildin the Alms house

[99]

The House Built for the Reception of the Poor of this Parrish Being Now finished According to Agrement is Received by the Vestry And Persuant to the Act of Asembly for that Purpose Made and Provided

it is Ordered that the Church Wardens of this Parrish at Chrismas Next or Some Convenient time Soon After Convei into the Said House All the Poor persons that now is or Hereafter Shall be Maintaind at the Parrish Expence there Be Supported

And it is further Ordered that Samuel Wallis then Be admited into the Said house As Overseer and Master And that he take Care of the Furniture And Provision{s} Which Shall be Provided for the Said Poor And Furthermoore that he Teach Eight poor Children Which Is to be Sent into the Said House by the Church Wardens To Read Rite &c. For All which Services The Said Samuel Wallis Is have and Receive from the Vestry of this Parrish Anully the Sum of Twenty Pounds Current Money His Own Children Accomadated And Liberty To take in And School ten Children besides the Poors Accordin as he Can Agree With there Parents &c Dureing the time As he Shall be Continued

And it is Further Ordered that the Church Wardens Find And Provide for the Said House Such and So many Beds Tables Chairs And other

Nessesires to furnish the The [*sic*] Said House As they Shall think Fitt

Truly Registered By   Sign^d William Webb
    Aaron Allmand Clk Vestry

[100]

At A Vestry held In Suffolk in the Poors house April the 7th 1755 for the Uper Parrish of Nansem^d County

Pressent   The Revd W^{im} Webb

M^{rss} Josiah Redik and Tho: Sumner. Ch: Wardens

M^{rss} David meade   Hening Tembtey ⎫
Daniel Pugh   Mills Redik   ⎬ Gentlemen Vestrymen
William Hunter   W^{im} Moore   ⎭

Tis Ordered that the money that Mr Josiah Redik Church Warden hath in his hands that he has Rec^d for fines Which is £8 : 01s Be distributed to the Poor Persons As followeth

	£	s
To William Lam	2	10
To Thos Jones	1	0
To the Widow Chapell	1	0
To Sarah Midcaf	1	0
To William Carter	0	17
To James Butler	0	17
To John Hansell	0	17

Which is the whole Sum £8 : 01

Mr David meade and Capt Hening Tembtey is apointed And Sworn Church Wardens for the Ensueing year in the Room of Mr Josiah Redik and Mr Thos Sumner

Tis Ordered that the Church Wardens do pay to the Above Several Poor Persons the Pertickualer Sums of money to them Alowed

Truly Registered   Sign^d By William Wibb
    By Aaron Allmand Clk Vestry

[101]

At A Vestry Held in the Court house In Suffolk Town Augst the 23^{thd} 1755 For the Uper Parrish of Nansemond County

Present The Revd William Webb
         Coln Lemuel Redick Josiah Redick
         David Meade Willis Redick
         Mills Redick Henry holand   Gentlemen
         William Baker Jacob Sumner   Vestrimen[53]
         John Ashbourn

Mr David Meade and Capt William Baker Is Apointed and Sworn Church Wardens untill [Easter ?][54] Next

Tis Ordered that the Church Wardens do Treat with the Vestry of Suffolk Parrish to See upon what Terms they will Agree To Joyn there Poor with ours In our Poors house before the Laying of our Parrish Leivie

Tis Ordered that the Vestry do Meet Again in this Town on Saturday the thirteenth day of September In order to apoint Posessioners For this Parrish

Truly Regisred by   Signd by Willm Webb
   Aaron allmand Clk Vestry

[102]

At A Vestry held In The Courthouse In Suffolk Town Septemb^r the 13th 1755 For the Uper Parrish of Nansemond County

Pressent the Revd William Webb Lemuel Riddick
          Josiah Ridick Willis Ridick David Sumner   Gentlemen
          Jacob Sumner Henry hollan John Ashbourn   Vestry men
          and David Mead

The Following Persons Are apointed to Procesion the Bounds of Land in this Parrish As Followeth to Witt

                In the Bounds   N° 1
        Matthias Jones   Robert Brown
                                N 2
        Richard godwin   Johnathan Nelms

---

[53] A new vestry had been elected by the freeholders and housekeepers of the Upper Parish in accordance with "An Act for dissolving the vestry of the upper parish in the county of Nansemond" (Hening, v. 6, p. 518-519), passed at the May 1755 session of the General Assembly.

[54] Cf. reference to their tenure on p. 104.

	N 3	
Christopher Norfleet		Elisha Norfleet
	N 4	
John Woodroop		Robert Lawrence
	N 5	
Thomas Godwin		Richard Matthews
	N 6	
Elisha Balard		Benjamin Forset
	N 7	
William Moore		Matthew Peirce
	N 8	
Thomas Winbourn		William Harrison
	N 9	
John Porter		James Couplan
	N 10	
James Rawls		Arthur Jones
	N 11	
Jesse Riddick		John Lawrenc Son of Michael
	N 12	
William howel		Samuel Watson
	N 13	
John Faulk		John Winbourn
	N 14	
James Holland		Solloman Hollan
	N 15	
Joshua Gardener		Moses Dardan
	N 16	
Simon Everit		Daniel Williams
	N 17	
Henry hollan		William Baker
	N 18	
William Cross		William Rogers Son of Robert
	N 19	
Joshua Spivy		James Brinkly

	N 20	
Thos Harrell		George Bains
	N 21	
William Hair		James Long
	N 22	
Richard Taylor		John Taylor
	N 23	
William Hunter		Edward pryor
	N 24	
John Rowntree		William Rown Tree
	N 25	
Josiah Riddick		William Acree
	N 26	
Joseph Parker		John Horton
	N 27	
Willis Riddick		Jos Stallings
	N 28	
Hugh Gouff		Robert Smith
Truly Registred By		Signd By William Webb
Aaron Allmand Clk Vestry[55]		

[103]

At A Vestry Held In the Court house in Suffolk Town Novembr the 20th 1755 For the Upr Parrish of Nansemond County

Pressent the Revd William Webb Lemuel Riddick Mills Riddick Willis Riddick William Baker William hunter John Ashburn Jacob Sumner Henry holland   Gentlemen Vestry Men

To the Revd William Webb his Sallary	16000
To Do An Allowance of 4 per Ct for Caskue & Do for Srinkage	1280
To Do An Allowance for A gleab	3000
To William Shekelton Clerk of Sumerton Chapell	1000
To Nickolas Maget Clerk of Notaway Chapell	1000
To Aaron Allmand Clerk of Suffolk Church	2000

---

[65] As the proceedings of this meeting were crowded onto one page, the attestations of the clerk and the minister were written, in that respective order, on the right-hand margin.

To D⁰ An Alowance of 4 per Ct For Caskue	80
To Ann howard over Charg⁴ a Leivie Last year	46
To Edward Cary over Charg⁴ 4 Leivies	140
To John gwin for keepin Rebeckah hynes 4 m⁰ˢ @ 800 per year	266
To William Moore for keeping Grace Amistead 3 ½ m⁰ⁿ @ 800 per year	234
To John Wilson for keeping Charles Stewart Seven Weeks	350
To Richard hynes for keeping Ann Hynes a year	800
To Michael Farow for Attending the Court as a Witness for the parrish	25
To John Jones For D⁰	25
To John hansell For D⁰	25
To Thoˢ Johnson Sexton of Suffolk Church	800
To the Shereif For Insolvents & a Depositum due from the Last year 52	1846
To Maj^r Williss Riddick Return⁴ an Insolvent from the year 1753	46
To Col^n Godwin For his Trouble at the Election of Vestry	362
To Be Sold by the Ch: Wardens at July Court For Cash	8500
	37825
To the Collector @ 6 per Ct	2269
	40094
1344 thydables at 30 per thidable Amounts to	40320
Due to the Parrish	226

[104]

Dr The Uper Parrish of Nansemond In Cash 1755

	£
To Frances Duke For Burying & Nursing a poor Woman	3 : 0 : 0
To Josiah Reddick his Acc^t as Ch: Warden for 1754	2 : 6 : 11½
To James Knight For Tending Johnson	1 : 11 : 1
To Mary Wiat For Nursing Cathrine Shaw	0 : 6 : 4
To Coln. Lemuel Riddick For Sundries Delivered the Poor	4 : 4 : 3
To Judith Perrit a Lame Woman	5 : 0 : 0
To Matthew Burley For makeing Benches for the Church	0 : 14 : 0
To John Wilson For Burying Charles Stewart	1 : 10 : 0

To Josiah Vaughan for mending the Plaistering of the Church	0 : 2 : 6	
To James Cary for makeing a Pew in Notaway Chapell	1 : 5 : 0	
To Josiah Vaughan for keeping Some poor people	0 : 7 : 6	
To Richard hynes For two Pair of Shoes for Ann hynes	0 : 8 : 0	
To John Warters For Iron work For the Poors house	1 : 16 : 6	
To John Barry For Burying Cathrine Shaw	1 : 10 : 0	
To Edward Giles For makeing Palmers Coffin	0 : 10 : 0	
To Docktor Brown For Medicines for Cathrine Shaw	3 : 13 : 4	
To Sarah Watkins For washing the Cirplis 3 times	0 : 7 : 6	
To James Gibson For Sundries for the Poors house	3 : 1 : 8	
To Thos Sumner his Acct as Church Warden 1754	36 : 4 : 3½	
To Samuel Wallis Ending the year First of January Next	20 : 0 : 0	
	£87 : 18 : 11	

By Mr David Meade Rendered in his Acct as Ch:
Warden And the Ball: is due to the Parrish   64 : 11 : 9¾

Tis Ordered that Mr David Mead Pay the Above Accots of with the money that he has in his hands as Far as it will go and when he Recives the Cash of the Ch: Wardens that the Tobacco will be Sold for then to discharge the others

Signd By William Webb

Truly Registred by Aaron Allmand Clk Vestry

[105]

At A Vestry held In Suffolk Town January the 17th 1756 For the Uper Parrish of Nansemd County

Pressent   The Revd William Webb
    Coln: Lemuel Redick   Josiah Redick ⎫
    Willis Redick   Mills Redick   ⎪   Gentn
    William Hunter   Henry holand   ⎬   Vestrymen
    Jacob Sumner   William Baker   ⎪
              John Ashburn   ⎭

Tis Ordered that Samuel Wallis be Continued in the Poors house the Ensueing year at Ten pounds Current money and that there is A woman as an asistant Imployd when Occasion Requires By the Church wardens and that he have Liberty to take in and School Fifteen Children Besides our Poor them Not Exceeding Eight

Tis ordered that that [sic] the Church Wardens take Cear to Buy and Provide Such Meteirals and other Instruments to Imploy the Said Poor People In Such work as Shall be thought Proper For the Benifit of the Parrish

Tis ordered that the Church Wardens do Advertise the Gleab Land In the Publick Papers For Sale Be fore Easter Next Alowing Twelve Months Credit to the Buyer

Sign^d by William Webb

Truly Registred By Aaron Allmand Clk Vestry

[106]

At A Vestry held at the Court house in Suffolk Town Febuary the 9th 1756 For the Uper Parrish of Nansemond County

Pressent the Revd William Webb
        David Meade & William Baker   Ch: Wardens
        William Hunter   Mills Redick
        Lemuel Redick   Josiah Redick   Jacob Sumner
        David Sumner   Henry holland   Gent: Vestrymen

This Vestry doth make Choice of Hening Tembtey Gent to be A Vestry man for this Parrish in the Room of John Ashburn Deceas^d

Signd By William Webb

Truly Entered by Aaron Allmand Clk Vestry

[107]

At A Vestry held In the Court house in Suffolk Town June the 5th 1756 For the Uper Parrish of Nansemond County

Pressent the Revd William Webb
        David Meade   Wi^m Baker   G^t Ch: Wardens
        Lemuel Reddick   Josiah Reddick
        Mills Reddick   John Rawls
        Wi^m Hunter   Henry holand
        Jacob Sumner   G^t Vestry Men

Mr David Meade and Capt William Baker Is Continued Church Wardens until Easter Next

Tis ordered that the Daughter Margaret hall Be put in the Alms house In Suffolk Town there to be Schoold

Tis Ordered that[56] Margaret hall have the Sum of £1..0..0 As Releif from this Parrish to Buy hir provisions out of the money that Coln. Lemuel Reddick has in his hands that he Received for a fine

Tis ordered that the Church Wardens pay to Charity Raiby towards Maintaining hir Son the Sum of £1..0..0 it Being in Consideration of his Mothers Keeping him of of [sic] the Parrish

Signd by W^{im} Webb

Truly Entered by Aaron Allmand Clk Vestry

[108]

Nansemond County sst

In obedience to an order Vestry held the 13th of Septem^{br} 1755 We have According met and Possesion^d the Land within our Bounds Capt Demsies[57] Sumner Land Possesiond Pressent Simon Femiley [?] & James Long and Absolam Butler Constant Harmons Land Done Pressent the Sam persons. Moses Harratts [sic][58] Land done Pressent the Same Persons James Longs Land done Pressent the Same. Edward Bakers Land p^s James Long & Nickolas Harmon Samuel Bakers Land done p^{rs} the Same Richard Taylors Land Done p^{rs} the Same Ephraim Peel^s Junr Land done p^s himself & John Baker Jacob Harrells Land done p^s himself & John Baker John Bakers Land done pr^s the Same Robert Peels Land done p^{rs} himself & Joseph Parker Jesse Peels Land done p^{rs} the Same Thomas Frazers Land p^{rs} the Same Jacob Sumners Land done p^{rst} the Same Cader Raby^s Land done p^{rst} the Same. Pharoah Felps Land done p^{rst} the Same Ephraim Peels Land done Pressent the Same

Richard Tayloe
John Tayloe

[109]

Persuant to an order of Vestry Dated Sept^{mbr} the 13th 1755 we the Subscribers being Apointed have Possesiond all the Bounds of Land Containd in the above order Begining at a Line Between Coln Lemuel Redick and Thomas Jones p^{rst} the Said Thos Jones a Line Between Thos Jones and John hare p^{rst} the afore Said Jones A Line Between Henry Couplan and George Keen p^{rst} the S^d George Keen and John Rawls a

---

[56] It appears that "of" was written after "that" and probably cancelled by a flourish of the first letter of "Margaret".
[57] The final "s" is faint as if erasure might have been intended.
[58] Probably intended for Harrell. Cf. return on p. 80.

Line Between henry Couplan & John hare p^rst Henry Copelan a Line Between henry Copelan & Robert Brewer p^rst John Rawls W^im Brewer Soloman Brewer Joseph Brewer and Jacob Brewer & Moses Brewer a Line Between William Colins & Robert Brewer p^rst John Rawls & William holand a Line Between Coln: Lemuel Reddick And John Rawls p^rs Jesse Rawls & Absolum Rawls a Line Between Coln Reddick & George Keen p^rst the Said Keen & Jesse Rawls a line Between John Everit & James Winbourn p^rst the Said John Everit a Line Between [...]⁵⁹ and Robert holland p^rst John Everit a Line Between Robert holan & the Orphans of William holan Deceas^d p^rst John Everit a Line Between John Rawls & Robert Brewer p^rst John Rawls & Jacob Brewer a Line Between John Rawls & the Orphans of Luke Rawls p^rst John Rawls & Jacob Brewer a Line Between John Rawls W^im Collins p^rst John Rawls & W^im holand a Line Between Wim holand & the orphans of Luke Rawls p^rst W^im holand a Line Between James Copelan & W^im holand p^rs Abraham Copelan and Jacob Brewer a Line Between the Orphans of Luke Rawls and the Orphans Wim holan p^rst John Winbourn & John Faulk a Line Between the Orphans of Wim holand and Henry holand p^rst John holand a Line Between James holand & Moses holand p^rst John Winbourn & John Faulk a Line Between Henry holand and James holand p^rst John holand a Line between John Faulk & John Winbourn p^rst W^im harrison & John harrison a Line Between W^im & John harrison & John Winbourn the Proprioters p^rst a Line Between Wim & John harrison & John Faulk the Proprioters p^rst a Line Between Wim & John harrison & John Winburn the Proprioters p^rst a Line Between Wim. & John harrison & James holand p^rst Wim & John harrison a Line Between James holand Senr & James holand Junr p^rst John Winburn & J^no Faulk a Line Between James holand & Joseph holand p^rst John Winbourn and John Faulk a Line Between John Winbourn & Wim Collins p^rst the Proprioters So Includeing all the above Said Bounds of Land posesiond peaceably and Quietly and no Objections made by

John Faulk
John Winbourn

[110]

In Obedeince to an order of Vestry we the Subscribers have possesiond All the Land Mentiond in the aforesaid order Jerimyah Godwins Land

---

⁵⁹ Name omitted in original.

Elisha Norfleets Land Gleab Land James Jones p^{rst} Gleab Land Mary Roberts Land Nickolas Perrits Land Johnathan Nelms Land Elisha Norfleet & James Jones p^{rst} Hening Tembties Land John Jones Land George Friths Land Christopher Sanders Land James Jones and Kedar Webb p^{rst} Mary Roberts Land David Nelms Land Peter Greens Land John Piners Land only them Selves p^{rst} Peter Mason^s Land Mary Roberts Land Elisabeth Thomas Land Johnathan Nelms Land Jerimyah Godwins Land only them Selves p^{rst} Joseph Godwins Land Thomas Godwin p^{rst}

            Richard Godwin
            Johnathan Nelms

  In Obedeince to An order Vestry of the Uper Parrish of Nansemond we the Procesioners Procesiond the Lands Mentioned in the Order of Vestry without Interruption March 1756.

            John Woodrop
            Robert Lawrence

[111]

  The Vestry of Nansemond County have Made an order that Moses Darden and Joshua Gardener Should procesion all the Land Between Black Water and Notaway to the Extent of the County Line And we have met according to the order and Procesiond the Bounds In peace and Quietness Possesiond Daniel Batens land in the Presence of Richard Williams Procesiond Thomas Edwards land [in] the pressence of Daniel Baten Procesiond Christopher Ronnelds Land in the p^{rst} of Daniel Baten Richard Williams Land posesiond in p^{rst} of Thomas Edwards John hays Land Procesiond in pst of Richard Williams James Masingel Returnd not Procesiond by Reason there was no one Apeard to See it done Michael Daughtrees Land in the p^{rst} of Jacob darden Robert Cars Land procesiond in the p^{rst} of Michael daughtrie Jacob dardens Land procesiond in pst of Michael daughtrie Moses dardens Land procesiond in the p^{rst} of Robert Car Car Darden Land Posesiond in the p^{rst} of Robert Darden Robert Dardens Land procesiond in p^{res} of Robert Darden Joshua Gardener Land procesiond in the p^{res} of Mathew gardener Mathew gardener Land procesiond in the p^{res} of James Daughtrie Coln. Johnathan Godwins Land procsiond in the p^{res} of Robert Darden Thos Lawrence Land procesiond in the p^res of Mathew Gardener James Gardener Land procesiond in the p^res of James Gardener George Lawrence Land procesiond in p^res of Michael Daughtrie

And Peaceably Procesiond by us

          Moses Darden
          Joshua Gardener

[112]

Nansemond County March the 10th 1756

In obedeince to the within Order Derected to us we have Procesiond the Several Lines within Mentiond Exum Lewis Line W^{im} Hart George Williams p^{rst} Simon Everits Line W^{im} Hart George Williams p^{rst} Robert Wests Robert Cars Junr Joseph herls Daniel Williams And William Alens in the pressence of Robert Car Junr Joseph hurl Robert West John hart & Moses hart George Williams Line John Spencers William Wiggins in the presence of William hart George Williams W^{im} Wigins John harts Line William harts & Moses harts in the pressence of W^{im} Wigins John hart W^{im} hart And Moses hart. James Carys Line and the Line that was Saml Warrens in the Pressence of Nath^a Cary Ja^s Cary

          Simon Everit
          Daniel Williams

In Obedience to an order of Vestry held at Suffolk Town Sept^{br} 13th 1755 We have met and Renewed all the Land Marks in the S^d order Mentiond the owners or Some persons for them p^{rst}

Mansel Turlington	For hunter & Turlington
Peter Wadkins	For Turlington & Brinkly
James March	For March & Scarbrough
William Hunter	For Scarbrough & Carnal
	For hunter and Hely
Christopher Norfleet	For Christopher Norfleet and
Joseph Skiner Son of John	For Thos Norfleet Son of Thos
Mace Duke	For Norfleet and Skiner
John Ballard	For Ballard and Carnal
Joseph Pearcy	For Spight and Pearcy
Henry Gwin Junr	For Gwin and Pearcy

James Copelan   For Pearcy and Newby
Jacob Bass   For Bass and Pearcy
                          For Demby and Gwin
                                    William Hunter
                                    Edward Pryer

[113]

In Obedience to An order of Vestry to us Directed we have processiond all the Bounds of Land in the Bounds No. 25 Vz
A line Between Henry Skiner & Edmund Pryor p^{rst} the proprioters and Joseph Price a Line Between Henry Skiner & John hamilton Pressent Henry Skiner Edmund Proyer and Joseph Price the Same Line Continued Between Hamilton and proyer p^{rst} Proyer & Henry Skiner & Joseph price A Line Between Edmund Pryer and Joseph Price the proprietors and Henry Skiner p^{rst} a Line Between the Revd W^{im} Webb & Joseph Price the Proprietors & Henry Skiner p^{rst} A Line Between the Revd Wim Webb & John Hamilton: Webb Henry Skiner and Joseph price p^{rst} a Line Between Joseph Price & James Constant Price Webb & Skiner p^{rst} Two Lines Between Joseph Price & John Dembey Junr Price Webb & Skiner Pressent A line Between the Revd W^{im} Webb & James Constant Joseph Price only p^{rst} A Line Between James Constant & Jotham Laseter Continued Between Jotham Lasiter & W^{im} Webb Joseph price p^{rst} only. a Line Between Moses Redick & Jotham Lasiter Riddick & Price p^{rst} a Line Between Wim Webb & John Giles M. Riddick & Price p^{rst} Two Lines Between Wim Webb & Mathew Buradal: proprioters p^{rst} and John Giles pressent A Line Between Moses Riddick & Josiah Riddick Continued Between Moses Riddick & John Watson Continued Between Moses Riddick and Mathew Buradall M: Riddick & Buradall and Wim Webb p^{rst} A Line Between Mathew Buradall & John Watson Buradall Moses Reddick & Wim Webb p^{rst} a Line between Mathew Buradall & Josiah Reddick Buradall & Moses Riddick & Wim Webb p^{rst} a Line between Mathew Buradall & Elisabeth Johns Buradall W^{im} Webb & Moses Reddick p^{rst} A Line Between John Watson & Josiah Reddick Buradall Wim Webb & Moses Riddick p^{rst} A line Between David Meade & Elisabeth Johns Continued Between Meade & W^{im} Acre Burdal only Present A Line Between W^{im} Acre & Elisabeth Johns Burdal p^{rst} a Line between David Meade & Josiah Reddick Continued Between Meade & hickmans Mathew Burdal Pressent. A line Between Meade & Thos Sumner A

line Between Hickman and Daniel pugh D⁰ Between Daniel Pugh & Lemuel Riddick: Riddick John Campbwell and James Stogdale p^{rst} Continued Between Lemuel Riddick & Ester Pugh Riddick & Stogdale p^{rst} a Line Between Daniel Pugh & Ester pugh D⁰ Between Lemuel Riddick & hickman D⁰ Between Mathew Parker & the Land Formerly James Pugh Parker p^{rst} A Line Between Mathew Parker & Ephraim Parker Both Pressent D⁰ Between Bates Formerly Spivy & Josiah Riddick Moses Rawlins p^{rst} the Same Line Continued Between Riddick & hickmans Land Moses Rawlings Pressent

              Josiah Riddick
              William Acre

[114]

Persuant to an order of Vestry Dated Septem^{br} the 13th 1755 We the Subscribers apointed in the Above Said order have Procesiond all the Bounds of Land Containd in the Said order Begining at a Line Between Jos: holands and Stephen Darden and Jos: holand in presence A line Between James holand and Stephen Dardan & Stephen Darden p^{rst} A line Between James holand and Jos: holand & Jos: Holand p^{rst} A line Between James holand & Soloman holand Jos. Holand p^{rst} A line Between Soloman Holand[60] Stephen Dardan in Pressence A line Between John Winburn & W^{im} Harrison W^{im} Harrison p^{rst} A line Between Christopher Sanders & W^{im} Harrison W^{im} Harrison & Moses Sanders in p^{rst} Line Between John Faulk & John King John Harrison in p^{rst} a line Between John King & John harrison Moses Sanders & John Faulk p^{rst} Line Between Christopher Sanders and John King W^{im} Harrison and Moses Sanders p^{rst} A line between John Winbourn & John Hedgbith John Hedgbith p^{rst} A line Between John hedgbith & Jos: Holand & John Hedgbith p^{rst} A Line between John Winburn & Jos: Holand Jos: holand p^{rst} A line between James Holand and John Carr & Nathan Car in pressence A line between Wim: Harrison & John Car and Nathan Car in pressence A line between Peter Butler & John King Peter Butler in pressence A line between Peter Butler & W^{im} Harrison Peter Butler in pressence A line Peter Butler Peter in pressence Line John Car John Car p^{rst} A line Between John Car John Car in pressence[61] line between W^{im} Butler & Nathan Wiat W^{im}

---

  [60] Apparently "&" was erased between "Soloman Holand" and "Stephen Dardan."
  [61] The statement about this line in the original shows no other name.

Butler p^rst a line between Jas: Johnson & Nathan Wiat both in presence Line between Joseph Holand & John Car Both in pressence line between[62] John Car & Jos: Holand and John Car in presence Line between John holan and Jos: Holand both in Pressence Line between Henry Johnson & John holand and W^im Johnson in Pressence Line between Henry Johnson & Jos: Holand Wim Johnson & Jos: Holand in pressence Line Between Henry Johnson And Wim. Johnson & Wim Johnson in pressence Line Between Jos: Holand And Wim Johnson both in Pressence. Line Between Jos: Holand & W^im Baker Jos: holand Pressent Line Between James Sumner & W^im Baker James Sumner in pressence Line Between Pricila Hedgbith & W^im Johnson J^os Holand in pressence Line Between James Sumner & Mary Fleming Ja^s Sumner & John Fleming in pressence Line Between Mary Fleming and W^im Baker and James Sumner & John Fleming in pressence

        James Holand
        Soloman Holand

[115]

Persuant To an order of Vestry Dated Septem^br the 13 1755 We the Subscribers apointed in the Above Said order have procesiond all the Bounds of Land Containd in the above Said order Begining at David Meade^s & John Milners Jethro darden in presence Line between David Meade and Charles Hedgbith Jethro darden & Charles hedgbith in p^rst Line Between Charels [sic] Hedgbith & John Milners Line Thos Cutchens and Milner John Garnes [sic][63] and Charles Hedgbith in Pressence Line Between Benjn Baker And John Milner and John Gardner & Charls Hedgbith p^rst Line between John Daughtrie and Benjn Baker and John daughtrie p^rst Line Between John daugtrie and Lucas daughtrie John daughtrie & Charles Hedgbith p^rst Line Between Thos Vaughan and Oliver Wiril Thos Vaughan in pressence Line between Wim Sanders & James Uzel James Uzel Wim Sanders in pressence Line Between W^im Vaughan and W^im Sanders Both in pressence. Line Between W^im Vaughan and Wim daughtrie Wim Vaughan in pressence Line Between Wim Vaughan and Jos: Holand Jos: Holand in pressence Line Between Elisabeth

---

[62] It appears that "Henry Johnson and John holand" was written after "between" and then erased.

[63] Possibly intended for John Gardner who appears in a similar relation in this return.

Vaughan and W.im Sanders W.im Vaughan in pressence Line Between Elisabeth Vaughan and John Whitfeild W^{im} Vaughan in pressence Line Between W^{im} Sanders and Mary Fleming W^{im} Vaughan & John Fleming p^{rst} Line Between Mary Fleming and Samuel Holand W^{im} Vaughan & John Fleming p^{rst} Line Between Henry holand & mary Fleming W^{im} Vaughan & John Fleming p^{rst} Line Between Wim Baker and Mary Fleming W^{im} Vaughan & John Fleming p^{rst} Line Between Stephen darden & Henry holand W^{im} Vaughan in pressence Line Between John Whitfeild and Henry holand W^{im} Vaughan in pressence Line Between Wim Holand and Henry holand W^{im} Holand in pressence Line Between John daughtrie and John Cutchens John daughtrie & John Cutchens p^{rst} Line Between Henry holand and Henry holand Wim Holand and Daniel Holand in pressence

Henry Holand
William Baker

[116]

In obedience To an order Vestry we the Subscribers have Procesiond [the bounds of land] Mentioned in the a fore Said Order John Butlers land John Simons Land W^{im} Osbourns Land only themselves pressent Mary Osburns Land W^{im} Mclenies Land W^{im} Parkers land. W^{im} Scotts Land Edward Taylors Land Hening Tembties Land Edward Elyes Land and W^{im} parker present John Elyes Land Thos Gay^s Land and W^{im} Kings Land Frances powels land Wim. Kings and Thos Gay^s pressent Hening Tembty and John Wiat Land James Copeland Land Frances powels and James parkers pressent. John Wilsons Land Daniel doughties Land John Holand Land John Bests Land W^{im} Beatmans Land James Holand and Jerimyah Godwin pressent Jerimyah Godwins Land and Mathias Jones Land Jean Bakers land Elijah Holand and John Barkley pressent John Barkleys Land and Thos Godwins land John Best and Wim Beatman pressent Robert Archers Land Jessy Elsberry Land Pressent Thos Godwin and Richard Matthews

Thomas Godwin
Richard Matthews

In Complyance to an order of Vestry dated the 13th of Septem^{br} 1755 We the Subscribers have procesiond all the Bounds of Land according to Order Begining at a line Between Widow parker and John Faulk Adam

Harrel and we being pressent and a line between John Faulk And John Hare in pressence of us and them and a line Between John hare and W^{im} Rawls in pressence of us and John hare and John Faulk and a Line Between W^{im} Rawls and Frances Rawls in pressence of us and John Hare and John Faulk a Line Between John Harel and W^{im} Rawls in the pressence of us and John Harrel and a line Between Wim Rawls and John porter Senr in Pressence of us and John Harrel and a Line Between the Widow Rawls and James Couplan In Pressence of us and a Line Between the Widow Rawls and John porter In Pressence of us and a line of John porters in pressence of us

         James Coupland
         John Porter

[117]

In Obedience to an order of Vestry In Suffolk Town dated Sept^{br} the 13 1755 We have procesiond all the Land in our Bounds Begining of Wim Waters & Michael Kings & Hening Tembteys and W^{im} Kings And Elisha Ballards & the Land of John and Henry Butler And W^{im} Kings & Thos Peirce^s Pressent W^{im} King Junr And Lawrence Moore & Jams Peirce and Land Between Wim King Junr And Lawrence Moore & James Peirce and also the Land Between Between [sic] W^{im} King & Abraham Lewis and Between W^{im} King and Michael King and also Between Michael King & Abraham Lewis And Thos Johnson p^{rst} W^{im} King Junr and also the land Between Wim Moore & Thos Johnson also the land Between Thos Johnson And Abraham Lewis and the Land Between W^{im} Moore and Abraham Lewis pressent Mathew Peirce & James Peirce Also the Land Between Mathew peirce & Abraham Lewis pressent James peirce also the Land Between Wim Moore & Thos peirce present James peirce and the land of John & Henry Butlers & John harris and the Land Between John King & John Harris Junr p^{rst} W^{im} Beasley and John Harris also Between W^{im} Beaseley & John King pressent John Harris and John Harris Junr also the Land Between John King and John Harris p^{rst} W^{im} Beaseley and John Harris Junr also the land Between John Harris and Thos Peirce and John Harris & John & Henry Butler pressent John Peirce & James peirce and W^{im} Beaseley & John Harris Junr Also the Land of John Kings and Edward Moores also the land Between Edward Moore & Thos Peirce p^{rst} John peirce & James peirce Also the land Between Thos peirce & John peirce p^{rst} James peirce Also the land Between Thos peirce & John peirce p^rst James peirce Also the land Between John peirce & peter Butler Also the land Between John Couplan and peter Butler p^rst John M:Clenney & John Copelan Junr Also the land Between John Couplan & John Car and W^im M:Clenney Also the land Between W^im Moore & John M:Clenney pressent John Copelan Junr also the land Between Michael King & Wim King pressent Wim King Junr Also the land Between Michael King And the land of W^im Waters^s p^rst W^im King Junr

William Moore
Matthew Peirce

[118]

Nansemond County ss

In Obedeince to an order of Vestry held the 13 of Septem^br 1755 We have Met and Procesiond all the Lands within our Bounds And no Objection Made but Being Neither of us Able to write Have Forgot the Names of the person pressent Do therefore Humbly Beg to be Excused From under our Hands

Hugh Goff
Robert Smith

Persuant to an Order of Vestry Dated Septem^br 13th 1755 We the Subscribers Have procesiond all the Bounds of Land Containd in the Said order Begining at Between John Rawls and James Copelan p^rst John porter & Abraham Copelan & David Rawls Thence a Line Between John porter & John Ballard in pressence of the Same a line between John porter and James Winburn pressent the Same a line Between John Harrison & Oliver Wirel pressent John Ballard and Henry Butler a line Between Moses Johnson and Jo^s Baker pressent the Said Baker and Christopher Norfleet a line Between the a Fore Said Norfleet and Joseph Baker in pressence of the Same a line between peter Watkinson And Ephraim Hunter pressent John Ballard & Henry Butler A line Between John Ballard and peter Watkison p^rst the Same A line Between John Skiner and Moses Johnson pressent the a fore Said John Skiner a line Between Oliver Wirrel & Ephraim hunter pressent the Same a line between Henry Butler & John Ballard pressent John Harrison a line Between W^im Harrison & John Harrison pressent John Ballard & Jesse Rawls a line Between James Copelan & James Winbourn p^rst Ja^s Winbourn & Thos Winbourn a line between Thos Winbourn & Ja^s Winbourn in pressence of the a fore Said

A line Between [. . .]⁶⁴ and W^im Harrison Junr p^rst as a fore Said a line Between W^im Harrison Senr & Wim Harrison Junr p^rst the a fore Said Includeing all the Bounds of Land peaceably & Quietly procesiond And no Objection Made

          William Harrison
          Thomas Winbourn

[119]

Persuant To an order of Vestry Dated Septemb^r the 13th 1755 We have Processiond the Lines as Followeth Vz

 Between James March & John hare Daniel March p^rst
 Between John hare & John Townsin Daniel March p^rst
 Between Odum & Daniel March Jacob Odum p^rst
 Betwen W^im and James purvis & Daniel March & Jacob Odum p^rst
 Between W^im Purvis & James Purvis Junr Daniel March p^rst
 Between Wim Purvis & John purvis Daniel March p^rst
 Between James Purvis & W^im Rodgers Son: Robt Wim purvis p^rst
 Between W^im Rodgers Son of W^im & James Savige W^im Purvis p^rst
 Between John purvis & W^im Rodgers Son of W^im W^im purvis p^rst
 Between John purvis & Benjamain Rodgers John Cross p^rst
 Between Wim Cross & W^im Rodgers Son of W^im John Cross p^rst
 Between Wim Cross & Benjamain Rodgers John Cross p^rst
 Between John Cross & Benjamain Rodgers Both p^rst
 Between John Cross & James Cross Benjamain Rodgers p^rst
 Between James Eliot & John Townsin James purvis p^rst
 Between James Savidge & W^im Rodgers Robert Rodgers p^rst
 Between David Sumner & James Eliot John hare p^rst
 Between Willis Redd[i]ck⁶⁵ & Daniel March Edward hare p^rst
 Between W^im Rodgers & Mary parker Richard Austin p^rst
 Between Wim Rodgers & Richard Roberts Richard Austin p^rst
 Between Richard Roberts & Elisabeth Rodgers Richard Austin p^rst
 Between Thos Sumner & Sarah Rodgers Richard Austin p^rst
 Between Lemuel Riddick & John Cross James Rawls p^rst
 Between Lemuel Riddick & Wim Cross James Rawls p^rst
 Between David Sumner & W^im Cross James Rawls p^rst

---

⁶⁴ Name omitted in original.
⁶⁵ This name seems either to omit the "i", although dotted, or, less likely, to be spelled "Reddik."

Between David Sumner & W^im Rodgers James Rawls p^rst
Between Lemuel Riddick & David Sumner W^im hearring p^rst

       William Cross
       William Rodgers

[120]

Nansemond County Septem^br the 13th In the year 1755

A Vestry Held and Apointed Jesse Reddick John Lawrence To Procesion all the Land Marks Between South Key Road & Sumerton Creek Road From the Redy Branch to the Carroliner Line. The Carroliner Line Possesiond Between W^im Baker & Benjamin Baker Abraham Reddick And Charles hedgbirth p^rst A Line Be[t]ween W^im Baker And Thos Car Abraham Reddick p^rst An Outside line of W^im Bakers Abraham Reddick p^rst An outside line of Abraham Reddicks W^im Baker & Benj^m Baker pressent. A Line Between Jesse Reddick & Abraham Reddick Joseph Rodgers pressent A Line Between Abraham Reddick & Thos Shivers Joseph Rodgers pressent An outside Line of John Butlers Abraham Reddick & Joseph Rodgers pressent A line Between Abraham Reddick & George Lawrencce Wim Baker pressent A line Between David Meade & John Lawrence Jethro Darden pressent A Line Between Thos Shivers & John Pendar John Lawrence pressent A Line Between Abraham Reddick & Thos Shivers John Lawrence p^rst A line Between John Lawrence and Thomas Shivers A line Between George Lawrence & John Lawrence them selves pressent A line Between John Lawrence and Paul Lawrence A Line Between George Lawrence & Paul Lawrence them selves pressent An outside Line of John Lawrence^s A line Between David Meade & John pendar Jethro Darden p^rst A line Between W^im Bryant & John Pendar A line of Jacob Dardens Includeing all the Land marks In our Bounds From Under our Hands

       Jesse Riddick
       John Lawrence

[121]

In obedience to an order Vestry Bearing Date the 13th of September 1755 We have Possesiond all the Land In our Bounds

At the Possesioning a Line Between Robert Baker & Richard Mathews p^rst Robert Baker A Line Between Richard Mathews & Mary Beaman pres^t Robert Baker & Absolum Beamon A line Between Robert Baker &

Mary Beamon pres^t Absolum Beamon & Robert Baker. A line Between Robert Baker & Mary Brewer press^t Robert Baker Henry Moore & John Brewer A line Between Mary Brewer & Pricelia Wright press^t Robert Baker Henry Moor & J^{no} Brewer. A line Between Pricelia Wright & Jo^s parker press^t Robt Baker J^{no} Brewer & Thos Beamon A Line Between J^{no} Northcot & Pricilia Wright press^t J^{no} Brewer Robt Baker & Thos Beama^r A line Between Rachel Brewer & Thos Mace press^t Robt Baker and Rachel Brewer A line Between Matthew witwell & Thos Mace press^t Robert Baker A Line Between[66] John Northcott & Thos Mace press^t Robt Baker A line Between Matthew witwell and J^{no} Northcot press^t Robt Baker Matthew Parker & Daniel pugh A line Between J^{no} Northcot & John Beamon press^t Robt Baker Matthew parker & Daniel Pugh A Line Between Matthew Parker & J^{no} Northcott press^t Matthew Parker J^{no} Beamon & Daniel Pugh A Line Between Ephraim Parker & J^{no} Northcott press^t Matthew Parker J^{no} Beamon & Daniel Pugh A line Between J^{no} mace & J^{os} Parker p^{rst} Robt Baker Matthew Parker J^{no} Beamon & Daniel Pugh A Line Between Matthew witwell & J^{os} Parker prs^t Robt Baker Matthew parker J^{no} Beaman & Daniel Pugh A Line Between Matthew witwell & Ephraim parker p^{rst} Matthew Parker J^{no} Beaman & Daniel Pugh. A Line Between Ephraim parker & Jo^s parker Present both parties A Line Between Matthew witwell & Matthew Parker Pressent Matthew parker J^{no} Beaman & Daniel Pugh A Line Between Matthew Parker & J^{no} Beaman p^{rst} both parties A Line Between Matthew witwell & John Beaman p^{rst} Matthew parker John Beaman & Daniel Pugh A Line Between Matthew witwell & Rachel Brewer p^{rst} Matthew Parker John Beaman & Daniel Pugh A Line Between Matthew witwell & Ester Pugh p^{rst} John Beaman

[122]

A Line Between Matthew witwell & John Beaman Pressent John Beaman & Daniel Pugh A Line Between John Beaman and Jo^s Parker present both parties A Line Between Matthew witwell and Joseph Parker pressent Daniel Pugh A Line Between John horton and Matthew witwell p^{rst} Daniel Pugh A Line Between Matthew witwell and John Mace pressent Thos Mace & Daniel Pugh A Line Between John Horton and John Mace

---

[66] It appears that "Matthew witwell" was written after "Between" and then erased.

pressent Daniel Pugh & Thos Mace A Line Between John Horton & W^{im} Woodward pressent Daniel Pugh Thos Mace & Wim Woodward A Line Between W^{im} Woodward & Joseph Parker pressent John Parker and Both Parties A Line Between Daniel Pugh & John Mace Pressent Daniel Pugh Thomas Mace & John parker A line Between John Northcot & John Mace Pressent Daniel Pugh Thos Mace & John Parker

        Joseph Parker
        John Horton

[123]

 At A Vestry Held In Suffolk Town Novem^{br} the 15 1756 For Laying & Assesing the Parrish Leivie

 Pressent the Revd Wim Webb Minister
   David Meade W^{im} Baker Church Wardens
   Lemuel Reddick Willis Reddick
   Hening Tembtey John Rawls & Josiah Reddick
   Gent^s Vestry Men

To the Revd Wim Webb his Salary	16000
To D^o 4 per C^t For Caskue & 4 per C^t on Srinkage	1280
To D^o an alowance for a gleab	3000
To William Shekelton Reader at Sum^t	1000
To Nickolas Maget D^o at Notaway	1000
To Aaron Allmand D^o at Suffolk	2080
To Thos Johnson Sexton	800
To Mary Rawls Sexton^s of Sumt for this & last year	600
To D^o for a well Bucket	20
To John Jenkens for Cleaning Round the Chapell	25
To Isaac Langston for Cuting Bushes on the Chapel land	50
To Coln. Jona: Godwin Ball. his acc^t for Insolvents	1231
To Jesse Reddick for a thithable gone to the wars	30
To Thos Wigens a thithable over Charg^d	30
To George Frith a Leivie for a person gone to the wars	30
To Hardy Rawls for the Same	30
To Wim Harrison for the Same	30
To John Hansel for a days atendance at Court for the parrish	25
To John Rawls for a Leivie over Charg^d Last year	30

To be Sold for Cash Next July Court to Discharge the Cash Debts	13000
	40291
To the Collector @ p per ct	2417
	42708
By 1322 Thithables @ 33 pounds of Tobacco per thithable Is	43626
Depositum due to the Parrish	918

[124]
Novembr 18th 1756
The Uper Parrish of Nansemond Dr In Cash

To Docktor Brown as per his Account	£ 1 : 2 : 6
To James Winbourn	6 : 3
To William Webb	8 : 9
To David Meade Ball: his Acct for the poors House &c	46 : 14 : 11
To Samuel Wallis For Keeping School &c	10
To Sarah Watkins for washing the Cirplis &c	8 : 6
To Judith Perrit a Poor woman	2 : 10
	£ 61 : 10 : 11

Tis ordered that the Sherreif Do Collect From Every Thithable in this Parrish thirty three pounds of Tobacco per thithable and there with Discharge the Several Debts this day Leivied &c

And that Mr Wallis Be Continued on the Same Terms as the Last Year

    Truly Registred   Signd By William Webb
        By Aaron Allmand Clk Vestry

[125]
At a Vestry Held In the Court House For the Uper Parrish of Nansemond Munday the 16 may 1757

    Pressent The Revd Wim Webb Minister
        David meade   W{im} Baker   Church Wardens
        Lemuel Reddick   Hening Tembtey Mils Reddick
        Josiah Reddick   Willis Reddick   W{im} Hunter
        & Jacob Sumner Gent. of the Vestry

W^im Baker Gent. render^d in an Account of a fine   £
   Received of Mary Coupland for a Bastard Child   2 : 10
Hening Tembtey for a Fine Rec^d of Mary Miles   2 : 10
By Africe Hedgbeth 17/3   17 : 3
Wim Baker for part of Keturah Holan^s fine & others   3 : 9 : 6
By David Meade for Mary osbourns fine   2 : 5

                                                £11 : 11 : 9

To Sarah Elis   £1 : 18 : 7½
To Widdow Hogard   1 : 18 : 7½
To Thomas Jones   1 : 18 : 7½
To Widdow Chappell   1 : 18 : 7½
To Sarah Hedgpeth   1 : 18 : 7½
To Widdow Watkins   1 : 18 : 7½

                              £11 : 11 : 9

    Benjamain Forset & Elisha Ballard procesioners Returnd there Acc^t Which is ordered to be Register^d also a Return of James Rawls and Arthur Jones.

    Willis Reddick & Henry Holand Is apointed Church Wardens till Easter Next Williss Reddick took the Oath In Vestry Before Josiah Reddick a Majestrate for this County

    Ordered that the persons Above Indebted pay the Several Sums So as a bove due to Willis Reddick Church Warden who is to Distribute the Several poor persons as afore Said

                              Signd: William Webb

[126 blank]

[127]

    In Obedience to An order of Court to us Directed We have In the Pressence of Elisha Ashburn & Josiah Reddick procesiond the Two New Lines Between James March & John Ashburn We have Also procesiond the two new Lines Between the Said James March and Peter Ashburn In the pressence of Elisha Ashburn Henry Gwin & Josiah Reddick the Said March Haveing Notice but would Not Apear

    July the 1st 1756

                              Benjamin Forset
                              Elisha Ballard

Persuant to an Order of Vestry Dated September the 13th 1755 We the Subscribers Being Apointed in the Said order Haveing procesion^d all the Bounds of Land there in Mention^d Begining at a line Between Coln Lemuel Reddick & Capt David Sumner p^{rst} Jacob Sumner & Isaac Langston. a Line Between Coln Lemuel Riddick & Jacob Langston p^{rst} William Herrand Isaac Langston A line Between John Boyt & William Boyt p^{rst} Jacob Langston. A Line Between W^{im} Boyt & Lidia Keen p^{rst} George Jones A Line Between John Hare Thomas Jones p^{rst} William Jarnagan. a Line Between John Hare & Hardy Rawls p^{rst} W^{im} Rawls. A Line Between Ja^s Couplan And Hardy Rawls p^{rst} the a fores^d proprioters A Line Between John Hare and James Coupland p^{rst} Hardy Rawls A Line Between James Couplan & John Rawls prst the a fore Said James Couplan. A line Between John Rawls & John Hare pressent James Coupland. A Line Between John Hare & W^{im} Jones p^{rst} James Coupland A Line Between John Rawls & Jacob Jones p^{rst} the Said Jacob Jones A Line Between John Rawls and Thomas Jones p^{rst} Thos Jones A Line Between Theophilus Jones and George Jones p^{rst} Jacob Jones & the propriot^{rs} A Line Between Isaac Langston & Arthur Jones p^{rst} Isaac Langston A Line Between James Rawls & Mary parker p^{rst} Abraham parker A Line Between James Rawls and Jacob Jones p^{rs} the proproters [sic]: all the Above Said Bounds of Land peaceably & Quietly procesioned and No objection made By us

James Rawls
Arthur Jones

[128]

At A Vestry Held In the Court house In Suffolk Town November the 29th 1757 For the Up^r Parrish of Nansemond County

Pressent the Revd William Webb Minis

Willis Riddick	Henry holand	Church wardens
Lamuel Riddick	Mills Riddick	Josiah Riddick
William Hunter	William Baker	Hening Tembtey
& David Sumner		

To the Revd William Webb Minist^r his Sallary	1 6000
To D^o An Alowance of 4 per Ct for Caskue & D^o for Srinkage	1280
To D^o An Alowance for a Gleab	3000
To Nickolas Maget Clerk of Notaway Chapel	1000

To William Shekelton D° of Sumerton D°	1000
To Aaron Allmand D° at Suffolk Church	2080
To John King a Leivie over paid in 1755	30
To John Giles for the Same	30
To Hening Tembtey Sherf for Insolvents this year	825
To Mary Rawls Sexton[s] of Sum[n] Chapell	300
To William Wigins Sexton of Notaway D° & grubing the yard	500
To Tho[s] Johnson Sexton of Suffolk Church	800
To Be Sold For Cash at July Court By the Church Warden[s] Towards Dischargeing the parrish Debts this day Leivied	20000
	46845
By Credd: the parrish with the Last years Depositum By Hening Tembtey Shrf	918
	45927
To the Collcet[r] at 6 per C	2756
	48683

Tis Ordered that Hening Tembtey Sherrf. Do Collect from Every Thithable in this parrish 38 pounds of Tobacco per thithable and therewith Discharge the parrish Debts this Day Brought In

on 1300 thithables Amounts to[67]	49400
Due to the parrish	717

Tis ordered that Hening Tembtey Sherrf Do Receive from Anthony Holaday the Sum of £35 it Being the Sum that he is to pay for the Gleab Land & the Said Hening Tembtey to pay it to the Church Wardens to Discharge the parrish Debts this Day Brought in

[129]

D[r] The uper parrish of Nansemond In Cash 1757

To Samuel Wallice his Account for Sundries	£ 1 : 6 : 6
To Jese Barret for makeing a Coffin	8
To Hening Tembtey Rendred In his Account of the Tobacco Sold And the Ballance is Due to him	4 : 15 : 8½

---

[67] This phrase is written in after a brace at the right of the latter part of the preceding paragraph.

To Lemuel Riddick his Account For Sundries For the poor	2 : 9 : 9	
To Dock. Tyre for Atending the poor at the poors house	12 : 18	
To Henry holand For Sundries Delivered the poor	2 : 5 : 4	
To James Holand For Carrying Tho⁸ parks to Dʳ Browns	12 : 6	
To Docʳ Robᵗ Brown For attending the poor at the poorˢ house	10	
To Thoˢ Sumner pᵈ mʳ Watson for Tallow & Burying Terel Brown	2 : 2 : 1¼	
To Majʳ Willis Riddick Rendred in his Accᵗ as Church Warden For Sundries For the poor &c	20 : 11 : 7½	
To James Gibson For Sundries Sold For the poor	2 : 19 : 3	
To John Watson For 2 Barrels pork for the poorˢ house	5 : 2 : 6	
To William Hunter For Sundries provision for the poorˢ house	6 : 10	
To Thoˢ Hamon Butcher For the poors House	4 : 8 : 8	
To Capᵗ William Baker his Accᵗ Due when he was Ch:Warden	3 : 10	
To Hening Tembtey for QRents for the Gleab Land	3 : 9½	
To Ann Nail Towards maintaining hir Child	2 : 10	
To Daniel Williams For work done at the Notaway Chapell	10	
To Coln: Lemuel Riddick	2 : 10	
For which he is to Let Thoˢ Jones have Nessaries of Liveing		
To Isabela Brown a poor Woman	2 : 10	

To Magaret Hall	£2 : 10	To Judith perrit	£2 : 10	5
To Walthoe Price	2 : 10	To Jean Savage	2 : 10	5
To Jean Wiat	2 : 10	To Sarah Ellis	2 : 10	5
To Ruth Chapel	2 : 10	To Mary Babb	2 : 10	5

Mʳ David meade Rendred in his Account as Church Wᵈ
   From November til June Last & the Ballance is
   Due to him   12 : 2 : 3
To Samuel Wallice Teacher at the poors house   10

                                            £ 130 : 5 : 11¾

                      Signᵈ By William Webb

Truly Registred By Aaron Allmand Clk Vestry

[130]

At A Vestry held for the Up{r} Parrish of Nansemond County at Suffolk Town on Easter Tuseday March the 28th 1758

Pressent the Revd Wim Webb Minister
    Willis Riddick Church Warden
    Mills Riddick   Josiah Riddick
    William Baker   Hening Tembtey } Gent{l} Vestry Men
    Lemuel Riddick

Henry Holand & Mills Riddick are Apointed Church Wardens Until Easter Next the Said Mills Sworn In Vestry and the Said Henry Not being pressent may be Sworn before Any Justice duly to Execute the Said office

Stephen Wright & Daniel Williams are Apointed Vestry men In the Room of William Hunter and David Sumner Gent{l} Who are Remov{d} out of this Colony

Ordered that Mr Baker & Mr Holand Agree with Some persons to Keep Ferry Over Notaway to the Chapel on Sundays & Bring In there Charge at the Next Leivie

Revd William Webb Mills Riddick Lemuel Riddick Josiah Riddick & Stephen Wright Gent{l} are Apointed Vissators of the poors house And they are to make Enquiry What Number of Children will be Nesasary to keep In the House how Many the master may take on pay And of them who are fit to Leave the House to Inform the Court In order to have them Bound to trade & all times to report to the Vestry the State & Condition they find the affairs of the House & to Se the Law And Orders of Vestry Punctaly fulfiled and they are to meet as often As they think Nesasary & any three of them at any time is Sufficient To make Any Such Inspection or Inquiry

    Truly Entred by   Sign{d} by William Webb
      Aaron Allmand Clk Vestry

[131]

At A Vestry Held In the Court house In Suffolk Town June the 12th 1758 For the Uper Parrish of Nansem{d} County

Press^t The Revd William Webb Minister
   Henry Holand   Mills Riddick   Church Wardens
   Lemuel Riddick   David Meade ⎫
   Josiah Riddick   Willis Riddick ⎪
   Jacob Sumner   Hening Tembtey ⎬ Gentlemen Vestry Men
   & William Baker ⎭

Tis ordered that the Tobacco that was Leivied for Dischargeing the Parrish Debts which was 20000^{lb} Be paid In money at 2^D per pound for all Such as have not Tobacco it Apearing To this Vestry that there will not be Tobacco to Discharge the Quantity above that was Leivied at the Laying the Last Parrish Leivie

   Truly Enter^d by   Sign^d by William Webb
   Aaron Allmand Cl. Vestry

[132]

At A Vestry Held for the uper Parrish of Nansemond July the 24th 1758

Pressent the Revd William Webb Minist^r
   Mills Riddick Gen^t Church Warden
   Willis Riddick   Hening Tembtey ⎫
   John Rawls   Jacob Sumner   ⎬ Gen^t Vestry men
   Josiah Riddick   David Meade   ⎭

William Moore is Apointed Vestry man in the room of William Hunter who has Remov^d out of this Colony

The Vestry being Sensible that there was a donation of 700 Acres of Land from William Cadogan in Trust of to Col: Thos Milner for the beter Support and Maintaining the poor of this parrish

Tis Ordered that the Church Wardens make Enquiry after the Said Donation and furnish themselves with all papers Relateing to the Same and Lay them before the Next Vestry and Consult a Lawyer if Necessary in order to the Recovery of the Same

                    Sign^d William Webb
   Truly Enterd by Aaron Allmand Clk Vestry

[133]

At A Vestry Held in Suffolk Town November the 29th 1758 For the Uper Parrish of Nansemond County

Pressent the Revd William Webb
    Mills Riddick Henry Holand Gen^t Ch: Wardens
    Williss Riddick Josiah Riddick ⎫
    John Rawls Stephen Wright ⎬ Gen^t Vestrymen
    William Baker Jacob Sumner ⎪
    Aded William Moore ⎭

To the Revd William Webb his Salary	16000
To D^o An Alowance of 4 per Ct for Caskue & D^o for Srinkage	1280
To D^o An Alowance for A Gleab	3000
To William Shekelton Clerk of Notaway Chapel	1000
To Aaron Allmand D^o of Suffolk Church	2000
To D^o an Alowance of 4 per Ct	80
To Nickolas Maget Clk of Notaway Chapel	1000
To Mary Rawls Sexton^s of Sumerton Chapel	300
To William Wigins Sexton at Notaway D^o	200
To Thos Johnson D^o of Suffolk Church	800
To Mosses Hart D^o of Notaway Chapel before Omited	200
To Hening Tembtey Sherreif for Insolvents	764
To D^o For Lamuel Riddicks Ticket	155
To Mary Rawls Alow^d a Leivie For a person took to the Army	30
To D^o For Cleaning the Chapel Ground	10
To 10^M pounds of Tobacco to be Sold by the Church Wardens at July Court For Cash Towards Dischargeing the Parrish Debts this day Brought in	10000
	36819
To the Colector @ 6 per ct	2209
	39028

Tis Ordered that Capt Thos Godwin Sherf do Colect From Every thithable in this parrish 30 pound of Tobacco per thithable   on 1329 thithes is   39870
And therewith Discharge the parrish Debts First Giveing Bond & Security as Useual to the Church Wardens For that purpose
                        Due to the Parrish[68]   842

---

[68] This phrase is written after a brace at the right of the latter part of the preceding paragraph.

[134]

D^r the Up^r Parrish of Nansemond in Cash 1758

To Jesse Riddick For provideing Necesasaries for a woman Deliver^d at his House	£ 2 : 5	s
To John Rawls for Blocking up the Chapell	1 : 15	
To Henry holand Ch: Warden for Sundries Deliver^d Mary Tucker	3 : 9 : 11	
To Capt Mills Riddick D^o Rendred in his Acc^t & the Ball Due to him	8 : 2 : 7	
To Thos Johnson for Diging a Grave to Inter [. . .]^{69} Wright	2 : 6	
To Dockt^r Robert Brown for medicines for Wilson & Woodson	13 : 5 : 8	
To Sarah Watkins for Washing the Cirplis 3 times @ 2/6	7 : 6	
To Richard Hynes for keeping Ann Hynes	13	
To D^o for Makeing a Coffin for Jesse farrow	8	
To Henry Holand for Sundries Deliver^d Grace Amistead	2 : 2 : 7	
To John Streeter for the hier of his Negrow woman at the poors house	4 : 10	
To Samuel Wallice his Account for Sundries for the poors house	3 : 14 : 6	
To D^o his Salary for one year as per Agreement	10	
To Ann O Neal Towards Maintaining hir Children	2 : 10	
To Sophia Berry D^o for D^o	2 : 10	
To D^o for 3 Months Boardin William pool @ 10/ per month	1 : 10	
To Thos Jones A poor Man	2	
To Ann Webb s^{nr} a poor Woman	2	
To William Brewer for work done on the well at holy Neck Chapell	1	
	£ 62 : 6 : 3	

---

^{69} Blank in original.

By Maj^r Willis Riddick Late Church Warden
Rendred in his Account and the Ball Due to
the parrish is   4 : 1 : 9½

    Parrish Debts   £ 58 : 4 : 6½[70]

[135]

    Orders of Vestry for 1758

Tis Ordered that the Church Yard in Suffolk Town be Inclos^d with good Lightwood posts and Rails in a Neat and work man Like maner And that Col^n Riddick Josiah Riddick Robert Brown Willis Riddick & Stephen Wright or Any three of them do Advertise the Said work to be Done to the Lowest Undertaker and agree with them assoon as it Conveniently Can be done

Tis Like wise ordered that A Chapell be Built on Thos Harrels Land of the Same Demensions of that at Notaway and that the Same be Compleated by the Last of October Next in A workman Like maner And that R^d William Webb Willis Riddick Mills Riddick Jacob Sumner and Stephen Wright or Any three of them do Agree with Thos Harrel for one Acree of Land to Build the Said Chapell on Like wise Any three of them do Advertise the Said Chapell to be Built by the Lowest Undertaker by the Time Afore Said

Dockt^r Robert Brown is apointed a Vestryman in the Stead of Mr David Meade Deceas^d

Henry Holand is this day Quallified as A Church Warden Until Easter Next

Capt Hening Tembtey haveing Received the Sum of Thirty pounds Five Shillings of Col: Anthony Holaday for the Gleab Land has paid the Same to Maj^r Willis Riddick Towards Dischargeing the parrish Debts

Tis Ordered that the Church Wardens do Aply to Col^n Anthony holaday for Codowgwans Will and have it Recorded

                                                 Sign^d by William Webb

Truly Enter^d by Aaron Allmand Clk Vestry

---

[70] The subtraction is in error: the amount in the pence column of the remainder should be 5½.

[136]

At A Vestry Held in Suffolk Town January the 1st 1759 For the Upr Parrish of Nansemond

Presst the Revd William Webb
    Capt Mills Riddick   Ch: Warden
    Coln: Lamuel Riddick   Stephen Wright ⎫
    Hening Tembtey   William Baker   ⎬ Gentl Vestry Men
    Josiah Riddick & John Rawls   ⎭

Whereas Mr Samuel Wallice hath been Imployd Some time past By the Vestry of this parrish to take Care of the poors house and to Educate the poor Children of the parrish and it Apearing to this Vestry that A Sufficient Number of Children Cannot be got to be Educated In the Said house and that Continueing the Said Mr Wallice Will be Runing the parrish to Expence without haveing the Desierd Good Efect it is therefore Ordered that the Church Wardens of this parrish Do Account with and Discharge the Said Mr Wallice on the Seventeenth of this Instant being the End of the year of his Said Service and that they Employ Some Sober Careful person to Look after the Said House Goods poor and other things Belonging to the Sd House And it is further Ordered that the Said Church Wardens Rent out Any Room or Rooms Belonging to the Said House that may be thought Not usefull for Such poor as Shall be Sent to the Said House for the Benifit and Advantage of the poor of this parrish Or to be Aplyed to Such other Charritable use or Uses as the Vestry Shall think proper

Whereas the Vestry formerly Ordered a Chapel to be Built on the Land of Thos Harrel and it Apearing that the Land of the Said Harrel is Entaild and Cannot make a Good Title to the Same

It is therefore ordered that the Said Trustees Aply to Jno Norfleet for the Like Quantity of Land and provide to Build a Chapel thereon According to the Demensions of the Said order

                                          Signd William Webb

Truly Enterd Aaron Allmand Cl: Vestry

[137]

At A Vestry Held at the Court house For the Uper Parrish of Nansemond County June the 24th 1759

Pressent   Revd William Webb   Josiah Riddick
Mills Riddick   Hening Tembtey
William Baker   Robert Brown   Stephen Wright
& John Rawls Gent^s Vestry Men

Mills Riddick & Stephen Wright Gent are Apointed Church Wardens for the Ensueing yeare

Mr Richard Webb Gent is Apointed A Vestry man to Supply the place of Henry Holland Deceas^d

Mills Riddick Church Warden Returnd an Account of £ 3 : 10/ In his hands Rec^d for fines

Ordered that out of the Same he pay the Sum of 25/ To Sarah Raiby and 25/ to Sarah Wright And 20/ to Jean Savage which is the whole of the Money In his hands Receiv^d for fines

William Webb

[138]

At A Vestry Held In Suffolk Town Septembr the 17th 1759 for the Uper Parrish of Nansemond County

Pressent the Revd William Webb Minister
Mills Riddick   Gent Church Warden
Lemuel Riddick   Josiah Riddick ⎫
Hening Tembey   William Moore ⎬ Gent Vestry Man
Jacob Sumner & Richard Webb   ⎭

Ordered that James Gibson & Thos Harrisson Procession all the Lands No 1 According to Law

Ordered that Christopher Roberts & Joseph Godwin procession All the Bounds of Land N° 2 According to Law

Ordered that William Norfleet & Edward Moore procession all the Bounds of Land N° 3 According to Law

Ordered that William Wilkinson & Aaron Allmand procession all the Bounds of Land in No: 4 According to Law

Ordered that Robt Archer & Edward Eley procession all the Land in Bounds No: 5 According to Law

Ordered that Jesse Battle & Elisha Ballard Procession all the Bound of Land in No: 6 According to Law

Ordered that William King & John Harrisson procession all the Land in Bounds No: 7 According to Law

Ordered that William Harrisson and John Winbourn[71] procession All the Land in Bounds No: 8 According to Law

Ordered that William Rawls and John Harrell Procession All the Land in Bounds No: 9 According to Law

Ordered that Isaac Langston and Jacob Jones Procession all the Land In Bounds No 10 According to Law

Ordered that James Norfleet & Thos Chivers Procession all the Lands In Bounds No 11 According [to] Law

Ordered that Hardey Rawls and Edward Howell Procession all the Land In Bounds No. 12 According to Law

[139]

Ordered that James Coupland Son of Henry and Moses Brewer Procession all the Bounds of Land No: 13 According to Law

Ordered that Stephen Dardan and James Sumner procession All the Land in Bounds No: 14 According to Law

Ordered that James Carr and Jacob Dardan Procession all the Land in Bounds No: 15 According to Law

Ordered that William Hart and Edward Cary Procession All the Land in Bounds No: 16 According to Law

Ordered that Daniel Holland and John Fleming Procession All the Land in Bounds No: 17 According to Law

Ordered that William Purvis and John Cross Procession all the Land in Bounds No. 18 According to Law

Ordered Henry Brinkley and John Melteir Procession All All [sic] the Land in Bounds No: 19 According to Law

Ordered that James Raiby and Joseph Hubbard Procession All the Land in Bounds No. 20 According to Law

Ordered that Joseph Smith and Job Harrell Junr Procession all the Land in Bounds No: 21 According to Law

Ordered that Job Harrell and John Baker Procession All the Land in Bounds No. 22 According to Law

Ordered that John Ballard and Joseph Skiner Procession All the Land in Bounds No. 23 According to Law

Ordered that John Wartridge and George Spivy Procession all the Land in Bounds No 24 According to Law

---

[71] The name, James Winburn, is subscribed to the return as recorded (See p. 138.)

Ordered that Matthew Barradal and Joseph Price Procession All the Land in Bounds No 25 According to Law

Ordered that John Brewer and William Woodward Procession All the Land in Bounds No. 26 According to Law

Ordered that John Cambwell and William Stallings Procession All the Land in Bounds No. 27 According to Law

Ordered that Richard parker & Joseph Horton Jun[r] Procession all the Land in Bounds No. 28 According to Law

James Gibson is Chosen A Vestry Man in the Room of Robert Brown Who hath Remov[d] out of the Parrish

William Webb

Truly Entered by Aaron Allmand Cl Vestry

[140]

At A Vestry Held in Suffolk Town for the Uper Parrish of Nansemond County November the 30th 1759

Pressent the Rev[d] William Webb

    Stephen Wright & Mills Riddick Ch: Wardens
    Willis Riddick William Baker Richard Webb ⎫ Gent
    Josiah Riddick Hening Tembtey   ⎬ Vestry
    John Rawls Lemuel Riddick   ⎭ Men

To the Rev[d] William Webb his Salary	16000
To D[o] An A Lowance of 4 per ct for Caskue & 4 for Srinkage	1280
To D[o] An Alowance for A Gleab	3000
To William Shekelton Clark of Holy Neck Chapell	1000
To Aaron Allmand D[o] of Suffolk Church	2000
To D[o] An A Lowance of 4 per Ct	80
To Nickolas Maget D[o] of Notaway Chapell	1000
To Mary Rawls Sexton[s] of Sumerton Chapell	300
To William Wiggins Sexton of Notaway	200
To Tho[s] Johnson D[o] of Suffolk Church	800
To Lemuel Riddick for his Tickets	121
To Cap[t] Tho[s] Godwin Sherreiff Ball: of his Last years Acco[t] For Insolvents &c	88
To John Rawls: Account	300
To Richard Hynes for Boarding & Maintaining Ann Hynes	800
	26969

To be Sold by the Church Wardens in July Court for Cash To Discharge the Cash Accounts &c	30000
	56969
To the Sherreiff for Collection @ 6 per Ct	3418
	60387
By 45 pounds of Tobacco on 1362 thithables Amounts To	61290
Depossitum Due to the Parrish	903

Ordered that the Sherreiff do Collect from Every thithable in this Parrish Fourty five pounds of Tobacco per thithable And therewith Discharge the Parrish Creddittors as Above Settled

John Jenkins is Apointed Sexton at Holy Neck Chapell in the Room of Mary Rawls

Stephen Wright Gent in Vestry Resign^d Being A Vestry man Being Upon his Removeal out of the County And Thomas Winbourn Is Elected in his Room

            William Webb

[141]

D^r the Uper Parrish In Cash 1759   £   S

To Mills Riddick Gent. Church Warden Ball: his Acc^o	0 : 3 : 0
To Stephen Wright Gent Church Warden	33 : 17
To Dock. James Tyre^s Acc^o	17 : 6 : 6
To Thos Hannoms Account	1 : 10 : 0
To Willis Riddick for paid Thos Jones Omited Last Year	2 : 10 : 0
To James Cary for Ferrying over Notaway one Year Due Last June	2 : 2 : 0
To Ephraim Lawrence for ferrying Over Notaway Since June Last to this Day	1 : 10 : 6
To Stephen Wright for Paid Wim Webb for Railing In the Church yard	21 : 0 : 4
To Ditto Paid for Intrest	0 : 16 : 3
	80 : 15 : 7

By the Tobacco Leivied for Dischargeing the Above Debts Tis ordered that the Church Wardens do Settle and pay of the Several Persons When they Receive the Money for the Tobacco When Sold

Sign^d William Webb

Mills Riddick ⎫
Richard Webb ⎬ Ch: Warden^s

Truly Entered Aaron Allmand C: Vestry

[142 blank]

[143]

A Return of John Cross & W^{im} Purvis to the Church Wardens of the Up^r Parrish of Nansemond County with the Account of the Lines Procession^d by us the Said J^{no} Cross & Wim. Purvis With the Names of the Person^s present at at [sic] the Same

The first Line was between Abraham parker & Wim Rogers Son of Joseph press^t Richard Parker & Hardy Parker

The Second Line between Abraham parker & James Long the Same pst

The third Between Wim Rogers & James Long the Same press^t

The fourth between Eliza Rogers & Col: Lamuel Riddick the Same pr^s

The Fifth Line between Eliza Rogers & W^{im} Rogers the Same press^t

The Sixth Between Col: Riddick & John Cross pres^t John Cole^s & Benjamain Rogers

The Seventh Line between Lamuel Riddick Wim Cross the Same press^t

The Eight Between Lemuel Riddick & W^{im} Rawls the Same pressent

The Ninth Line Between W^{im} Cross & W^{im} Rawls the Same pressent

The 10th line between Benj. Rogers & John Purvis J^{no} Cole & Wim Cross Pressnt

The 11th line between John purvis & Ja^s Purvis the Son of John purvis Junr the Same pressent

The 12th Line between John purvis & Wim Rawls the Same pressent

The 13th Line between W^{im} Rawls & W^{im} Rogers son of Robt the Same presst

The 14th Line between John Cross & Ja^s Cross Wim Cross pressent

The 15th Line between David Sumner & John Cross the Same pressent

The 16th Line between John Cross & Benj Rogers the Same pressent

The 17th Line between John Cross & Wim Cross the Same pressent

The 18th Line Between Wim purvis & Wim Rogers James purvis pressent

The 19th Line between Jas Purvis & Wim Purvis Wim Rogers pressent

The 20th Line between Wim Purvis & Jas Purvis son of John Junr Daniel March pressent

The 21st Line Between Wim Purvis & Daniel March Jno haire & Jas purvis prest

The 22d Line Between Daniel March & Abraham Odum the Same presst

The 23d Line Between Jas March & Jno haire Dan. March pressent

The 24 Line Between Jno Townsend & Jno haire the Same pressent

The 25 Line Between Ann Eliot & David Sumner the Same presst

The [. . .]⁷² Line Between Jno Townsend & Ann Eliot Jno Webb & Jno Lee pressent

The 26th Line Between Jas Purvis & Wim Rogers Procession[d] But forgot in Course

Witness our hands this 29th of January 1760

        Wim Purvis
        John Cross

[144]

At A Vestry Held in Suffolk Town April the 8 1760 for the Uper Parrish of Nansemond County

Pressent the Revd Wim Webb Minister
  Mills Riddick & Richard Webb Ch: Wardens
  Josiah Riddick   Hening Tembtey ⎫
  John Rawls   Wim Moor   ⎬ Gent Vestry Men
  James Gibson & Thos Winbourn ⎭

John Rawls is Apointed & Sworn Church Warden in the room of Mills Riddick

Richard Webb is Continued Church Warden for the Ensueing Year

       William Webb
       Richard Webb Ch: Warden
Truly Enterd by   John Rawls
  Aaron Allmand Cl: Vestry

---

⁷² Blank in original.

[145]

Pursuant To an Order of Vestry Dated Septembr the 17th 1759 We the Subscribers Apointed in the Said order have processiond all the Said Bounds of Land Containd in the Said order Begining at a Line Between Mr Benj: Baker & Lewis Daughterrie thence Oliver Vorrels Land presst the Said Oliver Vorrel & Lewis Daughterrie thence John Daughterries Land presst the Sd Jno Daughtire Oliver Vorrel & Lewis Daughtire the Land that Was Formerly John Milners processiond in pressence of Mr Cox one of the Proprioters of the Said Land & Thos Cutchens & Lewis Daughterie South Key Plantation Land was formerly Mr Meades processiond prest Jethro Dardan Thos Cutchens Land presst the Sd Cutchens & John Daughterie Holedays Land prest Lewis Daughterrie Edmund Fowlers Land presst Oliver Worrel Thos Vaughans Land the Sd Thos Vaughan & Oliver Worrell thence William Vaughans Land presst the Sd Wim Vaughan Wim Sanders And James Uzel Wim Sanderss Land prst the Said Wim Sanders Wim Vaughan & Jas Uzzil Jas Uzzils Land prst the Sd Uzzil & Wim Vaughn And Wim Sanders John Flemings Land prst John Whitfeild Cap: Baker Capt Wim Bakers Land prst Capt Baker & John Turlington Stephen Dardans Land prst the Sd Dardan & Jas Holland All the Land Belonging to the heirs of Henry Holland Deceasd processiond prs John Whitfeild John Whitfeild Land presst the Said John Whitfeid And Wim Sanders. Wim Hollands prest the Hollands one Land prest. Wim Vaughan & Wim Sanders

All the Bounds of Land Containd in the Above Mentiond Order Is Peaceably & Quietly processiond No objection made by Us the Subscribers

        Daniel Holland
        John Fleming

[146]

The Land Marks Renewd by George Spivy & John Watridge All done in Quiet procession from the pocowswon up the Dessart to the Cyprus Swamp Up the Ciprus to the Barbecue and to Newbies Road And down to Couplands Branch the persons all had Notice & Pressent as Would Come only Mr Josiah Riddick & Thos Newby Which we have done there Lines with John Demby Wim Savage Wim Roundtre & Wim Frost { Abraham Lassater & Jesse lassatir had Notice but Would Not Come the Lines between George Spivy & Robt Booth Between Robt Booth & Abraham Lassater Booth & Widdow Harrill Harril & Wm Roundtree. Roundtree & Abraham Lassater. Lassater & Josiah Riddick Riddick & Joshua & George Spivy & Thos Newby Newby & John Demby Demby & Jo^s price Between Boyce & Ja^s Sketo & Jesse Lassater Lassater & Boyce} Lassater & George Spivy Lassater & his Brother Abraham Lassater And great Abraham Lassater Jesse Lassater & Jo^s Booth Booth & Jotham Lassater Lassater & Great Abraham between Little and great Abraham Lassater Betw' Lassater Robt Roundtree Robt & John Roundtree Roundtree & John Wartridge & Ja^s Spivy James & George Spivy Betw' Ja^s Spivy & Abraham Lassater Lassater and John Roundtree[73]

In Obedience To An Order of Vestry Dated Septembr 17th 1759 We the Subscriber^s have procession^d the Land Agreeable to the Said Order without Any Interruption Certifie^d Under our hands This 10th Day of March 1760.

Joseph Godwin
Christopher Roberts

[147]

In Obedience to An Order of Vestry Granted Septemb^r the 17th 1759 We the Subscribers with the Inhabitants have procession^d the Bounds of Land Mention^d in the Order as followeth Wm Richards Land John Best^s Land Ja^s Hollands Land Eliz^a Hollands Land Wm Beatman^s Land Jerremiah Godwins Land Joseph Baker Land John Berkleys Land Thos Godwin^s Land Robt Archers Land Edward Elyes Land John Simon^s Land Wim. M: Clennys Land W^m parker^s Land James parker^s Land Edward Talors his Land Henning Tembtey^s Land not procession^d Round the Line Joyning to Edward Eley Entry not done Thos Gay^s Land Wm King^s Land Frances powels Land James Couplands Land Jonathan Nelm^s Land

The following Lands Not procession^d Wm Marshal Stakes Mr Robbins Henry hill Susanah Meade No Apearance

From Under our hands	Edward Eley
March the 10th 1760	Robert Archer

We have Renewed Col^n Riddicks Land Marks Arter Birt John Burts George Jones Jacob Jones Isaac Langstun Land marks James Harres Michal Jones was with us Besides the owner^s of the Land Wm Jones

---

[73] The braces in this paragraph are evidently intended for punctuation and seem to have no other significance.

John harres James Coupland Sarath Rights Ja^s Rawls the Owners of the Land was Evidence one for Another Arthur Jones Lide Keene And Hardey Rawls was in Pressence there is no objection^s By Any person within our Bounds

Isaac Langstun
Jacob Jones

[148]

Pursuant To An Order of Vestry Dated Septemb^r the 17th 1759 We the Subscribers have processiond all the Lands Contain^d In the Said Bounds Begining James Couplands Land process^d In the press. of Wm Harrisson John Rawls & Ja^s Coupland John porter^s Land process^d in the press. of Wm Harrisson & John Porter James Winbourn^s Land process^d in the pressence of Wm Harrisson & Thos Winbourn Thos Winbourn Land processiond in press of Benj^a Harrisson And Thos Winbourn[74] William Harrisson Ju^{nr} Land Procession^d in press of the Above S^d Harrisson & Winbourn Willm Harrisson^s Senr Land Process^d in the pressence of John Porter & John Skiner & Wim harrison John Harrisson^s Land Process^d in the press. of Benj^m Harrisson And Wim. Harrisson & John Harrisson Henry Butler & John Butler Land Process^d in the press of John Giles & Absolom bemon John Giles Land Process^d in the press. of Henry Butler & J^{no} Butler & John Giles Absolem Beamon^s Land Process. in the press of John Giles & Henry Butler & the Above S^d Bemon John Skiner^s Land Process. in the press. of Jo^s Baker & Absolem Bemon And John Skiner Jo^s Baker^s Land Process^d in the press. of John Skiner & Joseph Baker Also a peice of Land Belonging to Mosses Johnson left undone by the Reason he was out of the Goverment Includeing all the Land within the Said order Peaceably & Quietly Procession^d And no Objection^s Made By us the Subscribers

James Winbourn
William Harrisson

---

[74] The words "Thos Winbourn^s Land process^d in press.", which were written after "Thos Winbourn", were evidently intended to be canceled in toto, but the writer failed to strike out "in press."

[149]⁷⁵
In Obedience to An Order of Vest[   ]
We the Subscriber⁸ have Accordingl[   ]
Mentionᵈ in the Said Order E[   ]
James Right & Prisscila [   ]
To Wett the Line Bet[   ]
Pressent Jaˢ Gregorie & Mar[   ] the Lin[   ]
James Gregorie & R[   ]
And Thoˢ Sumn[   ]
And Robᵗ Bake[   ]
And Jaˢ Mour [   ]
Jaˢ Mour & [   ]
Pricila Wr[   ]
Pressᵗ [   ]
Robᵗ Bake[   ]
Robᵗ Bak[   ]
Parker [   ]
presˢᵗ [   ]
Ephrai[   ]
Line B[   ]
And Jo[   ]
The [   ]
The [   ]
The [   ]

[150]⁷⁶
[   ] Processionᵈ the Bounds
[   ]ing at the plantation Caled
[   ] by Jnº Butlers on the
[   ]amp thence up the
[   ] to the first Station
[   ]nds done between

---

⁷⁵ This page and the next page in the original (one leaf) have been mostly torn away, only parts of the upper halves remaining. The fragmentary return given here probably relates to bounds No. 26, John Brewer and William Woodward, processioners (See p. 132). A similar return is found on p. 116-118.

⁷⁶ See preceding footnote. The fragmentary return given here may relate to bounds No. 7, William King and John Harrison, processioners (See p. 130). A return showing most of these names is found on p. 113-114.

140 VESTRY BOOK OF THE UPPER PARISH

[   ]⁷⁷
[   ] King & the Widdow
[   ] Betwixt
[   ]nt
[   ]n Lewis
[   ]hael king
[   ] king
[   ] Moore
[   ]ears
[   ] Moore
[   ]twixt
[   ]son
[   ]
[   ]
[   ]
[   ]ing
[   ]

[151]

Whereas we the Subscribers was Ordered by a Vestry of this County of Nans[ed] Bearing date Septemb[r] the 17th 1759 that we Should procession all the Land Bounds therein Mention[d] which we have done peaceably begining on A Line of John Faulk[s] & John King & then a Line of the Afore s[d] faulk And Wim Harrisson in the press of Jn[o] Faulk Jn[o] Holand & Several others And then a Line of John Winbourn[s] & John Faulks & then a Line of Wim Harrisson[s] & the S[d] Winbourn in the press of John Harrisson & Ja[s] Holland And them selves then A line Jn[o] Winbourn[s] & Wi[m] Collins in the press of Ja[s] Winbourn And Josiah Winbourn then A Line of Tho[s] Jones & Josiah Riddick in the press. of the Afore s[d] Jones then A line of Henry Couplands & Th[os] Jones In the press of John hare & them selves then A line of John hare & Henry Coupland & Ja[s] Coupland in the press. of John hare & henry Coupland then A line of the S[d] Henry Couplan & George Keen in the press. of John hare & the Owner[s] then A line of Henry Couplands Mo[s] Brewer Both press[t] then A Line of Josiah Riddicks & George Keen In the press of Ja[s] Keen then A Line of George

---

⁷⁷ The words "& the Widdow Ashbourn", which appear at the end of this line, were struck out.

Keen and Frances Rawls in the press. of the Owners then A line of Fra. Rawls George Keen in the press of the owners themselves then a Line of Jno Rawls Francis Rawls in the press. of the Owners then a Line of Jno Rawls Wi^m Collins in the press of Jno Rawls Joshua Rawls then a Line of J^{no} Rawls Josiah Riddick in the press of Jno Rawls F^r Rawls then a Line of John Rawls & Gabriel Rawls in the press of John Rawls Junr then A Line of Jno Rawls & Wi^m. Collins John Rawls being press^t then A Line of Ja^s Hollands in the press of Josiah Winbourn Ja^s Holland then A Line of Ja^s Hollands John Winbourn in the press of Jno Holland Ja^s Holland then A Line of John Holland Ja^s Holland in the press of Wi^m Coupland Jno Holland then A Line of Ja^s Holland Daniel holland In the press of Jno Holland then A Line of Daniel Hollands Hy: Holland In the press. of Daniel holland Robt Holland then A line of Robt holands Henry holland in the press. of John Everrit Ja^s Holland then a Line of J^{no} Everrits Ja^s Winbourn in the press of Robt Holland Jno Everritt then A Line of Jno Everrit Elisha Coupland in the press of Jno Everritt Ja^s Coupland then A Line of Robt Holland Jno Holland in the press of Ja^s Holland Ja^s Coupland then a Line of Ja^s Couplands Jno Holland in the press. of Robt Holand Ja^s Coupland then a Line of Ja^s Coupland Wi^m Holland in the press of Wi^m Coupland Jno Holland then A Line of Wim Hollands Jno Holland in the press of Ja^s Coupland Wim Coupland then A Line of Gabriel Rawls Jno Rawls in the press of Wi^m Coupland Wim Holland then A Line of Mosses Brewer Gabriel Rawls in the press Two Last men

James Coupland
Mosses Brewer

[152]

In Obedience to An order of Vestry Dated Septemb^r the 17 1759 We the Subscribers have Procession^d all the Bounds of Land Mention^d in the Said Order Except Mills Riddicks Swamp Land which Cannot be done now it is so Wett

The Line Between Jotham Lassater and James Booth Jotham Lassater & James Booth presst

The Line between Ja^s Booth & Henry Riddick Ja^s Booth Henry Riddick Mills Riddick And John Price press^t The Line between Henry Riddick & Mills Riddick Henry Riddick Mills Riddick James Booth and John Price press

The Line between Mills Riddick & William Stallings Mills Riddick & Wm Stallings press

The Line Between Mills Riddick & Josiah Riddick Mills Riddick Press^t

The Line between Mills Riddick & Mosses Riddick Mills Riddick & Moses Riddick prest

The Line Between Mills Riddick & Isaac Lassater Mills Riddick & Isaac Lassater press^t

The Line Between Mills Riddick & Joseph Booth Mills Riddick Pressent

The Line Between James Stalling & Jo^s Stallings James [&] Joseph Stallings & Hezikiah Riddick Pres^t

The Line Between Jo^s Stallings & Hezikiah Riddick Jo^s Stallings & Hezakiah Riddick prest

The Line Between Hezakiah Riddick & Williss Riddick Williss Riddick press^t

The Line Between Williss Riddick & J^{no} Camwell Williss Riddick press^t

The Line Between Jno Cambwell & Aaron Lassater Aaron Lassater press^t

The Line Between J^{no} Cambwell & Josiah Riddick Mills Riddick & David Gwin press^t

The Line Between Josiah Riddick & Edward Bates Aaron Lassater & Thos Feild prest

The Line Between Aaron Lassater & Mills Riddick Aaron Lassater & Mills Riddick press^t

The Line Between Mills Riddick & Edward Bates Mills Riddick Aaron Lasater & Thos feild prest

The Line Between Wm Woodward & Daniel Pugh Wm Woodward Aaron Lassater Robert Noble & David Brown And Thos Feild Pressent

The Line Between Wm Woodward & Ester Pugh Wm Woodward Aaron Lassater Thos feild and David Brown Pressent

The Line Between Ester Pugh and Edward Bates Aaron Lassater and Thos Feild Pressent

John Cambwell
William Stallings

[153]

In Obedience to An order of Vestry Bearing Date Septem^{br} the 17th 1759 We have procession^d all the Lands in our Bounds Between the following Persons

A Line Between Christopher Norfleet Assia Duke Present both parties

A Line Mrs Meade & James March press^t John Driver Josiah Vaughan Thos Coulden A Line Between W^{im} Red & Ja^s March both parties press & Mansfeild Tarnington and Josiah Vaughan prest

A Line Between John Spight and Mansfeild Tarnington Press^t Wim Red & Ja^s March

A Line Between Between [sic] Mansfeild Tarnington & John Norfleet Pressent Both parties & Wim Red and James March

A Line Between Abraham Carnal and W^{im} Red prest Wim Red & Whitaker Red

A Line Between John Ballard & Jo^s Skiner pressent both parties

A Line Between James March and Mansfeild Tarnington present the Parties and W^{im} Waters Junr

A Line Between Thos Newby & Christopher Norfleet presst Christopher Norfleet Asia Duke And William Savage

A Line Between John Demby & Henry Gwin both parties Pressent

A Line Between Jo^s Skiner & Christopher Norfleet Aaron Duke And Christopher Norfleet Pressent

A Line Between Asia Duke and Joseph Skiner Pressent Christopher Norfleet and Asia Duke

John Ballard
Joseph Skiner

[154]

According To an Order of Vestry Dated September the 17 1759 We the Subscribers have Procession^d the Bounds of Land Betwixt J^{no} Downing And Elisha Norfleet press^t Elisha Norfleet John Best Likewise Betwixt J^{no} Richards And Mary Doughtie prest Mary Doughtie John Richards Elisha Norfleet John Best Likewise Betwixt John Best and John Downing press^t J^{no} Best Elisha Norfleet John Best Junr Likewise Betwixt John Best & Thos Sanders Pressent John Best Thos Sanders Elisha Norfleet Likewise Betwixt Elisha Norfleet and Thos Sanders John Best John Best Junr Likewise Betwixt Elisha Norfleet & W^{im} Norfleet pressent Elisha Norfleet

W:^m Norfleet John Best Tho:^s Norfleet John Jones Likewise betwixt Tho:^s Norfleet & William Norfleet pressent Tho:^s Norfleet & W:^m Norfleet John Jones John Best Likewise betwixt Tho:^s Norfleet and Christopher Norfleet pressent Tho:^s Norfleet Elisha Norfleet John Jones Likewise betwixt John Jones and John Streater Pressent John Jones & John Best Jun:^r Likewise betwixt John Streater & W:^m Norfleet pressent W:^m Norfleet John Jones John Best Kedar Webb Likewise betwixt George Frith & Tho:^s Sanders press Tho:^s Sanders Kedar Webb John Best Jun:^r Likewise betwixt Tho:^s Sumner & Samuel Jordan Pressent Tho:^s Sumner Samuel Jordan W:^m Babb Tho:^s Norfleet Likewise Betwixt Tho:^s Sumner and Tho:^s Norfleet pressent Tho:^s Sumner Tho:^s[78] Norfleet Christopher Norfleet Kedar Best Likewise betwixt Tho:^s Sumner & David Rice present W:^m Ward Tho:^s Sumner Likewise Betwixt Christopher Norfleet and Jerimiah Godwin press:^t Christo:^o Norfleet Wim Babb Likewise betwixt Jerimiah Godwin & Richard Webb press:^t Richard Webb W:^m Ward Wim Babb Likewise betwixt Jerimiah Godwin & Henning Temptey Pressent Richard Webb W:^m Ward Likewise betwixt Richard Webb and W:^m Ward present Richard Webb & W:^m Ward Likewise betwixt Richard Webb And W:^m Babb pressent Richard Webb & W:^m Babb W:^m Ward Likewise Betwixt Richard Webb & Edward Moore press:^t Richard Webb Edward Moore Wim Babb Likewise betwixt Richard Webb & Jer. Godwin Pressent Richard Webb W:^m Ward Likewise betwixt Jer. Godwin & Hening Tembtey pres:^t W:^m Ward Likewise betwixt Edward Moore and Jer. Godwin press:^t Wim. Ward Likewise betwixt Hening Tembtey & Edward Moore Press:^t Wim Ward Likewise betwixt Hening Tembtey & Jonathan Weaver Press:^t John Jones Likewise betwixt Edward Moore & Jonathan Weaver prest John Jones Likewise betwixt Johnathan Weaver & John Streater pres. John Jones

          Edward Moore
          William Norfleet

[155]

In obedience To an ord:^r of Vestry Held at Suffolk Town September the 17 1759 To us Directed we the Subscribers have Procession:^d all the

---

[78] The paper at this spot is blotched, and the two middle letters of this abbreviated name are almost illegible as if erasure might have been intended.

Land Marks Betwixt the Several Freeholders Within the District Mention^d in the S^d order As Under Stated Viz No: 22 No Objection

Im: Proprietors Names	Person Pressent
Dempsey Sumner	John Martain
Nickolas Harmon	Samuel Smith
Samuel Smith	Nickholas Harmon
Moses Harrel	Samuel Smith
John Smith	Samuel Smith & Steaven
Job Harrell	Samuel Smith & Steaven
Edward Baker	Samuel Smith
Richard Tayloe	
Saml Smith Son of Saml	
William Pearce	
Robert Peal	Joseph Parker
Ephraim Peal	Jacob Sumner
Ephraim Peal Junr	Joseph Peel
John Baker	Joseph Peel
Dempsy Sumner Exce^tr	
To Daihea Gorley	Kedar Raiby
Kedar Raiby	Jacob Sumner
Jacob Sumner	Jacob Sumner Kedar Raiby
Thos Frazier	Joseph Parker
Pharoh phelps	Joseph Parker
Dempsey Sumner	
Jesse Peal	

February the 2^d 1760
Job Harrell
John Baker

[156]

In Obedience to an order of Vestry Held at Suffolk Town Septem^br 17th 1759 We the Subscribers have been and Procession^d all the Lands in our District but John Wigins^s and he hath Stopt us and the Reason he does Say that he will go as his Draft of his Land does go for Somebody have Made a New Line betwixt Maj^r Willis Riddick and he Refuseth And forwarns us of doing of it and we do hereby Certify the same from Under our hands this the first day of January 1760

Samuel Sumner   Thos Harrell

William Sumner
John Night
John Raiby
Nickolas Raiby
Dempsey Wigins
Micajah Eliss
Henry Griffin
Lemuel Raiby
Thomas Brumton

Joseph Griffin
John Harrell
Joseph Peel
William Lamb
George Banns

James Raiby
Joseph Hubbard

[157]

In Obedience to an Order of Vestry held at Suffolk Town Septem^{br} 17 1759 To us Directed we the Subscribers have Procession^d all the Land Marks between the Several free holders within the District Mention^d in the Said Order under Certified

Im Proprioter^s Names	Persons Pressent
Adam Harrell	John Hare
John Hare	Adam Harrell
William Rawls	John Hare
James Harrell^s	William Bird
Edmund Birds	William Bird
Luke Harrells	James Harrell
William Birds	James Harrell
Charity Birds	William Bird
John Bird Son of W^m	John Bird
Jacob Bird	Jacob Bird
Richard Parker	
Aaron Bird	
Samuel Horton	
Jonathan Taylor	Edward Baker
Richard Taylor	Jonathan Taylor
Edward Baker	Johnathan Taylor
John Harrell	James Harrell
Joseph Smith	Samuel Baker
John Smith	Samuel Baker
	James Baker

James Baker   James Baker
Samuel Baker   James Baker
Job Harrell Junr   John Porter
Ann Webb
Soloman Rawls   Frances Duke
William Sumner   Joseph Baker
John Porter   Thomas Duke
Joseph Baker   Frances Duke
Frances Duke
Phillip Draper   Edward Perry
Thomas Duke
Thomas Guen

    No: 21 No Objection^s Made Febuary the 2 1760
          Joseph Smith
          Job Harrell jun^r

[158]

 Persuant to An Order of Vestry to us Directed we have Procesion^d & renew^d The Marks of the following Lands Viz A Line Between Jesse Battle & Elisha Ballard A Line Between Hening Tembtey & Elisha Ballard Pressent Nathaniel Pruden Richard Hynes & Wim Wright A Line Between Henry Wright & Hening Tembtey & Nathaniel Pruden And A Line Between Henry Wright & Nathaniel Pruden pressent Wi^m Moore Richard Hynes James Hynes & Wi^m Wright A Line Between Henry Wright & Ja^s Hynes and A pattent Line Between Abraham Velines And Richard Hynes and the Cross or Divideing Line Between Richard Hynes & Abraham Velines A Line between Mrs Meade & Ja^s March from Hunter^s Mill Swamp down by Josiah Vaughans press Josiah Riddick Wi^m Moore & Jos^h Gwin Three Lines Between John Ashburns Orphan And John March pressent Hening Tembtey & Josiah Gwin Two Lines between Ashburn^s Orphan and James March down to March & Ballards Corner pressent Hening Tembtey Josiah Gwin & Wi^m Moore A Line between Elisha Ballard & Ashburn^s Orphan to Dixon^s Old Corner pressent Hening Tembtey Wi^m Moore Elisha Ashbourn And James March A Line between Hening Tembtey & Nathaniel pruden Pressent Josiah Riddick Wi^m Moore & Elisha Ashbourn A Line between Abraham Velines & Ashburn^s Orphan & A short Line Between Elisha Ashburn & Veline^s & between Elisha

Ashburn & Henry Best And Between Elisha Ashburn & Ashburn^s Orphan And between Said Orphan and Mrs Meade to a Corner Small Hickory Pressent W^{im} Moore Josiah Vaughan James March & Others A Line Between Abraham Velines & Henry Best Pressent W^{im} Moore & Josiah Gwin A Line between W^{im} Moore & Thos Gwin Also the Line between Wim Moore & Mrs Meade and a Line between Mrs Meade and Thos Gwin press^t Josiah Gwin A Line between John Gwin & Josiah Gwin press^t Wim Moore & Wim Gwin A Line Between Josiah Gwin and Ashburns Orphan pressent Thos Gwin A Line between Benjamain Forset & Jesse Battle & Between Benjamain Forset & Elisha Ballard & between Benjamain Forset Frances Forset And between Benjamain Forset & Ja^s March Also Between James March & Frances Forset pressent James Letort And James March

Ballard & Battles return Processioning

[159]

Thomas Shivers & James Norfleet

A Line between Mrs Meade & John Pender Pender Pressent
A Line between John Pender & Mrs Crawford Pender Pressent
A Line between J^{no} Pender & Abraham Booth Pender Pressent
A Line Between Thos Shivers & Willis Parker
A Line Between Mrs Mead & J^{no} Lawrence Jethro Dardan present
A Line Between Paul Lawrence & George Lawrence Paul Pressent
A Line Between J^{no} Lawrence & George Lawrence J^{no} Pressent
A Line Between Capt Baker & Jesse Riddick
A Line Between J^{no} Lawrence & George Lawrence J^{no} Pressent
A Line Between James Norfleet & George Lawrence
A Line Between John Lawrence & Thos Shivers
A Line Between Jesse Riddick & Kedar Parker
A Line Between Thos Shivers and the King
A Line Between Jacob Dardan and the King
A Line Between Virginia & Carroliner
A Line Between Capt William Baker & John Lawrence

In Obedience to An Order of Vestry Held September the 17th 1759 We the Subscribers Apointed to Procession the Land in Patersons Neck Have Met and Procession^d all the Land in the said Bounds Except a Small Line between George Frith & Thos Milner Which they A Gree to make them selves No Line being to found Like wise A Line Between Aaron Allmand & the Land of Lucy No body Apearing for Lucy Likewise the Line between Joseph Dardan & Lucy No one Apearing for Lucy

William Wilkinson
Aaron Allmand

[160]

Persuant To An Order of Vestry Dated Septemb^r the 17th 1759 That we the Procession^{rs} (Edward Cary & William Hart) Have met And Procession^d all the Bounds of Lands in our Precints in peaceable Quiet Posscon

Simon Everits Land Procession^d in the pressence of Jno pope & Jo^s Cearle

John Pope^s Land Procession^d in the pressence of Simon Everit & Moses Hart

Robert Lawrence Land Procession^d in the pressence of Robt Car & John Everit

Joseph Cearl^s Land Procession^d in the pressence of Robt Lawrence Moses Hart

Daniel William^s Land Procession^d in the pressence of George William^s & Robt Lawrence

George Williams Land Procession^d in the pressence of Robt Lawrence & Jo^s Cearl

Moses Harts Land Procession^d in the pressence of John Hart & Robt Carr

John Harts Land Procession^d in the pressence of Benj Cary Moses Hart

William Harts Land Proces^d in the pressence Robt Car & John Everit

Edward Cary^s Land Proces^d in the pressence of Moses Hart & John Hart

James Cary^s Land Process^d in the pressence of John Hart & Moses Hart.

John Glovers Land Proces^d in the pressence of John Hart & Moses Hart

William Wiggin^s Land process^d in the pressence of Jo^s Cearl & George Williams

John Everits Land process^d in the pressence of Robt Lawrence Robt Carr

Exum Lewis Land process^d in the pressence of John Everit & Simon Everit

Martha Holand Land process^d in the pressence of Jo^s Cearl & Robt Carr

March the 8th 1760   Edward Cary
                            William Hart

[161]

Persuant to An Order of Vestry Dated Septemb^r the 17th 1759 That we the Processioners Between Black Water & Notaway River In Nansemond County (Jacob Dardan And James Carr have Met and Procession^d all the Bounds of Land in our precints In peacable & Quiet procession

   Daniel Battens Land Procession^d in the pressence of Thos Edwards

   William Hynes^s Land Process^d in the pressence of Richard Williams & Moses Dardan

   Thos Edwards Land Process^d in the pressence of Richard Williams & Mosses Dardan

   Richard William^s Land Process^d in the pressence of Wm Hynes & Mosses Dardan

   Charles binses [?][79] Land Not Procession^d by the Reason he did not Apear to Shew the Line

   Robt Carr^s Land Process^d in the Pressence of Richard William^s & Michael daughtrie

   Jacob Dardans Land Process^d in the Pressence of Richard Williams & Robt Carr

   Mosses Dardans Land Process^d in the Pressence of Robt Carr & Richard Williams

   John Bennets Land Process^d in the Pressence of Richard Williams & Thos Edwards

   Michael Daughtries Land Process^d in the Pressence of Mosses Dardan & Richard Williams

   James Carr^s Land Process^d in the Pressence of Robert Carr

   Charles Birdsong^s Land Process^d in the pressence Joshua Gardener & Matthew Gardener

   James Gardeners Land Process^d in the Pressence of Holand Dardan & Robert Dardan

---

[79] Probably intended for Bins.

Joshua Gardeners Land Process^d in the Pressence of Holand Dardan & Matthew Gardener

Matthew Gardeners Land Process^d in the Pressence of James Gardener & Robert Dardan

Jonathan Godwins Land Process^d in the Pressence of Jethro Dardan & Joshua Gardener

George Lawrence^s Land Process^d in the Pressence of Michael Daughtrie & Holand Dardan

Mary Dardans Land Process^d In the pressence of Matthew Gardener Holand Dardan[80]

Ann Dardans Land Procession^d In the Pressence of Matthew Gardener and Robert Dardan[81]

March the 8th 1759[82]   Jacob Dardan
                                   James Carr

[162]

At A Vestry Held In Suffolk Town Novemb^r the 28 1760 For the up^r Parrish of Nansemond

Pressent John Rawls Gen^t Church Warden

    Josiah Riddick   Mills Riddick
    Williss Riddick   William Moore   } Gent^m Vestrymen
    Hening Tembtey   Thos Winbourn
    Aded James Gibson

To the Revd William Webb his Salary for ¾ of the Year	15210
To William Shekelton Clark of Holy Neck Chapel	1000
To Aaron Allmand D^o of Suffolk Church	2000
To D^o An alowance of 4 per ct	80
To Nickolas Maget D^o of Notaway Chapel	1000
To John Genkins Sexton of Sumerton	200
To Wi^m Wigins D^o at Notaway	200
To Thos Johnson D^o at Suffolk Church	800
To Richard Hynes for Boarding Ann Hynes	1000

---

[80] This entry, evidently omitted in order, is written before a brace at the left of the names of the processioners.

[81] This entry, evidently omitted in order, is written before a brace at the left of the names of the processioners.

[82] This date should be 1760.

To Thos Godwin for Insolvents after the Last Years Depossitum Deducted	897
To be sold by the Church Wardens at July Court for Cash	25000
	47387
To the Collector at 6 per ct	2843
	50230

Tis Ordered that James Turner Gent Do Collect from Every Thithable in this Parrish 34 pound of Tobacco Per Thithable on 1490 Thithes is   50660
And therewith Discharge the Parrish Debts this day Brought in

Depossitum due to the Parrish   430
for Which the Sherreff is to Account for At the Laying the Next Parrish Leivie

Signd Josiah Riddick

[163]

The Uper Parrish Dr In Cash 1760

	£ s d
To Sarah Watkins for one Year & Ten Months Hier at the Poors house at £5 per Year & other Services	9 : 11 : 4
To Lemuel Riddick for Sundries for the poors house	3 : 1 : 3
To John Gwin for Boarding Wilson and Makeing a Lader for the Church	7 : 2 : 2
To Do for Makeing Cloths for Wilson	0 : 10 : 6
To Richard Hynes for makeing 2 Shifts for Ann Hynes	0 : 2 : 6
To Docktor Tyre his Account	8 : 15 : 9
To Do for Medicines for Bowsers Wife from the Lower parrish	14 : 16 : 1½
To William Horton for Nursing a poor Woman	1 : 10
To Hening Tembtey for Burrying A poor Woman	2 : 10
To William Howel for Boarding a poor Child	2 : 10
To the Widdow Perrit a poor Woman	1 : 10
To John Howel for Keeping a poor Child	1 : 10
To Majr Williss Riddick for 2 Bl Pork omited Last year	5 : 10
To the Revd Mr Colmer for a Sermon Preachd in the Church	2 : 3 : 4

To Ephraim Lawrence for ferrying over Notaway one Year   3 : 0 : 0

£64 : 2 : 11½

Mary Webb Administratrix of Richard Webb Late Church Warden rendered in his Account for Sundries Deliver^d the Poor in his Life time and the Ball. is due To the Parrish   64 : 9 : 7

Tis Ordered that the said Administratrix do pay the said Ball To Josiah Riddick

Josiah Riddick Gent is chosen Church Warden in the room of Richard Webb Deceas^d till Easter Next

Capt Edward Riddick is Chosen a Vestry man in the room of Richard Webb Deceas^d

Tis Ordered that James Gibson Jacob Sumner Mills Riddick do Veiw the Chapel at Norfleets And See Wheather it be done Agreeable to the Articles

Tis ordered that the Church Wardens do Aply to Mr Agnew and a Gree with him to Preach in our Church & Chapels

                 Signd Josiah Riddick Church Warden

Truly Entered by Aaron Allmand Clk Vestry

[164]

At A Vestry Held for the Uper Parrish of Nansemond County at the Court House December the 8th 1760

Pressent Lemuel Riddick   Josiah Riddick
         Mills Riddick   Willis Riddick
         Hening Tembtey   William Baker   } Gent Vestry Men
         William Moore   James Gibson
         & Jacob Sumner

The Revd Patrick Lunan is Receiv^d by this Vestry As Minister of this Parrish it is A Greed of by the Said Minister and Vestry that he Preach & Preform Divine Service Four times A Year at Notaway Chapel and Four times A Year at the Cyphres Chapel And the Rest of the year To Preach Two Sundays at Suffok Church Successively And one at the Holy

Neck Chapell and that Chrismas And Good Friday he Preach at Suffolk Church

>Patrick Lunan
>Lemuel Riddick
>Josiah Riddick
>Henning Tembtey
>W Baker
>W^im Moore
>Jacob Sumner
>Mills Riddick
>Williss Riddick

Truly Entered by Aaron Allmand Clk. Vestry

[165]

At A Vestry Held at Belsons Wrights Novembr. the 12th 1761 For the uper Parrish of Nansemond

Pressent The Revd Patrick Lunan
Josiah Riddick & John Rawls Gent Church Wardens
Lemuel Riddick Mills Riddick
Jacob Sumner   Thos Winbourn } Gen^t Vestry Men
James Gibson & W^im. Moore

To the Revd Patrick Lunan his Salary	16000
To D^o An Alowance of 4 per ct for Caskue & D^o for Srinkage	1280
To D^o An A Lowance for a Gleab	3000
To Nickolas Maget Clark of Notaway Chapel	1000
To Wim Shekelton D^o of Holy Neck	1000
To Aaron Allmand D^o of Suffolk Church And Keeper of the parrish Register	2000
To D^o An A Lowance of 4 per ct	80
To Thos Johnson Sexton of Suffolk Church	800
To John Jenkins D^o of Holy Neck Chapel And Keeping the Well Clean	250
To D^o for Puting 2 Blocks in the Chapel And finding a Bucket	30
To W^im Wigins Sexton of Notaway Chapel	200
To John Gwin for Boarding and Makeing Clothes for Wilson	900
	26540

This Vestry is Adjournd till Saturday The 12th of December[83]
                               Signd Patrick Lunan

[166]

At A Vestry Held at Belson Wrights Febuary the 12th 1761[84] To finish Laying the Parrish Livie (Begun Novembr the 12th 1761

Pressent Josiah Riddick & John Rawls Gent Ch: Wardns

Lemuel Riddick   Mills Riddick
Williss Riddick   Hening Tembtey   } Gent Vestry Men
Wim. Moore   James Gibson

	Pd Tobacco
Brought over	26540
To Richard Hynes for finding Some Necessasaries For Ann Hynes	300
To William Harrisson Junr a Levie over Chargd Last year	34
To the Sherreiff for Insolvents After deducting the Last years Depossitum	964
To be Sold by the Church Wardens at July Court For Cash	10000
	37838
To the Collector at 6 per Ct	2270
The Whole Parrish Debts in Tobacco Is	40108
Tis Ordered that James Turner Sherrff do Collect from Every thithable in this Parrish 29 pounds of Tobacco per thiheable on 1429 thithes is	41441
And therewith Discharge the parrish Creddittors	
Depossitum due to the Parrish	1333

Which the Sherrff is to Account for at the Laying the Next Parrish Levie
                               Signd Josiah Riddick Ch: Warden

---

[83] The next meeting, dated February 12, 1761 (*i. e.* 1762), which fell on Friday, carried on the business begun at this meeting. See following footnote.

[84] See footnote 83. The clerk apparently wrote 1762 and then erased and changed the last figure. It seems unlikely that he would have made the mistake of writing "Febuary" if the meeting had indeed been held on Saturday, December 12, 1761, unless, perhaps, he inadvertently gave the month of a delayed writing up of the book.

[167]
    Dr The Uper Parrish In Cash 1761

	£	s	d
To Wills Cowper for Cloathing Willm Powle	3	7	8
To James Gibson Paid a Woman for Cureing Powles Leg	2	0	0
To Dock^r Cohown for Nursing Eliza Booths Leg And other Services	14	11	9
To Lemuel Riddick Paid Daniel Pugh for A Lot Joyning the Church	12	10	0
To John Rawls as per his Account	1	10	0

Mr Josiah Riddick Church Warden rendred in his Account and the Ball is due to the Parrish £61 : 1 : 2

To Richard Hynes for Sundries for Ann hynes & Burying her	2	0	0
Tis Ordered that the Church Wardens do pay To David Sumner on Account of Christain Miles A Poor Woman for her Back Rent the Sum of	5	14	0
To Jacob Brantley for Keeping the Ferry Over Notaway one year	3	0	0
The Whole Parrish Debts in Cash is	£44	13	5
By Cash in Mr Josiah Riddicks hands	61	1	2
Ball Due to the Parrish	16	7	9

Benjamain Baker is Chosen A Vestry Man in the Room of Wim. Baker Deceas^d

                Signd Josiah Riddick Church Warden
Truly Enterd by Aaron Allmand Clk Vestry

[168]

At A Vestry Held at the house of Edmund Belson Wrights Saturday the 24th of April 1762

Pressent Hening Tembtey Mills Riddick
              Josiah Riddick   Willis Riddick   Gen^t Vestry Men
              Edward Riddick James Gibson
              Lemuel Riddick

James Gibson & Edward Riddick are Chosen Church Wardens Till Easter Next

Josiah Riddick Late Church Warden Rendred In an Account of Ten Shillings in his hands Which he Receiv^d for Swearing Ordered the Same be Paid to Mary Holland

Mr James Turner who was Appointed to Collect The Parrish Leivies on Giveing Bond & Security for the preformance Died without Giveing Such Bond Therefore Ordered that Samuel Swan Collect the Parrish Leivie on Giveing Bond & Security According to Law to the Church Wardens

    Coppy Test   James Gibson
        Aaron Allmand Clk Vestry   Edward Riddick

[169]

At A Vestry Held at Belson Wrights in Suffolk Town November the 15th 1762 For the Uper parrish of Nansemond

Pres^t James Gibson & Edward Riddick   Church Wardens
    Josiah Riddick   William Moore
    Benjamain Baker   Thos Winbourn   Gent. Vestry Men
    & Jacob Sumner

To the Revd Patrick Lunan his Salary	16000
To D^o an Alowance of 4 per Ct for Caskue & D^o for Srinkage	1280
To D^o An a Lowance for a Gleabe	3000
To Nickholas Maget Clk of Notaway Chapel	1000
To W^{im} Shekelton D^o of Holy Neck Chapel	1000
To Aaron Allmand D^o of Suffolk Church & Keeper of The parrish Register	2000
To D^o An Alowance of 4 per Ct	80
To John Cambel D^o at the Cyprus Chapel 14 Months at a thousand a Year	1200
To Thos Johnson Sexton of Suffolk Church	800
To John Genkins D^o of holy Neck & Cleaning the Well	250
To Wim Wigins D^o of Notaway Chapel	200
To Robt Booth D^o of the Cyprus 14 Months at 200 a Year	240
To John Gwin for Boarding Wilson	225
	27275
To be Sold by the Ch: Wardens at July Court for Cash	13000
	40275

By the Last Years Depossitum	1333	
To the Late Sherreiff for Insolvents	831	
Ball: Due to the parrish from the late Sherreiff	502	502
		39773
To the Collector at 6 per Ct		2387
		42160

Tis Ordered that Wim Moore Sherreiff do Collect
From Every thitheable in this parrish 29 pounds of
Tobacco per thitheable on 1465 thithes is   42485
And therewith Discharge the parrish Creddittors First
Giveing Bond & Security as Useal to the Church Warden[s]
    Depossitum Due to the parrish   325

        Signd James Gibson   Edward Riddick

[170 blank][85]

[171]

The Uper Parrish D[r] In Cash Novemb[r] the 15th 1762

	£	s
To Robt Booth for Blocking up the Chapel & Cuting down The Bushes	0 : 15 : 0	
To Richard Tayloe for Nursing a Sick Man	2 : 0 : 0	
To Ezekiah Norfleet for diging a Well at the Cyprus Chapel	1 : 0 : 0	
To Dock[r] Cohoon for Medicines & Attendance at the poors house	10 : 9 : 6	
To Jesse Jones for Burying A poor Man	1 : 10 : 0	
To Brittain Jones for Keeping the Ferry Over Notaway	3 : 0 : 0	
To John Hamilton for Keeping the orphans of Sarah Hamilton and his own Necessities	5 : 0 : 0	
	23 : 14 : 6	
By M[r] Josiah Riddick Late Ch: Warden rendred In his Account & the Ball Due to the parrish is	2 : 3 : 1½	

---

[85] The right-hand margin of this page is ruled with three vertical lines as if the page was intended for a financial statement, perhaps the one following which occurs with similar lines and better spacing on p. [171] of the original.

By Mr James Gibson pres^t Ch: Warden rendred in
his Account With the Tobacco that was Sold Last Yeare
And the Ball Due to the parrish is   8 : 14 : 3

$$ 10 : 17 : 4\tfrac{1}{2}$$
The Parrish is Indebted   12 : 17 : 1½

Tis Ordered that the Money due to the parrish from Mr Josiah Riddick be paid to the pres^t Ch: Wardens

Tis Ordered that if Any person should apply as an Organist and Should be takein in upon Subscription that the Ch: Wardens do apply to a proper person to put The Organ in Order

                      Signd James Gibson   Edward Riddick

Truly Entered by Aaron Allmand Clk Vestry

[172]

At a Vestry held in Suffolk Town Tuesday the 25th Octr 1763 for Appointing Processioners for the Different Districts in the upper Parish of Nansemond

Present
{
Ja^s Gibson Edwd Riddick Gen^t Chuc. War
The Revd Pat^r Lunan, Lem^l Riddick
Mills Riddick, Josiah Riddick
Willis Riddick, Henning Tembte
William Moore, Gen^t Vest^y Men
}

Order'd that Saml Cohoon, & Thos Harrison Procession all the Bounds of Lands N° 1 accord^g to Law

Ordered that Kedar Webb, & Peter Mason Procession all the Bounds of Lands N° 2 according to Law

Order'd that Thos Sumner, & Kedar Best Procession all the Bounds of Land N° 3 according to Law

Order'd that William Wilkinson, & Aaron Allmand procession all the Bounds of Lands N° 4 according to Law

Ordered that Thos Godwin & John Barkley processⁿ all the Bounds of Land N° 5 accord^g to Law

Ordered that Benja^a Forset, & Elisha Ballad processⁿ all the Bounds of Land N° 6 according to Law

Ordered that Willm King, & J^{no} Harrison procession all the Bounds of Land N° 7 according to Law

Ordered that Tho⁵ Winbourn & Absalom Beaman process︠n︡ all the Bounds of Land N⁰ 8 according to Law

Ordered that Will︠m︡ Rawls & Jn⁰ Harrel procession all the Bounds of Land N⁰ 9 according to Law

Ordered that Ja⁵ Rawls & Arth︠r︡ Jones procession all the Bounds of Land N⁰ 10 according to Law

[173]

Order'd that Tho⁵ Shivers, & Kedar Parker procession all the Bounds of Land N⁰ 11 according to Law

Order'd that Sam︠l︡ Watson & Jn⁰ Jenkins jun︠r︡ Process︠n︡ all the Bounds of Land N⁰ 12 according to Law

Order'd that Elisha Coupland & Jn⁰ Everitt procession all the Bounds of Land N⁰ 13 according to Law

Order'd that Ja⁵ Holland & Joseph Holland process︠n︡ all the Bounds of Land N⁰ 14 according to Law

Order'd that Moses Dardan, & Ja⁵ Carr procession all the Bounds of Lands N⁰ 15 according to Law

Order'd that Dan︠l︡ Williams & Joseph Curl Procession all the Bounds of Lands N⁰ 16 according to Law

Order'd that Dan︠l︡ Holland & Jn⁰ Flemming Procession all the Bounds of Lands N⁰ 17 according to Law

Order'd that Ja⁵ Purvis, & Will︠m︡ Cross Procession all the Bounds of Lands N⁰ 18 according to Law

Order'd that Solomon Riddick & Hump︠y︡ Griffin Process︠n︡ all the Bounds of Lands N⁰ 19 according to Law

Ordered that Jacob Sumner, & Henry Griffin Process︠n︡ all the Bounds of Lands N⁰ 20 according to Law

Order'd that Jeseph Baker, & Fran⁵ Duke Procession all the Bounds of Lands N⁰ 21 according to Law

Order'd that Rich︠d︡ Taylor, & Edw︠d︡ Baker Procession all the Bounds of Lands N⁰ 22 according to Law

Ordered that John Ballad & Will︠m︡ Red Procession all the Bounds of Lands N⁰ 23 according to Law

Order'd that Will︠m︡ Roundtree & Dan︠l︡ Lassiter Procession all the Bounds of Lands N⁰ 24 according to Law

Order'd that Matthew Parker, & Jacob Price procession all the Bounds of Lands N° 25 According to Law

[174]

Order'd that Jn° Horton & Jos. Parker Procession all the Bounds of Lands N° 26 according to Law

Order'd that Henry Bates & Willis Riddick Procession all the Bounds of Lands N° 27 according to Law

Order'd that Abraham Parker & Hardy Parker process^n all the Bounds of Land N° 28 According to Law

Sign'd { Pat^r Lunan / Ja^s Gibson / Edwd Riddick

Truely entered by Aaron Allmand Clk Vestry

[175]

At a Vestry held at Edmond B. Wrights in Suffolk January the 7th 1764 for the upper parrish of Nansem^d County

Present.   James Gibson   Gen^t Ch: Warden
            Lemuel Riddick   Williss Riddick
            Hening Tembtey   Josiah Riddick   } Gen^t Vestry men
            Benj^a Baker   Mills Riddick

To the Revd Patrick Lunan his Salary	16000
To D° An Allowance of 4 per Ct for Caskue & D° for Srinkage	1280
To D° An Allowance for A Gleab	3000
To Nicholas Maget Clk of Notaway Chapel	1000
To Wm Shekelton D° of Sumerton D°	1000
To Aaron Allmand D° of Suffolk Church And Keeper of the parish register	2000
To D° An alowance of 4 per Ct	80
To John Cambwel Clk of the Cyprus Chapell	1000
To Thos. Johnson Sexton of Suffolk Church	800
To John Jenkens D° at Holy Neck & Cleaning the Well	250
To W^m. Wigins D° at Notaway Chapell	200
To Robt Booth D° at the Cyprus D°	200
	26810

To be Sold by the Ch: Wardens at July Court for Cash	30000
	56810
By Last Years Depossitum	325
	56485
To the Collector at 6 per Ct After deducting the Last Years depossitum	3389
The parrish Debts	59874

Tis Ordered that the Church Wardens or Any other person whom they Shall Apoint after given Bond & Security as Useal do Collect from Every thitheable in this Parrish 40 pounds of Tobacco per thithe on 1501 Thithes Amounts To   60040

And therewith Discharge the parish Creddittors

Depossitum Due to the parish   166

[176]

Dr The Uper parish in Cash 1763

To John Jenkins for washing the Cirples	£ 0..2..6
To Samuel Wallis for John Orams Schooling & Wood	2..8..2
To Dock. Cohoon for Medicines & Attendance of Several poor persons &[86]	30..0..0
To Thos Gewin for Boarding Eliza Booth And Cureing her foot	5..0..0
To Abraham Spencer for Attendance & Dressing John Hobbys Leg	3..0..0
To Dock^r Jessey Brown for Salavateing Wm Pool & Eliz^a Haket &c If he will fully discharge his Account	25..0..0
To John Jones for Cleaning & takeing out the bruises out of the Comunion plate And Mending the Organ pipes	1..6..0
To Hanah Cotten for Nursing & dressing Eliz^a Hakets Leg	5..0..0
To Eliz^a Hanum for Cureing Kez Oram	2..10..0

---

[86] Doubtless intended for "&c".

To John Hamilton a poor man	6..0..0
To Mary Holan A poor Woman	3..0..0
To Christain Miles Towards paying her Rents &c	6..0..0
To Mary Hodey towards Maintaing her Child	2..0..0
To Anabel Williss a poor Woman	3..0..0
To Sarah rice for Keeping Susanah Waff	1..10..0
Mr James Gibson rendred in his Account As Church Warden and of the Tobacco Which was Sold Last Year And for Sundries Deliver^d the poor And the Ball. Due to him is	55..6..9
	£151..3..5

Sign^d James Gibson Ch: Warden

Truly Enter^d by Aaron Allmand Clk Vestry

[177]

In Obedience to An Order of Vestry Bearing Date October the 25th 1763 Begining at waters Old Feild
1 Line between Capt. Tembtey & Michael King
1 Between Michael King & Elisha Balard
1 Between Michael King & John King
1 Between Michael King & Jessey King
1 Between Wim King & Michael King
1 Between Michael King & John Butler
    In the press of John Butler Jessey King
1 Between Wm More & John Butler
1 Betwixt Wm More & Abraham Lewis
1 Betwixt Abraham Lewis & John Butler
1 Betwixt Abraham Lewis & Michael King
1 Betwixt Abraham Lewis & Jessey King
1 Betwixt John King & Josiah Vaughan
1 Betwixt Elisha Balard & Josiah Vaughan
1 Betwixt Henry Butler & Josiah Vaughan
    the people press^t Wm More John Butler Abraham Lewis Jo^s Vaughn
1 Betwixt Lemuel Holand Henry Butler
1 Betwixt Harisson sen^r & Henry Butler
1 Betwixt John Harisson Junr & Wm Beslee

The people pressent Lam. Holand & Henry Butler
1 Betwixt John pearce & Peter Butler
1 Betwixt Thos pearce & Peter Butler
1 Betwixt John pearce & Peter Butler
1 Betwixt John Harisson & Thos Pearce
1 Betwixt Jessey King & John Pearce
1 Betwixt Jessey King & Marthew pearce
1 Betwixt Marthew Pearce & Abraham Lewis
1 Betwixt Wim More & Thos Pearce
1 Betwixt Wim. More & Wim. Coupland
1 Betwixt Wim M.Cleney & Wim Coupland
1 Betwixt John Carr & John Coupland
1 Betwixt John Carr & Wim Maccleney
1 Betwixt James Johnson & Nathan Wiat
1 Betwixt Nathan Wiat Wim Butler

All these Lines Processd as Useal as Witness our hands

     William King John Harison

[178]

Persuant to An Order of Vestry Dated the 25th of Octobr 1763 We the Subscribers have Processiond all the Bounds of Land Containd in the order

Begining Thos Winborns Line and James Winborns In the pressence of Jas Winborn & John Porter John rawls Line in the Pressence of John porter & John Harrisson And Jas Couplans Line in the pressence of the Same John Porters Line in the pressence of the Same men John Harissons Line & Wim Harissons in the pressence of John Harisson & Wim Harisson Junr

John Balards Line in the pressence of the Same Joseph Bakers Line & Jessey Skiners in the pressence of Jos Baker & Jessey Skiner John Giles Line & Wim Batemans In the pressence of John Giles & Wim Bateman John Butler Line & Absolom Beamons in the pressence of John Giles And Absolom Beamon All the Land Within the Said Order peaceably & Quietly Processiond and No objections Made by No Man in our Bounds

         Thomas Winbourn
         Absolem Beamon

In Obedience to our Order of Vestry Dated Octob^r the 25th 1763 We the Subscribers have Processiond all the Land in Our District With Every Line therein Containd without Any Interruption the Inhabitants being pressent

Certify^d Under our hands this 13th Day of January 1764

Thos Godwin
John Barkley

[179]

Persuant to an Order of Vestry Dated October the 25th 1763 We the Subscribers Appointed in the Said order have Process^d all the Said Bounds of Land Containd in the Said order Begining at a Line Between Benj^a Baker And Lewis Daughterey press^t Line Between Crafford & Baker Joseph Gardener pres^t Line between Robert Whitfeild & David Meade Muls [?][87] Whitfeild press^t Line between John Daughterey and Crafford John Daughterey pres^t Line between Widow Cutchens & John daugtry John Daughterey pres^t Line between Edmond fowler & Oliver Worrell James Vaughan press^t Line between Oliver Worrell & James Vaughan Ja^s Vaughan press^t Line between James Vaughan & James Uzel Ja^s Vaughan pres^t Line Between Worl & Widdow Sanders Ja^s Uzel Pressent Line Between Sarah Sanders & Wm Vaughan Wm Vaughan press^t Line Between Wm Vaughan & Edward Howell And Line Between Daniel Holand & Wm Vaughan Wm Vaughan Present Line Between Widdow Vaughan & Widdow Sanders John Whitfeild press^t Line Between Wm Holand Sanders John Whitfeild Present Line Between John Harisson & Wm Holand Wim Holand Pressent Line Between Daniel Holand and John Harisson Edward Norfleet Samuel Norfleet press^t Line Between J^{no} Flemin And Sanders John Whitfeild press^t Line Between Widdow Baker And John Fleming Edward Norfleet & Sam. Norfleet pressent Line Between John Whitfeild and Christopher Norfleet John Whitfeild press^t Line Between Widdow Baker And Stephen Dardan Sam. Norfleet pressent Line Between Stephen Dardan and Christopher Norfleet Edward Norfleet & Samuel pressent Line Between Christo^r Norfleet and John Harrisson Sam. Norfleet & Edwd Norfleet Pressent All the Bounds of Land Con-

---

[87] This may be Meels.

taind in the Above Mentiond Order is peaceably & Quietly processiond And No Objections made by us the Subscribers

Daniel Holland
John Fleming

[180]

In Obedience to an order of Vestry Dated October the 25th We have Processiond All the Land Mentiond in the S^d order Without any Objections as Witness our hands

Kedar Webb
Peter Mason

Febuary the 10th 1764

In Obedeience to An Order of Vestry to us directed Dated Octob^r the 25th 1763 We the Subscribers have Procession^d the following Lines peaceably & Quietly begining at a Line between Thos Milner & Willm Wilkinson press^t both parties A Line between Thos Milner & George Frith the Line between John Lawrence formerly Kendals & Wm Wilkinson a Line between John Lawrence formerly Kendals & Aaron Allmand Pressent James Jones & Joseph Dardan then a Line between Robert Lawrence & Aaron Allmand press^t Robt Lawrence Jo^s Scott & John Lawrence then a Line Between John Lawrence^s Land whereon his New house Stands & Aaron Allmand So up to the head Line of Lucies Land press^t James Jones & Joseph Dardan then a Line between John Lawrence & James Jones press^t James Jones & Jo^s Dardan then a line between James Jones & John Jones press^t James Jones & Jo^s Dardan A Line between Nicholas Perritt & John Wilkinson^s Orphan A Line between Nicholas Perritt & John Lawrence A Line Between Nicholas Perritt & John Lawrence formerly Sam Lawrence In Pressence of John Lawrence Jo^s Scott Robt Lawrence All the above Lines We have peaceably & Quietly Process^d

Sign^d William Wilkinson
Aaron Allmand

[181]

At A Vestry held at Belson Wrights in Suffolk Town November the 16th 1764 For the up^r Parish of Nansemond County

Pressent   James Gibson   Church Warden
           Lemuel Riddick   Mills Riddick ⎫
           Hening Tembtey   Willis Riddick ⎬ Gent. Vestry Men
           Jacob Sumner   Wm Moore   ⎪
           Thos Winbourn   Josiah Riddick ⎭

To the rev^d Patrick Lunan his Salary	16000
To D^o an Alowance of 4 per c^t for Caskue & D^o Srinkage	1280
To D^o An Alowance for A Gleab	3000
To Wim Shekelton Clk at Sumerton Chapel	1000
To Aaron Allmand D^o at Suffolk Church & Keeper of the parish register	2000
To D^o An Allowance of 4 per ct	80
To John Cambwell D^o at the Cyprus Chapel	1000
To Thos Johnson Sexton of Suffolk Church	800
To John Jenkins D^o at Holy Neck	200
To Wm Wigins D^o at Notaway	200
To Robert Booth^s Exector^s D^o Late of the Cyprus	200
To the Sherreiff for Insolvents after deducting the Last Years depossitum & for 16 thithes Over Charg^d	1194
To be Sold by the Ch: Wardens at July Court for Cash as Useual	24000
	50954
To the Collector at 6 per ct	3058
	54012
Tis Ordered that the Sherreiff after Giveing Bond & Security as Useual do Collect from Every thithe in this parish 38 p^d of Tobacco on 1415 thites	53770
Ballance due to the Collector	242

[182]

   Dr The Uper Parish In Cash 1764

To John Hamilton A poor Man	£ 5 : 0 : 0
To Mary Holan A poor Woman	3 : 0 : 0
To Pricila Parker D^o	2 : 10
To Ana Willis D^o	2 : 10
To Christain Miles D^o	4 : 0 : 0

To Mary Babb D°	2 : 10 : 0
To Eliza Hanom for takeing Care of Sarah Brown	3 : 0 : 0
To Dock^r Cohoon for Medicines & attendance for the poor To be p^d to Ja^s Gibson	11 : 18 : 0
To James Hynes a poor Man	5 : 0 : 0
To Eliza. Stallins a poor Woman	5 : 0 : 0
Mr James Gibson rendred in his Account as Ch: Warden for Sundries Deliver^d the poor & by the Tobacco Sold Last Year and the Ball: due to the Ch: Warden is	87 : 13 : 5
	£132 : 1 : 5

Maj^r Willis Riddick is Chosen & Capt Thos Winbourn Church Warden^s & have takeing the Oath according to Law In the room of James Gibson & Edward Riddick

Hardy Parker is Apointed Clk of Holy Neck Chapel In the room of Wim Shekelton

Thos Johnson is Discharg^d from his duty in the Church as Sexton & that the Ch: Wardens Apoint Some other in his room

Mr Hening Tembtey Gent. one of the Members of this Vestry Came in to Vestry & Resign^d Serveing Any Longer as A Vestry Man he being to Old to Serve

Mr Jerimyah Godwin is Apointed to Serve in his room after being Qualify^d According to Law

    Truly Enter^d by   Sign^d Willis Riddick
      Aaron Allmand Clk Vestry   Thos Winbourn

[183]

A Greeable to an Order of Vestry Held for the Uper parish of Nansemond the 25 Octob^r 1763 We the Subscribers have Process^d the Bounds of Lands & Renew^d the Several Land Marks as directed in Said Order Quietly & without dispute in pressence of the parties Concern^d as Also Elisha Norfleet Edwd Moore Thos Fisher & Thos Norfleet

                                            Thos Sumner
                                            Kedar Best

A Greeable to An Order of Vestry Held for the uper parish of Nansem^d the 25th of Octob^r 1763 We the Subscribers have Procesion^d

the Lots of the Town of Suffolk as directed in the Said Order Quietly & Without dispute in pressence of Saml Fletcher John Stogdale John Narney & John Jones &c. Given Under our hands this 21st day of April 1764

        Saml Cohoon
        Thos Harison

Ordred to Obedience to an order of Vestry Held in Nansemond County bearing Date the 25 day of October 1763 We have Procession^d All the Land in Mention^d in the Said Order in the pressence of

Only the Land between Thos Fisher & Joshua Gardener is Not procession^d because the S^d fisher did Not Apear All in the Precints of our Order peaceably & Quietly done

{ Allbraxton Jones
Thos Edwards
Charles Hyes
Richard Williams
Jacob Dardan
Michael Daugterey
James Garner
Hollon Dardan
Joshua Garner }

Moses Dardan
James Carr
 Procssion Masters
March the 12 1764

[184]
March the 8th begining on John porters Line procession^d the said Line in the pressence of John porter procesion^d the Said Line between Between [sic] Thos Rawls John porter in the pressence of tho^s Rawls And the Line between Thos Price and the Said Thos Rawls procession^d And the Said Line between James Couplan & Thos Price process^d in the pressence of Abraham Couplan the Line between John porter and W^im Rawls process^d in the pressence of us the Line between John Harrell & me W^im Rawls process^d in the pressence of us The Line between Franes [sic]⁸⁸ Rawls and me W^im Rawls process^d In the pressence of us the Line between John hare & me Wim Rawls in the pressence of us John harrell the Line between John Faulk & John hare process^d in the pressence of John hare

---

⁸⁸ No doubt intended for Frances.

The Line between Abraham parker & John Faulk process^d being the Whole Concludeing Bounds by me

William Rawls
John Harrell

In Obedience to an Order of Vestry October the 25 1763 We the processioners Joseph Baker and Frances duke have process^d the Land between the Knuckle Swamp and Barbecue Swamp as Smiths Road runs and Sumerton Road Viz Begun at Jo^s Bakers Line Son of Ja^s Baker Press^t Job harrell Junr William Meltear Abrahams Couplans Line pres^t Ja^s Couplan And John Couplan John porters Line himself press^t between Gueing & Sumner press^t John price Josiah Meltear a Line between John Smith & Saml Baker press^t Job Harrell Demsey Smith Philip Drapers Deceas^d Line press^t John Couplan John hares line pres^t James Harrell Luke Harrell Edmun^d Burd Luke harrels Line press^t James Harrell John Harrell Concludeing the Whole Bounds in Quiet and peaceable Procession

Joseph Baker
Francis Duke

[185]

In Obedience to an Order of Vestry Bearing date the 25 October 1763 We the Subscribers have process^d all the Land Within our district

A Line between Asael duke & William Savage present both parties

A Line between Christopher Norfleet & Joseph Skiner press^t both parties

A Line between Joseph Skiner & John Ballard press^t both parties

A Line between John Ballard & Jo^s Perry press^t both parties

A Line between Jo^s perry & Willm Savage press^t Jo^s perry by Consent of W^{im} Savage

A Line between Lawren[c]e Blade & Jo^s perry Jo^s perry press^t by Consent of Blade

A Line between Henry Gwin & Lawrence Blade Jo^s perry press^t with Con[s]ent of both parties

A Line between Henry Gwin & John Ease press^t Wim Redd John Ease & Daniel Gwin

A Line between Jo^s Skiner & Aseal duke press^t both parties

A Line between John Norfleet & Mansfeild Tarlington pres^t both parties

A Line between Thos Healy & John Norfleet pres^t John Norfleet & W^{im} Redd

A Line between W^{im} Turlington & Thos Healy press^t Wm Turlington & W^{im} Redd

A Line between Mansfeild Turlington & W^{im} Redd press^t both parties

A Line between W^{im} Redd & Daniel March press^t Wm Redd & Whitaker redd by the Consent of March

A Line between Mansfeild Turlington & Danl March press^t both parties

A Line between Whitaker Redd & Abraham Carnal press^t Whitaker Red & John Ballard

A Line between Jo^s perry & Wm Turlington press^t both parties

A Line between John Ballard & W^{im} Turlington press^t both parties

A Line between Wm Redd & Wm Turlington press^t both parties

John Ballard
William Redd

[186]

At A Vestry Held for Nansem^d County Bearing date Octob^r the 25th 1763 I James Holland & Joseph Hollan Acted According to the directions & finds No failure Begining at a Line between John faulk & J^{no} king Both press^t Between John faulk & Will Harison both pressent then Between John King was formerly Call^d Bradleys but the true Owner is Not known then A Line between peter Butler And John King Then a Line between John Carr & John hollan Then a Line between Wm Harison Junr & John Carr a Line Between Joseph Holan & Moses Butler was formerly Calld Sanders^s A Line Between Jo^s Hollan & John Winbourn a Line between James Hollan & Soloman Hollan a Line between Jo^s hollan And Ja^s Hollan A Line between peter Butler & Wm Harison A Line between John Carr & Peter Butler a Line between Jo^s Hollan Junr & John Hollan a Line between Jo^s Hollan & Culbert Hedgberth A Line between Culbert Hedgberth & Jo^s Hollan one of the processioners a Line between Henry Johnson And Jo^s Hollan Senr a Line between Jo^s Hollan sen^r & Abraham Johnson a Line between the S^d Hollan and Hannah Baker a Line between Ja^s Sumner And John Flemings all persons being press^t

We the procession Masters Have a true return as far as possible Given under our hands this 8th Day of March 1764

          James Holland
          Joseph Holland

[187]

In Obedience to an Order of Vestry past Octob^r the 25 1763 We the Subscribers have Met & process^d all the Land in our precincts Maj^r Dempsey Sumners Land done press^t Job Harrell and Nicholas harmon Nicholas Harmons Land done press^t the Same John Smiths Land done press^t the Same Moses Harrels Land done press^t the Same Job Harrels Land done press^t the Same John Bakers Land press^t the Same Edward Bakers Land done press^t the Same Jacob Sumners Land done press^t Ephraim peal & Thos frasier Ephraim peals Land done press^t the Same Thos frasiers Land done press^t the Same Dempsey Sumners Land done press^t himself & Robt peal Robt peals Land done press^t the Same Wm Pearce^s Land done press^t himself and Saml Smith Samuel Smiths Land done press^t the Same Richard Tayloes Land done press^t the Same William Savage^s Land done press^t himself Samuel Bakers Land done press^t himself

         Richard Tayloe
         Edward Baker

[188]

In Obedience to An Order of Vestry Octob^r the 25th 1763 We have process^d the Line between francis forset & Danl March press^t Josiah Vaughan Wm Best the Line between Benj^a forsett And Daniel March press^t Josiah Vaughan Wm Best the Line between Mrs Mead & Daniel March the line Between Mrs Meade & John Ashbourn Orphan the Line Between Mrs Meade & Thos Gwin the Line between Mrs Meade and Willm Moore the Line between tho^s Gwin & Wm Moore press^t Josiah Vaughan & W^m pruden the Line between Thos Gwin & Josiah Gwin the Line between Josiah Gwin & John Ashbourns Orphan press^t Wm Wright And Wm Best Josiah Vaughan & W^m pruden The Line between Daniel March and John Ashbourns Orphan The Line between John Ashbourns Orphan and Henry Best The Line between Daniel March & Abraham Veline The Line between Hening Tembtey[89] the Line between Hening

---

[89] "The Line between Hening Tembtey", which seems to be incomplete, may be covered by the statement immediately following.

Tembtey and Henry Wright the Line between Hening Tembtey & W^m pruden The Line between Henry Wright and James Hynes the Line between Henry Wright and Nath Pruden^s Orphan the Line between Hening Tembtey & Nathaniel pruden^s Orphan In pressence of Wm Wright W^m pruden and Wm Bucker The Line between Elisha Ballard and Hening Tembtey The Line between Elisha Ballard & Jessey Battle the line Between Jessey Battle and Benj^a Forset in pressence of Jessey Battle and Daniel March the Line between Mrs Meade and Josiah Vaughan Press^t Josiah Gwin

            Benjamin Forsett
            Elisha Ballard

[189]

At A Vestry Held for the Uper parish of Nansemond County May 14 1752[90]

Press^t William Webb
  John Winbourn Wm Baker
  Lemuel Riddick Hening Tembtey
  Daniel Pugh Wm Moore & John Rawls
    Vestry Men

Ordered that John Winbourn Wm Baker Wm Moore & John Rawls or any three of them Sell the Land at Wickams And Sumerton in Such Lots or parcels as they Shall think fitt for Six Months Credditt[91]

Ordered that Wm Webb Hening Tembtey Daniel pugh And Thos Sumner or any three Sell the Gleab Land for Six Months Credditt[92]

Ordered that Wm Webb Daniel pugh Josiah Riddick And Lemuel Riddick or any three A Gree With Some Workmen to Build a house pursuant to the Act of assembly[93] Lately Made for that purpose Which

---

[90] See explanation of clerk at the end of the proceedings of this meeting. These proceedings should have been copied into the book before the meeting of October 14, 1752.
[91] See footnote 93.
[92] See footnote 93.
[93] "An Act to enable the Vestry of the upper parish in Nansemond County, to sell certain lands, and for other purposes therein mentioned" (Hening, v. 6, p. 266-268), passed at the February 1752 session of the General Assembly, authorized the vestry to sell certain lands devised for the benefit of the Upper Parish by will of William Cadowgan, dated January 1, 1675 (i. e. 1676), and to use the money from the sale of some of the lands to erect a poorhouse and for other charitable purposes. Cf. p. 84, 125, 128, and 196; also see account in Introduction, p. lv-lxiv.

House is to be A Greeable to the plan deliver^d to the Vestry this Day by Lemuel Riddick & Whereas Daniel pugh Gent hath this day offred to give three Acres of Land Near Suffolk Town for to Set the Said House on it is further Ordered that The Said persons Lay out the Said Land and take a Deed for The Same & Direct on What part of the Said Land the Said House Shall be built on

William Webb

Truly Enter^d by Aaron Allmand Clk Vestry

N B the reason the Above Orders Was Not Entered In Course they Were Mislaid in the Clk^s Office And Not found before

A. A

[190]

By An Order of Vestry Held at Suffolk Ordered that we the Subscribers should procession All the Land in Such Bounds therein Mention^d Begining on a Line of dempsey Sumners & John Jenkins then between Watson howell & the Said Sumner[94] then between John Jenkins & Dempsey Jenkins then between Dempsey Jenkins & Wm Jarnakin then between the Said Jarnakin & Wm Howell then between the Said Howell And John Jenkins then all the Lines between Dempsey Sumner And Wm Howell then between the Said Dempsey Sumner And Allice Rodgers then between Samuel Watson and Wm Howell then between Wm Edward Howell[95] then between Wm Howell & James Wigins then between the Said Wigins And Dempsey Sumner then between Jese Riddick and John pender then between Jese Johnson & the Said John pender Then between the Said Johnson and Jesse Riddick then between Wm Boyt and Moses Jones then between the Said Boyt And Thos Jones then between Henry & Moses Jones then Between Henry Jones & Stephen Howell then Between Henry Jones & Benj^a Baker then between Edward & Stephen Howell then between Lemuel Watson and Ely howell Then between Lemuel Watson & Edward Howell then between Mary Watson and Lemuel Watson then between Mary Watson & Moses Homes then between the Said Homes and Hardy Jones Then between Moses Homes and John Jones then between John & Henry Jones then between James Howard & Stephen Howell then between Benj^a Baker and Arthur Howell then between Lemuel Howard & Benj^a

---

[94] "Watson howell & the Said Sumner" may mean "[Samuel] Watson, [William] howell & the Said [Dempsey] Sumner."

[95] "W^m and Edward Howell" is doubtless intended.

Baker then between the Said Baker and Hardy parker then between Edward Howell & Benjamin[96] Then between the Said parker and Abraham Riddick then between S^d parker and Henry daughterey then between Abraham Riddick And James Wigins then between John Jenkins & Moses Jones then between Henry daughterey & Ja^s Wigins then between S^d Wigins and Edward Howell then between Sam. Watson & J^{no} Howell then between Wm Howell & Wm Jarnakin then between Sam Watson And Wm Howell then between the Said Watson dempsey Jenkins then between the S^d Watson & J^{no} Hare then between dempsey Jenkins & Harry Rawls then between the S^d Rawls & John hare all done peaceably And Quietly in pressence of the Owners of the Land by us the Subscribers

March the 12th 1764   Samuel Watson
              John Jenkins

[191]

At A Vestry Held at Belson Wrights in Suffolk Town Novembr the 28th 1765 for the Up^r Parish of Nansemond

Press^t Willis Riddick   Thos Winbourn Gen^t Ch: Wardens

Lemuel Riddick   Josiah Riddick
Jacob Sumner   Wm More   James Gibson &   } Gen^t Vestry men
Jeremyah Godwin

To the rev^d Patrick Lunan his Salary	16000
To D^o An Alowance of 4 per ct for Caskue & D^o for Srinkage	1280
To D^o An Alowance for A Gleab	3000
To Aaron Allmand Clk of Suffolk Church & keeper of the parish register	2000
To D^o An Alowance of 4 per Ct	80
To John Cambwel D^o at the Cyprus Chapel	1000
To D^o for Serveing as Sexton at the Same	200
To John Jenkins Sexton at Holy Neck D^o & keeping the Well & Cirples Clean	275
To D^o Omited Last Year	75
To Wm Wigins Sexton of Notaway Chapel	200
To Josiah Riddick Assigne of Thos Johnston for 4 M^o Service as Sexton	266

---

[96] Benjamin Baker is doubtless intended.

To Richard Leveston Sexton of Suffolk Church 8mo	534
To Elisha Dardan Clk of Notaway Chapel for 2 Years Service	2000
To the Sherreif Ball due as per his Account	432
To Col^n Riddick for Coppies of Six List thitheables	120
To Eley Brinkly a Leivy Over Charg^d Last year	38
To J^{no} Rawls Junr for D^o	38
To be Sold by the Ch: Wardens at July Court for Cash to Discharge the parish Creditors	12000
	39538
To the Collector @ 6 per ct	2372
	41910
28 per pole on 1518 thitheables	42504
Depositum Due to the parish	594

Tis Ordered that Capt Henry Riddick Sherreiff do Collect from Every thithable in this parish 28 p^d Tobacco After Giveing Bond & Security as Useual for that purpose & therewith Discharge the parish Creddittors

[192]

Dr The Up^r Parish In Cash 1765	£
To Coln. Riddick for 25 Bushels Meal for the poors House	3 : 2 : 6
To Capt Thos Winbourn his Acco^t for disbursments for the poor	6 : 0
To Richard Leviston his Acco^t for Sundries	1 : 10 : 6
To John Hamilton a poor Man	7 : 10
To Mary Holan a poor Woman	5 : 0
To Pricilia Parker D^o	2 : 10
To Anabil Willis D^o	2 : 10
To Christain Miles D^o	4 : 0
To Eliza. Stallins D^o	5 : 0
To Wm Bateman D^o	1 : 10
To James Hynes D^o	5 : 0
To Mrs Hanom for Dressings &c for Hoby & Brown	3 : 0
To James Gibson Ball. his Acco^t for the poor	72 : 10 : 2½

To Moses Jones for Keeping a poor Child	1 : 6 : 8
To John Ease for Keeping Jean Blade & her daughter in there Sickness	4 : 0
To Eliza. Parks a poor Woman	2 : 10
To Wm Gwin for Keeping the Orphan of Geo. Waff	6 : 0
	£132 : 19 : 10½
Maj^r Willis Riddick rendred In his Account as Ch: Warden & the Ball is due to the parish	24 : 3 : 4
	£108 : 16 : 6½

Tis Ordered that the Above disburstments to the Several poor persons be p^d to the Ch: Wardens & by him Laid out In Such Necessaryes as Will best Suit them

Capt Henry Riddick is apointed a Vestry man In the room of his father Deceas^d

Sign^d Willis Riddick ⎫ Ch:
Thos Winbourn ⎬ Wardens

Truly Entered by
   Aaron Allmand Clk Vestry

[193]

At A Vestry Held in the Court House in Suffo[l]k Septemb^r the 22^d 1766 for the Up^r Parrish of Nansem^d

Pressent Willis Riddick   Thos Winbourn Gen^t Ch: War^d

    Lemuel Riddick   Josiah Riddick
    Wm More   Jacob Sumner   Gent
    Ja^s Gibson & Edwd Riddick   Vestrymen

Tis Ordered that A petition be drawn up to the Revd Commissary Robinson[97] Seting forth the general behaviour & pray releif Against the Revd Patrick Lunan Which Pettion being drawn up by Lemuel Riddick With fourteen Charges[98] Alledg^d Against the Said Lunan & receiv^d in Vestry Was Approv^d of And ordered that Lemuel Riddick Wait on the Said Commissary with the Said petition & Cause the Said Lunan to be

---

[97] Rev. William Robinson, commissary or deputy in Virginia for the Bishop of London.

[98] For charges against Lunan, as given in a report on his case before the General Court in October, 1771, see Introduction, p. xli.

properly prosecuted thereon & Such Expences as May Arise by Occasion thereof is to be paid by the parrish

         Signd Willis Riddick
 Truly Enter^d by   Thos Winbourn Ch: Wardens
  Aaron Allmand Clk Vestry

[194]

At A Vestry Held at Belson Wright in Suffolk January the 14th 1767 for the Uper parrish of Nansem^d

Press^t Willis Riddick Thos Winbourn Gent Church Wardens
  Lemuel Riddick Ja^s Gibson Edwd Riddick ⎫ Gent
  Jeremyah Godwin Benj^a Baker Jacob Sumner ⎬ Vestry
  Henry Riddick Josiah Riddick   ⎭ Men

To the rev^d Patrick Lunan his Salary	16000
To D^o An Allowance of 4 per ct for Caskue & D^o for Shrinkage	1280
To D^o An Allowance for A Gleab	3000
To Aaron Allmand Clk of Suffolk Church & keeper of the parrish register	2000
To D^o An Allowance of 4 per ct	80
To John Cambwell Clk of the Ciprus Chapel	1000
To D^o as Sexton for the Same	200
To Dempsey Jenkins Sexton of Holy Neck Chapel & keeping the Well & Cirplus Clean	225
To Elisha Dardan Clk of Holy Neck	1250
To Richard Leviston Sexton of Suffolk	800
To Coln Riddick for Coppies of 6 Lists thithes	120
To Wm Shekelton for Serveing as Clk 6 M^o at Holy Neck	500
To Hardey Parker for D^o the other 6 Mo	500
To the Sherrff for Insolvents after deducting the Last Years depossitum	330
To Josiah Gwin for removeing Some poor out of the parrish	27
To be Sold by the Ch: Wardens at July Court for Cash to discharge the parrish Creddittors	25000
	52312
To the Collector at 6 per Ct	3140
	55452

Tis Ordered that Henry Riddick Sherrff do Collect from
Every thitheable in this parrish 35^{lb} Tobacco per thithe
on 1582 tithes   55370

& therewith discharge the parish Debts
  Due to the Sherreiff   82
[195]
D^r the Uper Parrish in Cash 1767   £
To John Hamilton a poor Man   7 : 0 : 0
To Jo^s Skeator D°   10 : 0 : 0
To Christain Miles a poor Woman   4 : 0 : 0
To Eliz^a Stallins D°   5 : 0 : 0
To Wm Bateman for Burying Mary Wiat to be paid to
 Henry Riddick   1 : 16 : 10½
To Ja^s Hynes A poor Man   5 : 0 : 0
To Eliz^a Parks A poor Woman   2 : 10
To Hezekiah Norfleet for diging a Well a bucket &
 Sweep & Blocking up the Chapel   2 : 2 : 6
To Eliz^a Booth for a Sheet for Mary Wiatt   0 : 10 : 0
To Mary Babb a poor Woman   2 : 10 : 0
To Richd Leviston for washing the Cirplus & burying
 Several poor people   2 : 2 : 6
To Dock^r Crothers for Medicines for the poor   1 : 14 : 1½
To George Kean for Keeping an orphan Child one Year   4 : 0 : 0
To Rachel Skeator for 3 ½ Bush: Meal for the poors house   0 : 10 : 6
To Jo^s Baker for Meal for the poors House   2 : 3 : 9
To Lemuel Riddick Assigne of Wm Gwin for Keeping
 the Orphan of George Waff 13 Months   6 : 10
To Mary Gwin for Makeing[99] for the Said orphan   0 : 6 : 3
To Wm Wigins A poor Man   2 : 0 : 0
To Ja^s Knight for Keeping Eliz^a Hacket   3 : 0 : 0
To Aaron Lassater for 60 Load of Wood   7 : 10
To Mrs Lassater for Some Service   0 : 5 : 0
Maj^r Willis Riddick rendred in his Account as
 Ch: Warden & the Ball is due to the S^d Ch: Warden
 Which is to be paid to James Gibson   104 : 7 : 8

---

[99] "Makeing clothes" is probably intended.

To Ja⁸ Newlan for Keeping John Butlers Child provided he gives Bond & Security to the Ch: Wardens that the S^d Child is Never to become burthensome to the parrish hereafter	8 : 0 : 0
	182 : 19 : 2
By Willis Riddick Ball. Last Year after being paid for Several Articles	22 : 5 : 10
	£160 : 13 : 4

[196]

Orders Made January the 14 1767

Capt Thos Winbourn this Day Came into Vestry & resign^d Serveing as A Vestryman Any Longer on Account of his removeal to Caroliner

Capt Edward Riddick has Like wise resign^d Serveing as A Vestryman Any Longer on Account of his Liveing So Inconvenient

Mr Thos Gilchrist & Mr David Meade is appointed Vestry men in there room

Jerimiah Godwin & Benj^a Baker is Sworn Church Wardens until Easter Next

Signd. Jerimiah Godwin
Ben Baker } Ch Wardens

Truly Enter^d by Aaron Allmand Clk Vestry

At A Vestry Held In Suffolk Town Decemb^r the 30 1767 for the uper Parish of Nansemond

Present Coln Lemuel Riddick Willis Riddick
James Gibson David Meade
Henry Riddick Thos Gilchrist
Josiah Riddick } Gentlemen Vestrymen

Jerimyah Godwin & Benjamin Baker Gen^t Ch: Wardens

Caried forward

[197]

1 Twas Ordered that Samuel Fletcher & John Narney Process^n all the Bounds of Land No 1 According to Law

2 Thos Sanders & William Pinner Proces^sn all the Bounds of Land N° 2 according to Law

3   William Ward & W[m] Norfleet Process[n] all the Bounds of Land No 3 According to Law
4   Thomas Milner & Nicholas Perritt Procession all the Bounds of Land No 4 According to Law
5   Wilkinson Godwin[100] & Stephen Archer Procession all the Bounds of Land No 5 According to Law
6   William Gwin & Tho[s] Gwin Procession all the Bounds of Land No 6 According to Law
7   William King & John Harrison Jun[r] Process[n] all the Bounds of Land No 7 According to Law
8   William Harison Jun[r] & John Norfleet Process[n] all the Bounds of Land No 8 According to Law
9   John Porter & Tho[s] Rawls Process[n] all the Bounds of Land No 9 According to Law
10 Isaac Langston & Arthur Jones Process[n] all the Bounds of Land N° 10 according to Law
11 Abraham Riddick & James Norfleet Process[n] all the Bounds of Land N° 11 According to Law
12 Henry Jenkins & Dempsey Jenkins Process[n] all the Bounds of Land No 12 According to Law
13 James Coupland & Zackariah Coupland Process[n] all the Bounds of Land N° 13 According to Law
14 James Holand & Joseph Holand Process[n] all the Bounds of Land N° 14 According to Law
15 Joshua Gardener & Holand Dardan Process[n] all the Bounds of Land No 15 According to Law
16 Edward Cary & George Williams Process[n] all the Bounds of Land N° 16 According to Law

                                        Carie[d] Over

[198]
Daniel Holand & John Fleming Procession all the Bounds of Land N° 17 According to Law
William Rawls & John Purvis Process[n] all the Bounds of Land N° 18 According to Law

---

[100] "Rich[d] W[n] [*i. e.* Wilkinson] Godwin" is subscribed to the return as recorded (See p. 185).

John Riddick & Eley Grifin Process[n] all the Bounds of Land N° 19 According to Law

Moses Harrel & James Raiby Process[n] all the Bounds of Land N° 20 According to Law

Soloman Rawls & Jacob Duke Process[n] all the Bounds of Land N° 21 According to Law

Robert Smith & Moses Horton Process[n] all the Bounds of Land N° 22 According to Law

William Tarlington & Joseph Skiner Process[n] all the Bounds of Land N° 23 According to Law

Robert Roundtree & John Wateridge Process[n] all the Bounds of Land N° 24 According to Law

William Frost & Matthew Parker Process[n] all the Bounds of Land N° 25 According to Law

John Cowper & John Brewer Process[n] all the Bounds of Land N° 26 According to Law

Mills Riddick & Hezekiah Riddick Process[n] all the Bounds of Land N° 27 According to Law

Willis Parker Drewry Rodgers Process[n] all the Bounds of Land N° 28 According to Law N° 28

The Vestry Continued

[199]

D[r] the uper Parish In Tobacco 1767

To the Rev[d] Patrick Lunan his Salary	16000
To D° an Alowance of 4 per ct for Caskue & D° for shrinkage	1280
To D° an Alowance for a gleab	3000
To Aaron Allmand Clk of Suffolk Church	2000
To D° an allowance of 4 per ct	80
To John Cambwell Clk of the Cyprus Chapel	1000
To D° as Sexton of the same	200
To Dempsey Jenkins D° at Holy Neck Chapel	200
To Elisha Dardan Clk at Holy Neck	1250
To Richard Leviston Sexton at Suffolk Church	800
To Ann Rawls a leivie overcharg[d] Last Year	35
To Tho[s] Winbourn for the same	35
To John Wilkins for the same	35

To Coln Riddick for Coppies 6 List of thithables	120
To the Sherreiff for Insolvents & a Ballance due Last year	1657
To Docktor Cohoon a Leivie overchargd 1763	29
	27721
To be Sold by the Church W^{ds} at July Court for Cash	20000
	47721
By Colⁿ Reddick By Joseph Scotts fine	500
	47221
To the Collector at 6 per ct	2834
	50055

Tis Ordered that Capt Henry Reddick Sherreiff do Collect from Every thithable in this parish 30^{lb} of Tobacco on 1626 Amounts To — 48780

Ball Due to the Collector — 1275

[200]

Dr The uper Parish in Cash Decemb^r the 30th 1767

	£
To George Kean for Keeping an orphan of Mary Lawrence	3 : 0 : 0
To Docktor Cohoon for Medicines for the poor	8 : 18 : 0
To Richard Leviston for Sundries	1 : 8 : 6
To James Knight for Keeping Elizabeth Hacket	3 : 0 : 0
To John Hamilton a poor Man	7 : 0 : 0
To Christian Miles a poor Woman	4 : 0 : 0
To Elizabeth Stallins D^o	5 : 0 : 0
To James Hynes a poor Man	5 : 0 : 0
To Mary Babb a poor Woman	2 : 10 : 0
To Pricilia Thomas a poor woman	4 : 0 : 0
To Wm Gwin for Keeping an Orphan of Geo Waff^s one Year	6 : 0 : 0
To Colⁿ Riddick for Wood for the poors house	9 : 2 : 6
To Maj^r Wilis Riddick for Wood for D^o 1765	14 : 9 : 3
Capt Jerimiah Godwin rendred in his acco^t as Church W^{dn} & by the Tobacco sold & the Ball is Due to the S^d Church Warden	17 : 3 : 4
Which Sum is to be paid to Mr James Gibson	

To Joseph Skeator a poor Man	5 : 0 : 0
	£95 : 11 : 7

Tis Ordered that Mr David Meade & Mr Thos Gilchrist Apply to Mr Attorney General & Mr Benj^a Waller & present them with the Alegations drawn up by the Vestry of this parish Against the Revd Patrick Lunan Minister of this parish And have there advice Concerning turning out the Said Lunan And the Said Mr Meade & Mr Gilchrist proceed according to the advice of the Said Attornies

Tis Ordered that the Church W^ds do Advertise the posting & Railing in the Church yard in Suffolk with good & Sufficient posts & Rails Suitable for that purpose which will be agreed on at the undertakeing & to Repair the Said Church to be Let to the Lowest undertaker Likewise to pale in a Garden for the poors House & repair the Said House all the above Work to be done in a Strong & Workman like Maner by the Lowest undertaker

Signd Ben Baker
Jerimiah Godwin

Truly Enter^d by
Aaron Allmand Clk Vestry

[201]

Thos Sanders & Wm Piners Return of Procession of Land Between frederick George & Robert Tucker Richard Wilkinson Godwin[101] & David Nelms & Joseph Thomas pres^t between the said Tucker & Jonathan Nelms between the said Nelms & Joseph Thomas & between Thomas & Christopher Roberts & between the said Roberts & Peter Mason & between the said Mason & Francis Pinner & between the said Pinner & Peter Green & between Wm Pinner & Thos Sanders & between the said Sanders & David Nelms & between Peter Mason & Jonathan Nelms & between the said Nelms & David Nelms & between the said Roberts and Spears Hollan & between Christopher Roberts & David Nelms Not Procession^d Between Jonathan Roberts & Benjamin Roberts & between Christopher Roberts & Benjamin Roberts not procession^d by Each party Not attending between Jerimiah Godwin & Elisha Norfleet & between the said Norfleet & Henry Hill & between the said Norfleet & Michal Farrow & between the said Farrow & Jonathan Roberts & between the said Roberts & Eleanor Nelms

---

[101] Richard Wilkinson Godwin appears to be one name.

& between the said Nelms & Peter Green and Between the said Green Kedar Webb & between Henning Tembtey & Henry Hill & between the said Hill & Jonathan Roberts & between Tembtey & Kedar Webb & between the said Webb & George Frith & between the said Frith & Thos Sanders & between the said Frith & Wm Pinner

Jerimiah Godwin   Elisha Norfleet } Present
Michal Farrow   Wm Nelms

In Obedience to an Order of Vestry held at Suffolk Decemb^r the 30th 1767 we the Subscribers have met & Process^d the Bounds according to our Orders with the parties Pres^t

William King
John Harison

In Obedience to an Order of Vestry Dated Decemb^r the 30th 1767 We the Subscribers have Process^d the Lands a Greeable to the s^d order without any Interruption   Certify^d under our hands this 10th day of March 1768

Richd W^n Godwin
Stephen Archer

[202]

Persuant to an Order of the up^r Parrish Vestry in the County of Nansem^d we the subscribers have process^d the Lands in our precint as ordered by the said Vestry as followeth the Line between Thos Milner & George Frith pres^t James Bascomb the Line between Geo^r Frith & Wm Wilkinson pres^t s^d Wilkinson Fra[n]cis Milner & Geo^r Frith the Line between Thos Milner & Wm Wilkinson pres^t S^d Wilkinson The Line Ge^o Frith & Jno Lawrence pres^t S^d Lawrence & Wm Wilkinson The Line between Jno Lawrence & Nicholas Perritt pres^t the Same The Line between Jno Lawrence & Wm Wilkinson pres^t Said Wilkinson & Francis Milner the Line between Joseph Scott & Ben Beal pres^t s^d Scott The Line between Eliz^a Norfleet & Jno Woodrop pres^t s^d Woodrop & James Lawrence The Line between Eliz^a Norfleet & James Lawrence Pres^t S^d Lawrence The Line between Christoph^r Godwin & Ja^s Lawrence pres^t the Same. The Line between Jo^s Scott & Moses Eley pres^t Scott & Eley. The Line between Jo^s Scott & Josiah Jordan pres^t the Same The Line between Jo^s Scott & John Lawrence S^d Scott John Lawrence & Moses Eley pres^t The Line between Jno Lawrence & Aaron Allmand pres^t S^d Lawrence & Allmand. The Line between Jno Lawrence & Robt Lawrence pres^t Jno

& Robt Lawrence. The Line between J^{no} Lawrence & Nicholas Perritt present the same. A Line between Jo^s Scott & John Lawrence said Scott And Lawrence agree to doo themselves. a Short Line between John Lawrence & Aaron Allmand adjoyning the Creek they both agree to be right but being Late In the Evening did not go upon it

Thos Milner
Nicholas Perritt

[203]

At a Vestry held at Suffolk March the 5th 1768

present Willis Riddick   James Gibson
       Josiah Riddick   Jerimiah Godwin } Gent
       Henry Riddick   David Meade   Vestry Men
       Thos Gilchrist

Ordered that in Concequence of an order of Vestry bearing date the 30th of decemb^r 1767 wherein it was ordered that David Meade & Thos Gilchrist apply to the Attorney Gen. & Mr Ge^o Wythe[102] for there advice concerning Prosecuteing the Revd Patrick Lunan Minister of this parish which advice being obtaind is that there is cause of prosecution & that the same can be supported by the Laws of this Country we do hereby appoint Mr David Meade to Empl[o]y such attornies as he may see fitt to manage said prosecution at the expence of this parish   Jerimiah Godwin

Pursuant to an Order of Vestry dated decemb^r the 30th 1767 We the subscribers appointed in the said order have procession^d All the said bounds of Land Contain in the said order all the bounds of Land contain in the above Mention^d is peaceably & Quietly process^d & no objection^s made by us the Subscribers

James Holland
Jo^s Holland

[204]

At a vestry Held at Belson Wrights in Suffolk town May the 13th 1768

Present Jerimiah Godwin Ch: Warden
       Colⁿ Lemuel Riddick   Willis Riddick
       Henry Riddick   Thos Gilchrist Wm More } Gent
       & James Gibson   Vestry Men

---

[102] The previous order (p. 184) had specified the Attorney General and Benjamin Waller.

Mr Thos Gilchrist & Capt Henry Riddick is appointed And sworn Church wardens in the room of Jerimiah Godwin & Benja Baker

Coln Riddick reports to this vestry that he has in his hands receivd for fines tis ordered that he pay the Same as followeth   £4 .. 7 .. 10

To Absolom parker a poor Man   2 .. 7 .. 10
To Mary Stallins a poor woman   2 .. 0 .. 0

Capt Henry Riddick reports that he has   1 .. 15 .. 0
Tis Ordered that he pay the same to
John Groves a poor Man

Mr James Gibson reports that he has in has [sic] hands   2 .. 0 .. 0
Tis ordered that he pay the same to Judey Willis a poor woman

Tis Ordered that Mr Josiah Riddick pay To Eliza Parks the sum of   £3 .. 0 .. 0
when he receives it of the fines

Tis Ordered that Majr Riddick pay out of Meltears fine
To Joseph Ellis   £2 .. 10 .. 0
To Ann Wigins   2 .. 10 .. 0
When he receives the Money

       Henry Riddick
       Thos Gilchrist

[205]

Persuant to an order of Vestry Dated the 30th of decembr 1767 We the subscribers have procesiond all the Bonds of Land contain in the order begining at John Everits Line. thence to Simon Everits Line thence to Daniel Williams Line thence to John Harts Line thence to Eliza Harts Line thence to Moses harts Line thence to James Carys Line thence to William Alins Line thence to the Vestry of Nansemd County We the subscribers have procesiond all the bounds of Land contain in the Order without any Objection by we the Subscribers

       Edward Cary
       George Williams

Abraham Lasiter & Jese Lasiters Land & he present George Spivy Land & he present Christain Spivy land & John price pres^t Moses Booth^s Land & John price present John Harrel Land & he present Wm Roundtree Land & he present Thos Newby^s Land & John Eas Land & he present david Gwin Land & James Bois present Jacob price land & he present Jame Bois land & he present James Sketo land & he present Henry Lawrance land And he present Joseph lasiter land & he present Joseph Booth land and he present Jotham lasiter land & he present Daniel lasiters land & he present John Roundtree^s land & he present Ja^s Spivy land & he pres^t John dilereace land & John ease present Quacus Lasiter land & he pres^t Josiah Riddick land & W^m roundtree pres^t Abraham lasiter Land & he prest Robt roundtree land & he present John Wateridge land & he present

    March the 14 day 1768

                                        Robert Roundtree
                                        John Wateridge

    Persuant to an order of Vestry held the 30th of Decemb^r 1767 We the Subscribers have Processiond distinckly and renewd all the Land Marks peaceably between each person in the presence of parties Concernd & some of the Inhabitants the Mentiond bounds begining at John porters Line & all the Land between sumerton road & Somerton Swamp up to the Knuckle swamp April the 11th 1768

                                        John Porter
                                        Thos Rawls

[206]

    By an Order of the Vestry bearing Date the 30th of decemb^r 1767 Ordered that John Riddick & Eley Griffin procession & renew all the lines from the Cyprus swamp to the Orapeak road & to the Country line & make there return to the Next Court To a line between John Brothers & John Brinkley John Brothers pres^t To a line between John Brinkley & Peter Brinkley John Brothers pres^t To a line between John Brothers & Peter Brinkley John Brothers pres^t

To a line between John Brothers & Luke sumner John Brothers pres^t
To a line between John Brothers & John Brinkley John Brothers pres^t
To a line between Luke Sumner & John Brinkley John Brothers pres^t
To a line between John Brinkly & Daniel Franklain Danl Franklain pres^t
To a line between John Brinkly & Edwd Arnal Danl Franklin pres^t

To a line between Danl Franklin & Edwd Arnal Danl Franklin pres^t

To a line between Edwd Arnal & Eleanor Franklin Danl Franklin Thos Wilkins pres^t

To a Corner tree between luke sumner & Eleanor Franklin Danl Franklin Thos Wilkins pres^t

To a line between Henry Brinkly & Eleanor Franklin Danl Franklin Thos Wilkins pres^t

To a line between Thos Wilkins & Henry Brinkly Thos Wilkins Danl Franklin pres^t

To a line between Thos Wilkins & Eleanor Franklin Thos Wilkins Danl Franklin pres^t

To a line between John Brothers & Eleanor Franklin John Brothers pres^t

To a line between John Brothers & Wm Sivels John Brothers pres^t

To a line between John Brothers & John Brinkley John Brothers John Brinkly prest

To a line between John Brinkly & Wm Brothers John Brinkly pres^t

To a line between John Brinkly & Shaderick Wilkins John Brinkly pres^t

To a line between Danl Franklin & Eleanor Franklin Tho Wilkins Eleanor Franklin pres

To a line between Wm Brothers & Shaderick Wilkins Wm Brothers Jo^n Wilkins pres^t

To a line between Shaderick Wilkins & Wm Sivils Shaderick Wilkins present

To a line between Wm Sivils & Henry Brinkly Shaderick Wilkins pres^t

To a Corner tree between Thos Wilkins & Wm Sivils Elean^r Franklin Sharderick Wilkins Wm Sivils Present To a line betewen Henry Brinkly & Luke sumner Henry Brinkly Pres^t To a line between Luke Sumner & John Riddick Henry Brinkly Pres^t

To a line between John Riddick & James Brinkly Ja^s Brinkly Henry Brinkly prest

To a line between Luke sumner & Ja^s Brinkly Ja^s Brinkly pres^t

To a line between Luke sumner & John Meltear Ja^s Brinkly prest

To a line between Henry Grifin & Hezekiah Norfleet Hezekiah Norflet prest

[207]

To a line between Hezekiah Norfleet & Christain Spivy Hezekiah Norfleet pres[t]
To a line between W[m] Spivy & Joshua Spivy Hezekiah Norfleet prs[t]
To a line between John Brinkly & Humphrey Grifin John Brinkly present
To a line between John Brinkly & Eley Brinkly John Brinkly pres[t]
To a line between Humphrey Grifin & Eley Brinkly John Brinkly pres[t]
To a line between John Brinkley & Soloman Riddick Soloman Riddick pres[t]
To a line between Soloman Riddick & Eley Brinkly So[l] Riddick Kader Brinkly prs[t]
To a line between Eley Brinkly & Eley Grifin Josh: Spivy Soloman Riddick pres[t]
To a line between Soloman Riddick & Joshua Spivy Jos[h] Spivy Jo[n] Brinkly prs[t]
To a line between Eley Grifin & Joshua Spivy Soloman Riddick Josh: Spivy pres[t]
To a line between John Riddick & Soloman Riddick Jo[n] Brinkly Josh: Spivy prest
To a line between Jo[n] Riddick & the King Jo[n] Brinkly Joshua Spivy present
To a line between Soloman Riddick & Eley Grifin Soloman Riddick prest
To a line between Soloman Riddick & the King Soloman Riddick pres[t]
To a line between W[m] Jones & the King Soloman Riddick pres[t]
To a line between Jo[n] Riddick & Soloman Riddick Jo[n] Brinkly Joshua Spivy prest
To a line between Jo[n] Riddick & Henry Grifin Jo[n] Brinkly Joshua Spivy prest
To a line between John Riddick & Humprey Grifin Joshua Spivy prest
To a line between Humphrey Grifin & Henry Grifin John Brinkly prest
To a line between Humphrey Grifin & Joshua Spivy Jo[n] Brinkly Josh: Spivy prest
To a line between Jo[n] Riddick & Jo[n] Brinkly Dan[l] Riddick present
To a line between Jo[n] Brinkly & Soloman Riddick Dan[l] Riddick prest

To a line between Eley Grifin & Wm Jones Wm Jones present
To a line between Jo^n Riddick & Wm Jones Wm Jones present
To a line between Wm Jones & the King Wm Jones present
To a line between John Brinkly & Wm Jones Wm Jones prest

John Riddick
Eley Griffin

[208]

In Obedience to an order of Vestry to us directed we have procesion^d all the Lands between Crany Creek & Parkers Creek to the desart as follows

1   A Line between the Orphan of Wm Woodward & the Land of Coln Lamuel Riddicks which he purchas^d from Wm Woodward
2   A line between the said Woodwards & sa[i]d Land of Coln Riddicks Purchas^d from W^m & John Horton
3   A Line between the s^d Woodward & John Horton
4   A line between the s^d Woodward & John Parker
5   A line between John parker & Coln Riddick
6   A line between John Parker & the land formerly theophilus pughs
7   3 Lines between the s^d Land of Mr Theophilus pugh & the land which Coln Riddick purchas^d from Matthew parker
8   2 Lines Between the s^d Land of Col^n Riddick^s & John parkers prest At the runing the afores^d Lines Coln. Riddick & Nathaniel Wright John Horton Ezekel Nelms & Thos Tallington
9   A line between the Land formerly Mr Theophilus pughs & the Land of Col^n Riddicks Purchas^d from W^m & John Horton
10 a line between the s^d Land & that Land which the s^d Coln Riddick purchas^d from Mr James Gibson
11 A Line between the s^d Land & the Land the s^d Coln Riddick purchas^d of John parker
12 A line between the s^d Land which the s^d Riddick purchas^d from John parker & the Land formerly Ephraim parker pres^t Coln Riddick & Nathaniel Wright
13 2 Lines between the Land formerly Mr Theophilus pughs & Abel Parkers
14 2 Lines between the Land formerly the s^d pughs & Jacob Morris
15 a Line between Jacob Morris & Jno Cowper

16   a Line between Abel parker & Jno Cowper
17   a Line between the land formerly Mr Theophilus pughs & Jno Cowper^s
18   2 Lines between the s^d Mr Pughs Land & John Brewers Land
19   a Line between the s^d Brewer^s & John Cowper
20   a Line between the s^d Brewers & Wm Wise

[209]
21   a Line between Wm Wise & John Cowper Wm Wise pres^t
22   a Line between David Barkers[103] Land & John Cowper Junr Land that he Lately purchas^d of Wm Wise
23   a Line between the s^d Baker & the Land formerly belonging to Francis Beaman present David Baker Wm Wise Elisha Manning This is as far as we Could proceed for the Water & Mier

John Cowper
John Brewer

Persuant to an order of Vestry of the up^r Parish of Nansem^d County bearing date the 30th of decemb^r 1767 we the subscribers have procesiond all the lands within the Bounds Specified by the s^d Order Except the swamp lands which are extream Wet Viz^t the lands of Mills Riddick pres^t Aaron Lasiter & Henry Bates also the lands of Aaron Lasiter pres^t Henry Bates also the lands of John Campel pres^t Aaron Lasiter & Henry Bates also the lands of Wilis Riddicks precint [sic] Aaron Lasiter & Henry Bates also the lands of Hezekiah Riddick pres^t Willis Riddick Aaron Lasiter & Henry Bates also the Lands of Margaret Stallings prs^t Willis Riddick & Aaron Lasiter Henry Bates & Ja^s Stallins also the Lands of Ja^s Staling prest Willis Riddick Aaron Lasiter & Henry bates Also the Lands of Josiah Riddick pres^t Willis Riddick Aaron Lasiter & Henry Bates & Henry Riddick also the Lands of Henry Riddick pres^t Josiah Riddick also the Lands of James Booth prest Henry Riddick & Josiah Riddick also the lands of Jotham lasiter pres^t Henry Riddick & Josiah Riddick

Mills Riddick
Hezekiah Riddick

---

[103] Baker was probably intended (see the next statement, numbered 23). The clerk apparently wrote "parkers" and then corrected only the first letter of the name. *Cf.* return on p. 235.

[210]

A return to the Vestry of the Mens Lands in our bounds procesion^d
Dempsie Sumners land done Robt Peal & Jese Peal present Robt Peals land done Jese & Robt peal pres^t Jesse Peals land done Robt peal & Jesse peal pres^t Thos frasure land done Thos frasure pr^t Ephraim peal land done Ephraim & Jo^s peal pres^t Jacob Sumner Land done Kedar Raiby & Dempsey Wigins pres^t Kedar Raiby land done Jacob sumner Dempsey Wigins pres^t Willis Wigins land done Jacob Sumner pres^t W,im Jones land done Jo^s Peal & Jacob sumner present Jese Peal Land done Ephraim peal & Jo^s Peal pres^t Jo^s Peals land done Ephraim peal & Jo^s Peal pres^t Norman Ellis Land done John Baker & Ephraim peal pres^t John Bakers land done John Baker & Ephraim peal pres^t Saml Bakers land done Saml Baker & John Smith pres^t Nicholas harmon Land done the s^d harmon present Moses Harrel land done Richard Turley pres^t Amos Rawls Land done Moses Harrel & Amos Rawls prest Job Harrel Land done Edwd Baker & Job Harrel present John Smith Junr Land done Amos Rawls Job Harrel Edward Baker John Smith pres^t John Smith Senr Land done John Smith pres^t Edwd Baker Land done Edwd Baker & Job Harrel pres^t Saml Baker Land done Job Harrel & Edwd Baker prest. Wm Savage Land done Wm Savage & Richard Tayloe pres^t Richd Tayloe Land done Richd Tayloe Land done [sic] Saml Smith & Wm Pearce present Wm Pearce Land done Saml Smith & Wm Pearce pres^t all done in peace & Quietness as our order directed March the 1st 1768

Moses Horton
Robt Smith

March the 10th 1768

Process^d all the Lines within our precint Quietly According to our orders by W^m & Thos Gwin Procesioners

[211]

In Obedience to an Order of Vestry held in Suffolk Decemb^r 30th 1767 We the subscribers have Proces^d all the Bounds Mention^d in the afors^d Order begining at Moses Brewers Line & Zacharias Couplans & George Keens. James Jones & Z. Couplands all in the Pressence of Moses Brewer than between Ja^s Keen & Moses Wateridge In presence of David Rawls & John Copeland between George Kean & Warteridge In the presence of Lemuel Keen & Moses Brewer between Arthur Jones & Ja^s

Jones in presence of Moses Brewer & John Porter & Ja^s Keen & John Porter & John Rawls in presence John Rawls & John Porter David Rawls & John Copelan Between John Rawls & John faulk in the presence of David Rawls than between Moses Brewer & John Rawls Will. Holland Ja^s Copeland all in the presence of John Rawls Junr thence between Absolom Holand & Robt & Daniel Holand & Henry Holand & Rob^{rt} & James Winbourn And Henry Holland all in the pressence of Wm Holland Thence between John Everitt & James Winbourn and Elisha Copelan & John Everitt in pressence of all parties thence between John faulk and John Winbourn & Jesse Collins & John daugtery & James Harris Josiah Winbourn & John faulk and Daughtery all in the pressence of of [sic] Jacob Hollan Benjamin Harris & Jesse Collins between Jesse Collins and John Winbourn thence between John faulk & James Harriss in Pressence of John Winbourn & John Harriss thence a line between John faulk & Jo^s Holland & Wm Holland And Daniel Holland all in the presence of Jacob Holland & Jesse Collins & Given under our Hands In the Year 1768

James Copeland
Zacharias Coupland

[212]

At A Vestry Held at Thos Brickles in Suffolk Town January the 25th 1769 For the up^r Parrish of Nansem^d

Pres^t Mr Thos Gilchrist & Henry Riddick Gen^t Ch: Wardens

Coln Lemuel Riddick   Will[i]s Riddick
Josiah Riddick   Ja^s Gibson   } Gent Vestry Men
Jerimyah Godwin & Ben Baker

To the Revd Patrick Lunan his Sallary	16000
To D^o an allowance of 4 per Ct for Caskue & D^o for Srinkage	1280
To D^o an Allowance for a Gleab	3000
To Aaron Allmand Reader at Suffolk Church	2000
To d^o An Allowance of 4 per Ct	80
To John Cambwel Reader at the Cyprus Chapel	1000
To d^o for Serveing as Sexton at the same	200
To Richard Leviston Sexton at Suffolk Church	800
To Elisha Dardan Reader at Holy Neck Chapel	1250
To Col^n Riddick for Coppies 6 List of tithes	120
To Capt Henry Riddick for Insolvents	1830
To D^o a Ball. Due Last year	1275

To Hezekiah Riddick a Leivie over charg^d last year	30
To be Sold by the Church W^{ds} at July Court for Cash	12000
	40865
To the Collector at 6 per Ct	2452
	43317
Tis ordered that James' Pitt do Collect from Every titheable in this Parish 26^{lb} of Tobacco on 1674 tithes after giveing Bond & Security as Useual And therewith discharge the Parish Creddittors	43524
Depossitum Due to the Parish	207

[213]

Dr The up^r Parish in Cash 1769	£
To Col^n Riddick for 89 Load of Wood for the poors house	11 : 2 : 6
To Ann Baker a poor Woman	2 : 0 : 0
To Dockt^r Cohoon for dressing Batemans Leg	0 : 7 : 6
To Richd Leviston for Burying Chance Chapman	0 : 10 : 0
To John Hamilton a poor Man	8 : 0 : 0
To Jo^s Skeatoe d^o	8 : 0 : 0
To Christain Miles a poor Woman	4 : 0 : 0
To Eliz^a Stallins d^o	8 : 0 : 0
To Ja^s Hynes a poor Man	5 : 0 : 0
To Eliz^a Parks a poor Woman	2 : 10 : 0
To Mary Babb d^o	2 : 10 : 0
To Wm Wigins a poor Man	2 : 0 : 0
To Ja^s Spivy for Nurseing & Burying Thos Jones	6 : 0 : 0
To Martin Goodwin for a Coffin for Chance Chapman	0 : 12 : 6
To Wm Harrell a poor Man	2 : 0 : 0
To Maj^r Riddick Paid Lasiter for a Bar^l Corn 1766	0 : 15 : 0
To Riddick & Cowper Assignee^s of Wm Gwin for his keeping the Orphan of George Waff	7 : 1 : 3
To Mary Gwin for makeing & mending for s^d orphan	0 : 10 : 0
To John Groves a Poor Man	5 : 0 : 0
Mr Thos Gilchrist rendred in his Account as Church W^d for disburstments for the Poor	21 : 8 : 2
	97 : 6 : 11

The up^r Parrish Credditt	
By Henry Riddick a Ball. from the Tobacco Sold last year	38 : 13 : 6
By Maj^r Willis Riddick for a former Ball	7 : 16 : 7
	46 : 10 : 1
Parish Indebted	50 : 16 : 10

Sign^d Thos Gilchrist
Henry Riddick

Truly Enter^d by Aaron Allmand Clk Vestry

[214]

At A Vestry held at Thos Brickels in Suffolk Town Octob^r the 19th 1769 for the up^r Parish of Nansem^d

Present Mr Thos Gilchrist   Henry Riddick Gen^{tn} C: Wardens

Col^n Lemuel Riddick   Willis Riddick
Benj^a Baker   Wm More   Ja^s Gibson } Gentm^n Vestry Men
Josiah Riddick   David Meade
Jacob Sumner

This Vestry has Strictly Examin^d the present state of the Poors House & are of Opinion that its Necessary to make Several Rules & orders for the well Goverment of the Same And has ordered that each Member Consider the mater relateing thereto and that the Vestry Meet again the 20th Novemb^r if fair or the first fair day After When the Parish Leivie will be laid And that proper Notice be given in Church

Tis Ordered That Wheras by an Act of asembly made In the twenty fifth year of his Late Majesties Reign Entitled an Act to enable the Vestry of the uper Parish of Nansem^d County to Sell Certain Lands And for other purposes therein Mentiond Several Lands Were Directed to be Sold and it appears that 700 Acres part of the Land therein Mention^d hath Not been yet Sold Ordered that the Church Wardens Inquire where the Said Lands Lie in Whose possesion the Same is And apply to Some Noted Attorney for his advice as to the title and make report to the Next Vestry[104]

Henry Riddick
Thos Gilchrist

---

[104] *Cf.* p. 173 and footnote 93.

[215]

At A Vestry Held at Thos Brickles in Suffolk Town Novemb^r the 22^d 1769 for the up^r Parish of Nansem^d

Present Mr Thos Gilchrist   Henry Riddick   G: Ch: W^{ds}
Col^o Lemuel Riddick   Willis Riddick   ⎫ Gent
Josiah Riddick   Ja^s Gibson   Wm Moore ⎬ Vestry
                                              ⎭ Men

To the Revd Patrick Lunan his Salary	16000
To d^o an allowance of 4 per ct for Caskue & d^o for srinkage	1280
To d^o an allowance for a Gleab	3000
To Aaron Allmand Reader at Suffolk Church & Keeper of the parish register	2000
To d^o an allowance of 4 per ct	80
To John Cambwell Reader at the Cyprus Chappell	1000
To d^o for Serveing as sexton at the Same	200
To Richd Leviston d^o at Suffolk Church	800
To Elisha Dardan Reader at Holy Neck	1250
To Col^o Riddick for Coppies 6 List of thithes	120
To Dempsey Jenkins sexton of Holy Neck for 2 Years	400
To D^o a Leivie overcharg^d 1767	30
To Nathaniel Fleming for 3 Leivies overcharg^d 1768	78
To the Sherreiff a Ball after deducting the last Years depositum and for Insolvents & Tikets	1376
To be sold by the Church W^{ds} at July Court for Cash	16000
	43614
To the Collector at 6 per Ct	2617
	46231
Tis Ordered that James Pitt Sherreiff do Collect from Each titheable in this parish 28 pounds of Tobacco per thith on 1688 Tithes a Mounts To	47264
Depossitum due to the Parrish	1033

[216]

Dr The up^r Parish in Cash 1769   £
To John Hamilton a poor Man   8 : 0 : 0

To Jos Skeatoe do To be pd to Mr Gilchrist	5 : 0 : 0
To Eliza Stallins a poor Woman	4 : 0 : 0
To James Hynes a poor Man	5 : 0 : 0
To Wm Wigins do	2 : 0 : 0
To Thos Gilchrist assignee of Wm Gwin for Keeping the orphan of Geo Waff	6 : 0 : 0
To Richd Leviston for washing the Cirplus & Sundries	1 : 5 : 0
To Hezekiah Norfleet for Cleaning the Chapel yard & Sundrie other services	1 : 0 : 0
To Samuel Wallice for Schooling some poor Children	6 : 0 : 0
To Dempsey Jenkins for Sundries work at the holy Neck Chappel	1 : 19 : 0
To Saml Smith for Keeping Edey peal 8 Months	5 : 0 : 0
To Colo Riddick for Wood for the poor house & flower	6 : 10 : 0
To James Knight for Boarding & Nurseing Ann Brown	1 : 0 : 0
Mr Thos Gilchrist rendred in his Account as Church Wd & by the Tobacco Sold & the Ballance Is Due to the said Church Warden	27 : 6 : 11¼
To Gibson & Granbury for Sundries for the poor	11 : 9 : 7
To Capt Henry Riddick Ball of his Account	0 : 19 : 5
To Martin Goodwin & Dempsey Riddick for Mending the poor house & Glaiseing the Church	4 : 0 : 0
To Thos Wilkins a poor Man	5 : 0 : 0
To Dockr Cohoon for Meddicines for the poor	12 : 11 : 6
	£114 : 1 : 5¼

George Spivy is appointed Clark at the Cyprus Chappell in the room of John Cambwell who by reason of his age & Infirmity is ordered to be discontinued

        Signd Henry Riddick ⎤ Church
          Thos Gilchrist ⎦ Wds

 Truly Enterd by
  Aaron Allmand Clk Vestry

[217]

At A Vestry held for the upr Parrish Nansemd Novembr the 22d 1769 This Vestry takeing into Consideration the present state order & Condition of the persons in the poors house & the regulations thereof have Come to Several resolutions thereupon to Wit

Resolved that the Said house at present is not under such goverm^t as the Law design^d & required and that at this time it is highly Necessary that proper & Legal rules & orders ought to be made And Established for the beter goverment of the same

Resolved that the Church Wardens of this parrish often liveing at a great distance from the Said house Cannot Conveniently attend so often as will be Necessary for the Inspection & well Goverment of the Same That a Certain Number of the Vestry Liveing Convenient to the s^d house be appointed as Visitors & them or a majority of them at least once in three Months To Visit Inspect & Inquire into the state & Condition of the Said house and the poor therein and the behaviour & actions of the overseer thereof & to make such rules & orders as they from Time to time shall think Necessary & Convenient The same Not being repugnant to the Law or any order of this Vestry And to report to the Next Vestry an account of there proceedings

Resolved that a proper person be appointed as an Overseer of the Said house Constantly to attend his duty as the Law requiers who is to have all the authority over the poor as is directed by the Act of assembly Intituled an Act for Imploying & beter Maintaining the poor[105] & the rules & orders of this Vestry

Resolved that it is the opinion of this Vestry that the Church W^{ds} of this Parrish assoon as conveniently Can be done procure at the Charge of the parrish as Much Wool Cotten flax Junck or other Matarials as may be Sufficient to Imploy the poor and all Vagarent People that may be Imploy^d in the poors house from time to time and What the Said persons may Earn or do shall be by the Overseer delivered or accounted to the Church Wardens & by them applyed to the benifitt of the Poor in the said house or as Shall otherwise be directed by the Vestry

Resolved that a Quantity of Tobacco be now Levied on The Titheables of this parrish to be Sold by the Church W^{ds} In July Next & the Money to be applyed towards defraying the Charge of the Said poor & to reimburse the Church W^{ds} What they may in the Mean time advance for the use & purposes aforesaid

Turn over

---

[105] Hening, v. 6, p. 475-478.

[218]

Pursuant to the said Several Resolves it is ordered That Thos Gilchrist Henry Riddick Co^{lo} Riddick James Gibson Maj^r Riddick David Meade Jerimyah Godwin be Visitors of this said House to Act & do agreeable to the Said Resolves

Ordered that the Visitors agree with a proper person to be overseer of the Said house to Act and do According To the Said Resolves agreeable to the direction of the Aforesaid Act of Assembly and every order of Vestry for that particualer purpose made or to be made And that he have and receive for his Care & Trouble besides all Necessary Expences a Sum Not exceeding Twenty Pounds per Anum

Sign^d Henry Riddick ⎫ Church
Thos Gilchrist ⎭ W^{ds}

[219]

At a Vestry held for the uper parrish of Nansem^d Saturday the 4th of Augst 1770

Present

Josiah Riddick	Willis Riddick	
Jacob Sumner	Jerimyah Godwin	Gentm^n
Henry Riddick	Benj^a Baker	Vestry Men
David Meade	Thos Gilchrist	

Patrick Lunan Clerk

David Meade & Jacob Sumner Gent. are apointed Church Wardens in the room of Henry Riddick & Thos Gilchrist

Capt Jerimyah Godwin Rendred his account of fines in his hands due to this Parrish Two pounds Ten Shillings

Col^o Riddick rendred his Account of fines due to this Parrish one pound Fifteen Shill

Mr Josiah Riddick rendred his Acco^t of fines in his hands due to this parrish Five pounds three shill & six pence

Ordered that the above Named Gentlemen pay the respective fines in there hands to the Church Wardens

Ordered that the Church Warden pay out of the above fines to Alice Rogers Twenty six Shill & Six pence To Mary Stallins Ann Baker Dorothy Meltier Wm Lamb Sarah harwood & Jean Wiat Twenty Seven Shill each wch makes out the whole of the above fines. Mr Josiah Granbury is elected a member of this Vestry in the Room of Mr Ja^s Gibson remov^d out of this Colony

Mr Josiah Riddick Came into the vestry & resign^d his office therein Mr Samuel Cohoon is elected in his room

Ordered that the Church Wardens employ Peter Pelham to Come here to take dimensions of two Barrils for the Organs of this Church in order to Send home to Mr James Gibson who Intends to Make a Complement of them to this parrish

The Church Wardens this day appointed took the oath according to Law

Sign^d Patrick Lunan

[220]

At a Vestry held at Saml Swans in Suffolk Town Novemb^r 26th 1770 for the up^r Parrish of Nansem^d

Present Jacob Sumner Gent Church W^d — Gent
Col^o Lemuel Riddick Henry Riddick Willis Riddick — Vestry
Benj^a Baker Thos Gilchrist Samuel Cohoon — Men

To the Revd Patrick Lunan his Sallary	16000
To d^o 4 per Ct for Caskue & d^o for Srinkage	1280
To d^o an Allowance for a Gleab	3000
To Aaron Allmand Clk Suffolk Church	2000
To d^o an allowance 4 per Ct	80
To George Spivy d^o at the Cyprus Chappell	1000
To Richd Leviston Sexton of Suffolk Church	800
To Elisha Dardan Reader at Holy Neck Chappell	1250
To Dempsey Jenken Sexton at d^o	200
To Hezekiah Norfleet d^o at the Cyprus d^o	200
To Col^o Riddick Coppies 6 List of tithes	120
To Wm Granbury over Charg'd 4 Leivies 1768	104
To St Brides Parrish for moveing Dan. Clark & family	700
To the Sherreif for Insolvents & Tikets after deducting the Last years depossitum	1087
To be Sold by the Church Wardens at July Court for Cash or Collected from the people at 2^d per lb	24000
	51821

To the Collector @ 6 per Ct	3109
	54930
Tis ordered that the Church W^ds Collect from Each Titheable in this Parrish 32^lb Tobacco per Titheable on 1741 thithes Amounts to	55712
after giveing Bond & Security as Useual for that purpose Depossitum due to the Parrish	782

Sign^d Jacob Sumner

[221]

Dr The Uper Parrish in Cash Novembr 26th 1770   £

To Colo Riddick for 85 Load Wood for the poor house @ 2/6	10 : 12 : 6
To do for 2 Quarters Lam 4/ To do for burying Cathrine Tyler £ 1 : 0 : 3	1 : 4 : 3
To Samuel Wallice for Schooling several poor Children	4 : 17 : 6
To Hannah Cotten for do Christain Bates & Wood	2 : 0 : 0
To Richd Leviston for Sundries for the poor & Washing the Cirplis	3 : 0 : 0
To John Miles overseer of the poors house 10 Mo^n & for Sundries	14 : 7 : 4
To Dock^r Cohoon for Medicines attendance &c. for the poor	37 : 4 : 9
To John Smith for Nurseing Ruth Smith in her Lying in	2 : 10 : 0
To Webb & Meridith for three Coffens for the poor	1 : 13 : 9
To Mr Thos Gilchrist Late Church W^d rendred in his Account & & [sic] by the Tobacco Sold & the Ball. due to Mr Gilchrist	37 : 5 : 8¾
To do for laying the hearths in the poors House	0 : 15 : 0
To Wills Cowper for Sundries for the poors house	23 : 17 : 2¾
To Capt Henry Riddick for 2½ barr^ls Corn for John groves	1 : 17 : 6
To Edwd Howel for Burying a poor Man	1 : 10 : 0
To Drewry Rogers for Keeping Eliz^a Colster in her lying in	1 : 10 : 0
To Josiah Vaughan for the Same	2 : 0 : 0
To John Groves a Poor Man	8 : 0 : 0

To Benj^a Baker paid Wm Howel for Clearing the Chapel y^d	0 : 7 : 6
To John Hamilton a poor Man	5 : 0 : 0
To Jo^s Skeatoe d^o	5 : 0 : 0
To Eliz^a Stallins a poor Woman	4 : 0 : 0
To William Wigins a poor Man	2 : 0 : 0
To Sarah Harrel a poor Woman	2 : 0 : 0
	172 : 13 : 0½

Sign^d Jacob Sumner

Truly Eentered Aaron Allmand Clk V:

[222]

At A Vestry held at Samuel Swans in Suffolk Town Feb the 2^d 1771 for the Up^r Parrish of Nansemond

Present Messrs David Meade Jacob Sumner Gen^t Church W^{ds}
    Col^o Lemuel Riddick Willis Riddick   ⎫ Gen^t
    Benj^a Baker Henry Riddick Josiah Granbury ⎭ V: Men

Whereas by an act of Asembly made in the twenty fifth year of the Reign of his Late Majesty Entituled an Act to enable the Vestry of the uper Parrish in Nansem^d County to Sell Certain Lands And for other Purposes therein mentiond[106] & by An other Act made in the twenty eight year of his Said Majestey^s reign Entituled an Act for disolveing the Vestry of the uper parish in the s^d County of Nansem^d[107] it was enacted by the first Act that a house Should be built in the Said parish for the receiption of the poor in the Said Parish and by the Last Mentiond Act the proceedings of the Vestry of the Said parish is Confirmd and whereas the Said Vestry Elected by Virtue of the said Act have made Several usefull Rules And regulations touching the Same yet the parishoners are dissatisfied at the Same and often Complaining of the Expence And the Vestry finding by experience that it does Not answer the end And design propoposed [sic] it is therefore ordered by this Vestry that the Church W^{ds} of this parish place the poor now in the s^d House as well as all Such as Shall become as Charge in this parish out to Such persons as to them Shall Seem Convenient to be paid for & Setled by this Vestry according to Law & it is further ordered that assoon as the poor Now in the Said house Can

---

[106] *Cf.* p. 173-174 and footnote 93.
[107] Hening, v. 6, p. 518-519.

Conveniently be Removed that the s^d House be rented out for the benifitt of the Poor of the Said parish and that Mr Josiah Granbury is desired to rent out the Same And it is further ordered that John Miles the Overseer of the Said House Shall be discharg^d from that office assoon as the s^d Poor shall be removed And that the person employed to find fier Wood for the S^d House shall Likewise be discharg^d It is Likewise ordered that the Church W^ds assoon as the poor is Removed out of the Said House do sell all the Household furniture that is in the S^d House belonging to the parish that is in the said House

This Vestry thinks its Necessary to purchase a Gleabe for the Minister of the Said parish & that Capt Mills Riddick has ofered his Lands for that purpose the Vestry not being full has adjournd till Munday the 11th Instant to Meet at the Useual place when they are to Consider the Same

             signd Jacob Sumner
 Truly entered   David Meade
  Aaron Allmand C: V:

[223]

At A Vestry held at Suffolk at the House of Saml Swans for the up^r Parrish of Nansem^d for the purpose of purchaseing A Gleab for the Incumbent of this Parrish the 11th of Feb 1771

Present David Meade Jacob Sumner Gen^tm C: Warden
    Willis Riddick Henry Riddick ⎫ Gen^tm
    Jerimyah Godwin Josiah Granbury ⎬ Vestry
    & Saml Cohoon   ⎭ Men

Whereas Capt Mills Riddick has ofered to Sell his Lands with the Apurtenances on the White Marsh to this parrish as a Gleab for the Incumbent thereof It is ordered that the Said Riddick Resurvey his Said Plantation and if the Surveior Shall return that the Said Land Contains the Number of Acres prescrib'd by Law Sufficient for A Gleab then & In such Case it is agreed by Said Vestry to pay unto Said Capt Riddick in Consideration of the same the Sum of of [sic] Five Hundred pounds Current Money In three payments Anualey as follow^s the first paym^t of one hundred & Sixty Six pounds thirteen shils & four pence to be made to S^d Mills Riddick in the Month of July in the year of our Lord one thous^d Seven hundred & Seventy two And the Seccond paym^t in the Month July in the year of Our Lord one thous^d Seven hundred & Seventy three With one years Lawful Intrest thereon & the third & last paym^t of the Like Sum of one Hundred & Sixty Six pounds thirteen Shils & four pence to be made in the Month of July In the year of our Lord one thous^d Seven hundred & Seventy-four with two years Legal Intrest theron & that Said Captn Mills Riddick has Agreed to deliver up the posession of the Said Land & premises on the Tenth Day of Decemb^r Next in Good Order & to Execute a deed Good & Sufficient for the Same

          Sign'd Jacob Sumner
Truly Enter'd   David Meade
  Aaron Allmand Clk V

[224]

At A Vestry held at Samuel Swans In Suffolk Town Decemb^r 23^d 1771 for the up^r Parish of Nansemond

Present Mr David Meade Gen^t Church W^d

Col^o Lemuel Riddick
Willis Riddick Benj^a Baker   } Gen^{tmen} Vestry Men
Henry Riddick Thos Gilchchrist [sic]
Samuel Cohoon

To Aaron Allmand Reader at Suffok Church & keeper of the Parish Register	2000
To d^o an Allowance of 4 per Ct	80
To George Spivi Reader at the Ciprus Chappell	1000
To Elisha Dardan d^o at Holy Neck	1250
To Rich'd Leviston Sexton at Suffolk Church	800
To Hardey Jarnagan d^o at Sumerton Chappell & washing the Curplis	250
To Hezekiah Norfleet d^o at the Ciprus Chappell	200
To Col^o Riddick for Coppies 4 Lists of tithes	80
To the Sherreiff for Insolvents & tikets after deducting the Last years depossitum	356
To be Sold by the Church W^{ds} at July Court for Cash or Collected from the people @ 2^d per lb	50000
To the Revd Patrick Lunan his Sallara	16000
To d^o an allowan[c]e 4 per ct for Caskue & d^o Srinkage	1280
To d^o an allowance for a Gleab	3000
	76296

Credditt By Colo Riddick 11 Leivies receiv^d from Vagarants Insolvents	352
	75944
To the Collector @ 6 per Ct	4560
	80504
Tis Ordered that the Sherreiff Collect from Every titheable In this parish 45 pounds Tobacco per tithe on 1774 tithes Amounts to	79830
Ballance due to the Sherreiff	00674

[225]

The up^r Parish D^r In Cash 1771

To Cathrine Johnson for Board of Edey Peale	5 : 10 : 0
To d^o for Attending John Hansel in his Sickness	0 : 12 : 0
To Thos Gwin for Board Susanah Nobles	2 : 2 : 6
To Wm Whitfeild for Repairs in the Church	1 : 8 : 3
To Richd Leviston his Account	0 : 10 : 0
To Samuel Cohoon for Medicines attendance &c	40 : 13 : 3
To James Adams	0 : 3 : 0
To Moses Brewer for Burying a poor Man	4 : 0 : 0
To Nicholas Perritt for keeping Mary Elsberry	3 : 15 : 0
To James Night for keeping Elizabeth Hacket	4 : 19 : 1½
To John Ease for attending Robt Warren in his Sickness	4 : 0 : 0
To Wm Webb for Mending the Organ Bellows &c	1 : 2 : 6
To Jacob Sumner Church W^d his Account	6 : 17 : 7
To Josiah Granburry	1 : 12 : 0
To d^o Assigne Sarah Woods	5 : 0 : 0
To Wells Cowper for Sundries deliv^d the poor	26 : 18 : 2
To Mary Parker for Cloathing & Board John Thomas Ending 23^d January Next	6 : 0 : 0
To Ruth Chappel for Board of Jean Blade & Eliz^a Blade	7 : 0 : 0
To Mary Stallins for Board Susanah Nobles	4 : 19 : 2
To Ann Baker a poor Woman	4 : 10 : 0
To Jean Wiatt	4 : 0 : 0
To Elizabeth Rountree	4 : 0 : 0
To Sarah Horton	4 : 0 : 0

To John Groves a poor man	12 : 0 : 0
To Ann Wigins a poor Woman	3 : 0 : 0
To John Hamilton a poor Man	5 : 0 : 0
To Joseph Skeatoe d^o	5 : 0 : 0
To Elizabeth Stallins a poor Woman	4 : 0 : 0
To Wm Stallins a poor Man	2 : 0 : 0
To Francis Piner for Board Eliz^a Conner	2 : 0 : 0
To Thos Norfleet for Nurseing John Hansel	5 : 0 : 0
To Capt Baker paid Dock^r Jesey Brown	5 : 9 : 8
To Col^o Reddick for 7 y^{ds} Linen Eliz^a Haket & a Load wood for the poors House	0 : 16 : 6
To John Wood for keeping Robt Abrams 3 Weeks	1 : 1 : 0
To Mr David Meade his Account	5 : 14 : 3
To Ja^s Brewer for keeping John Thomas	4 : 10 : 0
To Mr David. Meade for 2 Lawyers fees for this parish	10 : 0 : 0
To Capt Mills Riddick first paym^t for his Land	166 : 13 : 4
To John Best Junr for Schooling Bates	8 : 0
	£376 : 5 : 3½

[226]

Mr Thos Norfleet is Chosen a Vestry Man In the Room of Capt William Moore deceas^d

Tis Ordered that Aaron Allmand reader at Suffolk Church have Five Hundred pounds of Tobacco more then he formerly had for his Service In the Said Church as Long as he Continues Reader & behaves Well

        Sign^d David Meade Ch: W^d

Truly Enter'd by Aaron Allmand Clk V

[227]

No 1 tis Ordered that Wm Granbury & John Miles procession all the bounds of Land According to Law

No 2 Christopher Roberts & Joseph Thomas process^n all the bounds of Land According to Law

No 3 Willis Streater & Edward Moore process^n all the bounds Land according to Law

No 4 Robert Lawrence & Mosses Eley all the Bounds of Land according to Law

No 5   John Barkley & Wm Marshal Stakes[108] process^n all the Bounds of Land According to Law

No 6   John Ashbourn & Josiah Gwin procession all the Land According to Law

No 7   Francis Powel & Joshua king process^n all the Bounds of Land According to Law

No 8   Jesse Skiner & Absolem Beamon process^n all the bounds of Land According to Law

No 9   James Harrel & Leving Turlington process^n all the bounds Land According to Law

No 10   James Rawls & Arthur Boyet process^n all the bounds Land according to Law

No 11   Hardey Parker & Jacob Daughtrey process^n all the bounds of Land According to Law

No 12   Stephen Howel & John Eley process^n all the bounds Land according to Law

No 13   Elisha Coupland & John Everritt process^n all the Bounds Land According to Law

No 14   Jesse Collins & Soloman Holland process^n all the bounds of Land According to Law

No 15   Elisha Dardan & James Carr process^n all the bounds of Land According to Law

No 16   Dred Warren & Wm Hart process^n all the bounds of Land According to Law

No 17   John Whitfeild & Charles Vaughan process^n all the bounds of land According to Law

No 18   Edward Riddick & James Cross process^n all the bounds of land according to Law

N° 19   Daniel Riddick & Shadarach Wilkins process^n all the bounds of Land according to Law

No 20   Hezekiah Norfleet & Henry Griffin process^n all the bounds of Land According to Law

No 21   Joseph Baker & Francis Duke process^n all the bounds of Land According to Law

---

[108] The names, Joshua Barkeley and Wm Marshall Stokes, are subscribed to the return as recorded (See p. 210).

No 22   Richard Tayloe & Edward Baker process[n] all the bounds Land accord. to Law

No 23   Abraham Ballard & Edw[d] Norfleet process[n] all the bounds Land d[o]

No 24   William Rowntree & Daniel Lassater process[n] all the bounds Land d[o]

No 25   John Lester & Jacob price process[n] all the bounds Land d[o]

No 26   Col[o] Lemuel Riddick Tho[s] Turlington process[n] all the bounds d[o]

No 27   Willis Riddick Henry Riddick process[n] all the bounds d[o]

No 28   Abraham Parker & Willis Parker procession all the bounds of Land according to Law

        Signd. David Meade

Truly Enterd by Aaron Allmand Clk: V

[228]

Pursuant to an order of Vestry of Nansem[d] County We the Subscribers have process[d] the Line between W[m] Wilkinson & Tho[s] Milner they being pres[t] The Line between Tho[s] Milner & George Frith Frith & Nicholas perritt being pres[t] & Tho[s] Milner. the Line between George Frith & W[m] Wilkinson they & Nicholas perritt pres[t] the Line between Geo. Frith & Nicholas perritt they Tho[s] Milner & W[m] Wilkinson being pres[t] The Line between Aaron Allmand & John Lawrence from the Creek up they being pres[t] The Line between John Lawrence & Nicholas perritt they being pres[t] The Line between John Lawrence & Rob[t] Lawrence they being pres[t] The Line between Rob[t] Lawrence & Aaron Allmand they Jo[s] Scott & John Lawrence being pres[t] a Head Line between John Lawrence & Aaron Allmand they & Jo[s] Scott pres[t] the Line between John Lawrence & Jo[s] Scott they & Aaron Allmand pres[t] the Line between Benj[a] Beel & Jo[s] Scott they being pres[t] the Line between Moses Eley & Jo[s] Scott they being pres[t] the Line between Christopher Godwin & James Lawrence they being pres[t] The Line between Ja[s] Lawrence & Eliz[a] Norfleet they being pres[t] the Line between Eliz[a] Norfleet & Ann Woodrop they & James Lawrence pres[t] the Line between Ann Wodrop & Chris[to] Godwin they & James Lawrence pres[t] the line between Jo[s] Scott & John Lawrence they & Aaron Allmand pres[t]

        Robert Lawrence
        Moses Eley

[229]

In pursuance to an Order Vestry Dated for the Year 1772 We the Subscribers have process^d the Lines as followeth with the owners pressent The Line done betwixt Wm King & Francis powel & betwixt W^m king & Elisha ashbourn & betwixt W^m king & Elisha Ballard & betwixt Saml Cohoon & Elisha Balard the Line done betwixt W^m king & Joshua king the Line done betwixt Joshua king & James Newland the Line done betwixt Matthew peirce & Abraham Lewis The Line done betwixt Wm Moore & James pierce the Line done betwixt Wm Moore & John Macleney the line done betwixt Wm Moore & Peter Butler The line done betwixt Wm Macleney & Dempsey Car The line done betwixt John Copeland & Dempsey Car The line done betwixt Peter Butler & John Copeland The line done betwixt Francis Powel & Nathan Wiat The line done betwixt Wiat & Obediah Johnson the Line done betwixt W^m king & Samuel Cohoon the Line done betwixt Peter Butler & Peter Butler the line done betwixt Peter Butler & James peirce the line done betwixt Martha Peirce & Saml Cohoon the Line done betwixt James peirce & Saml Cohoon the Line done betwixt James peirce & Wm Moore the Line done betwixt Wm Moore & Saml Cohoon The Line done betwixt Saml Cohoon & Josiah Vaughan The Line done betwixt Josiah Vaughan & Henry Butler The Line done [betwixt] Josiah Vaughan & John Harison the Line done betwixt James peirce & John Harison the line done betwixt James peirce & Peter Butler The line done betwixt John Harison & David king the line done betwixt John Harison & John Harison the Line done betwixt John Harison & Charles king the Line done betwixt John Harison & Henry Butler

            Joshua king
            Francis Powel.

July 18th 1772

In Obedience to an Order of Vestry bearing Date December 23^d 1771 We the Subscribers have Processioned all the Land in Our Precint with every Line Contain'd therein the Inhabitents and Proprieters being present

            Joshua Barkeley
            Wm Marshall Stokes

[230]

Pursuant to an Order of Vestry Held at Suffolk Town December 23^d

1771 We the Subscribers being appointed In the s^d Order have processioned all the Bounds of Land Mentioned in the said Order with the proprieters present Peacably and Quietly and no objection made by any

Jesse Collins
Solomon Holland

In Obedience to an order of Vestry bearing Date December 23^d 1771 We the Subscribers have processioned all the Land In our precint with every Line Contain'd therein the Inhabitents being Present

Absolom Beamon
Jesse Skinner

1772 Pursueant all the Lands in our bounds with Content to the owners Thos Newbeys Lands Zachews Lasseters pres^t Wm Rowntrees land John Harrels Land Jethro Booth Land pres^t John Harrel & Moses Booth Zacke^s Laseters Lands Josiah Riddick Lands Wm Spivy Lands pres^t John Harrel Jesse Lasetor Lands James Boyces Lands Wm Rowntrees Lands David Gwins Lands Thos Willis Lands Jacob price^s Lands Henry Lawrence^s Lands James Skeetoes Lands pres^t Jacob price & James Boice & Jesse Lassetor John Watridge Lands Abraham Lasetors Lands John Rountrees Lands Robt Rountrees Lands Abraham Lasetor Son of Robt Lands Jotham Lasetor Lands Daniel Lasetors Lands another Tract of the Said Daniel Lands Purchas'd from Ja^s Spivy pres^t John Watridge Abraham Lasetor James Brewer Lands pres^t Zacke^s Lasetor Thos Newbey Joseph Lasetors Lands Jo^s Booths Lands Soloman Riddicks Lands Joseph Lasetor & Kedah Lasetor Wm Lasetor pres^t &c

Wm Rowntree
Daniel Lasator

[231]

1772 Process^d all the Lands in our bounds with Content to the Owners thereof a Line between John Knight & Luke Sumner A Line between John Knight & John Brinkley a line between John Knigh[t] & Charity Raiby a Line between Ja^s Knight & James Brinkley a Line between James Knight & John Riddick a Line between Ja^s Knight & Luke Sumner A Line between Ja^s Knight & Edwd Arnel a line between John Knight & Edwd Arnell a Line between John Knight & Ja^s Knight A Line between Thos Harrell & Dempsey Jones a Line between Thos Harrel & Henry

Raiby pres^t James Knight & John Knight Son a Line between Norman Johnson & Collins Johnson a Line between George Baanes [sic] & Isaac Lam a Line between James Raiby Isaac Lam a Line between Frue Raiby Ja^s Raiby a line between John Baker & Norman Johnson a Line between Norman Johnson & Ja^s Harrel a line between Norman Johnson & Thos Harell a Line between Ja^s Raiby & Norman Johnson a line between Collins Johnson & George Banns a Line between Sarah Harrel & Norman Johnson a Line between Ja^s Raiby & Sarah Harrel a Line between Thos Harrel & Sarah Harrell a Line between Thos Harrel & Hezekiah Norfleet a Line between Thos Harrel & Hezekiah Norfleet a Line between Thos Harrel & Henry Griffen a Line between Henry Grifen & Hezekiah Norfleet[109] pres^t Norman Johnson George Banns Isaac Lam & So on &c a Line between Luke Sumner & Elisha Sumner a Line between Ja^s Knight & Cajar Brinkley a Line between Luke Sumner & Cajer Brinkley a Line between John Powell & Cajer Brinkley a line between Luke Sumner & John Powel a Line between Powel & Wm Raiby a Line between Charity Raiby & John Powel a Line between Luke Sumner & Charity raiby a line between Henry Griffen & Luke Sumner &c Pres^t Luke Sumner Elisha Sumner John Knight

Hezekiah Norfleet
Henry Griffin

[232]

By an Order Dated Decemb^r 23^d 1771 We the Subscribers have process^d all the Lines in our bounds peaceably & Quietly without any Objection Viz^t a Line between Jesse Battle & Elisha Ballard in pressence of Jethro pruden a line between Benj^a Forset & Elisha Balard pres^t Jethro pruden a line between Benj^a Forset & Danl March in presence of Jessey Battle also a line between Danl March & Ann Forset also a line between Ann Forset & Ben Forset also a line between Elisha Balard & Elisha Ashbourn pres^t John Best A Line between Elisha ashbourn & W^m pruden pres^t Jessey Battle also a nother between Henry wright & Elisha Ashbourn pres^t Jessey Battle another between Rebeckah Hine & Elisha Ashbourn in presence of John Best a line between Rebeckah Hines & Peter Ashbourn in presence of James Newlan a line between Abraham Veline & Hardey Hine Hezekiah Veline A Line between Abraham Veline & Anth^o Holaday

---

[109] The clerk had written "a Line between" between Hezekiah Norfleet and Norman Johnson, and then incompletely erased the phrase and substituted "prest".

in presence of John Best a line between John Ashbourn & Antho Holaday in presence of John Best & Hezekiah Veline also a line between Peter Ashbourn & John Ashbourn also between Josiah Gwin and John Ashbourn also a line between David Meade & Josiah Vaughan pres^t John Bist also a line between Daniel March & John Ashbourn also a Line between Danl March & John Ashbourn also a Line between David Meade & Peter Ashbourn pres^t John Best a Line between Josiah Gwin & Thos Gwin pres^t John Best a Line between Josiah Gwin & Thos Gwin pres^t John Wilson a Line between Thos Gwin & Wm Moore pres^t Wm Copelan also a Line between David Meade & Wm Moore Wm Copelan pres^t also a line between David Meade & Wm Moore Wm Copelan pres^t a Line done betwixt Francis Powel & Jethro pruden & Wm Pruden the Line done between Jethro pruden & W^m pruden and Wm Wright the Line done betwixt Wm Wright & Rebeckah Hine

       John Ashbourn
       & Josiah Gwin

[233]

We the Subscribers Agreeable to an Order of Vestry held in Suffolk Decemb^r 23 1771 have mett & renew'd all the Land Marks In the Bounds of the Order Excepting a peice of a Line between Samuel Cohoon & Robt Tucker as Neither of the parties met all the Other Lines was process^d in the presence of the Inhabitants of the Said Lands without any Interruption by us

       Christ^{or} Roberts
       Joseph Thomas

In Obedience to an Order of Vestry held in Suffolk town Decemb^r 23^d 1771 We the Subscribers have process'd every Mans Land mention'd in our bounds with Satisfaction to the owners thereof themselves pres^t

       Willis Streator
       Edward Moore

In Obedience to an Order Vestry past 23 decemb^r 1771 we have met & proces^d all the Land in our Bounds Nicholas Harmons Land done pres^t John Smith & Moses Harrel Moses Harrels done pres^t the Same Amos rawls his Land done present the Same Job Harrels Land done present the Same Edward Bakers Land done pres^t the Same John bakers Land done pres^t Amos Rawls & John Baker Norman Gourleys done pres^t the Same

Edward Peels done pres^t the Same Colan Gorleys done pres^t the Same Samuel Bakers done pres^t Amos Rawls & Kaleb Savage Kaleb Savage^s done pres^t the Same Jacob Sumners done pres^t him Self & Jethro Sumner Thos frashers done prest the Same Cader Raibies done pres^t the same Wm Jones done pres^t the Same Joseph Ellis his Land done pres^t the Same Co^{lo} Dempsey Sumners done present himself & Jesse peel Jesse peels done pres^t the Same Wm Pearces done pres^t himself & Saml Smith Saml Smiths done pres^t the Same Richd Tayloes done pres^t the Same

Richd Tayloe
Edwd Baker

[234]

Persueant to an Order of Vestry Held in Suffolk 23 Decemb^r 1771 We the Subscribers have process^d all the bounds of Land in our precint in peaceable & Quiet procesion in pressence of the inhabitants as follows

Charles Hinis Land proces^d in pressence of Richd Williams & Moses dardan

Matt Edwards Land in presence of Soloman Edwards & John Carr
Soloman Edwards Land in presence of Jno Carr & Jno Batten
Richd Williams Land in pressence of Charles hines & Matt Jones
A Jones Land Land [sic] in pressence of Richd Williams & Moses dardan

James Carrs Land in pressence of Jno Carr & Moses Dardan
Jno Carrs Land in pressence of Matt Jones & Jacob Dardan
Moses Dardans Land in pressence of Jacob Darden & John Carr
Elisha Dardens Land in pressence of Jacob Darden & Matt Jones
James Gardeners Land in pres of Hollan Dardan & Matt Gardener
Robert Dardens Land in pressence of Ja^s Gardener & Hollan Darden
Holland Dardans Land in pres of Joshua Gardener & Matt Gardener
Matt Gardeners Land in pres of Ja^s Gardner Charles birdsong
Joshua Gardner Land in pres of Holland Darden & Matt Gardner
Charles Birdsong Land in pres of Matt Gardner & Ja^s Gardner
Wm Lawrence' Land in pres of Jacob Darden Joshua Gardner

The Land that formerly belong^d to Thos Fisher deceas^d in pressence of Holland Dardan and Joshua Gardner

The above has been duly preform'd by us the Subscribers

Elisha Dardan
James Carr

[235]

Pursuant to Order of Vestry for the up^r Parish Nansem^d County we the Subscribers have process^d John Harts Land in pres of Simon Everitt Dread Everit. Titus Cars Land in pres of John Everitt Robt Car Simon Everits Land in pres of John Everitt Dre^d Evtt

Robt Cars Land in pres of Joshua Car Josiah Williams
John Everitts Land in pres of Robt Lawrence Dred Everitt
Robt Lawrence^s Land in pres of John Everitt Robt Carr
John Williams Land in pres of Thos Baile abrames Jo^s Carr
William Allins Land in pres of William Curle John Williams
Wm Curles Land in pres of Rich^d fortune Joshua Carr
George Williams Land in pres of Edwd Cary William Curle
Thos Wiggins Land in pres of Wm Curle Josiah Williams
Thos Bailies Abrames Land in pres of Edwd Cary Wm Curle
Edward Cary^s Land in pres of Thos Bal^s Abrames Wm Curle
John Dardans Land in pres of Wm Battle Wm Curle
Wm Battles Land in pres of John Williams Josiah Williams
Ann Cary^s Land in pres of Wm Battle John Hart

Etheldred Warren
Wm Hearte

[236]

By Submission to y^r Vestry & Church Wardens of the Up^r Parish Nansem^d County Virgin^a be it known that we Abraham Ballard & Edward Norfleet have process^d in the Year of our Lord Christ 1772 first the Line between Joseph Perritt & Wm Turlington the S^d Jo^s Perritt pres^t Next between the Said Perritt & Abraham Ballard each partie pres^t & agreed

then between the said Jo^s Perritt & Jo^s Skiner the Said Jo^s perrit pres^t only

then between the S^d Perritt & Acey Duke Perritt pressent
then between S^d Perritt & Thos Newbey the S^d perritt pres^t only
then between S^d Perritt & Magaret Hall each parties present & Satisfied
then between S^d Perritt & Jonas Mercer the S^d Perritt present only to Shew the Lines Mercer Satisfied

then between S^d Perritt & Isaac Lasetor each parties pres^t & Satisfied
then between Isaac Lasetor & Henry Gwin each parties pres^t And Satisfied

Then between Isaac Lasetor & Jonas Mercer the said Lasetor present & Henry Gwin

Then between David Gwin & Jonas Mercer John rawls appointed to Shew the Lines

Then between Henry Gwin & David Gwin Henry Gwin And John rawls Present

then between David Gwin & Sarah Jones Henry Gwin & John Rawls present. then between Wm Turlington & Ja^s Adams Wm Turlington & Jo^s Sketor pres^t then between David Meade & Ja^s Adams Wm Turlington & Jo^s Sketoe pres^t then between David Meade & Mansfield Turlington Wm Turlington pres^t only. then between Abraham Balard & Wm Turlington Wm Turlington pres^t to shew the Line then between Jo^s Skiner & Christo Norfleet each pres^t then between S^d Skiner & Acey duke each partie pres^t then between Chris Norfleet & Acey Duke each partie pres^t then between Acey duke & Th^{os} Newbey & Acey duke Jo^s Skiner & Chris. Norfleet pres^t then between Jo^s Skiner & Abraham balard each partie pres^t then between Edwd Norfleet & Wm Turlington Edwd Norfleet & Wm Reade pres^t then between Edwd Norfleet & Wm Reade each partie pres^t & Satisfied Then between dan^l March & Wm Reade Wm Reade had Notice Jno Ja^s appointed to Shew the Line then between the S^d March & Mansfield Turlington Mansfield Turlinton & John James pres^t then between Edwd Norfleet & Abraham ballard Each partie pres^t & Satisfied. The Last line between Chris Norfleet & Thos Newbey The Said Norfleet & Jo^s Skiner present

[237]

In Obedience to an Order of Vestry bearing date Decemb^r 23^d 1771 to us directed We have proces^d the Lands in the bounds therein mentiond as Follows

A Line between the Gleab Land & Aaron Lasitor in presents of the Revd Patrick Lunan & the Said Lasiter Saml Carr & David Campbell

A line between Aaron Lasitor & John Campbell in pressence of S^d Lasetor David Campbell Saml Carr Rev^d P Lunan

A Line between John Campbell & Willis Riddick in pres^t s^d Riddick D: Campbell

A line between Willis Riddick & Hez Riddick in pressence of Said Willis riddick David Campbel & Aaron Lasetor

A Line between Hezekiah Riddick and Magaret Stallings in presenc of Saml Carr Wm Stallings & Josiah Riddick

A line between Margaret Stallings & James Stallings in presence of Wm Stallings & Josiah Riddick

A Line between Wm Stallings & Ja^s Stallings in pressence of the Said Wm Stallings and Josiah Riddick

A Line between Wm Stallings & Josiah riddick in pres^nc of the parties

A Line between Henry Riddick Miriam Ridick in pres^s Jo^h Riddick & Saml Carr A Line between Henry Riddick & Ja^s Booth in pressence of Josiah riddick Saml Carr & Henry Booth

A Line between Ja^s Booth & Jotham Lasetor in presents of the parties

A Line between Henry Riddick & Jo^s Booth Called the old pattent line on the West Side pocoson in presence of Saml Carr Jo^s Ridick H. Booth

A Line between Jo^s Booth & Meriam Riddick in pres Sam Car Hen Booth

A Line between Jotham Lasetor & Meriam Riddick in pres Sam Car H: Booth

A Line between Soloman Riddick & Amos Riddick in pres S: Carr H: Booth

A Line between Amos Riddick & Moses Riddick pres^t S: Carr Henry Booth

A Line between Josiah Riddick the elder & Danl Riddick Wm Stallings Josiah Riddick Junr & Amos Riddick

A Line between Josiah Riddick sn^r & Wm Stallings in presents of Said Stallings & Amos Riddick & Josiah Riddick

A Line between Josiah Riddick sn^r & Ja Stallings in pres of Wm Stallins & Josiah Riddick sn^r A Line between Magarett Stallings and John Campbell in pres of Wm Stallings and Josiah Riddick

A Line between Josiah Riddick Senr and John Campbell in presents of David Campbell Saml Carr & Aaron Lasetor

          Willis Riddick
          Henry Riddick

[238 and 239 blank]

[240]

At A Vestry Held in Suffolk Town Novemb^r 25th 1772 for the up^r Parish of Nansem^d County

Pressent Messrs David Meade Jacob Sumner Gent C: Wardens
Colo Lemuel Riddick Willis Riddick ⎫
Benjamin Baker Jerimyah Godwin ⎬ Gentmn Vestry Men
Henry Riddick Saml Cohoon & Thos Norfleet ⎭

To Aaron Allmand reader at Suffolk Church & Keeper of the Parish Register	2500
To do an Allowance of 4 per ct	100
To George Spivy reader at the Ciprus Chappell	1000
To Elisha Darden do at Holy Neck do	1250
To Wm Whitfield Sexton of Suffolk Church from the first Feb. 1772 to this day @ 800 per year	665
To the administratrix of Richd Leviston late Sexton of Suffolk Church	135
To Hardey Jarnagan do at Sumerton Chappell	250
To Hezekiah Norfleet do at the Ciprus do	200
To John Baker a Leivie overcharg'd Last year	45
To be Sold by the Church Wds at July Court for Cash or Collected from the people at 2d per lb	70000
	76145
To the Collector at 6 per Ct	4569
	80714

Tis Ordered that the Church Wardens or whoom they Shall apoint after giveing Bond & Security As Useual for that purpose Collect from every tithable in this parrish 46lb Tobacco on 1777 tithes   81742
And therwith discharge the parrish Creddittors
     Depossitum due to the parrish   1028

[241]

It is the opinion of this Vestry that no Tobacco be Leivied for the Revd Patrick Lunan present Minister of this parish on Account of his Ill behaviour and Neglect of duty in the Churches In which Opinion Colo Lemuel Riddick dissents

Colo Lemuel Riddick & Samuel Cohoon is appointed & Sworn Church Wardens for the Ensueing year

Wills Cowper is appointed a Vestry man in the room of Thoˢ Gilchrist

This Vestry a Greeˢ to reverse an order made bearing Date Febuary 2ᵈ 1771 Concerning Renting out the poors House and that the Said house be restablished as formerly A Greeable to the Act of Assembly relateing to the Said House

Tis Ordered that the Church Wᵈˢ provide Furniture and Necessaries As Shall Seem to them Convenient for the poors House & employ the poor in Such Work as they Shall think proper

[242]

The Upʳ Parrish of Nansemᵈ Dʳ In Cash Novemᵇʳ 25ᵗʰ 1772

To Hardey Jarnagan for Grubing the Chappell Yard	£ 0 : 15 : 0
To James Bates for Several articles & work done on the Gleab to be paid to Willis Riddick	1 : 19 : 6
To Dockʳ Cohoon for Medicines & attendance on the poor	12 : 17 : 6
To Henry Bates for finding wood for the poors House 7 Months to be paid to Willis Riddick	3 : 0 : 0
To Charles Ruther Constable in Norfolk for Conveing Danˡ Clark & Family back	5 : 5 : 0
To Thoˢ Norfleet for Necessaries for Hansel	2 : 8 : 2
To Webb & Meridith for Several Coffins for the Poor	2 : 0 : 0
To John Richards for Boarding the Orphan of Brounds 9 Mᵒ	4 : 10 : 0
To Wᵐ Whitfield for Sundris work done in the Church	2 : 8 : 0
To John Ease for keeping Robᵗ Abrams	8 : 12 : 6
To Dᵒ for Edey Peels Board	5 : 10
To Dᵒ for Board & Funeral of Elizabeth Meltears Child	2 : 10
To Thoˢ Willis for Board Robᵗ Lowrey	4
To Thoˢ Turlington for A Sheet to bury John Groves	9
To Norman Johnson for Moses Raibies diet 3 Months	1 : 5
To Luke Baker for 5 Barˡˢ Corn found Charity parker & Children	3 : 15
To Sarah Wood for Nurseing Rogers 11 days for which she is to be allow'd her rent	
To James Night for Nurseing & Burying Elizᵃ Haket	4
To James Adams for Carrying a Lunatick person to WᵐˢBurg Omited Last Year	3

To the administratrix of Richd Leviston for filling up Several Graves & burying Bethel Rogers	10	
To D^o for 6 Weeks board of Richd Miller & 5 of Saml MCfarn	4 : 19	
To Wm Dixon for makeing a Coat & Bretches for Hansell	7 : 6	
To James Campbel for work done on the Gleab	3	
To Wills Cowper Ball. his Account for Sundries for the poor	61	9¾
To John Miles ball. his Acc^t as overseer of the poors house 1770	3	
To Hezekiah Norfleet for a Frame for the Well & Cleaning the Chappell yard	3 : 5	
To Mary Stallings for Board Susanah Nobles	3 : 10 : 10	
	£ 147 : 17 : 9¾	

[243]

To Amount Brought forward	147 : 17 : 9¾	
To James Pugh for Work done on the Organ	5 : 10	
To Wm Alegree for Tuneing the Organ & finding Locks	5 : 4 : 6	
To Hardey Jarnagan for maintaining the orphan of Ann Homes 10 Months & 10 Days @ £ 6 per Ann	5 : 3	
To Thos Craighead for a Coffen for Hester Bates	10	
To Wm Granbury for Hinghes & Bolts for the Gleab	10 : 6	
To Elizabeth Parks a poor Woman	4 : 10	
To Jacob Sumner for Sundries for the poor	1 : 19 : 10	
To Ann Baker a poor Woman	4 : 10	
To Jean Wiat D^o	4	
To Sarah Horton D^o	4	
To John Groves^s Widdow	4	
To Ann Wiggins a poor Woman	3	
To John Hamilton a poor Man	7 : 10	
To Joseph Skeatoe d^o	5	
To Elizabeth Stallins a poor Woman	4	
To Wm Stallins a poor Man	4	
To Capt Mills Riddick the Seccond payment for the Gleab & Intrest thereon	175	

To Mary Parker for Board John Thomas & Cloathes from the 23ᵈ Jan till now at £ 6 per Ann	5	
To Charles Raibey for Sundries & Cureing Moses raiby of the dropsie	5 : 5	
To Daniel Peck a poor Man	2	
To Keziah Groves Rent one Year to be paid to Colᵒ Riddick	2	
To John Weatherley for keeping Robᵗ Abrams 1 Month	: 13	

£ 401 : 3 : 7¾

Signd   Lemuel Riddick } C : Wᵈˢ
            Samuel Cohoon

Truly Enterd by Aaron Allmand C : V

[244]

At A Vestry Held at Samul Swans in Suffolk Town January 2ᵈ 1773 for the Upʳ Parrish of Nansemᵈ County

Presᵗ Colᵒ Lemuel Riddick Samˡ Cohoon Gentᵐⁿ Ch : Wᵈˢ
    Colᵒ Willis Riddick Henry Riddick } Gentlemen Vestry Men
    David Meade Jerimiah Godwin
    Thoˢ Norfleet & Wills Cowper

It is the opinion of this Vestry that the Church Wᵈˢ Refuse the Revᵈ Patrick Lunan admittance in any the Churches or Chappels in this parish to preform divine Service on Account of his Ill behaviour & Neglect of duty

Colonel Lemuel Ridᵈ Colᵒ Willis Riddick & Thoˢ Norfleet Gentlemen desiers to be Enter'd dessenters from the above Opinion

Tis Ordered that the Church Wᵈˢ do pay out of the   70000ˡᵇ
of Tobacco that was Ordered to be Sold at July Court
as followeth

To Michael King Last Sherreiff for Insolvents Tikets & Ball due Last year	4456
To George Frith a Leivie over Charg'd Last year	45
	4501

Tis Ordered that the Church Wᵈˢ receive from Michael king the Sum of £ 3..1..3 due from him to the parish it being the difference in what Tobacco he Collected Last year at 2ᵈ per lb

And Pay to Mʳ David Meade the Sum of £ 15..19..9 it being the Ball due to him after giveing Credditt for the Sale of Last years Tobacco

Mʳ Willis Streator is appointed a Vestry man In the room of Mʳ Josiah Granbury deceasᵈ

        Signd Lemuel Riddick
        Samˡ Cohoon

[245]

At a Vestry held at Samuel Swans in suffolk Decembʳ 20ᵗʰ 1773

Present Colⁿ Lemuel Riddick Samˡ Cohoon Gentⁿ Ch: Wardens
    Colⁿ Willis Riddick Henry Riddick Thomas Norfleet ⎫ Gentⁿ
    Wells Cooper Willis Streater Benjamin Baker ⎬ Vestry
    & Jeremiah Godwin   ⎭ Men

To Aaron Allmand reader at suffolk Church & Keeper of the Parrish register	2500
To do An allowance of 4 per Cent	100
" George Spivy reader at the Cyprus Chapel	1000
" Elisha Darden do at Holy Neck	1250
" William Whitfield sexton at suffolk Church	800
" Hardy Jarnagan sexton at sumerton Chapel	250
" Hezekiah Norfleet sexton at the Cyprus Chapel	200
" The Sheriff for Insolvents after deducting the Last years depossitum	1772
" Colⁿ Riddick for Copy of 6 List of Tithes	120
" John Robbins Constable allow'd 3 Levies for the years 70: 71 & 72	128
	8120
The Upper Parrish of Nansemond Cʳ	
By Colⁿ Riddick for 8 Insolvents	368
	7752
To be sold by the Ch: Wardens at July Court or Collected from the People at 10/ per Cᵗ[110]	90000
	97752

---

[110] The clerk has written "reversed" in the margin at the beginning of this entry, and "These Sums are all reversed," at the end of this and several following

To the Collector at 6 per C^t	5865
	103617

Tis ordered that the Ch: Wardens or whom they shall appoint do collect from every Tithable in this Parrish 58 lb of Tob^o or to recieve from the People at 10/ per C^t in Lieu of Said Tob^o 58 lb Tob^o on 1779 Tithes   is   103182

Ballance due the Collector		435
The Parrish D^r 7752 lb Tobacco at 10/ is	£ 38 .. 15 ..	2½

[246]

Dr The Upper Parrish of Nansemond in Cash Decemb^r 20th 1773 Col^n Riddick rendered in his Acc^t as Ch: Warden for

	£	S	d
sundry disburstments for the Poor and the Bal^l due him is	126	15	3
To Doct^r Cohoon for Medicines per his Acc^t	50	1	9
" Wells Cowper for 3 y'ds Linen		4	6
" William Whitfield for Work done in the Church & burying some Poor Persons	3	9	1
" William Webb for Coffins	1	15	
" David Meade bal^l his Acc^t Last Vestry	16	14	10½
" Meriam Riddick for Keeping Sebiah Fields In her Lying In	2	10	
" Ann Leviston for board of Miller & McFarron	8	0	6
" Hardy Jarnagan for board of Riddick Homes	1	10	
" Luke Baker for 28 bushels Corn	3	10	
" Ruth Reade for Attending Sarah Scarbord In her Lying In	2	10	
" John Groves for Keeping John Thomas one year	2	10	
" Mary Baker a Poor Woman to be p^d to Sarah Jordan	2	10	
" John Richards for Keeping Jethro Bound	6		

entries, but between them and the column of figures. Braces before and after the entries apparently indicate that these statements apply to the sums from 90000 to 435. Since these entries and sums seem to be correct and in order, the statements probably applied to the form in which the figures were originally written before being copied into the vestry book.

To Hardy Rawls for Keeping Absolom Jones's Child ¾ of a year at £ 3	2 : 5
" Ann Baker a Poor Woman	4 : 10
" Charity Parker do	3
" Daniel Peck a Poor Man	2
" Keziah Groves a Poor Woman	3
" Jean Wiat do	4
" Joseph Skeatoe a Poor Man	5
" Elizabeth Stallins a Poor Woman	3
" William Stallins a Poor Man	3
" Mary Stallins a Poor Woman	2
" Mary Scutchins do	2
" Capt Mills Riddick for his Last paym^t for the Glebe	166 : 13 : 4
" Interest thereon from not known	
	£ 428 : 9 : 3½
Bro^t Over 7752^{lb} Tob^o @ 10/	38 : 15 : 2½
	467 : 4 : 6
To the Collector at 6 per Ct	28 : 0 : 8½
	£ 495 : 5 : 2½

[247]

Col^n Lemuel Riddick Came into Vestry this day after serving this Parrish as a Vestry Man 40 Years has resigned on Acc^t of his Age & Infirmities

Mr Andrew Meade & Mr John Riddick is appointed Vestry Men in the Room of Col^n Lemuel Riddick & Mr David Meade Gent^n the one having resigned & the other remov'd out of this County

Capt Wells Cooper & Mr Thomas Norfleet are appointed & sworn Ch: Wardens in the room of Col^n Riddick & Doct^r Cohoon

Wells Cowper
Thomas Norfleet

    Truly Enterd by Aaron Allmand Clk Vestry

At a Vestry held at Mr Samuel Swans in Suffolk Town March 15th 1774 for the Upper Parish of Nansemond County

Pres.t Cap.t Wells Cooper Thomas Norfleet Gent.n Ch: Wardens
    Col.n Willis Riddick Henry Riddick Willis Streator ⎫ Gentlemen
    John Riddick Benj.n Baker Jeremiah Godwin   ⎬ Vestry
    Jacob sumner   ⎭ Men

M.r John Riddick is Qualified as a Vestry Man and has taken the Oath in Vestry According to Law

Tis orderd that the Ch: Wardens do apply to & agree with the Reverend M.r John Agnew to preach once a Month at Suffolk Church & also at the Cyprus Chapel & to agree with the Reverend M.r Burgess to preach once a Month at the Holy Neck Chapel

Tis order'd that the Ch: Wardens do purchase Tobacco to pay the several parrish Creditors their several sums due in Tobacco

This Vestry agrees to reverse an order made last Vestry bearing date 20.th of Decemb.r 1773 relating to the Collection of the Parrish Levies it was then order'd that the Collector should recieve from every Titheable in this Parrish 58 lb of Tob.o per tithe or recieve from the People at 10/ per C.t but it is now ordered that the Collector recieve from each titheable in this Parrish the sum of Five shillings & seven Pence Or 56 lb of Tobacco

on 1779 Tithes is   £ 496 . . 12 . . 9
                         495 . . 5 . . 2½

Ball.e due the Parrish   1 . . 7 . . 6½

To James Booth overcharg'd a Levie in the year 1772 46 lb Tob.o
    Truly Enterd by   Signd Wills Cowper
        Aaron Allmand C: V   Tho.s Norfleet

[248]

At a Vestry held at sam.l swan's in suffolk Dec.r 17, 1774 for the Upper Parrish of Nansemond

Pres.t Wells Cooper & Thomas Norfleet Gent.n Ch: Wardens
    Capt.n Henry Riddick Benj.n Baker   ⎫
    Willis Streator Jacob Sumner Jerimiah   ⎬ Gent.n Vestry men
    Godwin John Riddick & Willis Riddick   ⎪
    & samuel Cohoon   ⎭

To Aaron Allmand reader at Suffolk Church & Keeper
    of the Parrish Register as per Agreem.t   20

To ditto for Extra Services 6 days	2 : 5	
To George spivy reader & sexton at syprus Chapel	9 : 12	
To John Glover reader at Holy Neck	8	
To Wm Whitfield sexton at suffolk Church	6 : 8	
To ditto for Sundries for the Church & burying some poor	3 : 2 : 2	
To Doct^r Cohoon his Acc^t for Medicines for the poor	30 : 10 : 6	
To Captn Wells Cowper rendered in his Acct as Church Warden for Sundries for the poor & the Ballance due him Is	90 : 10 : 8	
To Elizabeth Fletcher for Attending Sarah Woods	2 : 10	
To Mary Stallins a poor Woman	2	
To John Richards for keeping Bond's Child 11 Months & 10 days	5	
To Arthur Boy'd for Keep^g Riddick Holmes	3	
To Silas Siers for Nurs^g Mary Robinson	2 : 4	
To Wm Nelms for Burying Rebecca Morris	1 : 10	
To James Campbell for Coffins &c	4 : 10	
To Wm Webb for 2 Coffins for Hansel & S. Woods	1 : 7 : 6	
To Francis Duke for Coffin & Grave	10	
To John Baker a Levie Overcharg'd	7 : 8	
To Col^n Lemuel Riddick for Copy 4 List of Tithes	10	
To Joseph Skeatoe a poor Man	8	
To the Reverend John Agnew for 5 Sermons	10	
To Luke Baker for 5½ bls Corn for Charity Parker	2 : 15	
To ditto for Keep^g Ann Baker one Year	4 : 10	
To Jean Wiat a poor Woman	4	
	£ 223 : 2 : 6	

[249]

Brought forward	223 : 2 : 6	
To Elizabeth Stallins a poor Woman	3	
To William ditto Man	3	
To Jno Lester for Nursing a Child	2	
To Ruth Reade do. Sarah Scarboard	2	
To Mary Groves for Keep^g Jno Thomas one year	2 : 10	
To Ann Thomas a poor Woman	4	

To Daniel Peck a poor Man	3
To Mary Scutchins do Woman	4
To Captn Kinchen Godwin for Insolvents	12 : 11 : 4½
To Sarah Moore for her Rent to be paid Captn Baker	2
To Dorothy Melteir a poor Woman	1 : 10
To Matthew Parker for 4 Load of Wood for the poor	8
To be Levied for the Use of the Parrish &c	100
To discharge the Interest of the Ch: Warden's Bond to Captn Mills Riddick to be paid to Mr Jno Riddick	17 : 8 : 8
	£ 380 : 10 : 6½
To the Collector at 6 per Cent	22 : 16 : 9[111]
	403 : 7 : 3½
Tis order'd that the Ch: Wardens or whom they shall appoint do Collect from Every Tithable in this parrish 4/7 On 1758 Tithes	402 : 17 : 6
Ballance due the Collector	9 : 9½

Tis order'd that the Poors house be discontinued As it is the Opinion of this Vestry that it be rather an Incumberance to the Parrish & that the said House be rented out by the Ch: Wardens & the furniture sold

                                        Wills Cooper
Truly Enter^d Thomas Norfleet
   Aaron Allmand Clk Vestry

[250]

At a Vestry held at Mr Thomas Langstons March 21st 1775

Present Mr Wills Cowper   Mr Thomas Norfleet Gent^n Ch: Wardens
    Messrs Henry Riddick, Benjamin Baker, Samuel Cohoon
    Jeremiah Godwin & John Riddick Gent^n Vestry Men

This Vestry has reciev'd the Reverend Wm Andrews as Minister of this Parrish for one Year and agrees to pay him the sum of £ 128 Current Money for Services hereafter Mentioned, He is to perform One Sunday at Suffolk Church, One Sunday at Holy Neck & the Next Sunday at

---

[111] This calculation is slightly in error as to pence.

Suffolk Church, And the Next Sunday at the Cyprus Chapel and so to Continue the year out, Good friday and Christmas to preach at Suffolk Church.

Tis Ordered that Captn Wills Cooper do pay the Reverend Mr Duncan the Sum of £ 6 for 3 Sermons preach'd at Suffolk Church & Cyprus Chapel

At a Vestry held for Laying the Parrish Levie it was omitted to ossess what Quantity of Tobacco the people shoud pay in Lieu of 4/7 tis now order'd that the people may pay the Sum of 4/7 or 46 lb Tobacco per tithe

Tis Order'd the Church Wardens apply to Mr Lunan to give up the Gleab & to have it put in repair for the Reverend Wm Andrews As it appears to this Vestry that it is of not much Use to the said Mr Lunan and that there is much danger of the House being destroy'd by fire and of its going to ruin On Account of some person to Live in it it appearing that Mr Lunan is Seldom at home and in Case he refuses to give up the Gleab to take possession

                                    Wills Cowper
Truly Enter'd   Thomas Norfleet
    Aaron Allmand Clk Vestry

[251]

At a Vestry held at Mr Tho: Langstons in Suffolk Septr 30th 1775

Present Capt Wills Cowper Mr Thomas Norfleet Gent Ch: Wardens
        Capt Jeremiah Godwin Col: Willis Riddick Doct: Samuel Cohoon Mr Thos. Norfleet Mr John Riddick Mr Jacob Sumner & Mr Andrew Meade Gent Vestry Men

Tis Orderd that the Ch Wardens do pay to the Reverend Patrick Lunan the sum of £ 100 the Money that was Levied Last fall &c In June 1777 to pay the sum of £ 100 more and in June 1778 to Recieve the Last payment of £ 100 more Exclusive of Interest Which makes the sum of £ 300 Likewise to discharge the said Lunan of all costs that may or shall accrue from Lawsuits that are Commenc'd by the Parrish against the said Lunan on his giving a proper Relinquishment of all Immunities emoluments or Claims that he the said Lunan hath or ever shall have in or against this parrish as a Minister

                                          Wills Cowper
                                          Thomas Norfleet

Septr 30th 1775 The Reverend Patrick Lunan, claiming to be Rector of the Upper parish in Nansemond, appeared this day in Vestry, & hereby Relinquishes all Right, Title & Claim as Rector of the said Parish

          Pat: Lunan

Witness Present
 Willm Cowper
 Thomas Langston
Truly Enterd Aaron Allmand Clk Vestry

[252]

At a Vestry held at Suffolk Decemb^r 19th 1775 for the Upper Parish of Nansemond

 Present Capt Wills Cowper Mr Tho. Norfleet Gent. Ch: Wardens
  Col^o Willis Riddick Messrs Henry Riddick Ben: Baker
  Willis Streator Jacob Sumner Sam: Cohoon Jeremiah
  Godwin & John Riddick Gent: Vestry Men

To the Rev^d Wm Andrews his Salary as per Agreement due in April	128		
To Aaron Allmand Reader at Suffolk Church &c	20		
To ditto for Extra Services	15		
To Geo: Spivey former Clk of Cyprus Chapel	9 : 12		
To John Glover Clk at Holy Neck	8		
To John Frith a Levie overcharged Last year		4 : 7	
To Doct Cohoon his Acct for Medicines for the Poor	22	6	
To Capt Wills Cowper Ball: his Acct	29 : 8 : ¾		
To Wm Whitfield Sexton at Suffolk & keeping the Chu: Linen	7 : 10		
To do Burying the poor &c	4 : 17 : 2		
To Tho: Norfleet his Acct as Ch Warden	1 : 15 : 3		
To Henry Gwin for keep^g Sarah Ease one year after deducting £ 2..13..3 for Sundries brot. from Poors House	4 : 17		
To Wm Webb for 4 Coffins for the Poor	2 : 10		
To Thos Gwin for keep^g & burying Ebenezer Garland	1 : 15 : 7		
To Wm Nelms for Board Abenezer Garland	2 : 2 : 6		
To the Executors of Col: Lem: Riddick for Copy 4 List Tithes	13 : 4		

To James Bates for Work done at the Gleab	5 : 11 : 3
To Margaret Hall for Nursing Martha Willis	1 : 10
To Alexander Ross for Cloaths for M^rs frazior	1 : 5
To Will. Cowper for Meal & Remov^g a poor family	1 : 2 : 6
To Jesse Lassetor Boarding Thos. Brown Bennitts	10
To Joseph Holland Keeping Sarah Moore	2
To Ann Thomas a Poor Woman	5
To Joseph Skeatoe a Poor Man	10
To Eliz^th Stallins a Poor Woman	3
To Mary Scutchings do	4
To Dorothy Miltier do	1 : 10
	288 : 19 : 8¾

[253]

Brought forward	288 : 19 : 8¾
To Dempsey Baker for board Ann Baker	5
To Jean Wiat a Poor Woman	4
To Mills Howel for Cleaning Chapel Yard	1 : 17 : 6
To Will Pugh Sheriff for Insolvents & ball: Last year	13 : 1 : 10½
To John Everitt for keep^g Eliza. Holland 2 Mths & 12 days	3 : 10
To Catherine Johnston for do Mrs Hedgbeth one year	10
To Thomas Langston 3 times Acting as Clk of Chapel	1 : 10
To be Levied for the Use of the Parrish	100
	£ 427 : 19 : 1¼
To the Collector at 6 per Cent	25 : 13 : 6½
	453 : 12 : 7¾
Tis Orderd that the Collector Recieve from Each Titheable in this Parrish the Sum of 5/ on 1819 Tithes Amounts to	454 : 15
& to discharge the Parrish Creditors Due the Parish	£ 1 : 2 : 4¼

Capt Henry Riddick & Mr John Riddick are appointed and Sworn Ch Wardens in the Room of Messrs Wills Cowper & Thomas Norfleet

The Revd Will: Andrews is Recieved as Minister of this Parrish
To Daniel Peck a poor Man £ 5 to be paid of the £ 100

              Henry Riddick
              John Riddick

[254]

1775 Cont^d

	No.
Tis Orderd that Dempsey Riddick & Geo: Sparling procession all the bounds of Land	1
Christopher Roberts Junr & Joseph Thomas	2
Henning Webb & Samuel Nelms	3
Joseph Scott & Jas Lawrence	4
John Best Junr & Will Stakes	5
Ezekiel Virlines & Thos Gwinn	6
Will: King & John King	7
John Giles & Joseph Skinner	8
John Porter & Benjn Turlington	9
Arthur Jones Junr & Will Jarnagan	10
David Howell & Will Glover	11
Hopkins Howell & John Jones	12
Zachariah Coupland & William Holland	13
Joseph Holland & Stephen Darden	14
John Carr & Holland Darden	15
John Everitt & John Hart	16
Thos Holland & John Flemings	17
Arthur Smith & Will Davidson	18
John Brothers & John Brinkley	19
Thomas Harrell Junr & Henry Raiby	20
John Smith & Jacob Duke	21
Edward Baker & William Pearce	22
John Ballard & Abram Ballard	23
Zacheus Lassitor & Moses Booth	24
Robert Riddick & Will Midcap	25
Dempsey Baker & John Brewer	26
Josiah Riddick & Amos Riddick	27
Abraham Coles & Israel Beamon	28

            Henry Riddick
Truly Enterd   John Riddick
 A. Allmand C: Vestry

[255]

Pursuant to an order of Vestry held in Suffolk Dec[r] 19th 1775 We the Subscribers have processiond & Renew'd Each persons Land Mark in our precint with the Approbation of parties therein Concern and in peace & quietniss

        Jacob Duke
        John Smith

We the Subscribers have processiond all the bound of Land According to Order of the Vestry held 19th Dec[r] 1775 at Suffo:

        Will. Davidson
        Arthur Smith

In obedience to an Order of Vestry from Suffolk Dec[r] 19th 1775 We the Subscribers have processiond all the Lands Included in the Order with the Owners present

        Will: King
        John King

We the subscribers have processiond all the Lands within our bounds peacably and quietly

        John Ballard
        Abraham Ballard

We the Subscribers have Processiond all the Lands within our bounds peaceably and Quietly

        John Giles
        Joseph Skinner

Pursuant to an order of Vestry Dated Decemb[r] 19th 1775 We the subscribers have met & processiond all the Bounds of Land in our precinct between Black Water & Nottoway river in peaceable possession in presence of the Inhabitants

Given Under our hands this 10th day of August Anno Domino [?] 1776

        Holland Darden
        John Carr

Agreeable to an Order of Vestry We the subscribers have Renewd all the Land marks in our district peaceably without any Interruption

        John Best Jun[r]
        William Stakes

[256]

The Account of the Land that Zaccheus Lassetor and Moses Booth hath processiond with the names of the persons present in our bounds from Newbys Road down the Barbique & down the Cyprus Swamp to the desart down the desart to the Pocoson up the Pocoson to Couplands Branch between William Roundtree & Thos Newby Wm Roundtree present Between Aramas [?] Duke & Newby Roundtree & Duke present Zaccheus Lassetor & Duke present Between Edwd Bower & Newby Brewer present between Brewer & Joshua Noshar [?]^{112} ditto present between Wm Roundtree & David Gwin & Noshar [?]^{113} present Between James Boyce & Henry Larrence Boyce present Between Boyce & James Skeato both present betwen Skeato & Larrence Lassetor present Benjn Boyce & Ja^s Skeato both present between Skeato & Lawrence Joseph Lassetor present between Joseph Booth & Joseph Lassetor both present Jesse Lassetor & Joseph Ellis both present between Wm Roundtree & John Harrell Wm Roundtree present between John Harrell & Moses Booth both present John Harrell & Jethro Booth both present between Daniel Lassetor & Newby Lassetor between Daniel Lassetor & Geo. Spivey between Spivy & Jesse Lassetor Jos. Skinner present between Daniel Lassetor & Abram Lassetor ditto present between John Roundtree & Daniel Lassetor & Abram Lassetor John Roundtree present between John Roundtree & Widow Roundtree ditto present between Abram Lassetor Senr & Widow Roundtree Robt Lassetor present between Abram Lassetor & Jotham Lassetor Ditto present between Abram Lassetor Daniel Lassetor & Jesse Lassetor ditto present between Wm Roundtree & Jacob Price Roundtree present

             Zaccheus Lassetor
             Moses Booth

[257]

In obediance to an order of Vestry dated Decemb^r 19th 1775 We the Subscribers have met & processiond the following Lines Viz

A Line between John Brothers & John Brinkley Shad^k Wilkings present Between Jno. Brinkley & Jno. Wilkins & between Jno. Brothers

---

[112-113] The rendering of these surnames is little more than a guess. They are probably the same name although they appear dissimilar. The first also looks like "hackar," "hacken," "hoshar," or some other spelling; the second, "Nothar," or "Hoshar."

& John Wilkings Shad. Wilkins prest. between Luke Sumner & John Wilkins Thos Wilkins present between John Brothers & John Brinkley Shad. Wilkins prest. between John Brinkley & Luke Sumner Thos Wilkins prest. between Daniel Frankline & John Brinkley between Daniel Frankline & Edwd Arnal & between Ellener Frankline & Edwd Arnal between Luke Sumner & John Riddick & between Henry Brinkley & Luke Sumner Shad. Wilkings present Between Ellener Frankline & Luke Sumner Henry Brinkley present Between Wm Sivels & Ellener Frankline & between Wm Sivels & Henry Brinkley Wm Sivels prest. between Shad. Wilkings & Wm Sivels & between Shad. Wilkings & Daniel Riddick between Shad. Wilkins & John Barr between John Brinkley & Wm Brothers between John Brinkley & Wm Brinkley between Wm Brinkley & Daniel Riddick between Shad. Wilkins & John Brinkley Shad. Wilkings present between Daniel Riddick & John Barr between John Barr & John Brinkley Daniel Riddick present between Wm Brothers & John Brothers Shad. Wilkins pres^t between James Brinkley & John Riddick Mills Brinkley present between Luke Sumner & John Meltier John Me[l]tier pres^t between Henry Griffin & John Riddick & between Henry Griffin & Humphrey Griffin between Henry Griffin & Hezekiah Norfleet Henry Griffin present betwen John Brinkley & Kadah Brinkley between Kadah Brinkley & Solomon Riddick between Solo. Riddick & John Brinkley between John Brinkly & John Brinkley between John Brinkley & Humphrey Griffin between John Brinkley & Humphrey Griffin between John Griffin & Eli Griffin between John Brinkley & Solo. Riddick between John Brinkly & Joshua Spivey John Brinkley present. between Eli Griffin & Solo. Riddick Humphrey Griffin pres^t between Eli Griffin & Wm Jones Eli Griffin present between Solo. Riddick & Joshua Spivey between Joshua Spivey & Humphrey Griffin between Humphrey Griffin & John Riddick Humphrey Griffin present A Line between John Riddick & Soloman Riddick John Riddick pres^t a Line between soloman [?]^{114} Riddick & John Brinkley John Brinkley pres^t Line between John Brinkley & William Jones Elisha Griffin prest Line between John Riddick & William Jones Ely Griffin pres^t

John Brothers
John Brinkly

---

[114] Or John. The clerk apparently wrote "John," and then partially erased and roughly corrected it.

[258]

In obedience to an Order of Vestry to us directed we have processiond all the Land Marks between Craney Creek & Parkers Creek to the Desart as follows

    a Line between David Baker & Wm Cowper
    a Line between David Baker & Daniel Baker
    a Line between David Baker & James Briggs
    a Line between Daniel Baker & James Briggs
    a Line between David Baker & Moses Slater
    a Line between Moses Slater & James Gregory
    a Line between David Baker & James Gregory
    a Line between David Baker & Daniel Baker

Present Wm Cowper David Baker Daniel Baker James Briggs & Moses Slater

    a Line between Edwd Riddick & Thos Turlington
    a Line between Edwd Riddick & David Sumner
    a Line between Edwd Riddick & Richd Woodward
    a Line between Richd Woodward & Prisilla Anderson
    a Line between Priscilla Anderson & Edwd Riddick
    a Line between Richd Woodord & Leavin Turlington

Present Thos Turlington Ezekiah Riddick & Leavin Turlington, a Line between John Brewer & David Sumner

    a Line between John Brewer & Wm Cowper
    a Line between John Brewer & Charles Cason present Dempsey hollowell a Line between Dempsey Baker & Wm Cowper in Dispute we have Left all the swamp Land unprocessiond on Acct of its being so very Wet Likewise a Line between John Brickle & Leavin Turlington also a Line between the said Brickle & Wm Pugh on Acct of Mr Brickles not Attending

                                    Demse [?] Baker
                                    John Brewer

[259]

In Obediance to an Order of Vestry Dated Decemb^r 19, 1775 We the Subscribers have processiond the following Lands pocessiond Geo Williams Lines in presence of Wm Hart Dred Everitt & Simon Williams Likewise John Everitts in presence of same men also Simon Everitts in presence of Titus Carr, also Edwd Cross in presence of Dred Everitt & John Bonood[?] also Robt Carrs in presence Robert Lawrenc[e][115] & Thos Abrams also Wm Allen in Presence of Edwd Cary & Dred Warren also John Harts in presence of Etheldred Warren Wm Hart & Wm Battle also Wm Curles in presence of Exum Curle & Robt Carr also Edwd Cary's in presence of Whittleton & Dred Warren also Wm Harts on River pres^t Wm Hart, Wm Battle also Mrs Carys in presence of Wm Hart & Dred Warren also Wm Battles in presence of the same also Capt John Darden in presence of Same also Thos Gwaltney present John Everitt also Mourning Williams pres^t Josiah Williams also Robert Lawrence pres^t Robt Carr & Thos Abrams

In processioning the Line between Mourning Williams & Wm Hart Mourning Williams refused to have one Line processiond & Wm Hart another in Presence of Robt Carr Josiah Williams & John Williams

John Everitt
John Hart Senr

[260]

At a Vestry held at Suffolk February 11th 1777 for Upper Parrish

Present Capt Henry Riddick & Mr John Riddick Gent: Ch. Ward^s Col. Willis Riddick Maj^r Jeremiah Godwin Capt Saml Cohoon Capt Ben Baker & Capt Wills Cowper Gent. Vestry men

To the Revd Willm Andrews his Salary 6 Months	£ 64
" Aaron Allmand reader at Suffo. Church & Keeper of the parrish Register	20
" Ditto for Extra services three times & a Levie allow'd	1 : 7 : 6
" John Glover Reader at Holy neck	8
" Joshua Spivey ditto at sumeton (Cyprus)	8
" W. Whitfield sexton suffo. & burying several Soldiers	11 : 1
" Henry Gwin for Keeping Sarah Ease one year	7 : 10
" Jos. Holland ditto Sarah Moore & her son Levie	6

---

[115] This name, which occurs at the end of the line, may have had its final letter crumbled off at the edge of the page.

To John Brothers for Keep^g Eliz Stallins one year	3	
" Mary Scutchins a poor Woman	4	
" Dorothy Meltier Ditto	1 : 10	
" Ann Baker Ditto	5	
" Joseph Skeatoe a poor Man	10	
" John Everitt for Nursing & bury^g Elizth Holland	1 : 10	
" Edwd Brewer for keep^g Mary Hedgbeath one year	10	
" Ditto for Ditto Mary Henry 3 Months	1 : 5	
" Arthur Jones for Ditto Eliz Bailey 5 Mths	2 : 16	
" Wm Boy'd Ditto Martha Rogers 7 do	2 : 10	
" Elisha Cowpland for sundries p^d the poor by Capt Riddicks Order	3 : 15 : 8	
" Michael Jones a poor man	7 : 10	
" Maj^r Jerim^h Godwin for sund^s found Pris^a Gardner	1 : 2	
" Wm King for nursing & burying Abram Lewis	5 :	1 : 10
" Ann Leviston for burying a poor man	6	
" Judith Stallins for Keep^g Sussanah Nobles 3 mths	2 : 10	
" Robert Owens ditto an orphan of Emanuel Walker	1 : 10	
" Elizth Fields ditto Mary Anderson 1 months	8 : 4	
" John Giles ditto Judith Willis 7 months	6	
" Tho. Gwin ditto Teagul Nelson 14 moths	2 : 19 : 2	
" Hardy Jarnagan sexton 18 mths & washing Surplus 4 times	2 : 4 : 4	
" Sarah Wright sexteness holy neck 2 years	3 : 6 : 8	
" John Whimmer for Keep^g Eliz. Willis & John Goodman three months	11	
Carried forward	£220 : 17 : 6	

[261]

Brought forward	£220 : 17 : 6
To Charity Harculus a poor Woman	3
" Sarah Kean for Keep^g an orphan one year	4
" Capt Wills Cowper for 30 Lights Glass for Gleab	18 : 9
" Wm Meltier for Keep^g 2 orphans 10 Months	5
" Mary Groves ditto John Thomas 2 years	4
" Rachael Skeatoe a Poor Woman	1 : 10

To Jacob Daughtree for Keep^g Robt Abrams & mak^g his Cloaths	10 : 3 : 6	
" Doct. Cohoon for Medicines for the poor	47 : 18 : 6	
" Daniel Peck a poor Man	6	
" Willis Streator for a pair shoes for Daniel Peck to be paid out of the £ 6 6/ price		
" Mary Henry a poor Woman	3	
" Robert Abrams a poor Man	10	
" Patr. Lunan his second payment	100	
" Levied for the Use of the parrish	100	
" Mr Littlepage for Copies of 5 List of Tithes	10	
" Wm Whitlock for Nurs^g Priscilla Gardner 4 weeks	1 : 12	
" Sheriff for Insolvents after deducting the Last years Depositum	13 : 12 : 8	
	£532 : 2 : 11	
By Capt Henry Riddicks Account as Ch Warden & the Ballance due the Parrish is	66 : 15	
	465 : 7 : 11	
To the Collector at 6 per Cent	27 : 18 : 5	
	493 : 6 : 4	
T'is order'd that the Ch Warden or whom they shall appoint after giving bond and security as usual do collect from every Titheable in this Parrish the sum of 5/9 on 1733 Tithes amounts to	498 : 4 : 9	
Ballance due the Parrish	4 : 18 : 5	

Capt John Brickle Mr John Driver & Mr Christo Roberts sen^r is appointed vestry men in the Room of Mr Tho. Norfleet dec^d Mr Andrew Meade remov'd & Mr Jacob sumner resign'd

    Truly Enterd
        Aaron Allmand Clk Vestry

[262]

    At a Vestry held at Suffolk January 17th 1778 for Upper Parrish of Nansemond

Present Henry Riddick   John Riddick Gen* Ch Ward*
Willis Riddick   Jeremiah Godwin   Wills Cowper, Samuel
Cohoon John Brickle & John Driver, G V. Men

To Aaron Allmand Reader at Suffo. Church	20
To Ditto for Extra Services	: 15
To Ditto for ½ bush* Nails for the Church	2 : 10
To John Glover Reader at Holy Neck	8
To Joshua Spivey do. at Cyprus	8
To Wm Whitfield Sexton Suffo Church	7 : 10
To John Ashburn for Repairing the Church	49 : 1 : 5
To Joseph Lassetor for Nursing &c. D Wiggins	6
To Ann Baker a Poor Woman	7 : 10
To Doct^r Cohoon for Medicines for the Poor	27 : 9
To Capt Henry Riddick ChW^n Due him per Acc^t	14 : 9 : 8
To James Knight for Keep^g &c. Eliza Raiby	7
To Henry Gwin D° Sarah Ease	3 : 11
To Joseph Elsberry D° Priscilla Garland	10
To Henry Gwin D° Small's Child	3
To Edward Brewer for Nurs^g & Burying Mary Hegebeth	16
To Ann Hower D° Martha Willis	13 : 11 : 1½
To Robert Owens D° Walkers Child	7 : 10
To James Butler a Poor Man	12
To Saml Butler for Keep^g Stephen Butlers Child	6
To Patrick Lunan his Last payment	100
To John Brothers for Keep^g Eliza Stallins	7 : 10
To Mary Scutchins a Poor Woman	4
To Joseph Skeatoe a Poor Man	12 : 10
To Michael Jones Ditto	7 : 10
To Sarah Jones Sextoness Holy Neck	1 : 13 : 4
To Charity Herculas a Poor Woman	7 : 10
To Mary Henry Ditto	6
To Robert Abrams " Man	10
To Thos Gwin for Nursing &c Tegal Nelson	5
To Coll° W Riddick for ½ Bll Corn	7 : 6
	£ 391 : 18 : ½

To the Quaker & Baptists &c free from Church
Expences 145 Tithes at 13 ¾ d Each[116]   8 : 5 : 1¾

£ 400 : 3 : 2¼

[263]

Am{t} bro{t} forward   400 : 3 : 2¼
To the Sheriff @ 6 per C{t}   35 : 4 : 4[117]
         Depossitum   151 : 11 : 5¾

586 : 19

Order{d} the Shff collect for every Titheable in this parrish the sum of Seven shill{gs} on 1677 Tithes Am{ts}   586 : 19

Christo Roberts Josiah Riddick & John Cole are appointed V{y} Men in the room of C Roberts decd Willis Streator removd & Wills Cowper resignd. John Brickle & John Driver Gen{t} are appointed Ch Ward{s} in room of Henry Riddick & John Riddick

Aaron Allmand C V.   John Driver } Ch W.
                      John Brickle }

A Vestry held Suffo. 28th Decr 78.
Pres{t} Revd Wm Andrews
    John Driver & John Brickle G. C W.
    Willis Riddick   Henry Riddick   Jeremiah Godwin
    John Riddick   Josiah Riddick & C. Roberts, G. V. M.

To the rev{d} W. Andrews his Salary   400
Aaron Allmand reader Suffo. &c   25 : 7 : 6
John Glover ditto Holy Neck   8
Wm Whitfield Sexton Suffo. & 2 bottles Wine for Sacram{t}   11 : 2
Christian Spivey sextoness Cyprus Chapel   3
Sarah Wright do. Holy Neck   3

---

[116] Dissenters had been exempted by law from taxes and levies for the support of the Established Church. However, this act (Hening, v. 9, p. 164-167), passed at the October 1776 session of the General Assembly, provided that vestries should include dissenters in making assessments to pay all salaries and arrears of salaries of ministers to January 1, 1777, to carry out existing commitments, and to continue poor relief as usual.

[117] This is 6% of 586:19, the amount to be collected by the sheriff.

John Jinkins for Grub⁸ Chapel Yard	9
Wᵐ Pugh for fixing a Bell to the Church	9
	£ 468 : 9 : 6
To Doctʳ Cohoon for Medicines for the Poor	43 : 4
John Cowpland for Keepᵍ Zach. Butler	10
Arthur Jones do. Elizth Bailey	20
Sarah Best do. John Waters	9 : 10
Catherine Johnston do. Martha Rodgers	20
John Giles do. Wᵐ Ashwell 4 Mths	10
Jaˢ Wright do. Riddick Jones 15 "	18
	£ 130 : 14

[264]

Amᵗ broᵗ Over	£ 130 : 14
To Martha Frith for Coffin & Sheet for Ann Nail	5
Ann Baker a poor Woman	20
James Knight for 2 yʳˢ rent for Isaˡ Browne	5
James Butler a poor Man	20
Joseph Skeatoe ditto	25
Michˡ Jones do	15
John Brothers for Keepᵍ Eliz. Stallins	10
Mary Henry a Poor Woman	10
Elizth Lewis do.	15
Sarah Ellis do	9 : 10
Joseph Elsberry for Keepᵍ Elizth Garland 1 yʳ	15
John Wood do Robert Abrams	5
Majʳ Henry Riddick do Willis Dyson 1 yʳ	18
John James do Sarah Ease 1 yʳ	20
John Giles do Robᵗ Abrams 3 Mths	9
	332 : 4
To the Collector at 6 per Cᵗ	19 : 19
	352 : 3

Orderd the shff after giving Bond & Security as usual for that Purpose Collect for every Titheable in this parrish 4/3 on 1677 Tithes Am^ts   356 : 7 : 3

D. Due the Parrish   £ 4 : 4 : 3

Orderd the Ch Wardens do advertise & sell the Poors House & the Land belong to it to the Highest Bidder, & that John Driver & John Brickle be Continued Ch W. the Ensuing year

John Brickle ⎫
John Driver ⎬ C W.

A. Allmand C V.

[265]

Lands procession'd by Jos. Scott & Ja^s Lawrence Febr^y 76. Ann Woodrop & Christopher Godwin. Ann Woodrop & Cordall Norfleet. James Lawrence and Cordall Norfleet Christo Godwin & Ja^s Lawrence. Moses Eley and Jos. Scott. Josiah Jordan & Jo^s Scott Benjamin Beal & Jo^s Scott. Robert Lawrence & John Lawrence. Jo^s Scott & John Lawrence. Nicholas Perritt & John Lawrence. Geo. Frith & Nicholas Perritt Geo. Frith & Thos Milner Thos Milner & Wm Wilkinson Wm Wilkinson & Geo. Frith. John Lawrence and Wm Wilkinson. Robert Lawrence & John Lawrence. Aaron Allmand & John Lawrence. Aaron Allmand & Robert Lawrence Aaron Allmand & John Lawrence. John Lawrence & Jo^s Scott

Jos. Scott
James Lawrence

At a Vestry held at Suffo. Decr 30th 79
Pres^t Jno Brickle & John Driver Ch W^s
  Willis Riddick. Henry Riddick. Josiah Riddick.
  Jno Cole   Saml Cohoon   G. V. Men

Twas Orderd That Wm Jones & Nich^s Jones procession all the Bounds of Land N° 1 Fred^k George & Peter Green N° 2. Wm Whitlock & Benjn Hill N° 3. Thos Milner & Wm Wilkinson N° 4. Joseph Baker & Jethro Bateman N° 5—John Ashburne & Hardy Hynes N° 6—Joshua King & Ja^s Pierce N° 7—Absolom Beamon & Abram Ballard N° 8—John Hair & Bryant Hair N° 9—Isaac Langston & Hardy Rawls N° 10—Henry Jones & Hardy Parker N° 11 David Howell & Mich^l Howell

Nº 12—Elisha Coupland & Jaˢ Coupland Nº 13 Wᵐ Baker & Henry Holland Nº 14—Wᵐ Hart & Jnº Everitt Nº 15—Jordan Williams & Wᵐ Carr Nº 16—Jos. Holland & Danˡ Holland Nº 17—Hardy Cross & Thoˢ Smith Nº 18—Daniel Riddick & Jnº Barr Nº 19—Jethro Riddick & Jaˢ Griffin Nº 20—Elisha Duke & Jonathan Baker Nº 21—Jnº Langston & Caleb Savage Nº 22—Majʳ Turlington & David Gwin Nº 23—Wᵐ Roundtree & Thoˢ Duke Nº 24—Jaˢ Bates & Jacob Lawrence Nº 25—Richard Woodard & Levin Turlington Nº 26—Henry Riddick & Willis Riddick Nº 27—Willis Parker & David Parker Nº 28

Carried Over

[266]

John Driver Actᵍ Ch Warden, render'd his Accᵗ for 1778 and the Ball. due the parrish is	£ 149 .. 7 .. 7
& his Accᵗ for 1779 due the parrish	1283 .. 15 .. 8
which sum of 1283 .. 15 .. 8 Mʳ Driver paid into the Hands of Jos[i]ah Riddick now actᵍ Ch Warden	
Orderd, The Ch Wardens pay to	
Aaron Allmand	£ 25 .. 7 .. 6
John Glover	8
Wᵐ Whitfield	11 .. 2
Christian Spyva £ 3 Sarah Wright £ 3	6
Wᵐ Pugh £ 9 .. 0 .. 0. Edwᵈ Riddick £40	49
Wᵐ Eley for Insolvents 51 Tithes @ 4/3	10 .. 16 .. 9
Jacob Byrd for Keepᵍ Francis Walker a Child	20
Ben. Baker per Accᵗ	132 .. 4
Doctʳ Cohoon for Medicines for the Poor	£ 365 .. 0 .. 0
Mary Matthews for Nursᵍ Mary Oddy	120
Thoˢ Gwin for buryᵍ do	20
Lemˡ Kean for Keepᵍ Eliz. Bailey	56
John Giles for do Rob. Abrams	127 .. 16
Arthʳ Jones for Sundries for M. Jones	120
Margᵗ Hall for Nursᵍ Charity Cuningham	40
Charles Burket for a Coffin for a Poor Woman	10
Michˡ Jones a Poor Man	145
James Butler do	100

Jos. Elsberry for Keep^g Eliz. Garland	100
Henry Riddick per Acc^t	220
John James for Keep^g Sarah Ease	80
Margaret Hall a Poor Woman	25
Aaron Allmand C. Vestry	100

Orderd, That the Shff collect for every Titheable in this Parrish 15/ On [...][118] Tithes Amounts to [...][119]

Wm Pugh is appointed V. Man in the room of Willis Streator remov'd out of the Parrish[120]

Josiah Riddick & Christo Roberts are appointed Ch Ward^s the Ensuing year

Josiah Riddick

Truly Enterd A. Allmand C V.

[267]

Pursuant to an Order of Vestry held at suffolk Decr 30th 79, We have peaceably & quietly processiond each Mans Land in our Precinct with approbation & in Presence of each person therein Concern'd, except Kedar Booth & John Turlingtons Lands who absolutely refuse to have their Lands Processiond. We have certified the same to the Ch Wardens agreeable to Order

Elisha Duke
Jonathan Baker

Febr^y 14th 1780.

A Return to the Vestry of Nansemond County. Procession'd in presence of One Owner or both Or a person sent in their Room all the Lines Peaceably On the upper Side of the Road from Jarnagans Bridge to Porters Bridge to the extent of the County

Joseph Baker
Jethro Bateman

All the Lines within the Bounds of Our Order are processioned peaceably & quietly

John Ashburne
Hardy Hynes

---

[118] Blank in original.
[119] Blank in original.
[120] Cf. meeting of January 17, 1778, p. 240, where a vestryman seems to have been appointed in the place of Willis Streator, removed. The book shows no service by William Pugh as vestryman.

In Obedience to an order Vestry we have process^d as follows V^z
A Line between Ja^s Lawrence & John Cowper both present
A Line between Robt Jordan & Ann Woodrop Rob Jordan Ja^s Lawren[c]e prs^t
A Line between Ja^s Lawrence & Robt Jordan both present
D^o between Jo^s Scott & Mosses Eley both pres^t
D^o between Josiah Jordan Jos Scott Thos davis & Moses Eley pres^t
D^o between Jo^s Scott & Ben Beal Jo^s Scott press^t
D^o between Thos Milner & Martha Frith Martha & John frith prest
D^o between Martha Frith Junr & Wm Wilkinson John Frith press^t
D^o between Thos Milner & Wim Wilkinson both prest
D^o between Martha Frith Ju^r Nicholas perritt John frith & N: Perrit pr^t
D^o between Nich^o Perritt & John Lawrence N: Perritt pres^t
D^o between Amey Lawrence & John Lawrence N: Perritt prest
D^o between Amey Lawrence & Aaron Allm^d A. Allmand prest
D^o between Aaron Allmand & John Lawrence A Allmand prest
D^o between Jo^s Scott & John Lawren[c]e Jo^s Scott prest

Thos Milner
Wm Wilkinson

Witnes our hands this 11th March 1780

[268]

This is to certify that this is a true acc^t of all the Land in the bounds between Pughs Mill Creek & Katons Creek William Heaftons Land. David Bakers Land. Moses Riddicks Land. Demsey Bakers Land. Wm Coopers land. John Brewers land John Brickle & James Turlingtons Land. all procession'd In presence of the Owners

Richard Woodard
Leving Turlington

At a Vestry held in the Town of Suffolk for the upper Parish of Nansemond County Decm^r 28th 1780.

> present Capt Josiah Riddick, and Capt Christopher Roberts, Church Wardens: Col^o Henry Riddick Col^o Willis Riddick, Capt John Brickle, Mr John Driver, & Mr John Riddick Gentlemen Vestrymen

George Callis is appointed Clerk to this Vestry in the room of Aaron Allmand who has removed Out of this County

Ordered that the Church Wardens Sell the Houses &c on the Glebe assoon as Convenient to the best advantage

Capt Josiah Riddick and Capt Christopher Roberts are Chosen Church Wardens to Act the ensuing Year

Signed

Test   Josiah Riddick   } C: Wardens
   George Callis, Clerk Vestry   Christopher Roberts }

[269]

At a Vestry held in the Town of Suffolk for the upper Parish of Nansemond County Decm^r 17th 1781

>present Major Josiah Riddick and Capt Christopher Roberts Church Wardens. Col^o Henry Riddick, Doctor Samuel Cohoon Mr John Riddick Capt John Brickle & Capt John Coles Gentlemen Vestry-men

Ordered that the Church Wardens for the ensuing
year pay unto Major Josiah Riddick for the balance
of his acco^t Including his last years Accompt   £ 44 .. 5 .. 3
Capt Christopher Roberts for Pork for John Hoggard   1 .. 8 .. 8
Ann Hosier for boarding a Sick Woman including
what was levied for her last year   2 .. 10
                                                         £ 48 .. 3 .. 11

Capt John Brickle in Vestry resigned his office of Vestryman

Capt Robert M. Riddick Mr Elisha Darden & Capt Willis Riddick Gentlemen are appointed Vestrymen

Signed

Test   Josiah Riddick   } C: Wardens
   George Callis, Clerk Vestry   Christopher Roberts }

[270]

A a Vestry held in the Town of Suffolk for the upper Parish of Nansemond March 14th 1782

Present Major Josiah Riddick Church Warden, Col⁰ Henry Riddick M\ John Riddick Cap\ John Coles Major Jeremiah Godwin Cap\ Robert M. Riddick Cap\ Willis Riddick Gentlemen Vestry-men

M\ John Driver Gentleman is appointed a Vestry man[121]

The Upper Parish of Nansemond D\

To Amount brought forward as levied Decm\ 17\ 1781	£ 48 .. 3 .. 11
To John Giles for Boarding Robert Abrams &c	10
To John Riddick for Sundries per Acco\	3
To William Bird for boarding Mary Wills 2 Years	16
To Joseph Ellsbury for boarding Betsey Garland	1
To James Butler a poor man for Support	7 .. 10
To Arthur Jones for House Rent for Michael Jones	2
To Michael Jones a poor man for Support	8
To Elizabeth Wills for Boarding Judith Grimes	3 .. 10
To Mary Hubbard a poor Woman for Support	3
To John James for boarding Sarah Ease	8
To Levin Talington for boarding Catherine Mercer	2
To Edward Brewer a poor man for Support	7 .. 10
To Ann Baker a poor Woman for d⁰	2
To Patience Hoggard a poor Woman for d⁰	7 .. 10
To Major Josiah Riddick for Am\ of his Acco\ Supply'd the poor	4 .. 2 .. 6
To M\ Patrick Lunan for burying a poor Woman	12 .. 6
To George Callis for Acting as Clerk of the Vestry last year	5
	138 .. 18 .. 11
To The Sheriffs Commissions at 6 per C\ on £275	16 .. 10
To A Depositum in the hands of the Church Wardens	119 .. 11 .. 1
	£275

Ordered that the Sheriff Collect from each Tithe in this Parish the Sum of Three Shilling in Specie Computed to be 1500 Tithes   £275[122]

---

[121] One John Driver had been appointed vestryman on February 11, 1777 (see p. 238), subsequently serving in that office and as churchwarden.

[122] 1500 tithables at 3 s. each would be £225.

Cap.t Robert M Riddick and Cap.t John Coles Gentlemen are Chosen Church Wardens to act the ensuing Year

Signed

Truly Entered   Robert M. Riddick
  George Callis, Clerk Vestry   John Coles   } C: Wardens

[271]

At a Vestry held in the Town of Suffolk for the upper Parish of Nansemond, January 16.th 1783

    present Cap.t Robert M. Riddick and Cap.t John Coles, Church Wardens. Col.o Henry Riddick Maj.r Jeremiah Godwin Maj.r Josiah Riddick M.r Christopher Roberts & M.r Willis Riddick Gentlemen Vestry men

The upper Parish of Nansemond D.r

To Rebecah Gomer for boarding a helpless Woman	£ 3 .. 15
To Hardy Cross for burying a poor Woman	1 .. 9 .. 3
To Joseph Baker for boarding Rachel Hines	8
To Joseph Holland for boarding John Pierce &c	23 .. 8 .. 2
To John Ease for boarding Sarah Ease	8
To James Butler a poor man for Support	7 .. 10
To Joseph Baker for Sundries furnish'd James Butler	2
To Sarah Winburne for boarding Elizabeth Bailey	1 .. 5
To Thomas Gwin for boarding John Hudson	3 .. 10
To Mary Hubbard a poor woman for Support	3
To Ann Baker D.o for D.o	2
To Margaret Hall D.o for D.o	2
To David Gwin for boarding Jeremiah Anthony	4
To Ditto for boarding Mary Gwyn	12
To Aaron Allmand for acting Clerk of the Vestry in 1780	5
To Judith Duke for boarding Richard Webb	5
To Arthur Jones for Sundries furnished Michael Jones & wife	6
To William Bird for boarding Mary Wills	8
To Peter Butler for boarding John Pierce	2 .. 10
To Willis Cowling for Cash advanced a sick man	1 .. 7
To George Callis for acting Clerk last year	5
	£ 114 .. 14 .. 5

To Sherriffs Commissions on 1320 Tithes @ 1/6. £ 99 @ 6 per C^t	5..18..10
To A Depositum in the hands of the Church Wardens	71.. 5.. 4
	£ 191..18.. 7

C^r

By A Depositum in the hands of the Church Wardens for last year	92..18.. 7
By 1320 Tithes in this Parish @ 1/6	99
	£ 191..18.. 7

Ordered that the Sherriffe Collect for every Tithe in this Parish, the Sum of One Shillings & Six pence in Specie; and pay the same into the hands of the Church Wardens

Capt Robert M. Riddick and Capt John Coles are chosen Church wardens to act the Ensuing year

Signed

Test   Robert M. Riddick } Church wardens
   George Callis.   John Coles
   Clerk Vestry

[272]

At a Vestry held in the Town of Suffolk for the upper Parish of Nansemond; February 11th 1784.

    Present Capt Robert M. Riddick, and Capt John Coles; Church Wardens Major Jeremiah Godwin Capt Willis Riddick & Capt Christopher Roberts Vestrymen

The upper Parish of Nansemond D^r	
To Joseph Baker for boarding Rachel Hines	£ 10.. 0.. 0
d^o for Sundries furnished James Butler	7..10.. 0
d^o for provision for Danl Butler	1.. 0.. 6
To Margaret Hall for boarding Jamima Jones	11.. 0.. 0
To Ferebee Skeator for boarding Ann Johnson	1..10.. 0
To Mary Hubbard a poor Woman for Support	6.. 0.. 0
To William Wright for boarding Elias Eley	5.. 0.. 0
To Joseph Holland for boarding John Pierce	10.. 0.. 0
To Sarah Winburne for boarding Elizabeth Bailey	8.. 0.. 0

D° for keeping Eliz² Baileys Child never more to be any expence	8 .. 0 .. 0
D° for keeping Sarah Parker Child One month	0 .. 15 .. 0
To Jesse Holland for burying a poor Woman	1 .. 2 .. 0
To Henry Winburne for keeping Elizabeth Baileys Child	0 .. 15 .. 0
To John Ease for keeping Sarah Ease	10 .. 0 .. 0
To Jacob Bass for keeping Kindred Lee	6 .. 0 .. 0
To Thomas Harrard for boarding Zilla Harrard	10 .. 0 .. 0
To Ann Baker a poor Woman for Support	8 .. 0 .. 0
To David Gwyn for boarding Mary Gwyn	10 .. 0 .. 0
To Arthur Jones for boarding Michael Jones & wife	25 .. 0 .. 0
To William Bird for boarding Mary Wells	8 .. 0 .. 0
To Kedar Booth for balance of boarding a Child 2 years	3 .. 5 .. 9
To Mary Lassitor for boarding Christian Stallions & Child	15 .. 0 .. 0
To Richard Alderman for boarding Ann Johnson	3 .. 0 .. 0
To Mourning Hines a poor Woman for Support	6 .. 0 .. 0
To Richard Terry a poor man for d°	7 .. 0 .. 0
To George Callis for keeping Elizabeth Lewis	6 .. 0 .. 0
D° for acting Clark of the Vestry Last year	5 .. 0 .. 0
	£ 192 .. 18 .. 3

[273]

At a Vestry held in the Town of Suffolk, for the upper Parish of Nansemond April 14th 1784.

> present Capt Robert M. Riddick, Church Warden:
> Col° Henry Riddick, Major Jeremiah Godwin, Doctor Samuel Cohoon, Capt Willis Riddick, Mr John Riddick, and Mr Christopher Roberts, Vestrymen

This Vestry approves of the business done by the former Vestry on the 11th day of February Last and the whole business is hereby confirmed

The Amount brought forward which is	£ 192 .. 18 .. 3
To Capt Robert M. Riddick for John Gregory's Tithes overcharged	1 .. 15 .. 0
d° his Own twice charged 10 Tithes @ 1/6	0 .. 15 .. 0
To John Rawls for Sundries furnished Mary Brewer	2 .. 4 .. 9

To Zachariah Copeland for Sundries furnished Michael Jones	2..0..0
d° for Sugar furnished a poor Child	0..8..5
To George Callis for keeping Dan¹ Butler & Child	10..0..0
To Sarah Ellis a poor Woman for Support	3..0..0
To Mary Brewer d° d°	3..0..0
To Jean Smith d° d°	3..0..0
To William Pugh Sheriffe for 34 Insolvents @ 1/6	2..11..0
To Isaac Langston for keeping Sarah Keen	5..0..0
To Henry Winburne for burying a poor Child	1..0..0
To Mourning Hines for keeping a poor Child 4 Weeks	0..10..0
To Edward Baker for keeping Elizabeth Peel 3 months	3..0..0
To John Whimmer for boarding & nursing Eliz^a Moore	3..0..0
To Christian Parker a poor Woman for Support	3..0..0
	£ 237..2..5
To the Church Warden for Cimmissions on £ 285..5 @ 6 per Cent	17..2..4
To a Depositum, in the hands of the Church Wardens, due the Parish	53..13..0½
	£ 307..17..9½
C^r	
By 1630 Tithes in this Parish @ 3/6	£ 285..5..0
By Balance in the hands of Capt Robert M. Riddick	22..12..9½
	£ 307..17..9½

Ordered that Capt Robert M. Riddick pay in to the hands of the Church Wardens for the present year the Sum of £ 22..12..9½ which is the balance due the Parish from him, agreeable to acco^t settled

Nathaniel Norflett is chosen a Vestry man

Ordered that the church Wardens, or who they may appoint: Collect from Each Tithe in this Parish, the Sum of Three Shillings and Six pence in Specie, and there with discharge the Parish Debts

[274]

Ordered that William Riddick & John Miles Procession all the bounds of Land N° 1. Thomas Nelmes & Samuel Godwin n° 2. Archer Nelmes

& Nathaniel Norflett n° 3. Thomas Roberts & Sawyer Lawrence n° 4. John Bateman & Lewis Best n° 5 Peter Ashburne & Robert Willis n° 6. James McClenny & Stephen Pierce n° 7 Abram Ballard & John James n° 8. John Hare & William Faulk n° 9 Hardy Rawls & John Copeland n° 10. Henry Jones & Hardy Parker n° 11. Edward Howell Junr & Michael Howell n° 12. Jesse Copeland & Willoughby Jenkins n° 13 Henry Holland & Edward Baker n° 14. Jordan Williams & John Carr n° 15 William Hart & Etheldred Warren n° 16. Joseph Holland & James Holland n° 17 Hardy Cross & Thomas Smith n° 18. Daniel Riddick & John Barr n° 19 Jethro Riddick & James Griffin n° 20. Reuben Smith & John Smith n° 21 John Langston & Caleb Savage n° 22. John Coles & Major Turlington n° 23 William Roundtree & Thomas Duke n° 24. Moses Riddick & William Midcalf n° 25 John Brewer & James Turlington n° 26. Hezekiah Riddick & Uriah Stallions n° 27 Willis Parker & David Parker n° 28. Zachariah Copeland & David Holland n° 29 being all the Land which lays between the Cappell [sic] Roads; which has before been neglected. Demsey Baker & Markum Owens, n° 30. being the Land which lays between Summerton Road & the Mare Branch Road; & so to the extent of the County and Country Line, which has before been neglected

Col° Henry Riddick and Capt Willis Riddick are chosen, and Sworn Church Wardens to act the ensuing year

Sign'd Henry Riddick
Willis Riddick } C. Wardens

Truly Entered
George Callis Clk Vestry

We Thomas Nelmes & Samuel Godwin hath Processioned all the Land Marks within Our bounds according to Order of Vestry   Jany 4th 1785

Thomas Nelmes
Samuel Godwin

[275]

We Nathaniel Norflet & Archer Nelmes, hath Processioned all the Land-Marks; within Our district agreeable to the Order of the Vestry

Nathaniel Norfleet
          his
Archer X Nelmes
         mark

Agreeable to an Order of the Vestry of Nansemond County Dated April 14th 1784 for the upper Parish of said County, We the Subscribers have Processioned the Land as follows Viz. Alexander Woodrope's, himself present William Wilkerson Senr Alex^r Woodrope & Joseph Laurence present. Capt John Cowper's Moses Eley & Alexander Woodrope present. Joseph Laurence's orphan himself present. Moses Eley's himself & Joseph Pritlow present Joseph Scott's Joseph Pritlow & Moses Eley present, Benjamin Beals's Joseph Pritlow present, John Laurence's Joseph Pritlow present, Josiah Jordan's Senr Joseph Pritlow present, Aaron Allmand's himself and Joseph Pritlow, Thomas Roberts's himself & Sawyer Lawrence present, Nicholas Perry's Thomas Pinner present, John Lawrence's Thomas Pinner present, Sawyer Lawrence's Thomas Pinner present, Jessee Hodges's himself and Thomas Pinner present, Thomas Milner's himself & Wilkerson Senr present, William Wilkerson's himself & Thomas Milner & Jesse Hodges present,

Given under Our hands this 9th day of June 1784

       Thomas Roberts
       Sawyer Lawrence

We John Bateman, & Lewis Best, have Processioned all the Land in Our bounds: agreeable to the Order of the Vestry:—Decm^r 31st 1784

       John Bateman
       Lewis Best

We Peter Ashburn & Robert Willis, hath Processioned all the Land marks; within Our bounds agreeable to the order of the Vestry Jany 1st 1785

       Peter Ashburn
       Robert Willis

[276]

Agreeable to an order of the Vestry for the upper Parish of Nansemond bearing date April 14th 1784. We the Subscribers have renewed all the Land marks within Our precinct In presence of the Inhabitants given under Our hands this 10th day of January 1785

       James McClenny
       Stephen Pierce

Pursuant to an order of Vestry; We the Subscribers appointed in the said order, have processioned all the s^d bounds of Land contained in the s^d order; begining at a Line Between Benjamin Baker, and Lewis Daughtrey. all the bounds of Land contained in the above mentioned order, is peaceably and Quietly processioned; and no Objection made:— By us the Subscribers Decm^r 20th 1784

Joseph Holland
James Holland

By an Order of a Vestry, held at Suffolk April 14th 1784 We the Subscribers; have processioned all the bounds of Land within the above mentioned Order, in the presence of the Inhabitance peaceable, and Quietly: and in the presence of us:— Decm^r 20th 1784

his
Henry X Holland
Mark
Edward Baker

In Compliance with an order of Vestry held in Suffolk the 14th of April 1784. We have processioned all the Land in our bounds in peace & Quietness in presence & with the approbation of the Parties therein concerned

Reuben Smith
John Smith

[277]

In obedience to an order of Vestry held at Suffolk Town April 14th 1784. To us Directed; We the Subscribers have processioned all the Land Marks, Between the Several free Holders within the District mentioned in the s^d Order, and no Objection made; Certified under Our hands.

Demsey Baker
Markum Owens

Pursuant to an Order of Vestry held at Suffolk April 14th 1784 We the Subscribers have processioned all the bounds of Land in Our precinct in the presence of the Inhabitants and no objection made Given under Our hands

Edward Howell
Michael Howell

Pursuant to an Order of Vestry to us Directed bearing date 14th April 1784 We have met and processioned all the bounds of Land Specified in said Order in peaceable and quiet proccession in presence of the Inhabitants. Given under Our hands this 8th day of January 1785.

         Henry Jones
         Hardy Parker

October 9th 1784 Processioned all the Land marks with in our District agreeable to the order of Vestry in presence of the Inhabitants peaceable and Quietly Given under Our hands

         Hardy Cross
         Thomas Smith

In Obedience to an Order of the Vestry for processioning the Bounds of Land, from the Sypruss Swamp, on the East Side of Orapeak Road to the Country Line Complyed with agreeable to an Order Given under Our hands

         Dan¹ Riddick
         John Barr

[278]

At a Vestry held in the Town of Suffolk February 21st 1785

 Present Henry Riddick, and Willis Riddick, Church Wardens;
    Jeremiah Godwin, John Coles, Ro. M. Riddick, Josiah
    Riddick, and John Riddick Gentlemen Vestrymen

The upper Parish of Nansemond Dr	
To John McCabe for 8 months board &c Susanna Nelmes	£ 8
To Doctr J. Hay for amt of his accot for the poor	10 .. 1
To Elisha Darden for Sundries furnished Sarah Bembra	19 .. 8½
To Joseph Baker for Keeping James Butler & wife	13 .. 5
To John Butler for burying his Mother &c	1 .. 5
To Susannah Jucely for keeping Ann Baker	8
To Joseph Holland for Keepg & Clothg John Pierce 6 Months	7 .. 1
To Henry Winburne for Keepg & Clothg Elizabeth Bailey	8 .. 19 .. 6
To John Kenny for Keeping Elizabeth Moore	3 .. 12

To Peter Butler for Keep^g & Cloth^g John Pierce 6 Months	7..7	
To Mourning Hines a poor Woman for Support	6	
To John Ease for Keeping Sarah Ease	10	
To William Bird for Keeping Mary Wills	8	
To David Gwyn for Keeping Mary Gwyn	10	
To Robert Willis for Keep^g Eliz^a Moore 42 days	2..10	
To Capt Willis Riddick for Keep^g Isbell Brown 9 Months	9	
To Africa Darden for 3 Levies Over charged	10..6	
To Amey Darden for 2 Levies Over charged	7	
To Jethro Riddick for Sundries furnished Mary Hubbard	4	
To Arthur Jones Senr for Keeping Michael Jones	12..10	
To William Wright for Keeping Rachel Hines	10	
To John Webb for board & nursing David Webb	6	
To George Callis for acting Clark Last year	5	
To John Rawls for 3 Levies over charged	10..6	
To Mary Lassiter for Keeping Christian Stallions & Child	15	
To Mary Hubbard a poor Woman for Support	10	
To Sarah Ellis d^o d^o	3	
To Mary Brewer d^o d^o	4	
To Isaac Langston for Keeping Sarah Keen	5	
To Edward Baker Dec^d for Keep^g Eliz^a Peel 21 Days	15	
To Thomas Harrod for Keep^g Zilla Harrod	10	
To Patience Hoggard a poor Woman to pay her Rent	3	
To Mary Stallions a poor Woman for Support	3	
To Thomas Adams for 85 Insolvents @ 3/6	15..8	
To Col^o Henry Riddick C. Warden for balance of his acco^t	3..10	
	£ 222..5..0½	

[279]

		d
The upper Parish of Nansemond D^r		
To amount brought up	£ 222..5..0½	
To Commissions on £288..4..6 at 6 per Cent	17..5..10½	
To a Depositum in the hands of the Church Wardens	48..13..7	
	£ 288..4..6	

C.^r^
By 1647 Tithes in this Parish @ 3/6   £ 288 .. 4 .. 6

Ordered that the Church Wardens, or Who ever they may appoint, Collect from each Tithe in this parish, the Sum of of [*sic*] Three Shillings and Six pence; and therewith Discharge the Parish Debts.

Col^o^ Henry Riddick and Capt Willis Riddick are Chosen Church Wardens to Act the Ensuing Year.

         Sign'd   Henry Riddick ⎫
Truly Enter'd   Willis Riddick ⎬ C. Wardens
  George Callis Clk Vestry   ⎭

At a Meeting of the Gentlemen Chosen by Ballot of the free Inhabitant of this upper Parish of Nansemond; agreeable to a late Act of Assembly;[123] to Serve as Vestrymen for the said Parish The s^d^ Meeting held in the Town of Suffolk April 18th 1785

Present, Henry Riddick, Willis Riddick, Josiah Riddick, Robert M Riddick, John Riddick, Jethro Riddick, Richard Baker, Demsey Sumner, John Giles, William King, & Abram Parker, Gentlemen

We the Subscribers above mentioned; do profess ourselves to be Members of the Protestant Episcopal Church; and do promise to be conformable to the Doctrine, Discipline, and Worship of the Same. Sign'd by Henry Riddick, Willis Riddick, Richd Baker, Demsey Sumner, John Riddick, Jethro Riddick, John Giles, William King, Josiah Riddick, Robert Moore Riddick, Abram Parker.[124]

George Callis is appointed Clark to this Vestry.

Willis Riddick and Richard Baker are Chosen to attend the Convention which is to be held at Richmond as Delagates[125]

It is recommended by this Vestry; that the Church Wardens do Advertise to procure a Minister for this parish

---

[123] Hening, v. 11, p. 532-537: "An act for incorporating the Protestant Episcopal Church", passed at the October 1784 session of the General Assembly. The act stipulated that "no person shall be allowed to vote who does not profess himself a member of the Protestant Episcopal Church, and actually contribute toward it[s] support"; and that the elected vestrymen should be members of the Protestant Episcopal Church.

[124] The act specified also (p. 535) that the elected vestrymen should "previous to their entering on the office of vestrymen, subscribe in vestry to be conformable to the doctrine, discipline, and worship of the Protestant Episcopal Church."

[125] This convention to organize the Protestant Episcopal Church in Virginia met May 18-25, 1785.

Col⁰ Henry Riddick and Capt Willis Riddick are again Chosen Church Wardens this present Year

                          Signed Henry Riddick ⎫
Truly Entered   Willis Riddick ⎬ C. W
    George Callis Clk Vestry

[280]

At a Vestry held in the Town of Suffolk, for the upper Parish of Nansemond, October 11th 1785.

    present Willis Riddick, Gentleman Church Warden, Josiah Riddick, Jeremiah Godwin, Richard Baker, Robert M. Riddick, William King, Demsey Sumner, John Giles, and Jethro Riddick, Gentlemen Vestry men

Ordered that Each of the Vestrymen assist in the numbering the Episcopalians in the upper Parish of Nansemond; and present a Subscription to the people professing that Religion; in order to See what Sum of Money can be raised, and make report of their Success to the next Vestry

Ordered that the Church Wardens pay Willis Riddick Six Pounds for his attendance on the Convention, as a Delagate

Ordered that the Church Wardens pay Richard Baker Six Pounds Ten Shillings for his attendance on the Convention as a Delagate

Wills Cowper is Chosen a Vestry man in the room of Col⁰ Henry Riddick Decd

                          Signed Willis Riddick C W.
Truly Entered
    George Callis Clk Vestry

[281]

At a Meeting of the Overseers of the Poor[126] for Nansemond County November 17th 1786

    Present Willis Everitt, Mills Minton, Thomas Allmand, Joseph Baker, Zacheriah Copeland, Jethro Riddick and Archd Richardson

---

[126] Overseers of the Poor had by law taken the place of vestries with respect to public poor-relief and various other duties.

To Col Josiah Riddick for a Ballance Henry Riddick's a/c as Church Warden	2 : 3 : 3
Margaret Smith an infirm person[127]	2 : 5
Judith Sullivant an infirm Woman	3
Elizabeth Allmand Ditto	7 : 10
Ann Pierce	2
James Heffeton	1 : 5
Charity Myars for keeping Orphan Child	6
Margaret Welch a poor Woman	3
Mary Graham Ditto	3
Mary Churchwell Ditto	3
George Cummings D°	6
Susanah Jucely Keeping a Sick Woman	3 : 3 : 9
The Widow Allmond keeping a poor Orphan	3
Henry Winborne keeping E. Bailey & two Children	10 : 10
Zacheriah Copeland Ditto	10
Mourning Hines infirm person	6
Mary Brewer D°	4
Zacheriah Copeland, for Polly Hubbard	1 : 10
Jonathan Cross furnish'd Sundry poor	1 : 17 : 7
Lydda Keene, for keeping Sarah Keene	2 : 10
Doct^r Joseph Hay per Acc^t	4 : 10
Willis Everitt for Alexander Thompson £ 10	
D° D° Elizabeth Benn 14	
D° D° Rachael Nail 10	
D° D° Orphans E Smith 16	£ 50
William Weatherly for Julia Campbell	12
Barsilla Harrell poor person	10
John Ease for Sarah Ease	12
Jacob Price for Henry Price	10 : 0
Jacob Duke for Michael Jones	12 : 10
Benj^a Duke for William Duke	5
Hardy Duke for John Duke	5
Abram Lassetor for Betty Duke	5 : 10
Jethro Riddick for Jimimah Jones	12

---

[127] The next entry, which was struck out, is "James Howard for keeping Orphan Ch."

James Bates for Isbell Brown	12
Jethro Taylor for Rachael Hines	8
Saml Barkley for John Price	12
car^d over	£242 : 14 : 7

[282]

	S d
Brought Over	£242 : 14 : 7
Joseph Elsbery for Jethro Holland	5
John Simons —— Elizabeth Lewis	10
William King —— John Terry	4 : 10
William Roberts —— —— Evans[128]	6
John Giles —— —— Bishop	5
Levin Stakes —— poor woman	3 : 5
Josiah Cowling —— House Rent	2 : 6 : 8
David Gwinn —— Mary Gwinn	12
Mrs Darby —— poor person	3
Joseph Baker —— Sarah Whimmer	6 : 0
Jethro Riddick —— Beck Lassetor	8
D^o —— Harrel [?]	12 : 6
Mary Lassetor for Orphan	6
A. Richardson per Acc^t	1 : 7 : 6
Ditto acting as Clerk	5
	£320 : 16 : 3
S d	
Com^s on £320 : 16 : 3 @ 6 per C^t	19 : 4 : 11½
	£340 : 1 : 2½
Depositum Due the parrish after the Collection is compleated	42 : 5 : 9½
	£382 : 7
2185 Tithables @ 3/6	382 : 7

Orderd that the Sheriff Collect three Shillings & Six pence per tithable

---

[128] The number of dashes (some omitted) in this and the following entries varies. At least one is in lieu of "for", but it is impossible to say whether the last dash in this and the following entry is used instead of a repetition of "John". On the whole, such a deduction seems unwarranted in view of the apparent carelessness with which the account is done.

for the above purposes and account with the persons intitled to receive the Same, according to Law

       Teste A Richardson Clk

[283]

At a Meeting of the Members of the Protestant Episcopal Church, in the Upper parrish of Nansemond County, convend, by notice of Willis Riddick, (late Church Warden, for the said parrish) in the Town of Suffolk, for the purpose of Electing a Vestry, the poll was taken and conducted by Archibald Richardson, at the request of the Said Willis Riddick, who was Sick, and unable to attend: when the following Gentlemen ware unanimously Elelected [sic] Vestry Men, for the parrish aforesaid to wit

  Jeremiah Godwin Senr
  Willis Riddick
  John Riddick
  John Giles
  Jethro Riddick
  Robert Moore Riddick
  Henry Harrison
  Riddick Hunter
  Hardy Parker
  Robert Cowper
  Josiah Riddick
  William King

Suffolk September 13th 1790
  Certifyed by A Richardson

I certify that the above persons were Lawfully chosen to serve as Trustees & Vestery Men for the upper parrish of Nansemond County

       Willis Riddick C. W.
        Turn Over

[284]

We hereby bind & oblige ourselves to be conformable to the Doctrin Dicipline and government of the protestant Episcopal Church of Virginia

       Willis Riddick
       Robert Cowper

Josiah Riddick
Henry Harrisson
John Giles
Jethro Riddick
Riddick Hunter

Suff⁰ April the 21ˢᵗ 1791

At a meeting of the Vestry of the upper parrish of Nansemond County.
Present Willis Riddick, Robert Cowper, Josiah Riddick, Henry Harrison, John Giles Jethro Riddick, Riddick Hunter & Robert M. Riddick

[285]

Ordered that Josiah Riddick, & Robert Cowper be appointed Church Wardens

Ordered that Mʳ John Vaughn be appointed Vestry men in the Room of Majʳ Jeremʰ Godwin deceas'd

Ordered that the Church Wardens take an Accoᵗ of the Church property in this Parrish both real & personal & make an immediate Report thereof to the Treasurer of the Convention, also that he be informd that at present there is no minister in this parrish

Ordered that the Church Wardens do collect by Subscription what Money they can to be sent to the Treasurer of the Convention to be apply'd to the Generall purposes of the church agreeable to the requisition of the last Convention

Ordered that Mʳ Archᵈ Richardson & Docter Joseph Hay be appointed to represent this parrish, as Laymen in the next convention to be held at Richmond in May Next.

Ordered that each Vestryman with the Church Wardens open Subscriptions for the purpos of Raising Money for to

[286]

Repair the Church & Chappills of this Parrish

Josiah Riddick } C. W.
Robᵗ Cowper }

[287]

Agreeable to appointment, we processioned and renewed all the land Marks in Our bounds that was Shewn or we Could find, a Line between

John Daughtry & Newman, present John Daughtry, between John Giles & Newman pres^t Giles, between Beaman & Norfleet in their presence. between Norfleet & Coles pres^t Beaman, between Cole & Cole pres^t Beaman, between Beaman & Giles in their presence, by agreem^t of Abraham Ballard and John Giles, that we should make a new line between them in presence of Absolem Beaman, sen^r to be an Esthableshed Line between them between Daughtry & Porter in their presence, between Daughtry & Holland in their presence, between Porter & Holland in their presence, between Holland & Copland pres^t Copland, between Copland & Norfleet, pres^t Copland, between Norfleet & Holland, pres^t John Norfleet & Stephen Shepherd, between Norfleet & Shepherd in their presence, between Norfleet & Porter pres^t Norfleet & Shepherd between Porter & Shepherd pres^t Norfleet & Shepherd, between John Giles and Benjamin Baker pres^t Benj^a Baker, James Baker & Sol^o Rawles Junr between Giles & Coles pres^t Giles & Abs Beaman, Senr between John & William Porter pres^t John Porter, between John Porter & John Rawles pres^t Porter, between John Porter & David Rawles pres^t John & David Rawles, between Rawles & Council pres^t John & David Rawles, between John & David Rawles in their presence

James Norfleet
Lemuel Council

Peaceably processioned all the bounds of Land from the Going Wickam Swamp, to the County Line so to Kingsale Swamp, thence up the Swamp to the first Station, with the Names of Persons pres^t Eine Whitfield, Lewis Daughtry, Robert Daughtry, Adam Cutchins, James Holland, Arthur Howell, Michael Howell, Charles Vaughan, Job Saunders, James Saunders, John Saunders, Nathl Tatman, Sol^o Whitfield, Henry Norfleet, Henry Harrisson, & Thomas Holland

James Vaughan
John Holland

We the Processioners have Processioned all the Lines in the bounds N° 28, to the best of our knowledge Witness our hands this 10th day of Feby 1793

Riddick Hunter
Thomas Smith

INDEX

Superior figures indicate the number of times the same personal names occur on pages containing processioning records.

———, Ephrai[ ], 139.
———, Jo[ ], 139.
———, Mar[ ], 139.
———, Prisscila, land processioned, 139.
———, R[ ], 139.

Abingdon Parish, Gloucester Co., minister of, xxxiv.
Abjuration, oath of, administered to vestryman, 23, 45.
Abrames, Thos. Bailie (Baile), land processioned, 215; present at processioning, 215.²
Abrams, Robert, 207, 219, 221, 238, 239, 241, 243, 247.
Abrams, Thos., present at processioning, 236.²
Accounts, *see* Churchwardens; Doctors; Fines; Poor persons; Upper Parish, Nansemond County.
Acre (Acree), William, land processioned, 109²; processioner, 101, 110.
Acts, assessing dissenters, 240 (note); concerning boundaries of parish, xiv, xiv (note), xv (note), xvi, xvi (note), xvii, xvii (note), xxiii, 15, 15 (note); concerning incorporation of Protestant Episcopal Church, lxviii, lxx, lxxi, 257 (note); concerning ministers, xxiii, xxiv; concerning poor, lix, 199; concerning tobacco, 14, 14 (note), 18; concerning vagrants, lv; confiscatory, lxxiv; copies of, 56; establishing religious freedom, lxix; for building poorhouse, lxiv, 84, 97, 173 (note), 203, 219; for dissolving vestry of Upper Parish, xx, lvii (note), 99 (note), 203; for establishing Suffolk, li (note); for relief of sufferers in loss of Nansemond Co. records, liii (note); for suppressing Quakers, xxv; limiting credit to any one person, xlii (note); of toleration, xxvii; relating to church repealed, lxxiii; to enable vestry to sell certain lands, 173, 173 (note), 196, 203; Two Penny, xxxvii-xxxviii, xxxviii (note), xli (note).
See also Bills; General Assembly; Laws.
Adams, James, 206; land processioned, 216²; paid for services, 219.
Adams, Thomas, 256.
Adkins (Addkins), Richard, paid for services, 13, 21.
Administrator, of Judith Bromegom, 86.
Administratrix, of Richd. Leviston, 218, 220; of Richard Webb, 153.
See also Executors.
Adultery, minister solicit women to commit, xli.
Advertisement, for bids for building chapel, lv, 128; for bids for building church, 20, 46; for bids for enclosing churchyard, 128; for bids for work on Suffolk Church and poorhouse, 184; for minister for Upper Parish, lxix, 257; election of vestrymen, xx; of sale of glebe land, 104; of sale of poorhouse and land, lxiv, 242.
Agnew, Rev. John, minister of Suffolk Parish, xxxvii; services in Upper Parish, xxxviii, xliii, xliv, 153, 225, 226.
Agreements, between vestry and Capt. Mills Riddick, 204; for building almshouse, 84, 85; for building Brick Church, 54.
See also Contractor; Contractors.
Agur, ———, minister, Nottoway Parish, xlv (note).
Albemarle Parish, Sussex Co., Rev. Wm. Andrews, minister of, xlvi; parish register of, xlviii (note); vestry book of, xlvi (note).
Alderman, Richard, paid for services, 250.
Alegree, Wm., paid for services, 220.
Alen, William, *see* Allen, William.

Alesbury, Phillip, land processioned, 35. See also Elsbury, Philip.
Alexandria, Va., Protestant Episcopal Theological Seminary, *see* Protestant Episcopal Theological Seminary.
Allegiance, oath of, xxvi, xliv (note).
Allen (Alen, Alin, Allin), William, land processioned, 108, 187, 215, 236.
Allmand (Almand, Almond), Aaron, allowance to, 132, 151; clerk of Brick Church, 56, 85; clerk of Middle Chapel, 53, 56, 85; clerk of Suffolk Church, 90, 95, 101, 121, 126, 132, 151, 154, 157, 161, 167, 175, 178, 182, 201; clerk of vestry, 92, 93, 94, 95, 97, 98, 99, 101, 103, 104, 105, 119, 123, 124, 125, 128, 129, 132, 134, 135, 153, 154, 156, 157, 159, 161, 163, 168, 174, 177, 178, 180, 184, 196, 198, 203, 207, 209, 221, 224, 225, 227, 228, 229, 231, 238, 242, 243, 244, 248; keeper of parish register, 154, 157, 161, 167, 175, 178, 197, 218, 222, 225, 236; land processioned, 149, 166^3, 185, 186, 209^3, 242^3, 245^4, 253; present at processioning, 209^2; processioner, 130, 149, 159, 166; reader at Suffolk Church, 118, 194, 197, 205, 207, 218, 222, 225, 229, 236, 239, 240, 243; tobacco levied for, 87.
Allmand, Elizabeth, indigent person, 259.
Allmand, Thomas, overseer of poor, 258.
Allmond, Mrs. ———, paid for services, 259.
Almond, James, land processioned, 79.
Almshouse, *see* Poorhouse.
American Loyalists . . . (book), xliv (note), xlvi (note), xlvii (note), xlviii (note), xlix (note).
American Revolution, xxi, xxxii, lxiv; claims for losses suffered by reason of, xlix.
Amistead (Amisted, Amsted), Grace, *see* Armstead, Grace.
Anderson, Mary, indigent person, 237.
Anderson, Priscilla (Prisilla), land procesioned, 235^2.
Andrews, Rev. William, chaplain at Yorktown, xlvii; chaplain to Portsmouth garrison, xlvii; charged with treason, xlviii, xlix; claim for losses suffered by American Revolution, xlix; death threatened to, xlvi; glebe to be put in repair for, xlv; letter to governor, xlviii (note); licensed by Bishop of London for New York, xliv; minister of Albemarle Parish, xlvi; minister of Nottoway Parish, xlv (note); minister of Portsmouth Parish, xlvii; minister of Upper Parish, xliv, xlvi, 227, 228, 231, 240; returns to Great Britain, xlix; salary of, 229, 236, 240.
Anglican Church, *see* Church of England; Established Church; Protestant Episcopal Church.
Anthony, a Portuguese, 53.
Anthony, Jeremiah, indigent person, 248.
Apprentice fee, 49.
Archer, Robert, land processioned, 35^4, 73^1, 112, 137; present at processioning, 73^3; processioner, 3, 130, 137.
Archer, Stephen, processioner, 181, 185.
Armstead (Amistead, Amisted, Amsted, Annstead, Anstead, Armsted), Grace, indigent person, 12, 13, 17, 21, 26, 45, 49, 52, 56, 57, 85, 96, 102, 127.
Army, allowance for tithable in, 126. *See also* War.
Arnall (Arnal, Arnel, Arnell), Edward, land processioned, 37, 188, 189^2, 211^2, 234^2.
Arnold, Gen. Benedict, xlvii.
Ashbourn, Mrs. ———, 140 (note).
Ashburn (Ashborn, Ashborne, Ashbourn), Elisha, land processioned, 30, 147, 148^2, 210, 212^3; paid for services, 52, 57, 86; present at processioning, 120^2, 147^2; processioner, 24, 30, 59, 68.
Ashburn (Ashbourn, Ashburne), John, deceased, 104; his orphan's land processioned, 147^3, 148^2, 172^4; land processioned, 30, 68, 120, 213^5; overcharge refunded, 90; paid for services, 239; processioner, 208, 213, 242, 244; reimbursed, 91; vestryman, 99, 101, 103, 104.
Ashburn (Ashbourn, Ashburne), Peter, land processioned, 120, 212, 213^2; processioner, 252, 253^2.

Ashwell, Wm., indigent person, 241.
Assembly, *see* General Assembly.
Assessment bill, for support of Christian denominations, lxix.
Atheists, conduct of ministers confirm, xxviii.
Attorney-General, allegations against Rev. Patrick Lunan presented to, xl, 184, 186.
See also Randolph, John.
Attorneys, *see* Lawyers.
Auction, petition to sell glebe and poorhouse at, lxiv; poorhouse to be sold at, 242; tobacco to be sold at, 27, 47.
Austin, Richard, land processioned, 115; present at processioning, 115³.
Averi, Alexander, land processioned, 80.
See also Evera, Alexander.

Baanes, George, *see* Bains, George.
Babb, ———, indigent child, 13, 21.
Babb (Bab), Mary, indigent person, 94, 123, 168, 179, 183, 195.
Babb, R., indigent person, 16.
Babb, Richard, land processioned, 31².
Babb (Balb), William, land processioned, 31, 31 (note), 144²; present at processioning, 144⁴; processioner, 3.
Back Street, Suffolk, name changed, li.
Back Swamp, chapel to be built on, liii, 28.
Badge, indigents on relief required to wear, lx.
Bailey, Elizabeth (E., Eliz.), indigent person, 237, 241, 243, 248, 249, 250, 255, 259.
See also Baly; Bayley.
Bains (Baanes, Banns), George, land processioned, 212³; present at processioning, 146; processioner, 25, 101.
Bake[ ], Robt., 139.
Baker, ———, land processioned, 75, 165.
Baker, Capt. ———, 207, 227; land processioned, 70, 75, 148; present at processioning, 70, 136.
See also Baker, William (sometimes designated captain or colonel).
Baker, Col. ———, money in custody of, 97; to select location for chapel, 87; vestryman, deceased, 94.
See also Baker, William (sometimes designated captain or colonel).
Baker, Mrs. ———, land processioned, 165².
Baker, Ann, indigent person, 195, 200, 206, 220, 224, 226, 230, 237, 239, 241, 247, 248, 250, 255.
Baker, Benjamin (Ben., Benja., Benjm., Benjn.), accounts of, 243; churchwarden, 180, 183, 187; land processioned, 111², 116, 136, 165, 174², 175², 254, 263²; present at processioning, 116; reimbursed, 203; vestryman, 156, 157, 161, 178, 194, 196, 200, 201, 203, 205, 218, 222, 225, 227, 229, 236.
Baker, Daniel, land processioned, 235⁴.
Baker, David, land processioned, 192, 192 (note), 235⁷, 245; present at processioning, 192.
Baker, Dempsey (Demsey), land not processioned, 235; land processioned, 245; paid for services, 230; processioner, 231, 235, 252, 254.
Baker, Edward, deceased, 256; land processioned, 38, 71, 80, 105, 145, 146, 172, 193², 213; present at processioning, 146, 193²; processioner, 65, 80², 160, 172, 209, 214, 231, 252, 254; reimbursed, 251.
Baker, Hannah, land processioned, 171.
Baker, James, 170; land processioned, 33, 34³, 35², 38, 38 (note), 147²; present at processioning, 146, 263; reimbursed, 12, 248.
Baker, Jane, land processioned, 73³, 74.
Baker, Jean, 95; land processioned, 112.
Baker, John, land processioned, 38², 80, 105, 145, 172, 193², 212, 213; present at processioning, 80², 105², 193, 213; processioner, 8, 131, 145; reimbursed, 218, 226.
Baker, Jonathan, processioner, 243, 244.
Baker, Joseph (Jeseph, Jos., Josept), land processioned, 34, 69, 114², 137, 138, 147, 164², 170; overseer of poor, 258; present at processioning, 69, 138², 147; processioner, 25, 34, 64, 160, 170², 208,

242, 244; reimbursed, 179, 248, 249, 255, 260; son of James, 170.
Baker, Luke, reimbursed, 219, 223, 226.
Baker, Mary, indigent person, 223.
Baker, Richard, vestryman, lxix, 257, 258.
Baker, Robert, land processioned, 116², 117; present at processioning, 116, 117¹²; processioner, 10.
Baker, Samuel, land processioned, 34³, 38 (note), 80, 105, 170, 172, 193², 214; present at processioning, 80, 146², 147.
Baker, William (sometimes designated captain or colonel), accounts of, 50, 54, 57, 123; churchwarden, 88, 89, 91, 93, 94, 95, 99, 104, 118, 119; deceased, 95, 156; land processioned, 29², 31, 32, 33, 69, 72³, 75², 111², 112, 116², 136², 148; member of committee to sell devised land, 173; present at processioning, 69, 116²; processioner, 100, 112, 243; report on location for chapel, 88; trustee for building chapel, 28; vestryman, 19, 23, 24, 26, 45, 49, 55, 87, 99, 101, 103, 121, 124, 125, 126, 129, 130, 132, 153, 154, 173.
Baker, Wm., jr., present at processioning, 72².
Baker, prominent family in Upper Parish, xix.
Baker's Mill Run, 9, 10, 65, 66.
Balb (Babb), William, land processioned, 31, 31 (note).
Balfour (Balfoure), Rev. William, minister of Upper Parish, xxxvi-xxxvii, 12, 14, 15, 16.
Ballard (Balard), Abraham (Abram, Abrm.), land processioned, 30, 215², 216², 263; processioner, 24, 30, 209, 215, 231, 232, 242, 252.
Ballard (Balard, Ballad), Elisha, land processioned, 68³, 82², 113, 147³, 148, 163², 173², 210², 212²; processioner, 100, 120², 130, 148, 159, 173.
Ballard (Balard, Ballad), John, land processioned, 68, 69², 76³, 108, 114², 143, 164, 170²; present at processioning, 114³, 171²; processioner, 131, 143, 160, 171, 231.
Ballard's Corner, 147.

Ballot, vestrymen chosen by, 257.
Baly, Jno., present at processioning, 71.
See also Bailey; Bayley.
Bandy, James, processioner, 25, 33.
Banns, George, *see* Bains, George.
Baptists, levy on, 240.
Barbecue (Barbacu, Barbacue, Barbcue, Barbicure, Barbique) Swamp, 8, 9, 34, 64, 65, 66, 83, 136, 170, 233.
Barfield, John, present at processioning, 30.
See also Bearfield, John.
Barkeley, Joshua, processioner, 208 (note), 210.
Barker, David, land processioned, 192, 192 (note).
Barkley, John, land processioned, 35⁴, 73², 112; present at processioning, 112; processioner, 75, 159, 208.
See also Berkley, John.
Barkley, Saml., reimbursed, 260.
Barr, John, land processioned, 234²; processioner, 243, 252, 255.
Barradal, Matthew, processioner, 132.
See also Buradall, Mathew.
Barret, Jese, paid for services, 122.
Barry, John, paid for services, 103.
Bascomb, James, present at processioning, 185.
Baskervill, Hamilton P., *Andrew Meade of Ireland and Virginia* . . . (book), xviii (note), xix (note).
Bass, Jacob, land processioned, 109²; paid for services, 250.
Bastard children, women fined for having, 29, 55, 120.
See also Childbirth; Orphans.
Bateman, Jethro, processioner, 242, 244.
Bateman, John, processioner, 252, 253².
Bateman, William, indigent person, 176, 195; land processioned, 35, 164²; paid for services, 179; processioner, 24, 35.
See also Beatman, William.
Baten, *see* Batten.
Bates, Christian, indigent child, 202, 207.
Bates, Edward, land processioned, 81⁴, 110, 142³.
Bates, Henry, paid for services, 219;

present at processioning, 192⁸; processioner, 161.

Bates, Hester, indigent person, 220.

Bates, James, processioner, 243; reimbursed, 219, 260.

Bates, John, paid for services, 230.

Batten (Baten), Daniel, land processioned, 33, 69, 107, 150; present at processioning, 69², 107².

Batten, Jno., present at processioning, 214.

Battle, Elisha, present at processioning, 30.

Battle, Jesse (Jessey), land processioned, 147, 148, 173³, 212; present at processioning, 212²; processioner, 130, 148.

Battle, William, land processioned, 4, 30², 59, 215, 236; present at processioning, 215², 236².

Bawls (Rawls), William, land processioned, 34, 34 (note).

Bawls (Rawls), William, jr., land processioned, 34, 34 (note).

Bayley, Rev. Thomas, xxx, xxxi.

See also Bailey; Baly.

Beal (Beel), Benjamin, land processioned, 185, 209, 242, 245, 253.

Beaman, ———, land processioned, 263²; present at processioning, 263².

Beaman (Beamon, Bemon), Absalom (Absolem, Absolom, Absolum), land processioned, 138², 164²; present at processioning, 116, 117, 138²; processioner, 160, 208, 211, 242.

Beaman, Absolem (Abs.), sr., present at processioning, 263².

Beaman, Francis, land processioned, 192.

Beaman (Beamon), John, land processioned, 117⁸; present at processioning, 117⁸.

Beaman (Beamon), Mary, land processioned, 116, 117.

Beaman (Beamon), Thos., present at processioning, 117².

Beamon, Israel, processioner, 231.

Beamon

See also Bemond.

Bearfield, John, land processioned, 70.

See also Barfield, John.

Beasley (Beaseley, Beslee), Wim., land processioned, 83, 113, 163; present at processioning, 113³.

Beatman, William, land processioned, 72², 112, 137; present at processioning, 73², 112.

See also Bateman, William.

Beaverdam (Beverdam, Bever Dam) Swamp, 4, 9, 10, 11, 60, 65, 66, 67, 80.

Beckett, Rev. J. (or Thomas), xxxvii (note), 19, 22.

Bed (Bead), 55.

Beds, for almshouse, 97.

Beel, Benjamin, *see* Beal, Benjamin.

Bell, Gertrude, indigent person, 52.

Bell, for new church, l, li, 47, 241.

Bembra, Sarah, indigent person, 255.

Bemon, Absalom, *see* Beamon, Absalom.

Bemond, Nathanill, processioner, 10.

See also Beaman Beamon.

Benches, for church, 102; for Middle Chapel, 21.

Benn, Elizabeth, indigent person, 259.

Bennet, John, land processioned, 150.

Bennett, Rev. Thomas, leader of Independent congregation, xxiv.

Bennitts, Thos. Brown, indigent person, 230.

Berkley, John, land processioned, 137; processioner, 59.

See also Barkley, John.

Berry, Sophia, indigent person, 127.

Beslee, Wim., *see* Beasley, Wim.

Best, Henry, land processioned, 148², 172.

Best (Bist), John, land processioned, 31, 35², 72, 73, 112, 137, 143⁴; paid for services, 90, 91; present at processioning, 72⁵, 73², 82, 112, 143³, 144³, 212², 213⁵; processioner, 24, 35.

Best, John, jr., present at processioning, 143², 144²; processioner, 231, 232; teacher, 207.

Best, Kedar, present at processioning, 144; processioner, 159, 168.

Best, Lewis, processioner, 252, 253².

Best, Sarah, paid for services, 241.

Best, Wm., present at processioning, 172⁸.

Bible, for new church, li, 93; formerly used in Suffolk Church, lxxiv.

Bids, for building chapel, lv, 128; for

building church, 20, 46; for enclosing churchyard, 128; for work on Suffolk Church and poorhouse, 184.
Bills, for dissolving vestry, xx; for establishment of poorhouse in Bruton Parish, lix; for raising money by lottery, lxxiii; for religious freedom, lxv; for support of Christian denominations, lxv, lxix. *See also* Acts; General Assembly; Laws.
Binse (Bins), Charles, 150, 150 (note).
Bird, Aaron, land processioned, 146.
Bird, Barna, indigent person, 91.
Bird, Charity, land processioned, 146.
Bird, Edmund, land processioned, 71, 146.
Bird, Jacob, land processioned, 146.²
Bird, John, land processioned, 71; paid for services, 91; present at processioning, 71.
Bird, John (son of Wm.), land processioned, 146².
Bird, William, land processioned, 34, 146; paid for services, 247, 248, 250, 256; present at processioning, 146². *See also* Burd; Byrd.
Birdsong, Charles, land processioned, 150, 214; present at processioning, 214.
Birt, Arter, land processioned, 137. *See also* Burt.
Bishop, ———, indigent person, 260.
Bishop, ministers to present evidence of ordination by English, xxvi.
Bishop of London, xliv; commissary in Virginia for, xxv, 177 (note); letters to, xxviii, xxx, xxxi, xxxv, xxxvi.
Bist, John, *see* Best, John.
Blackwater River, xvii, 7, 33, 62, 87, 107, 150, 232; petition of inhabitants over, liv, 87.
Blade, Eliza., indigent person, 206.
Blade, Jean, indigent person, 177, 206.
Blade, Lawrence, land processioned, 170².
Blair, James, controversy with Gov. Francis Nicholson, xxxiv; deputy in Virginia for Bishop of London, xxv; letter to Bishop of London, xxx.
Blake, ———, land of, 84.
Blake, George, indigent person, 52.
Bland, Richard, and "Two Penny" act, xli (note); in case of vestry vs. Rev. Patrick Lunan, xli; *To the Clergy of Virginia* (book), xlii (note).
Blith, Jno., *see* Blythe, John.
Blocks, for Middle Chapel, 21; horse, 12, 50.
Bly, Harrell, reader at Middle Chapel, 47.
Blythe (Blith), John, indigent person, 12, 17, 21, 26.
Bodkin, Jane, coffin for, 13.
Bodys, ———, land processioned, 31.
Boice, James, *see* Boyce, James.
Bois, James, *see* Boyce, James.
Bolts, for glebe, 220.
Bond, ———, 226.
Bond, Susanah, indigent person, 97. *See also* Bound.
Bond, collector of parish levy to give, 14, 18, 22, 46, 54, 58, 87, 92, 126, 157, 158, 162, 167, 176, 179, 195, 202, 218, 223, 225, 230, 238, 240, 242; contractor to give, 85; custodian of child to give, 180; interest on churchwarden's, 227; trustees of poorhouse to give, 84.
Bonood, John, present at processioning, 236.
Book of Common Prayer, formerly used by Suffolk Church, lxxiv; purchased, li, 93; Puritan refuses to use, xxiv.
Booth, Abraham, land processioned, 148.
Booth, Eliza, indigent person, 156, 162; paid for services, 179.
Booth, Henry (H., Hen.), present at processioning, 217³.
Booth (Boothe), James, land processioned, 39², 80, 81², 141, 161, 197, 212; present at processioning, 141; processioner, 11; reimbursed, 225.
Booth, Jethro, land processioned, 211, 233.
Booth, Joseph, 44; land processioned, 41, 43³, 137², 142, 188, 211, 217², 233.
Booth, Kedar, paid for services, 250; refuses to have land processioned, 244.
Booth, Moses, land processioned, 188, 233; present at processioning, 211; processioner, 231, 233².
Booth, Robert, executors of, 167; land processioned, 43², 136², 137; sexton at Cyprus Chapel, 157, 158, 161, 167.

Boothe, ———, land processioned, 75².
Bound, Jethro, indigent person, 223.
  See also Bond.
Boundary, of Chuckatuck, Lower and Upper parishes, xv, xv (note); of Isle of Wight and Nansemond counties, xiv (note), xv, xvi (note); of Isle of Wight, Upper Norfolk and Lower Norfolk counties, xiv, xiv (note); of Upper and Suffolk parishes, xvi, xvii; of Virginia and North Carolina, xvi, xvii, xix, xxix, liii (note), 116, 148.
  See also Processioning of land.
Bower, Edwd., land processioned, 233.
Bowser, Mrs. ———, indigent person, 152.
Boyce, ———, land processioned, 137².
Boyce, Benjn., land processioned, 233.
Boyce (Boice, Bois, Boys), James, land processioned, 44, 188, 211, 233²; present at processioning, 188, 211.
Boyd, ———, 43.
Boyd, Arthur, paid for services, 226.
Boyd (Boyt, Boyte, Byte), William, land processioned, 36, 75, 78, 121², 174²; paid for services, 237; present at processioning, 36, 75.
Boyet, Arthur, processioner, 208.
Boyt, Ann, indigent person, 17, 21.
Boyt, Edward, land processioned, 75², 78; processioner, 5.
Boyt (Boyte), John, 36; land processioned, 121.
Boyt, Thomas, present at processioning, 78.
Boyte, Moses, land processioned, 36.
Boyte, Rebeaco, land processioned, 36.
Bradley, ———, 171.
Bradly, John, land processioned, 29, 35.
Branches, *see* names of particular branches: Copeland's; Meadow; Redy.
  See also Creeks; Rivers; Runs.
Brandy, 93.
  See also Liquor.
Brantley, Jacob, ferryman, 156.
Brantun, Thomas, land processioned, 37².
Breeches, for indigent person, 220.
Brewer, Edward, indigent person, 247; paid for services, 237, 239.

Brewer, Jacob, present at processioning, 106⁴.
Brewer, James, land processioned, 211; paid for services, 207.
Brewer, John, land processioned, 192³, 235³, 245; present at processioning, 117¹; processioner, 66, 132, 139 (note), 182, 192, 231, 235, 252.
Brewer, Joseph, present at processioning, 106.
Brewer, Mary, indigent person, 250, 251, 256, 259; land processioned, 117².
Brewer, Moses (Mos., Mosses), land processioned, 140, 141, 193, 194; paid for services, 206; present at processioning, 106, 193²; processioner, 131, 141.
Brewer, Newby, land processioned, 233.
Brewer, Rachel, land processioned, 117³.
Brewer, Robert, land processioned, 76², 106³.
Brewer, Soloman, present at processioning, 106.
Brewer, William, paid for services, 127; present at processioning, 106.
Brewer's Creek, formerly Duke's Creek, xvii, xvii (note).
Brick, almshouse built of, 84.
Brick Church, *see* Church.
Brickle, John (sometimes designated captain), churchwarden, 240, 242; land not processioned, 235²; land processioned, 245; resigns from vestry, 246; vestryman, 238, 239, 246.
Brickle (Brickel), Thos., vestry held at home of, 194, 196, 197.
Bridges, *see* names of particular bridges: Jarnagan's; Knuckle Swamp; Porter's; Yeats, Robt.
Briggs, James, land processioned, 235³.
Brinkley, Cajar, land processioned, 212³.
Brinkley (Brinkly), Eley, land processioned, 37³, 190¹; present at processioning, 37; reimbursed, 176.
Brinkley (Brinkly), Henry, land processioned, 37⁵, 189⁵, 234²; present at processioning, 37³, 189², 234; processioner, 131.
Brinkley (Brinkly), James, land processioned, 37³, 189⁴, 211, 234; present at

processioning, 37², 189; processioner, 8, 100.
Brinkley (Brinkly), John, land processioned, 37⁵, 38, 188⁶, 189⁶, 190⁷, 191, 211, 233², 234¹⁴; present at processioning, 190⁹; processioner, 231, 234.
Brinkley (Brinkly), Kader (Kadah), land processioned, 234²; present at processioning, 190.
Brinkley, Michall (Micall), land processioned, 10, 37, 38.
Brinkley, Mills, present at processioning, 234.
Brinkley, Peter, land processioned, 37⁴, 188².
Brinkley, William, land processioned, 234²; present at processioning, 37.
Brinkly, ———, land processioned, 108.
Brinkly, Mary, indigent person, 21, 27.
British, Virginia invaded by, lxvii.
British Public Record Office, xxxiii (note), xxxiv (note), xxxv (note), xliv (note).
Bromegom, Edwd., administrator, 86.
Bromegom, Judith, administrator of, 86.
Brothers, John, land processioned, 188⁸, 189⁵, 233², 234²; paid for services, 237, 239, 241; present at processioning, 188²; processioner, 231, 234.
Brothers, Richard, land processioned, 37³, 38⁴.
Brothers, Wm., land processioned, 189³, 234.
Brounds, ———, orphans of, 219.
Brown, ———, 176.
Brown, Dr. ———, 96, 103, 119.
Brown, Ann, indigent person, 198.
Brown, David, present at processioning, 142².
Brown, Fenol, indigent person, 22.
Brown, Isabela (Isal., Isbell), indigent person, 123, 241, 256, 260.
Brown, Jesse, land processioned, 33.
Brown, Dr. Jesse (Jesey, Jessey), accounts of, 91, 97, 162, 207.
Brown, Joell, indigent person, 17.
Brown, Robert, processioner, 99.
Brown, Dr. Robert, accounts of, 21, 50, 86, 91, 123, 127; vestryman, 128, 130, 132.
Brown, Sarah, indigent person, 168.
Brown, Terel, indigent person, 123.
Brown, Thomas, present at processioning, 39, 82².
Brumton, Thomas, land processioned, 146.
Brunswick Co., St. Andrew's Parish in, xxxix.
Bruton Parish, petition for poorhouse for, lix.
Bryant, William, land processioned, 116; present at processioning, 70.
Brydon, Dr. G. MacLaren, x, xxxi (note).
Bucker, Wm., present at processioning, 173.
Bucket, 118, 179.
Buntley, ———, indigent person, 96.
Buradall (Buradal), Mathew, land processioned, 109⁹; present at processioning, 109³.
See also Barradal, Matthew.
Burd, Edmund, present at processioning, 170.
See also Bird; Byrd.
Burgess (Burges), Rev. Henry John, substitute at Holy Neck Chapel, xliii, xliii (note), 225.
Burgesses, see House of Burgesses.
Burials, of indigent persons, 12, 16, 21, 50, 52, 53, 55, 56, 86, 87, 91, 96, 97, 102, 103, 123, 152, 156, 158, 179, 195, 202, 219, 220, 223, 226, 229, 237, 239, 243, 247, 248, 250, 251; of soldiers, lxvi, 236; sheets for, 179, 219, 241.
See also Coffins; Deaths; Funerals; Graves.
Burket, Charles, paid for services, 243.
Burley, Matthew, paid for services, 102.
Burt, John, land processioned, 137.
See also Birt.
Burtell, Rev. James, minister of Upper Parish, xxxiv.
Busskin, Mourning, 1.
Butcher, 123.
See also Meat; Pork.
Butler, ———, land processioned, 68.
Butler, Absolam, land processioned, 105.
Butler, Danl., indigent person, 249, 251.

Butler, Henry, land processioned, 83², 113³, 114², 163, 210²; present at processioning, 114, 138³, 164; processioner, 60, 83.
Butler, James, indigent person, 98, 239, 241, 243, 247, 248, 249, 255; land processioned, 82⁴; present at processioning, 82.
Butler, John, 60, 139, 180; land processioned, 29, 31, 69², 70, 74, 75, 82, 83, 112, 113³, 116, 138, 163², 164; present at processioning, 138, 163; processioner, 60, 83; reimbursed, 255.
Butler, Moses, land processioned, 171.
Butler (Buttler), Peter, land processioned, 30², 68², 71, 72, 83, 110⁶, 114², 164³, 171³, 210⁵; paid for services, 13, 16, 248, 256; present at processioning, 71; processioner, 4.
Butler, Saml., paid for services, 239.
Butler, Stephen, indigent person, 239.
Butler, William, deceased, 45; land processioned, 29, 83, 110, 164; present at processioning, 111; vestryman, 1, 12, 14, 15, 16, 18, 19, 20, 23.
Butler, Zach., indigent person, 241.
Byrd, Aaron, land processioned, 34.
Byrd, Edward, land processioned, 34².
Byrd, Jacob, land processioned, 34; paid for services, 243.
Byrd, John, land processioned, 34.
Byrd, John, jr., land processioned, 34.
Byrd, John, sr., 34.
Byrd, Col. William, comments on religion in Nansemond Co., xxix; *Histories of the Dividing Line Betwixt Virginia and North Carolina*, xix (note), xxix (note); *History of the Dividing Line, Run in the Year 1728*, liii (note).
See also Bird; Burd.
Byte, John, 36.
See also Boyt, John.

Cadowgan (Cadogan, Codowgwan), William, certain properties of, devised to Upper Parish, lv, lvi, lxiii, 125, 173, 173 (note); land of, to be surveyed, lvii, 84; will of, to be obtained and recorded, 128.

Cairnes, Alexander, processioner, 58; to build pew in church gallery, li, 88, 93.
Calendar of Virginia State Papers and Other Manuscripts (book), xlvii (note), xlviii (note), xlix (note), lxv (note), lxvi (note).
Calf, 68.
Callis, George, clerk of vestry, 246, 247, 248, 249, 250, 252, 256, 257, 258; reimbursed, 250, 251.
Camm, Rev. John, sent to England about "Two Penny" act, xxxvii.
Campbell, David, present at processioning, 216⁴.
Campbell (Campbel), James, paid for services, 220, 226.
Campbell (Cambel, Cambell, Camble, Cambwel, Cambwell, Campble, Campbwell, Campel, Camwell), John, clerk, Cyprus Chapel, 157, 161, 167, 175, 178, 182, 198; land processioned, 39², 81⁶, 142², 192, 216², 217²; paid for services, 57, 85; present at processioning, 39², 81³, 82³, 110; processioner, 132, 142; reader, 18, 20, 45, 52; reader, Cyprus Chapel, 194, 197; reader, Summerton Chapel, 47; reader, Upper Chapel, 49; sexton, Cyprus Chapel, 175, 178, 182, 194, 197.
Campbell, Julia, indigent person, 259.
Campbell, Nathl., paid for services, 13.
Capitol Landing, petition for poorhouse at, lix.
Car, Dempsey, land processioned, 210².
Car, Joshua, present at processioning, 215².
Car, Nathan, present at processioning, 110².
Car, Robert, jr., land processioned, 108².
Car, Robert, sr., land processioned, 33.
Car, Thos., land processioned, 116.
See also Carr; Kerr.
Carl, Joseph, land processioned, 33.
See also Cearl; Curle.
Carnal, ———, land processioned, 108².
Carnal (Carnall), Abraham, land processioned, 143, 171²; processioner, 24.
Carr, James, land processioned, 150, 214;

processioner, 131, 150, 151, 160, 169, 208, 214.

Carr (Car), John, land processioned, 29^2, 72^4, 110^6, 111^3, 114, 164^2, 171^3, 214; present at processioning, 72, 214^4; processioner, 231, 232, 252; reimbursed, 12.

Carr, Jos., present at processioning, 215.

Carr (Car), Robert, land processioned, 33, 69, 107, 150, 215, 236; present at processioning, 69, 107, 149^4, 150^4, 215^2, 236^2.

Carr (Car), Saml. (S.), present at processioning, 216^2, 217^9.

Carr (Car), Titus, land processioned, 215; present at processioning, 236.

Carr, Wm., processioner, 243.

See also Car; Kerr.

Carter, William, indigent person, 98.

Cary, Mrs. ———, land processioned, 236.

Cary, Ann, land processioned, 215.

Cary, Benj., present at processioning, 149.

Cary, Edward, clerk, Nottoway Chapel, 95; land processioned, 149, 215, 236; present at processioning, 215^2, 236; processioner, 131, 149, 150, 181, 187; reimbursed, 102.

Cary, James, ferryman, 133; land of, as site for chapel, 88, 89; land processioned, 33, 108^2, 149, 187; paid for services, 96, 103.

Cary, James, jr., clerk of vestry, 52, 54, 57.

Cary, Natha., present at processioning, 108.

Cason, Charles, land processioned, 235.

Catechism, only Church of England, to be taught, xxvi.

Cearl (Cearle), Joseph, land processioned, 149; present at processioning, 149^2, 150.

See also Carl; Curle.

Chain bearer, 90.

Chairs, for almshouse, 97.

Chamberlayne, Dr. C. G., v, x.

Champion, Rebecca (Reb.), indigent person, 13, 17.

Chapel (Chappel), Ruth, indigent person, 123; paid for services, 206.

See also Chapell, Mrs. ———

Chapel land, 34; deed for, recorded, 50; processioned, 30.

Chapel Road, cleared, 56, 85; land on, processioned, 62, 252.

Chapell (Chappell), Mrs. ———, indigent person, 98, 120.

See also Chapel, Ruth.

Chapels, at Norfleets, 153; blocked up, 127, 154, 158, 179; building of, liv, 87, 89, 128, 129; hinges for, 57; location of, lii; minister neglects duties at, 16; ornaments of, removed to Suffolk, lii, 91; readers at, 16, 18, 27, 52; repair of, 52, 262; sextoness, 50; tarred, 87; yard cleaned, 118, 198, 203, 219, 220, 230, 241.

See also names of particular chapels: Cypress; Holy Neck; Lower; Middle; Nottoway; Somerton; Union; Upper.

Chaplain, at Yorktown, xlvii; to garrison in Portsmouth, xlvii; to Virginia Regiment, xxxviii (note).

Chapman, Chance, indigent person, 195.

Chesapeake Bay, lxv.

Childbirth, 12, 127, 202, 223.

See also Bastard children; Children.

Children, allowance for education and maintenance of, xxi, lvii; almshouse trustees to report on indigent, 124; bastard, 29, 55, 120; bound out, lxi, 124; provided for, 12, 13, 21, 57, 85, 86, 105, 152, 177, 180, 239, 243, 250, 251; school in almshouse for, lviii, lx, 97, 103, 104, 119, 123, 129; taken to court, 86.

See also Orphans; Schools; Teaching.

Chivers, Thos., processioner, 131.

See also Shavass; Shiffers; Shivers.

Christmas, xlvi, 12, 90, 96, 97; services at Suffolk Church on, xliv, 153, 154, 228.

Chuckatuck Parish, xiii (note), xv (note), xxxiii, xxxiv, lx; boundaries of, xv (note); debate at church in, xxxiv; formerly West Parish, xv; minister of, xxx, xxxiii, xxxiv, xxxv, xxxvii, lviii (note); united with Lower as Suffolk,

INDEX 275

xvi; vestry book of, xiii; vestry of, fined, xv, xxvi.
See also Lower Parish, Nansemond Co.; Suffolk Parish; West Parish.

Church, R. W., x.

Church, bell for, l, li, 47, 241; benches for, 102; building of, l, li, 46, 53, 54, 88, 89; clerk of, 56, 85, 90, 95, 101, 122, 126, 132, 151, 154, 157, 161, 167, 175, 178, 182, 201; communion cloth in, li, lxxiv, 86; demolished, lxxiv, lxxiv (note); erected in Suffolk, xxi; galleries in, 46, 47, 93; glazed, 198; ladder for, 91, 152; linen of, 229; lot adjoining purchased, li (note), 156; marble font in, li, lxxiv, 86; ministers of xliii, xliv, 225, 226, 231; money for building, 17, 22, 23, 27, 46, 47, 50, 53, 57; nails for, 239; old brick, xlix, lii, 2, 3, 47, 48, 58, 82; organ for, li, 86, 91; ornaments, l, li, lii, 46, 89, 91; petition to raise money to rebuild, lxxii, lxxiii; pew in gallery of, li, 88, 89; plans for, xlix, 19, 20; readers at, 18, 118, 194, 197, 205, 207, 218, 222, 225, 229, 236, 239, 240, 243; repairs to, 45, 91, 103, 184, 206, 219, 239, 262; services at, 153, 154, 227; sexton of, lxvi, 50, 52, 56, 85, 90, 96, 102, 122, 126, 132, 151, 154, 157, 161, 167, 168, 176, 178, 182, 194, 197, 201, 205, 218, 222, 226, 229, 236, 240, 243; site for, xlix, 20, 46, 48; yard of, 12, 128, 133, 184, 243.
See also Chapels; St. Paul's Church, Suffolk.

Church of England, established in Nansemond County, xxiii; formalism and rationalism of, xxxii; ministers required to conform to orders and constitutions of, xxiii, xxvi; Rev. Patrick Lunan ordained according to rites of, xli; religious decline in, xxv; rites and doctrine of, xxii; slandered by Quaker teachers, xxviii; successor to, in Virginia, lxviii; vestrymen required to subscribe to the doctrine and discipline of, xxvi.

See also Established Church; Protestant Episcopal Church.

Church Road, cleared, 45; land on, processioned, 3, 30, 58.

Church Street, Suffolk, li.

Churchwardens, 1, 2, 11, 12, 14, 15, 16, 17, 18, 19, 20, 23, 24, 26, 27, 28, 29, 45, 48, 49, 51, 54, 55, 67, 68, 83, 85, 87, 88, 89, 92, 93, 94, 98, 99, 104, 118, 119, 120, 124, 125, 126, 129, 130, 132, 134, 135, 151, 153, 154, 155, 157, 159, 161, 167, 168, 175, 177, 178, 184, 194, 197, 198, 200, 203, 204, 218, 221, 222, 225, 227, 228, 229, 236, 239, 240, 242, 245, 248, 249, 250, 252, 255, 257, 258; accounts of, 13, 17, 22, 23, 27, 29, 50, 53, 54, 56, 57, 58, 85, 86, 87, 90, 91, 92, 93, 94, 97, 98, 102, 103, 123, 128, 130, 133, 153, 156, 157, 158, 159, 163, 168, 177, 179, 180, 183, 195, 198, 202, 206, 207, 223, 226, 229, 238, 239, 243, 247, 249, 251, 256, 259; apprentice fee given by, 49; chosen, 1, 15, 18, 23, 29, 48, 51, 55, 68, 88, 94, 99, 104, 120, 124, 128, 130, 135, 153, 156, 168, 180, 187, 200, 218, 224, 230, 240, 244, 248, 249, 252, 257, 258, 262; Chuckatuck Parish fined for not swearing in, xv, xxvi; collectors of parish levy, 22, 27, 162, 202, 218, 223, 227, 238, 251, 257; deaths of, 95, 153; fines to, 15, 200; glebe land processioned by order of, 77; interest on bond of, 227; oaths administered to, 1, 15, 18, 23, 48, 94, 120, 168, 180, 201, 218, 224, 230; order poorhouse discontinued and rented for benefit of poor, lxiii, 203, 204; persons refusing to have land processioned certified to, 2, 3, 4, 5, 6, 7, 8, 9, 10, 11, 58, 59, 60, 61, 62, 63, 64, 65, 66, 67; processioners report to, 134; sheriffs and tobacco collectors give bond and security to, 14, 18, 46, 54, 87, 92, 126, 157, 158; to advertise and sell poorhouse, lxiv, 242; to advertise for minister, 257; to advertise sale of glebe land, 104; to answer petition of inhabitants of Upper Parish, l; to change manager of poorhouse, 129; to deed galleries in new church, 46, 47; to convey indigent persons to poorhouse, 97; to dispose of poorhouse furniture, 227; to establish title to glebe land, 88; to get deed for lot for poorhouse, 84; to have glebe land surveyed, 84; to inform convention of lack of minister, 262; to interview minister, 153; to inventory church property, 262; to investigate donation of land, 125; to obtain and record Cadowgan's will, 128; to pay delegates to convention, 258; to pay for work on new church, 88; to pay Lunan, 228; to persuade Lunan to relinquish glebe, xlv, 228; to prepare deed for land for church, 20, 46; to present gift to minister, 19; to provide for poorhouse, 97, 104, 199, 219; to purchase tobacco, 225; to raise money to repair church and chapels, 262; to sell tobacco, 17, 22, 23, 27, 47, 50, 53, 57, 86, 87, 90, 102, 103, 122, 126, 133, 152, 155, 157, 162, 167, 176, 178, 183, 195, 197, 199, 201, 205, 218, 222; to supply money for building Holy Neck Chapel, 28; to report on certain lands, 196; to sell houses, etc. on glebe, lxvii, 246; to serve minister with order, 16; to survey land at Wickham, 84; to treat with Suffolk Parish for caring for poor, 99; tobacco levied for poorhouse, 96; vs. John Norfleet (Norpleet), 92; vs. Capt. Lewis Merideth, 17; vs. ―――― Narney, 95.

Churchwell, Mary, indigent person, 259.

Circuit Court, of Suffolk, xiii.

Clark, Danl. (Dan.), 201, 219.

Cleeves, John, land processioned, 37[4]; present at processioning, 37.

Cleny, William, land processioned, 29. *See also* McClenney, William.

Clergy, and "Two Penny" act, xxxviii (note), xli (note); discontinuance of levies for support of, lxv; Meade's criticism of, xxxii; religious and moral decline of English, xxxii. *See also* Ministers.

Clerks, of churches and chapels, xxi. *See also* Readers; names of clerks: Allmand, Aaron; Callis, George; Campbell, John; Cary, Edward; Cary, James, jr.; Darden, Elisha; Fry, Robert; Glover, John; Jackson, Christopher; Maget, Nicholas; Norfleet, Edward; Parker, Hardy; Rambow, Isaac; Richardson, Archd.; Riddick, Lemuel; Sheckleton, William; Skinner, Henry; Spivey, George; Webb, Richard.

Cloth, Communion, 86.

Cloth, country, 45. *See also* Cotton; Flax; Linen; Oznaburg.

Clothes, for indigent persons, 24, 49, 52, 56, 57, 86, 91, 96, 152, 154, 156, 220, 221, 230, 238. *See also* Oznaburg; Shoes.

Coat, for indigent person, 220.

Coffield, Edwd., processioner, 10.

Coffins, for indigent persons, 13, 27, 96, 103, 122, 127, 195, 202, 219, 220, 223, 226, 229, 241, 243. *See also* Burials; Deaths; Funerals; Graves.

Cohoon (Cohown), Samuel (Saml.) (sometimes designated captain or doctor), accounts of, 156, 158, 162, 168, 183, 195, 198, 202, 206, 219, 223, 226, 229, 238, 239, 241, 243; churchwarden, 218, 221, 222, 224; land not processioned, 213; land processioned, 210[6]; processioner, 150, 169; vestryman, 201, 204, 205, 218, 225, 227, 228, 229, 236, 239, 242, 246, 250.

Cole, John (Jno., Jon.), land processioned, 71[3]; paid for services, 17, 21; present at processioning, 134; sexton, 50, 52, 56, 85.

Cole, John, jr., land processioned, 71; processioner, 8.

Coles, ――――, land processioned, 263[2].

Coles, Abraham, processioner, 231.

Coles (Cole), John (Jno.) (sometimes designated captain), churchwarden, 248, 249; present at processioning, 134; processioner, 252; vestryman, 240, 242, 246, 247, 255.

Collation, of clergymen, xxxix (note).

Collings, Frans., provided for by parish, 12.
Collins, Jesse, land processioned, 194^2; present at processioning, 194^2; processioner, 208, 211.
Collins (Colins, Collans, Collings), William (Wim.), land processioned, 35^3, 73^4, 76, 106^3, 140, 141^2; present at processioning, 35.
Colmer, Rev. Davis, chaplain, xxxviii, xxxviii (note), 152.
The Colonial Church in Virginia (book), see Goodwin, Edward Lewis.
Colonial Churches in the Original Colony of Virginia, 2d ed., rev. and improved, lxxiii.
Colonial Churches of Tidewater Virginia (book), see Mason, George Carrington.
The Colonial Clergy of Virginia (book), xxxi (note), xxxiv (note), xxxv (note), xxxvii (note), xxxviii (note), xxxix (note), xlvi (note), xlvii (note).
Colster, Eliza., indigent person, 202.
Commissary in Virginia for Bishop of London, xxv, 177 (note).
See also Blair, James; Robinson, William.
Commission of Enquiry into the Losses and Services of the American Loyalists, xlviii (note), xlix.
Commission, paid collectors of parish levy, 13, 17, 22, 46, 50, 53, 57, 86, 96, 102, 119, 122, 126, 133, 152, 155, 158, 162, 167, 176, 183, 195, 197, 202, 206, 218, 223, 227, 230, 238, 240, 242, 247, 249, 251, 256, 260.
Communion cloth, li, lxxiv, 86.
Communion plate, 162.
Compass heads, windows in church to have, 55.
Conaway, Jno., indigent person, 55, 56.
Confiscatory act of 1802, lxxiv.
Connell, Marjorie, x.
Conner, Eliza., indigent person, 207.
Conner (Connar), Elizabeth, xlviii (note).
Constables, 219, 222.
Constant, James, land processioned, 109^3.
Contractor, required to give bond, 85.

Contractors, *see* Pugh, Daniel; Riddick, Josiah.
See also Agreements.
Conventions of Protestant Episcopal Church, *see* Protestant Episcopal Church.
Conyears (Cunyerds), land so called, not processioned, 43, 77.
Cooling's (Coolings) Creek, xv (note).
Cooper, *see* Cowper.
Coor, Henry, processioner, 5.
See also Core.
Coors, 5, 61.
Copelan (Couplan), Abraham, land processioned, 170; present at processioning, 106, 114, 169.
Copelan (Coupland, Cowpland), Elisha, land processioned, 141, 194; processioner, 160, 208, 243; reimbursed, 237.
Copelan (Couplan, Coupland), Henry, 131; land processioned, 76^3, 105, 106^2, 140^4; present at processioning, 76.
Copelan, John, jr., present at processioning, 114^2.
Copeland (Copland, Coupland), Francis (Fran.), branch, *see* Copeland's Branch.
Copeland (Copelan, Coplan, Couplan, Coupland), James (Jas.), land processioned, 35^4, 36^2, 44^4, 60^2, 68^4, 73^2, 74^4, 78^2, 106^2, 112^2, 113^2, 114^4, 121^8, 137^2, 138^2, 141^3, 164^2, 169^2, 194^2; present at processioning, 35^2, 44^{14}, 68^2, 78^2, 109^2, 121^4, 140^2, 141^8, 170^2; processioner, 25^2, 44^2, 100^2, 113^2, 131, 141^2, 181^2, 194^2, 243^2.
Copeland, Jesse, processioner, 252.
Copeland (Copelan, Couplan, Coupland, Cowpland), John, 55, 68, 88, 241; land processioned, 29^4, 68^2, 82^2, 83^3, 114^4, 164, 210^4; present at processioning, 83^2, 170^4, 193^2, 194^2; processioner, 252.
Copeland (Couplan, Coupland), Zachariah (Zacharias), land processioned, 193^2; overseer of poor, 258; processioner, 181, 194, 231, 252; reimbursed, 251, 259.
See also Coupland.
Copeland's (Copland's, Coupland's) Branch, 9, 10, 65, 66, 136, 233.

Copland, ———, land processioned, 263²; present at processioning, 263².
Core, Thos., land processioned, 70.
Core, Thomas, jr., land processioned, 31.
Core, Thomas, sr., land processioned, 31⁸.
See also Coor.
Corn, 93, 195, 202, 219, 223, 226.
Cornelus, ———, indigent person, 85, 86.
Cornelus (Cornelas), Sarah, indigent person, 90, 91, 96.
Cornwallis, General, xlvii.
Corpse (Corps), 52.
Cotten, Hannah (Hanah), paid for services, 162, 202.
Cotter, Elizabeth, paid for services, 55.
Cotter, Garrot (Garritt), paid for services, 17, 50.
Cotton, 199.
Coulden, Thos., present at processioning, 143.
Council, ———, land processioned, 263.
Council, Lemuel, processioner, 263.
Council, authorized to silence nonconformists, xxvi; case of Rev. Wm. Andrews before, xlviii; meeting of, 54; petition of inhabitants of Upper Parish to, 1; Puritan minister summoned before, xxiv; Rev. T. Bayley charged before, xxxi; vestrymen members of, xviii.
See also General Court.
Council Journals from Decr 1st 1781 to [November 16th 1782] (book), xlviii (note).
County court, xxviii; and indigent children, lxi, 86, 124; church property and revenue to be reported to, lxviii; of King George, xxxi; orders regarding processioning, xxi, 2, 35, 120; petition in, against Rev. Patrick Lunan, xlii (note); to issue warrants for transgressors of laws, xxvii; tobacco sold at, 22, 47, 50, 53, 57, 86, 90, 96, 102, 122, 126, 133, 152, 155, 157, 162, 167, 176, 178, 183, 195, 197, 199, 201, 205, 218, 221, 222; vestrymen judges of, xviii; witnesses in, paid for services, 102, 118.
County levy, lxx.

Coupland, Mary, fined for having bastard child, 120.
Coupland, William, deceased, 51; vestryman, 45.
Coupland, Wim., land processioned, 164²; present at processioning, 141⁴, 213³.
See also Copelan; Copeland.
Court of Oyer and Terminer, churchwardens to appear before, 1.
Courthouse, sale of tobacco at, 47; vestry held at, 12, 16, 18, 98, 99, 101, 104, 119, 121, 124, 129, 153, 177.
Courts, *see* Circuit Court of Suffolk; County court; Court of Oyer and Terminer; General Court.
Cow, 68.
Cowling, Josiah, reimbursed, 260.
Cowling, Willis, reimbursed, 248.
Cowper, John (Jno.), land processioned, 191, 192⁴, 245; processioner, 182, 192.
Cowper, Capt. John, land processioned, 253.
Cowper, John, jr., land processioned, 192.
Cowper, Robert, churchwarden, 262; oath signed by, 261; vestryman, 261, 262.
Cowper (Cooper), Willm. (Will., Wm.), land processioned, 235³, 245; paid for services, 230; witness to Lunan's renunciation, 229.
Cowper (Cooper), Wills (Wells) (sometimes designated as captain), accounts of, 156, 202, 206, 220, 223, 226, 229; churchwarden, 224, 225, 227, 228, 229, 230; resignation of, 240; vestryman, 219, 221, 236, 239, 258.
Cowper & Riddick, assignees of Wm. Gwin, 195.
Cowpland, *see* Copelan; Copeland.
Cox, ———, land processioned, 136.
Crafford, ———, land processioned, 165².
See also Crawford.
Craighead, Thos., paid for services, 220.
Craney (Crany) Creek, 191, 235.
Crawford, Mrs. ———, land processioned, 148.
See also Crafford.
Creeks, *see* names of particular creeks: Brewer's; Craney; Duke's; Everits;

Gumbs's; Indian; Keatons; Parkers; Pugh's; Somerton.
See also Branches; Rivers; Runs.
Cromwell's Party, member of, xxiv.
Cross, Edwd., land processioned, 236.
Cross, Hardy, paid for services, 248; processioner, 243, 252, 255.
Cross, James (Jas.), land processioned, 134; processioner, 208.
Cross, John, land processioned, 34^2, 79^2, 115^4, 134^5; present at processioning, 70, 115^3; processioner, 7, 63, 131, 134, 135.
Cross, John, sr., processioner, 80.
Cross, Jonathan, reimbursed, 259.
Cross, William (Willm., Wim., Wm.), land processioned, 79, 115^4, 134^2; present at processioning, 79^3, 134^3; processioner, 100, 116, 160.
Crothers, Dr. ———, accounts of, 179.
Cummings, George, indigent person, 259.
Cuningham, Charity, indigent person, 243.
Cunyerds, see Conyears.
Curle, Exum, present at processioning, 236.
Curle (Curl), Joseph, processioner, 25, 33, 160.
Curle, William, land processioned, 215, 236; present at processioning, 215^6.
See also Carl; Cearl.
Customs, act for preventing frauds in, 114 (note).
Cutchens, Mrs. ———, land processioned, 165.
Cutchens (Cuchin, Scutchins), John, land processioned, 32^4, 70^2, 112.
Cutchens (Cuchins), Thos., land processioned, 70; present at processioning, 111, 136^2.
Cutchins, Adam, present at processioning, 263.
See also Scutchens; Scutchins.
Cypress (Cyphres, Cyprus, Syprus) Chapel, clerk of, 157, 161, 167, 175, 178, 182, 198, 201, 229; reader at, 194, 197, 205, 218, 222, 226, 236, 239; schedule for divine services at, 153, 227; sexton of, 157, 158, 161, 167, 175, 178, 182, 197, 201, 205, 218, 222, 226; sextoness of, 240, 243; site and dimensions of, liv, 128; temporary minister at, xliii, xliv, 225, 226; well at, 158.
Cypress (Sipress, Sipruss, Sipruss, Sypruss) Swamp, lv, 8, 9, 64, 66, 136, 188, 233, 255.

Darby, Mrs. ———, 260.
Dardan, Ann, land processioned, 151.
Dardan, John, land processioned, 215.
Dardan, Mary, land processioned, 151.
Darden, Africa, reimbursed, 256.
Darden, Amey, reimbursed, 256.
Darden (Dardan, Durden), Carr (Car), land processioned, 33, 69, 107; present at processioning, 69; processioner, 7.
Darden (Dardan), Elisha, clerk, Holy Neck Chapel, 178, 182; clerk, Nottoway Chapel, 176; land processioned, 214; processioner, 208, 214; reader, Holy Neck Chapel, 194, 197, 201, 205, 218, 222; reimbursed, 255; vestryman, 246.
Darden (Dardan), Holland (Holand, Hollan), present at processioning, 150, 151^3, 214^3; processioner, 181, 231, 232.
Darden (Dardan, Durden), Jacob, land processioned, 33, 69, 107, 116, 148, 150; present at processioning, 69, 107, 169, 214^4; processioner, 7, 131, 150, 151.
Darden (Dardan), Jethro, present at processioning, 70 111^2, 116^2, 136, 148, 151.
Darden, Capt. John, land processioned, 236.
Darden (Dardan), Joseph, land processioned, 149; present at processioning, 79^5, 166^4.
Darden (Dardan, Durden), Moses (Mosses), land processioned, 33^2, 69, 107, 150, 214; present at processioning, 71, 150^4, 214^3; processioner, 100, 107, 108, 160, 169.
Darden (Dardan, Durden), Robert (Robt.), land processioned, 33, 69, 107; present at processioning, 107^3, 150, 151^2; processioner, 62, 69.
Darden (Dardan), Stephen (Stephin), land processioned, 29, 32^3, 69, 71^2, 110^4,

112, 136², 165²; paid for services, 90, 96²; processioner, 25, 30, 131, 231.

Darnal, Robert, indigent person, 53.

Daughtery, ———, land processioned, 194.

Daughtrey (Daughtree), Jacob, paid for services, 238; processioner, 208.

Daughtrie, James, present at processioning, 107.

Daughtrie, Lucas, land procesioned, 111.

Daughtrie (Daughtree, Daugterey, Dawtery), Michael (Michaell, Michal), land processioned, 33, 69, 107, 150; present at processioning, 69², 107², 108, 150, 151, 169.

Daughtry, ———, land processioned, 263².

Daughtry (Daughtree, Daugtry), Bryan (Bryant, Bryun), land processioned, 32², 70, 75, 76.

Daughtry, Bryun, jr., land processioned, 32.

Daughtry, Bryun, sr., land processioned, 32.

Daughtry (Daughterey, Daughtree), Henry, land processioned, 75², 175²; present at processioning, 75; processioner, 25, 31, 61, 75.

Daughtry (Daughterey, Daughterie, Daughterrie, Daughtire, Daughtree, Daughtrey, Daughtrie, Daugtery, Daugtrie, Daugtry), John, land processioned, 29, 32⁴, 70, 111², 112, 136, 165², 194, 263; present at processioning, 136, 165; processioner, 63, 69, 70, 70 (note).

Daughtry (Daughterey, Daughterie, Daughterrie, Daughtire, Daughtree, Daughtrey), Lewis, land processioned, 32², 69, 70, 136, 165, 254; present at processioning, 136³, 263.

Daughtry, Robert, present at processioning, 263.

Daughtry (Daughtrie), William (Wim.), land processioned, 111; present at processioning, 76.

Davidson, Will, processioner, 231, 232.

Davis, Thos., present at processioning, 245.

Deaths, of churchwardens, 95, 153, 258; of collector of parish levy, 157; of sexton, 218; of vestrymen, 15, 23, 45, 51, 57, 94, 104, 128, 130, 156, 177, 207, 222, 238, 240, 262.

See also Burials; Coffins; Funerals; Graves.

Declaration of Independence, xlvii.

Declaration of Rights, religious liberty in, lxv; violated by incorporation law, lxx.

Deeds, for chapel lands, 28, 50; for galleries in new church, 47; glebe, lxiii, 205; for land for new church, 20, 46; for land for poorhouse, 84, 174.

Dembey, John, jr., land processioned, 109.

Demby, ———, land processioned, 109.

Demby, John, land processioned, 136, 137², 143.

Denbigh, John, land processioned, 39.

Denby, John (Jno.), land processioned, 43⁴; paid for services, 13, 17, 21; present at processioning, 83.

The Desert (Desart), 9, 10, 66, 136, 191, 233.

Devoll, William, land processioned, 74, 75².

Dilereace, John, land processioned, 188.

Dismal Swamp, lv.

Dissenters, assessed for ministers' salaries, etc., 240 (note); Established Church challenged by, xxxi; in Upper Parish, xxxii, 240; strongest in poorer counties, xxix; taxation of, for benefit of church abolished, lxv, lxvi.

See also Baptists; Independent Congregation; Presbyterians; Puritans; Quakers.

Dixon, William, notice in regard to Rev. Patrick Lunan, xlii (note), xliii (note).

Dixon, Wm., paid for services, 220.

Dixon's Old Corner, 147.

Doctors, services for the poor, 13, 16, 17, 21, 47, 50, 53, 56, 57, 86, 91, 97, 103, 123, 127, 152, 156, 158, 162, 168, 179, 183, 195, 198, 202, 206, 219, 223, 238, 239, 241, 243, 255, 259.

See also Brown, Jesse; Brown, Robert; Cohoon, Samuel; Crothers, ———; Edmonson, Thomas; Fanin, ———; Fleming, Wm.; Gourlay, Arthur; Hay,

Joseph; Purdie, John R.; Tembtey, Hening; Tyre, James; Wright, Christopher.

Doors, in Nottoway Chapel, 89.

Doughtie (Doughtey), Daniel, land processioned, 30^2, 31^3, 35, 112.

Doughtie, Edward (Edwd.), reimbursed, 13, 17, 21; vestry held at home of, 1, 15.

Doughtie (Doughte, Douthtie), Mary, land processioned, 72^2, 143; paid for services, 45, 49, 52, 56, 86.

Downing, John, land processioned, 143^2.

Dragon (Draggon) Swamp, 64.

Draper, Philip (Phillip), land processioned, 34, 147, 170; present at processioning, 34.

Drew, John, land processioned, 33.

Driver, John, accounts of, 243; churchwarden, 240, 242, 243; present at processioning, 143; vestryman, 238, 239, 247, 247 (note).

Driver, Thos., paid for services, 13.

Dropsy, 221.

Dudle, John, indigent person, 91.

Dues, Rebeckah, fined, 93.

Duke, Aaron, present at processioning, 143.

Duke, Acey, land processioned, 215, 216^3.

Duke, Aramas, land processioned, 233.

Duke, Aseal (Asael), land processioned, 170^2.

Duke, Assia (Asia), land processioned, 143^2; present at processioning, 143.

Duke, Benja., reimbursed, 259.

Duke, Betty, indigent person, 259.

Duke, Elisha, processioner, 243, 244.

Duke, Francis (Frances, Frans.), land processioned, 34; paid for services, 102, 226; present at processioning, 147^2; processioner, 25, 34, 64, 160, 170^2, 208.

Duke, Hardy, reimbursed, 259.

Duke, Jacob, processioner, 182, 231, 232; reimbursed, 259.

Duke, John, processioner, 25; reimbursed, 259.

Duke, Judith, paid for services, 248.

Duke, Mace, present at processioning, 108.

Duke, Thomas (Thos.), land processioned, 34, 147; present at processioning, 147; processioner, 25, 243, 252.

Duke, William, indigent person, 259.

Duke's Creek, xvii (note).

Duncan, Rev. William, xliv, xliv (note), 228.

Dunmore, Lord, lxv.

Dunn, Joseph B., *The History of Nansemond County, Virginia*, xiii (note), xxiv (note), xxv (note), xxviii (note), lxv (note), lxvi (note), lxvii (note), lxxiv (note).

Durden, *see* Dardan; Darden.

Dyal, ———, indigent person, 96.

Dyson, Willis, indigent person, 241.

Ease (Eas), John, land processioned, 170^2, 188^2; paid for services, 177, 206, 219, 248, 250, 256, 259.

Ease, Sarah, indigent person, 229, 236, 239, 241, 244, 247, 248, 250, 256, 259.

East Parish, establishment of, xiv, xiv (note); glebe appropriated to, xxiii; name changed to Lower Parish, xv.

See also Lower Parish, Nansemond Co.

Easter, churchwardens terms expire on, 1, 15, 18, 23, 29, 48, 51, 55, 68, 95, 99, 104, 120, 124, 128, 153, 156, 180.

Easter Tuesday, vestry held on, 23, 48, 124.

Easter week, lxviii.

Eckenrode, H. J., *The Revolution in Virginia*, xlviii (note), lxv (note), lxvii (note), lxxi (note); *Separation of Church and State in Virginia . . .*, xxiii (note), xxiv (note), xxv (note), xxxii (note), xl (note), lxviii (note), lxix (note), lxx (note), lxxi (note), lxxii (note), lxxiii (note).

Edmonson, Dr. Thomas, accounts of, 56.

Education, *see* Children; Grammar school; School; Teaching.

Edwards, Matt, land processioned, 214.

Edwards, Soloman, land processioned, 214; present at processioning, 214.

Edwards, Thomas (Thos.), land processioned, 33, 69, 107, 150; present at processioning, 107, 150², 169; processioner, 62, 69.
Election, of vestrymen, xx, lxviii, lxix, lxxii, 99 (note), 257, 261.
Eley (Elye), Edward, land not processioned, 137; land processioned, 112, 137; present at processioning, 35, 73⁹; processioner, 3, 130, 137.
Eley, Elias, indigent person, 249.
Eley, James, land processioned, 76; present at processioning, 76; processioner, 5.
Eley (Elye), John, land processioned, 35², 73², 112; processioner, 208.
Eley, Michael, land processioned, 35, 75²; present at processioning, 73².
Eley, Moses (Mosses), land processioned, 185, 209, 242, 245, 253; present at processioning, 185, 245, 253²; processioner, 207, 209.
Eley, Wm., 243.
Eliot, Ann, land processioned, 135².
Eliot, James, land processioned, 115².
Eliss, Micajah, land processioned, 146.
See also Ellis.
Elizabeth City County, Nansemond County formed from, xiv; New Norfolk County formed from, xiv.
Elizabeth River, lxv.
Elizabeth River Parish, minister of, xxiv.
Ellet, James, land processioned, 79.
Ellis, Joseph, land processioned, 214, 233; payment to, 187.
Ellis, Norman, land processioned, 193.
Ellis (Elis), Sarah, indigent person, 120, 123, 241, 251, 256.
See also Eliss.
Elsberry, Jessy, land processioned, 112.
Elsberry (Ellsbury, Elsbery), Joseph, paid for services, 239, 241, 244, 247, 260.
Elsberry, Mary, indigent person, 206.
Elsbury, Philip, land processioned, 73².
See also Alesbury, Phillip.
Elye, see Eley.
Episcopal Church, see Protestant Episcopal Church.
Established Church, challenged by dissenting sects, xxxi; clergymen of, and "Two Penny" act, xxxvii, xxxviii, xxxviii (note); disestablishment of, lxv; dissenters and support of xxviii, xxxii, 240 (note); effect of war on, lxviii; result of political and social revolution on, lxv.
See also Church of England; Protestant Episcopal Church.
Evangelical denominations, growth of, in Virginia, lxv.
See also Dissenters.
Evangelical revival, spread of, xxxii.
Evans, ———, indigent person, 260, 260 (note).
Evera, Alexander, land processioned, 38.
See also Averi, Alexander.
Evera, Wilm., present at processioning, 38.
Everard's Mill, xvi.
Everat, Wm., land processioned, 71².
Everits Creek, 3, 59.
Everitt (Everit), Dred (Dread), present at processioning, 215², 235, 236.
Everitt (Everit, Everrit, Everritt), John (Jno.), land processioned, 76², 106, 141², 149, 187, 194², 215, 235; paid for services, 237; present at processioning, 106², 141², 149², 150, 215³, 236; processioner, 160, 208, 231, 236, 243.
Everitt (Everit, Evrit), Simon, land processioned, 33, 108, 149, 187, 215, 235; present at processioning, 149, 150, 215; processioner, 100, 108.
Everitt, Willis, overseer of poor, 258; reimbursed, 259.
Executive Journals of the Council of Colonial Virginia, xvi (note), xxviii (note), xxxi (note), l (note).
Executive Papers, xlviii (note).
Executors, of Daihea Gorley, 145; of Capt. Danl. Pugh, 15; of Col. Lemuel Riddick, 229; of Robert Booth, 167; of Rev. William Balfoure, xxxvii, 16.
See also Administrator; Administratrix.

Fanin, Dr. ———, accounts of, 91.
Farrow (Farrum), Elizabeth (Eliza.), paid for services, 12, 21, 26, 52.

Farrow, Jesse, indigent person, 127.
Farrow (Farow), Michael (Michal), land processioned, 184²; present at processioning, 185; witness for Upper Parish, 102.
See also Forrer, Mikel.
Faulk, John (Jno.), land processioned, 71, 76, 106, 110² 112, 113², 140⁴, 169, 170, 171, 194⁴; present at processioning, 71³, 76, 106⁴, 113; processioner, 100, 106.
Faulk, William, processioner, 252.
See also Folks; Foulks.
Fees, act concerning, 14 (note); apprentice, 49.
Felps, Pharoah, see Phelps, Pharoah.
Femiley [?], Simon, present at processioning, 105.
Ferry, at Suffolk, 87, 96; over Nottoway River, liv, 124, 133, 153, 156, 158.
Ferryman, 87, 96, 133, 153, 156, 158.
Field (Feild), Thomas (Thos.), present at processioning, 81⁴, 142⁵.
Fields, Elizth., paid for services, 237.
Fields, Sebiah, indigent person, 223.
Fines, Capt. Danl. Pugh's executors to report on, 15; for breach of laws, xxvii; for offenses against morality and church discipline, xviii; on masters of vessels, xxv; on minister, xxxi; on vestry, xv; paid, 1, 29, 55, 88, 93, 120, 183; payments made out of, 1, 29, 55, 105, 187; report on, 29, 55, 98, 130, 157, 187, 200.
Fire, houses on glebe destroyed by, lxiv, lxvi.
Fisher, Thos., land formerly belonging to, processioned, 214; land not processioned, 169; present at processioning, 168.
Flat Swamp, 60.
Flax, 199.
Fleming (Flemming), Isaac, land processioned, 29 (note), 32, 69, 72.
Fleming (Flemin, Flemings, Flemming), John, land processioned, 136, 165², 171; present at processioning, 111², 112⁴; processioner, 131, 136, 160, 166, 181, 231.

Fleming, Mary, land processioned, 111², 112⁴.
Fleming, Nathaniel, reimbursed, 197.
Fleming (Flemin, Flemings, Flemming), Dr. Wm., accounts of, 57, 86, 91, 97.
Flemming, William, present at processioning, 69.
Flesmny (doubtless intended for Fleming), Isaac, land processioned, 29, 29 (note).
Fletcher, Elizabeth, paid for services, 226.
Fletcher, Samuel (Saml.), present at processioning, 169; processioner, 180.
Flint, Isabella (Issabella), payment made to, 29, 55.
Flour, 198.
See also Meal.
Folks, John, land processioned, 44²; present at processioning, 44⁵.
See also Faulk; Foulks.
Font, marble, li, lxxiv, 86.
Foot, 162.
Forbes, Rev. Alexander, indictment of some ministers, xxxi; on clerical salaries, xxx; minister of Upper Parish, Isle of Wight Co., xxviii.
Forrer, Mikel, land processioned, 31; present at processioning, 31.
See also Farrow, Michael.
Forset, ———, land processioned, 68.
Forset, Ann, land processioned, 212².
Forset (Forsett), Benjamin (Benja., Benjamain), land processioned, 148⁴, 172, 173, 212²; processioner, 100, 120², 159, 173.
Forset, Francis, land processioned, 172; present at processioning, 68.
Forsett, Frances, land processioned, 30², 148².
Fortune, Richd., present at processioning, 215.
Foulks, Anne, land processioned, 29.
See also Faulk; Folks.
Fowler, Edmund (Edmond), land processioned, 136, 165.
Fox, George, founder of Society of Frends, xxvii.
Francis Copeland's Branch, see Copeland's Branch.

Frank, a Portuguese, 53.
Franklin (Franklain, Frankline), Daniel (Danl.), land processioned, 188, 189², 234²; present at processioning, 188, 189⁵.
Franklin (Frankline), Eleanor (Eleanr., Ellener), land processioned, 189⁷ 234³; present at processioning, 189.
Franklin (Frankley), Peter, land processioned, 37³; present at processioning, 37.
Frasier (Frasher, Frasure, Frazer, Frazier), Thomas (Thos.), land processioned, 105, 145, 172, 193, 214; present at processioning, 172.
Frazier, Robt., indigent person, 21.
Frazior, Mrs. ———, indigent person, 230.
Freeholders, appointed processioners, xxii; petition for dissolving vestry, xix, xx; vestry elected by, xx, 99 (note).
Freshet, 33.
Frith, George (Geo.), 118; land processioned, 42², 77, 78, 107, 144, 148, 166, 185³, 209⁴, 242³; present at processioning, 78; reimbursed, 221.
Frith, John, present at processioning, 245³; reimbursed, 229.
Frith, Martha, land processioned, 245²; paid for services, 241; present at processioning, 82.
Frith, Martha, jr., land processioned, 245².
Frost, Gertrude, 29.
Frost, William (Wm.), land processioned, 136; processioner, 182.
Fry, Robert, clerk, paid for services, 12.
Funerals, of child, 219; of indigent person, 21, 27.
See also Burials; Coffins; Deaths Graves.
Furniture, for poorhouse, lxiii, 97, 219; in poorhouse to be sold, lxiii, 204, 227.

Gallery, in wing of church, 46, 47, 93; pew in, li, 88, 89.
Garden, of poorhouse, 184.
Gardener (Gardiner, Gardner), James (Jas.), land processioned, 69, 108, 150, 214; present at processioning, 69, 151, 214².

Gardener, Joseph, present at processioning, 165.
Gardener (Gardiner, Gardner), Joshua, land processioned, 107, 151, 169, 214; present at processioning, 69, 150, 151, 214²; processioner, 100, 107, 108, 181.
Gardener, Mathew (Matt., Matthew), land processioned, 107, 151, 214; present at processioning, 107, 108, 150, 151³, 214⁴.
Gardiner, Jas., jr., land processioned, 69.
Gardner (Garnes), John, present at processioning, 111, 111 (note).
Gardner, Priscilla (Prisa.), indigent person, 237, 238.
Garland, Ebenezer, indigent person, 229.
Garland, Elizth. (Betsey), indigent person, 241, 244, 247.
Garland, Priscilla, indigent, person, 239.
Garnagan, George, see Jarnagan, George.
Garner, James, land processioned, 33, 169.
Garner, Joshua, land processioned, 169.
Garnes (Gardner), John, present at processioning, 111, 111 (note).
Gay, Charles, present at processioning, 74.
Gay, Thomas (Thos.), land processioned, 35³, 74⁶, 112, 137; present at processioning, 112.
General Assembly, order Chuckatuck vestry fined, xv; petition to, for dissolving vestry of Upper Parish, xix, xx; petition to, relating to dividing line between Suffolk and Upper parishes, xvi; petitions to, in defense of incorporation of Episcopal Church, lxxi; proposition to, from Quakers in Nansemond County, xxviii; report to, by jury of inquest in Nansemond County, xxvi; vestry of Suffolk Parish dissolved by, lx.
See also Acts; Bills; Council; House of Burgesses; House of Delegates; Laws.
General Court, charges against Rev. Patrick Lunan in, xl, 177 (note); destruction of records of, xlii; ecclesiastical jurisdiction of, xli, xlii.
See also Court of Oyer and Terminer.

Genkins, John, *see* Jenkins, John.
George, Frederick (Fredk.), land processioned, 184; processioner, 242.
Gewin, Thos., *see* Guen, Thos.; Gwin, Thos.
Giblin, John, paid for services, 56, 87.
Gibson, James, 156, 179, 183, 201; accounts of, 103, 123, 159, 163, 168, 176, 187; churchwarden, 156, 157, 158, 159, 161, 167, 168; land processioned, 191; on commitee to inspect chapel, 153; on poorhouse board of visitors, 200; processioner, 130; vestryman, 132, 135, 151, 153, 154, 155, 156, 175, 177, 178, 180, 186, 194, 196, 197, 200.
Gibson & Granbury, accounts of, 198.
Gilchrist, Thomas (Thos.), 198; accounts of, 195, 198, 202; churchwarden, 187, 194, 196, 197, 198, 200; on poorhouse board of visitors, 200; to employ attorneys to prosecute Lunan, xl, 184, 186; vestryman, 180, 186, 201, 205, 219.
Giles, ———, land processioned, 263^2.
Giles, Edward, land processioned, 43; paid for services, 91, 96, 103.
Giles, John, conforms to doctrines, etc., of Episcopal Church, 257, 262; land processioned, 109, 138^2, 164^2, 263^4; patroller, 90; present at processioning, 109, 138^2, 164; processioner, 231, 232; reimbursed, 122, 237, 241, 243, 247, 260; vestryman, 257, 258, 261, 262.
Gladman, ———, indigent person, 13, 16.
Glass, for windows in chapel, 89.
Glebe, allowance to minister in lieu of, 16, 26, 45, 49, 52, 55, 85, 90, 95, 101, 118, 121, 126, 132, 154, 157, 161, 167, 175, 178, 182, 194, 197, 201, 205; attorney to establish title to, 88; hinges and bolts for, 220; houses, etc., on, to be sold, lxvii, 246; petitions relating to, lvi, lxiv, lxvi; processioned, 41, 42, 77, 107, 216; purchased, lxiii, 204, 207, 220, 224; quitrents for, 13, 27, 46, 50, 123; Rev. Patrick Lunan requested to relinquish, xlv, 228; suit to determine bounds of, 92; surveyed, 90; to be sold, lvii, 83, 104, 122, 128, 173, 173

(note); trees on, 91; vestry held for purchasing, 204; work done on, 219, 220, 230.
Gloucester County, Abingdon Parish, xxxiv.
Glover, John, clerk, Holy Neck Chapel, 229; land processioned, 149; reader, Holy Neck Chapel, 226, 236, 239, 240, 243.
Glover, Will, processioner, 231.
Godwin, Christopher (Christophr.), land processioned, 185, 209^2, 242^2.
Godwin, James H., xiii (note).
Godwin, Jeremiah (Jeremh., Jeremyah Jerimh., Jerimiah, Jerimyah, Jerremiah) (sometimes designated captain, major, or senior), accounts of, 183, 200; churchwarden, 180, 184, 186, 187; death of, 262; land processioned, 31^2, 35^3, 41^2, 42^4, 43, 72^2, 73^2, 77, 106, 107, 112, 137, 144^5, 184; on poorhouse board of visitors, 200; order prosecuting Lunan signed by, xl; present at processioning, 82, 112, 185; reimbursed, 237; vestryman, 168, 175, 178, 194, 200, 204, 218, 221, 222, 225, 227, 228, 229, 236, 239, 240, 247, 248, 249, 250, 255, 258, 261.
Godwin, Col. Jonathan (Johnathan, Jona.), 95, 102, 118; land processioned, 107, 151.
Godwin, Joseph, 43; land processioned, 77, 107; processioner, 58, 77, 130, 137.
Godwin, Capt. Kinchen, 227.
Godwin, Margaret Joanna, land processioned, 79.^{2}.
Godwin, Richard, processioner, 99, 107.
Godwin, Richard Wilkinson, present at processioning, 184, 184 (note); processioner, 181, 181 (note), 185.
Godwin, Samuel(processioner, 251, 252^2.
Godwin, Thomas (Thos.), 152; land processioned, 35^2, 73^2, 112, 137; present at processioning, 73^3, 107, 112; processioner, 100, 112, 159.
Godwin, Capt. Thos., sheriff, 126, 132.
Goff (Gouff), Hugh, land processioned, 71; processioner, 101, 114.
Gomer, Rebecah, indigent person, 248.

Gooch, Gov. William, letters to Bishop of London, xxxi, xxxv, xxxvi.
Good Friday, xliv, 154, 228.
Goodman, John, indigent person, 237.
Goodwin, Edward Lewis, *The Colonial Church in Virginia*, xxiv (note), xxv (note), xxxii (note), xxxiii (note), xxxiv (note), xxxv (note), xxxvi (note), xxxvii (note), xxxix (note), lviii (note).
Goodwin, Martin, paid for services, 195, 198.
Gorley (Gorely, Gorlay), Arthur (Arthor), land processioned, 38, 80; processioner, 25.
Gorley, Colan, land processioned, 214.
Gorley, Daihea, land processioned, 145. *See also* Gourley.
Gornagan, George, *see* Jarnagan, George.
Gouff, Hugh, *see* Goff, Hugh.
Gouldie, Robert, processioner, 2.
Gourley (Goarlay, Gourlay, Gourly), Dr. Arthur, accounts of, 13, 27, 47, 53, 56.
Gourley, Norman, land processioned, 213. *See also* Gorley.
Graham, Mary, indigent person, 259.
Grammar school, conducted by Rev. Wm. Andrews, xliv; of College of William and Mary, xxxviii. *See also* School.
Granbury (Granburry), Josiah, deceased, 222; payment to, 206; to rent out poorhouse, 204; vestryman, 200, 201, 203, 204.
Granbury, Wm., processioner, 207; reimbursed, 201, 220.
Granbury & Gibson, accounts of, 198.
Grand jury, *see* Jury.
Graves, filling up several, 220; for indigent persons, 27, 127, 226. *See also* Burials; Coffins; Deaths; Funerals.
Great Bridge, battle of, lxv; damage done in, lxvi.
Green, Mrs. ——, indigent person, 56.
Green, Elizabeth, indigent person, 45, 49, 52, 53.

Green, Peter, land processioned, 42^3, 77, 107, 184, 185^2; processioner, 242.
Green, Rev. Roger, xxxiii.
Green, Sarah, fined, 93.
Gregorie, James, present at processioning, 139^2.
Gregorie, John (also designated captain), vestryman, 2; vestryman taken into Suffolk Parish, 14-15.
Gregory, James, land processioned, 235^2.
Gregory, John, 250.
Gregory, Rev. John, minister of Upper Parish, xxxiii.
Gregory family, xvii (note).
Griffin, Elisha, present at processioning, 234.
Griffin (Grifin), Ely (Eley, Eli), land processioned, 190^3, 234^4; present at processioning, 234; processioner, 182, 188, 191^2.
Griffin (Grifen, Griffen, Grifin), Henry, land processioned, 146, 189, 190^3, 212^3, 234^3; processioner, 160, 208, 212.
Griffin (Grifin), Humphrey (Humphry, Humpy.), land processioned, 37^3, 38^4, 190^5, 234^5; paid for services, 27; present at processioning, 37, 234; processioner, 160.
Griffin, Humphry, jr., present at processioning, 37^2.
Griffin, James (Jas.), processioner, 243.
Griffin, John, land processioned, 234.
Griffin (Griffing), Joseph, land processioned, 37^2, 38; present at processioning, 146; processioner, 8.
Grimes, Judith, indigent person, 247.
Groves, John, 220; indigent person, 187, 195, 202, 207, 219; paid for services, 223.
Groves, Mrs. John, indigent person, 220.
Groves, Keziah, indigent person, 221, 224.
Groves, Mary, paid for services, 226, 237.
Gueing, ——, land processioned, 170.
Guen, Thomas, land processioned, 147. *See also* Gwin, Thos.
Gumbs's [Creek?], 10, 66.
Gwaltney, Thos., land processioned, 236.
Gwin, ——, land processioned, 108, 109.
Gwin (Gwinn, Gwyn), David, land

processioned, 188, 211, 216³, 233; paid for services, 248, 250, 256, 260; present at processioning, 142, 170; processioner, 243.
Gwin (Gwinn), Henry, 88, 94; indigent person, 91; land processioned, 143, 170², 215, 216³; paid for services, lii, 91, 229, 236, 239; present at processioning, 83, 120, 216; processioner, 25, 33; sexton, Middle Chapel, 13, 16, 21, 26, 27, 46, 50, 52, 56, 85.
Gwin, Henry, jr., present at processioning, 108.
Gwin (Gwinn), John, 17; land processioned, 30², 68², 148; paid for services, 12, 21, 27, 45, 50, 52, 56, 85, 90, 95, 102, 152, 154, 157; present at processioning, 30; processioner, 59, 68.
Gwin, Josiah (Josh.), land processioned, 148², 172², 213³; paid for services, 178; present at processioning, 68, 147³, 148², 173; processioner, 208.
Gwin (Gwinn, Gwyn), Mary, indigent person, 248, 250, 256, 260; paid for services, 96, 179, 195.
Gwin (Gewin, Gwinn), Thos., land processioned, 34, 148³, 172³, 213³; paid for services, 162, 206, 229, 237, 239, 243, 248; processioner, 181, 193, 231.
See also Guen, Thomas.
Gwin, William (Wm.), 195; paid for services, 177, 179, 198; present at processioning, 68, 148; processioner, 181, 193.

Hacket (Hackett, Haket), Elizabeth (Eliza.), indigent person, 21, 162, 179, 183, 206, 207, 219.
Hacket, Margaret, 13.
Hains, Ann, 23, 29.
Hair, Bryant, processioner, 242.
Hair, Thomas, land processioned, 31².
Hair, William, land processioned, 34; processioner, 101.
Hairs, Mary, indigent person, 50.
See also Hare.
Hall, Margaret (Magaret), indigent person, 104, 105, 123, 215, 244, 248; paid for services, 230, 243, 249.

Hall, Mosses, processioner, 7.
Hamilton (Hamleton), John, indigent person, 163, 167, 176, 179, 183, 195, 197, 203, 207, 220; land processioned, 40², 109³; paid for services, 158.
Hamilton, Sarah, indigent person, 158.
Hamon, Thos., butcher for almshouse, 123.
Hannom, Thos., accounts of, 133.
Hanom, Mrs. ———, paid for services, 176.
Hanom (Hanum), Eliza., paid for services, 162, 168.
Hansel (Hansell), ———, indigent person, 219, 220, 226.
Hansel (Hansell), John, indigent person, 98, 206, 207; land processioned, 31³; paid for services, 118; present at processioning, 82; witness for Upper Parish, 102.
Hanton, Jacob, 33.
Harculus, Charity, *see* Herculas, Charity.
Hare, Edward (Edwd.), present at processioning, 72³, 115.
Hare (Hair, Haire, Heair), John, land processioned, 34², 36, 44, 76, 78, 79, 105, 106, 115,², 121,⁵, 135², 140, 146, 169², 170, 175²; present at processioning, 78, 80, 115, 135, 140, 146³; processioner, 4, 60, 242, 252.
Hare, Judith, 29.
Hare, Luke, plantation processioned, 4.
Hare, Moses, 29.
See also Hair.
Harel, *see* Harrel; Harrell.
Harmon, ———, 47.
Harmon, Mrs. ———, indigent person, 97.
Harmon, Constantine (Constant), land processioned, 80, 105.
Harmon, Nicholas (Nickolas), land processioned, 145, 172, 193, 213; present at processioning, 105, 145, 172.
See also Hamon; Hannom; Hanom.
Harrard, *see* Harrod.
Harratt, Moses, *see* Harrell, Moses.
Harrel [?], ———, 260.
Harrel, Sarah, indigent person, 203; land processioned, 212².
Harrell (Harrel), Adam, land proces-

sioned, 34, 146; present at processioning, 34, 112, 113, 146.
Harrell, Barsilla, indigent person, 259.
Harrell, Jacob, land processioned, 105.
Harrell (Harrel), James (Jas.), land processioned, 34, 146, 212; present at processioning, 146², 170²; processioner, 208.
Harrell (Harrel), Job, land processioned, 80, 145, 172, 193, 213; present at processioning, 38², 80, 170, 172, 193²; processioner, 9, 131, 145.
Harrell, Job, jr., land processioned, 147; present at processioning, 170; processioner, 131, 147.
Harrell (Harel, Harrel), John, land processioned, 38, 80, 113, 146, 169, 188, 211, 233³; present at processioning, 113, 146, 169, 170, 211²; processioner, 131, 160, 170.
Harrell (Harrel), Luke, land processioned, 146, 170; present at processioning, 170.
Harrell (Harrel), Moses, land processioned, 38, 80, 105 (note), 145, 172, 193, 213; present at processioning, 80, 193, 213; processioner, 64, 182.
Harrell (Harrel), Thomas (Thos.), land of, for chapel, liv, 128, 129; land processioned, 43², 211², 212⁵; present at processioning, 43; processioner, 101, 145.
Harrell, Thomas, jr., processioner, 231.
Harrell, Wm., indigent person, 195; land processioned, 44.
Harrill, Mrs. ———, land processioned, 137².
Harris, Benjamin, present at processioning, 194.
Harris (Harres, Harriss), James, land processioned, 194²; present at processioning, 137.
Harris (Harriss), John, land processioned, 113¹; present at processioning, 113², 194.
Harris, John, jr., land processioned, 113; present at processioning, 113².
Harris (Harriss), Mary, indigent person, 13, 17, 21, 26, 45, 52.

Harris (Harriss), Wm., jr., processioner, 60.
Harrison (Harisson), ———, sr., land processioned, 163.
Harrison, Mrs. ———, land processioned, 38.
Harrison (Harrisson), Benja., present at processioning, 138².
Harrison, Gov. Benjamin, letter to, xlviii (note); pardon signed by, xlix (note).
Harrison, Henry, present at processioning, 263; vestryman, 261, 262.
Harrison (Harrisson), James (Jas.), present at processioning, 69², 71, 72.
Harrison (Harison, Harisson, Harrisson), John, 83; land processioned, 29², 68², 69, 71, 72, 106⁴, 114², 138, 164³, 165⁵, 210⁶; present at processioning, 71, 106, 114, 140, 164; processioner, 4, 130, 139 (note), 159, 164, 185.
Harrison (Harisson, Harrisson), John (Jno.), jr., land processioned, 69, 163; present at processioning, 69; processioner, 181.
Harrison (Harrisson), John, sr., present at processioning, 68.
Harrison (Harison, Harrisson), Thos., processioner, 130, 159, 169.
Harrison, Rev. Thomas, xxiv.
Harrison (Harison, Harisson, Harrisson), William (Wim., Wm.), 118; land processioned, 29², 68, 69, 71³, 72, 76², 106⁵, 110, 114, 140, 164, 171²; present at processioning, 71, 106, 110², 138⁵; processioner, 4, 34 (note), 69, 100, 115, 131, 138.
Harrison (Harison, Harisson, Harrisson), William (Wim., Wm.), jr., 155; land processioned, 69, 115², 138, 171; present at processioning, 164; processioner, 181.
Harrison (Harrisson), Willm. (Wim.), sr., land processioned, 115, 138.
Harrod, Adam, present at processioning, 71.
Harrod (Harrard), Thomas, paid for services, 250, 256.

INDEX 289

Harrod (Harrard), Zilla, indigent person, 250, 256.
Hart, Eliza., land processioned, 187.
Hart (Harte), John, land processioned, 33, 108^2, 138, 149, 187, 215, 236; present at processioning, 108, 149^1, 215; processioner, 63, 231.
Hart, John, sr., processioner, 236.
Hart, Mary, land processioned, 33.
Hart, Moses (Mosses), land processioned, 108^2, 149, 187; present at processioning, 108, 149^6; sexton, Nottoway Chapel, 126.
Hart (Hearte), William (Wim., Wm.), land processioned, 33, 108^2, 149, 236^2; present at processioning, 108^2, 235; 236^2; processioner, 25, 33, 131, 149, 150, 208, 215, 243, 252.
Harvey, Sir John, charged with silencing a minister, xxxiii.
Harwood, Sarah, indigent person, 200.
Haslip (Haslep), John, processioner, 26, 30.
Hawks, Francis L., *A Narrative of Events Connected with the Rise and Progress of the Protestant Episcopal Church in Virginia,* xxiii (note), xxiv (note), xxv (note), lxxi (note).
Hay, John, land processioned, 69, 107.
Hay, Dr. Joseph, accounts of, 255, 259; delegate to church convention, 262.
Heafton, William, land processioned, 245.
Healy, Thos., land processioned, 171^2. See also Hely.
Hearring, Wim., present at processioning, 116. See also Herrand, William.
Hearths, laid in poorhouse, 202.
Hedgbeath (Hegebeth), Mary, indigent person, 237, 239.
Hedgbeth, Mrs. ———, indigent person, 230.
Hedgbeth, Africe, 120.
Hedgbirth (Hedgbith), Charles (Charels, Charls), land processioned, 111^4; present at processioning, 111^2, 116.
Hedgbirth, Wim., indigent person, 91.
Hedgbith, Pricila, land processioned, 111.
Hedgpeth, ———, 29.

Hedgpeth (Hedgberth, Hedgepeth, Hedgpath), Culbert (Culbirt), 29; land processioned, 70, 71, 72, 171^2; processioner, 6.
Hedgpeth (Hedgepeth), Henry, land processioned, 29, 72^3; present at processioning, 72.
Hedgpeth (Hedgbith, Hedgepeth), John, land processioned, 32^3, 110^4; present at processioning, 29, 71^3.
Hedgpeth, Sarah, indigent person, 120.
Heffeton, James, indigent person, 259.
Hely, ———, land processioned, 108. See also Healy.
Hening, William Waller, *The Statutes at Large,* xiii (note), xiv (note), xvi (note), xvii (note), xx (note), xxi (note), xxii (note), xxiii (note), xxiv (note), xxv (note), xxvi (note), xxvii (note, xliii (note), li (note), liii (note), lv (note), lvi (note), lx (note), lxiv (note), lxvi (note), lxvii (note), lxix (note), lxx (note), lxxi (note), lxxii (note).
Henry, Mary, indigent person, 237, 238, 239, 241.
Henry, Patrick, xxxviii (note).
Henry, William (Wm.), land processioned, 34, 80.
Herculas (Harculus), Charity, indigent person, 237, 239.
Herl (Hurl), Joseph, land processioned, 108^2.
Herrand, William, present at processioning, 121. See also Hearring, Wm.
Hickman, ———, land processioned, 109, 110^3.
Hickmons, 81.
Hill, Benjn., processioner, 242.
Hill, Henry, land not processioned, 137; land processioned, 184, 185^2.
Hines (Ilinis), Charles, land processioned, 214; present at processioning, 214.
Hines (Hine), John, land processioned, 68; processioner, 2.
Hines, Mourning, indigent person, 250, 251, 256, 259.

Hines, Rachel, indigent person, 248, 249, 256, 260.
Hines, Sarah, fined, 55.
See also Hyes; Hynes.
Hinges, for chapel, 57; for glebe, 220.
Hobby, John, indigent person, 162.
Hobgood, Henry, land processioned, 74.
Hoby, ———, 176.
Hodey, Mary, indigent person, 163.
Hodges, Jesse (Jessee), land processioned, 253; present at processioning, 253.
Hoes, 93.
Hogard, Mrs. ———, indigent person, 120.
Hoggard, John, indigent person, 246.
Hoggard, Patience, indigent person, 247, 256.
Holan, Keturah, fined, 120.
Holand, Absolom, land processioned, 194.
Holand, Elijah, present at processioning, 112.
Holand, Lemuel (Lam.), land processioned, 163; present at processioning, 164.
Holand, Martha, land processioned, 150.
Holand, Moses, land processioned, 106.
Holand, Samuel, land processioned, 112.
See also Hollan; Holland.
Holeday, ———, land processioned, 136.
Holladay (Holaday), Anthony (Antho.) (sometimes designated captain or colonel), burgess, xx; churchwardens apply to, for will, 128; land processioned, 212, 213; glebe land purchasbd by, 122, 128; sheriff, 46, 50, 53.
Hollan, Spears, land processioned, 184.
Holland, ———, land processioned, 263^4.
Holland (Holand), Daniel, land processioned, 141^2, 165^2, 194^2; present at processioning, 112, 141; processioner, 131, 136, 160, 166, 181, 243.
Holland, David, processioner, 252.
Holland, Eliza. (Elizth.), indigent person, 230, 237; land processioned, 137.
Holland (Holand, Hollan), Henry (Hy.), 77; accounts of, 123, 127; churchwarden, 120, 121, 124, 125, 126, 128; deceased, 130; land processioned, 6, 29, 71^2, 76^2, 106^2, 112^3, 136, 141^2, 194^2; plantation of, 6, 62; present at processioning, 70, 76^2; processioner, 100, 112, 243, 252, 254; vestryman, 99, 101, 103, 104.
Holland, Henry, jr., land processioned, 32^3, 69, 76.
Holland, Henry, sr., 29; land processioned, 76.
Holland (Hollan), Jacob, present at processioning, 194^2.
Holland (Holand, Hollan), James, land processioned, 6, 71^3, 72, 76^2, 106^4, 110^4, 137, 141^5, 171^2; paid for services, 123; present at processioning, 29, 72^4, 73^2, 112, 136, 140, 141^3, 263; processioner, 30, 72, 100, 111, 160, 171, 172, 181, 252, 254.
Holland, James (son of Henry), land processioned, 77^2.
Holland, James (son of John), land processioned, 77; processioner, 25.
Holland (Holand), James, jr., land processioned, 106; processioner, 62.
Holland (Holand), James, sr., land processioned, 106.
Holland, Jesse, paid for services, 250.
Holland, Jethro, indigent person, 260.
Holland (Holan, Holand, Hollan), John, 25, 77; land processioned, 29, 33, 35^6, 71^2, 72^4, 73, 111^2, 112, 141^4, 171^2; present at processioning, 72^2, 73, 106^2, 140, 141^4; processioner, 63, 263.
Holland (Holan, Holand, Hollan), Joseph (Jos.), land processioned, 29^2, 32, 69, 71^2, 72^{11}, 76, 77, 106, 110^7, 111^8, 171^4, 194; present at processioning, 110^2, 111; processioner, 6, 72, 160, 171, 172, 181, 231, 243, 252, 254; reimbursed, 230, 236, 248, 249, 255.
Holland (Hollan), Joseph (Jos.), jr., land processioned, 171; processioner, 62.
Holland (Hollan), Jos., sr., land processioned, 171^2.
Holland (Holan), Mary, indigent person, 157, 163, 167, 176.
Holland (Holan, Holand), Robert (Robt.), land processioned, 76^2, 106^2, 141, 194; present at processioning, 76^2, 141^4.

Holland (Holand, Hollan), Soloman (Solloman, Solomon), land processioned, 110³, 171; present at processioning, 71²; processioner, 100, 111, 208, 211.
Holland, Thomas (Thos.), present at processioning, 263; processioner, 231.
Holland (Holan, Holand), William (Will., Wim., Wm.), land processioned, 69, 76⁴, 106⁷, 112², 136², 141², 165³, 194²; present at processioning, 76, 106², 112, 141; processioner, 231.
Holland, William, sr., land processioned, 32.
See also Holan; Holand.
Hollaway, Joseph, land processioned, 35.
Hollowell, Dempsey, present at processioning, 235.
Holmes, *see* Homes.
Holy Neck Chapel, 61; building of, 28; clerk of, liii, 85, 90, 132, 151, 154, 157, 168, 178, 182, 229; derivation of name, liii; reader at, 194, 197, 201, 205, 218, 222, 226, 236, 239, 240, 243; schedule for divine services at, 153, 154, 227; sexton at, 133, 154, 157, 161, 167, 175, 178, 182, 197, 201; sextoness at, 85, 237, 239, 240, 243; substitute minister at, xliii, xliv, 225; Upper Chapel superseded by, liii, well at, 127, 154, 157, 161, 175, 178; work done at, 198.
Homes, Ann, indigent person, 220.
Homes, Moses, land processioned, 174³.
Homes (Holmes), Riddick, indigent person, 223, 226.
Homes, William, land processioned, 75.
Hood, Sarah, 12.
Horse blocks, 12, 50.
Horten, Margaret, indigent person, 16.
Horton, John, land processioned, 117², 118, 191²; present at processioning, 191; processioner, 101, 118, 161.
Horton, Joseph, land processioned, 71; present at processioning, 71; processioner, 30.
Horton, Joseph, jr., processioner, 26, 132.
Horton, Moses, land processioned, 71; processioner, 182, 193.
Horton, Samuel (Saml.), land processioned, 146; present at processioning, 71.
Horton, Sarah, indigent person, 206, 220.
Horton (Horten), William (Wm.), land processioned, 191²; paid for services, 13, 17, 21, 26, 45, 50, 52, 152; processioner, 8.
Hosier, Ann, paid for services, 246.
See also Hower, Ann.
Housden, Rev. William, minister of Chuckatuck Parish, xxxiii.
House of Burgesses, xix; reject proposition of Quakers, xxviii; representatives in, from Nansemond Co., xx; vestrymen members of, xviii.
See also Petitions.
House of Delegates, Committee for Religion of, lxiv, lxiv (note); Committee of Propositions and Grievances of, lxxiii.
See also Petitions.
Housekeepers, act enabling, to elect vestrymen, xx; vestry elected by, xx, 99 (note).
See also Freeholders.
Howard, Ann, reimbursed, 102.
Howard, James (Jas.), 259 (note); land processioned, 76³, 174; present at processioning, 76²; reimbursed, 52.
Howard, Lemuel, land processioned, 174.
Howard, Peter, land processioned, 76²; present at processioning, 76².
Howard, Thomas, land processioned, 35², 75, 76²; present at processioning, 76.
Howel, Mills, paid for services, 230.
Howell, Arthur, land processioned, 174; present at processioning, 263.
Howell, David, processioner, 231, 242.
Howell (Howel), Edward (Edwd.), land processioned, 75⁴, 165, 174³, 174 (note), 175²; paid for services, 202; processioner, 61, 75, 131, 254.
Howell, Edward, jr., processioner, 252.
Howell, Ely, land processioned, 174.
Howell, Hopkins, processioner, 231.
Howell, James, land processioned, 75².
Howell (Howel), John (Jno.), land processioned, 175; paid for services, 152.
Howell, Michael (Michl.), present at

processioning, 263; processioner, 242, 252, 254.
Howell (Howel), Stephen, land processioned, 174²; processioner, 208.
Howell, Watson, land processioned, 174.
Howell (Howel), William (Wm.), 36; land processioned, 36, 75², 78, 174⁶, 174 (note), 175²; paid for services, 152, 203; present at processioning, 75, 78; processioner, 100.
Hower, Ann, paid for services, 239.
See also Hosier, Ann.
Hubbard, Joseph, processioner, 131, 146.
Hubbard, Mary, indigent person, 247, 248, 249, 256.
Hubbard, Polly, indigent person, 259.
Hudson, John, indigent person, 248.
Hughes, Rev. Thomas, xxxiv.
Hunter, ———, land processioned, 108².
Hunter, Capt. ———, 60.
Hunter, Ephraim, land processioned, 69, 114².
Hunter, Riddick, processioner, 263; vestryman, 261, 262.
Hunter, William (Wim.), accounts of, 123; present at processioning, 83, 108; processioner, 9, 101, 109; vestryman, 94, 95, 98, 101, 103, 104, 119, 121, 124, 125.
Hunter's Mill Swamp, 147.
Hunter's Plantation, 4.
Hurl, Joseph, *see* Herl, Joseph.
Hyes, Charles, present at processioning, 169.
See also Hines, Charles.
Hynes (Hine), Ann (An), indigent person, 86, 90, 96, 102, 103, 127, 132, 151, 152, 155, 156.
Hynes (Hine), Hardy (Hardey), land processioned, 212; processioner, 242, 244.
Hynes (Hine), James (Jas.), indigent person, 168, 176, 179, 183, 195, 198; land processioned, 147, 173; present at processioning, 68, 147.
Hynes (Hine), Rebecca (Rebeckah), 68; indigent person, 90, 91, 95, 96, 101; land processioned, 212², 213.
Hynes (Hine), Richard (Rich., Richd.), 90; land processioned, 68², 147²; paid for services, 86, 90, 96, 102, 103, 127, 132, 151, 152, 155, 156; present at processioning, 147².
Hynes, William (Wim.), land processioned, 150; present at processioning, 150.
See also Hines.

Independent congregation, Nansemond County, xxiv.
Indian Creek, 3, 59.
Indigent persons, *see* Poor persons; Poorhouse.
Induction, of ministers, xxv, xxxiv, xxxix, xxxix (note).
Insolvents, 12, 17, 21, 27, 46, 50, 53, 57, 85, 90, 96, 102, 118, 122, 126, 132, 152, 155, 158, 167, 178, 183, 194, 197, 201, 205, 206, 221, 227, 238, 243, 251, 256.
Ireland, xliv.
Iron work, for almshouse, 103.
Isle of Wight County, xvi, xvii (note), xxx, xxxiii; assessors book for 1778, xliv; boundary of, xiv, xiv (note), xv, xvi (note); Lower or Newport Parish of, xxx; proposal of inhabitants of Lower Parish of, xv, xv (note); Upper Parish of xxviii.

Jackson, Christopher (Christo.), clerk, 21; land processioned, 40²; list of tithables by, 13, 17, 45.
James, John (Jno.), indigent person, 85; paid for services, 241, 244, 247; present at processioning, 216²; processioner, 252.
James River, xiv.
Jarnagan (Garnagan, Gornagan), George, land processioned, 36, 78.
Jarnagan, Hardey (Hardy), paid for services, 220, 223; sexton, 205, 218, 219, 222, 237.
Jarnagan, William (Will), present at processioning, 121; processioner, 231.
Jarnagan's (Jernagan's) Bridge, 3, 58, 59, 82, 244.
Jarnagan's (Jernagan's) Bridge Run, 4, 59.

Jarnakin, Wim., land processioned, 174², 175.
Jassey, Robert, processioner, 10.
Jefferson, Thomas, in case of vestry vs. Rev. Patrick Lunan, xl-xlii.
Jefferson's Reports (book), xl (note), xli (note), xlii (note).
Jenkins, Charles, land processioned, 76.
Jenkins (Jenken), Dempsey, land processioned, 174, 175²; processioner, 181; reimbursed, 197; sexton, Holy Neck Chapel, 178, 182, 197, 198, 201.
Jenkins, Henry, processioner, 181.
Jenkins (Genkins, Jenkens, Jinkins), John (Jno.), 6, 6 (note); land processioned, 5, 61, 75, 174², 175; paid for services, 96, 118, 162, 241; processioner, 175; sexton, Holy Neck Chapel, 133, 154, 157, 161, 167, 175; sexton, Somerton Chapel, 151.
Jenkins, Jno., jr., land processioned, 160.
Jenkins, Willoughby, processioner, 252.
Jerico, 81.
Jinkins, John, *see* Jenkins, John.
Joanes, *see* Jones.
Job, Samuel (Saml.), land processioned, 32; paid for services, 85, 86.
Johns, Mrs. ———, land processioned, 40.
Johns, Elisabeth, land processioned, 109³.
Johns, Sarah, fined, 29, 55; land processioned, 40²; paid for services, 45, 49, 53, 56; transportation provided for, 50.
Johns, Wm., paid for services, 12, 13.
Johnson, ———, indigent person, 97.
Johnson, ———, paid for services, 102.
Johnson, Abraham, land processioned, 171.
Johnson, Ann, indigent person, 249, 250.
Johnson, Cathrine, paid for services, 206.
Johnson, Collins, land processioned, 212².
Johnson, Henry, land processioned, 29, 72, 111³, 171.
Johnson, James (Jas.), land processioned, 29, 83³, 111, 164.
Johnson, Jese, land processioned, 174².
Johnson, John, land processioned, 79.
Johnson, Moses (Mosses), land processioned, 114², 138.
Johnson, Norman, land processioned, 212¹; paid for services, 219.
Johnson, Obediah, land processioned, 210.
Johnson, Thos., land processioned, 113²; paid for services, 127; sexton, 90, 96, 102, 118, 122, 126, 132, 151, 154, 157, 161, 167, 168.
See also Johnston, Thos.
Johnson, William (Wim., Wm.), land processioned, 29², 72, 111⁴; present at processioning, 111².
Johnston, Catherine, paid for services, 230, 241.
Johnston, Thos., sexton, 175.
See also Johnson, Thos.
Jones, A., land processioned, 214.
Jones, Absolom, 224.
Jones, Allbraxton, present at processioning, 169.
Jones (Joanes), Arthur (Arter), 78; land processioned, 36, 78, 121, 193; paid for services, 237, 241, 243, 248, 250; present at processioning, 36, 78, 138; processioner, 100, 120, 121, 160, 181; reimbursed, 247.
Jones, Arthur, jr., processioner, 231.
Jones, Arthur, sr., paid for services, 256.
Jones, Brittain, ferryman, 158.
Jones, Dempsey, land processioned, 211.
Jones (Joanes), Frederick (Featherick, Fredireck), land processioned, 36, 78; processioner, 25, 36.
Jones (Joanes), George, land processioned, 36, 78, 121, 137; present at processioning, 121.
Jones, Hardy, land processioned, 174.
Jones, Henry, land processioned, 75⁵, 76, 174⁴; processioner, 62, 77, 242, 252, 255.
Jones (Joanes), Jacob, land processioned, 36, 78, 121³, 137; present at processioning, 78, 121; processioner, 25, 36, 131, 138.
Jones, James, land processioned, 166³, 193, 194, 195; paid for services, 90; present at processioning, 42, 43, 107², 166².
Jones, Jamima (Jimimah), indigent person, 249, 259.

Jones, Jesse, paid for services, 158.
Jones, John, land processioned, 31, 42^2, 77^3, 107, 144^2, 166, 174^2; paid for work, 162; present at processioning, 82, 144^5, 169; processioner, 2, 231; witness in court for Upper Parish, 102.
Jones, M., indigent person, 243.
Jones, Mathias (Matt, Matthias), land processioned, 112; present at processioning, 214^3; processioner, 58, 99.
Jones (Joanes), Michael (Mical, Michal, Michl.), 36; indigent person, 237, 239, 241, 243, 247, 248, 250, 251, 259; land processioned, 36; present at processioning, 137.
Jones, Moses, land processioned, 174^2, 175; paid for services, 177; present at processioning, 76.
Jones, Rev. Nicholas, xxxiv, xxxv.
Jones, Nichs., processioner, 242.
Jones, Riddick, indigent person, 241.
Jones, Sarah, land processioned, 216; sextoness, 239.
Jones, Theophilus, land processioned, 36, 78, 121; paid for services, 17, 21; present at processioning, 78^2; processioner, 5.
Jones (Joanes), Thomas (Thos.), 93, 94, 133; indigent person, 22, 98, 120, 123, 127, 195; land processioned, 5, 6, 36, 61, 62, 75, 76, 78, 103^3, 121^3, 140^2, 174; processioner, 6, 77; plantation, 6.
Jones, Thos., jr., processioner, 62.
Jones, Virginia, x.
Jones (Joanes), William (Wim., Wm.), land processioned, 36, 78, 121, 137, 190, 191^8, 193, 214, 234^3; processioner, 242.
Jordan, Josiah, land processioned, 185, 242, 245.
Jordan, Josiah, sr., land processioned, 253.
Jordan, Mary, indigent person, 16, 21, 27.
Jordan, Robt., land processioned, 245^3.
Jordan, Samuel, land processioned, 30, 144^2.
See also Saml. Jordan's Point.
Jordan, Sarah, 223.

Jordan, Thos., present at processioning, 68.
Journal of the House of Delegates . . . of Virginia, lxxiii (note).
Journals of the House of Burgesses of Virginia, xv (note), xvi (note), xx (note), xxvii (note), xxviii (note), xxxviii (note), li (note), lvi (note), lix (note), lx (note).
Jucely, Susannah, paid for services, 255, 259.
Judges, vestrymen as, xviii.
Junk, 199.
Jury, grand, xxvii; of inquest, xxvi.
Justice, churchwarden sworn in by, 124.

Keatons (Katons, Keetons) Creek, 10, 66, 245.
Kean, Sarah, paid for services, 237.
Keen (Kean, Keene), George, land processioned, 76, 78, 105^2, 106^2, 140^3, 141^2, 193^2; paid for services, 179, 183; processioner, 6.
Keen, Jas., land processioned, 140, 193; present at processioning, 194.
Keen, John, present at processioning, 76^2.
Keen (Kean), Lemuel (Leml.), paid for services, 243; present at processioning, 193.
Keen (Keene, Ken), Lydia (Lide, Lidia, Lydda), land processioned, 36, 121; present at processioning, 138; reimbursed, 259.
Keen, Sarah, indigent person, 251, 256.
Keene, Mrs. ———, payment made to, 29.
Kelly, Mary, indigent person, 27.
Kendal, ———, 166.
Kenny, John, paid for services, 255.
Kerr (Karr), John, land processioned, 83^2; paid for services, 26, 50.
See also Car; Carr.
King, ———, 140.
King, Charles, land processioned, 210.
King, David, land processioned, 210.
King, Jesse (Jessey, Jessy), land processioned, 163^3, 164^2; present at processioning, 73, 74^2, 82^2.
King, John, 83; land processioned, 29, 83, 110^4, 113^3, 140, 163^2, 171^4; present

at processioning, 113; processioner, 231, 232; reimbursed, 122.
King, Capt. John, land processioned, 71^2.
King, Joshua, land processioned, 210^2; present at processioning, 73^2, 74^2; processioner, 208, 210, 242.
King, Michael ([ ]hael, Michaell), 140; land processioned, 68, 82^2, 113^3, 114^2, 163^7; sheriff, 221.
King, Michael, sr., land processioned, 4, 59.
King, William (Will., Wm.), land processioned, 35, 74^3, 82^5, 83^2, 112, 113^4, 114, 137, 163, 210^5; paid for services, 237; present at processioning, 82^4, 112; processioner, 130, 139 (note), 159, 164, 181, 185, 231, 232; reimbursed, 260; to conform to doctrines of Episcopal Church, 257; vestryman, 257, 258, 261.
King, Wim., jr., land processioned, 113; present at processioning, 113^2, 114^2.
King, The, land processioned, 148^2, 190^3, 191.
King George County Court, minister fined by, xxxi.
King's Bounty for Virginia, recipients of, xxxiv, xxxiv (note), xxxv, xxxvi, xxxvii, xxxix, lviii (note).
Kingsale (Kingsail, King Saile, King Sale) Swamp, 6, 7, 32, 62, 63, 263.
Knight (Night), James (Jas.), land processioned, 211^5; paid for services, 102, 179, 183, 198, 206, 219, 239, 241; present at processioning, 212^2.
Knight (Night), John, land processioned, 146, 211^5; present at processioning, 212.
Knight, John (son of James), present at processioning, 212.
Knuckle (Kneukle, Knuckel) Swamp, 5, 7, 8, 11, 34, 44, 60, 63, 64, 67, 170, 188.
Knuckle Swamp Bridge, 67.

Lacitor, Abraham (son of John), 43.
Lacitor, John, 43, 44; land processioned, 43, 44.
Lacitor, John, sr., land processioned, 43^2.
Lacitor, James, jr., processioner, 25.
Lacitter, James, land processioned, 37^2; processioner, 37, 38.

See also Lasetor; Lasiter; Lassater; Lassetor; Lassiter.
Lackey, Mary, land processioned, 30.
Lacy (Lacey), James (Jas.), paid for services, 17, 22, 85, 86, 90, 91, 96.
Ladder, for church, 91, 152.
Lakey, Wm., land processioned, 68.
Lam, Isaac, land processioned, 212^3.
Lamb (Lam), William (Wm.), 94, 98; indigent person, 200; present at processioning, 146.
Land, adjoining church purchased, 156; devised to Upper Parish, lv, lvi, lxiii, 84, 125, 173, 173 (note); for chapels, 28, 50, 88; for glebe, 204, 207, 220, 224; for new church, 46, 48; offered for poorhouse, 84, 174; to sell certain, 173, 173 (note), 196, 203.
See also Glebe; Processioners of land; Processioning of land.
Land grants, xv, xv (note), xxxiii.
Land patents, 84, 95, 147, 217.
Landing, John, present at processioning, 30.
Landing, William, land processioned, 70^2.
Langston (Langstun), Isaac (Isac), 36; land processioned, 78, 121^2, 137; paid for services, 118, 251, 256; present at processioning, 121; processioner, 61, 78, 131, 181, 242.
Langston (Langstone, Longston), Jacob, 36; land processioned, 36, 78, 121; present at processioning, 36, 121; processioner, 5, 61, 78.
Langston, John (Jno.), 27; land processioned, 36; processioner, 243, 252.
Langston, Mical, 36.
Langston, Thomas, paid for services, 230; vestry held at home of, 227, 228; witness, 229.
Larrans; Larrence; Laurence, *see* Lawrance; Lawrence.
Lasetor (Lacitor), Abraham (son of Robert), land processioned, 43^2, 211.
Lasetor, Kedah, present at processioning, 211.
Lasetor, Wm., present at processioning, 211.
Lasiter, ———, 195.

Lasiter, Quacus, land processioned, 188.
Lassater, Mrs. ———, paid for services, 179.
Lassater, Abraham (called Great Abraham), land processioned, 137³.
Lassater, Abraham (called Little Abraham), land processioned, 137.
Lassater (Lasetor), Isaac, land processioned, 142², 215², 216.
Lassetor (Lacitor, Lasater, Lasetor, Lasiter, Lasitor, Lassater, Lasseter, Lassetor), Aaron, 179; land processioned, 39⁴, 81⁴, 82⁴, 142⁴, 192², 216⁴; patroller, 90; present at processioning, 142⁸, 192¹⁴, 216², 217²; processioner, 67, 82.
Lassetor (Lacitor, Lasetor, Lasiter, Lasitor, Lassater, Lassiter), Abraham (Abra., Abram.), land processioned, 43⁴, 136², 137¹², 188⁴, 211², 233⁶; present at processioning, 43³, 211; processioner, 9, 65; reimbursed, 259.
Lassetor, Abram, sr., land processioned, 233.
Lassetor, Beck, indigent person, 260.
Lassetor (Lasator, Lasetor, Lasiter, Lassater, Lassiter), Daniel, land processioned, 188, 211, 233⁵; processioner, 160, 209, 211.
Lassetor (Lacitor, Lasetor, Lasiter, Lassater, Lassatir), Jesse (Jese), land processioned, 43¹⁰, 44⁴, 136², 137⁸, 188², 211², 233⁶; paid for services, 230; present at processioning, 44, 211.
Lassetor (Lasetor, Lasiter), Joseph, land processioned, 188², 211², 233²; paid for services, 239; present at processioning, 211, 233.
Lassetor (Lacitor, Lasetor, Lasiter, Lassater), Jotham, land processioned, 41⁴, 43⁴, 80⁴, 109⁶, 137⁴, 141², 188², 192², 211², 217⁴, 233²; processioner, 26.
Lassetor (Lassiter, Lassitor), Mary, 260; paid for services, 250, 256.
Lassetor, Newby, land processioned, 233.
Lassetor (Lacitor, Lasetor), Robert (Robt.), 43, 211; present at processioning, 233.
Lassetor (Laseter, Lasetor, Lasseter, Lassitor), Zaccheus (Zacheus, Zachews, Zackes), land processioned, 211; present at processioning, 211², 233; processioner, 231, 233².
Lassiter, Jas., sr., paid for services, 17.
See also Lacitor; Lacitter.
Law suits, churchwardens vs. Capt. Lewis Merideth, 17; churchwardens vs. John Norfleet, 92; churchwardens vs. Narney, 95; churchwardens vs. Rev. Patrick Lunan, 186; Lunan discharged of costs of, 228.
Lawrance, Ann, land processioned, 79²; present at processioning, 79.
Lawrance, Thos. (son of Michl.), present at processioning, 69.
Lawrence, Amey, land processioned, 245².
Lawrence, Ephraim, ferryman, 133, 153.
Lawrence (Lawrance), George (Geo.), 25; land processioned, 31, 70², 108, 116³, 148⁴, 151; present at processioning, 70¹.
Lawrence (Larrans, Larrence, Lawrance), Henry, land processioned, 31², 43,² 44², 188, 211, 233³; processioner, 7.
Lawrence, Jacob, processioner, 243.
Lawrence (Lawrance), James (Jas.), land processioned, 185², 209², 242², 245²; present at processioning, 185, 209², 245; processioner, 3, 231, 242.
Lawrence (Laurence, Lawrance), John, land processioned, 31, 33, 70, 79², 116⁵, 148⁵, 166⁷, 185⁴, 186³, 209⁶, 242⁸, 245⁴, 253²; present at processioning, 70⁵, 78, 79⁴, 116², 166, 209; processioner, 61, 70, 116².
Lawrence, John (son of George), processioner, 25.
Lawrenc[e], John (son of Michael), processioner, 100.
Lawrence (Laurence), Joseph (Jos.), present at processioning, 253²; processioner, 24, 33.
Lawrence, Mary, indigent person, 183.
Lawrence (Lawrance), Michael (Michal, Michl.), 69, 100; land processioned, 31², 33, 70³.
Lawrence (Lawrance), Paul, land processioned, 70², 116², 148; present at processioning, 70².

INDEX 297

Lawrence (Lawrance), Robert (Robt.), land processioned, 79, 149, 166², 185, 186, 209², 236, 242³; present at processioning, 149⁴, 166, 215, 236; processioner, 59, 79, 100, 107, 207, 209.
Lawrence (Lawrance), Samuel (Sam), 166; land processioned, 79²; present at processioning, 78, 79⁸.
Lawrence, Sawyer, present at processioning, 253; processioner, 252, 253.
Lawrence (Lawrance), Thomas (Thos.), land processioned, 31², 33, 69, 107; present at processioning, 69².
Lawrence, Wm., land processioned, 214.
Laws, enforced by vestries, xviii; for regulation of Quakers or other separatists, xxvii; relating to Established Church, xxvi; warrants for transgressors of, xxvii.
See also Acts; Bills; General Assembly.
Lawson, Epaphroditus, patent granted to, xv (note).
Lawyers, consulted as to certain lands, 196; employed to establish title to glebe land, 88; employed to prosecute Rev. Patrick Lunan, xl, xli, 186; fees of, 207; to be employed in recovery of land, 125.
Leach (Leatch), John, *see* Leitch, John.
Lecturer, minister employed as, xxxv.
Lee, Jno., present at processioning, 135.
Lee, Kindred, indigent person, 250.
Leg, 57, 162.
Leitch (Leach, Leatch), John (Jno.), indigent person, 45, 49, 52, 56, 86.
Lester, John (Jno.), paid for services, 12, 16, 21, 226; processioner, 209.
Lester, Rachell (Rachal), land processioned, 40²; paid for services, 27.
Letort, James, present at processioning, 148.
Letters, from Comm. James Blair to Bishop of London, xxx; from Gov. Gooch to Bishop of London, xxxi, xxxv, xxxvi; from Rev. Alexander Forbes to Bishop of London, xxviii; from Rev. Wm. Andrews to governor, xlviii (note).
Leviston, Ann, paid for services, 223, 237.

Leviston (Leveston), Richard (Richd.), accounts of, 176, 179, 183, 195, 198, 202, 206; administratrix of, 218, 220; sexton, 176, 178, 182, 197, 200, 205.
Levy, *see* County levy; Parish levy.
Lewis, ———, 140.
Lewis, Abraham, land processioned, 113³, 163⁴, 164, 210; present at processioning, 163.
Lewis, Abram, indigent person, 237.
Lewis, Elizabeth (Elizth.), indigent person, 241, 260.
Lewis, Exum, land processioned, 108, 150.
Liberty Spring Christian Church, lii (note).
Library Board of Virginia, *see* Virginia State Library.
Lightwood, 23, 48, 93, 128.
Linen, 207, 223; church, 229.
Liquor, 13.
See also Brandy.
"A List of the Counties, Parishes and present Ministers of Virginia . . .," xxxv (note).
"A list of the Parishes in Virginia," June 30, 1680, xxxiii.
"A List of the Parishes, Ministers, Tithables, Clergy, &c . . . in Virginia, July the 8th 1702," xxxiii (note).
"A List of the sev^ll parishes within this her Matys Colony of Virginia with the names of the present Ministers thereof," xxxiv (note).
Littlepage, ———, 238.
Liturgy, whole, to be read, xxvi.
Locks, for organ, 220.
London, Bishop of, *see* Bishop of London.
Long, James, land processioned, 71, 80, 105², 134²; present at processioning, 80², 105; processioner, 101.
Long, John (Jno.), paid for services, 21; processioner, 10.
Longston, Jacob, *see* Langston, Jacob.
Lord's Supper, *see* Sacrament.
Lots, *see* Land; Processioning of land.
Lottery, committee to prepare bill authorizing, lxxiii.
Lower Chapel, disappearance from vestry records, lii; improvements on, 12.

Lower Norfolk County, xxxiii; Elizabeth River Parish in, xxiv; formed from New Norfolk County, xiv.

Lower Parish, Isle of Wight Co., for adding part of Upper Parish of Nansemond Co. to, xv, xv (note); minister of, xxx.

Lower Parish, Nansemond Co., xxxiii, 152; formerly called East Parish, xv; land grant in, xv; minister of, xxxiii, xxxiv, xxxv; part of Suffolk Parish formerly known as, lx; united with Chuckatuck as Suffolk, xvi.
See also Chuckatuck Parish; East Parish; Suffolk Parish.

Lower Suffolk Parish, see Suffolk Parish.

Lowrey, Robt., indigent person, 219.

Lowther, Thomas (Thos.), land processioned, 70^3, 75; present at processioning, 70.

Loyalists, royal governor supported by, lxv.

Lucy (Lucie), ———, land processioned, 149^2, 166.

Lunan, Rev. Patrick, allegations against, xl, xli, 184; allowance in lieu of glebe, 154, 159, 161, 167, 178, 182, 194, 197, 201, 205; at processioning, 216; at vestry meetings, xxxix, 154, 159, 200, 201; charges against, xxxix, xlii (note), xliii, 177, 184; concerning prosecution of, xl, 186; Jefferson's report on case of vestry vs., xl; paid for burial, xlvi, 247; paid for relinquishment of rectorate, xlv, 228, 238, 239; processioning orders signed by, 161; received as minister of Upper Parish, xxxviii, 153; refused admittance to churches and chapels, xliii, 221; rejected by vestry of St. Andrew's Parish, xxxix; relinquishes rectorate, xlv, 229; requested to relinquish glebe, xlv, 228; salary of, xliii, 154, 159, 161, 167, 175, 178, 182, 194, 197, 201, 205, 218.

Lunatic, taken to Williamsburg, 219.

McCabe, John, reimbursed, 255.

M:Clenney (Macleney), John, land processioned, 114, 210; present at processioning, 114.

McClenney (Maccleney, M.Cleney, Macleney, Mclenie, M:Clenney, M:Clenny, McClenney, Mackclenny), William (Wim., Wm.), land processioned, 29, 35, 74^2, 83^2, 112, 114, 137, 164^2, 210; present at processioning, 74.
See also Cleny, William.

McClenney, James, processioner, 252, 253.

Mace, John (Jno.), land processioned, 117^3, 118^2.

Mace, Thomas (Thos.), land processioned, 117^3; present at processioning, 117, 118^4.

Mcfarn, Saml., indigent person, 220.

McFarron and Miller, 223.

McGovern, Mrs. Frances, x.

McIlwaine, Henry R., *The Struggle of Protestant Dissenters for Religious Toleration in Virginia,* xxiv (note), xxv (note), xxvii (note), xxviii (note), xxix (note), xxxi (note), xxxii.

Mackclary, Jonah, land processioned, 37^2.

Mackenzie, Rev. John, minister of Suffolk Parish, xxxvii.

Maget (Magett, Maggett), Nicholas (Nickolas), clerk, Nottoway Chapel, 94, 95, 101, 121, 126, 132, 151, 154, 157, 161; reader, Nottoway Chapel, 118.

Main Street, Suffolk, lviii, 84.

Mainer, ———, land processioned, 76.

Manning, Elisha, present at processioning, 192.

Map, of Upper Parish, l.
See also Plots.

March, ———, land processioned, 108.

March, Daniel (Dan., Danl., Danniel), land processioned, 34^2, 79^2, 115^2, 135^2, 171^2, 172^5, 212^2, 213^2, 216; present at processioning, 115^5, 135^2, 173; processioner, 25.

March, James (Jas.), church to be erected on property of, xlix, 20; land processioned, 30^5, 34, 115, 120^2, 135, 143^3, 147, 148^2; present at processioning, 68^2, 83, 108, 143^2, 147, 148^2.

March, John (Jno.), land processioned, 68^6, 147^2.

Mare Branch Road, 252.

Marriage, liberalization of law of, lxv; report on, by jury of inquest, xxvi; to be solemnized by lawful ministers, xxvi.

Martain, John, present at processioning, 145.

Maryland, xxix.

Masingel (Massigal), James, land not processioned, 107; land processioned, 69.

Mason, George Carrington, *Colonial Churches of Tidewater Virginia*, xlix (note), lii (note), liii (note), lv (note), lxxiv (note).

Mason, Peter, land processioned, 42², 77, 107, 184²; paid for services, 56; processioner, 58, 77, 159, 166.

Massigal, James, *see* Masingel, James.

Matthews, Mary, paid for services, 243.

Matthews (Mathews), Richard (Richd.), 93; land processioned, 116²; present at processioning, 112; processioner, 100, 112.

Maxwell, William, editor of *The Virginia Historical Register*, lxvii (note).

Meal, for poor, 176, 179, 230. *See also* Flour.

Meat, for poorhouse, 202. *See also* Butcher; Pork.

Medicine, for the poor, 13, 16, 17, 21, 47, 50, 53, 56, 57, 86, 91, 97, 103, 123, 127, 152, 156, 158, 162, 168, 179, 183, 195, 198, 202, 206, 219, 223, 226, 229, 238, 239, 241, 243, 255, 259.

Meade, ———, land processioned, 70, 136.

Meade, Mrs. ———, land processioned, 143, 147, 148⁵, 172⁴, 173.

Meade, Andrew, vestryman, 224, 228, 238.

Meade (Meed, Meede), Col. Andrew (And., Andr., Andw.), sketch of, xviii-xix; vestryman, 1, 2, 12; deceased, 15.

Meade (Mead, Meede), David, accounts of, 103, 119, 120, 123; churchwarden, 98, 99, 104, 118, 119; deceased, 128; land processioned, 30⁵, 31², 40⁷, 68⁴, 70, 109⁵, 111², 116²; member of committee on erection of church, l, 46; to have gallery in new church, l, 47; vestryman, 15, 19, 20, 22, 45, 48, 55, 67, 83, 85, 88, 89, 92, 94, 95, 98, 99, 125.

Meade, David, accounts of, 207, 222, 223; churchwarden, 200, 203, 204, 205, 207, 209, 218; land processioned, 165, 213⁴, 216²; member of poorhouse visitors, 200; to employ attorneys to prosecute Lunan, xl, 184, 186; vestryman, 180, 186, 196, 200, 221, 224.

Meade, Susanah, land not processioned, 137.

Meade, Bishop William, *Old Churches, Ministers and Families of Virginia*, vii, vii (note), xiii, xiii (note), xviii, xviii (note), xxx (note), xxxi (note), xxxii, xxxii (note), xxxiv (note), xxxv (note), xxxvi (note), xxxvii, xxxvii (note), xxxix (note), lxxiii (note).

Meadow Branch, 4, 6, 60, 62.

Meltear, ———, fined, 187.

Meltear, Elizabeth, indigent person, 219.

Meltear, Josiah, present at processioning, 170.

Meltear, William, present at processioning, 170.

Melteir (Meltier, Miltier), Dorothy, indigent person, 200, 227, 230, 237.

Melteir (Meltear, Meltere, Meltier), John, land processioned, 37, 189, 234; processioner, 131.

Mercer, Catherine, indigent person, 247.

Mercer, Jonas, land processioned, 215, 216².

Meridith, Capt. Lewis, suit against, 17.

Meridith and Webb, *see* Webb and Meridith.

Metcalf (Midcaf, Midcalf, Midcef), Sarah, indigent person, 55, 88, 94, 98.

Midcalf (Midcap), William (Will), processioner, 231, 252.

Middle Chapel, lii; benches and blocks for, 21; bids for new church advertised at, 20; cleaned, 16; clerk of, 14, 53, 56, 85; identified with "the" chapel, liii; reader at, 47; repaired, 26; road to, cleared, 21; services at, lii, 47; sexton, 13, 16, 21, 26, 27, 46, 50, 52, 85; spring and yard at cleared, 21;

vestry to be held at, xxxvi, 15, 15 (note).
Miles, Christain, indigent person, 156, 163, 167, 176, 179, 183, 195.
Miles, Edward, paid for services, 49, 52, 53, 85; vestry held at home of, 47, 48.
Miles, Harmon, indigent person, 91.
Miles, John, overseer of poorhouse, lxii, lxiii, 202, 204, 220; processioner, 207, 251.
Miles, Mary, fined, 120; indigent person, 91.
Mill, 31.
Miller, Richd., indigent person, 220.
Miller and McFarron, 223.
Milner, Francis, present at processioning, 185^2.
Milner, John (Jno.), 14, 96, 136; land processioned, 32^2, 70, 111^3; surveyor, 95; vestryman taken in Suffolk Parish, 14-15.
Milner, John, jr., processioner, 2.
Milner, Thomas (Thos.), land processioned, 78^2, 148, 166^2, 185^2, 209^2, 242^2, 245^2, 253; present at processioning, 78, 79, 209^2, 253; processioner, 33, 181, 186, 242, 245.
Milner, Thomas, jr., processioner, 24.
Milner, Col. Thomas, parish land held in trust by, 125.
Miltier, Dorothy, *see* Melteir, Dorothy.
Ministers, advertised for, lxix, 257; and vestries incorporated, lxviii; appeal for veto of "Two Penny" act, xxxvii; charges against, xxviii, xxx, xxxi, xxxii, xxxv, xxxvi, xxxix, xl, xli, xlii (note), xliii, 16, 177, 184; church to remove unworthy, lxviii; collation of, xxxix (note); convention notified of need for, 262; difficult to obtain, xxiii, xxv, xxix, xxx, lxix; employed by vestries, xviii; glebes and maintenance for, xxvi, 204; law concerning, xliii; lay readers in absence of, xxi; no tribunal to punish, xl; of Upper Parish, xxxii-xlvi, lxix, lxxii, 178, 221, 229, 257, 262; presentation and induction of, xxv, xxxiv, xxxix, xxxix (note); Puritans apply for, xxiii;

salaries of, xxx, xlvii, lxvi; ordination of, xxvi, xxxvi, xliv; to conform to Church of England, xxiii, xxvi.
See also Chaplain; Clergy; Readers; Visitation, right of. *See also* names of ministers: Agnew, John; Agur, ———; Andrews, William; Balfour, William; Bayley, Thomas; Beckett, J. (or Thomas); Bennett, Thomas; Burgess, Henry John; Burtell, James; Camm, John; Colmer, Davis; Duncan, William; Forbes, Alexander; Fox, George; Green, Roger; Gregory, John; Harrison, Thomas; Housden, William; Hughes, Thomas; Jones, Nicholas; Lunan, Patrick; Mackenzie, John; Owen, Gronow; Rainsford, Giles; Rudd, William; Smith, Joseph; Story, Thomas; Wallis, Samuel; Webb, William; White, George; Willie, ———; Wood, John.
Minton, Mills, overseer of poor, 258.
Minutes of the Council and General Court of Colonial Virginia (book), xxv (note).
Money, almshouse building paid for in, 84, 97; almshouse overseer paid in, 97, 103; Bible and prayer books paid for in, 93; church in Suffolk paid for in, 88, 89; due to poor of parish, 67; Episcopalians enumerated in order to raise, 258; fines paid in current, 1, 29, 55, 98, 130; for building Holy Neck Chapel, 28; for purchase of church ornaments, 46, 89; glebe paid for in, 204; minister's salary paid in, 227, 228; paid for insolvents, 227, 238, 243, 251, 256; parish debts paid in, 1, 29, 47, 50, 53, 54, 56, 57, 58, 86, 91, 92, 96, 98, 102, 119, 120, 122, 123, 127, 133, 152, 156, 158, 168, 176, 179, 195, 198, 202, 206, 207, 219, 220, 221, 223, 224, 226, 227, 229, 230, 236, 237, 238, 239, 240, 243, 247, 248, 249, 250; parish levy paid in, 125; to raise by lottery, lxxiii; to repair church and chapels, lxxii, 262; tobacco sold for, 17, 22, 23, 27, 46, 47, 50, 53, 57, 86, 87, 90, 96, 102, 103, 119, 122, 126,

133, 152, 155, 157, 162, 167, 176, 178, 183, 195, 197, 199, 201, 205, 218, 224. *See also* Commission; Pistoles; Tobacco.
Moore, ———, 88, 140.
Moore (Moor), Edward, land processioned, 31, 83, 113^2, 144^4; present at processioning, 82, 168; processioner, 24, 130, 144, 207, 213.
Moore, Eliza., indigent person, 251, 255, 256.
Moore (Moor), Henry, present at processioning, 117^2.
Moore, John, processioner, 2.
Moore, Lawrence, land processioned, 113^2.
Moore, Levie, indigent person, 236.
Moore, Sarah, indigent person, 227, 230, 236.
Moore (Moor, More), William (Willm., Wim., Wm.), accounts of, 53, 55, 56, 57, 85, 86, 90, 91, 96, 102; churchwarden, 51, 54, 55, 67, 68, 83, 85, 87; deceased, 207; land processioned, 29, 30^3, 35, 44, 68^2, 82^5, 113^3, 114, 148^2, 163^2, 164^2, 172^2, 210^5, 213^3; on committee for location for chapel, 87, 88; on committee to sell devised land, 173; present at processioning, 147^5, 148^3, 163; processioner, 100, 114; sheriff, 158; vestryman, 51, 88, 89, 92, 93, 95, 98, 125, 126, 130, 135, 151, 153, 154, 155, 157, 159, 167, 173, 175, 177, 186, 196, 197. *See also* Mour.
Morgan, Olive, fined, 93.
Morris, Jacob, land processioned, 191^2.
Morris, Rebacca, indigent person, 226.
Mour, Jas., 139. *See also* Moore.
Myars, Charity, indigent child, 259.

Nail, Ann (An), fined, 55; indigent person, 123, 241; paid for services, 91. *See also* O'Neal, Ann.
Nail, Rachael, indigent person, 259.
Nails, for church, 239.
Nansemond County, x, xvii, xix, xx, 105, 107, 108, 114, 116, 140; boundary with Isle of Wight Co., xiv (note), xv, xvi (note); burgesses, xviii, xx, lix; clerk, xxvii; county line, 3, 4, 6, 7, 32, 59, 60, 62, 63, 107, 252, 263; destruction of local public records of, xiii, liii (note); dissenters in, xxxi; dividing line between Suffolk and Upper parishes in, xvi; early religious services in, xxiii, xxxiii; early settlements in, xiii; formation of, xiv, xiv (note); invaded by British, lxvii; land grant in, xxxiii; magistrate, 120; name of Upper Norfolk County changed to, xiv; original manuscripts and petitions of, lxiv (note), lxvii (note), lxx (note), lxxi (note), lxxiii (note); overseers of the poor for, lxx, 258; Puritans in, xxiii, xxiv; Quakers in, xxvii, xxviii; religious conditions in, xxvi, xxvii, xxix, xxx.
Nansemond River, xiii (note), xv (note), xvi, xvii, xvii (note), xxxiii; Southern Branch of, 3, 30, 58, 82; Western Branch of, xv (note), xvi, xvii, xvii (note), xlix, 2, 58.
Narney, ———, suit against, 95.
Narney, John, present at processioning, 169; processioner, 180.
Nash, Rebeckah, 1.
Natson, Mical, *see* Watson, Michl.
Negroes, lxv; minister solicits women to fornication, xli; work of woman compensated, 127.
Nelmes, Archer, processioner, 251, 252^3.
Nelmes, Susanna, indigent person, 255.
Nelmes, Thomas, processioner, 251, 252^2.
Nelms (Nelmes), David, land processioned, 35, 42^5, 72, 107, 184^3; paid for services, 13, 56; present at processioning, 184.
Nelms, David, jr., land processioned, 42, 77; paid for services, 49, 52, 86.
Nelms, David, sr., land processioned, 77.
Nelms, Eleanor, land processioned, 184, 185.
Nelms, Ezekel, present at processioning, 191.
Nelms, Jonathan (Johnathan, Jona.), land processioned, 42, 43, 77, 107^2, 137, 184^4; processioner, 24, 43, 99, 107.
Nelms, Samuel, processioner, 231.

Nelms, William (Wm.), land processioned, 77; paid for services, 226, 229; present at processioning, 185.
Nelson, Teagul (Tegal), indigent person, 237, 239.
New, ———, *see* Newby, Thomas.
New England, xxix, 12.
New Norfolk County, xiv.
New York, minister licensed for, xliv.
New York City, held by British, xlix (note); minister goes to, xlviii, xlix.
Newby, ———, land processioned, 83, 109.
Newby, Edward, indigent person, 50.
Newby (Newbey), Thomas (Thos.), land processioned, 43^5, 136, 137^2, 143, 188, 211, 215, 216^2, 233; present at processioning, 43^2, 211.
Newby's (Newbie's, Nubies, Nuby's) Road, 9, 65, 136, 233.
Newland (Newlan), James (Jas.), 180; land processioned, 210; present at processioning, 212.
Newman, ———, land processioned, 263^2.
Newport Parish, Isle of Wight Co., *see* Lower Parish, Isle of Wight Co.
Newsom, *see* Nusom.
Newspapers, sale of glebe land advertised in, 104.
Nicholson, Gov. Francis, controversy with Commissary James Blair, xxxiv.
Night, John, *see* Knight, John.
Noble, Robert, present at processioning, 142.
Nobles, Susanah (Sussanah), indigent person, 206; paid for services, 220, 237.
Nonconformists, *see* Dissenters.
Norfleet, ———, land processioned, 108, 263^7.
Norfleet (Nofleet), Christopher (Christo, Christor.), deceased, 57; land processioned, 30, 31^2; processioner, 24; trustee for building chapel, 28; vestryman, 15, 18, 19, 20, 24, 28, 48, 49, 52, 54.
Norfleet, Christopher (Chris., Christo.), land processioned, 108^2, 114, 143^5, 144^3, 165^3, 170, 216^3; present at processioning, 82, 83, 114, 143, 144, 216; processioner, 100.

Norfleet, Cordall, land processioned, 242^2.
Norfleet, Cordial, present at processioning, 79^4.
Norfleet, Edward (E., Edwd.), clerk of vestry, 11, 12, 14, 16, 20; deceased, 23; reader, 16; reimbursed, 13; vestryman, 1, 2, 12, 14, 15, 16, 18, 19, 20.
Norfleet, Edward (Edwd.), land processioned, 216^2; present at processioning, 165^4, 216; processioner, 209, 215.
Norfleet (Norflet), Elisha, land processioned, 77, 107, 143^6, 184^2; present at processioning, 41, 82, 107, 143^4, 144, 168, 185; processioner, 100.
Norfleet, Eliza., land processioned, 185^2, 209^2.
Norfleet, Elizabeth, land processioned, 79, 79 (note).
Norfleet, Henry, present at processioning, 263.
Norfleet, Hezekiah (Ezekiah), land processioned, 189^2, 190^2, 212^2, 234; paid for services, 158, 179, 198, 220; present at processioning, 190; processioner, 208, 212; sexton, 201, 205, 218, 222.
Norfleet, James, land processioned, 148^2; processioner, 131, 181, 263.
Norfleet (Norflet, Norflit, Norpleet), John (Jno.), land processioned, 31^4, 41^3, 143, 170, 171^2; land of, for chapel, lv, 129; present at processioning, 263; procesioner, 181; suit against, 92; vestryman, xxi, 1, 2, 12, 14, 16, 18, 24, 26.
Norfleet (Norflet, Norflett), Nathaniel, processioner, 252^3; vestryman, 251.
Norfleet, Samuel, present at processioning, 165^5.
Norfleet (Norflet), Thomas (Tho., Thos.), 108, 219; accounts of, 229; churchwarden, 224, 225, 227, 228, 229, 230; death of, 238; dissents from vestry, xliii, 221; land processioned, 30, 31^3, 43, 144^6; paid for services, 207; present at processioning, 144^2, 168; processioner, 58, 82; vestryman, 207, 218, 221, 222, 228.
Norfleet, Thos. (son of Thos.), land processioned, 108.
Norfleet, William (Wm.), land proces-

INDEX 303

sioned, 31³, 143², 144⁴; present at processioning, 82; processioner, 3, 130, 144, 181.
Norfleet family, prominent in Upper Parish, xix.
Norfleets, chapel at, 153.
Norfolk, lxv; constable, 219; destruction of, lxvi.
Norfolk County, xlvii; Portsmouth Parish in, xlviii (note).
Norris, John, present at processioning, 70.
North Carolina, dividing line between Virginia and, xvi, xvii, xix, xxix, liii (note), 116, 148.
See also Processioning of land.
Northcott, Capt. ———, paid for services, 91.
Northcott (Northcot), John (Jno.), land processioned, 117³, 118; processioner, 66.
Noshar, Joshua, land processioned, 233².
Nottoway (Notaway) Chapel, clerk of, 94, 95, 101, 121, 126, 132, 151, 154, 157, 161, 176; ferry to, 124; ornaments for, 91; payments for work done at, 96, 123; petition for, liv, 87; pew in, 103; reader at, 118; services at, 153; sexton of, 122, 126, 132, 154, 157, 161, 167, 175; site and dimensions of, liv, 88, 89, 128; tobacco levied for building, 90.
Nottoway Parish, Southampton Co., ministers of, xliv, xlv (note).
Nottoway (Notaway) River, xvii, 7, 33, 63, 87, 88, 107, 150, 232; ferry over, liv, 124, 133, 153, 156, 158; petition of inhabitants over, liv, 87.
Nusom, Richard, land processioned, 38³.

Oaths, administered to churchwardens, 1, 15, 18, 23, 48, 94, 120, 168, 180, 201, 218, 224, 230; administered to vestrymen, 15, 16, 19, 23, 45, 225; of Abjuration, 23, 45; of Allegiance, xxvi, xliv (note); of clerk of vestry, 54; of Supremacy, xxvi.
Odam (Odome, Odum), Abraham, land processioned, 34, 79, 115, 135; paid for services, 51, 52.

Odam, James, present at processioning, 79.
Oddy, Mary, 13, 243.
Odum, Jacob, present at processioning, 115².
Official Letters of the Governors of the State of Virginia (book), xlvii (note).
O'Neal (Oneil), Ann, fined, 88; indigent person, 127.
See also Nail, Ann.
Operation, performed on woman, 21.
Oram, John, 162.
Oram, Kez, indigent person, 162.
Orapeak Road, 8, 64, 188, 255.
Ordination, of ministers, xxvi, xliv.
Organ, for new church, li, 86, 91; in Suffolk Church, lxxiv; repairs to, 159, 162, 201, 206, 220.
Organist, 159.
"Oronoko" tobacco parishes, xxx.
Orphans, 49, 90, 96, 158, 177, 179, 183, 195, 198, 219, 220, 237, 259, 260; land of, processioned, 76, 106, 147, 148, 166, 172, 173, 191, 253.
See also Children.
Osborn (Ozburn, Soborn), Samuel, land processioned, 35, 74.
Osbourn (Ozborn), William (Wim.), land processioned, 75, 112; present at processioning, 74.
Osbourn (Osburn), Mary, fined, 120; land processioned, 112.
Osburn, Sarah, 94.
Osheal, Col. ———, paid for services, 12.
Osheal, Daniel, land processioned, 73.
Osheal, Elizabeth, paid for services, 56.
Osheal, John, land processioned, 35.
Overseers of the poor, lxv, lxix, lxx, 258.
Overseers of poorhouse, lviii, 97, 103, 200, 220; dismissed, lxi, lxiii, 129, 204; rules and orders for, 199; salary of, lxii, 200; to conduct school in, lviii, lx, lxi, 97, 103; to have woman assistant, 103.
See also Miles, John; Wallis, Samuel.
Owen, Rev. Gronow, minister of St. Andrew's Parish, xxxix (note).
Owens, Markum, processioner, 252, 254.

Owens, Robert, paid for services, 237, 239.
Ozborn (Ozburn), *see* Osborn; Osbourn; Osburn.
Oznaburg (Ozenbrigs), 93.

Pain, Richd., indigent person, 45, 57. *See also* Payn, Richard.
Palmer, ———, indigent person, 103.
Palmer, Ann, indigent person, 48.
Palmer (Palmmer), John, indigent person, 52, 57, 85.
Palmer, Joseph, 49.
Palmer, Truman, 49.
Pardon, granted Rev. William Andrews, xlix, xlix (note).
Parish levy, 14, 18, 22, 27, 46, 50, 54, 57, 86, 87, 91, 92, 96, 102, 118, 119, 122, 126, 133, 152, 155, 158, 162, 167, 176, 179, 183, 195, 197, 202, 206, 218, 223, 225, 227, 228, 230, 238, 240, 242, 244, 247, 249, 251, 257, 260; allowance in, for benefit of poor children, lvii (note), lix; and poorhouse, lxii, lxiv, 199; collectors of, 14, 17, 18, 22, 27, 46, 54, 92, 119, 122, 126, 133, 152, 155, 157, 158, 162, 167, 176, 179, 183, 195, 197, 202, 206, 218, 223, 225, 227, 230, 238, 240, 242, 244, 247, 249, 251, 257, 260; collectors to give bond and security for, 14, 18, 22, 46, 54, 58, 87, 92, 126, 157, 158, 162, 167, 176, 179, 195, 202, 218, 223, 225, 227, 230, 238, 240, 242; glebe land to be surveyed before, 84; paid in money, 125. *See also* County levy; Money; Salaries; Taxes; Tithables; Tobacco; Wages.
Parish register, delivered to minister, 29; keeper of, 20, 86, 87, 154, 157, 161, 167, 175, 178, 197, 205, 218, 222, 225, 236; of Albemarle Parish, xlviii (note); of persons receiving relief, lx; of processioners' returns, xxii, 24, 120. *See also* Vestry book.
Parishes, dividing Upper Norfolk County into, xiv, xv (note), xxiii; history in acts of Assembly, xiii; in colonial Virginia, v, xxiii; incorporation of ministers and vestries of, lxviii, lxxi;

law for poorhouses in, lviii, lix; ministers in, xxiii, xxv, xxvi, xxix, xxx, xxxi; new, organized, xxxii; petitions for adding parts of Upper Parish to other, xvi; processioning in, xxvi, 2; unequal value of tobacco in, xxix, xxx. *See also* names of particular parishes: Abingdon; Albemarle; Bruton Parish; Chuckatuck; East; Elizabeth River; Lower, Isle of Wight Co.; Lower, Nansemond Co.; Nottoway; Portsmouth; St. Andrew's; St. Bride's; St. George's; South; Suffolk; Upper, Isle of Wight Co.; Upper, Nansemond Co.; Upper Suffolk; West.
Parker (Parkor), ———, 34, 139.
Parker, Mrs. ———, land processioned, 112.
Parker, Abel, land processioned, 191, 192.
Parker, Abraham (Abram), land processioned, 134^2, 170; present at processioning, 121; processioner, 161, 209; to conform to doctrines of Episcopal Church, 257; vestryman, 257.
Parker, Absolom, indigent person, 187.
Parker, Charity, indigent person, 219, 224, 226.
Parker, Christian, indigent person, 251.
Parker, David, processioner, 243, 252.
Parker, Ephraim (Epharim), land processioned, 41^2, 110, 117^3, 191.
Parker, Francis, land processioned, 71^2, 78.
Parker, Hardy (Hardey), clerk, Holy Neck Chapel, 168, 178; land processioned, 175^3; present at processioning, 134; processioner, 161, 208, 242, 252, 253; vestryman, 261.
Parker, James, present at processioning, 74^3, 112.
Parker, John, 88; land processioned, 35, 74^3, 191^6; present at processioning, 118^3.
Parker, Joseph (Jos.), land processioned, 117^6, 118; present at processioning, 80, 105, 145^3; processioner, 101, 118, 161.
Parker, Kedar, land processioned, 148; processioner, 160.
Parker, Mary, land processioned, 115, 121; paid for services, 206, 221.

Parker, Matthew (Mathew), 227; land processioned, 41², 110², 117³, 191; present at processioning, 117³; processioner, 161, 182.
Parker, Peter, land processioned, 71⁴.
Parker, Pricila (Pricilia), indigent person, 167, 176.
Parker, Richard (Richd.), land processioned, 36, 71², 146; present at processioning, 71, 134; processioner, 132.
Parker (Parkor), Robert, land processioned, 34², 36, 44, 71³, 78.
Parker, Samuel (Saml.), present at processioning, 74⁴, 75³.
Parker, Sarah, indigent person, 250.
Parker, Willis, land processioned, 148; processioner, 182, 209, 243, 252.
Parker, Wim., land processioned, 112, 137; present at processioning, 112.
Parkers Creek, 191, 235.
Parks, Elizabeth (Eliza.), indigent person, 177, 179, 187, 195, 220.
Parks, Thos., indigent person, 123.
"Parsons' Cause", xxxviii (note).
Passport, minister asks for, xlviii.
Patents, see Land patents.
Patrollers, paid for services, 90.
Pattersons (Patersons) Neck, 3, 59, 148.
Payn, Richard, 93.
See also Pain, Richd.
Peal, William (Wilm., Wm.), land processioned, 38², 71², 80; present at processioning, 80.
See also Peel.
Pearce, John, land processioned, 38, 164³; present at processioning, 82, 83².
Pearce, Thos., land processioned, 82⁵, 83, 164²; present at processioning, 82³, 83.
Pearce, William (Wilm., Wm.), land processioned, 80, 145, 172, 193, 214; present at processioning, 38, 193²; processioner, 80², 80 (note), 231.
See also Peirce; Pierce.
Pearcy, ———, land processioned, 108², 109².
Pearcy, Joseph, present at processioning, 108.
Peck, Daniel, indigent person, 221, 224, 227, 231, 238.

Peel (Peal, Peale), Edey, indigent person, 198, 206, 219.
Peel, Edward, land processioned, 214.
Peel, Elizabeth, indigent person, 251, 256.
Peel (Peal), Ephraim (Epharem), land processioned, 38², 80, 105, 145, 172, 193; present at processioning, 80, 172, 193.
Peel (Peal), Ephraim, jr., land processioned, 105, 145.
Peel (Peal), Jesse (Jese), land processioned, 80, 105, 145, 193², 214; present at processioning, 193², 214.
Peel (Peal), Joseph (Jos.), land processioned, 193²; present at processioning, 145², 146, 193³.
Peel (Peelle), Joshua, land processioned, 34²; processioner, 25, 34.
Peel (Peal, Peele), Robert (Robt.), land processioned, 38², 80, 105, 145, 172, 193²; present at processioning, 80, 172, 193²; processioner, 9.
See also Peal.
Peirce, John, land processioned, 29, 113², 114; present at processioning, 113².
Peirce, Martha, land processioned, 210.
Peirce, Thos., land processioned, 113⁶.
See also Pearce; Pierce.
Pelham, Peter, 201.
Pender (Pendar, Pinder), John, fined, 93; land processioned, 31, 70, 75², 116³, 148³, 174².
Pender, Poll, land processioned, 34.
Perrit, Mrs. ———, indigent person, 152.
Perrit, Judith, indigent person, 102, 119, 123.
Perritt, John, land processioned, 82.
Perritt, Joseph, land processioned, 215¹¹.
Perritt (Perit, Perrit), Nicholas (Nicholus, Nickolas, Niclous), land processioned, 42³, 77, 79, 107, 166², 185, 186, 209², 242², 245³; paid for services, 91, 206; present at processioning, 41, 78, 79⁴, 209²; processioner, 181, 186.
Perry, Edward, present at processioning, 147.
Perry (Perrey, Pery), Joseph, land pro-

cessioned, 43², 44³, 170⁴, 171; processioner, 9, 65, 83².

Perry, Nicholas, land processioned, 253.

Perry, William Stevens, *Papers Relating to the History of the Church in Virginia* . . ., xxv (note), xxviii (note), xxix (note), xxx (note), xxxi (note), xxxiv (note), xxxvii (note).

Petitions, complaining of behavior of Rev. Patrick Lunan, xxxix, 177; concerning payment for property in Suffolk, li (note); for dissolving vestry, xix, xx; for dividing Upper Parish, xvi; in county court against Rev. Patrick Lunan, xlii (note); in defense of Protestant Episcopal Church, lxxi; in regard to incorporation of Protestant Episcopal Church, lxx, lxxi; of inhabitants of Suffolk Parish, lxx; of inhabitants over Blackwater and Nottoway rivers, liv, 87; praying relief against order of vestry, l; regarding poorhouse for Bruton Parish, lix; relating to glebe, lxiv, lxvi; to raise money to rebuild church, lxxii, lxxiii; to sell certain lands, lvi; to sell poorhouse, lxiv.

Pews, in gallery of new church, li, 88; in Nottoway Chapel, 103.

Phelps (Felps), Pharoah (Pharoh), land processioned, 105, 145.

Pierce, Ann, indigent person, 259.

Pierce (Peirce), James (Jams, Jas.), land processioned, 113², 210⁶; present at processioning, 113³, 114; processioner, 242.

Pierce, John, indigent person, 248, 249, 255, 256.

Pierce (Pearce, Peirce), Matthew (Marthew, Mathew), land processioned, 113, 164², 210; present at processioning, 75, 113; processioner, 100, 114.

Pierce, Stephen, processioner, 252, 253.

Pierce, Wm., processioner, 65.

See also Pearce; Peirce.

Pinner (Piner), Francis, land processioned, 184², 207.

Pinner (Piner), John (Jon), land processioned, 42², 77, 107; present at processioning, 43.

Pinner, Thomas (Thos,), land processioned, 79; present at processioning, 253³; processioner, 59, 79.

Pinner (Piner), William (Wm.), land processioned, 184, 185; processioner, 180, 184.

Pistoles, xxxvii, 19, 22.

Pitt, James, sheriff, 195, 197.

Plantations, *see* names of particular plantations, or names of owners: Hare, Luke; Holland, Henry; Hunter's Plantation; Jones, Thomas; Smith, Richard; South Key Plantation; Walter, William; White Marsh.

Plaster, of church repaired, 103; for almshouse, 84.

Plots, copy of, 96.

See also Map.

Poquoson (Pocoson, Pocosson, Pocowswon), 9, 66, 80, 136, 217, 233.

Pool, William (Wim.), 127, 162.

Pipes, of church organ, li, lxxiv, 162, 201.

Poor persons, act for employing and better maintaining, lix; burial of, xlvi, 12, 16, 21, 50, 53, 56, 86, 87, 91, 96, 97, 102, 103, 152, 156, 158, 179, 195, 202, 206, 223, 226, 229, 236, 237, 239, 243, 247, 248, 250; cared for by vestry, xviii; clothes for, 24, 49, 52, 56, 57, 86, 91, 96, 152, 154, 156, 220, 221, 230, 238; coffins for, 13, 27, 96, 122, 127, 202, 219, 220, 223, 226, 229, 243; corn for, 202; cow and calf for, 68; doctors and medicine for, 13, 16, 17, 21, 47, 50, 53, 56, 57, 86, 91, 97, 103, 123, 127, 152, 156, 158, 162, 168, 179, 183, 195, 198, 202, 206, 219, 223, 226, 229, 238, 239, 241, 243, 255; graves for, 27, 127; land donated for benefit of, lv, lvi, 125, 173 (note); leg made for, 57; moved out of parish, 178; overseers of, for Nansemond County, lxx, 258; receiving relief, required to be registered, lx; rent paid for, 156, 163, 219, 221, 227, 241, 247, 256, 260; report on money due to, 67; shoes for, 26, 45,

103, 238; sundries for, 102, 123, 153, 156, 163, 168, 179, 198, 202, 220, 226, 237; wood for, 227.

Poorhouse in Bruton Parish, petition for, lix.

Poorhouse in Upper Parish, act for building, lxiv, 84, 97, 173, 173 (note), 203, 219; actions of old vestry binding on new, xx, lvii (note); butcher for, 123; Daniel Pugh to donate land for, lvii, 84, 174; furniture for, lxiii, 97, 204, 219, 227; hearths laid in, 202; inmates to work for parish, 104; iron work for, 103; located in Suffolk, lviii, lxiv, 84, 174; negro woman hired to, 127; order of vestry discontinuing, lxii, lxiii, 203, 204, 227; order of vestry reestablishing, lxiii, 219; overseers of, lviii, lx, lxi, lxii, lxiii, 97, 103, 129, 199, 200, 202, 204, 220; plan for building, lvii, lviii, 84, 92, 173, 174; repaired, 97, 184, 198; rules and regulations for, lxi, lxii, 196, 199, 203; school conducted in, lviii, lx, lxi, 97, 103, 104, 119, 123, 124; Suffolk Parish asked to coöperate in, xxi, lx, 99; sundries, etc., for, 97, 103, 119, 122, 123, 127, 152, 158, 176, 179, 183, 195, 198, 202, 207, 219, 220; to be sold, lxiv, 242; tobacco levied for building, 96; tobacco levied for expenses of, lxii, 199; vestry held at, 98; visitors for, lxi, lxii, 124, 199, 200; woman assistant for, lx, 103, 152.

Poorhouses, law authorizing establishment of, lviii-lix.

Pope, John, land processioned, 33, 149; present at processioning, 149.

Pork, 123, 152, 246.
See also Meat.

Porter, ———, land processioned, 263^1.

Porter (Poorter), John, land processioned, 4^2, 34, 36, 44^4, 60^2, 68^2, 113^2, 114^2, 138^2, 147, 164, 169^4, 188, 194^2, 263^5; present at processioning, 44, 69, 114, 138, 147, 164^2, 170, 194; processioner, 25, 100, 113, 181, 188, 231.

Porter, John, jr., present at processioning, 44.

Porter, John, sr., land processioned, 44, 113.

Porter, William, land processioned, 263.

Porter's (Poorters) Bridge, 2, 3, 58, 59, 244.

Portsmouth, lxv; chaplain to garrison at, xlvii; damage done in, by troops, lxvi; occupied by British, lxvii.

Portsmouth Parish, Norfolk County, xlviii (note); minister of, xlvii.

Portuguese, two provided for, 53.

Powell (Powel), Francis (Frances, Francies), land processioned, 35^2, 74^2, 112, 137, 210^2, 213; present at processioning, 73, 74^6, 112; processioner, 208, 210.

Powell (Powel), John, land processioned, 212^4.

Powle, William, indigent person, 156.

Prayer books, *see* Book of Common Prayer.

Precincts, Upper Parish divided into, xxi, xxii, 2, 3, 4, 5, 6, 7, 8, 9, 10, 11, 24, 25, 59, 60, 61, 62, 63, 64, 65, 66, 67, 68, 180, 181, 182, 207, 208, 209, 231, 242, 243, 251, 252.

Presbyterians, mentioned, xxx.

"The present State of Virginia for the year 1714 with respect to the Countys in particular", xxxiv (note).

"The present State of Virginia with respect to the Colony in General", 1726, xxxiv (note).

"The present State of Virginia with respect to the Colony in General Anno 1729", xxxv (note).

Presentation, of clergymen, xxxiv, xxxix, xxxix (note).

Price, Henry, indigent person, 259.

Price, Jacob, land processioned, 188, 211, 233; present at processioning, 211; processioner, 65, 83^2, 161, 209; reimbursed, 259.

Price, John, indigent person, 260; present at processioning, 141^2, 170, 188^2.

Price, Joseph (Jos.), land processioned, 39, 40, 43^2, 109^4, 137; present at processioning, 109^3; processioner, 132.

Price, Thomas (Thos.), land processioned, 40², 43, 169².
Price, Walthoe, indigent person, 123.
Pritlow, Joseph, present at processioning, 253⁶.
Privy Council, charges against Sir John Harvey in, xxxiii.
Processioners of land, 2, 3, 4, 5, 6, 7, 8, 9, 10, 11, 24, 25, 26, 29, 30, 31, 32, 33, 34, 35, 36, 37, 38, 39, 41, 43, 44, 58, 59, 60, 61, 62, 63, 64, 65, 66, 67, 68, 69, 70, 71, 72, 75, 77, 78, 79, 80, 82, 83, 99, 100, 101, 105, 106, 107, 108, 109, 110, 111, 112, 113, 114, 115, 116, 118, 120, 121, 130, 131, 132, 134, 135, 136, 137, 138, 139 (note), 141, 142, 143, 144, 145, 146, 147, 149, 150, 151, 159, 160, 161, 164, 165, 166, 168, 169, 170, 171, 172, 173, 175, 180, 181, 182, 184, 185, 186, 187, 188, 191, 192, 193, 194, 207, 208, 209, 210, 211, 212, 213, 214, 215, 217, 231, 232, 233, 234, 235, 236, 242, 243, 244, 245, 251, 252, 253, 254, 255, 263; appointed by vestries, xxi, 2; directions given to, 2, 3, 4, 5, 6, 7, 8, 9, 10, 11, 58, 59, 60, 61, 62, 63, 64, 65, 66, 67; to report to vestry, xxii.
Processioning of land, 2-11, 24-26, 29-44, 58-67, 68, 69-83, 105-118, 120-121, 130-132, 134-135, 136-151, 163-166, 168-173, 174, 184-186, 187-194, 209-217, 232-236, 242, 244-245, 252-255, 262-263; done every fourth year, xxi; parish divided into precincts for, xxi, xxii, 2, 3, 4, 5, 6, 7, 8, 9, 10, 11, 24, 25, 59, 60, 61, 62, 63, 64, 65, 66, 67, 68, 180, 181, 182, 207, 208, 209, 231, 242, 243, 251, 252; persons refusing, 2, 3, 4, 5, 6, 7, 8, 9, 10, 11, 58, 59, 244; recorded in vestry book, xxii; to country line, 7, 8, 9, 11, 31, 63, 64, 65, 67, 70, 188, 252, 255, 263. *See also* Land.
Protestant Episcopal Church, x, xxv, xxvi; act for sale of glebes and related property, lxxiv; acts relating to, repealed, lxxiii; conventions of, lxix, lxxi, lxxii, 257, 257 (note), 258, 262; incorporation of, lxviii, 257 (note); law incorporating, repealed, lxv, lxx, lxxi, lxxii; petitions in defense of, lxxi; required to report property and revenue, lxviii; vestrymen promise to conform to doctrine and discipline of, 257.
See also Church of England; Established Church.
Protestant Episcopal Theological Seminary, original parish records in, v, vii.
Pruden, Jethro, land processioned, 213²; present at processioning, 212².
Pruden (Prudent), Nathaniel (Nath., Nathanl), land processioned, 30², 68³, 147², 173².
Pruden, Wm., land processioned, 173, 212, 213; present at processioning, 172², 173.
Pruer, Robert, reimbursed, 52.
Pryor (Proyer, Pryer), Edmund, land processioned, 109³; present at processioning, 109.
Pryor (Pryer), Edward, present at processioning, 83; processioner, 101, 109.
Public Record Office, *see* British Public Record Office.
Pugh, ———, land processioned, 30².
Pugh, Daniel (sometimes designated captain or colonel), accounts of, 13, 15; churchwarden, 1, 2, 11, 12, 13, 14, 15; deceased, 15.
Pugh (Pught), Daniel (sometimes designated captain), accounts of, 50, 53, 54, 55, 56, 58, 86, 87, 88, 89; churchwarden, 51, 54, 55, 67, 68, 83, 85, 87; land processioned, 39, 40⁴, 41⁴, 82³, 110³, 118, 142; lot purchased from, 156; offers land for poorhouse, lvii, 84, 174; on committee on erection of new brick church, l, 20, 46; on committee on erection of poorhouse, 84, 173; on committee to sell glebe land, 173; present at processioning, 39³, 41, 82, 117¹⁴, 118⁴; processioner, 25, 41, 66; to build new church, li, 54, 55; to examine accounts of John Watson, 92; vestryman, 15, 16, 18, 19, 23, 24, 26, 28, 45, 48, 49, 51, 88, 89, 92, 93, 94, 95, 98, 173.
Pugh, Esther (Easter, Ester, Hester),

land processioned, 39^2, 40^3, 41^2, 81^3, 82^2, 110^2, 117, 142^2.
Pugh, James, land formerly belonging to, processioned, 110; paid for services, 220.
Pugh, Theophilus, land processioned, 191^5, 192^2.
Pugh, Theos., reimbursed, 12.
Pugh, William (Will, Wm.), land not processioned, 235; payments to, 241, 243; sheriff, 230, 251; vestryman, 244.
Pugh's Creek (Pugh's Mill Creek), xvi, 10, 66, 245.
Pulver (Purvis), John, processioner, 63, 63 (note).
Purdie, Dr. John R., xiii (note).
Purdie & Dixon, publishers of *The Virginia Gazette,* xlii (note).
Puritan Revolution, xxiv.
Puritans, Nansemond County, xxiii, xxiv.
Purvis, ———, fined, 93.
Purvis (Purves), James (Jas.), indigent person, 45; land processioned, 34^2, 79^2, 115^2, 135^2; present at processioning, 115, 135^2; processioner, 160.
Purvis, James, jr., land processioned, 115.
Purvis, James (son of John, jr.), land processioned, 134, 135.
Purvis (Purves), John, land processioned, 34^2, 79, 115^3, 134^3; processioner, 63 (note), 80, 181.
Purvis, John, jr., 134, 135.
Purvis, William (Wim.), land processioned, 79, 115^3, 135^4; present at processioning, 79, 80, 115^3; processioner, 131, 134, 135.

Quakers, decline of, xxxii; distrained for refusing to pay church dues, xxviii; in Nansemond County, xxvi, xxviii; in Upper Parish, xxxii, 240; in Virginia, xxiv; laws relating to, xxv, xxvii; letter relating to, xxviii; literature of, prohibited, xxv; proposition to the General Assembly, xxviii; slander Church of England, xxviii; William Byrd comments on, xxix.
See also Story, Thomas.
Quitrents, lvi, 13, 27, 46, 50, 57, 93, 123.

Raby's Swamp, 9, 64, 65.
Rack, Richard (R., Richd.), indigent person, 13, 17, 21, 26, 45, 49, 53.
Ragged Islands, xv (note).
Raibey, Charles, paid for services, 221.
Raiby, Charity, indigent person, 105; land processioned, 211, 212^2.
Raiby, Eliza., indigent person, 239.
Raiby, Frue, land processioned, 212.
Raiby, Henry, land processioned, 212, 213; processioner, 231.
Raiby (Raby), James (Jas.), processioner, 64, 131, 146, 182; land processioned, 212^3.
Raiby, John, land processioned, 146.
Raiby (Raibie, Raby), Kedar (Cader), land processioned, 38^2, 80, 105, 145, 193, 214; present at processioning, 145^2, 193.
Raiby, Lemuel, land processioned, 146.
Raiby (Raibie), Moses, indigent person, 219, 221.
Raiby, Nicholas, land processioned, 146.
Raiby, Sarah, indigent person, 130.
Raiby, Wm., land processioned, 212.
Rainsford (Ransford), Rev. Giles, xxxiv, xxxiv (note).
Rales, Jon, 48.
See also Rawls, John.
Rambow, Isaac, clerk, Middle Chapel, 14; reader, 16.
Rand, ———, plans for church by, 46.
Randolph, John, attorney-general, xli, xlii.
Ransford, Rev. Giles, *see* Rainsford, Rev. Giles.
Rawles, ———, land processioned, 263.
See also Rales; Rawls.
Rawlins, ———, vestry held in home of, 28, 44.
Rawlins (Rawlings), Moses, land processioned, 81^2, 82; present at processioning, 110^2; processioner, 67, 82.
Rawls, Mrs. ———, land processioned, 113^2.
Rawls, Absolum, present at processioning, 106.
Rawls, Amos, land processioned, 193^2, 213; present at processioning, 193, 213, 214.

Rawls, Ann, reimbursed, 182.
Rawls (Rawles), David, land processioned, 263³; present at processioning, 114, 193, 194².
Rawls, Frances (Fr., Fra., Francis, Franes, Franses), land processioned, 36, 113, 141⁴, 169.
Rawls, Gabriel, land processioned, 141⁸.
Rawls (Ralls), Hardy (Hardey), 118; land processioned, 78, 121²; land purchased from, 28; paid for services, 86, 224; present at processioning, 78, 121, 138; processioner, 131, 242, 252.
Rawls, Harry, land processioned, 175².
Rawls, James (Jas.), land processioned, 78, 121², 138; present at processioning, 78, 115², 116; processioner, 100, 120, 121, 160, 208.
Rawls, Jesse, present at processioning, 106², 114.
Rawls (Ralls, Rawles), John (Jno.), 93; accounts of, 87, 88, 118, 127, 132, 156, 250, 256; churchwarden, 135, 151, 154, 155; land processioned, 36, 68, 75, 76², 78, 106⁷, 121⁴, 141⁹, 164, 194⁴, 263²; on committee to sell land, 173; present at processioning, 68, 76², 78, 105, 106³, 138, 216³, 263; processioner, 25; trustee for building chapel, 28; vestryman, 57, 67, 83, 85, 87, 93, 95, 104, 118, 125, 126, 129, 130, 132, 135, 173.
Rawls, John (Jno.), jr., present at processioning, 141, 194; reimbursed, 176.
Rawls, John (son of Thos.), 94.
Rawls, Joshua, present at processioning, 141.
Rawls, Luke, orphans' land processioned, 76, 106³.
Rawls (Ralls), Mary, allowances to, 126; paid for services, 51; sextoness, 50, 52, 90, 96, 118, 122, 126, 132, 133.
Rawls (Rawles), Ruth, sextoness, 56, 85.
Rawls, Soloman, land processioned, 147; processioner, 182.
Rawls (Rawles), Solo., jr., present at processioning, 263.
Rawls (Rawles), Thomas (Thos.), land processioned, 44², 169³; present at processioning, 44²; processioner, 181, 188.

Rawls, William (Willm., Wim., Wm.), 34, 34 (note); land processioned, 113⁴, 134⁴, 146, 169⁴; present at processioning, 44², 121; processioner, 60, 131, 160, 170, 181.
Rawls (Rawles), William, jr., 34, 34 (note); processioner, 4.
Rawls, Wm., sr., land processioned, 44.
Rawls (Rawles), Wm. (son of John), land processioned, 44².
Rawls (Rawles), William (son of Wm.), 44.
See also Rales; Rawles.
Reade, Ruth, paid for services, 223, 226.
Reade, Wm., land processioned, 216; present at processioning, 216.
Readers, lay, xxi.
See also Clerks; names of readers: Allmand, Aaron; Bly, Harrell; Campbell, John; Darden, Elisha; Glover, John; Maget, Nicholas; Norfleet, Edward; Rambow, Isaac; Sheckleton, William; Skinner, Henry; Spivey, George; Spivey, Joshua.
Redy Branch, 116.
Redd (Red), Whitaker, land processioned, 171; present at processioning, 143, 171.
Redd (Red), William (Wim.), land processioned, 143³, 171⁴; present at processioning, 143², 170, 171²; processioner, 160, 171.
Rent, for indigent persons, 156, 163, 219, 221, 227, 241, 247, 256, 260.
Revolution, see American Revolution.
Reynols (Ronnelds), Christopher (Christor), land processioned, 69, 107.
Rice, ———, 30.
Rice, David, land processioned, 30², 31², 144.
Rice, David, sr., present at processioning, 82.
Rice, Sarah, paid for services, 163.
Rice, William, processioner, 11.
Richards, John, land processioned, 143²; paid for services, 219, 223, 226.
Richards, Wim., land processioned, 137.
Richardson, Archd. (A.), clerk of vestry,

260, 261; delegate to church convention, 262; overseer of poor, 258.
Richmond, church convention held in, lxviii, lxix, 257, 262.
Riddick, ——— (father of Capt. Henry), vestryman, deceased, 177.
Riddick, Capt. ———, 237.
Riddick (Reddick), Col. ——— (probably Col. Lemuel), 183; accounts of, 176, 183, 195, 198, 200, 202, 205, 206, 207, 222, 223; land processioned, 106, 134, 137; lists of tithables furnished by, 86, 176, 178, 183, 194, 197, 201, 222; on committee on enclosing churchyard, 128; on poorhouse board of visitors, 200; report on fines, 187.
Riddick, Majr. ———, accounts of, 187, 195; on poorhouse board of visitors, 200.
Riddick (Reddick), Abraham, land processioned, 31^3, 70^4, 75^3, 116^5, 175^2; present at processioning, 75^3, 116^4; processioner, 25, 61, 70, 181.
Riddick, Amos, land processioned, 217^2; present at processioning, 217^2; processioner, 231.
Riddick, Daniel (Dan.), land processioned, 217, 234^3; present at processioning, 190^2; processioner, 208, 243, 252, 255.
Riddick, Dempsey, paid for services, 198; processioner, 231.
Riddick, Edward (Edwd.) (sometimes designated captain), churchwarden, 156, 157, 158, 159, 161, 168; land processioned, 235^4; payment to, 243; processioner, 208; resignation of, 180; vestryman, 153, 156, 177, 178.
Riddick (Redik), Henry (sometimes designated captain, major, colonel), 179; accounts of, 187, 194, 196, 198, 202, 238, 239, 244, 256, 259; churchwarden, 187, 194, 196, 197, 198, 200, 230, 231, 236, 239, 240, 252, 255, 257, 258; deceased, 258; land processioned, 141^4, 192, 217^4; on poorhouse board of visitors, 200; paid for services, 97, 241; present at processioning, 80^2, 81, 192^3; processioner, 209, 217, 243;

sheriff, 176, 179, 183; to conform to doctrines of Episcopal Church, 257; vestryman, 177, 178, 180, 186, 201, 203, 204, 205, 218, 221, 222, 225, 227, 229, 240, 242, 246, 247, 248, 250.
Riddick, Hezekiah (Ezekiah, Hez., Hezakiah, Hezikiah), land processioned, 142^3, 192, 216, 217; present at processioning, 142, 235; processioner, 182, 192, 252; reimbursed, 195.
Riddick, James, present at processioning, 81.
Riddick, Jean, land processioned, 37^3.
Riddick (Reddick), Jesse, 118; land processioned, 37^2, 116, 148^2, 174^2; paid for services, 127; processioner, 64, 100, 116^2.
Riddick, Jethro, overseer of poor, 258; processioner, 243, 252; reimbursed, 256, 259, 260; to conform to doctrines of Episcopal Church, 257; vestryman, 257, 258, 261, 262.
Riddick, John (Joh., Jon.), accounts of, 247; churchwarden, 230, 231, 236, 239, 240; land processioned, 39^3, 81^2, 189^2, 190^7, 191, 211, 234^4; present at processioning, 217^2, 234; processioner, 182, 188, 191; to conform to doctrines of Episcopal Church, 257; vestryman, 224, 225, 227, 228, 229, 240, 246, 247, 250, 255, 257, 261.
Riddick (Reddick, Redick, Redik, Ridick), Josiah (Josah, Josia) (captain, major, colonel), 50, 175, 259; accounts of, 57, 85, 92, 93, 94, 97, 98, 102, 156, 157, 158, 159, 187, 200, 246, 247; and erection of poorhouse, lvii, lviii, 84, 85, 93, 173; churchwarden, 88, 89, 92, 93, 94, 95, 98, 99, 152, 153, 154, 155, 156, 243, 244, 245, 246, 247, 262; land processioned, 40^2, 81, 109^4, 110, 136, 137^2, 140^2, 141, 142^3, 188, 192, 211, 217; magistrate, 120; on almshouse board of visitors, 124; on committee for building church, l, 46; on committee for enclosing churchyard, 128; present at processioning, 40, 41, 120^2, 147^2, 192^3, 217^1; processioner, 101, 110, 231; resignation of, 201; to conform to doc-

trines of Episcopal Church, 257; tobacco collector, 54, 58; vestry held at house of, 23; vestryman, 23, 24, 26, 28, 45, 48, 49, 51, 52, 54, 55, 67, 83, 85, 87, 99, 103, 104, 118, 119, 121, 124, 125, 126, 129, 130, 132, 135, 151, 153, 156, 157, 159, 161, 167, 173, 175, 177, 178, 180, 186, 194, 196, 197, 200, 240, 242, 248, 255, 257, 258, 261, 262.

Riddick, Josiah, jr., present at processioning, 217.

Riddick, Josiah, sr., land processioned, 217^5.

Riddick (Reddick, Redick), Lemuel (Lamuel, Lem., Leml.) (sometimes designated captain, major, colonel), 126, 132, 179; accounts of, 47, 51, 53, 58, 86, 90, 91, 102, 123, 152; burgess, xx, lix; charges against Lunan, xxxix, 177; churchwarden, 45, 48, 49, 51, 99, 154, 218, 221, 222; clerk of vestry, 20, 23, 24, 26, 28, 29, 47, 52; copies of acts and lists by, 56, 226; dissents from vestry, xliii, 218, 221; executors of, 229; fines paid out by, 29; land processioned, 39^2, 69, 70^2, 78, 79^3, 81^2, 105, 106, 110^6, 115^2, 116, 121^2, 134^3, 191^{10}; member almshouse board, 124; oaths administered to, 29; present at processioning, 191; processioner, 2, 24, 209; resignation of, 224; to build private gallery in church, l, 46; trustee for building chapel, 28; vestryman, xxi, 2, 12, 14, 15, 16, 19, 20, 23, 24, 26, 28, 54, 55, 101, 104, 118, 119, 121, 124, 125, 129, 130, 132, 153, 154, 155, 156, 159, 161, 167, 175, 177, 178, 180, 186, 194, 196, 197, 201, 203, 205, 218.

Riddick, Lemuel, jr., present at processing, 70.

Riddick (Reddick, Redick, Redik), Mills (Miles, Mils) (sometimes designated captain), 46, 227; accounts of, 17, 22, 27, 29, 47, 50, 53, 54, 127, 130, 133; churchwarden, 15, 16, 18, 19, 20, 23, 24, 26, 27, 28, 47, 124, 125, 126, 129, 130, 132, 134, 135; land not processioned, 141; land of, purchased for glebe, lxiii, 204, 207, 220, 224; land processioned, 39^2, 80, 81^2, 141^2, 142^{14}, 192; on almshouse board of visitors, 124; on committee for building chapel, 128, 153; present at processioning, 141, 142; processioner, 11, 182, 192; tobacco collector, 22, 27; vestryman, 15, 45, 48, 49, 51, 52, 85, 88, 89, 94, 95, 98, 99, 101, 103, 104, 119, 121, 124, 151, 153, 154, 155, 156, 159, 161, 167.

Riddick (Ridick), Miriam (Meriam), land processioned, 217^4; paid for services, 223.

Riddick (Redick), Moses, land processioned, 41, 109^6, 142^2, 217, 245; present at processioning, 109^9; processioner, 25, 41, 66, 252.

Riddick, Robert, processioner, 231.

Riddick, Robert (Ro.) M. (Moore) (sometimes designated captain), accounts of, 251; churchwarden, 248, 249, 250; to conform to doctrines of Episcopal Church, 257; vestryman, 246, 247, 255, 258, 261, 262.

Riddick, Samuel, present at processioning, 81^2.

Riddick (Redik), Solomon (Soloman), land processioned, 190^{12}, 211, 217, 234^4; patroller, 90; present at processioning, 39^3, 190^3; processioner, 160.

Riddick, William, processioner, 251.

Riddick (Reddick, Redick, Redik, Ridick), Willis (Wilis, Williss) (captain, major, colonel), 102, 219, 256; accounts of, 50, 96, 123, 128, 133, 152, 177, 179, 180, 183, 196, 239; churchwarden, 120, 121, 124, 168, 175, 177, 178, 252, 255, 258; delegate to church convention, lxix, 257, 258; dissents from decision of vestry, xliii, 221; land processioned, 39^2, 81^4, 115, 142^4, 192, 216^3; land not processioned, 145; on committee for building chapel, 128; on committee for enclosing churchyard, 128; present at processioning, 192^4; processioner, 26, 39, 101, 161, 209, 217, 243; sheriff, 87, 92; to conform to doctrines of Episcopal Church, 257; tobacco collector, 92; vestryman, 99, 101, 103, 118, 119, 125, 126, 132, 151, 153, 154, 155, 156, 159,

161, 167, 180, 186, 194, 196, 197, 200, 201, 203, 204, 205, 218, 221, 222, 225, 228, 229, 236, 239, 240, 242, 246, 247, 248, 249, 250, 261, 262.
Riddick & Cowper, assignees of Wm. Gwin, 195.
Riddick family, prominent in Upper Parish, xix.
Right, James, land processioned, 139.
Right, Sarath, land processioned, 138. *See also* Wright.
Rivers, *see* names of particular rivers: Blackwater; James; Nansemond; Nottoway; Roanoke. *See also* Branches; Creeks; Runs.
Roads, cleared, 45, 50, 52, 56; from Brick Church to Jarnagan's Bridge, 58, 82; from Brick Church to Porter's Bridge, 58; from Jarnagan's Bridge to Porter's Bridge, 3, 59; from Thos. Jones to John Jenkins, 61; to Middle Chapel, 21; to the chapel, 62. *See also* names of particular roads: Chapel; Church; Mare Branch; Newby's; Orapeak; Searum; Smith's; Somerton; Somerton Creek; South Key.
Roanoke River, settlement on, xxxiii.
Robbins, ———, land not processioned, 137.
Robbins, John, constable, 222.
Roberts, Benjamin, land not processioned, 184^2.
Roberts, C., deceased, 240.
Roberts, Christopher (Christor.), land processioned, 184^4; processioner, 130, 137, 207, 213.
Roberts, Christo., sr., vestryman, 238.
Roberts, Christopher, jr., processioner, 231.
Roberts, Christopher (Christo.) (sometimes designated captain), churchwarden, 244, 245, 246; vestryman, 240, 248, 249, 250.
Roberts (Roberds), James, land processioned, 71^2; processioner, 67, 71.
Roberts, Jonathan (Jona.), land processioned, 41^3, 42^5, 77, 184^2, 185; present at processioning, 77; processioner, 24, 43.

Roberts, Mary, land processioned, 107^3.
Roberts, Richard, land processioned, 115^2.
Roberts, Thomas, land processioned, 253; processioner, 252, 253.
Roberts, William, paid for services, 260.
Robinson, Mary, indigent person, 12, 226.
Robinson, Morgan Poitiaux, *Virginia Counties* . . ., xiv (note).
Robinson, William, deputy in Virginia for Bishop of London, 177, 177 (note); petition concerning Rev. Patrick Lunan presented to, xxxix; powerless to discipline or punish clergy, xl.
Rodes, John, land processioned, 73, 74^2, 75; present at processioning, 73^2, 74^3.
Rodgers, ———, 34.
Rodgers, Allice, land processioned, 174.
Rodgers, Drewry, processioner, 182.
Rodgers, Elisabeth, land processioned, 115.
Rodgers, Sarah, land processioned, 115.
Roger, Jethro, present at processioning, 79.
Rogers, ———, indigent person, 219.
Rogers, Alice, indigent person, 200.
Rogers (Rodgers, Rodgerz, Rogger), Benjamin (Benj., Benjamain), land processioned, 34, 79^2, 115^3, 134^2; present at processioning, 79, 115, 134.
Rogers, Bethel, indigent person, 220.
Rogers, Drewry, paid for services, 202.
Rogers, Eliza, land processioned, 134^2.
Rogers (Rodgers, Roggers), John, land processioned, 34, 71^2, 75^2; processioner, 11, 67, 71.
Rogers (Rodgers, Roggers), Joseph (Jos.), 134; land processioned, 75^3; present at processioning, 75, 116^3; processioner, 5.
Rogers (Rodgers), Martha, indigent person, 237, 241.
Rogers (Rodgers, Roger, Rogers, Roggers), Robert (Robt.), 100, 115, 134; land processioned, 75, 79; present at processioning, 75, 79^2, 115; reimbursed, 52.
Rogers (Rodgers, Roger, Roggers), William (Wim., Wm.), land processioned, 34^2, 71, 79^2, 115^3, 116, 134^2, 135^3;

present at processioning, 30, 135; processioner, 116.
Rogers (Rodgers), William (Wim), son of Robert (Robt.), land processioned, 100, 115, 134.
Rogers, Wim., son of Joseph, land processioned, 134.
Rogers (Rodgers), Wim. (son of Wim.), land processioned, 115^2.
Ronnelds, Christopher, *see* Reynols (Ronnelds), Christopher (Christor).
Ross, Alexander, paid for services, 230.
Roundtree, Mrs. ———, land processioned, 233^2.
Roundtree (Rountree, Rowntree), John, land processioned, 43^4, 137^3, 188, 211, 233^2; present at processioning, 233; processioner, 9, 101.
Roundtree, Newby, land processioned, 233.
Roundtree (Rountree, Rowntree), Robert (Robt.), land processioned, 43^3, 137^2, 188, 211; processioner, 25, 43, 182, 188.
Roundtree (Rowntree, Rown Tree), William (Willm., Wim., Wm.), land processioned, 136, 137^2, 188, 211^2, 233^3; present at processioning, 188; processioner, 101, 160, 209, 211, 243, 252.
Rountree, Elizabeth, indigent person, 206.
Rudd, Rev. William, xxxiv.
Runs, *see* names of particular runs: Baker's Mill; Jarnagan's Bridge; Spight's.
See also Branches; Creeks; Rivers.
Russell, Charles, land processioned, 71^3.
Ruther, Charles, constable, 219.

Sacrament, xli, 47, 240.
Sailor, 17.
St. Andrew's Parish, Brunswick Co., ministers of, xxxix, xxxix (note).
St. Bride's Parish, 201.
St. George Parish, Spotsylvania County, Vestry Book, 1726-45, xxxvi (note).
St. George's Parish, Spotsylvania Co., minister, xxxvi.
St. Paul's Church, Suffolk, vii, lxxiv, lxxiv (note).
Salaries, levies for ministers', discontinued, xlvii, lxvi; of clerk, 12; of clerk of Brick Church, 85; of clerk of Cyprus Chapel, 157, 161, 167, 178, 201, 229; of clerk of Holy Neck Chapel, 85, 90, 132, 151, 154, 157, 178, 229; of clerk of Middle Chapel, 14, 85; clerk of Nottoway Chapel, 95, 126, 132, 151, 154, 157, 161; of clerk of Suffolk Church, 90, 95, 101, 122, 126, 132, 151, 154, 157, 161, 167, 175, 178, 182, 201; of clerk of Somerton Chapel, 14, 161, 167; of clerk of Upper Chapel, 52, 56, 95; of clerk of vestry, 12, 16, 20, 57, 248, 250, 256; of master of Grammar School, xxxviii; of minister, xxxvii, xliii, xliv, 12, 16, 26, 45, 49, 52, 55, 85, 89, 90, 95, 101, 118, 121, 132, 151, 154, 157, 161, 167, 175, 178, 182, 194, 197, 201, 205, 218, 227, 229, 236, 240; of overseer of poorhouse, lviii, lx, lxii, 97, 103, 127, 200, 202; of reader at Cyprus Chapel, 194, 197, 205, 218, 222, 226, 236, 239; of reader at Holy Neck Chapel, 194, 197, 205, 218, 222, 226, 236, 239, 240, 243; of reader at Middle Chapel, 47; of reader at Nottoway Chapel, 118; of reader at Somerton Chapel, 16, 47, 118, 236; of reader at Suffolk Church, 118, 194, 197, 205, 218, 222, 225, 229, 239, 240, 243; of reader at the chapel, 45; of reader at the church and chapel, 20; of reader at Upper Chapel, 12, 49, 50; Rev. Alexander Forbes on clerical, xxx.
See also Wages.
Salivation, 27, 86.
Saml. Jordan's Point, 87.
Sanders, ———, 171.
Sanders, ———, land processioned, 165.
Sanders, Mrs. ———, land processioned, 165^2.
Sanders (Sander), Christopher (Chris., Christepher, Christo., Christor, Chrstopher), 12, 17; land processioned, 29, 31^3, 42^3, 71, 77, 107, 110^2.
Sanders, Moses, present at processioning, 82, 110^3.
Sanders, Sarah, land processioned, 165.
Sanders, Thos., land processioned, 143^3,

144², 184², 185; processioner, 180, 184.
Sanders, William (Wim., Wm.), land processioned, 32⁴, 33, 69, 111², 112², 136²; present at processioning, 136⁴; processioner, 25, 32, 33.
Sap, Mary, indigent person, 26, 45, 50, 52.
Saunders, James, present at processioning, 263.
Saunders, Job, present at processioning, 263.
Saunders, John, present at processioning, 263.
Savage, Caleb (Kaleb), land processioned, 214; present at processioning, 214; processioner, 243, 252.
Savage (Savidge, Savige), James, land processioned, 115²; present at processioning, 79.
Savage, Jean, indigent person, 97, 123, 130.
Savage, William (Wim.), land processioned, 79, 136, 170², 172, 193²; present at processioning, 143.
Scarbord, Sarah, indigent person, 223, 226.
Scarbrough, ———, land processioned, 108².
Schenectady, N. Y., Rev. William Andrews at, xliv.
School, at poorhouse, lviii, lx, lxi, 97, 103, 104, 119, 123, 124, 129.
See also Children; Grammar school; Teaching.
Scott, Exum (Exam), 3, 3 (note); land processioned, 79; present at processioning, 79².
Scott, John, paid for services, 57, 91.
Scott, Joseph (Jos.), fine of, 183; land processioned, 185⁴, 186, 209⁴, 242⁵, 245⁶, 253; present at processioning, 74², 166², 209²; processioner, 231, 242.
Scott, Mourning, land processioned, 79.
Scott, Sarah, land processioned, 74³.
Scott, William (Wim., Wm.), land processioned, 35, 74², 112.
Scutchens (Scutchin), Thomas, land processioned, 32².

Scutchins (Scutchings), Mary, indigent person, 224, 227, 230, 237, 239.
See also Cutchens.
Searum Road, 7, 64.
Security, collector of parish levy to give, 14, 18, 22, 46, 54, 58, 87, 92, 126, 157, 158, 162, 167, 176, 179, 195, 202, 218, 223, 225, 230, 238, 240, 242; custodian of child to give, 180.
See also Bond.
Sextons, *see* names of sextons: Booth, Robert; Campbell, John; Cole, John; Gwin, Henry; Hart, Moses; Jarnagan, Hardey; Jenkins, Dempsey; Jenkins, John; Johnson, Thos.; Jones, Sarah; Leviston, Richard; Norfleet, Hezekiah; Rawls, Mary; Rawls, Ruth; Spivey, Christian; Spivey, George; Taylor, Susana; Whitfield, William; Wiggins, William; Wright, Sarah.
Shavass, Jeen, land processioned, 34.
See also Chivers; Shiffers; Shivers.
Shaw, Cathrine, indigent person, 102, 103.
Sheckleton (Shekelton, Shettleton, Shickleton, Shitleton, Shittleton), William (Wm.), clerk, Holy Neck Chapel, 85, 90, 132, 151, 154, 157, 168, 178; clerk, Nottoway Chapel, 126; clerk, Somerton Chapel, 101, 122, 161, 167; clerk, Upper Chapel, 52, 56, 95; present at processioning, 69; reader, Somerton Chapel, 118; reader, Upper Chapel, 12.
Sheets, for burials, 179, 219, 241.
See also Burials.
Shepherd, Samuel, *The Statutes at Large of Virginia*, lxxiii (note).
Shepherd, Stephen, land processioned, 263³; present at processioning, 263².
Sheriffs, act defining duties of, 14 (note), 18; allowance to, for insolvents, 155, 158, 167, 183, 197, 205, 222, 238; allowance to, for tickets, 197, 201, 205, 222; collect parish levy, 14, 17, 18, 46, 57, 87, 92, 96, 119, 122, 126, 133, 152, 155, 157, 158, 167, 176, 179, 183, 195, 197, 206, 240, 242, 244, 247, 249, 260; to advertise election of vestrymen, xx; to collect fines, xxvii.

See also names of sheriffs: Godwin, Capt. Thos.; Holladay, Anthony; King, Michael; Moore, William; Pitt, James; Pugh, William; Riddick, Henry; Riddick, Willis; Tembtey, Dr. Hening; Turner, James; Wright, Edward.

Shettleton (Shickleton), William, *see* Sheckleton, William.

Shiffers, Thomas, land processioned, 31^2; processioner, 31.
See also Chivers; Shavass; Shivers.

Shitleton (Shittleton), William, *see* Sheckleton, William.

Shivers, Thomas, land processioned, 70^3, 75^3, 116^4, 148^4; present at processioning, 70^3, 75^3; processioner, 7, 25, 160.
See also Chivers; Shavass; Shiffers.

Shoes, 26, 45, 103, 238.

Siers, Silas, paid for services, 226.

Simons, Augustin, land processioned, 74.

Simons (Simon), John, land processioned, 35, 112, 137; present at processioning, 74; reimbursed, 45, 52, 260.

Sivels, Wm., land processioned, 189^5, 234^4.

Skeato (Skeetoe, Sketo), James, land processioned, 137, 188, 211, 233^2.

Skeatoe (Skeator, Sketor), Joseph (Jos.), indigent person, 179, 184, 195, 198, 203, 207, 220, 224, 226, 230, 237, 239, 241; present at processioning, 216^2.

Skeatoe (Skeator), Rachel, indigent person, 237; paid for services, 179.

Skeator, Ferebee, paid for services, 249.

Skiner, ———, land processioned, 108.

Skinner (Skiner), Henry, 40; clerk, Somerton Chapel, 14; land processioned, 40^2, 109^3; present at processioning, 109^6; processioner, 10; reader, Somerton Chapel, 16; reimbursed, 13.

Skinner (Skiner), Jesse (Jessey), land processioned, 164^2; processioner, 208, 211.

Skinner (Skiner), John, 33, 108; land processioned, 69^2, 114, 138^2; present at processioning, 69, 83, 138^1; processioner, 24.

Skinner (Skiner), Joseph (Jos.), land processioned, 143^2, 170^3, 216^3; present at processioning, 216^2, 233; processioner, 131, 143, 182, 231, 232.

Skinner (Skiner), Joseph (son of John), present at processioning, 108.

Slater, Moses, land processioned, 235^2.

Slatter, Kesiah, 68.

Slaughter, Philip, *History of St. George's Parish, in the County of Spotsylvania, and Diocese of Virginia,* xxxvi (note).

Small, ———, 239.

Smith, Arthur, processioner, 231, 232.

Smith, Charles, 84.

Smith, Demsey, present at processioning, 170.

Smith, E., 259.

Smith, Jean, indigent person, 251.

Smith, John, 38; land processioned, 34, 80, 145, 146, 170, 172; paid for services, 202; present at processioning, 193^2, 213; processioner, 231, 232, 252, 254.

Smith, John, jr., land processioned, 193.

Smith, John, sr., land processioned, 193^2.

Smith, Joseph, land processioned, 146; processioner, 131, 147.

Smith, Rev. Joseph, Gooch's criticism of, xxxv, xxxvi; minister Upper and Chuckatuck parishes, xxxv.

Smith, Margaret, indigent person, 259.

Smith, Martha, land processioned, 38.

Smith, Reuben, processioner, 252, 254.

Smith, Richard, plantation occupied by, 70; present at processioning, 70.

Smith, Robert (Robt.), land processioned, 71^2; processioner, 101, 114, 182, 193.

Smith, Ruth, indigent person, 202.

Smith, Samuel (Samuell, Saml.), indigent person, 12; land processioned, 145, 172, 214; paid for services, 198; present at processioning, 145^4, 172, 193^2, 214; processioner, 25, 38.

Smith, Saml. (son of Saml.), land processioned, 145.

Smith, Thomas (Thos.), processioner, 243, 252, 255, 263.

Smithfield, Va., xiii (note).

Smith's Road, 8, 9, 11, 34, 64, 65, 67, 170.

Society for the Propagation of the Gospel, xliv.
Society of Friends, see Quakers.
Soldiers, burial of, lxvi, 236; damage done by, lxvi.
Somerton, land at, devised, lv, lvi, 173, 173 (note); Upper Chapel located near, liii.
Somerton (Sommorton, Summerton, Sumrt., Sumrton) Chapel, lii, 89; clerk of, 14, 101, 122, 161, 167; formerly known as Upper Chapel, liii, liii (note); reader, 16, 47, 118; services at, lii, 47; sexton, 151, 205, 218, 222; sextoness, 16, 96, 118, 122, 126, 132; well cleaned, 96.
Somerton Creek, 5, 61.
Somerton (Sumerton, Summerton) Creek Road, 61, 116.
Somerton (Sumerton, Summ., Summerton, Summorton, Summn., Sumn., Sumrton) Road, 4, 5, 8, 9, 11, 34, 44, 60, 64, 65, 67, 83, 170, 188, 252.
Somerton (Summerton, Sumn., Sumrton) Swamp, 4, 5, 44, 60, 61, 188.
South Key Plantation, processioned, 136.
South Key (Keey) Road, 5, 6, 60, 61, 62, 116.
South Parish, formation of, xiv; name changed to Upper Parish, Nansemond Co., xiv, xv.
South Quay, depot for foreign trade, lxv.
Southampton County, Nottoway Parish in, xliv, xlv (note); territory added to, xvii, liv.
Sparling, Geo., processioner, 231.
Spencer, Abraham, paid for services, 162.
Spencer, John, land processioned, 108.
Spight, ———, land processioned, 108.
Spight, John, land processioned, 143.
Spight, Mary, 68, 88.
Spight's (Speight's, Spikes') Run, 4, 59, 83.
Spivey (Spivy, Spyva), Christian (Christain), land processioned, 188, 190; sextoness, 240, 243.
Spivey (Spivi, Spivy), George (Geo.), clerk, Cyprus Chapel, 198, 201, 229; land processioned, 43, 136, 137^3, 188,

233^2; processioner, 65, 131, 136; reader, Cyprus Chapel, 205, 218, 222, 226; sexton, Cyprus Chapel, 226.
Spivey (Spivy), James (Jas.), 211; land processioned, 137^3, 188; paid for services, 195; processioner, 25, 43.
Spivey (Spivy), Joshua (Josh, Joshula), land processioned, 37^4, 37 (note), 43, 190^7, 234^3; present at processioning, 190^8; processioner, 37, 38, 100; reader, Cyprus Chapel, 236, 239.
Spivey (Spivy), Joshua, jr., processioner, 25.
Spivey (Spivy), Thomas, land processioned, 39^2, 40^4.
Spivy, ———, former land of, processioned, 110.
Spivy, Moses, processioner, 64.
Spivy, Wm., land processioned, 190, 211.
Sprague, William B., *Annals of the American Pulpit* (book), xliv (note).
Spring, church to be erected near, 20; cleaned, 21, 27, 50, 52, 56, 85; road to cleared, 45.
See also Well.
Stakes, Levin, reimbursed, 260.
See also Stokes.
Stallings (Staling, Stallins), James (Jas.), land processioned, 142^2, 192, 217^3; present at processioning, 192.
Stalling, John, present at processioning, 39.
Stallings (Stallins, Stallions), Joseph (Jos.), land processioned, 39^3, 81^3, 142^4; present at processioning, 40^3; processioner, 101.
Stallings, Joseph, jr., present at processioning, 39^3.
Stallings, Magaret, land processioned, 192, 217^2.
Stallings (Stallins, Stallions), Mary, indigent person, 187, 200, 224, 226, 256; paid for services, 206, 220.
Stallings (Stallins), William (Wm.), indigent person, 207, 220, 224, 226; land processioned, 39^3, 81^3, 142^2, 217^4; present at processioning, 217^5; processioner, 132, 142.

Stallings, Wm., jr., present at processioning, 39.
Stallins, Elizabeth (Eliza.), indigent person, 168, 176, 179, 183, 195, 198, 203, 207, 220, 224, 226, 230, 237, 239, 241.
Stallins, Judith, paid for services, 237.
Stallions, Christian, indigent person, 250, 256.
Stallions, Uriah, processioner, 252.
Steaven, ———, 145.
Stewart, Charles, indigent person, 102.
Stogdale, James, present at processioning 110^2.
Stogdale, John, present at processioning, 169.
Stokes (Stockes, Stocks), John, land processioned, 35^1.
Stokes, Thomas (Thos.), land processioned, 72, 73^2, 74.
Stokes (Stakes), Wm. Marshal (Marshall), land not processioned, 137; processioner, 208, 208 (note), 210.
See also Stakes.
Story, Thomas, Quaker, xxxiv.
Streater (Streator, Streeter), John (Jno.), land processioned, 144^3; paid for services of negro woman, 127; present at processioning, 70, 78, 79^2.
Streater (Streator), Willis, processioner, 207, 213; reimbursed, 238; vestryman, 222, 225, 229, 240, 244.
Stringfield, Richard, land processioned, 33.
Suffolk, burned by British, lxvii; church ornaments brought to, 91; Church Street in, li; circuit court of, xiii; courthouse in, 98, 99, 101, 104, 121, 124, 177; damage done in, by state troops, lxvi; depot of military supplies, lxv; establishment of, xvii, li (note); ferry at, 87, 96; land in, processioned, 2, 24, 58, 169; Main Street in, lviii, 84; meeting to elect vestry held in, 261; new brick church built in, xxi, l, li, 46, 48, 54; poorhouse in, lvii, lviii, lxiv, 84, 92, 98, 104, 174; post for colonial troops, lxv, lxvi; tavern in, xlii (note); Union Chapel in, lxxiv (note); vestry held at home of Edmund (Edmond) Belson Wright in, 154, 155, 156, 157, 161, 166, 175, 178, 186; vestry held at home of Saml. Swan in, 201, 203, 204, 221, 222, 224, 225; vestry held at home of Tho. Langston in, 227, 228; vestry held at home of Thos. Brickle in, 194, 196, 197; vestry held in, 1, 14, 18, 19, 20, 23, 24, 26, 44, 48, 49, 51, 54, 55, 67, 83, 85, 87, 88, 89, 92, 93, 94, 95, 98, 99, 103, 108, 113, 118, 124, 125, 129, 130, 132, 135, 144, 145, 146, 151, 159, 174, 180, 185, 186, 193, 210, 214, 215, 216, 217, 229, 232, 236, 238, 240, 242, 244, 245, 246, 248, 249, 250, 254, 255, 257, 258; Western Avenue in, lii.
Suffolk Parish, Nansemond Co., vii, lxxiv; adding part of Upper Parish to, xvi, xvii, xvii (note), lii, 15 15 (note), 24, 25; and relief of poor, xxi, lx, lxx, 99; minister of, xxxvii; Lower and Chuckatuck parishes united as, xiii (note), xvi; vestry of, xiii (note), xix, lx, 14, 15; vestry book of, xiii, xiii (note).
See also Chuckatuck Parish; Lower Parish, Nansemond Co.
Suffolk Parish, Nansemond County, Virginia, Vestry Book, 1749-1856, xxxvii (note).
Sugar, 251.
Sullivan, Judith, indigent person, 259.
Sumner, ———, land processioned, 170.
Sumner, Capt. ———, land processioned, 30.
Sumner, David (sometimes designated captain), 156; land processioned, 78, 79, 115^2, 116^2, 121, 134, 135, 235^2; present at processioning, 78^2; vestryman, 99, 104, 121, 124.
Sumner, Dempsey (Dempsie, Dempsy, Demsey, Demsie) (sometimes designated captain, major, colonel), executor, 145; land processioned, 105, 145^2, 172^2, 174^4, 193, 214; to conform to doctrines of Episcopal Church, 257; vestryman, 257, 258.

Sumner, Elisha, land processioned, 212; present at processioning, 212.

Sumner, Jacob, accounts of, 206, 220; churchwarden, 200, 201, 202, 203, 204, 205, 218; land processioned, 38[2], 105, 145, 172, 193, 214; on committee for building chapel, 128; on committee to inspect chapel, 153; present at processioning, 80, 121, 145[3], 193[3]; processioner, 160; resignation from vestry, 238; vestryman, 99, 101, 103, 104, 119, 125, 126, 153, 154, 157, 167, 175, 177, 178, 196, 200, 225, 228, 229.

Sumner, James (Jas.), 22; land processioned, 29, 38, 72[5], 111[4], 171; present at processioning, 71[3], 72, 111; processioner, 131.

Sumner, Jethro (Jothro) (sometimes designated captain), accounts of, 13, 17, 22, 23, 27, 50; churchwarden, 1, 2, 11, 12, 14, 15, 16, 17, 18, 19, 20, 23, 24, 26, 27; deceased, 68; land of, desired for church site, l, li (note), 46, 47; land processioned, 30[5], 34, 34 (note), 40; on committee on new church, l, 46; vestryman, 48, 49, 51, 54, 55.

Sumner, Jethro, present at processioning, 82, 214.

Sumner, Luke, land processioned, 188[2], 189[3], 211[2], 212[5], 234[6].

Sumner, Mrs. Margaret (Margret), l, li (note), 46, 47.

Sumner, Robert, present at processioning, 79.

Sumner, Samuel, processioner, 145.

Sumner, Thomas (Thos.), 139; accounts of, 103; churchwarden, 95, 98; land processioned, 109, 115, 144[5]; on committee to sell glebe land, 173; present at processioning, 82, 144; processioner, 159, 168; reimbursed, 123; vestryman, 68, 83, 89, 92, 93, 94.

Sumner, William, land processioned, 146, 147.

Sumner family, prominent in Upper Parish, xix.

Supremacy, oath of, xxvi.

Surplice, 47, 51, 52, 56, 85, 91, 96, 103, 119, 127, 162, 175, 178, 179, 198, 202, 205, 237.

Survey, of glebe land, 83, 84; of land offered for glebe, lxiii, 204; of land of Blake and Cadowgan, lvii, 84.

Surveyors, lvii, 83, 91, 95, 204.

Surveyor's chain, men paid for carrying, 90.

Sussex Co., Albemarle Parish in, xlvi.

Swamps, *see* names of particular swamps: Back; Barbecue; Beaverdam; Cypress; Dismal; Dragon; Flat; Hunter's Mill; Kingsale; Knuckle; Raby's; Somerton; Wickam.

Swan, Samuel, tobacco collector, 157; vestry held at home of, 201, 203, 204, 221, 222, 224, 225.

Sweep, for well, 179.

"Sweet Scented" tobacco parishes, xxx.

Tables, for almshouse, 97.

Talington (Tallington), *see* Turlington.

Tallow, 123.

Talor, Edward, *see* Taylor, Edward.

Tar, 23, 24, 48, 88.

Tarlington (Tarlinton, Tarnington), *see* Turlington.

Tarrascoe Neck, xv (note).

Tatman, Nathl., present at processioning, 263.

Tavern, in Suffolk, xlii (note).

Taxes, act concerning, 14 (note); for religious purposes discontinued, xxxii, xlvii, lxv, lxvi; levied by vestries, xviii; minister subjected to double, xliv (note); proposition of Quakers relating to, xxviii.

See also Parish levy; Tithables.

Taylor, ———, leg made for, 57.

Taylor (Talor), Edward (Edwd.), land processioned, 35, 75, 112, 137; present at processioning, 74[4], 75.

Taylor, Jethro, reimbursed, 260.

Taylor (Tayloe), John, land processioned, 71; processioner, 101, 105.

Taylor (Tayloe), Jonathan, land processioned, 80, 146[2].

Taylor (Tayloe), Richard (Richd.), land processioned, 71², 80, 105, 145, 146, 172, 193, 214; paid for services, 158; present at processioning, 80, 193; processioner, 25, 38, 101, 105, 160, 172, 209, 214.

Taylor, Robert (Robt.), indigent person, 56, 57; salivation of, 86.

Taylor (Tayloe), Susana (Susanah), land processioned, 38; sextoness, 13, 16, 21, 26, 45, 49.

Teaching, lxi, 162, 198, 202; at almshouse, 97, 103, 104, 119, 123, 124, 129. *See also* Best, John, jr.; Children; Cotten, Hannah; Grammer school; School; Wallis, Samuel.

Tembtey (Tembey, Tembte, Tembtie, Tembty, Temptey, Temty), Dr. Hening (Harning, Henning) (sometimes designated captain), 123; acts in sale of glebe land, 128, 173; churchwarden, 98; land processioned, 31⁵, 35², 41², 68, 73³, 74, 77², 107, 112², 113, 137, 144⁴, 147³, 163, 172, 173⁴, 185²; paid for services, 13, 21, 152; present at processioning, 82, 147³; sheriff, 122, 126; vestryman, 15, 16, 18, 20, 23, 24, 48, 49, 67, 85, 88, 92, 94, 95, 98, 104, 118, 119, 121, 124, 125, 129, 130, 151, 153, 154, 155, 156, 159, 161, 167, 168, 173.

Terry, Emily, x.

Terry, John, indigent person, 260.

Terry, Richard, indigent person, 250.

Test, subscribed to by vestryman, 16, 23, 45.

Thomas, Ann, indigent person, 226, 230.

Thomas, Elisabeth, land processioned, 107.

Thomas, John (Jon., Jno.), indigent person, 206, 207, 221, 223, 237; land processioned, 32², 42, 43², 77; paid for services, 226; present at processioning, 42².

Thomas, Joseph, land processioned, 184²; present at processioning, 184; processioner, 207, 213, 231.

Thomas, Pricilia, indigent person, 183.

Thompson, Alexander, indigent person, 259.

Tibbs, John, indigent person, 56.

Tickets, allowance for, 126, 132, 197, 201, 205.

Tithables, allowance for, gone to wars, 118; assessed for parish expenses, 14, 18, 22, 27, 46, 50, 51, 54, 57, 86, 87, 91, 92, 96, 102, 119, 122, 126, 133, 152, 155, 158, 162, 167, 176, 179, 183, 195, 197, 202, 206, 218, 223, 225, 227, 228, 230, 238, 240, 242, 244, 247, 249, 251, 257, 260; dissenting, in Upper Parish, 240; listed, 13, 17, 45, 50, 53, 56, 86, 90, 176, 178, 183, 194, 197, 201, 205, 222, 226, 229, 238, 243; taxed for poorhouse, 199.

See also Parish levy; Taxes.

Tobacco, act regarding levies, etc., in, 14 (note); allowed minister in lieu of glebe, 16, 26, 45, 49, 52, 55, 85, 90, 95, 101, 118, 121, 126, 132, 154, 157, 161, 175, 194, 197, 201; casks, allowance for, 12, 16, 45, 49, 52, 55, 85, 90, 95, 101, 102, 118, 121, 132, 154, 157, 161, 167, 175, 178, 182, 194, 197, 201, 205; clergy's remonstrance against payments in lieu of, xxxviii; collectors of, 14, 14 (note), 17, 18, 22, 27, 46, 47, 54, 58, 87, 92, 126, 157, 158, 162, 167, 176, 179, 195, 202, 218, 223, 225, 230, 238, 240; levied for building chapel, 90; levied for building church, l, 17, 22, 23, 27, 46, 47, 50, 53, 57; levied for parish debts, 14, 18, 22, 27, 46, 50, 54, 57, 86, 87, 91, 92, 96, 102, 119, 122, 126, 133, 152, 155, 158, 162, 167, 176, 179, 183, 195, 197, 202, 206, 218, 223, 225, 228; levied for poorhouse, lxii, 96, 199; not provided for Lunan's salary, xliii, 218; order of vestry relating to collection of, 223, 225; oronoco, xxx; paid for insolvents, 12, 17, 21, 27, 46, 50, 53, 57, 85, 90, 102, 118, 122, 126, 132, 152, 155, 158, 167, 178, 183, 194, 197, 201, 205, 221, 227, 238; poor, and clergy, xxix; purchased to pay debts due in, 225; shortage of, 125; sold to buy church organs, 86; sold to discharge cash accounts, 86, 87, 102, 103, 122, 126, 133, 152, 155, 162, 167, 176,

178, 183, 195, 197, 201, 205, 218, 221, 222, 224; sweet scented, xxx; unequal value in parishes, xxx.
See also Commission; Money.
Toleration Act of William and Mary, xxvii.
Torlington (Torlinton), *see* Turlington.
Townsend (Towsin), John (Jno.), land processioned, 115², 135².
Trade, children from poorhouse to be taught a, lxi, 124.
Treason, minister accused of, xlviii, xlix.
Treaty of Peace, 1783, xlix (note).
Trees, 37, 148, 189; on glebe marked, 91.
Trustees, as successors to vestries, lxxi.
Tucker, ———, 43.
Tucker, Majr. ———, 77.
Tucker, Mary, indigent person, 127.
Tucker, Robert (Robt.), land not processioned, 213; land processioned, 184².
Tucker's Neck, 21.
Tunstall, Robert B., x.
Turley, Richard, present at processioning, 193.
Turlington, ———, land processioned, 108².
Turlington, Major ———, processioner, 243, 252.
Turlington, Benjn., processioner, 231.
Turlington, James, land processioned, 245; processioner, 252.
Turlington, John, present at processioning, 136; refuses to have land processioned, 244.
Turlington (Talington), Levin (Leavin), Leving), land processioned, 235²; paid for services, 247; processioner, 208, 243, 245.
Turlington (Tarlington, Tarlinton, Tarnington, Torlington, Torlinton), Mansfield ((Mansel), land processioned, 143³, 170, 171², 216²; present at processioning, 40⁷, 83, 108, 143⁴.
Turlington (Tallington), Thos., land processioned, 235; paid for services, 219; present at processioning, 191, 235; processioner, 209.
Turlington (Tarlington), William (Wim., Wm.), land processioned, 171⁵,

215, 216³; present at processioning, 216²; processioner, 182.
Turner, James, death of, 157; sheriff, 152, 155.
Two Penny Acts, clergy and, xxxvii-xxxviii, xxxviii (note), xli (note).
Tyler, Cathrine, indigent person, 202.
Tyre, Dr. James, accounts of, 123, 133, 152.

Union Chapel, Suffolk, lxxiv (note).
Upper Chapel, clerk, 52, 56, 95; identified with Somerton Chapel, liii, liii (note); new, lii, liii, 47; readers, 12, 49, 50; repairs on, 86, 87; sextoness, 13, 21, 26, 45, 49, 50, 52, 90.
Upper Norfolk County, divided into parishes, xiv, xv (note), xxiii; formed from New Norfolk County, xiv; name changed to Nansemond Co., xiv; Puritans in, xxiii.
Upper Parish, Isle of Wight Co., minister of, xxviii.
Upper Parish, Nansemond Co., act of dividing, xvi, xvii, xvii (note), 15, 15 (note); and convention of Protestant Episcopal Church, lxxii, 257, 262; area of, xv, xv (note), xvii; as Upper Suffolk Parish, vii, lxxiv; debts of, in cash, 1, 29, 47, 50, 53, 54, 56, 57, 86, 91, 92, 94, 96, 98, 102, 119, 120, 122, 123, 127, 133, 152, 156, 158, 168, 176, 179, 195, 198, 202, 206, 207, 219, 220, 221, 223, 226, 227, 229, 230, 236, 237, 238, 239, 240, 241, 243, 244, 247, 248, 249, 250, 251, 256, 259, 260; debts of, in tobacco, 12, 13, 16, 17, 20, 21, 22, 26, 27, 45, 46, 49, 50, 52, 53, 55, 56, 57, 85, 86, 90, 95, 96, 102, 118, 119, 121, 122, 126, 132, 151, 152, 154, 155, 157, 158, 167, 176, 178, 194, 197, 201, 205, 218, 222, 225; dissenters in, xxxii, 240; end of ministry of Established Church in, xlvi; formation of, xiii; formerly called South Parish, xiv, xv; land grant in, xv; map to be made of, l; petitions of, xvi, xix, xx, l, lvi, lxiv, lxvi, lxxi, lxxii, lxxiii; prominent families in, xix; properties de-

vised to, lv, lvi, lxiii, 125, 173, 173 (note); Quakers in, xxvii, xxviii, xxix; religion in, xxii-xxxii; ruinous condition of, lxxii-lxxiv; to raise money for repairs on church and chapels in, lxxii, 262; to survey certain lands in, lvii, 83, 84; witnesses in court for, 102, 118. *See also* Chapels; Church; Ministers; Parish levy; Parish register; Poorhouse; Precincts; Processioners; Processioning of land; Tithables; Vestry of Upper Parish, Nansemond Co.; Vestry book.

Upper Suffolk Parish, vii, lxxiv.

Uzzell (Uzel, Uzell, Uzzil), James (Jas.), land processioned, 33, 69, 111^2, 136^2, 165; present at processioning, 136^2, 165; processioner, 25, 32, 33.

Vagrants, act concerning, lv.
Van Schreeven, W. J., x.
Vaughan, Mrs. ———, land processioned, 165.
Vaughan, Charles, present at processioning, 263; processioner, 208.
Vaughan, Elisabeth (Elizh., Elizth.), land processioned, 32^2, 69, 111, 112^2.
Vaughan, James, land processioned, 165^4; present at processioning, 165; processioner, 263.
Vaughan, Josiah, 147; land processioned, 163^4, 173, 210^3, 213; paid for services, 96, 103, 202; present at processioning, 143^2, 148, 172^4.
Vaughan (Vaughn), Peter, indigent person, 85, 90, 91, 96.
Vaughan (Vaughn), Thomas, land processioned, 33, 70, 111^2, 136^2.
Vaughan (Vaughn), William (Wim., Wm.), land processioned, 32^3, 33, 69, 111^3, 136^2, 165^5; present at processioning, 112^3, 136^3.
Vaughn, John, vestryman, 262.
Veline (Velines), Abraham, land processioned, 147^4, 148, 172, 212^2.
Veline, Hezekiah, present at processioning, 212, 213.
See also Virlines.
Vestries, and ministers incorporated,

lxviii; and right of visitation, xlii; dissolved by law, lxviii; duties and powers of, xiv, xviii, xxi, xxvi, lv, lix, lxviii; election of, lxviii; members of, as civil officers and judges, xviii; members of, to take oath of supremacy, xxvi; new, successors to former, lxxi, lxxii; processioners appointed by, 2; processioners to report to, xxi, xxii; to meet legal demands promptly, lxviii, lxix.

Vestry book, of Albemarle Parish, Sussex Co., xlvi (note); of Chuckatuck Parish, Nansemond Co., xiii; of Suffolk Parish, Nansemond Co., xiii, xiii (note); of Upper Parish, Nansemond Co., v, xiii, xiii (note), xix (note), xxi (note), xxii, xxii (note), xxxii (note), xxxvi (note), xxxvii (note), xxxviii (note), xxxix (note), xl (note), xliii (note), xliv (note), xlv (note), xlvi (note), xlix (note), l (note), li (note), lii (note), liii (note), lv (note), lvi (note), lvii (note), lviii (note), lx (note), lxi (note), lxii (note), lxiii (note), lxiv (note), lxvi (note), lxvii (note), lxix (note), lxx (note), lxxii (note).

See also Parish register.

Vestry of Chuckatuck Parish, Nansemond Co., fined, xv.

Vestry of Suffolk Parish, Nansemond Co., xiii (note), xix, lx, 14, 15.

Vestry of Upper Parish, Nansemond Co., actions against Rev. Patrick Lunan, xxxix, xl, xliii, xlv, 177, 184, 186, 218, 221, 228, 238, 239; agreements with ministers, 153, 227; and new church, xlix, l, 19, 20, 46, 48, 54, 128; and poorhouse, lvii, lviii, lx, lxi, lxii, lxiii, lxiv, 84, 97, 124, 129, 173, 174, 196, 199, 200, 203, 204, 219, 227, 242; clerks of, 11, 12, 14, 16, 20, 24, 26, 29, 47, 52, 54, 55, 57, 67, 68, 85, 92, 98, 99, 101, 103, 104, 105, 119, 123, 124, 125, 128, 129, 132, 134, 135, 153, 154, 156, 157, 159, 161, 163, 168, 174, 177, 178, 180, 184, 196, 198, 203, 209, 221, 224, 225, 227, 228, 229, 231, 238, 242, 244, 246, 247, 248, 249, 250, 252, 256,

257, 260, 261; committees for building chapels, liv, lv, 28, 87, 88, 128, 129, 153; deaths of members, 15, 23, 45, 51, 57, 94, 104, 128, 130, 156, 177, 238, 240; ferries operated by, liv, 87, 96, 124, 133, 153, 156, 158; for dissolving, xix, xx, lvii (note), 203; investigate behavior of Rev. Wm. Balfour, xxxvi, 15, 16; land adjoining church purchased by, li (note), 156; meetings of, xxi, xxii, xxvii, xxxix, xl, xliii, xliv, xlv, xlix, l, li, lii, liv, lvi, lviii, lxiii, lxvi, lxvii, lxviii, lxix, lxx, lxxi, lxxii, 1, 2, 12, 14, 15, 15 (note), 16, 18, 19, 20, 23, 24, 26, 28, 44, 48, 49, 51, 54, 55, 67, 83, 85, 87, 88, 89, 92, 93, 94, 95, 98, 99, 101, 103, 104, 118, 119, 121, 124, 125, 129, 130, 132, 135, 151, 153, 154, 155, 156, 157, 159, 161, 166, 173, 175, 177, 178, 180, 186, 194, 196, 197, 198, 200, 201, 203, 204, 205, 217, 221, 222, 224, 225, 227, 228, 229, 236, 238, 240, 242, 245, 246, 248, 249, 250, 255, 257, 258, 262; members conform to doctrine and discipline of Episcopal Church, lxix, lxxii, 257, 261; members taken into Suffolk Parish, xix, 14, 15; to serve as trustees and vestrymen, lxxii, 261; elected, xx, 99 (note), 257; orders in regard to old brick church, 47, 48; payments on land for glebe, 207, 220, 224; petition relating to glebe, lxiv, lxvi; processioners appointed, 2, 3, 4, 5, 6, 7, 8, 9, 10, 11, 24, 25, 26, 58, 59, 60, 61, 62, 63, 64, 65, 66, 67, 99, 100, 101, 130, 131, 132, 159, 160, 161, 180, 181, 182, 207, 208, 209, 231, 242, 243, 251, 252; report to, on devised land, 125; report to, on selling glebe land, 83; resignations of members, 168, 180, 201, 224, 238, 240, 246; to enumerate Episcopalians, lxix, 258; to raise money for church and chapels, 262; to sell certain lands, lvi, 173, 173 (note), 196, 203; vestrymen chosen, 15, 16, 19, 23, 45, 51, 57, 68, 94, 104, 124, 125, 128, 130, 133, 156, 168, 177, 180, 200, 201, 207, 219, 222, 224, 225, 238, 240, 244, 246, 247, 251.

See also Churchwardens; Parish levy; Upper Parish, Nansemond Co.

Virginia, commissary in, for Bishop of London, xxv, 177 (note); damage done by troops of, lxvi; democratic revolution in, lxiv; dividing line between North Carolina and, xvi, xvii, xix, xxix, liii (note), 116, 148; growth of dissenters in, xxxi; invaded by British, lxvii; Jefferson on patronage and kinds of parochial establishments in, xlii; King's Bounty for, xxxiv, xxxiv (note), xxxv, xxxvi, xxxvii, xxxix; nonconformists required to leave, xxiii, xxiv; recognition of Toleration Act in, xxvii; settling of, on Roanoke River, xxxiii; spread of population in, xxxi.

The Virginia Gazette, notice regarding Rev. Patrick Lunan, xlii (note).

The Virginia Historical Register, lxvii (note).

Virginia Local Public Records: Housing Conditions in the Offices of the Clerks . . . (book), xiv (note).

The Virginia Magazine of History and Biography, vii (note), xv (note), xvii (note), xxiv (note), xxxi (note), xxxiii (note), xxxv (note), xxxvi (note), xxxvii (note), xliv (note), xlviii (note).

Virginia Regiment, chaplain to, xxxviii (note).

Virginia State Bar Association, xiv (note).

Virginia State Land Office, *Patents* (book), xv (note).

Virginia State Library, Board of, x, xiv (note); Nansemond County manuscripts in, lxvii (note); Nansemond County petitions in, lxiv (note), lxx (note), lxxi (note), lxxiii (note); parish record books in, v; parish record books, published by Board of, v.

Virlines, Ezekiel, processioner, 231. *See also* Veline.

Visitation, right of, xli, xlii.

Visitors, for poorhouse, lxi, lxii, 124, 199, 200.

Vorrel, Oliver, *see* Worrell, Oliver.

Wadkins, Peter, *see* Watkins, Peter.
Waff (Worf), George (Geo.), ferryman, 87, 96; orphan of, 177, 179, 183, 195, 198.
Waff, Susanah, indigent person, 163.
Wages, of sexton of Brick Church, 50, 52, 56, 85; of sexton of Cyprus Chapel, 157, 161, 167, 178, 194, 197, 205, 218, 222, 226; of sexton of Holy Neck Chapel, 154, 157, 161, 167, 178; of sexton of Middle Chapel, 13, 16, 21, 26, 46, 50, 52, 56, 85; of sexton of Nottoway Chapel, 126, 132, 151, 154, 157, 161, 167; of sexton of Somerton Chapel, 151, 205, 218, 222; of sexton of Suffolk Church, 90, 96, 126, 132, 151, 154, 157, 161, 167, 178, 194, 197, 201, 205, 218, 222, 226, 229, 236, 239, 240, 243; of sextoness of Cyprus Chapel, 240, 243; of sextoness of Holy Neck Chapel, 85, 237, 239, 240; of sextoness of Somerton Chapel, 16, 96, 118, 126, 132; of sextoness of Upper Chapel, 13, 21, 26, 45, 50, 52, 56, 90. *See also* Salaries.
Wainwright (Weignright), Benjamin, land processioned, 42^2, 77.
Walker, ——, 239.
Walker, Emanuel, 237.
Walker, Francis, 243.
Walkins, Peter, *see* Watkins, Peter.
Waller, Benjamin, allegations against Lunan presented to, xl, 184.
Wallis (Wallice), Samuel, accounts for sundries for poorhouse, 122, 127; overseer and teacher in poorhouse, lviii, lx, lxi, 97, 103, 104, 119, 123, 129; poor children taught by, lxi, 162, 198, 202; salary of, 103, 119, 123.
Wallis (Wallice), Rev. Samuel, minister of Chuckatuck Parish, xxxiv, xxxiv (note), lviii (note).
Walter, William, plantation of, 4, 60.
War, allowance for tithables gone to, 118.
See also Army.
Ward, Joshua, paid for services, 17.
Ward, William (Wim.), land processioned, 30, 31^2, 144; present at processioning, 144^7; processioner, 181.
Warren, Etheldred (Dred), present at processioning, 236^3; processioner, 208, 215, 252.
Warren, Robt., indigent person, 206.
Warren (Warran), Saml., land processioned, 33, 108.
Water table, 54, 55.
Wateridge (Wartridge, Waterridge, Watridge), John, land processioned, 43^2, 137, 188, 211; present at processioning, 211; processioner, 131, 136, 182, 188.
Wateridge, Moses, land processioned, 193^2.
Waters (Warters), John, indigent person, 241; paid for services, 103.
Waters, Wim., land processioned, 113, 114.
Waters, Wim., jr., present at processioning, 143.
Water's Old Field, 163.
Watkins, Mrs. ——, indigent person, 120.
Watkins (Wadkins, Walkins), Peter, present at processioning, 68, 83, 108.
Watkins, Sarah, paid for services, 91, 96, 103, 119, 127, 152.
Watkinson (Watkison), Peter, land processioned, 114^2.
Watson, John, accounts of, 92, 123; land processioned, 40, 41^2, 75, 78, 109^3; to have pew in gallery of church, li, 88, 93.
Watson, Jonathan, indigent person, 51, 52.
Watson, Lemuel, land processioned, 174^3.
Watson, Mary, land processioned, 174^2.
Watson (Natson), Michl. (Mical), present at processioning, 36, 75.
Watson, Samuel (Saml.), land processioned, 75^3, 174, 175^4; processioner, 100, 160, 175.
Weatherley (Weatherly), John, land processioned, 33; paid for services, 221.
Weatherly, William, reimbursed, 259.
Weaver, Jonathan, land processioned, 144^3.
Webb, Mrs. ——, paid for services, 47.

INDEX

325

Webb, Ann, indigent person, 127; land processioned, 147.
Webb, David, indigent person, 256.
Webb, Henning, processioner, 231.
Webb, James, land processioned, 34³.
Webb, John, land processioned, 34²; present at processioning, 135; reimbursed, 256.
Webb, Kedar, land processioned, 185³; present at processioning, 107, 144²; processioner, 159, 166.
Webb, Mary, administratrix of Richard Webb, 153.
Webb, Richard (Richd.), 153; churchwarden, 134, 135; clerk of vestry, 54, 55, 57, 67, 68, 85, 86, 87, 88, 89, 90, 92; indigent person, 248; land processioned, 31⁵, 144¹⁰; paid for services, 13, 17, 21, 26, 45, 50; present at processioning, 144; processioner, 58, 82; vestryman, 130.
Webb, Thos., land processioned, 34.
Webb, William (not identified as minister), 119; land processioned, 109²; paid for services, 133, 206, 223, 226, 229; present at processioning, 109¹.
Webb, Rev. William, allowances to, 26, 45, 49, 52, 85, 90, 95, 101, 118, 121, 126, 132; and "Two Penny" act, xxxvii; land processioned, 109³; master of Grammar School, xxxviii; member of almshouse visitors, 124; on committee for building chapel, 128; on committee for building church, l, 46; on committee for erection of almshouse, 84, 85, 173; on committee to sell glebe land, 173; paid for searching for patent, 95; parish register delivered to, 29; preaches in Suffolk Parish, xxxvii; present at meeting of vestry, 26, 28, 45, 48, 49, 51, 54, 55, 67, 83, 85, 87, 88, 89, 92, 93, 94, 95, 98, 99, 101, 103, 104, 118, 119, 121, 124, 125, 126, 129, 130, 132, 135, 173; proceedings of vestry signed by, 29, 47, 48, 49, 51, 54, 55, 67, 68, 85, 87, 88, 89, 92, 93, 94, 95, 98, 99, 101, 103, 104, 105, 119, 120, 123, 124, 125, 128, 129, 130, 132, 134, 135; processioning orders signed by, 67; received as minister, 24; salary of, 26, 45, 49, 52, 55, 85, 90, 95, 101, 118, 121, 126, 132, 151; signs order for building chapel, 28; to examine accounts of John Watson, 92.
Webb and Meridith, 202, 219.
Weeks, Archilus, land processioned, 32.
Weeks, Stephen B., *Southern Quakers and Slavery* . . ., xxv (note), xxvii (note), xxviii (note), xxix (note).
Weignright, Benjamin, *see* Wainwright, Benjamin.
Welch, Margaret, indigent person, 259.
Well, at chapel, 179; at Cyprus Chapel, 158; at Holy Neck Chapel, 127, 154, 157, 161, 175, 178; at Somerton Chapel, 96; bucket for, 118, 179; repaired, 220; sweep for, 179.
See also Spring.
Wells, Mrs. ———, widow of Samuel, 29.
Wells, Mary, indigent person, 250.
Wells, Samuel, 29.
See also Wills.
West, Robert, land processioned, 108².
West Parish, establishment of, xiv, xiv (note); name changed to Chuckatuck Parish, xv.
Western Avenue, Suffolk, lii.
Whale, Ruth, indigent person, 24; payment made to, 29.
Whaleyville, lii (note).
Wharton, Joseph, land processioned, 34.
Wharton, William, land processioned, 34².
Whimmer, John, paid for services, 237, 251.
Whimmer, Sarah, indigent person, 260.
Whinard, Sarah, indigent person, 13, 17.
White, Baker, land processioned, 32².
White, Rev. George, xxxiii.
White Marsh, land and plantation on, for glebe, lxiii, 204, 207, 220, 224.
Whitfeild, Muls (?), present at processioning, 165.
Whitfeild, Robert, land processioned, 165².
Whitfield, Eine, present at processioning, 263.
Whitfield (Wheatfield, Whitfeild), John, land processioned, 32³, 69, 112², 136²,

165^2; present at processioning, 136^2, 165^3; processioner, 63, 69, 70, 208.
Whitfield, Solo., present at processioning, 263.
Whitfield, Thomas, land processioned, 32^5.
Whitfield (Whitfeild), William (W., Wm.), paid for services, 206, 219, 223; sexton, 218, 222, 226, 229, 236, 239, 240, 243.
Whitlock, Wm., paid for services, 238; processioner, 242.
Whitney, Joseph, indigent person, 56, 86.
Whittleton, ———, present at processioning, 236.
Wiat (Wiatt), Jean, indigent person, 123, 200, 206, 220, 224, 226, 230.
Wiat, Mary, indigent person, 179; paid for services, 102.
See also Wyatt.
Wickam (Wicham) Swamp, 7, 32, 63, 263.
Wickham's, land at, lvi, lvii, 84, 173.
Wiggins (Wigins), Ann, indigent person, 187, 207, 220.
Wiggins, D., indigent person, 239.
Wiggins (Wigins), James, land processioned, 174^2, 175^3; present at processioning, 75.
Wiggins (Wigens), Thos., land processioned, 215; reimbursed, 118.
Wiggins (Wiggin, Wigins), William (Wim., Wm.), indigent person, 179, 195, 198, 203; land processioned, 33, 108^2, 149; present at processioning, 108; sexton, 122, 126, 132, 151, 154, 157, 167, 175.
Wigins, Dempsey, land processioned, 146; present at processioning, 193^2.
Wigins, John, land not processioned, 145.
Wigins, Willis, land processioned, 193.
Wigmore, ———, indigent person, 56.
Wilkerson (Wilkason), William, land processioned, 38, 253.
Wilkerson, William, sr., land processioned, 253.
See also Wilkinson.
Wilkins (Wilkings), John (Jon.), land processioned, 233, 234; present at processioning, 189; reimbursed, 182.

Wilkins (Wilkings), Shadarach (Shad., Shaderick, Shadk., Sharderick), land processioned, 189^4, 234^4; present at processioning, 189^2, 233, 234^4; processioner, 208.
Wilkins, Thomas (Thos.), indigent person, 198; land processioned, 37^2, 189^4; present at processioning, 189^5, 234^2; processioner, 8.
Wilkinson (Wilkison), John, land processioned, 78, 166; present at processioning, 78, 79^3.
Wilkinson, William (Willm., Wim., Wm.), land processioned, 166^2, 185^3, 209^2, 242^3, 245; present at processioning, 185, 209, 245; processioner, 130, 149, 159, 166, 242, 245.
See also Wilkerson.
Will, of William Cadowgan, lv, lvi, 128, 173 (note).
William and Mary College, convocation of clergy at, xxxviii (note); Grammar School of, xxxviii.
William and Mary College Quarterly Historical Magazine, xxxvii (note), xxxix (note), xliv (note); 2d series, xvi (note).
Williams, Daniel (Danl.), land processioned, 33, 108, 149, 187; paid for services, 123; processioner, 100, 108, 160; vestryman, 124.
Williams, George (Geo.), land processioned, 33, 108^2, 149, 215, 235; present at processioning, 108^2, 149^2; processioner, 181, 187.
Williams, John, present at processioning, 215^2, 236; land processioned, 215.
Williams, Jordan, processioner, 243, 252.
Williams, Joshaa, land processioned, 33.
Williams, Josiah, present at processioning, 215^3, 236^2.
Williams, Mourning, land processioned, 236.
Williams, Richard (Richd.), land processioned, 33, 69, 107, 150, 214; present at processioning, 69^3, 107^2, 150^7, 169, 214^2.
Williams, Robt., present at processioning, 69.

Williams, Simon, present at processioning, 235.
Williams, Thomas (Thos.), paid for services, 12, 45, 52^3, 57, 85.
Williamsburg, xliv, 54, 219; idle persons in, lix; lunatic taken to, 219; minister employed as lecturer in, xxxv.
Willie, Rev. ———, minister of Albemarle Parish, xlvi.
Willis, ———, indigent person, 53; land processioned, 38.
Willis (Williss), Anabel (Ana, Anabil), indigent person, 163, 167, 176.
Willis, Eliz., indigent person, 237.
Willis, Judith (Judey), indigent person, 187, 237.
Willis, Martha, indigent person, 230, 239.
Willis, Robert, paid for services, 53, 256; processioner, 252^2.
Willis, Thos., land processioned, 211; paid for services, 219.
Wills, Elizabeth, paid for services, 247.
Wills, Mary, indigent person, 247, 248, 256.
See also Wells.
Wilson, ———, indigent person, 57, 85, 127, 152, 154, 157.
Wilson, Jane, indigent person, 86.
Wilson (Willson), John, indigent person, 95, 96; land processioned, 35^1, 36, 72^3, 112, 213; orphan, 90; paid for services, 102.
Winbourn (Winborn, Winborne, Winburn), James, 119; land processioned, 76^2, 106, 114^2, 138, 141, 164^2, 194^2; present at processioning, 140; processioner, 60, 60 (note), 69, 138.
Winbourn (Winberne, Winborn, Winborne, Winbourne, Winburn), John (Jno.), churchwarden, 29, 45, 48, 49; land processioned, 29^2, 71^7, 76^5, 106^4, 110^3, 140^3, 141, 171, 194^3; on committee for building chapel, 28; on committee to sell devised land, 173; present at processioning, 76^4, 77^2, 106^4, 194; processioner, 100, 106, 131, 131 (note); vestryman, 1, 14, 15, 16, 18, 19, 23, 24, 26, 28, 54, 55, 83, 85, 87, 89, 92, 95, 173.

Winbourn, John, jr., processioner, 25.
Winbourn (Winborne), Jno., sr., land processioned, 69.
Winbourn, Josiah, land processioned, 194; present at processioning, 140, 141.
Winbourn, Robert, land processioned, 194.
Winbourn (Winborn, Winborne), Thomas (Thos.) (sometimes designated captain), accounts of, 176; churchwarden, 168, 175, 177, 178; land processioned, 68, 114, 138^2, 164; present at processioning, 68, 114; processioner, 100, 115, 160, 164; reimbursed, 182; resignation of, 180; vestryman, 133, 135, 151, 154, 157, 167.
Winburne (Winborne), Henry, paid for services, 250, 251, 255, 259.
Winburne, Sarah, paid for services, 248, 249.
Windows, in new chapel, 89; in new church, 55.
Wine, for sacrament, 240.
Winfrey, Martha, x.
Wise, J. C., vii (note).
Wise, Wm., land processioned, 192^4; present at processioning, 192.
Witnesses, in court for Upper Parish, 102, 118; to renunciation of Rev. Patrick Lunan, 229.
Witwell, Matthew, land processioned, 117^{12}.
Woddrap, Jno., executor, 16.
See also Woodrop, John.
Women, assistants at poorhouse, lx, 103, 127, 152; fined, 29, 55, 88, 93, 120; minister solicits to fornication, xli.
Wood, 162, 179, 183, 195, 198, 202, 204, 207, 219, 227.
Wood, John, paid for services, 207, 241.
Wood, Rev. John, minister of Lower Parish, xxxiii.
Wood (Woods), Sarah (S.), 1, 206, 219, 226.
Woodly, Thos., land processioned, 33.
Woodrop, Ann, land processioned, 209^2, 242^2, 245.
Woodrop (Woodroop, Woodrope, Woodroph), John, land processioned, 79^2,

185; present at processioning, 79³; processioner, 100, 107.
See also Woddrap, Jno.

Woodrope, Alexander (Alexr.), land processioned, 253; present at processioning, 253.

Woodson, ———, 127.

Woodward (Woodard, Woodord), Richard, land processioned, 235³; processioner, 243, 245.

Woodward, William (Wim., Wm.), land processioned, 82², 118³, 142⁴, 191⁴; processioner, 132, 139 (note).

Wool, 199.

Worf, George, *see* Waff, George.

Worrell, John, present at processioning, 69, 136².

Worrell (Vorrel, Wirel, Wiril, Wirrel, Worl), Oliver, land processioned, 32, 33, 69, 70, 111, 114², 136, 165³; present at processioning, 136⁴.

Wrench, Rachel, indigent person, 12.

Wright, ———, grave for, 127.

Wright, Dr. Christopher, land processioned, 40²; paid for services, 16, 17, 21, 50; present at processioning, 41; processioner, 24.

Wright, Edmund (Edmond), Belson, vestry held at home of, 154, 155, 156, 157, 161, 166, 175, 178, 186.

Wright, Edward (Edwd.), sheriff, 14, 17, 18, 21.

Wright, Henry, land processioned, 30², 68⁴, 74, 147³, 173³; paid for services, 45; processioner, 4, 75.

Wright, Henry, jr., land processioned, 35; processioner, 59.

Wright, Jas., paid for services, 241.

Wright, John, list of tithables by, 50, 53.

Wright, Nathaniel (Nathanll., Nathll.), 12, 17; present at processioning, 191².

Wright, Pricilia (Pircelia, Pricila), 139; land processioned, 117³.

Wright, Sarah, indigent person, 130; sextoness, 237, 240, 243.

Wright, Stephen, churchwarden, 130, 132, 133; on almshouse board of visitors, 124; on committee for building chapel, 128; on committee on enclosing churchyard, 128; vestryman, 124, 126, 129, 130, 133.

Wright, William (Wm.), land processioned, 213²; present at processioning, 68, 147², 172, 173; reimbursed, 249, 256.

Wright, Capt. Wm., vestryman, 12; vestryman taken into Suffolk Parish, 14-15.
See also Right.

Wyatt (Wiat, Wyat), John, land processioned, 35⁶, 73, 74², 112; present at processioning, 74².

Wyatt (Wiat, Wyat), Nathan, land processioned, 83, 110, 111, 164², 210²; paid for services, 52.
See also Wiat.

Wythe, George, in case of vestry against Rev. Patrick Lunan, xl, xli, 186.

Yeats, Robt., bridge, 6, 62.

Yeats, Wm., reimbursed, 12.

Yorktown, chaplain at, xlvii.

www.ingramcontent.com/pod-product-compliance
Lightning Source LLC
Chambersburg PA
CBHW020637300426
44112CB00007B/140